FINANCIAL INCLUSION IN INDIA

FINANCIAL INCLUSION IN INDIA

Issues and Challenges

Editors

Siddaraju V.G.

Ramesh

Centre for the Study of Social Exclusion and Inclusive Policy University of Mysore

GYAN

Financial Inclusion in India: Issues and Challenges

ISBN : 978-81-212-1182-6

Published in 2013 in India by
Gyan Publishing House
23, Main Ansari Road, Daryaganj,
New Delhi - 110002
Phones : 23282060, 23261060
Fax : (011) 23285914

E-mail: books@gyanbooks.com
website: gyanbooks.com

Laser Type Setting : Rajender Vashist, Delhi
Printed at : Chawla Offset Printers, Delhi

Contents

Foreword

When Professor Theodore Schultz wrote the famous treatise on Transforming Traditional Agriculture, he was arguing the necessity of shifting from low level equilibrium to a higher level with the help of enhancing the quality of capital. But the vital point missed out then was that the access to resources has been always skewed in all the developing economies. India is more intensely affected due to our social system. The access to resources in India has always been skewed in favour of a few upper castes and this did not happen just in the process of development but through a sinister design perpetuated through irrational social order. Poverty, lack of employment opportunities, ownership of productive resources and persistent dependence syndrome perpetuates unabated. As all assets are distributed skewly and the development can only be achieved by providing them a clear access to investible resources and productive assets, credit becomes inevitable. Most of the discussions on credit delivery points out failure of the institutional systems to reach these most deserving groups.

Rural credit system in India has come under review in three different contexts. First, the review was taken in the context of liberalization wherein, it was felt necessary to augment the operations of financial market in the economy and inclusiveness. The imperfect development of credit market operated as the main driving force for such review. Second, more or less, at the same time, many studies brought out clearly that the trends in capital formation in the rural economy are becoming adverse and therefore, in order to boost up the capital formation, it was felt necessary to provide new impetus to rural credit structure. The third provocation for reforms in credit market came from the severe distress expressed by the weaker sections in various parts of the country. A good number of studies and activists' groups have argued to correct the inefficiency of rural credit to reach the neediest and reduce the presence of informal money market. In this context, it was felt necessary to understand inclusiveness of rural credit structure in order to bring out its weaknesses and need for corrections, if any. This is accomplished in light of the findings of various committees starting from All India Rural Credit Survey headed by Gorewala to the Expert Committee on Rural Credit and Advisory Committee on Flow of Agricultural Credit headed by Prof. Vyas. The analysis brings out a few important factors. First, it comes out clearly that the policy for collateral and the process of arriving at bankability of the project needs to be reviewed. Pledge financing, credit for marketing, introduction of negotiable warehousing system are now essential to be included in the formulation of credit policy. The financial health of credit institutions indicates matters of concern. in the presence of a few authoritative reports during the process of reforms on credit reforms that include Narasimham Committee as well as Vyas Committee reports. Two important questions need to be addressed to in this seminar viz., (i) what kind of financial environment and inclusive policies are prevailing in the State that face most critical situation? and (ii) which are the important and distilled guidelines of the reform process that would be useful in this context?

Karnataka has always stayed on the forefront of accepting and implementing the process of reform despite various constraints. It is also a State where, capital formation in non-agricultural sector has been quite strong whereas, the same in agricultural sector has slowed down. The impact of this situation on the agricultural sector is two-fold: First, the savings generated in the economy are siphoned out naturally towards high value added sectors and agricultural sector is last to have claim on such resources. Second, there are a good number of initiatives in the sector that require large capital intensity and therefore, capital scarcity is felt immensely. In Karnataka, the budget has provided to cover the loss in interest of banks when the co-operative sector charges at 6 per cent instead of the prevailing rate of interest. But, subsidisation of one institution as against others may create imbalances in rural credit structure. We have also noted that in the State Self-Help Groups have worked hand in hand with Watershed Development Committees and that has proved exceptionally successful both in credit management as well as natural resource conservation. It is necessary to highlight the success of these experiments and boost them up to achieve better results. That goes along with the emergence of new generation of moneylenders. Rural credit structure in Karnataka has been developed over the years and it indicates a good number of variations. In this seminar the question of inclusiveness needs is analysed in detail by the researchers and they also brought forth the development in rural credit structure in the State and its growth during recent past. The question of inclusiveness in this context became centripetal.

I am sure the issues raised by the paper writers will evoke interest for further analyses and take us to a few policy leads.

Prof. R S Deshpande
Director
Institute for Social and Economic Change
Bangalore, Karnataka

Preface

The prediction of Millennium Development Goals of U.N. i.e. "growth with equity" clearly envisages that the growth spree of the globe in the 21st century has left some people behind the time. Handful of the global populace are still languishing in the vicious circle of poverty and are cast aside by those who are economically stronger and swifter in the sway of globalization and liberalization. For sustenance/better growth of the world, the deprived sections should be dragged into the mainstream of growth. This is because of the fact that poverty any where is a grave threat to prosperity everywhere. Over the last several decades, the banking sector in the country has taken significant steps to achieve profitability, financial stability and competitiveness to cater to the increasing demand for financial services. However, much of the benefits accrued due to the growth in banking services have been limited to a minority of the total population of the country. Banks have not been able to reach a vast segment of the population particularly in the rural areas and take even basic banking services to the underserved and disadvantaged masses for various reasons. Banks have confined to only areas around their branch network whereas the need for cheap and timely credit transcends the boundaries of these branches to remote areas which lack even basic infrastructure. In India, only 34 per cent of population engaged in formal banking and it has approximately 135 million financially excluded households and the second highest number after China. Further, the real rate of financial inclusion in India is also very low and about 40 per cent of the bank account holders use their accounts not even once a month. It is universally opined that the resource poor need financial assistance at reasonable costs and that too with uninterrupted pace. However, the economic liberalization policies have always tempted the financial institutions to look for more and more greener pastures of business ignoring the weaker sections of the society. In India, the financially excluded sections comprise largely rural masses comprising marginal farmers, landless labourers, self-employed and unorganized sector enterprises, urban slum dwellers, migrants, ethnic minorities and socially excluded groups, senior citizens and women. Some of the important causes of relatively low extension of institutional credit in the rural areas are risk perception, cost of its assessment and management, lack of rural infrastructure, and vast geographical spread of the rural areas with more than half a million villages, some sparsely populated.

Financial services actively contribute to the humane and economic development of the society. This led to social safety net and protects the people from economic shocks. Hence, each and every individual should be provided with affordable institutional financial products/services popularly called "Financial Inclusion". Financial Inclusion, both as a topic and as a movement, has attracted global attention in recent years. Financial inclusion may be defined as the process of ensuring access to financial services and timely and adequate credit where needed by vulnerable groups such as weaker sections and low income groups at an affordable cost. Financial products and services are identified as basic banking services like deposits accounts, institutional loans, access to payment, remittance facilities and also life and non life insurance services. Financial inclusion is contemplated as a crucial means to achieve inclusive growth in the economy during the 11th Five Year Plan. It is a powerful instrument for reducing poverty and income disparities among the people in the country. Financial inclusion is necessary to enable the weaker sections of the society to participate in the formal financial system as they are otherwise disadvantaged sections and low-income groups. Further, the 12th Five Year Plan has also adopted "faster, Sustainable and more Inclusive growth" as the key development paradigm. Further, India being a sovereign, socialist, secular, democratic, republic, it is imperative on the policies of the government to ensure equitable growth of all sections of the economy. It is essential for any economy to aim at inclusive growth involving each and every citizen in the economic development progression. In this context, that financial inclusion should be aimed at inclusive growth in the Indian context.

This is a collection of research papers presented in the national level conference entitled "Financial Inclusion in India: Issues and Challenges" conducted by the Centre for Study of Social Exclusion and Inclusive Policy (CSSEIP), University of Mysore, Karnataka held on 9th and 10th October, 2012. Centre would like to thank Indian Council of Social Science (ICSSR), New Delhi for its funding support and all contributors in this conference. We also thank our beloved Vice Chancellor Prof. V.G Talawar for his never ending encouragement and support. We also gratified to the Registrar for his logistic prop up. I take this opportunity to express my heartfelt thanks to all the authors who have enriched the book by contributing their learned papers. We thank to Dr. Nanjunda D.C, and Dr. Dinesha P T faculty members of CSSEIP, University of Mysore for their support. We acknowledge all others who have supported and assisted directly and indirectly for completion of this work. We are also indebted to the Gyan Publishing House, New Delhi for publishing this edited volume.

Editors

Dr. SIDDARAJU V.G

Reader-cum-Deputy Director

CSSEIP, University of Mysore, Mysore.

and

Dr. RAMESH

Professor-cum-Director

CSSEIP, University of Mysore, Mysore.

List of Contributors

Prof. M. Ramanjaneyulu, Professor of Economics, Bangalore University, Bangalore -560056.

Prof. K.E. Sreeramapa Rtd. Professor of Economics, Mysore University, Mysore.

Mr. Nagesh, Reserch Scholar, DOS in Economics and Cooperation Mysore University, Mysore.

Prof. S. N. Tripathy, Professor of Economics, Gokhale Institute of Politics And Economics (Deemed University), BMCC Road, Pune-411004, Maharashtra.

Prof. M.G. Basavaraja, Professor, Department of Economics, University of Mysore, Sir M. Visveswaraya P.G Centre, Mandya - 571402, Mysore.

Dr. S. R Keshava, Faculty, Post Graduate Department of Economics, Bangalore University, Bangalore-560056.

Prof. Odeyar D. Heggade, Professor, DOS In Economics, University of Mysore, Sir M.V. PG Centre, Tubinakere, Mandya District, Karnataka.

Dr. Vighneswara Swamy, Associate Professor, IBS-Hyderabad.

Mr. Jnaneshwar Pai Maroor, Senior LecturerJustice K.S. Hedge Institute of Management, NMAMIT, Nitte.

Dr. Ashalatha K., Associate Professor, Justice K.S. Hedge Institute of Management, NMAMIT, Nitte.

Dr. N. Maruti Rao, Associate Professor, PG Dept. of Business Administration Rani Channamma University, Belagavi.

Vishwanath Talwar, Research officer, ICSSR Project, PG Dept. of Business Administration Rani Channamma University, Belagavi.

Dr. M. Indira, Professor, Department of Economics and Cooperation, University of Mysore, Mysore.

Mr. C. Anand, Research Scholars, Department of Economics and Cooperation, University of Mysore, Mysore.

Dr. V. Ramakrishnappa, Reader-cum-Deputy Director, Centre for the study of Social Exclusion and Inclusive Policy (CSEIP), Mangalagangothri, Mangalore University, Mangalore-574199.

N Krishne Gowda, PhD Scholar, Department of Economics, Mangalore University, Mangalore-574 199

Dr. Santhosh Areekkuzhiyil, Asst. Professor, Govt. Brennen College of Teacher Education, Thalassery, Kannur, Kerala-670101

Prajisha. K., Guest Faculty, Dept. of Commerce, Govt. College Mokeri, Mokeri. PO., Kozhikode Dist., Kerala

Dr. S. Mahendra Kumar, Associate Professor, DOS in Economics and Cooperation, Manasagangotri, University of Mysore, Mysore.

S. Srinivasa, Research Scholar, DOS in Economics and Cooperation, Manasagangotri, University of Mysore, Mysore.

H.S. Niranjana Babu Reddy, Assistant Professor, Govt. First Grade College, T.Narasipura, Mysore

Dr. Ashoka M.L., Assistant Professor, DOS Commerce, Manasagangothri, University of Mysore, Deepu PG Centre, JSS College, Mysore.

Rajesh R., Research Assistant, Centre for the Study of Social Exclusion and Inclusive Policy (CSSEIP), Research Scholar, Department of Applied Economics, Cochin University of Science and Technology, Kochi-22, Kerala.

Dr. P.P. Sajimon, Asst. Professor in Economics, PG Department of Economics, St. Aloysius College (Autonomous), Mangalore-3.

Dr. Siddaraju V.G., Reader *cum* Deputy Director, Centre for the Study of Social Exclusion and Inclusive Policy, Humanities Block, Manasagangothri, University of Mysore, Mysore-570006.

Dr. Huchhe Gowda, Assistant Professor, Department of Studies in Economics, Rani Channamma University, Vidyasangama, P.B.N.H-4, Belagavi-591156.

Dr. B.T. Ramappa, Associate Professor and Head, Department of Economics, Tunga Mahavidyalya, Thirthahalli, Kuvempu University, Karnataka, ramappaeco@gmail.com.

Dr. Ramakrishna, Post Doctoral Fellow, Institute of Development Studies, University of Mysore, Manasagangothri, Mysore-570006. Karnataka.

Dr. K.V.Aiahanna, Professor of Development Studies, Institute of Development Studies, University of Mysore, Manasagangothri, Mysore-570006. Karnataka.

M.V. Dinesha, Assistant Professor, DOS in Economics and Cooperation University of Mysore, Mysore.

Mr. Rajendraprasad, Lecturer, Govt. PU College, Ponnampete, Kodagu.

Dr. Navitha Thimmaiah, Assistant Professor, Department of Economics and Co-operation, University of Mysore, Mysore.

Anitha C.V., Research Scholar, Department of Economics and Co-operation, University of Mysore, Mysore.

Dr. B.P. Mahesh Chandra Guru, Professor and Chairman, DOS in Communication and Journalism, University of Mysore, Manasagangotri, Mysore, Karnataka.

Dr. C.K. Puttaswamy, Assistant Professor, DOS in Communication and Journalism, University of Mysore, Manasagangotri, Mysore, Karnataka State.

Nagaraju, Research Scholar, DOS in Political Science, University of Mysore, Manasagangotri, Mysore, Karnataka.

Shashikala, Teacher Fellow, DOS in Economics and Co-operation, Manasa Gangothri, Mysore.

Dr. H.R. Uma, Associate Professor, DOS in Economics and Co-operation, Manasa Gangothri, Mysore.

Dr. Mahesh R., Associate professor, B.N. Bahadur Institute of Management Sciences,University of Mysore, Mysore-570006.

Sri. Shamanth N., Lecturer in Business Management, Vidya Vikas First Grade College, Mysore-570010.

Dr. P.N. Udayachandra, Registrar and HOD of Commerce, SDM College (autonomous) Ujire.

Mr. Vishal Pinto, Research Scholar, SDM College (autonomous) Ujire.

Sunil D'souza, Research Scholar, Department of Studies in Commerce, Post Graduation Centre, Hassan.

Dr. M. Chandramma, Assistant Professor, Department of Studies in Commerce, Mangalore University, Mangalagangotri-574199.

Dr. Raghrama A., Professor, Chairman and Dean, Department of Studies in Commerce, Mangalore University Mangalagangotri-574199.

Mahadevaswamy, MDOS in Commerce, Manasa Gangotri, University of Mysore, Mysore.

Dr. Sajan C.P., University Evening College, University of Mysore, Mysore.

Dr. G. Kotreshwar, DOS in Commerce, Manasa Gangotri, University of Mysore, Mysore.

Prakruthi A.R., Research Scholar, DOS in Law, University of Mysore.

Mamatha Kyatannanavar, Research Scholar, DOS in Law, University of Mysore.

Naveen Chandra C.B., Research Scholar, DOS in Law, University of Mysore.

Dr. B.H. Suresh, Professor, DOS in Commerce, Manasagangotri,University of Mysore, Mysore-570006, bhsmysore@yahoo.in.

Ms. Amrutha Varshini, VJRF-UGC, DOS in Commerce, Manasagangotri, University of Mysore, Mysore-570006.

Dr. M. Dhanabhakyam, Assistant Professor, School of Commerce, Bharathiar University, Coimbatore.

Swapna Kurian, Research Scholar, School of Commerce, Bharathiar University, Coimbatore.

P.T. Dhamayanthi, Asst. Professor in Commerce, Government First Grade College Hullahalli, Nanjanagud Taluk, Mysore District.

Dr. P.T. Bharathi, Asst. Professor in Geography, Maharaja's College, Mysore.

Raghavendra, Lecturer in Economics, Dr. N.S.A.M. First Grade College, Nitte. and PhD Research Scholar, Rayalaseema University, Kurnool (AP).

Dr. V. Basil Hans, Associate Professor and HOD of Economics, and Dean, Faculty of Arts, St Aloysius Evening College, Mangalore – 575003.

Dr. M. Dhanabhakyam, Asst. Professor, Dept. of Commerce, Bharathiar University Coimbatore- 641046.

M. Kavitha, Research Scholar, Dept. of Commerce, Bharathiar University, Coimbatore- 641046.

Ramaprakasha N., Faculty, Department of Business Administration Maharaja's College and University Evening College, University of Mysore, Mysore - 570005.

Dr. Mohan Kumar T.P., Asst. Professor, Poojabhagavath PG Centre, Mysore.

R. Ramya, Faculty and Coordinator, Mother Teresa PU College, Mysore.

R. Nakul, Assistant Manager, Chamundeshwari Sugar Pvt. Ltd.

Dr. O.D. Heggade, Professor of Economics, University of Mysore, Sir M.V.P.G. Centre, Mandya.

Puttaraja, FDP Teacher Fellow, DOS in Economics and Co-operation, University of Mysore.

Dr. Dinesha P.T., Lecturer cum Asst. Director, Centre for the Study of Social Exclusion and Inclusive Policy, University of Mysore, Mysore, Karnataka 570006.

Kiran Kumar P., Assistant Professor, Department of Economics, Rani Channamma University Belgaum-591156, Karnataka.

Dr. Rajendraprasad N.L., Lecturer, University Evening College, Mysore.

Sri. Oscar Abhishek, Lecturer in Business Management,Vidya Vikas First Grade College, Mysore-570010.

R. Nagabhushan, Asst Prof in Economics, Govt First Grade_College, Kuvempunagar, Mysore.

Kempe Gowda G.N., Research Scholars, DOS in Economics and CooperationUniversity of Mysore, Mysore.

Nadeesha H.K., Research Scholar, DOS in Economics and Cooperation, University of Mysore, Mysore.

Bhavya Shri B., Lecturer at Vidya Vikas, Institute of Engineering, P.G. Center for Commerce, Mysore.

1

Impact of Institutional Credit on Agriculture and Rural Development In India - An Assessment of Financial Inclusion

M. Ramanjaneyulu, K.E. Sreeramapa **and** *Nagesh*

Introduction

> "Where enterprise leads, finance follows, there by economic development creates demand for a specific type of financial arrangements" — **Johon Robinson (1952)**

The institutional credit for agriculture and allied sectors has been a continuous phenomenon of an increasing the production and employment in India. The several policies and programmes have also been working towards enhancing the economic activities in rural development. In spite of numerous efforts by governments and institutional efforts, half of the India is not use of formal financial services and half of them are in unbanked. Only 55 per cent of the population have deposit accounts, and as low as 9 per cent have credit accounts with banks. Moreover, only one Bank Branch constitutes per 14,000 people. Out of six lakh villages in India rural branches of Scheduled Commercial Banks including Regional Rural Banks number at least 33,495 which comprised of only 5.58 per cent coverage of villages. Another important indicator that only 20 per cent of population has the access of Life Insurance Corporation and only 9.6 per cent of the population has non life insurance coverage. Just 18 per cent had the debit cards and less than 2 per cent has credit cards (Financial Inclusion: Dr. K.C. Chekravarthy, Deputy Governor, RBI, Sept. 2011).

Financial inclusion has a multiple dimensions like credit, savings, financial services or products, financial capability, financial education which are expected to influence penetration and percolation of wide coverage among the different sections of society and in turn contribute to enhance production, employment and income. Credit delivery has been a significant priority of Reserve Bank of India. In this pursuit, formal credit faculties have been expended by Scheduled Commercial Banks, Cooperative Banks and Regional Rural Banks etc. The challenge of Financial Inclusion is to covering all sections of society under umbrella of financial transaction activities of Financial Inclusion Plan of Banks. The importance of Financial Inclusion Plan and expanding the scope of business correspondent model improving credit delivery procedures of small, medium, and large farming communities and micro small enterprises and also the use of information technology and communication solutions. The Indian Bank's Associations revised the guidelines on the priority sector lending were issued on July 20, 2012, in which overall target under priority sector is retained at 40 per cent and targets for both direct and indirect agricultural lending have also been kept unchanged.

The flow of credit to agriculture sector is concerned; a target of 4,750 billion for agriculture credit in 2011-12 was announced in the Union Budget. Against this target banks including cooperative banks and RRBs disbursed to the extend of 5,110 billion accounting 108 per cent of the target as at the end of March 2012, the government has fixed a target of 5,750 billion for distribution to agriculture by all agencies. Banks have also been asked to step up direct lending to agriculture and credit to small and marginal farmers.

NSSO data represent that 45.9 million farmer households in the country (51.4%) out of a total of 89.3 million households do not access credit, either from institutional or non –institutional sources. The main reason for financial exclusion is the lack of a regular or substantial income. The financial inclusion is characterised primarily as either general access to loans or access to savings accounts.

According to World Bank (2008) a report states, "Financial inclusion, or broad access of financial services, is defined as an absence of price or non price barriers in the use of financial services."

According to Chekravarthy financial inclusion means, "it is the process of ensuring access to appropriate financial services and products needed by all sections of the society in general and vulnerable groups such as weaker sections and low income groups in particular at an affordable cost in a fair and transparent manner by mainstream institutional players".

According to C. Rangarajan (January 2008) there is an increasing gap with an increased range of personal finance options for a segment of high and upper middle income groups and significantly large sections of population who lack access to even the most basic banking services. This is termed as 'financial inclusion'. These people mainly living on low income, can not access main stream financial products such as bank accounts, credit, remittances and payment services, financial advisory services, insurance facilities etc. A basic no frills banking account for making and receiving payments, a serving product suited to the pattern of cash flow of a poor household, money transfer facilities, small loans and overdrafts for productive, personal and other purposive insurance etc. Banking technology transformed into the channels like Automated Teller Machines (ATMs) credit/ debt cards internet banking, online money transfers etc. The technology is also restricted to certain segment of society and it has increasingly sophisticated customer segmentation, which create targeting sections of the market and leading to restricted access to financial services for the some groups.

Reserve Bank of India also defined the financial inclusion that implies the provision of financial services like credit card, remittance and overdraft facilities for the rural poor. Financial inclusion helps to increase credit deposit ratio, encroach of un banked areas, opening branches in those areas and improves the inadequate flow of credit to agriculture. Micro Small Medium enterprises, handicrafts, and handloom sectors were cited as areas of concern and more loans to farmers.

The intend of financial inclusion, the RBI in 2005 advised the banks to make available a basic banking No-Frills (NF) account with low or nil minimum stipulated balances and charges. These NF Accounts, similar to savings accounts of banks were to improve the outreach of the financial services to vast sections of the population. The Union Finance Minister Pranab Mukherejee said "Financial inclusion is a necessary for economic growth. Out of the six lakh habitats, only 13 per cent have debit cards and 2 per cent carry credit cards. The facilities like issue of General Purpose Credit Cards (GCCs), small doses of overdraft, loans, savings, Electronic Benefit Transfer (EBT) i.e. payments for National Rural Employment Guarantee Scheme (NREGS), or government schemes, Micro insurance are being initiated.

Usha Thorat (2006) said that introduction of IT enabled financial inclusion would facilitate easy payments to beneficiaries under various schemes of the state and central governments.

Objectives

The present paper entitled "Impact of Institutional Credit on Agriculture and Rural Development in India – A measure of Financial Inclusion" comprised of the following objectives. They are:

1. To examine and estimate the performance of institutional credit providers and its influence on agriculture and rural development.
2. To examine the performance of SHG Bank Linkages and Regional Rural Banks.
3. To estimate the direct finance to farmers on the size of land holdings.
4. To estimate agriculture and allied sector GDP by Loans and advances from PACS, SCARDBs and PCARDBs.

Hypotheses

The hypotheses have been framed based on the above objectives:

1. Loans extended by RRBs, Cooperative Banks, Scheduled Commercial Banks positively influencing agriculture and allied sectors in the rural economy.
2. Loans and advances of PACS, SCARDBs, and PCARDBs are contributing growth of agriculture and allied sector in rural areas.
3. Direct finance to farmers based on the size of land holdings also influencing positively to increase the production.

Methodology

This article is based on the secondary data from the latest Reserve Bank of India report on Statistics of Indian Economy. The data has been collected from 1991-92 to 2010-11 comprised of 20 years. Log Linear Multiple Regression Analysis has been used to estimate the coefficients of independent variables such loans extended by Regional Rural Banks, Cooperative Banks, Scheduled Commercial Banks and loans also extended by Primary Agricultural Cooperative Societies, State Cooperatives Agricultural and Rural Development Banks etc.based on the size of landholdings of the farmers. All these financial institutions extending credit facilities delivery mechanism which are directly influencing the production of agriculture and allied activities in the country. Log linear regression model is specified below:

$$\text{Ln AGDP}_t = \beta_1 + \beta_2\text{Ln (CRRBs)}_{2t} + \beta_3\text{Ln (OLCCOS)}_{3t} + \beta_4\text{ Ln (OLSCBs)}_{4t} + \beta_5\text{ Ln (OLRRBs)}_{5t} + u_t \text{ ....} \quad (1)$$

$$\text{Ln AGDP}_t = \beta_1 + \beta_2\text{ Ln (PACS)}_{5t} + \beta_6\text{ Ln (SCARDBs)}_{6t} + \beta_7\text{ Ln (PCARDBs)}_{7t} + u_t \text{ ....} \quad (2)$$

$$\text{Ln AGDP}_t = \beta_1 + \beta_2\text{ Ln (Below 2.5 Acre) 2t} + \beta_3\text{ Ln (Between 2.5-5.0 Acre)}_{3t} + \beta_4\text{ Ln (Above 5.0 Acre) 4t} + u_t \text{ ....} \quad (3)$$

In the above equations $\beta_1 + \beta_2$ terms equal to parameters and u equals random disturbance term

Dependent Variable: Agriculture and Allied Sector GDP at constants prices 2004-05.

Independent Variables:

CRRBs = Credit of Regional Rural Banks

OLCCOS = Outstanding Loans of Credit Cooperative Societies

OLSCBs = Outstanding Loans of Scheduled Commercial Banks

OLRRBs = Outstanding Loans of Regional Rural Banks

Below 2.5 Acre, Between 2.5-5.0 Acre and Above 5.0 Acre of land possessed by farmers

PACS = Primary Agricultural Cooperative Societies

SCARDBs = State Cooperatives Agricultural and Rural Development Banks

PCARDBs = Primary Cooperative Agriculture and Rural Development Banks.

Result-1

Table 1: Regression on direct loan of RRBs, Cooperatives Banks, Scheduled Commercial Banks and credit of RRBs

S.No.	*Indicators*	*Coefficients*	*t-Values*	*P. Values*
1.	Credit of Regional Rural Banks	.246	1.289	.216
2.	Outstanding Loans of Credit Cooperative Societies	-.040	-1.225	.238
3.	Outstanding Loans of Scheduled Commercial Banks	-.105	-1.285	.217
4.	Outstanding Loans of RRBs	.048	.203	.842
	Constant	5.175	27.202	.000
	R Square	97.7 %		
	F- Statistic	171.860		
	P-Value	0.000		

Expected GDP of agriculture and allied sector value of dependent variable conditional upon the independent variables fixed values such as credit of RRBs, loan of Cooperative banks, loans of Scheduled commercial banks and loans of RRBs comprised of 0. 246, minus 0.040, minus 0.105 and 0.048 respectively. The partial regression coefficients measure the change in the mean value of dependent variable per unit change in the explanatory variable holding other variables are constant. The multiple coefficient determination R square the average rate of actual GDP of agriculture. The partial regression coefficient of 0.246 means that by holding other three variables constant, the rate of average increase by about 2.46 per cent for every one unit increase in the outstanding credit of RRBs. Like wise by holding the outstanding loans of RRBs, the coefficient value of cooperatives minus 0.048 implies that the actual agriculture GDP decreased by 4.8 per cent for every one percentage point decrease in the anticipated or expected rate of agriculture and allied sector in rural areas. The R square value 0.977 means that all explanatory variables to gather accounts for about 97 per cent of the variation in the actual GDP of agriculture and allied sector, a fairly high amount of explanatory power since the R square can at most be one.

Result 2:

Table 2: Regression on the Loans and advances of PACS, SCARDBs and PCARDBs

S.No.	*Indicators*	*Coefficients*	*t-Values*	*P. Values*
1.	Primary Agriculture Cooperative Societies	.199	4.633	.000
2.	State Cooperative Agriculture and Rural Development Bank	.021	1.514	.148
3.	Primary Cooperative Agriculture and Rural Development Bank	-.038	-.573	.574
	Constant	4.905	61.299	.000
	R Square		93%	
	F- Statistic		76.372	
	P-Value		0.000	

All explanatory variables considered together explain about 93 per cent of variation in the agriculture and allied sectors of GDP in India. The coefficients associated with different explanatory variables are found to significant at different probability levels. The coefficient associated with the Primary Agricultural Cooperative Societies comprised of 0.199, State Cooperative Agriculture and Rural Development Bank with .021 and Primary Cooperative Agriculture and Rural Development bank shows a negative coefficient i.e. -.038, which shows that 19.9 per cent and 2.1 per cent increase and 3.8 per cent decrease in Agriculture and allied sector GDP.

The analysis of the determinants of GDP of Indian agriculture and allied sectors reveals that outstanding loans of from Primary Agriculture Cooperative Societies, State Cooperative Agriculture and Rural Development Bank and Primary Cooperative Agriculture and Rural Development Bank are important factors determining GDP of agriculture and allied sectors.

Result 3

All explanatory variables considered together explain about 94 per cent of variation in the agriculture and allied sectors of GDP in India. The coefficients associated with different explanatory variables are found to significant at different probability levels. The coefficient associated with the land below 2.5 acre comprised of minus.366, between 2.5 to 5.0 acre constitutes .143 and above 5.0 acre with 0416 which means that 36.6 per cent decrease by very small holdings such as below 2.5 acre, nearly 14.3 per cent increase by 2.5 to 5.0 acre of land holdings and 41.6 per cent increase by the landholdings of above 5.0 acre.

Table 3: Regression on the direct finance to farmers on the size of land holdings

S.No.	*Indicators*	*Coefficients*	*t-Values*	*P. Values*
1.	Below 2.5 Acre	-.366	-1.827	.085
2.	Between 2.5-5.0 Acre	.143	.435	.669
3.	Above 5.0 Acre	.416	1.515	.148
	Constant	4.812	22.636	.000
	R Square	94%	-	-
	F- Statistic	88.266	-	-
	P-Value	0.000	-	-

The analysis of the determinants of GDP of Indian agriculture and allied sectors reveals that outstanding loans of attained from the farmers of landholdings of 2.5 to 5.0 acre and above 5.0 acre are important factors determining GDP of agriculture and allied sectors.

Accounts and Deposits of Scheduled Commercial Banks and Population

Table 4 represents the deposits of Scheduled Commercial Banks according to population. The penetration of accounts and deposits in rural is also an important factor of financial inclusion. The number of accounts has been increasing from 5.45 per cent in 1992 to 12.25 per cent in 2010. But it has registered the growth rate of accounts in 2009 at 18.84 per cent in rural areas. The number of accounts in rural area during 2010 is about 30 per cent which is higher than that of semi urban (26%), urban (21%) and metropolitan (23%) respectively. In case of deposits, metropolitan registered the highest share ie.57 per cent, which is followed by 21 per cent in urban, 13 per cent in semi-urban and only 9 per cent in rural areas. The outstanding deposits in rural areas have been at the level of stagnation i.e 154.29 per cent in 1992 and it has slightly increased 15.51 per cent in 2010. The maximum percentage increase took place at 20.23 per cent in 1997, nearly 19.92 per cent in 2008 and 19.93 per cent in 2009 respectively. The lowest rate of growth registered at 5.04 per cent during 1995.

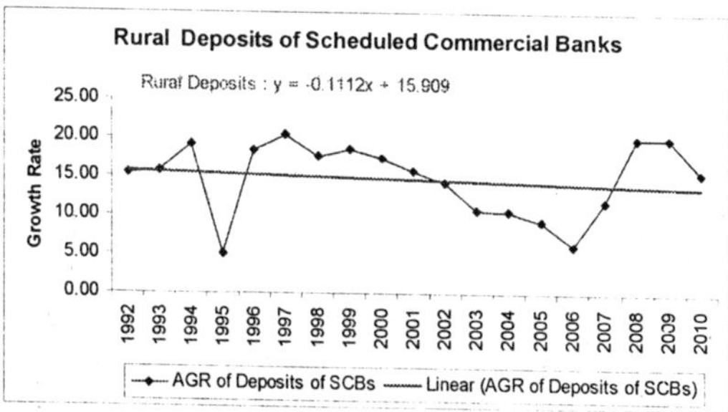

Table-4 : Deposit of Scheduled Commercial Banks - According to Population Group

(Amount in Rupees crore) *(No. of Accounts in Thousands)*

Years	Rural				Semi-urban		Urban		Metropolitan	
	No. Accounts	*AGR*	*Amount Outstanding*	*AGR*	*No. of Accounts*	*Amount Outstanding*	*No. of Accounts*	*Amount Outstanding*	*No. of Accounts*	*Amount Outstanding*
1991	108876		31009.80		98084	41439.17	80889	49140.02	67342	78979.37
1992	114808	5.45	35749.70	15.29	101949	46591.38	83449	55289.40	69553	99476.73
1993	117814	2.62	41409.73	15.83	104023	53584.61	87256	63934.92	70618	116921.21
1994	121299	2.96	49331.14	19.13	108502	63035.46	93032	74248.54	74046	137361.38
1995	109944	-9.36	51819.62	5.04	108129	71464.36	88828	84128.74	83134	171761.42
1996	112904	2.69	61313.17	18.32	109416	83187.34	88452	95565.57	81238	186053.47
1997	116693	3.36	73769.70	20.32	110129	98045.13	88645	112577.67	81112	216163.87
1998	120060	2.89	86706.41	17.54	110705	115644.26	88536	134897.34	80731	259220.60
1999	122660	2.17	102697.07	18.44	112376	136052.49	89533	160181.05	81339	299238.47
2000	125852	2.60	120539.19	17.37	114109	161972.42	89831	188963.44	83023	349944.64
2001	131723	4.67	139431.36	15.67	116400	186188.00	92769	217832.75	87137	405981.19
2002	133000	0.97	159423.46	14.34	117394	214990.39	94622	255478.10	94975	493501.37
2003	136733	2.81	176502.39	10.71	117537	241756.68	96099	290503.36	95711	567433.27
2004	138760	1.48	195081.71	10.53	120651	268216.92	99571	330295.74	98176	717679.01

Table 4 : (contd...)

(Amount in Rupees crore) *(No. of Accounts in Thousands)*

Years	*Rural*				*Semi-urban*		*Urban*		*Metropolitan*	
	No. of Accounts	*AGR*	*Amount Outstanding*	*AGR*	*No. of Accounts*	*Amount Outstanding*	*No. of Accounts*	*Amount Outstanding*	*No. of Accounts*	*Amount Outstanding*
2005	141908	2.27	213104.11	9.24	125198	295685.40	101376	374891.03	98310	863133.51
2006	139570	-1.65	226061.18	6.08	121664	302212.81	106172	430813.23	117692	1132087.02
2007	149663	7.23	253013.69	11.92	132808	357395.14	113422	532592.21	123306	1454043.47
2008	168034	12.27	303423.04	19.92	148361	430279.71	128021	657699.02	137241	1858544.40
2009	199695	18.84	363910.19	19.93	169725	529758.39	142272	822913.61	150611	2205398.63
2010	224155	12.25	420337.72	15.51	189457	614047.18	152323	944992.24	168934	2581651.91

Source : Basic Statistical Returns of Scheduled Commercial Banks in India, DSIM.

Note : Data as on last Friday of June from 1980 to 1989 and as on 31st March from 1990 onwards.

Self-Help Group Bank Linkage Programme

The poor households in rural areas under SHGs are engaging in micro enterprises which are linked to their livelihood. The micro enterprises as a lot of potential and a source of employment, easy to entry, low level of capital to invest, micro credit support to SHGs with other extension supports such as skill up gradation, enhancing abilities, along with necessary infrastructure and marketing support which helps SHGs to cross the barriers that keep them below poverty line.

An innovative credit facility the self help Group (SHGs) approach introduced in 1992 to link poor people with banks exclusively women groups. This approach does not involve any subsidy. SHGs have been perceptible and desirable changes in the living standards of SHG members in terms of ownership of assets, borrowing capacities, income generating activities, income levels and increase in savings. The table 5 represents number of SHGs, Bank loan and refinance for its members. From 2006-07 onwards, data on number of SHGs financed by banks and bank loans are inclusive of Swarnajayanti Gram Swarozgar Yojna (SGSY) and extending groups receiving loans repeatedly.

Table 5 : Self-Help Group-Bank Linkage Rogramme

(Amount in Rupees crore)

Year (End - March)	*No. of SHGs Financed by Banks*		*Bank Loan*		*Refinance*	
	During the year	*AGR*	*During the year*	*AGR*	*During the year*	*AGR*
1992-93	255		0.29		0.27	
1993-94	365	43.14	0.36	24.14	0.19	-29.63
1994-95	1502	311.51	1.79	397.22	1.67	778.95
1995-96	2635	75.43	3.62	102.23	3.53	111.38
1996-97	3841	45.77	5.78	59.67	4.99	41.36
1997-98	5719	48.89	11.92	106.23	10.74	115.23
1998-99	18678	226.60	33.31	179.45	30.70	185.85
1999-00	81780	337.84	135.91	308.02	98.04	219.35
2000-01	149050	82.26	287.89	111.82	250.61	155.62
2001-02	197653	32.61	545.47	89.47	395.76	57.92
2002-03	255882	29.46	1022.33	87.42	622.30	57.24
2003-04	361731	41.37	1855.53	81.50	705.40	13.35
2004-05	539365	49.11	2994.26	61.37	967.80	37.20
2005-06	620109	14.97	4499.00	50.25	1067.70	10.32
2006-07	1105749	78.32	6570.00	46.03	1292.86	21.09
2007-08	1227770	11.04	8849.26	34.69	1615.50	24.96
2008-09	1609586	31.10	12253.51	38.47	2620.03	62.18
2009-10	1586822	-1.41	14453.30	17.95	3173.56	21.13

Source : NABARD.

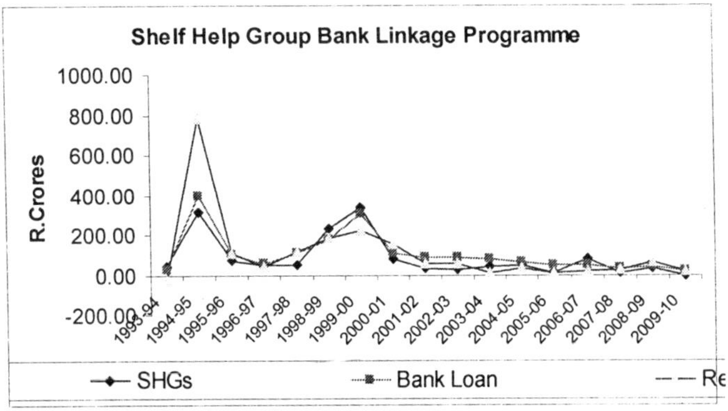

Banking Indicators of Regional Rural Banks

Table 6 envisaged the important indicators of Regional Rural Banks and

Table 6: Important Banking Indicators - Regional Rural Banks – Outstanding

(Rupees crore)

Years	*Demand Deposits*	*Time Deposits*	*Aggregate Deposits*	*AGR*	*Bank Credit*	*AGR*
1990-91	941	3619	4560		3497	
1991-92	1044	4227	5271	15.59	3951	12.98
1992-93	1093	5277	6370	20.85	4451	12.66
1993-94	1394	6651	8045	26.30	5024	12.87
1994-95	2115	8733	10848	34.84	6201	23.43
1995-96	2475	10895	13370	23.25	7289	17.55
1996-97	2947	14025	16971	26.93	8544	17.22
1997-98	3805	17173	20977	23.60	9687	13.38
1998-99	4688	20740	25428	21.22	11016	13.72
1999-00	5105	24946	30051	18.18	12663	14.95
2000-01	6098	29897	35995	19.78	15211	20.12
2001-02	7305	35189	42494	18.06	18033	18.55
2002-03	8513	39131	47644	12.12	21359	18.44
2003-04	10727	42663	53390	12.06	25057	17.31
2004-05	12757	45529	58286	9.17	31651	26.32
2005-06	17355	46840	64195	10.14	36050	13.90
2006-07	20003	61617	81620	27.14	48420	34.31
2007-08	21022	73390	94412	15.67	57417	18.58
2008-09	24353	89475	113828	20.57	64011	11.48
2009-10	28710	107104	135814	19.32	79086	23.55
2010-11	33663	123039	156702	15.38	94626	19.65

Source: Reserve Bank of India , NABARD.

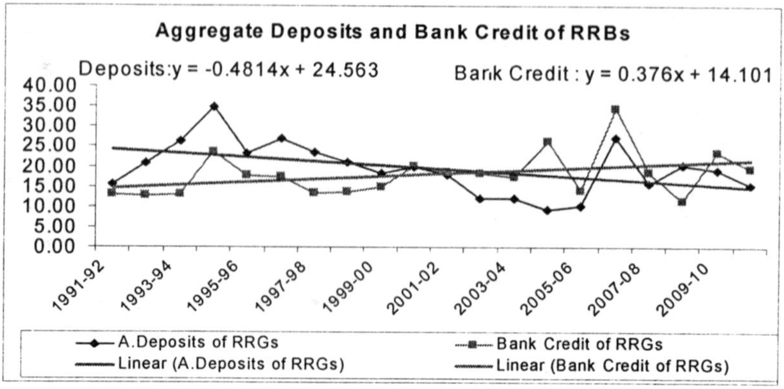

its outstanding deposits and credit for rural development. It shows the time deposits are higher than that of demand deposits. The annual growth of aggregate deposits over a period of 20 years from 1991-92 to 2010-11 have registered at non increasing level indicating extent of stagnation of deposits in RRBs for rural development. This shows even though they are meant for development, deposit rate has not been satisfactory level. In terms of bank credit of RRBs, a continuous increasing level from 12.98 per cent in 1991-92 to 19.65 per cent in 2010-11 and the highest growth has recorded at 34.31 per cent in 2006-07 and the lowest in 2008-09. Therefore, the credit of RRBs has been increasing level due to several governmental efforts to extend credit facilities to rural people in India.

Direct Institutional Credit for Agriculture and Allied Activities

Table 7 presents the institutional credit for agriculture and allied activities both in short and long term. As high as 70 per cent growth rate in loans issued registered in 2005-06 by scheduled commercial banks and 77 per cent in 1991-92 and 66.23 per cent in 2004-05 by Regional Rural Banks. The direct institutional credit of RRBs has been the strong support for agriculture and allied activities in rural areas. Outstanding loans of Scheduled Commercial Banks accounted for 71 per cent share, and only 18 per cent loans by Cooperative Banks and 11 per cent share of loans by RRBs respectively. Annual growth rate of outstanding credit by RRBs has been continuously increasing during 1990-91 to 2009-10.

Table-7 : Direct Institutional Credit For Agriculture And Allied Activities

(Short-term and Long-term) (Rupees crore)

Year	*Loans Issued*								*Loans Outstanding*							
	Co-operatives	*AGR*	*SCBs*	*AGR*	*RRBs*	*AGR*	*Total*	*AGR*	*Co-operatives*	*AGR*	*SCBs*	*AGR*	*RRBs*	*AGR*	*Total*	*AGR*
1990-91	4819		4676		335		**10188**		10531		17032		1753		**29316**	
1991-92	5797	20.29	4806	2.78	596	77.91	**11538**	13.25	12176	15.62	16981	-0.30	1984	13.18	**31142**	6.23
1992-93	6484	11.85	4960	3.20	698	17.11	**12530**	8.60	13769	13.08	18288	7.70	2206	11.19	**34263**	10.02
1993-94	8484	30.85	5400	8.87	752	7.74	**15013**	19.82	15316	11.24	19113	4.51	2560	16.05	**36988**	7.95
1994-95	9876	16.41	7408	37.19	1083	44.02	**18773**	25.04	16810	9.75	20920	9.45	3009	17.54	**40738**	10.14
1995-96	12483	26.40	9274	25.19	1381	27.52	**23692**	26.20	19126	13.78	23427	11.98	3467	15.22	**46020**	12.97
1996-97	13254	6.18	10675	15.11	1748	26.57	**26345**	11.20	20556	7.48	26327	12.38	4038	16.47	**50921**	10.65
1997-98	14159	6.83	11537	8.07	2103	20.31	**28656**	8.77	21390	4.06	28445	8.04	4683	15.97	**54518**	7.06
1998-99	15099	6.64	14663	27.10	2515	19.59	**32697**	14.10	22199	3.78	29819	4.83	5389	15.08	**57408**	5.30
1999-00	25678	70.06	16350	11.51	2985	18.69	**45534**	39.26	41950	88.97	33442	12.15	5991	11.17	**81383**	41.76
2000-01	27295	6.30	16440	0.55	3966	32.86	**48187**	5.83	46135	9.98	38270	14.44	7249	21.00	**91654**	12.62
2001-02	30569	11.99	18638	13.37	4546	14.62	**54195**	12.47	52110	12.95	45106	17.86	8286	14.31	**105502**	15.11
2002-03	34040	11.35	25256	35.51	5879	29.32	**65175**	20.26	59064	13.34	53804	19.28	10261	23.84	**123129**	16.71
2003-04	40049	17.65	36203	43.34	7175	22.04	**83427**	28.00	71403	20.89	68103	26.58	11721	14.23	**151228**	22.82

Table 7 (contd...)

Year	*Loans Issued*								*Loans Outstanding*							
	Co-operatives	*AGR*	*SCBs*	*AGR*	*RRBs*	*AGR*	*Total*	*AGR*	*Co-oper-atives*	*AGR*	*SCBs*	*AGR*	*RRBs*	*AGR*	*Total*	*AGR*
2004-05	45009	12.38	48367	33.60	11927	66.23	**105303**	26.22	78822	10.39	95519	40.26	16709	42.56	**191050**	26.33
2005-06	48123	6.92	80599	66.64	15300	28.28	**144021**	36.77	82327	4.45	135603	41.96	21510	28.73	**239439**	25.33
2006-07	54019	12.25	115266	43.01	20228	32.21	**189513**	31.59	89443	8.64	169018	24.64	27452	27.62	**285913**	19.41
2007-08	57643	6.71	113472	-1.56	23838	17.85	**194953**	2.87	65666	-26.58	202796	19.98	33216	21.00	**301678**	5.51
2008-09	58787	1.98	160690	41.61	26499	11.16	**245976**	26.17	64045	-2.47	256119	26.29	37367	12.50	**357531**	18.51
2009-10	74938	27.47			34640	30.72	.		76480	19.42	309442		46282	23.86	.	

Source: Reserve Bank of India , NABARD.

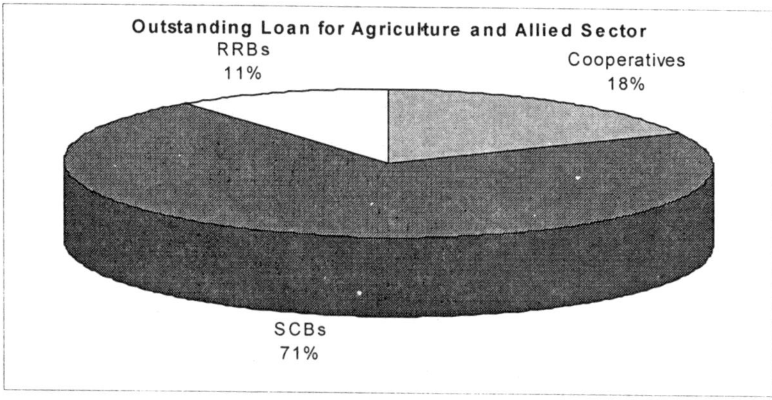

Loans and Advances of PACS, SCARDBs and PCARDBs

Table 8 represents loans and advances of Primary Agricultural Credit Societies, State Cooperative Agriculture and Rural Development Bank and Primary Cooperative Agricultural and Rural Development Banks in the country. A maximum of 73 per cent outstanding loans are covered by PACS during 1009-10, nearly 16 per cent share is covered by SCARDBs and only 11 per cent PCARDBs respectively.

As for as annual growth rate of Primary Agricultural Credit Societies are concerned, a maximum of 91.66 per cent registered in 1999-2000, but overall period of 20 years it is not conducive growth for agriculture and rural development. So far as SCARDBs and PCARDBs are demonstrated very well in the first 10 years, latter their role in extending loans and advances has been at declining trend.

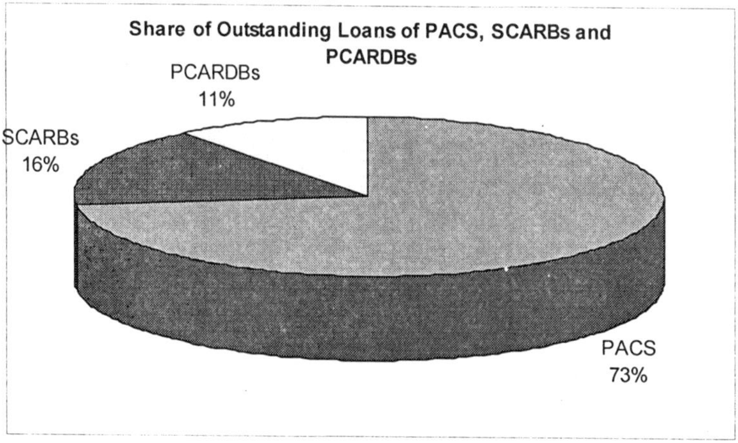

Table 8: Loans and Advances of PACS, SCARDBs and PCARDBs

(Numbers in million; Amount in crore)

Years	*PACS*				*SCARDs*				*PCARDBs*			
	Loan	*AGR*	*Outstanding*	*AGR*	*Loan*	*AGR*	*Outstanding*	*AGR*	*Loan*	*AGR*	*Outstanding*	*AGR*
1990-91	4311		6486		384		1348		376		2014	
1991-92	5575	29.32	8177	26.07	300	-21.88	30	-97.77	444	18.09	2143	6.41
1992-93	6223	11.62	10245	25.29	415	38.33	1906	6253.33	542	22.07	2480	15.73
1993-94	7158	15.02	9399	-8.26	469	13.01	2091	9.71	612	12.92	2701	8.91
1994-95	8312	16.12	9996	6.35	566	20.68	2500	19.56	651	6.37	2709	0.30
1995-96	10552	26.95	12980	29.85	1798	217.67	6857	174.28	1219	87.25	4098	51.27
1996-97	11292	7.01	13345	2.81	2151	19.63	8016	16.90	1455	19.36	4936	20.45
1997-98	12137	7.48	13994	4.86	2295	6.69	9182	14.55	1593	9.48	5840	18.31
1998-99	12743	4.99	14894	6.43	2437	6.19	10442	13.72	1692	6.21	6819	16.76
1999-00	23662	85.69	28546	91.66	2532	3.90	11598	11.07	1818	7.45	7574	11.07
2000-01	25698	8.60	34522	20.93	2586	2.13	12596	8.60	1866	2.64	8276	9.27
2001-02	30770	19.74	40779	18.12	2746	6.19	14110	12.02	2045	9.59	10005	20.89
2002-03	33996	10.48	42411	4.00	2962	7.87	15333	8.67	2151	5.18	10809	8.04
2003-04	35119	3.30	43873	3.45	2942	-0.68	16221	5.79	2197	2.14	11336	4.88

Table 8 (contd...)

(Numbers in million; Amount in crore)

Years	*PACS*				*SCARDs*				*PCARDBs*			
	Loan	*AGR*	*Outstanding*	*AGR*	*Loan*	*AGR*	*Outstanding*	*AGR*	*Loan*	*AGR*	*Outstanding*	*AGR*
2004-05	39211	11.65	48785	11.20	2291	-22.13	17404	7.29	2506	14.06	12633	11.44
2005-06	42920	9.46	51779	6.14	2907	26.89	17678	1.57	2296	-8.38	12870	1.88
2006-07	49613	15.59	58620	13.21	2436	-16.20	18644	5.46	1970	-14.20	12179	-5.37
2007-08	57643	16.19	65666	12.02	2221	-8.83	18327	-1.70	1822	-7.51	11800	-3.11
2008-09	58787	1.98	64045	-2.47	2585	16.39	16279	-11.17	2045	12.24	11229	-4.84
2009-10	74935	27.47	76480	19.42	3205	23.98	16999	4.42	2465	20.54	11512	2.52

Source : National Bank for Agriculture and Rural Development, National Federation of State Co-operative Banks.

Direct Finance to farmers based on size of landholdings

Table 9 presents SCBs Direct Finance to Farmers according to size of land holdings in India. Number of accounts of the farmers' up to 2.5 acre constitutes 36 per cent of the total, the farmers with 2.5 acre to 5.0 acre land who possessed 30 per cent of accounts and the farmers above 5 acres comprised of 34 per cent during 2008-09 in India. In the same manner the direct finance to farmers also expressed that a maximum of the farmers above 5 acre landholders attained 46 per cent of the share of finance and the group of farmers up 2.5 acre and farmers between 2.5 acre to 5.0 acre have the share of 27 per cent each. Up to 2.5 acre farmers accounts are more but attained less share of finance by the SCBs during 2008-09, but a continuous increase of growth rate in finance has registered positively. Even in case of the farmers between 2.5 acre to 5.0 acre who are more in the share of accounts than in direct finance and its growth rate also continuously increasing trend. In case of the farmers above 5 acres who are more share in finance than that of number of accounts.

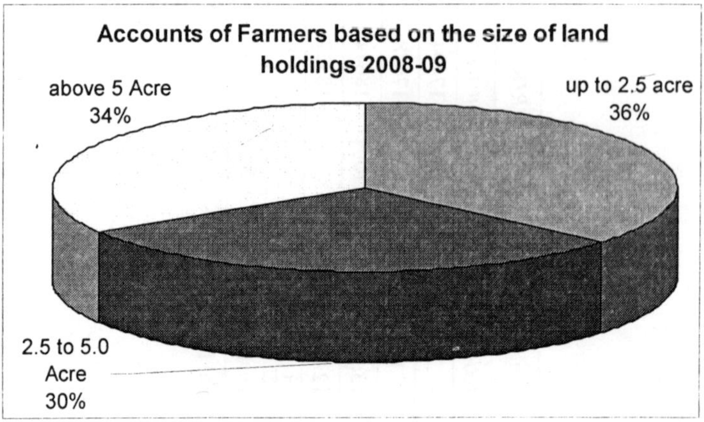

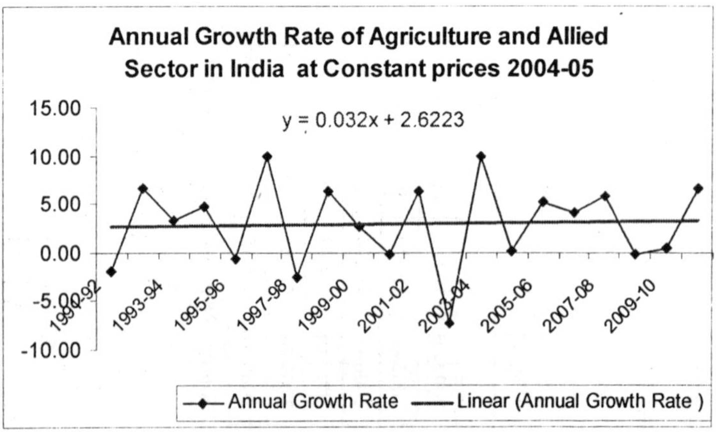

Table 9 : Scheduled Commercial Banks' Direct Finance to Farmers According to Size of Land Holdings (Outstanding) Short-Term and Long-Term Loans

(Number of accounts in thousands; Amount in crore)

Years (end-June)	*Up to 2.5 Acres*			*Above 2.5 acres*			*Above 5 Acres*			*Total*		
	Number of Accounts	*Amount*	*AGR*	*Number of Accounts*	*Amount*	*AGR*	*Number of Accounts*	*Amount*	*AGR*	*Number of Accounts*	*Amount*	*AGR*
1990-91	6137	2895	-	4346	2870	-	3563	6624	-	**14045**	**12389**	-
1991-92	6063	3239	11.88	4439	3050	6.27	3669	7058	6.55	**14170**	**13346**	7.72
1992-93	6057	3437	6.11	4460	3328	9.11	3878	7444	5.47	**14395**	**14210**	6.47
1993-94	6007	3595	4.60	4282	3411	2.49	3637	7902	6.15	**13926**	**14908**	4.91
1994-95	5463	3889	8.18	4047	3659	7.27	3492	8359	5.78	**13002**	**15906**	6.69
1995-96	5557	4326	11.24	4255	4295	17.38	3461	9265	10.84	**13273**	**17885**	12.44
1996-97	5296	4894	13.13	4219	5033	17.18	3575	10469	13.00	**13090**	**20396**	14.04
1997-98	4890	5058	3.35	4034	5442	8.13	3354	11752	12.26	**12278**	**22252**	9.10
1998-99	4408	5511	8.96	3711	5680	4.37	3389	12651	7.65	**11507**	**23842**	7.15
1999-00	4544	6185	12.23	3777	6445	13.47	3379	14719	16.35	**11700**	**27349**	14.71
2000-01	4600	7215	16.65	3689	7308	13.39	3555	16963	15.25	**11844**	**31486**	15.13
2001-02	4902	8759	21.40	3961	9686	32.54	3394	19083	12.50	**12257**	**37529**	19.19

Table 9 : (contd...)

(Number of accounts in thousands; Amount in crore)

Years (end-June)	Up to 2.5 Acres			Above 2.5 acres			Above 5 Acres			Total		
	Number of Accounts	Amount	AGR	Number of Accounts	Amount	AGR	Number of Accounts	Amount	AGR	Number of Accounts	Amount	AGR
2002-03	4749	9813	12.03	4092	11316	16.83	3835	23831	24.88	**12676**	**44961**	19.80
2003-04	6086	14805	50.87	4806	13974	23.49	4377	28786	20.79	**15268**	**57565**	28.03
2004-05	7299	20499	38.46	5874	20759	48.55	5274	37218	29.29	**18447**	**78476**	36.33
2005-06	8239	29719	44.98	6677	29255	40.93	6321	52769	41.78	**21237**	**111743**	42.39
2006-07	9954	37336	25.63	7548	37815	29.26	6985	64810	22.82	**24487**	**139961**	25.25
2007-08	11345	46457	24.43	9512	46631	23.31	8739	80956	24.91	**29596**	**174044**	24.35
2008-09	11708	60199	29.58	9570	59792	28.22	10884	99349	22.72	**32162**	**219340**	26.03

Source : National Bank for Agriculture and Rural Development, National Federation of State.

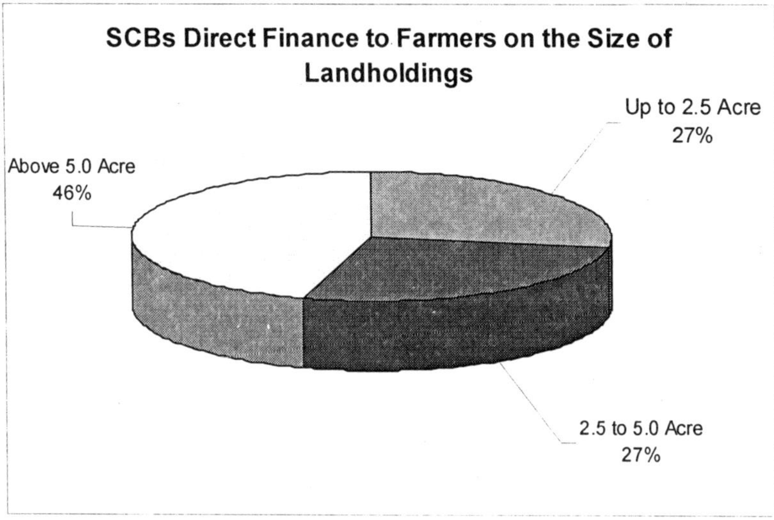

Conclusions

The institutional credit has more significant role to promote the economic activities in agriculture and allied activities in rural areas. The evidence shows that increasing demand can be seen in terms of penetration of number of accounts in the banks. The log linear regression analysis revealed that inducing rural households through formation and nurturing self help groups, RRBs, SCBs, COOBs, providing credit facilities for agriculture and rural development activities would positively influence financial inclusion from credit facility and other rural development programme perspectives. Collectively, all the independent variables influence on the size of financial inclusion with reference to loans and credit explaining 97 per cent of variation, Primary Agriculture Credit Societies, State Cooperative Agriculture and 'Rural Development Bank explaining 73 per cent variation, and credit on the size of land holding at 74 per cent variation respectively. The F-test also found to be significant at one per cent level, which suggests that there exits a strong association between the financial inclusion and the selected set of independent variables.

There is need to establish Financial Literacy and Credit Counseling Centers to provide free financial literacy, education and credit counseling in rural and semi urban areas. Revival of Rural Co-operative Credit Structure is a need of improvement in legal and institutional reforms in a democratic self reliant and efficient functioning to improve the quality financial services.

References

1. Asli Demirguc-Kunt and Klapper, L. (2012) "Measuring Financial Inclusion", Policy Research Paper, 6025, World Bank, April.

2. Nirupam Mehratro, V. Puhazhendhi, Gopakurmarn Nair, B.B. Shahoo (2009) "Financial Inclusion- An Overview" NABARD of Economic Analysis and Research, Mumbai.
3. Priya Basu (2005) World Bank and the National Council of Applied Economic Research, New Delhi.
4. Rangarajan.C (2008) Report of the Committee on Financial Inclusion, New Delhi.
5. RBI (2011) Handbook of Statistics on Indian Economy, 2010-11 Mumbai.
6. Smt. Usha Thorat, Deputy Governor, Reserve Bank of India as circulated at the Annual Banksers's Conference 2006, Hyderabad on November 4, 2006.
7. World Bank Report (2008), Finance for all, Policies and Pit falls in Expanding Access,
8. Report on An Evaluation of State Implementation Models (March 2011) Delivering Financial Inclusion Services to Rural Citizens through the Common Service Centers.

2

Financial Inclusion of the Poor through Rural Credit for Inclusive Growth

S.N. Tripathy and *M.G. Basava Raja*

Introduction

The significance of provision for credit as an instrument for socio-economic change is being widely recognised. Despite high density of rural retail outlets of formal financial institutions the presence of informal lenders continued to exist in spite of their exorbitant interest rates and other terms of credit. This is mainly due to their proximity, feel at ease, and all time access and purpose free credit. As of late 1990s about 34 per cent of the rural households, particularly economically weaker sections, are indebted to the money lenders and their lending was rarely for any productive investments. For any kind of economic activity some sort of financial service is indispensable no matter how rudimentary it is. A wide network of rural bank branches have been involved in implementing a wide variety of poverty alleviation programmes, nevertheless a sizeable number of poor remain outside the fold of the formal banking system and perhaps it could be due to the fact that the deposit and loan products are not ideally suited to meet the most immediate needs of the poor. The existing land tenure system and collateral based lending policies of the formal financial institutions also elude a large number of marginal farmers in the rural area. Besides, other major problems with the rural environment faced by these institutions are the lower spatial density of clients, irregular cash flows, lower human capital, bad debts, limited economic opportunities, high transaction costs in small lending, high perceived risks and so on. Owning to the poor performance of formal institutions in providing financial services to the rural areas and the poorer sections of the society, the Government of India contemplated in the late eighties to promote another apex bank to take care of financial needs of the poor, informal sector and rural areas. At that point of time NABARD initiated a search for alternative methods to fulfill the financial needs of the rural poor and informal sector. The decline of cooperatives in the sixties and seventies is widely attributed to the government's direct promotional role, their artificial propping up through subsidies and undue interference in management. As a result the NABARD wanted to develop the new channel, which is free from government subsidies and interference. Meanwhile, development workers across the country have been targeting "groups" of the poor and disadvantaged as a bulwark against social inequities. The consequent social capital is the only capital that the poor can rely on and use (not without cost) as a hedge against their resource deficient condition and powerlessness. Despite the decline of the cooperatives, the search for an appropriate community-based structure continued and women's groups called self-help groups (SHGs) emerged in the late eighties and the early nineties around rotating mutual savings and credit, as a stable and viable alternative. In its search for alternative channels to reach the un-reach, the NABARD found SHGs as an interesting and effective means to provide the banking services to 'so called' 'un-bankable' people. The NABARD initiated the pilot project of SHG bank linkage in the year 1992. Soon it became regular banking program and an important component in the priority sector lending. Since then the growth of bank linkage has been phenomenal. The number of groups linked has doubled every year for about a decade and the loan amount has doubled every year for more than a decade, between 1992-93 and 2003-04 (NABARD). Though the growth rate has decelerated a little in recent years, the absolute loan amount has been increasing by higher amounts year after year.

The credit policy for the poor involves many practical difficulties arises from operation followed by financial institutions and the economic characteristics and financing needs of low-income households. For example, commercial banking institutions require that borrowers have a stable source of income out of which principal and interest can be paid back according to the agreed terms. However, the income of many self employed households is not stable. A huge number of micro loans are needed to serve the poor, but banking institution prefers dealing with big loans in small numbers to minimise administration expenses. They also look for collateral with a clear title - which many low-income households do not have. In addition bankers tend to consider low income households a bad risk imposing exceedingly high information monitoring costs on operation. The impact of microfinance on poverty reduction has been measured in terms of several dimensions, such as improved income, employment and household expenditure, and reduced vulnerability to economic and social crisis. These measurements have tended to focus on a specific geographic area, an institution or a small client group and are difficult to generalise or draw conclusions that reach across borders, income levels, gender or socio-economic status. 'Micro Finance' (MF) in recent decades occupied a very important position in India as well as other parts of South East Asia since the formal financial institutions[1] were not able to cater completely to the small and frequent credit needs of most of the poor. Microfinance assumed prominence in some developing countries like Bangladesh, Brazil, and India in the 1970s. In India, microfinance has been in existence in some form or the other for several centuries. Traditional moneylenders have been providing credit to those in needs and the money lending activity still continues to be a very important aspect of rural financial landscape. In the middle and later part of 1970s, some NGOs in collaboration with National Bank for Agriculture and Rural development (NABARD) initiated the Self Help Group (SHG) Model for delivering microfinance. The SHG model became very popular and was widely replicated by various other NGOs. NGOs played the role of facilitators, provided capacity building services to the groups and helped them by providing bank linkages with an active support from NABARD. Thus, the failure of formal institutions to provide the credit to the poor, the alternative models were on search that finally 'micro finance' took its course and shape has taken place after the task force suggested to form a study group in 1987 and accepted its some recommendations. The year 1992 is a land mark in history of micro finance movement in India because the National Bank for Agricultural and Rural Development (NABARD) undertook a pilot project which designed Self help group (SHG) - bank linkage programme (SBLP)[2]. Recently, the Micro finance MFIs have widened their scope that involve various activities including poverty alleviation programme, but one of the ILO studies found that MFIs succeeded only where the legal framework was in place[3]. Nevertheless, MFIs play an important role as financial intermediaries in microfinance sector. MFIs mainly operate under four legal frames as under:

(i) NGO MFIs – Registered under Societies Registration Act, 1860 and/ or Indian Trust Act, 1880.

(ii) Cooperative MFIs – Registered under State Cooperative Societies Act or Mutually Aided Cooperative Societies Act (MACS) or Multi-State Coop. Societies Act, 2002.

(iii) NBFC MFIs- Registered under Section 25 of Companies Act, 1956 (Not for profit).

NBFC MFIs - Incorporated under Companies Act, 1956 and registered with RBI:

The above state of affairs above supplemented a new dimension in the rural credit delivery system viz., the intermediation of a local institution between the formal financial institution and the individual borrower by offering various financial services. These intermediaries are mostly Non-Governmental Organisations. What is implied by intermediation in this context is the to various functions and services like promoting saving habits, programme linkages with higher level constituents, imparting training and education, providing external funding wherever indispensable, identifying economic activities at the local level, making credit available so as to improve the economic and social conditions of the poor.

The purview of livelihood finance also embraces agricultural and business development services like productivity enhancement, risk mitigation, other than insurance (such as vaccination of livestock), local value addition, and alternate market linkages. In its fold it also covers institutional development services like-forming and strengthening of various producer organisations such as self-help groups, water users' associations, forest protection committees, credit and commodity cooperatives, panchayats.

Thus, it is evident from the foregoing analysis that social banking in India has a long history in terms of expanding rural bank branches, priority sector targeting and lending, subsidy oriented credit programme, and interest rate policies etc. to serve the economically weaker rural households. But such programmes could make only very little impact on poverty alleviation. The myth that poor households are not credit worthy or able to save has been negated by the emergence of NGO sponsored micro credit and saving programme commonly known as Self Help Groups (SHGs) which came into existence during early 90s. Subsequently these groups got linked with banks for financial services. The NGOs play the role of a financial intermediary between the group and the banks. The credit extended to the group facilitate investment opportunities both individually and collectively, diversification of economic activities and reduce the dependence on informal money lenders who offer high cost loans.

Finance Facility to MFIs

RBI had issued a guideline[4] to all scheduled commercial banks including RRBs in 2000 for providing financial help to MFIs, since then, MFIs have been availing bulk loans from banks for on-lending to SHGs and other small borrowers. The recent data stated that during 2008-09, 10 Public Sector Commercial Banks, 10 private sector Commercial Banks, 4 foreign Commercial Banks, 9 Regional Rural Banks (RRBs) had reportedly financed to MFIs for on-lending for microfinance activities. During the year 2008-09, the banks financed 581 MFIs with bank loans of Rs. 3,732.33 crore as against 518 MFIs with bank loans of Rs. 1,970.15 crore during 2007-08, thus achieving a growth rate of 12.2% (No. of MFIs) and 89.4% (Bank Loans disbursed to MFIs). As on 31 March 2009, the outstanding bank loans to 1915 MFIs was Rs. 5009.09 crore as against Rs. 2748.84 crore to 1109 MFIs as on 31 March 2008. So, in in terms of disbursement the bank-MFIs partnership has achieved new horizon and outlook for reaching credit to the poor beneficiaries.

Microfinance, as defined by the National Bank of Agriculture and Rural Development (NABARD), is the "provision of thrift, credit and other financial services and products of very small amounts to the poor in rural, semi-urban or urban areas for enabling them to raise their income levels and improve living standards" (Nanda 1999). It encompasses a wide variety of schemes, including savings, insurance, credit and other risk management instruments (Ananth and George 2003) that are usually extended by banks, microfinance institutions (MFIs) or non-governmental organisations (NGOs). In recent decades, there has been much interest generated in the field of microfinance, as it has been accepted as a tool to alleviate poverty, particularly in developing nations.

Vulnerability of the Rural Poor and the Rationale for Microfinance

Banks must continue to play a crucial role in the rural outreach and must promote rural friendly banking plans. In this context, microfinance allows rural communities to reduce their vulnerability. Vulnerability is defined by the World Bank as the "risk of experiencing poverty and the probability of being exposed to a number of other risks such as violence, crime and natural disasters" (Shalizi, Chomitz et. al. 2003). Risk can afflict the poor, particularly rural communities, through natural disasters, illness, death in the family, lack of skills in the operation of enterprises and through social factors such as the caste system in India (Duggal, Ananth et al. 2002). The only way to lower the risk that the rural poor face would be to reduce their vulnerability through the use of microfinance to engage positively in capacity building. The Indian government has established the National Bank for Agriculture and Rural Development (NABARD) that oversees the linkage of banks and other microfinance institutions and the rural population. The NABARD supports banks to lend to the rural population while providing subsidised refinancing support. In addition, the Reserve Bank of India (RBI), India's central bank, requires that all commercial banks, regional rural banks and co-operatives allocate 40 per cent of their total advances to sectors such as agriculture, small and micro-enterprises, housing loans and microfinance loans, with one per cent specifically allocated to the weakest sectors of the population. types of microfinance institutes. In the initial stage, the group is in the formed of a modified rotating saving and credit association. The group members contribute a specified amount each month (approximately one day's wage) and the savings are allowed to accumulate for approximately six months. After six months, members can borrow from it at an interest rate specified by the NGO and any amount borrowed has to be repaid (Aniket 2005).

The Microfinance as an Alternative

As an alternative to the traditional paradigm, several experiments have been made in the last three decades in the developing countries the world over in order to innovate institutional structures to cater to the need for financial services for low-income populations. Financial services have been provided to an increasing number of low income people because of developments in microfinance. Microfinance refers to that part of financial sector that responds to the financial demand of low-income households. It has now emerged as an effective system for provision of financial services to the poor households, more specifically micro-enterprises. Several variants of microfinance technologies have evolved in the last two decades as also a wide range of institutions. Basically microfinance refers to small scale financial services for both credit and deposits - that are provided to people who farm, fish or herd; operate small or micro enterprises where goods are produced, repaired or recycled or traded; provide services; work for wages or commissions; gain income from renting out small amounts of land, vehicles, draft animals, or machinery and tools; and to other individuals and local groups in developing countries, in both urban and rural areas. The range of services is expanded in the Asian Development Bank (ADB) definition which defines microfinance as the provision of a broad range of services such as deposits, loans, payment services, money transfers, and insurance to poor and low income households and their micro-enterprises. Urban and rural clientele of microfinance are usually located in areas that have a high population density and low income people often engaged in non-farm activities. Generally it is observed that microfinance borrowers tend to be engaged in commercial activities such as street vending. Non-farm business activities generate more regular income and permit repayment in frequent and small installments. As farm sector activities have relatively longer and less stable production cycles few microfinance institutions lend exclusively for agricultural activities. Thus, the microfinance revolution that came to the fore during 1980s and 1990s had largely been an urban phenomenon in most parts of Africa and Latin America. Even where it had entered the rural areas, as in parts of Asia, it confined itself essentially to rural micro-enterprises. As such mainstream agricultural finance remained outside the light of microfinance.

Self Help Groups (SHG s) Banks Linkage Programme

After an action programme in mid eighties, which showed that the credit delivery mechanism for SHGs is effective and can be accepted by the banking system SHG-Bank linkage programme was launched as a pilot project in 1992 for forming and financing SHGs across the country. SHG Bank linkage programme by innovating a novel way of banking with the poor has provided them access to the financial services in a reasonably shorter time and low costs. The National agricultural policy stipulates promotion of micro- Credit as an effective tool for alleviating poverty and development of Self- Help Groups (SHG) Bank linkage system as a supplementary mechanism for bringing the rural poor in to the formal banking system.

The Self Groups (SHGs) shall no more be seen as a cost effective delivery channel for the banks to reach the rural poor. Instead, it is necessary to acknowledge their ability to mobilise resources, undertake income generating activities both individually and collectively, control over economic resources, build linkages with other organisations for their financial and other services. What is intended here is to demonstrate the decisive role played by such financial intermediaries in achieving upliftment of the poorest of the poor in the rural areas through group-based approach. The role of intermediary is very critical in the sense that majority of the rural folks have hardly any asset base and therefore undertaking any viable economic activity at the individual level is very remote. Under such conditions, the first and foremost step of an MFI is in identifying appropriate economic activities at the group level which suit the local conditions and are feasible with the targeted group. Many models and projects have been developed in recent years to simultaneously address the problem of rural poverty, employment, gender issues, empowerment and a host of other related issues. However, such attempts by and large have turned out to be highly optimistic. The role of MFI is very critical in formulating a sustainable program. Very often the target group is mainly women in the rural areas and any sustainable individual activities for them seldom exist. Therefore in most cases they need services in terms of developing technical know-how for developing micro enterprises and production, marketing tie-ups, training, skill development along with credit and saving portfolios. Such strategies were found to have better edge over others. As women's group exclusively dominates the SHGs in general, their empowerment both on the economic and social front is one of the greatest opportunities in the main stream of development activities. Very many such models have been tried out in the past and what is presented below is one such model with proven benefits to the poorest of the poor in the rural areas.

As has been stated earlier, in India, it was in February 1992, NABARD launched a pilot project to link such Self Help Groups (SHGs) with banks. The project was a great success and soon developed into the SHG-bank linkage programme. Under the programme, a group of 15 to 20 persons, generally women from rural areas voluntarily come collectively and form a group. The members should belong to the same social strata and share a common ideology. Economic welfare of all members should be among their aims. The members save a fixed amount at regular intervals, generally monthly, and the collected savings are then used by one or more members of the group who borrow the money and return it later along with interest at predetermined rates. The group determines its internal lending policy as well as interest rates.

After the group has been in existence for some months, it opens a savings bank account with a bank. The bank watches the operations in the account for some time. After it is satisfied about the operations in the account and the credentials of the group, the bank considers the group for lending purposes. The group is eligible for borrowing from the bank in a multiple of its savings. The bank lends to the group, which, in turn, gives loans to its members in accordance with the group's policy. At this stage the group is said to be credit linked, or simply linked, to the bank.

While group formation may take place at the initiative of the members themselves, experience has shown that NGOs, who have a rapport with the people, are better placed to from groups of people for this purpose. Besides helping in formation, these organisations play a useful role in guiding the groups and enabling them to deal with banks and use their funds prudently. Further, some banks have also taken the initiative and formed such SHGs.

Under the SHG-bank linkage programme, three different models of lending have emerged. In the first model, the bank takes the initiative to form the groups, nurture them, open their savings accounts and provide them credit. In the second model, while the groups are formed and nurtured by government, NGOs or community based organisations, the credit facilities are provided by the bank. In the third model, the NGOs that formed and nurtured the groups also act as financial intermediaries. Under this model, banks lend to these intermediaries for onward financing to the groups or their members. In certain areas where a very large number of groups have been financed by banks, intermediate agencies like federations of SHGs have come up as links between banks and the groups. The banks finance these federations which, in turn, finance their member groups. So far, the second model has remained the most popular with over 70 per cent of the total SHGs financed falling under this category.

The 'Task Force on Supportive Policy and Regulatory Framework for Micro-Finance' constituted by NABARD (National Bank for Agriculture and Rural Development) defines "micro-finance as the provision of thrift, saving, credit and financial services and products of very small amounts to the poor in rural, semi-urban and urban areas for enabling them to raise their income levels and improve their standard of living". The emphasis of support under micro-finance is on the poor in 'pre-micro-enterprise' stage for building up their capabilities to handle larger resources. This perception is quite significant, keeping in view the limitations of any approach of micro-enterprise development to help the poorest of the poor for self-employment (Awasthi, 1994 and 1996). The Task Force has not specified limit for the 'small' amount of financial services envisaged.

In a holistic perspective micro-finance is a process of social intermediation and building social capital. Process of social intermediation is an investment that is made for development of both human resources and institutional capital to make marginalised groups self-reliant in preparing them to engage in formal financial intermediation. According to Elaine and Barton (1998), social intermediation is a financial intermediation with a capacity building component, aimed at those sectors of society that lack access to credit and savings facilities. It can be understood by transformation of beneficiaries into clients or customers and creation of local institutions that bridge the gap between the formal financial institutions and marginalised groups. The concept of social capital is the key theoretical element in social intermediation, derived from the anthropological and sociological literature. According to Pischke (1991) micro-finance is primarily social as the Latin root of credit is to believe or entrust.

NABARD supported SHG – Bank linkage program, making it as the largest microfinance program in the world. The SHG movement has successfully addressed major issues related to economic, social and political empowerment of poor women. SHG federations, promoted by the SHGs themselves, have emerged as formal institutions to address those issues that the individual SHGs are not able to deal with on their own. While the growth of the SHG federations is largely confined to South India, there are clear indications of a large number of SHG federations being promoted in other parts of India as well. Moreover, experience shows that microfinance can help the poor to increase income, build viable businesses, and reduce their vulnerability to external shocks. It can also be a powerful instrument for self-empowerment by enabling the poor, especially women, to become economic agents of change (Tripathy, 2009).

Table 1: Micro-finance in India at a glance

Population of India	1.1 billion
Number of population below international poverty line	77 million=34.7%
Un-banked low-income "occupational segments"	250 million
Micro-finance services potential client outreach	350 million
Annual growth in micro-finance services	40 million
Micro-finance loan portfolio	50%
Total number of active borrowers	2 billion
Total number of micro-finance institutions (MFIs)	1.6 million

Source: Micro finance in India, CIA fact book, 2007 Ghate, 2006, Oxford policy management, 2006.

The financing to SHGs is a unique contribution to methods of development intervention for social and economic changes that relies on peoples' own resources and gradually supplements its resources from the banking system. It builds on the collective decision making, capacity of people and utilises such a capacity for all round development of the people and the area.

Banks have found in SHGs a reliable credit delivery mechanism which is cost–effective. Concerned, as they are, with the imperative need for avoiding Non Performing Assets, lending through SHGs is accepted as a safer means of reaching out to the poor, especially in rural areas. The Committee on Financial Inclusion (Chairman: Dr. C. Rangarajan, 2008) has aptly pointed out that "The process of ensuring access to financial services and timely and adequate credit where needed by vulnerable groups such as weaker sections and low income groups at an affordable cost". Financial Inclusion is a Public Private Partnership initiative for providing access to the main stream banking services for Below the Poverty Line (BPL) Citizen of India. Basically, it means that even lower strata of society with less disposable income should also have bank accounts, can get immediate credit as well as avail the benefits of financial advisory services. The people who have been covered for this are:

1. underprivileged people in rural areas like farmers.
2. underprivileged people in urban areas like labourers, domestic help.
3. unemployed.
4. physically challenged.

Emerging Challenges

The phenomenal expansion of the programme in the last 4 to 5 years, has thrown many challenges:

System for Monitoring of SHGs

The general reports on the progress of SHGs show statistics of growth and spread of SHGs without questioning the process and internal health of SHGs. There is a need to pay considerable attention to this aspect for developing healthy and sustainable groups. For this purpose, there is a need to establish a separate SHG Monitoring Cell in every State. The cell should have direct links with district and block level monitoring systems. The cell should collect both quantitative and qualitative information.

Capacity Building of SHG Members

Currently, there is a significant emphasis on capacity building for bankers, NGOs and government officials involved in promoting and financing SHGs. The time has come when there is a need to focus on capacity building of SHG members as many of the SHGs are maturing and the business level of the groups is increasing.

A Task Force could be set up to review the existing capacity building programmes for SHG members and suggest innovative approaches in addressing the capacity building needs. The task force should also suggest ways of monitoring the capacity building programmes. Routine or poor training is worse than no training.

SHGs as self managed units: It has been observed that groups, in case there is withdrawal of promoting institutions, tend to slip in their performance. The solution lies in nurturing of group upto a point where it becomes self managed and independent of promoting institutions. This implies setting up of proper accounts keeping and auditing, credit management, etc.

NABARD is implementing a pilot project 'Computer Munshi' in five districts – four districts in Jharkhand and one district in Orissa. The project envisages entrusting the task of maintaining SHG accounts, preparation of relevant reports for use by the groups as well as bankers by training a skilled youth from local communities as a Computer Munshi (CM). The trained individual is equipped with a computer and software to serve 100 to 300 SHGs. The results of the pilot project have been quite encouraging.

There are also other examples of trained para accountants cum facilitators paid by the groups who successfully keep the records and the accounts of the groups. It is recommended that such practices may be studied, documented and replicated in other regions through identification and training of group based accountants cum facilitators. This would help in providing stability and continuity to groups essential for sustained micro finance lending in future.

Regional Imbalances

There are regional imbalances in the spread of SHGs. A cursory glance at the banks' penetration ratio into rural households (the percentage of rural households availing banking services out of total rural households) among the States reveals that there is a positive co-relation between this ratio and the number of SHGs in operation in States. This underlines the need for expanding the SHG network in the States, where the banking penetration ratio is very low. It is recommended that based on the Census 2001 data, 100 districts having the highest percentage of the deprived rural households, can be selected and special strategies need to be designed for increasing the number of SHGs in the identified districts.

Special surveys and analytical studies should be undertaken in such regions to identify factors effecting spread and sustainability of SHGs. There will also be a need to invest more in capacity building programmes in these areas. For this, It will be essential to build training capabilities in these regions by identifying or promoting new training institutions that may be trained and guided by training institutions of excellence in other areas.

SHG Lending and Agriculture

The SHGs have been quite active in disbursing small doses of credit but their foray into agriculture per se is somewhat limited. They have excelled in providing micro credit for activities allied to agriculture sector but the loans made for crop cultivation and land based activities are comparatively less. In line with the Budget announcements for the year 2006-07, a separate line of credit for financing Farm Production and Investment activities through matured SHGs has been introduced by NABARD in addition to existing refinance facility available to banks.

Livelihood Promotion among Members of SHGs

Of the total groups financed by banks, there are over four lakh SHGs which are more than three years' old and are well stabilised in their credit and savings operations. Members of these mature SHGs are now in a position to scale up and diversify their income generating activities. Many of the NGOs are trying to promote micro enterprises among SHG members. But the experience is very limited. The critical constraining factor is that SHG members face a lot of problems in marketing of their produce. There is a need to evolve a methodology for promoting micro enterprises among SHG members that can be replicated on a large scale. With this view, NABARD is implementing a pilot project in nine districts spread over nine States with a view to evolving a replicable methodology. The lessons from these interventions need to be documented and disseminated.

It is proposed that SHGs need to offer wide range of saving products so as to capture the enormous demand for savings that remains unmet. SHGs can be encouraged to collect savings on daily basis from their members on the lines of daily deposit schemes being implemented by the banking system. SHGs can consider paying higher rate of interest on these deposits and the rate of interest could be even to the level at which SHGs borrow from the commercial banks.

Micro finance and the SHG-bank linkage program has been the appropriate remedy for mitigating the problems of the poverty-stricken people by their own way of self-help and collective action. In deed, it is heartening to note that more and more committed professionals have demonstrated their interest to renovate the whole structure and to make it more beneficial to the rural poor, who are the actual target people. Thus, not only does a comprehensive approach to poverty reduction (for example, providing credit along with primary health and education) create positive synergies that are more likely to break the cycle of impoverishment, but the regular meetings of microfinance groups provide an effective delivery mechanism for other social services (Tripathy, 2009).

The geographical out reach of micro-finance need to be enhanced in view of mounting disparity in accessing micro-finance particularly in eastern and northern India There has been extremely limited coverage of micro finance in these regions.

Since micro finance has to address the livelihood problem only peripherally, we need to deepen and broaden the outreach through livelihood finance, which is a comprehensive approach to promote sustainable livelihoods for the poor. It includes financial services like-savings, credit both short and long-term, for investment in natural resources: land, water, trees, livestock, energy; insurance for the lives and livelihoods of the poor, covering health, crops and livestock.

Currently, only about 38% of bank branches are in rural areas providing coverage to 40% of the country's population. Though strides have been made in expansion of bank branches from around 8700 at the time of bank nationalisation in 1969 to present number of 85,300, rural areas have only 32,000 branches. To address this shortfall I had given a target in 2010 to all banks, to provide appropriate banking facilities to habitations having population in excess of 2000 by March, 2012 using various models and technologies including branchless banking through Business Correspondents. The Banks have worked out their plans accordingly. We intend to cover at least 73,000 new habitations with a population of 2000 and above and we will open at least 5 crore new accounts by March 2012. For the year 2010-11, we need to set a target of rollout in 20,000 villages.

Considering the present context, there is a need for a forum to share the experience of diverse stakeholders, to identify the lessons that could be learnt, to identify the good practices, to understand the expectations of the representatives of the SHG federations and to discuss ways by which the SHG federation model could be up-scaled to sustain the SHG movement and to come up with a set of recommendations for the consideration of policy makers, planners and practitioners.

While public sector banks have achieved substantial broadening in branch outreach, their effectiveness has been constrained by high cost and inefficiencies, inadequate incentive structures, limited staff and inadequate technology use. Further, while cooperative credit structures and microfinance institutions demonstrate proximity to client and ability to customise services, their ability to scale up and effectively manage risks remains weak. However, technology today has become an enabler for improving the reach of banks to the unbanked at an affordable price. Mobile banking has the potential of changing lives in a way that may be difficult to imagine.

There are three models being followed in the area of Micro Finance in India:

In model 1, banks themselves take up the work of forming and nurturing the self help groups, opening their accounts and providing them with bank loans. Up to March 2006, about 20% of SHGs financed were from this category.

In model 2, where SHGs are formed by formal agencies other than banks, NGOs and others, but directly financed by banks, have occupied the major share with 74% of the total number of SHGs as on 31 March 2006.

Model 3 consists of SHGs financed by banks using NGOs and other agencies as financial intermediaries. The share of cumulative number of

SHGs linked to this model is relatively small i.e. 6 per cent. As per the information available 90% of the SHG linked to banks were women SHGs. For the purpose of providing Micro Finance, not only the SHGs were linked to Bank, but also they link to RRBs and Cooperative Banks.

Up to the year 2005-06, nearly 44362 branches of 547 banks have participated in the SHG-Bank Linkage programme. All the 27 public sector banks and 20 private sector banks and the cooperative banks had participated in this linkage programme. SBI credit linked the highest number of SHGs followed by the Indian Bank and Canara Bank. During that year, IOB, PNB, Andhra Bank, Bank of India, Bank of Baroda registered impressive growth in SHG-Bank Linkage.

As the Report of the Committee on Financial System (Narasimham Committee) observed in 1991, the end result was the disturbing growth in over dues, which not only hampered the recycling of scarce resources of banks, but also affected the profitability and viability of the financial institutions. The Government sponsored schemes witnessed extremely poor recovery rates. Improper utilisation of subsidy was exceedingly high and repayment ethics were thrown to the winds. The Government's disastrous Agricultural Debt Relief Scheme of 1989 put the final nail in the coffin; and has been considered as one of the major impediments to poor recovery and credit discipline. Thus, RRBs encounter multifarious problems due to their peculiar nature and tasks involved. The main issues are as follows:

1. Poor recovery rate and the resultant, mounting losses.
2. Delay in decision making on account of different agencies being involved in the management process.
3. Capital inadequacy.
4. Staff incompatibility as they find it difficult to cope with rural surroundings and business opportunities.
5. Restrictions in respect of deposit mobilisation and scope for investment.

With regard to microfinance, undoubtedly, it is an important development tool. While overall economic impact is still hard to demonstrate, this could be because MFIs have not invested sufficiently in data collection and impact assessments, and also because few MFIs have achieved the scale they need to start showing up in national accounts. An evaluation of microfinance programmes should not be based simply on how profitable, or even sustainable they are, but how cost-effective they are in realising their development objectives. At a minimum, microfinance brings crucial financial services to the poor at market rates.

Concluding Remarks

Successful poverty alleviation requires a multi-pronged strategy, and microfinance should be part of that strategy. It is an important contributor to achieving the MDGs. Women's empowerment is perhaps the most complex, and potentially the most powerful of these goals, and microfinance clearly helps drive female empowerment.

In its more than six decades of independence, India has waged a long battle against hunger and poverty. Two hundred years of colonial rule built a country incapable of meeting the basic needs of its own population. To remedy this situation, the policies adopted by the Indian government after Independence were a broad mix of state-led market-based policies, leaning towards heavy interventionism and high levels of economic protection for key domestic industries. This 'import substitution' model was unevenly implemented, and while some industries and sectors benefited, the government was never fully able to wean itself from the influence of powerful Indian elites and their vested interests. Over time, these elites, combined with international pressure, pulled the Indian economy towards an open market. This economic liberalisation crept slowly into India's economy throughout the 1970s and 1980s. But in 1991, precipitated by high levels of debt, India officially committed to full-fledged neo-liberal reforms when the Indian government signed onto World Bank and International Monetary Fund loans.

The two central components of these neo-liberal policies have been the liberalisation of India's private sector and a reform of the public sector. The claim advanced by key members of India's elites, and by the World Bank, was that the Indian economy needed to be set on a more sustainable path. More than a decade later, the Indian government claims vindication for its direction, with higher levels of income, reduced poverty, and a booming information technology sector—areas that have come under criticism abroad for its success in welcoming 'outsourced' jobs.

In India there are more than 250 million people still live below the official poverty line. Most of them live in rural areas, working on small plots of marginal lands or as laborers on larger farms. The public services meant to ensure a basic standard of welfare have been dismantled or rendered ineffectual, and the private sector has not reached out to those most in need of goods and services.

The most common understanding of microfinance is that microfinance provides poor families with very small loans (micro credit) to enable them to take up income generating activities or start small business enterprises. Traditionally, microfinance focused on providing a very standardised credit product. Today, it includes a broad range of services like credit, savings, insurance etc. Micro-finance is an area which is looked upon as a very effective tool for poverty eradication. By getting access to finance, the poor people are able to start their own micro-enterprise that helps increase their incomes and paves the way for their availability of consumption and reduce risks.

There is need to change the rural mindset on agro-exports. A farmer as well as a laborers working in the field should be made to think about export and quality of the product. The industry should provide agro-business services to the farming community. A rural infrastructure development fund, adequate flow of credit to agriculture is some of the steps in this direction can support the landless labourers, small and marginal farmers.

Despite growth rate attained by the Indian economy in the recent years, the benefits of economic growth have not percolated to the poorer sections. The fundamental objectives of planning such as reduction in poverty, unemployment and regional disparity instead of being mitigated have been accentuated over the periods. The poorer sections have been deprived of growth which demonstrates that equity aspect have been undermined at the cost of economic growth. It has been found out that the poverty alleviation programmes in India are confined to a set of targeted intervention and couldn't substantially affect poverty. Growth is not penetrated so as to ameliorate the socio-economic conditions of the poor tribes, scheduled castes and other depressed sections of the society. The incidence of poverty is more concentrated among the groups. Not withstanding planned efforts, the poverty percentage in India is 28% in 2004-05. National Family Health Survey-3 indicates that almost 46% of the children in 0-3 group suffered from malnutrition in 2005-06 which declined by 1% as it was 47% in 1998 (NFHS-2).

The ultimate objective of planned development is to ensure human well-being through sustained implementation in quality of life of people, particularly the poor and the poorer segment of population. The development of human resources contributes to sustained growth and provides employment opportunities to the people. Unfortunately, the indicators of human development such as literacy and education, maternal and infant mortality rate depicts slow ad tardy improvement as a result, India continues to lag behind several Asian counties. Despite a literacy level of 64% (2001 census) the number of illiterate people exceeds 304 million making India the country with the largest number of illiterate persons in the world. Life expectancy at birth is 63.9 years for males and 66.9 years for females in 2005-06 which is below the life expectancy of 72 of China. India's maternal and infant mortality rates are much higher than those of countries in East Africa indicating poor access to essential health services.

The 11th five year plan aptly emphasised on inclusive growth oriented policies combined with policies ensuring broad based per capita income growth benefiting all sections of society.

The inclusiveness involves four different attributes they are income opportunity, to exploit capability, access and security. The opportunity aspect focuses on generating more and more opportunities to the people which focus on their income. The capability aspect concentrates on providing the means for people to create and enhance their capabilities in order to exploit available opportunities.

The access attributes highlight on providing the means to bring opportunity and capabilities together. Finally, the security component provides the means for the people to protect themselves against a temporary or permanent loss of livelihood. Effective implantation of government sponsored schemes aimed at the weaker sections of the society such as National Rural Employment Guarantee Act (NREGA), National Rural Livelihood Mission (NRHM) would also accelerate the process of inclusiveness of poverty stricken community in the process of growth.

There has been dominance of unorganised sector (about 90%) which comprised of agriculture and allied sector activities, small and micro enterprises, weavers, artisans, craftsmen. There is an urgent need for expansion in the scope and courage of social security measures for these unorganised workers so that they can be assured of a minimum level of social protection and ensure their contribution for growth. The provision of infrastructure especially in rural areas can be a catalyst of inclusive growth through better delivery of social services to the common man.

Empowering the poor through the provision of education, health and financial inclusion and building their capacity, addressing the deprivations of the poor will go along way in paving the way for inclusive growth.

Notes

1. After nationalisation banks in 1969 and in 1980, the formal institutions (public sector banks) had undertaken branch expansion program, and sidelined the credit need of the poor people.
2. The pilot project was launched by NABARD after extensive consultations with Reserve Bank, commercial banks and non-Governmental Organisations (NGOs) with the following objectives: (i) to evolve supplementary credit strategies for meeting the credit needs of the poor by combining the flexibility, sensitivity and responsiveness of the informal credit system with the strength of technical and administrative capabilities and financial resources of the formal credit institutions; (ii) to build mutual trust and confidence between the bankers and the rural poor; and (iii) to encourage banking activity, both on the thrift as well as on credit sides, in a segment of the population that the formal financial institutions usually find difficult to cover.
3. Technical Intervention Area Summary Notes: TIA-3, ILO, September 2002, Micro Finance Interventions.
4. RBI guidelines issued vide its circular dated 18 February 2000, to all scheduled commercial banks including RRBs.

References

1. Ananth, B. and S. A. George (2003), Scaling up Micro Financial Services: An Overview of Challenges and Opportunities, icicisocialinitiatives.org

2. Aniket, K, (2005), Self Help Groups: Use of Modified ROSCAs in Microfinance, Economics. Edinburgh, University of Edinburgh.
3. Awasthi, Dinesh N. (1994), "Promoting Group Entrepreneurship" in Gautam Raj Jain and Debmuni Gupta (ed.) New Initiatives in Entrepreneurship Education and Training, Ahmedabad: Entrepreneurship Development Institute of India.
4. Awasthi, Dinesh N. (1996). "Rural Entrepreneurship Development: Relevance, Approach and Issues". Working Paper, Ahmedabad: Entrepreneurship Development Institute of India.
5. Ghate, P, (2006), Oxford policy management, Micro finance in India: A state of the sector report.
6. Duggal, B., B. Ananth, et. al. (2002), Micro Finance: Building the Capacities of the Poor to participate in the Larger Economy, icicisocialinitiatives.org
7. Elaine, Edgcomb and Barton, Laura (1998), "Social Intermediation and Microfinance Programmes: A Literature Review", USA: Micro-Enterprises Best Practices. The SEEP Network.
8. Nanda, Y.C. (1999), Summary and Recommendations of the Task Force on Supportive Policy and Regulatory Framework for microfinance, NABARD.
9. Pischke, J.D. Von (1991), Finance at the Frontier: Debt Capacity and the Role of Credit in the Private Economy. Washington D.C.: World Bank.
10. Report of Working Group on: Gender Issues, Panchayat Raj Institutions, PublicPrivate Partnership, Innovative Finance and Micro Finance in Agriculture, For the Eleventh Five Year Plan (2007 – 2012) Volume One, Government of India, Planning, Commission January, 2007.
11. Shalizi, Z., K Chomitz, et al (2003), World Development Report 2003: Sustainable Development in a Dynamic World. Washington, D.C., the International Bank for Reconstruction and Development / the World Bank.
12. Tripathy, S.N (2009), "Finance for Rural Development: Interface with Microfinance, Manglam Publications, Delhi.

3

Financial Inclusion in Excluded Indian Economy: A Tuff Terrain India Needs to Travel!

S.R. Keshava

Introduction

The key driver of Indias vision of an inclusive economy is Financial Inclusion. Inclusive growth aims at including everyone, more so the excluded class in the process of development. It is the holistic development process on the foundations of equity and justice. It seeks to cement the divisions in the society. The important objectives of inclusive growth are reduction in poverty and disparities of income as well as ensuring the minimum standard of living for every individual. Empirical evidence has revealed that countries with large proportion of population excluded from the formal financial system also show higher poverty ratios and higher inequality (Chakrabarty, 2011). The access to finance by the poor and vulnerable groups is recognised as a pre requisite for poverty reduction and social cohesion. Hence financial inclusion has become an integral part of the efforts to promote inclusive growth of India.

Financial inclusion is imperative for the overall development of the economy. It is the holistic approach of development with human face. The important definitions of Financial Inclusion are:

Definition and Meaning of Financial Inclusion

'Financial inclusion may be defined as the process of ensuring access to financial services and timely and adequate credit where needed by vulnerable groups such as weaker sections and low income groups at an affordable cost' (Rangarajan committee (2006).

'Financial inclusion, broadly defined, refers to universal access to a wide range of financial services at a reasonable cost. These include not only banking products but also other financial services such as insurance and equity products' (Raghuram Rajan Committee, 2007).

'Financial Inclusion is the process of ensuring access to appropriate financial products and services needed by all sections of the society in general and vulnerable groups such as weaker sections and low income groups in particular, at an affordable cost in a fair and transparent manner by regulated mainstream institutional players' Chakrabarty K.C. (2011).

Financial inclusion is providing financial services at an affordable cost. It is not just to access credit, but also fetch various financial services and products though banking system. The various financial services include savings, loans, insurance, payments, remittance facilities and financial counseling/advisory services by the formal financial system.

In India, at present the Finance ministry of Government of India strongly feels that financial Inclusion in the first instance is to provide the Bank account to all the citizens of India.

Goal of Financial Inclusion

The major goal of financial inclusion is to provide access to financial products and services like bank accounts, affordable credit facilities, savings products, remittances and payment services, insurance, healthcare, mortgage, financial advisory services and entrepreneurial credit, at an affordable cost to the vast sections of underprivileged, disadvantaged and low income groups.

United Nation Lists out the goals of financial Inclusion as:

1. Access at a reasonable cost of all households and enterprises to the range of financial services for which they are 'bankable'. These include savings, short and long-term credit, leasing and factoring, mortgages, insurance, pensions, payments, local money transfers and international remittances.
2. Sound institutions, guided by appropriate internal management systems, industry performance standards, and performance monitoring by the market, as well as by sound prudential regulation where required.
3. Financial and institutional sustainability as a means of providing access to financial services over time.
4. Multiple providers of financial services, wherever feasible, so as to bring cost-effective and a wide variety of alternatives to customers. This can include number of combinations of private, non-profit and public providers. Source: Promoting Financial Inclusion.

Importance of Financial Inclusion in India

Financial inclusion aspires three 'A's namely (1) Accessibility (2) Affordability and (3) Availability of financial products to the citizens of the country. Financial Exclusion have made it 'NA' namely (1) Non- Accessibility, (2) Non-Affordability and (3) Non-Availability of financial products to two third of India's population. It leads to massive poverty and unemployment in the economy. Money lenders squeeze interest from the borrowers. Corruption will be rampant. Government schemes will not reach the designated beneficiaries. The end result is that economic development of the Indian economy is hampered.

The financial inclusion helps to end corruption and implement the welfare schemes of government efficiently. The government wants to electronically transfer the benefits directly to the beneficiary. Direct subsidies, aid, grant, funds in the social security pension can be directly deposited to the illiterate masses accounts through the electronic benefit transfer.

Financial Exclusion in India

The financially excluded sections largely comprise marginal farmers, landless labourers, oral lessees, self employed and unorganised sector enterprises, urban slum dwellers, migrants, ethnic minorities and socially excluded groups, senior citizens and women. While there are pockets of large excluded population in all parts of the country, the North East, Eastern and Central regions contain most of the financially excluded population (Thorat Usha, 2007).

Many measurements are used, in order to know the extent of financial exclusion in India, The important among them being Geographical and demographical penetration of banking services, Financial Inclusion Index (FII), intra and intra region wise financial inclusion, Level of indebtedness and Non indebtedness among farmers and social groups,

Geographical and Demographical Penetration of Banking Services

Geographic penetration is measured in terms of number of bank branches per 1000 sq. km. More number of banks in a square kilometer indicates lesser distances to be travelled to reach the nearest physical bank outlets. Demographic penetration refers to per capita availability of a bank branch. More the number of branches per lakh population, higher the financial services to the people.

Comparison of India with the leading nations of the world and its BRIC group will be able to give us the clear idea about the geographical and demographic penetration of banking services in India.

Table 1: Geographical and demographical penetration of banking services

	Geographical penetration	*Demographic penetration*
Country	No. of Branches per 1000 sq.km.	No. of braches per 100000 people
Korea	65.02	13.4
U.K	45.16	18.35
USA	9.81	30.86
Brazil	3.05	14.59
India	**22.57**	**6.3**
Indonesia	10	8.44
China	1.83	1.33
Russia	0.19	2.24
Median Number	**4.80**	**8.5**

Source: RBI (2009), Financial Inclusion, an Overview, Occasional Paper, RBI, Mumbai.

India when compared with the rest of the world is a moderate economy in terms of financial inclusion. In geographical penetration India with 22.57 branches is above the median number of 4.8 branches per 1000 square kilometer. Korea, UK, fare better than India. In the case of Demographic penetration, India with 6.3 branches is lesser than median number of 8.5 branches per lakh persons for India. Economies like Korea, UK, USA and Brazil and Indonesia fair better than India. A higher value connotes fewer clients per branch, so that there will be easy and better banking services.

Region-wise Financial Inclusion in India

India, when seen through its different regions, one can find wide disparity even in the financial exclusion. In the region analysis Northern (80%), Southern (66%) followed by western (60%) is above the National average of 59% adult population having savings accounts. The eastern region (34%), North eastern Region (37%) and Central Region (52%) is having less than national average of 59% adult population having savings accounts. Hence 41% of adult population in the country is unbanked. In rural areas the coverage is 39% against the 60% in the urban areas. This figure is arrived with the assumption that each adult is having only one saving account. But in reality, all of us are aware, majority of the educated and elite have more than one savings account at various banks.

In case of the loan accounts, the extent of exclusion of adult population in India, from the credit markets is too vast. On an average, only 14% of adult population had loan accounts. Adult population in the Southern region (25%) had more than national average of 14% loan accounts; whereas North

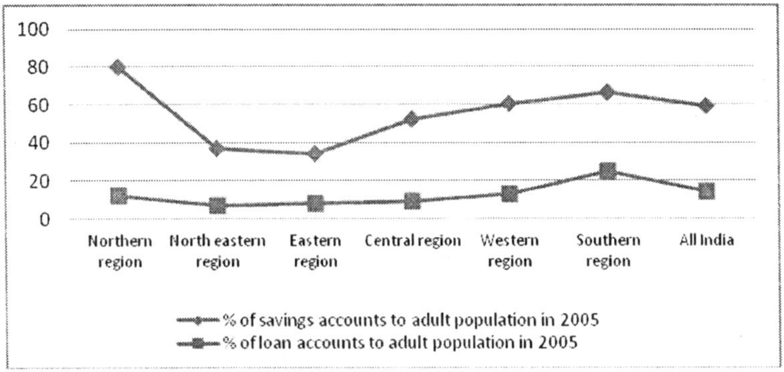

Chart 1

Source: Smt. Usha Thorat (2007), Deputy Governor, Reserve Bank of India, Speech at the HMT-DFID Financial Inclusion Conference, Whitehall Place, London, UK on 19 June 2007.

eastern Region (7%), the eastern region (8%), Central Region (9%), Northern (12%), and western (13%) were below the national average.

Financial Exclusion in Rural India

In India, there are 203 million households. Out of which 147 million are in rural areas. Among them 89.3 million are farmer households. 51.4% of farm households do not have access to formal or informal source of credit. 73% of them do not have access to the formal source of credit. Similar data is not available for non farm and urban households (NSSO, 59th Round). This clearly implies that magnitude of financial exclusion is rural India is very seviour.

Level of Exclusion Across Regions

The total number of farm households is 893.50 lakh in India. 434.24 lakh households i.e., 48.60% of them are indebted. In other words 459.26 lakh households, i.e., 51.40% of households are indebted. The most disturbing part of it is that only 243.96 lakh households, i.e., 27.30% of households have taken the loan from the formal or institutional source of credit. 649.54 lakh households are excluded from the formal or institutional source of credit. It conveys the fact that 72.70% of the households are left out from the formal source of credit.

Table 2: Level of indebtedness across regions (No. of Farmer Households (HH) in lakhs)

Region	*Total HH*	*Indebted HH (% to total HHs)*	*Non indebted HH (% to total HHs)*	*Indebted to formal sources (% to total HHs)*	*Excluded to formal sources (% to total HHs)*
Northern	109.46	56.26 (51.40)	53.2 (48.60)	27.423 (25.05)	82.04 (74.95)
North Eastern	35.40	7.04 (19.90)	28.36 (80.10)	1.448 (4.09)	33.95 (95.9)
Eastern	210.61	84.22 (40.00)	126.39 (60.00)	39.467 (18.74)	171.14 (81.26)
Central	271.33	113.04 (41.60)	158.29 (58.40)	60.814 (22.41)	210.52 (77.5)
Western	103.66	55.74 (53.70)	47.92 (46.30)	45.586 (43.98)	58.07 (56.02)
Southern	161.56	117.45 (72.70)	44.11 (27.30)	69.072 (42.75)	92.49 (57.25)
Group of Uts	1.48	0.49 (33.10)	0.99 (66.90)	0.15 (10.14)	1.33 (89.86)
All India	**893.50**	**434.24 (48.60)**	**459.26 (51.40)**	**243.96 (27.30)**	**649.54 (72.70)**
NE, C and E regions	517.34	204.30 (39.49)	313.04 (60.51)	101.73 (19.66)	415.61 (80.34)
Share to All India (%)	57.90	47.05	68.16	41.70	63.99

Source: Report of the Committee on Financial Inclusion (2008), Government of India

The most excluded from the formal sector of credit belongs to North East(95.91%), Eastern Regions (81.26%) and Central (77.59%). In total 80.34% of households do not get the credit from institutional source from these three regions. On the other hand relatively southern and western regions are relatively less excluded. It is mainly because of relatively better levels of access to formal credit, due to the availability of more branches, banking habits and relatively a better banking infrastructure.

Level of Exclusion Across States

In India 459.26 lakh households (51.4%) are excluded from formal as well as non formal sources of credit. The proportion of non-indebted farmer households was most pronounced in Meghalaya 95.9% followed by Arunachal Pradesh 94.1%, Uttaranchal 92.8% and Assam 81.9%. Relatively the most least excluded are Andhra Pradesh 18%, Tamil Nadu 25.5%, Punjab 34.6%, Kerala 35.6% and Karnataka 38.4.

Table 3: Level of Indebtedness Across States

State/Region	*Non-indebted farmer HH**		*State/Region*	*Non-indebted farmer HH**	
	Lakh	*%*		*Lakh*	*%*
Northern	53.21	48.7	Jharkhand	22.34	79.1
Haryana	9.11	46.9	Orissa	22.09	52.2
Himachal Pradesh	6.03	66.6	West Bengal	34.53	49.9
Jammu & Kashmir	6.43	68.2	**Central**	158.29	58.4
Punjab	6.38	34.6	Chhattisgarh	16.50	59
Rajasthan	25.26	47.6	Madhya Pradesh	31.09	49.2
North Eastern	28.36	80.4	Uttar Pradesh	102.38	59.7
Arunachal Pradesh	1.15	94.1	Uttaranchal	8.32	92.8
Assam	20.51	81.9	**Western**	47.92	46.3
Manipur	1.61	75.2	Gujarat	18.20	48.1
Meghalaya	2.44	95.9	Maharashtra	29.72	45.2
Mizoram	0.60	76.4	**Southern**	44.11	27.3
Nagaland	0.51	63.5	Andhra Pradesh	10.84	18.0
Tripura	1.19	50.8	Karnataka	15.52	38.4
Sikkim	0.36	61.2	Kerala	7.82	35.6
Eastern	126.39	60.0	Group of UTs	0.99	66.9
Bihar	47.42	67.0	All India	459.26	51.4

Note: *Non indebted to both formal and non formal source of credit.
Source: Report of the Committee on Financial Inclusion (2008), Govt of India.

Level of Indebtedness Across Category of Farmers

From our general understanding we know that poor farmers require more credit. Generally marginal and small farmers require credit for their cultivation. They are poor and hence depend more on credit for their farming requirements. Farmers are generally categorised as marginal, small, semi medium, medium and large farmers.

51.4% of farmers are excluded from both formal and non formal credit. Out of which 55% of the marginal farmers, 49% of small farmers, 41.8% of semi-medium, 34.9 of medium, 33.6% of large farmers are excluded from both formal and non-formal sources of credit.

Table 4: Level of Non-indebtedness : Across Marginal/Small Farmer Households

Category of farmer HH	*Size class of land owned (Ha) (no. lakhs)*	*Total farmer HHs*	*Non indebted farmer HHs (no. lakh)*	*Exclusion by form and non form sources (%)*
Marginal	<1.00	589.06	324.04	55.0
Small	1.01 – 2.00	160.60	78.68	49.0
Semi-medium	2.01 – 4.00	93.50	39.10	41.8
Medium	4.01 – 10.00	42.58	14.84	34.9
Large	10.00 +	7.76	2.60	33.6
All sizes		893.50	459.26	51.4

Source: Report of the Committee on Financial Inclusion (2008), Government of India.

Level of Non-indebtedness across Social Groups

The highest levels of non-indebtedness to both formal and non-formal sources are observed among Scheduled Tribes (ST) with 63.7%, followed by Scheduled Castes (SC) with 49.8%. they are not only excluded socially, but economically too.

Table 5: Level of Non-indebtedness: Across Social Groups

Households	*ST*	*SC*	*OBC*	*Others*	*All*
Total no. of farmer HH (lakh)	119.24	155.93	370.43	247.90	893.50
Non-indebted farmer HH (lakh)	75.94	77.60	179.96	125.76	459.26
Proportion of non-indebted farmer HH (%)	63.69	49.77	48.58	50.73	51.40

Source: Report of the Committee on Financial Inclusion (2008), Government of India.

ST Constitute 13.34% of farm households, out of which 63.69% are excluded from any formal and non formal credit. SC constitutes 17.45% of farm house holds; out of which 49.77% of farmers are excluded from both forms of credit.OBC constitute 41.45% of farm households, out of which 48.58% of farmers were excluded from both the form of credit. Others constitute 27.74% of farm households, out of which 50.73 were excluded from both the form of credit.

India's Existing Financial Infrastructure

India have 62,828 public sector branches, 15777 RRB Branches, 11842 private bank branches, 318 foreign bank branches and 55 local area banks (Economic Survey 2011-12). But only 37.2 per cent of all the commercial banks are working in rural areas, where 68.84 per cent of people are residing in the rural areas in India (2011 Census).

In order to cater short term credit, there are 31 state cooperative banks with 992 branches, 373 district central cooperatives banks with 12233 branches and 95663 primary agricultural credit societies with a membership base of around 126 million members by 31 March 2010. Along with it, in order to cater long term credit there are 20 state cooperative agriculture and rural development banks with 864 branches and 696 primary cooperative agriculture and rural development banks in the country.

But going by any indicator of financial inclusion, India is lagging behind. The 'Nationalisation of banks, massive expansion of branch network in rural areas, mandatory directed credit to priority sectors of the economy, subsidised rates of interest and creation of RRBs and NABARD are some of the notable measures in this direction. Though these measures resulted in impressive gains in rural outreach and volume of credit, the structure built up was 'quantitatively impressive but qualitatively weak'. We still have a long way to go to fully realise the original objectives of inclusive growth' Chakrabarthy (2012).

A careful observation of India's banking infrastructure with that of growing India's population, It will be clear that it is neither quantitatively impressive nor qualitatively. In both the terms, it is inadequate and weak. Villages Brick and Mortar branches have expanded tenfold. In 1969 there were 8000 branches. Today the branches have reached 80000. The growth, purchasing power has increased. So is disparity and poverty! India's populations have increased from 51 crores (1969) to 121 crores (2011). India still lives in her villages with 68.84% of people living in rural areas (2011 Census). India have 6, 38,588 inhabited villages. The following are some of the most disturbing figures:

- By 2010, there were 72,825 financially excluded villages.
- 51% farmers did not seek credit from institutional or non institutional sources.
- 40% of Indians have check in accounts.
- Only 59% adult population has bank accounts in urban areas.

- Only 39% adult populations in rural areas have bank account.
- 80% of Indian population is without life, health and non life insurance cover.
- Only 10% Indians have life insurance cover.
- Only 0.6% has non life insurance.
- Only 13% Indians have debit cards.
- Only 2% Indians have credit cards.
- Only 17 Credit Accounts per 100 persons with all the institutions (June 2007).
- Only 54 Savings Accounts per 100 persons with all the institutions (June 2007).
- Only 13% individuals are availing loans from the banks in the income bracket of less than Rs. 50,000.
- Critical Exclusion in terms of credit is manifest in 256 districts across 17 states and 1 UT (Dadra and Nagar Haveli).
- 63.7% of farm households belonging to scheduled Tribes and 49.77% of farm households belonging to Scheduled Castes are excluded from both the formal and informal credit.

Even these disturbing figures are not the truth. Many accounts opened are dormant. Hardly they transact in these account, not utilise the financial services. Few have numerable accounts and they add to total number of accounts. In order to evolve the first Financial Inclusion Index, a survey was conducted to find out the extent of reach of banking services in 100 countries. India was ranked 50th among 100 nations. According to Financial Inclusion Index Only 34% of Indian individuals have access to or receive banking services. The following chart depicts the penetration of banks in India. The ideal bench mark of OECD is compared with India's existing infrastructure. India is lagging behind the OECD Bench mark, in case of Branches per one lakh people, ATMs per one Lakh people, Deposit accounts per 1000 people and Loan account per 1000 people. Whereas in case of Branches per 1000 km^2. Indian banks has attained the OECD bench mark.

Penetration of Banks in India

Indicators	*2005*	*2006*	*2007*	*2008*	*2009*	*Bench mark (OECD)*
Branches per 100000 peoplea	6.33	6.37	6.35	6.60	6.33	10-69
ATMs per 100000 people	1.63	1.93	2.4	3.28	4.3	47-167
Deposit accounts per 1000 people	432.11	442.87	459.52	467.35	n.a	976-1671
Loan accounts per 1000 people	71.42	78	83.59	89.03	n.a	248-513
Branches per 1000 km^2	22.99	23.46	24.13	25.49	26	1-159
Trends in operating Exp/Ratios						
Operating exp. (% of total assets)	2.1	2.1	1.9	1.8	1.7	
Deposits per account (Rs)	37421.7	43108.3	50020.2	55873.9	59517.3	
Advances per account (Rs)	149378.2	177190.2	206168.8	225907.5	258751.3	
Urban + Metro Business/ total Business (%)	71.99	74.97	76.70	76.83	77.63	

Source: FICCI, 'Promoting Financial Inclusion' can the constraints of political economy be overcome.

Different Options to attain Financial Inclusion

Basically 'Financial inclusion' can be thought of in two ways. One is exclusion from the payments system –i.e. not having access to a bank account. The second type of exclusion is from formal credit markets, requiring the excluded to approach informal and exploitative markets (Thorat Usha 2007). There are different options to attain the Financial Inclusion. The important among them are Bank led model, SHG-MFI Model, Bank, NBFI Model.

Bank Led Model

RBI is giving more priority to the bank led model for financial inclusion. The scheduled commercial banks, public sector banks, private banks, foreign banks, RRBs, cooperative banks are to play a important role in Financial Inclusion. Primarily commercial banks perform the function of accepting the deposits from public and lending the money to public. In the initial phase of financial inclusion of unbanked areas, if these basic functions are performed, then it will pave the way for providing further financial services.

The technology driven bank led model will make it more effective. Technology and Brick and Mortar banks are not substitutes, but complementary to each other. One cannot replace the other. Hence the technology based click and mouse as well as the traditional brick and mortar is needed for financial inclusion. The masses still have faith in brick and mortar structure of bank rather than technology driven financial inclusion. It is primarily due to low financial literacy. Hence the mixture of both will lead to successful and effective financial inclusion of unbanked areas.

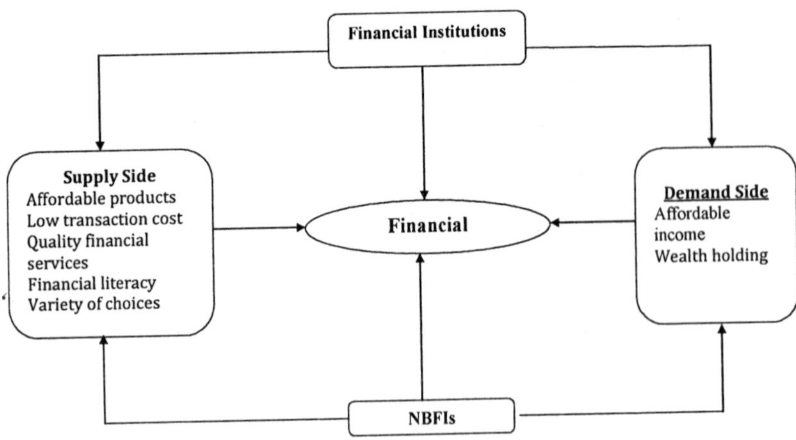

Source: Author has written the chart based on the readings on the subject.

SHG – Micro Finance Model

Microfinance facilitates Financial Inclusion very effectively. Microfinance is recognised as a cost effective and sustainable way of taking the banking system to the rural poor. The broad principle behind microfinance initiatives is: (i) to act as a cost effective avenue for the formal financial sector to expand its coverage of poor; (ii) to develop effective collateral substitutes; (iii) to emphasise on the poor masses, both rural and urban, especially women; and (iv) to focus on the objectives of macro-economic growth. Indirectly, microfinance improves schooling, health and women's empowerment (Chakrabarthy 2012).

Microfinance can be dispensed through commercial banks, RRBs or Micro Finance Institutions. The micro credit can be delivered through these institutions directly. It can also be distributed through the self help groups linked to the financial institutions.

Self help groups can be utilised for the effective penetration of Financial Inclusion. Self help groups members can be asked to identify the non account holders and convince them to open the account. The SHG members can be given financial incentive for the same.

Banks and NBFI Model

The Non Banking Financial Intermediaries can be used to penetrate financial inclusion in banked areas. These institutions can be of a greater help in the developing countries. But unfortunately, at present these intuitions are not considered in financial inclusions due to conflicting interest.

Steps Undertaken by the Government to Attain Financial Inclusion

Since 2005, Financial Inclusion has become RBI's policy Priority. Government of India constituted two committees to recommend the strategy and action plan for achieving financial inclusion. The first was in 2006 on Financial Inclusion under the chairmanship of Mr. C. Rangarajan. The second committee was on Financial Sector Reforms in 2007 under the chairmanship of Dr. Raghuram G. Rajan.

The central government, based on the recommendations of the Rangarajan Committee set up two funds namely:

1. Financial Inclusion Fund (FIF) for meeting the cost of development and promotional interventions of financial inclusion and
2. Financial Inclusion Technology Fund for meeting the cost of technology adoption for financial inclusion.

Both the funds were proposed with the corpus of 500 crores. But by 2010 each had a size of Rs. 50 crores with contributions from Government of India, RBI and NABARD in the ratio 40:40:20 (Promoting Financial Inclusion FICCI). Based on the recommendations of the both committees many initiatives are undertaken by the government including the BC model.

In order to promote the financial inclusion in India, the Government of India, RBI, IRDA, PFRDA (for micro pensions) have developed regulations and guidelines for strengthening financial inclusion. RBI has taken many measures to expand banking in India like no frill accounts, overdraft in savings bank account, Kisan Credit Cards, liberalised branch expansion, allowing the business facilitators and business correspondent to facilitate the banking in unbanked areas, usage of technology based products and services like Prepaid cards, Mobile banking, ATMs, e-banking etc.

A special drive has been initiated for cent per cent financial inclusion in the districts with maximum concentration of Scheduled Castes, Scheduled Tribes and minorities.

The financial inclusion has received special emphasis in the growth strategies of India recently. In recent years, development programmes is being implemented with equal or more stress on inclusive aspects particularly financial inclusion dimensions in rural areas. The following are some of the important measures/initiatives adoped by RBI in India to ameliorate the financial exclusion in rural areas (Thorat, Usha, 2007; Leeladhar V, 2005; Committee on Financial Inclusion, 2008).

No Frill Accounts

Since November 2005, RBI asked the commercial banks to open the savings account with 'no frills'. It refers to the savings account either with 'nil' or very low minimum balance. There will be no other charges involved in opening and maintaining the account. This was made with the noble intention of making the accounts accessible to vast sections of the unbanked population.

Overdraft Facility on no Frill Accounts

RBI has directed the private and public sector banks to give a certain limited over draft facility to its no frill accounts customers. The no frill accounts are established to benefit the poor and neglected masses. This direction is a milestone towards achieving the Financial Inclusion. Regional Rural Banks also has been directed by RBI to allow limited overdraft facilities to 'no frills' accounts, without any collateral.

Government has initiated the programme called as 'Swabhimaan' to boost the opening of the no frill accounts, by the customers in the unbanked areas.

Know Your Customer (KYC)

RBI had introduced the KYC for the purpose of customer identification, monitoring of accounts and reporting of suspicious transactions to the appropriate authorities. The KYC guidelines define the customer as a person or entity that maintains an account or has a business relationship with the bank.

But for the poor, illiterate downtrodden individual opening of bank account was a tedious job. It involved cumbersome procedure along with the introducer signature and account number. The underprivileged, poor, depressed hardly were unable to get an introducer, leave alone fulfilling the procedure.

Since August 2005 RBI simplified the procedure and relaxed know your customer (KYC) requirements for small accounts. Any evidence of customer's identity and address proof were considered as sufficient for opining the account. A customer of the bank with six months satisfactory transaction can now be the introducer for opening the account. This simplified procedure is available to those who intend to keep a balance not exceeding Rs. 50, 000 and credits in the accounts not exceeding Rs.100000/- in a year.

Since 2011 job cards of MGNREGA and AADHAAR is also considered for opening the account without any hassles. Aadhaar is a 12-digit unique number which the Unique Identification Authority of India (UIDAI) will issue for all residents. The number will be stored in a centralised database and linked to the basic demographic and biometric information including a photograph, ten fingerprints and the iris of each individual. Over a period of five years (beginning 2010) the Authority plans to issue 600 million UIDs.

Business Correspondents

RBI has permitted commercial banks to engage business correspondents as intermediaries for providing financial services in unbanked areas. In January 2006, banks were permitted to utilise the services of non-governmental organisations (NGOs/SHGs), micro-finance institutions and other civil society organisations as intermediaries in providing financial and banking services through the use of business facilitator and business correspondent (BC) models. It is ICT based agent bank model. It is done through handheld electronic devices, mobiles, mini ATM etc. Link to mobile or hand held connectivity devices ensure that the transactions are recorded in the bank's books on real time basis. Some State Governments are routing social security payments as also payments under the National Rural Employment Guarantee Scheme through such smart cards.

The business correspondents would go to door to door to deliver the financial services in unbanked areas. Initially RBI proposed and delivered four basic products and services namely savings account, recurring deposits, remittance product, kisan credit card (KCC), general purpose credit card (GCC). SBI tried to peep into the interior of Andhra Pradesh by mobile business correspondents, who travel on bikes. Domestic commercial banks have deployed 58,361 BCs in 76,081 villages by 31 March 2011.

KCC

The Kisan Credit Card (KCC) scheme aims to provide financial support to farmers to meet their different financial requirements, including the purchase of seeds and inputs for agriculture. It requires a very limited documentation. Account holders under this scheme are allocated a card and a pass book which contains their credentials and also serves as an authentic identification document. The KCC provides a line of credit for 3 years, with the review of the transactions every year. The farmer is having flexible repayment options. The three-year Personal Accident Insurance is added bonus to the card holders.

General Credit Card (GCC)

RBI in 2005 introduced General Credit Card (GCC) scheme for non-agricultural clients of banks in rural and semi-urban areas. Women clients' are given preference while distributing GCC. The upper ceiling of the credit is Rs. 25, 000 in GCC.

Simplified Branch Expansion

Since 2009, scheduled commercial banks are permitted to open their branches freely under general permission, subject to permitting. It has been permitted in the areas, where less than 50,000 populations are residing.

In case of North Eastern States and Sikkim domestic scheduled commercial banks can open new branches in rural, semi urban and urban areas without permission, subject to reporting.

25 per cent Branches in Unbanked Rural Areas

RBI in order to improve the banking penetration in unbanked areas has directed the banks to open at least 25% of the total number of branches in the unbanked rural areas.

Financial Literacy Programmes (FLP)

Financial illiteracy is the stumbling block in furthering financial inclusion in India. 570 million people are in age group of 0-25, every year large section of people enter into workforce. Hence Financial Inclusion will be of great importance at this juncture.

RBI has undertaken the FLP to educate children and youngsters about the basic banking transactions. Broachers which explain the banking basics are distributed freely to children in primary schools and colleges. A survey reveals that the worldwide average age of introducing financial literacy to children is 11.3 years. Hence this scheme is expected to make positive impact on Financial Inclusion.

The other important features of the FLP are:

- Broachers about the financial inclusion are printed in the respective regional Languages.
- Banks are directed to print all the concerned material used by retail customers in the regional language.

- A multilingual website was launched by the Reserve Bank on 18 June 2007. It is in 13 languages on all issues concerning banking.
- The information about Financial Inclusion in particular and the banking information in general were disseminated to various target groups. It included school going children and college going youths, women, rural and urban poor, defense personnel and senior citizens.

Jagruthi

In order to create awareness among general public about the financial inclusion drive, the National Stock Exchange of India (NSE) and India Post have together initiated the programme. It is called as Jagruthi.

National Mission of Financial Inclusion

Government is contemplating implementing a National Mission on Financial Inclusion (NAMFI) comprising representatives from all stakeholders The Mission will be responsible for suggesting the overall policy changes required for achieving the desired level of financial inclusion, and for supporting a range of stakeholders – in the domain of public, private and NGO sectors - in undertaking promotional initiatives.

Financial Inclusion Road Map of Banks

RBI in January 2010 advised all the commercial bank to prepare a concrete road map for financial inclusion of their respective banks. Hence forth the banks has prepared their planned targets for financial for the year 2011, 2012 and 2013. Along with the individual road maps of financial inclusion of the respective banks, the RBI also fixed the targets for each financial year. The important targets fixed by the RBI for the banks is summarised in the table 7.

(Chakrabarty, K.C. (2011) Deputy Governor, Reserve Bank of India at the FICCI – UNDP Seminar on "Financial Inclusion: Partnership between Banks, MFIs and Communities" at New Delhi on October 14, 2011).

Progress of Financial Inclusion

The progress attained by Bank led financial inclusion is as follows:

- As on June 2011, 7.91 Crore No-frills accounts have been opened by banks with outstanding balance of Rs. 5, 944.73 Crore. These figures, respectively, were 4.93 Crore and Rs. 4257.07 Crore in March 2010. Till March 2012, more than 50 million no frill accounts were opened.
- Himachal Pradesh, Goa and Uttarkhand have achieved 100% financial inclusion.
- Karnataka: Kodagu and Chikamagalur have become financial inclusive
- Banks up to June 2011 has opened banking outlets in 1.07 lakh villages from 54,258 as on March 2010. Out of these, 22,870 villages

Table 7

S.N.	Particulars	March 10-Actual	March 11-Actual	June 11-Actual	March 12-Target	Mar 13-Target
1	Villages Covered - Grand Total (2+3+4 = 5+6)	54258	100183	107604	218574	352269
2	Villages Covered - Total Branches	21475	22662	22870	24995	26440
3	Villages Covered - Total BCs	32684	77138	84274	192249	323699
4	Villages Covered - Total Other Modes	99	383	460	1330	2130
5	Villages Covered >2000	27353	54246	59640	86806	91440
6	Villages Covered <2000	26905	45937	47964	131768	260829
7	Urban Locations covered through BCs	433	3757	4524	6068	8614
8	No Frill A/Cs (No. in Lakh)	493.27	739.36	790.86	1125.06	1582.93
9	Amount in No Frill A/Cs (Amt in Crore)	4257.07	5702.94	5944.73	7449.86	8871.55
10	No Frill A/Cs with OD (No. in Lakh)	1.31	6.32	9.34	183.61	286.54
11	No Frill A/Cs with OD (Amt in Crore)	8.34	21.48	37.42	1008.04	1636.32
12	KCCs-Total-No. in Lakh	176.3	201.91	202.89	276.59	350.36
13	KCCs-Total-Amt in Crore	98749.5	132352	136122	144686	172775
14	GCC-Total-No. in Lakh	4.73	10.83	10.7	37.34	61.23
15	GCC-Total-Amt in Crore	753.49	2328.36	2356.25	4266.13	6715.07
16	ICT Based A/Cs-through BCs (No. in Lakh)	125.42	295.41	338.36	641.73	1014.74
17	EBT A/Cs-through BCs (No. in Lakh)	74.81	146.51	164.6	249.07	368.96

have been covered through brick and mortar branches, 84,274 through BC outlets and 460 through other modes like mobile vans, etc.

- Up to June 2011, banks had provided 9.34 lakh Over Drafts amounting to Rs. 37.42 Crore. The figures, respectively, were 1.31 lakh and Rs. 8.34 Crore in March 2010.
- Interest rate on the facility is completely deregulated.
- As on June 2011, banks had provided credit aggregating Rs. 2, 356.25 Crore in 10.70 lakh General Credit Card (GCC) accounts.
- As on June 30, 2011, the total number of KCCs issued has been reported as 202.89 lakh with a total amount outstanding to the tune of 1, 36,122.32 Crore.
- Overall, customer protection (including price transparency, collection practices and over-indebtedness) continues to be the primary focus in financial intermediation.
- By November 2009, there were 23 micro-insurance products offered by 13 insurance companies, accounting for 28% of new business. Life micro-insurance policies cover around 15 million lives, which is about 13% of the 120 million excluded households.
- The PACS, supported by District Central Cooperative Banks, are probably one of the largest rural financial systems in the world providing financial services (savings as well as credit) to 132 million members and 46 million borrowers through more than 95,000 societies.

Long Way to Go!

RBI has admitted that the progress in Financial Inclusion is not satisfactory. RBI deputy governor K.C. Chakrabarty who represented RBI in a panel discussion in Washington on 25 April 2012 has accepted the fact that financial Inclusion in India is not still satisfactory. He said "While excellent work (on financial inclusion) is being done in some pockets, in many other areas the progress is not satisfactory and there is a need to broad base the achievements."

India Post is also looking to diversify its activities and leverage on its huge network of post offices, the postman's intimate knowledge of the local population and the enormous trust reposed in him. Banks are entering into agreements with India Post for using post offices as agents for branchless banking. An ICRIER study by Mandira Sarma [Sarma 2009] placed India at a low 29th rank (out of 55 countries) on an Index of Financial Inclusion with a value of 0.2.

Concerns and Challenges

The important concerns and challenges to attain Financial Inclusion in India are listed as follows:

- Low financial literacy.
- Meeting the different financial needs of the poor and under privileged masses in the unbanked areas.
- Customer centric approach for the large sections of poor, downtrodden and excluded society in both rural and urban India and gaining their confidence.
- Reducing and lowering the transaction cost.
- Adopting appropriate technology.
- Developing the supporting infrastructure in remote villages in unbanked areas.

CRISIL report (2011) on financial inclusion lists three big challenges of Financial Inclusion. They are (1) high cost (2) lack of robust technology (3) lack of awareness.

CRISIL has pointed out that bankers need paradigm shift in thinking process on Financial Inclusion. They should see it as an opportunity rather than an obligation.

CRISIL stresses that the key for the success of Financial Inclusion to work on innovative business strategies. It would help in developing a delivery model which revolves around appropriate product design, technology and minimal use of manpower to make the Financial Inclusion more profitable.

Financial inclusion should be made to sustain itself. It should be implemented on commercial lines rather than as government sponsored obligation.

Sinha Janmejaya (2010) had given a five point agenda for Financial Inclusion. They are :

1. Increasing overall consciousness of the need for financial inclusion;
2. Increase in wireless and broadband connectivity in the rural areas to support rural banking;
3. Spread of financial literacy programmes;
4. Greater experimentation for financial inclusion through business correspondents, self-help groups, etc.
5. Greater collaboration between the key stakeholders in the banking system.

Opportunity Galore

The bankers in India should not feel it as just as an social obligation, but a great business opportunity. I am reminded of story of a sales man who was deputed to sell the footwear in Africa. The sales man after visiting the Africa returned back immediately and reported there is no market for the footwear in Africa, as majority walk bare footed. When an enterprising sales man was sent, he after seeing Africa immediately sent a wire message that he has found a great potential market as nobody is wearing the foot ware in African Villages. It is the perception that matters. If bankers in India sense it as a great business opportunity, then they will succeed in penetrating the Financial Inclusion in unbanked areas. With an apt business strategy, banking business will expand tremendously. Telecom sector got it with mobile revolution. Surplus rural income can be converted into an investment for the economy. Recent studies have found increasing consumption expenditure in rural India. Hence there is tremendous potential for business growth in unbanked areas. Vast population, vast new market along with providing financial services for rural India should be viewed as a great opportunity. '*Financial inclusion,* prima facie, needs to be viewed as "money at the bottom of the pyramid" and business models should be so designed to be at least self-supporting in the initial phase and profit-making in the long run' Chakrabarty (2011).

Policy Suggestions

The important policy suggestions are as follows:

1. Brick and mortar branches should be established in every village panchayat.
2. Joint accounts in the name of husband and wife or parents and children should be encouraged initially.
3. Adequate infrastructure in term of Business Correspondents with broad band connectivity to every village along with uninterrupted power supply should be provided.
4. Business Correspondents should be a localite, who is familiar with the land and people help to further the cause of financial inclusion. BC should be trained properly and also give them a suitable remuneration.
5. Post office and Post man should be used in appropriate and effective way. The post office, like in western countries should play a multifaceted role. It is the need of the hour.
6. Change the mindset of the banker and try to implement the financial inclusion on minimum profit lines. Though it should work on commercial lines, it should not exploit the poor, weak and ignorant people.
7. Focus should be on area specific models rather than a one size fits all approach.
8. Government of India is planning to provide a mobile phone to all families below BPL. Use it for mobile banking; let the mobile number help to transact the banking operation. Every time BC collects the money and enters the money into e book of bank. Immediately the acknowledgement of the same should come as SMS to the depositor.

Conclusion

The future of India lies in the success of Financial Inclusion. Hence all the stake holders, academicians, researchers, policy makers, bankers join together and do their part for the successful Financial Inclusion of unbanked areas and its people. The universities and colleges should adopt few unbanked villages and convince and cajole them to open the account and use the financial services.

Bibliography

1. Chakrabarty, K.C. (2011) Deputy Governor, Reserve Bank of India at the FICCI – UNDP Seminar on "Financial Inclusion: Partnership between Banks, MFIs and Communities" at New Delhi on October 14, 2011
2. Thorat Usha (2007), 'Financial inclusion – the Indian experience', Deputy Governor of the Reserve Bank of India, at the HMT-DFID Financial Inclusion Conference 2007, London, 19 June 2007.
3. Chakrabarty K.C. (2009), Deputy Governor, RBI. "Banking : Key Driver for Inclusive Growth", Address at the Mint's 'Clarity Through Debate' series on August 10th, 2009 at Chennai.
4. Chakrabarty K.C. (2009), Deputy Governor, RBI. "Furthering Financial Inclusion through Financial Literacy and Credit Counseling", Address at launch of Federal Ashwas Trust, Kochi, Kerala.
5. Rangarajan,C. (2008), Report of the Committee on Financial Inclusion.
6. Keshava SR (2012) Inclusive Growth in India: Challenges and Opportunities, Presented at UGC Sponsored National Seminar on Inclusive Growth in India: Progress and Challenges held on 14th Feb, 2012 at Department of Economics, University of Kerala.
7. Keshava SR(2012) An analysis of the Changing face of Indian Banking Sector' Presented at UGC Sponsored National Seminar on Macro Economic Development in India Since 2000 held on 1st March 2012 at Department of Applied Economics, Cochin University of Science and Technology, Kochi.
8. FICCI (Federation of India Chambers of Commerce and Industry), (2011), 'Promoting Financial Inclusion can the constraints of political economy be overcome,' Publication M-CRIL Knowledge Partner and FICCI, New Delhi. www.ficci-banking.com
9. Report of Commission on Financial Inclusion (2008), Government of India.
10. Reserve Bank of India, (2009), Financial Inclusion, An overview, Occasional Paper, 48, Mumbai.
11. Financial Inclusion not satisfactory: RBI, News Paper, ENS Economic Bureau Posted: Thursday, April 26, 2012 at 0024 hrs IST.

4

Financial Inclusion Among Rural Women in Mandya District: An Empirical Study

Odeyar D. Heggade

Defining the Concept of Financial Inclusion

The C. Rangarajan Committee Report (2008) has defined the concept of Financial Inclusion as "the process of ensuring access to financial services and timely and adequate credit where needed by vulnerable groups such as weaker sections and low income groups at an affordable cost" That means financial inclusion implies more and access to all individuals to institutional credit and financial services for the purpose of productive and social purposes. The Rangarajan Committee (2008: p. 1) observes that:

"The essence of financial inclusion is in trying to ensure that a range of appropriate financial services is available to every individual and enabling them to understand and access those services. Apart from the regular form of financial intermediation, it may include a basic no frills banking account for making and receiving payments, a savings product suited to the pattern of cash flows of a poor household money transfer facilities, small loans and overdrafts for productive, personal and other purposes, insurance (life and non-life) etc."

The term 'financial exclusion', the opposite of 'financial inclusion' is defined by the Dr. Rangarajan Committee (2008: p. 1) as under: "There is a growing divide, with an increased range of personal financial options for a segment of high and middle income population and a significant large section of the population who lack access to even the most basic banking services. This is termed "financial exclusion". These people, particularly, those living on low incomes, cannot access mainstream financial products such as bank accounts, credit, remittances and payment services, financial advisory services, insurance facilities etc.,"

FINANCIAL INCLUSION

The idea of financial inclusion is very powerful and socially important. The achievement of financial inclusion helps to promote personal/individual economic development/empowerment as well as social empowerment/

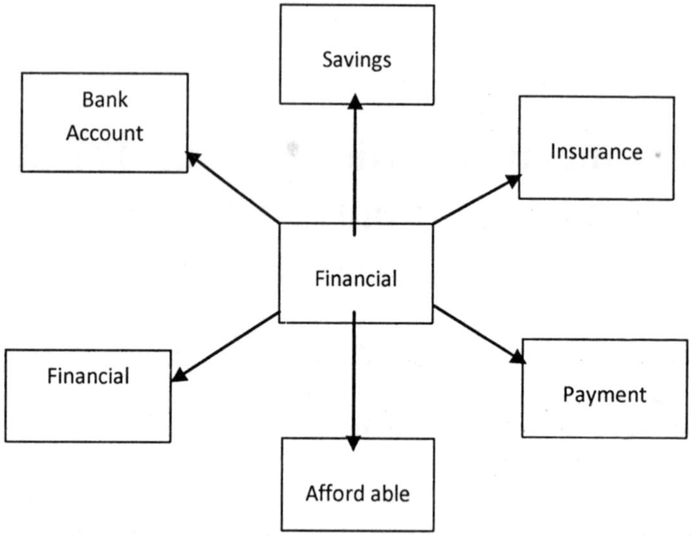

development. This all important aspect is explained by Dr. C. Rangarajan Committee Report (2008; pp. 34) as under: "... the term financial inclusion is perceived in different ways under different contexts". There is a view that only access to credit is treated as financial inclusion where as the other view inclusion by banks and other institutions must target, apart from personal/ private "investment requirements of individuals and groups, the universal public investment requirements necessary for development of infrastructure, social sector services, public utilities and productive forces / capacity building efforts, etc. Thus, financial inclusion may well be all about money and finance, but with the ultimate objective of directly abolishing the state of social exclusion in the economy".

The study on Financial Inclusion by the UN (2006) has set the following as its main goals:

(a) Access at a reasonable cost of all households and enterprises to the range of financial services for which they are "bankable", including savings, short-term payments, local money transfers and international remittances.

(b) Sound institutions, guided by appropriate internal management system's industry performance standards and performance monitoring by the market, as well as by sound prudential regulation where required.

(c) Financial and institutional sustainability as a means of providing access to financial services over time.

(d) Multiple providers of financial services, wherever feasible, so as to bring cost-effective and a wide variety of alternatives to customers (which could include any number of combinations of sound private, non-profit and public provider).

Statement of the Problem – An Analysis of Financial Exclusion

The need for and significance of financial inclusion is advocated in the recent past throughout the World. Further its need is more and widely felt in the developing countries including India. The roots of financial exclusion exist in the need for reducing and if possible eliminating the problem of 'financial exclusion'. The problems of poverty and unemployment, use of internet and e – banking, geographical distance and social exclusion all have resulted in financial exclusion of the rural people including poor and the women.

On account of the seasonality of agriculture, the cash flows and cash highly influenced by climate conditions and credit is, therefore, essential for rural families. The unavailability of credit from formal institutions and the lack of money circulating with rural society are important reasons why poverty among the rural poor is perpetuated (Remenyi 1991: 44-45). In the rural areas, lending often implies servicing a client that requires small loans at any given time and that lives dispersed over a large area without adequate infrastructure and information. These circumstances inevitably increase transaction costs and make lending institutions, if present at all in rural areas, target large and medium-sised enterprises higher income households and bigger farmers (Tilakaratne 1996:1). Community based credit schemes are one example of using indigenous institutions and social mechanisms to bring about development.

In this an attempt is made to analyse the:

(a) Socio economic characteristics of the rural women;

(b) The behavior of the rural women regarding financial inclusion;

(c) The perceptions of rural women about the prospective benefits of financial inclusion; and

(d) The Problems of Financial Inclusion of the rural women in a dry land agricultural region.

The Background

The Mandya District is located towards south of Bangalore urban district. It is 80 kms. away from Bangalore city/and 40 kms. towards the north of the Mysore city on the Bangalore Mysore State highway. The Mandya District is predominately an agricultural district with a small degree of rural industries and modern small scale industry growth.

The Mandya district has seven taluks namely Mandya, Maddur, Nagamangala, Malavalli, K.R. Pet, and Srirangapatna, however, the case study villages namely Hemmanahally, Yaraganahalli, Hulaganahalli are located on the banks of river Simsha in Maddur Taluk. Basically Hulaganahalli village has wetland agriculture and other two villages namely Hemmanahalli, Yaraganahalli have dry land agriculture.

There is one post office and panchayat raj institution (local) at Hemmanahalli village which is a larger village than the other two case study villages.

There is one Agricultural Credit Co-operative Society in Hemmanahalli which provides banking facility to the other two case study villages as well. This indicates that the farmers of Yaraganahalli and Hulaganahalli lack leadership and awareness regarding the significance of Co-operative credit and marketing.

There are 200 households in Hulaganahalli, 500 households inYaraganahalli and 650 households in Hemmanahalli village; all the three villages are predominately inhabited by the Vokkaligas (that is farmers/ the cultivating class), the schedule caste (the Ex untouchabbs) and a number of other highly backward caste which are ranked low in terms of social status in Hindu Order.

Socio Economic Characteristics of Rural Women

The important socio economic characteristics of the respondents (rural women) are briefly stated below:

1. Total numbers of 100 rural women respondents are selected for the field study. One rural woman from each or sample household is selected for interview purpose. These women belong to all the 3 case study villages Hemmanahalli, Yaraganahalli, Hulaganahalli. Of this 25 respondents each are selected from Yaraganahalli and Hulaganahalli villages whereas the remaining 50 selected from the larger village namely Hemmanahalli.
2. The total sample of 100 rural women respondent belong to different age groups (Table 1) and different caste groups (Table 2).

Table 1: Age-wise Distribution of Respondents (in year)

Sl. No	*Age*	*No. of Respondents*
1	20-30	22
2	30-40	34
3	40-50	24
4	50-60	17
5	60-70	3
	Total	100

Source: Field Survey.

Table 2: Caste-wise Distribution of Respondents (in numbers)

Sl. No.	*Caste*	*No. of Respondents*
1.	Vokkaliga	28
2.	SC	23
3.	ST	3
4.	Oil Hnskers	6
5.	Gold Eith Lingayitha	8
6.	Fisher men	11
7.	Washer men	6
8.	Baebers	5
9.	Carpent	4
10.	Lingayith	4
11.	Potters	2
	Total	**100**

Source: Field Survey.

Out of sample of 100 rural women comprise relatively young women (54%) and the remaining 46% are middle aged and old women above 40 to 50 years. Nearly 34 women are in the age group of 30 to 40 years and 20 younger women are in the age group of 20 to 30 years (Table 1).

Table 2 shows a caste wise distribution of 100 women respondents. Our sample includes greater number of Vokkaliga (22), Schedule Caste (23), Fisher men (11), women and a small number of other minority and backward caste women. This selection is based on the total number of households of the various Hindu caste groups. Based on this reasoning we have drawn more number of Vokkaliga and SC women in relation to their large number in case study villages.

On an average each family of the respondent has two children whereas small number of aged women respondents it was found that they have 3 children. This trend was observed in both the Vokkaliga and Scheduled Caste households.

This field data showed that about 15 sample households are landless. Of this 5 landless families belong to Vokkaliga group and the remaining 10 landless families are scheduled caste. Altogether these landless and highly marginal farmer families are economically very poor.

Of the 100 respondents 44 of them earn Rs. 500 to 1000 per month; this group is economically the poorest. About 43 respondents earn between 3000 to 4000 per month; whereas 8 respondents earn 5000 to 6000; 3 respondents earn between 7000 to 8000 and only two respondents earn 8000 to 10,000 per month. two very important points showed be noted here; (1) a total number of 87 sample respondents who earn less than 18,000 or per year are the absolute poor and 8 respondents who earn between 8000 to 12,000 per year are relatively poor.

The employment activity under taken by the rural sample women and their households is irregular and they work as agricultural laborers household maid servants and manual workers in the nearby semi urban areas. Since their employment is un stable, their income flows are also irregular and unstable. Thus we find poverty traps repeating with 3 to 6 months frequency.

The sample rural women have expressed diverse views about the source of inspiration and motivation to take up jobs out of 100 sample rural women 53 have reported that their husbands have motivated them to take up a job; 39 rural women were motivated by their children: 6 war advised by their own parents and 2 rural women have made independently the decision to take up job. This trend regarding decision to undertake an occupation clearly reveal that the rural women live under the control and influence of other family members (mostly men). The rural women are not used to make decision to take up occupation independently. In other words, this clearly shows that the awareness of the rural women about the linkage between jobs, income and improvement in standards of living are unknown.

Financial Inclusion- Behaviour of the Rural Women

Banking Habits and Motivation

The banking habits denote the frequency and use of the banking instruments and facilities by the bank customers. To do so, the user of the banking services should possess a bank account. A bank account may be a savings account, a current account and fixed deposit account or recurring deposit account. The banking habits include the loans and advances given by the bank or taken by the bank costumer; the use of banking instrument which facilitate various kinds of money transfers like the purchase of a demand draft, purchase of bankers cheque, with travelers cheques across a bank counter, or the Automatic Teller Machine (ATM) by the use of credit cards or debit cards) and use of mobile banking services in India. At present Airtel mobile company provides mobile banking services.

Some of the important banking habits and factors motivating the rural women to use bank services are briefly explained below:

- India has relatively more diversified financial institutional structure. It has Commercial Banks (28) in Public Sector and a large number of small and medium sised to indigenous and foreign private banks. To meet the credit needs of the farmers there are over 1 lakh agricultural credit cooperative societies and more than 200 Regional Rural Banks in India.

- The nationalised banks like Canara Bank, Syndicate Bank, State Bank of India, State Bank of Mysore, Indian Over seas Bank, Punjab National Bank etc and Kaveri Kalpathru Grameen Bank branches are operating in Mandya District. There is a branch of State Bank of Mysore at Somanahalli located 2 kms. away from Hemmanahalli village. Of the 100 sample rural women, nearly 23 of them have their bank accounts in State Bank of Mysore Somanahalli, another 18 women are members of the private banks; and 18 women have bank accounts through the SHGs and the remaining rural sample women have bank account with RRBs and other banks. All these financial institutions are located at a distance of 3 kms. (at Maddur Town) from the case study villages.
- Nearly 90 out of 100 sample rural women are partially aware of economic uses of the position of the bank account. Out of 100, rural women, 88 of them have said that a bank account is essential to save money. Only 2 of the rural women have reported that a bank account is useful to use other types of banking and financial services; and whereas the remaining 10 rural women have expressed the view that they are ignorant about it. It is interesting to note that none of the 100 sample rural women have expressed the view that the banks are useful to take loans and advances for different production and consumption purpose.
- The occupation wise distribution of 100 sample rural women speaks about women disempowerment; since 93 of them are only the housewives and occasionally work on family farms. The remaining women work as agricultural labourers, tailors and manual workers in industries. This indicates that a large number of women being housewives do not have independent sources of income.
- Of the 100 sample rural women, 29 of them have reported to have savings deposits in Commercial Banks, Post office and Self-Help Groups that means a large majority of the sample rural women (71) do not have any savings neither do not have savings deposits. This situation indicate the great degree of financial exclusion prevailing among rural women; and it should be noted that agricultural regions with low growth potential credit face greater financial exclusion among the poor like women, children, landless agricultural workers etc. For example it may be noted that none of the 100 sample rural women have used money lenders as a source of holding bank deposits.
- It is interesting to note that of the 100 sample rural women, a small number of them save for children's education (19); and 5 of them save

for addressing health problems of the family members; whereas 40 rural women have said that they save for creating economic security for their future and 36 of them have said that they saved to meet the old age requirements. This shows that the rural poor do not save with the purpose of investment in human resource development of their children. In other words, the rural poor do not have either the habit to save or desire or motivation to save for creating a prospective economic security and HRD opportunity for their children.

- The researcher has tried to ascertain the reasons for not working by the rural women; 10 women said that they have health problems; 48 of them said that they do not have family support; 28 sample women reported that they are not interested in work and of 14 sample women give the reason that they have more number of children to take care. (3 to 5 children)
- In our case study villages (Hemmanahalli,Yaraganahalli, Hulagenahalli) there are no branches of the public and private sector banks as well as non bank financial institutions. The populations of the 3 villages being farming communities are not able to lobby for obtaining a bank branch. Of the 46 rural women having bank accounts, 36 of them have opened their savings accounts in different nationalised banks located in Maddur town and remaining 10 rural women have opened saving accounts in primary credit cooperative society and a few others in the private banks at the Maddur town. A few more women have said that they would soon open savings accounts in near future since they are the beneficiaries under empowerment programmes for the poor like SHGs, MGNREGP, rural housing and old age pension scheme.
- A 46 sample rural women having bank accounts travel 4 and 6 kms to visit a bank branch located at Somanahalli, Shivapura and Maddur town. These semi-urban centres are located on the Bangalore, Mysore state highway.
- Of the 46 banks savings deposit holders, 29 of them have said that they have more than one savings account. Some of them have opened bank savings accounts in public and private sector as well as in the NBFI's. The purpose of opening savings account in more than one financial institutions is to approach bankers to obtain small loans (ranging between 10 to 20 000).
- 54 sample rural women who belong to the group of financially excluded (they do not have bank account)
- Belong to occupational and social categories like landless labourers (25), agricultural labourers (20), and the remaining 9 members work irregularity in rural public works, agriculture and allied activities.
- Of the 100 sample rural women, 76 of them deal with money lenders

whereas the remaining 24 of them deal with money lenders, trader money lenders and rich farmers. 100 of the total sample rural women have also reported that very occasionally they borrow money from friends and relatives at a low rate of interest (2 per cent per month) such borrowings are an secured loans in the range of 1000 5000.

- Out of 100 samples, 84 of the village women are in the habit of keeping deposits of taking loans and advances from the agents of unorganised financial sectors. This speculation resembles the banking habits of the people of medieval Europe. It may be noted that out of 100 sample women, 72 of them only take loans. These rural women do not have any savings to keep deposits with traders and money lenders since they are economically poor.
- Our sample of 100 rural women have reported that the scheduled banks in both private and public sector demand mortgages as securities for providing loans. Thus a large number of rural women approach rich farmers, money lenders and trader money lenders to meet their credit needs. This data analysis shows that the continuation of poverty, partriarchical values on one hand and the traditional security oriented lending practice on the part of bankers on the other hand, is responsible for the problem of financial exclusion of the rural poor. The bankers in general ask for gold or silver ornaments, agricultural land, house and household assets, pump sets, agricultural implements as the security or mortgages. Most of these assets are absent with the rural women. These assets and wealth are officially documented as the properties in the name of the male head of the family. Thus, the female members of the rural households are unable to take loans and advances from organised as well as the unorganised financial sectors agents. In this sense, the poor women become 'un bankable' (not credit worthy in the traditional banking).
- The trader money lenders, rich farmers and money lenders charge interest at the rate of 10 per cent per month on the loans and advances given by them. It implies that these money lenders charge exorbitant interest per year on the loans and advances given. In this sense borrowing from unorganised sector money markets is very exploitative.
- The rural farmers, self employed persons are eligible for loans from commercial banks, cooperative society and regional rural banks. These categories of rural borrowers (men or women) are allowed to take loans under different farmers loans scheme (5000 to 1 Lakh). In general the rural borrowers, both men and women complain against bankers that bankers in general, do not allow them to borrow up to the sanction credit limit.

- In Karnataka state the government is providing short term agricultural loans at an annual interest of 1 per cent and 3 per cent under crop loan scheme and agricultural land scheme. These short term loans are disbursed through the network of cooperative credit institutions. Our samples of 100 rural women are aware about these term loans schemes. However they are of the view that the rural women should be provided loans at zero interest to reduce the gender gap and access to institutional credit. The sample rural women are mostly unaware of the institutional loan sources for the rural households. Only 13 rural women out of 100 have reported that they have come to know about formal sources of loans through newspapers, cooperative credit society, banks, farmers information centers and friends and relatives.
- 87 respondents have expressed the view that illiteracy and fatal attitude are the sole reasons for their ignorance (63 rural women have expressed this view); the remaining 24 respondents have expressed the view that since they do not have radio, T.V. at home they are unable to get information about sources of loans; and further, these 24 women have also said that they do not have opportunities or courage to interact with bank officers and PRI officials. This is because if women take self-initiative to interact with such officials their character and chastity are doubted by family members or the villagers. Therefore most of the rural women are not courageous to interact with bank and PRI officials.
- Of the 100 sample rural women, about 20 of them are aware about ATMs and the use of bank checks. The remaining 80 per cent of the sample rural women are unaware of different bank services like ATMs, mobile banking and use of bank instruments for money transfer (MT, DD/ Traveler check, over draft etc.). Thus Reserve Bank of India has accepted the scheme of bank correspondent (BCs) or bank facilitators as intermediary to promote financial inclusion process among the poor, both men and women, in both rural and urban areas. This scheme was implemented in 2009. About 98 rural women of our sample said that they are unaware of BC or BF models of financial inclusion. That means the initiatives under financial inclusion schemes are not widely published. The publicity of the initiatives for financial inclusion is very essential and socially desirable.
- The rural women in general and 100 sample women in particular have expressed that the bonafides of the BC or BF according to the RBI scheme the retired village post master, secretary of the cooperative society, school teachers and other educated persons may be appointed as agents of BC or BF. One of the important functions of the BC or BF is to mobilise the savings of the poor including women and deposit it into their savings accounts in the schedule commercial

banks and cooperative bank/RRBs.

- Kisan credit cards is a new banking instrument which ensures easy flow of specific credit amount to the farmers. It is a useful credit programme. Out of 100 sample rural women 98 of them are unaware of credit cards. This is partly due to the fact that the landless rural women are not eligible to receive credit cards. Therefore, most of the rural women are unaware of the advantages of the kisan credit cards.
- About 43 of the respondent rural women who have bank accounts, did not felt the need for using the banking facility or financial services. Because they felt that they are extremely poor and their children work and live in the same place. Thus these women did not felt the need for using banking facilities.
- The rural poor women are indifferent towards rural development programmes they are invalid as workers seeking employment or farmers seeking agricultural subsidy. Thus to avail benefits under various rural development programmes women shall possess or open bank account. Of the 100 sample respondents 24 of them have opened bank accounts with a view to seek benefits under rural development programmes. Of these 24 women, 10 rural women have benefited under NREGP, 11 rural women have benefited under agricultural loans waiver scheme, agricultural subsidies for buying chemical fertilizer and agricultural implements and 3 of respondents have opened bank account since they were beneficiaries under rural housing programme.
- We have tried to ascertain the motivation of rural women to open bank savings account in the recent past. Out of 100 sample, 55 of them have reported that they have opened bank accounts very recently (during March 2012) 55 of the women members of the SHGs have opened bank account being motivated by the women groups; whereas 11 rural women have said that opening an bank account is essential for achieving women economic empowerment; whereas 4 of the women respondents have reported that their respective husbands have motivated and cooperated with them to start savings accounts in banks. Thus based on this data, it maybe said that there is increasing awareness about the need for and significance of women economic empowerment. However the awareness about financial inclusion as a means of achieving women economic empowerment is very low and highly inadequate.

Problems Identification or Social Barriers for Women Financial Inclusion – Adverse Effects of Caste Biased and Male Biased Values

- There are many social barriers for women's financial inclusion in rural areas. Most of which vary from caste biased and male biased values as well as practices and gender discriminations. We have tried to ascertain how the sociological factors are responsible for financial exclusion in rural India. Out of 100 sample rural women, 45 of them have reported patriarchy and female subjugation as the basis of the problem of women's financial exclusion. Of this 45 rural women, 24 of them have said that negligible or non-participation in economic growth by rural women has been the strong factor contributing to women's financial exclusion. Secondly 11 women have said that patriarchical values are prohibiting women participation in economic and financial transactions. Thirdly, the husband and other members of the family (both men and women) are against the women participation in economic and financial matters. Fourthly, high transaction cost, bankers and money lenders passive approach to women customer, the dependency syndrome are responsible for women not approaching banks for loans and advances. 9 out of 100 rural women respondents have said that caste tribunals and village caste committee discourage them from working outside the village; and the families also discourage village women to take up wage employment in towns or cities and deal with banks independently. All women respondents have said that to exercise control over women reproductive and patriarchical behaviour and to impose for their social control over women are deprived of participating in empowerment process.

- Almost all rural women respondents have said that the government has started certain initiatives to empower women. It is satisfactory to note that women are more aware and need radical change in awareness regarding social economical life to achieve the goal of women economic empowerment. Out of 100 respondents, 26 rural women belong to rural rich and elite households. Thus, these women have reported that they have sufficient freedom to act economically independently; whereas their counterparts (74 poor women) do not enjoy such high level of socio economic and cultural freedom. There is a slow and gradual transition from shackles to freedom for the women belonging to the rural elite families. These 26 rich family women have said that the have sufficient freedom to open a bank account to become members of a cooperative milk society or a caste association. These rural rich women are gradually able to achieve liberation from the patriarchical values.
- There is a gradual transition in the attitude of rural women about social interaction; nearly 94 out of 100 rural women have said that they do not believe and trust the BC or BF who are proposed as the agent between banks and the prospective bank customers. These women have reported that caste control on mobility of village women has loosened and in other words no more today caste is a major barrier for interaction of rural women with the outside world.

Effects of Financial Inclusion on Rural Women

The process of financial inclusion has many direct and indirect facilities or effects on the life of rural women. This positive effect of both socio economic developments on one hand and cultural emancipation of the rural women on the other hand. The income effects of inclusion process on rural women help them to achieve their educational empowerment as it leads to women's cultural empowerment. This way the processes of financial inclusion of women create the necessary potential for the total women emancipation, liberation and freedom. Whereas other after effects of financial inclusion on rural women could be indentified. Some of these effects maybe stated as under:

1. The rural women in general have not developed confidence in the role of BC's and BF over the past 3 or 4 years; out of 100 sample respondents only one of the women said that she has started believing the BC's and BF as agents of financial inclusion.
2. 6 out of 100 sample respondents said that they are able to undertake wage employment, self employment along with their household work; 5 sample respondents have reported that they are earning from outside employment is economically helping their family. Therefore their social status has improved in the eyes of her husband and other family members; that means women economic empowerment improves her social empowerment; 9 sample respondents have reported that some kind of banking office should be setup in our major villages. 57 out of 100 sample respondents have said that their knowledge and about others bank transaction and other financial matters is gradually improving.
    - The women participation in financial inclusion has benefited the family substantially. The rural women in the recent past were able to become members of the group, share their life experience, discuss collective as well as individual problems and find solutions; all the remaining including SC and ST women have reported that their access to bank credit has increased; a good number of rural women respondents have reported that they have saved some of amount of money in their savings deposits; further, these poor rural women have opened recurring deposits accounts in the banks for their daughters marriage and sons education.
    - The rural poor women have said that nationalised banks are most suited financial institution for transaction; this was the response of 56 sample rural women 6 of the interviewed sample women have said that private banks, private chit funds and private companies, are more useful and suitable in providing

banking services. One each of the respondents has said that post offices and RRBs are also suitable. The ignorant rural women are not able to visualise the dynamic and flexible role of post offices in delivering financial services. This ignorance on the part of rural women has prompted them to transact with money lenders rather than with post offices.

- 88 out of 100 rural respondents selling milk since they have undertaken dairying; the remaining small number of rural women is involved in selling fruits and vegetables and other agricultural produces. Only 3 of the sample women are running small petty shops.
- When the rural women employed outside the family, get exhausted with double day work burden. They are being partly helped by their husbands and sister in-law respectively.
- Of the total 100 sample rural women, 63 of the respondents have said that they participate in family level decision-making regarding financial matters and children education as well as their behavior. All the 100 rural women have reported that they are not at all consulted in the purchases of property, gold and silver or purchases regarding festivities and celebrations.
- There is wide spread social backwardness in agricultural communities; thus the male members of the rural households are highly aggressive and arrogant. In case of protests by women, it leads to series of quarrels and domestic violence. It is also unfortunate that women head of the family also think like men.
- Major conflict between rural women barrowers and money lenders are not reported.
- The case study villages (Hemmanahalli, Yaraganahalli, Hualaganahalli) are well connected by road to the nearby Maddur town, which is taluk head quarters.

Conclusion

None of the rural women respondents or their family members are practicing money lending occupation; nearly 75% of the village money lenders do not keep any record of transactions. There are 20 Self Help Groups, as is well known most suitable for the provision for micro finance in developing countries like India. In fact they are the pioneers of financial inclusion process in rural India.

Smita Nirbachita Badajen, Haripriya Gundimed observe rightly that : "Micro-finance is the provision of thrift, credit and other financial services and products of very small amounts to the poor for enabling them to raise their income levels and improve their living standards (RBI, 2005). Microfinance has profound implications not just from a finance perspective, but also from the perspective of economic development. Microfinance consisting of micro credit, micro savings and micro insurance, is regarded as an important tool to reduce risk, poverty and vulnerability of common people. Microfinance is one of the most remarkable socio-economic developments in the present era. The micro finance sector started getting recognition in India after the launch of the self help group linkage model in the year 1992. Self Help group linkage model is one of the indigenously developed and successfully operated models of Micro-finance in India. Under this model, the SHGs are financed by bank without any collateral, peer group pressure is considered as collateral by the lenders. SHG led micro finance approach also helps to reduce the burden of heavy transaction cost faced by formal financial institution in India. Further, various empirical studies also found that micro finance through SHG bank linkage programme has enabled the SHG members to improve their socio economic status through the availability of various micro finance services. Thus, Micro-finance through self help group bank linkage model can provide sustainable mechanism to meet the unmet financial needs of un-banked poor".

References

Report of the Committee on Financial Inclusion in India (Chairman: C. Rangarajan) (2008), Government of India.

Thorat, Usha (2008), "Speech an Financial Inclusion and Information Technology", Vision 2020-India Financial Services Sector.

World Bank (2008), "Banking the Poor", Measuring banking Access in 54 Economics, Washington, DC.

World Bank (2008), "Finance for All? Policies and Pitfalls in Expanding Access, World Bank Policy Research Paper, World Bank.

5

Does Directed Bank Credit Cause Inclusive Growth? –An Evidence From Indian Banking

Vighneswara Swamy

Introduction

Amartya Sen (2000) convincingly argued that poverty is not merely insufficient income, but rather the absence of wide range of capabilities, including security and ability to participate in economic and political systems. Joseph. E. Stilglitz opines that, if economic growth is not shared throughout society then development has failed. Accordingly, there is felt a need for policy support in channelling the financial resources towards the economic up-liftment of resource poor in any developing economy. These large numbers of poor are required to be provided with much needed financial assistance in order to sail them out of their poverty conditions.

Inclusive Growth

Economic growth is a topical phenomenon in human history which was set in motion with the industrial revolution. There is ample theoretical literature in development economics that looks at credit from a market failure perspective. A fundamental implication of misplaced markets is that *inequality* in the distribution of income or wealth plays a central role in many development problems (Ray Debraj, 1998).

Proper distribution of income among the population in an economy is an essential prerequisite for achieving sustainable economic growth. The table 1 below presents certain considerate information on the evolution of the distribution of income in some selected countries. It appears that income distribution has worsened in Bangladesh, China, and India, countries that have experienced rapid growth in the last two decades. Whereas in Brazil, where per capita income stagnated over the last two decades, income distribution has enhanced as an outcome of the end of hyperinflation (which penalised the poor disproportionately) and the implementation of redistributive programs. In Chile, Indonesia, and Morocco, the income distribution has remained relatively stable.

Table 1: Gini Coefficients of Selected countries (times 100)

Country	*Year-1*	*Year-2*	*Gini in Year-1*	*Gini in Year-2*
Bangladesh	1991-92	2005	28.27	33.20
Brazil	1990	2004	60.68	56.99
Chile	1990	2003	55.52	54.92
China	1990	2004	33.50	46.90
India	1993-94	2004-05	31.52	36.76
Indonesia	1993	2004	34.63	34.76
Morocco	1990-91	1998-99	39.20	39.46
Tanzania	1991	2000-01	33.83	34.62

Source: World Bank, World Development Indicators 2007.

Development economists and states have often been for a long time interested in the relationship between financial development and economic growth especially in the period which is known as the era of the Washington Consensus. A growing GDP is an evidence of a society getting its collective act together for progress. As its economy grows, a society becomes more strongly organised, more compactly interwoven. Growth is good, Sustained high growth is better and Sustained high growth with inclusiveness is best of all. Inclusive growth in the economy can only be achieved when all the weaker sections of the society including agriculture and small scale industries are nurtured and brought on par with other sections of the society in terms of economic development. Equitable growth is indeed an imperative for inclusive growth.

The major development challenge is to make the growth inclusive. Policies for inclusive growth are vital components of majority of government strategies for sustainable growth. Commission on Growth and Development (2008) notes that inclusiveness–a concept that encompasses equity, equality of opportunity, and protection in market and employment transitions – is an essential ingredient of any successful growth strategy. Three pillars of inclusive growth are; (i) Maximise economic opportunities (ii) Ensure economic well-being and (iii) Ensure equal opportunities to economic opportunities (Ifzal Ali, 2007). An inclusive growth strategy encompasses the key elements of an effective poverty reduction strategy and, more importantly, expands the development agenda. As a poverty reduction strategy, developing inclusive financial systems should be given priority, which is financially and socially sustainable (Amit K. Bhandari, 2009). Indeed concept of Inclusive growth is millions of years old in the Indian Context.

The well acceptable inclusive growth can be realised when there is commensurate financial development with a focus on inclusiveness.

Financial Development

If the 1950s, 60s and 70s were the 'golden age of capitalism' for the industrialised world, then in much part of the developing world the same period can be phrased as the 'age of developmental state' (Marglin and Schor, 1990; Wade, 1990). In many of the developing world, state was seen as general agent of development and state intervention in the area of policy and prescriptions for enabling faster economic development and consequent inclusive growth (Gerald Epstein and Ilene Grabel, 2007). Beginning with Ricardo and through Marx, Schumpeter, Gerschenkron and Rostow, various theories of growth have been propounded. The ideas of development economics (Paul Krugman, 1995) were once regarded as revolutionary and important and commanded both great intellectual prestige and substantial real-world influence. In developing countries economic transformation is surely the most important and perhaps the most complex of all economic issues(Ray Debraj, 1998).

The Finance-Growth Nexus is an established source of debate among economists. From the time when the seminal work of Patrick (1966), which first hypothesised a bi-directional relationship between financial development and economic growth, enormous empirical literature has developed testing this hypothesis (Levine, 1997). Since the groundbreaking contributions of King and Levine (1993a, b), economists have shown renewed interest in the finance–growth nexus. It is indeed irrefutable that considerable part of the differences in long run economic growth across countries can be elucidated by disparity in their financial development (King and Levine, 1993; Levine and Zervos, 1998, Demirguc-Kunt and Maksimovic (1998) and Rajan and Zingales, 1998). Beck, Demirguc-Kunt, Laeven and Levine (2006) use Rajan and Zingales (1998) approach, which provides supplementary evidence that financial development increasingly props up the growth of smaller firms which constitute largely the priority sector lending in the case of Indian Financial sector. Recent survey evidence suggests that access to finance has a direct nexus with faster rates of innovation and firm dynamism consistent with the cross-country finding that finance promotes growth through increase in productivity (Ayyagari, M., Demirgüç-Kunt, A. and Maksimovic, V, 2007b, Levine, 1998, 1999). Further, it has also been revealed that financial development plays a significant role in moderating the impact of external shocks on the domestic economy (Beck, T., Lundberg, M. and Majnoni, G, 2006 and Raddatz, C, 2006).

Table 2: Cross-country Trends in Household Credit (Per cent)

Item	*Emerging Europe*	*Emerging Asia*	*Latin America*	*Mature Markets*	*All countries*	*India**
Household credit as percentage to GDP	12.1	27.5	9.2	58.0	29.2	9.9
Share of household credit in total private sector credit	38.9	31.4	35.7	41.5	37.5	24.5
Share of housing loans in total household credit	27.9	54.2	37.5	77.5	52.9	52.7

Data pertains to year 2005, *Data pertains to 2005-06.
Source: IMF-2006 and Report on Currency and Finance in India, (Credit Market in India), RBI.

Deprived of savings accounts and bank loans, the poor also often lack secure title to their physical assets. Without property rights and the means to enforce them, they may struggle to obtain a loan from a formal financial institution. This reduces their access to credit, which makes it harder for them to start a business or expand one (Table 2).

Credit to private sector plays a significant role in the expansion of credit to different segments of an economy. In the developed economies (United Kingdom and United States of America) where inclusive growth has been on the rise we find a consistent increase in credit to private sector (Figure 1). Among the emerging economies Thailand has been showing a great surge in this direction.

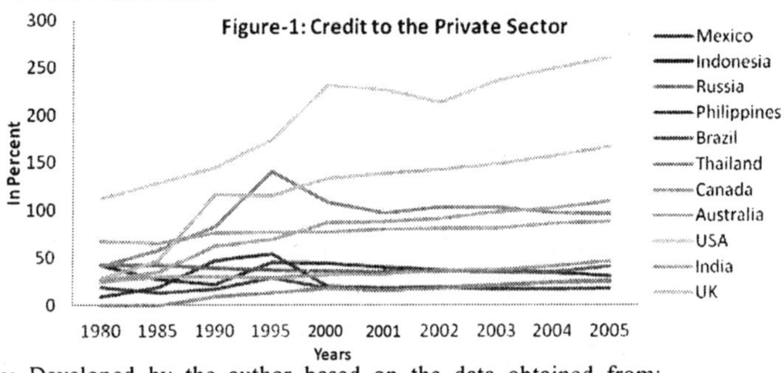

Source: Developed by the author based on the data obtained from:
1. World Development Indicators, Online Database, World Bank and Reserve Bank of India.
2. Report on Currency and Finance in India, (Credit Market in India), RBI.

Economies with higher levels of financial development experience faster reduction of poverty. Levine, (1998), (1999) and Beck, Demirguc-Kunt and Levine (2007) have noticed a positive effect of finance on poverty reduction. This has been further explained by an extensive body of literature including Deininger and Squire (1998), Dollar and Kraay (2002), White and Anderson (2001), Ravallion (2001) and Bourguignon (2003). In an often cited cross-country study, Kraay (2004) proves that growth in average incomes explains 70 per cent of the variation in poverty reduction (as measured by the headcount ratio) in the short run, and as much as 97 per cent in the long run. Lopez and Servén (2004) suggest that for a given inequality intensity, the poorer the country is, the more vital is the growth component in explaining poverty reduction. To substantiate further, the recent endogenous growth literature, building on 'learning by doing' processes, assigns a special role to finance (Aghion and Hewitt, 1998 and 2005, Banerjee and Newman, 1993; Galor and Zeira, 1993; Aghion and Bolton, 1997).

Besides debate concerning the role of finance in economic development, economists have also debated the relative importance of bank-based and market-based financial systems for a long time (Golsdmith, 1969; Boot and Thakor, 1997; Allen and Gale, 2000; Demirguc-Kunt and Levine, 2001). Joseph Schumpeter argued in 1911 that banks play a pivotal role in economic development. According to this view, the banking sector alters the path of economic progress by affecting the allocation of savings and not necessarily by altering the saving rate. Largely, the Schumpeterian view of finance and development highlights the impact of banks on productivity growth (Schumpeter, Joseph A, 1934)*. Banking sector can wield a positive influence on the overall economy, and hence is of broad macroeconomic importance (Bonin and Wachtel, 1999, Jaffe and Levonian, 2001, Rajan and Zingales, 1998, Wachtel, 2001).

It is established that better developed banks and markets are closely associated with faster growth (Levine, Loazya and Beck, 2000; Loayza and Ranciere (2002); Christopoulos and Tsionas, 2004). Improved functioning of banks can be able to boost resource allocation and hasten growth (Boyd and Prescott 1986; Greenwood and Jovanovic 1990; King and Levine 1993; Levine, R. and S. Zervous 1998). Correspondingly, by aiding risk management, improving the liquidity of assets available to savers, and by lowering trading costs; banks can enliven investment in potential economic activities (Obstfeld 1994; Bencivenga and Smith 1991; Greenwood and Smith 1997). Banks do exercise significant and causal impact on productivity growth, which feeds through to overall GDP growth. The long-run association between prioritised banking and both capital growth and private savings are more tenuous

---

*Recent theoretical models have carefully documented the links between banks and economic activity. By economising the costs of acquiring and processing information about firms and managers, banks can influence resource allocation.

(Levine, Ross; Loayza, Norman; and Beck, Thorsten,1999). It is also ascertained by some researchers that the size of the banking sector can be safely considered a good predictor for future growth, especially when focusing on long term projects (Andrea Vaona, 2005).

Intermediation costs in financial sector of an economy can be considered as one of the indicators of efficiency of financial development. Figure-2 presents the intermediation cost of banks of major Asian countries. The calibrated deregulation of the banking systems and the entry of several private and foreign banks in some of the economies has gradually induced greater competition, prompting banks to alter their business strategy and management practices which, along with technological developments, led to overall improvement in efficiency. This was reflected in the intermediation cost (operating expenses as percentage to total assets), which decelerated from 2.77 per cent in 1996 to 2.11 in 2006. Notwithstanding this improvement, intermediation cost of banks in India is still high in comparison with other countries. There is, thus, scope to bring it down to the level of intermediation cost of banks in other Asian countries.

Figure 2: Intermediation Cost of Banks of Major Asian Countries

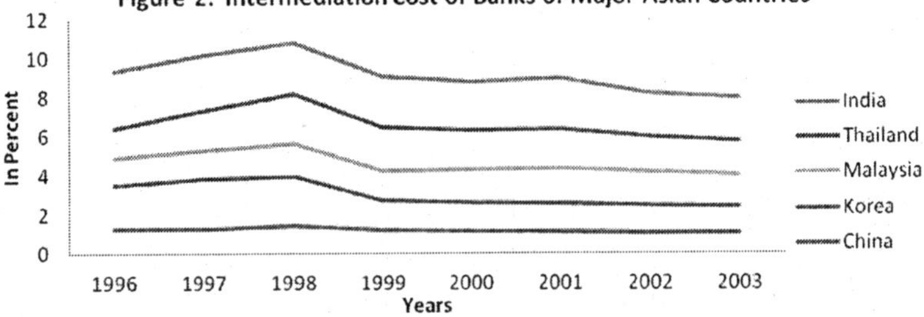

* Intermediation cost represents operating expenses as percentage to total assets.

Source: Developed by the author based on the data obtained from the following sources

1. Mohan (2006c).
2. Report on Trend and Progress of Banking in India, various issues, Reserve Bank of India.
3. Report on Currency and Finance in India, (Credit Market in India), Reserve Bank of India.

Even though finance prospers on market discipline and fails to contribute to development process effectively in the presence of interventionist policies, governments undoubtedly have an exceptionally vital role to play in promoting well-functioning financial systems (Aslý Demirgüç-Kunt, 2008). Table 3 presented here below illustrates the interventionist approaches of some governments in credit deployment towards achievement of economic growth and equity.

Table 3: Global Experiences of Government Interventions in Credit Deployment for Economic Development

Country	*Schemes*	*Experience*	*Current Status*
Brazil	Sectorally directed credit (quantity controls) combined with lower than market interest rates (price controls), or budgetary or off budget support, often funnelled through publicly owned banks.	Directed credit failed to meet intended targets, with better-off farmers capturing much of the subsidies.	
China	Lending quotas for State-owned Banks and price control schemes.	Large NPLs, political biases, and difficulties in monitoring.	Experimenting with switchover to micro financing actively since 2000
India	A target of 40 per cent of net bank credit has been stipulated for lending to the priority sector by domestic commercial banks.	The priority sector lending is fraught with targeting problem, though asset quality has not been a major issue.	Continues
Indonesia	Special credit scheme (KUK) - Pakjan 90 and Pakmei 93.	Characterised by high defaults	The emphasis has gradually shifted to microfinance
Nepal	'Intensive Banking Programme (IBP)' based on the 'Area Development Approach' and provides credit to all the beneficiaries within a specific geographical area		Deprived sector lending is proposed to be continued.
Pakistan	Mandatory credit targets for agriculture since 1972.	Agricultural credit in volume terms has increased	Legal and regulatory systems have been put in place to provide an enabling environment
Philippines	Banks are required to allocate an amount equivalent to at least 25 per cent of their loanable funds for agricultural credit,		Carried out by government financial institutions (i.e. Land Bank of the Philippines, Development Bank of Philippines, etc).

Source: Draft Technical Paper by the Internal Working Group on Priority Sector Lending, RBI, 2005.

The dynamic involvement of government thus makes certain the superior functioning of the banking sector, which sequentially has a growth enhancing effect (Arun and Turner, 2002b, Denizer, Desai and Gueorguiev, 1998, Gerschenkron, 1962, La Porta, Guiso et al., 2004a, b, 2006; Usai and Vannini,

2005; Jappelli et al., 2005). Governments play an important role in building effective and inclusive financial systems and policies to make finance work for development (Aslý Demirgüç-Kunt, 2008, La Porta et al. 1998). Directed credit programme involving loans on preferential terms and conditions to priority sectors was a major tool of development policy in both developed and developing countries in the 1960s, 1970s and mid-1980s. Japan and other East Asian countries have focused on directed credit programmes. Of course, a few countries like Nepal, Pakistan, and Philippines continue to prescribe directed credit requirements. A few economies in transition like Peoples Republic of China (PRC), Kyrgyz Republic, and Vietnam do not have directed credit requirements as such, but do have certain comparable programmes. In Korea, directed credit programmes were more extensive than in Japan and amounted to over 50 per cent of total lendable resources in the 1970s, though they fell to around 30 per cent of the total lendable resources of the financial system in the 1980s following the rise in the relative share of finance companies and other non-bank financial intermediaries. In China, policy-based lending amounted to about a third of total bank credit. A distinguishing feature of policy-based finance in Japan and Korea was the close degree of monitoring and supervision of the allocation and utilisation of preferential funds. Both countries promoted close consultation, coordination and information exchange between the government and the private sector (Internal Working Group on Priority Sector Lending, (2005).

Indian Scenario

Indian economy is primarily agricultural based and agriculture continues to be a major sector in terms of its contribution to national income. The farmers constitute an important segment of rural India. Agriculture is a major sector of Indian economy as 67 per cent of the working population is employed in it and almost 78 per cent of the farmers are small and marginal farmers. The farmers in general and small and marginal farmers in particular, do not have capital or ability to invest in agriculture. Similarly, Small Scale Industries, Rural Cottage Industries, Tiny Industries, Small Business Enterprises, Professionals and Self Employed in rural areas, retail traders, education, housing, weaker sections and other sections needed and still need prioritised financial assistance in view of the apathy of the commercial banks in helping these sections of the society. Year on year growth in GDP as well as Bank Credit in India is presented in Figure 3.

Figure 3: Year on Year Growth in GDP and Bank Credit in India

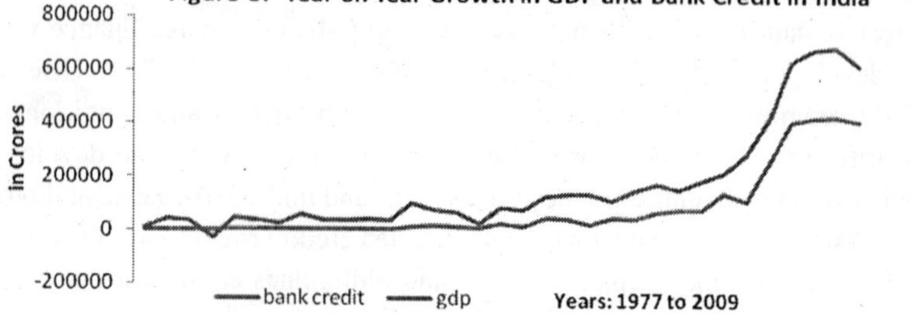

Source: Figure developed based on the data from Reserve Bank of India Publications

A well-developed financial system can help an economy grow by mobilising savings, allocating funds to investment, and redistributing risk. But the pattern of financial sector maturation varies considerably among countries. The trend of Bank Credit and GDP in India is captured in Figure 4.

Figure 4: Bank Credit and GDP in India

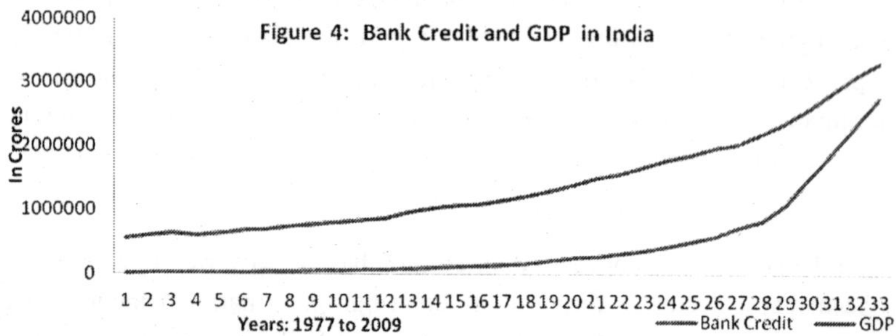

Source: Figure developed based on the data from Reserve Bank of India Publications.

In order to achieve equitable growth in the economy there is need for continued focus on priority sector lending in India. Public policy in India has consistently conferred a pivotal role for bank lending in the process of economic development. Post-independence and post nationalisation banking progress in India (Table 4) has received encomium in literature on the constructive role played by bank lending in the process of economic development (Figure 5).

Table 4: Select Macro-Indicators of Indian Banking

Indicators	*1992-93*	*2008-09*
1. Population (in mn)	872	1138
2. Per capita income* (in Rupees)	7698	33299
3. Gross Domestic Product (constant prices) (in Crores)	792150	4303654
5. No. of Scheduled Commercial Banks (SCBs)	76	80
6. SCB branches	75821	64608
7. SCB Rural and Semi-urban branches	33025	36204
8. No. of Automated Teller Machine (ATMs)	-NA-	43651
9. Bank Assets (in Crores)	385778	52,41,330
10. SCB Gross Advances (in Crores)	151982	30,00,906
11. SCB Deposits (in Crores)	268572	40,63,203
12. SCB Net Profit (in Crores)	(-)4150	52,771
13. Priority Sector Lending (in Crores)	59097	1,68,506
14. SCB Loans A/Cs under SHG-Bank Linkage Program SBLP(in 000s)	0.255	2831
15. SCB Loans O/S under SBLP (in Crores)	0.29	16,149
16. No. of Regional Rural Banks (RRBs)	196	86 **
17. RRBs Assets (in Crores)	9860	145824
18. RRB Deposits (in Crores)	6960	117984
19. RRB Advances (in Crores)	4474	69030
20. RRBs Profit (in Crores)	(-) 311	1830
21. No. of Cooperatives		97782
22. No. of Kisan Credit Cards Issued (Numbers in million)	-	84.6
23. Financial Assistance Sanctioned and Disbursed by Financial Institutions (in Crores)	-	88,973
24. No. of No-frill accounts (bank accounts)	-	33,024,761

Source: Compiled by the author from various Reserve Bank of India Publications

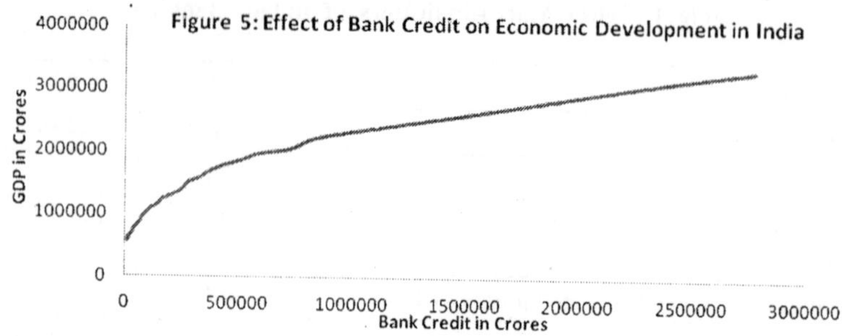

Source: Figure developed based on the data from Reserve Bank of India Publications

* One Crore is equivalent to Ten Million Indian Rupees

According to World Bank (2006), the government of India's justifiable concern with the inclusiveness of economic growth can be addressed by focusing on expanding the regional scope of economic growth, expanding access to assets and thriving markets and expanding equity in the opportunities. In this background, we notice that the twin objectives of the nationalisation of banks were rapid branch expansion and the channelling of credit in tune with the main concerns of the five-year plans. To achieve these objectives, the newly nationalised banks received quantitative targets for the expansion of their branch network and also for the proportion of credit they had to extend to priority sector in the economy (Arun and Turner, 2002a; Bhide, Prasad and Ghosh, 2001; Ganesan, 2003; Hanson, 2001; Joshi and Little, 1997; Kumbhakar and Sarkar, 2003; Reddy, 2002b). Furtherance to the nationalisation of banks, the priority sector lending target was raised to 40% (Arun and Turner, 2002a; Hanson, 2001; Ganesan, 2003; Kumbhakar and Sarkar, 2003). The rationale behind directed credit is mainly to viaduct the gap between private and social benefits, whilst high investment risk of the projects and problems of information asymmetry discourage lending to small and medium sised firms. Use of policy-based lending, in addition to other forms of industrial assistance (e.g. lower taxes, grants, etc.), is premised on the argument that the main constraint facing new or expanding enterprises is their limited access to external finance at reasonable terms and conditions (Internal Working Group on Priority Sector Lending, (2005). Directed credit programmes involving small subsidies overcome this constraint. The system of directed credit programmes has clearly contributed to an expansion of credit in the directions that were considered necessary (Narasihmam, 2002). Bell and Rousseau (2001) have explained that financial institutions in India have had an instrumental role in influencing the overall economic performance. Burgess and Pande (2003 and 2004) and Burgess, Pande and Wong (2004) have concluded that the directed bank lending (under which priority sector lending is regulated) has indeed helped in reducing poverty across Indian states.

Priority sector lending by commercial banks in India is monitored by Reserve Bank of India through periodical returns received from them. Performance of banks under this criterion is rigorously reviewed in the various fora set up under the Lead Bank Scheme (at State, District and Block levels). Directed lending in the Indian banking sector have been guided by the recommendations of various expert committees (Gupta Committee, Vyas Committee, Samal Committee and Working Group (Chairman: C.S. Murthy) on Priority Sector Lending (2005). The guiding principle of the revised guidelines on lending to the priority sector has been to ensure adequate flow of bank credit to those sectors of the society/economy that impact large segments of the population and weaker sections, and to the sectors that are employment-intensive such as agriculture, and tiny and small enterprises.

The importance of this study lies in the fact that India being a socialist, democratic republic, it is imperative on the policies of the government to ensure equitable growth of all sections of the economy. Priority sector lending in a socialistic economy is very important as it directly affects the economic conditions of the resource poor. It is universally opined that the resource poor need financial assistance at reasonable costs and that too with uninterrupted pace. However, the economic liberalisation policies have always tempted the financial institutions to look for more and more greener pastures of business ignoring the weaker sections of the society. It is essential for any economy to aim at inclusive growth involving each and every citizen in the economic development progression. It is in this context that a study has to be made to understand the importance of priority sector lending in ensuring the inclusive growth in the Indian context.

On a perusal of the available literature on directed lending, it is felt that in the backdrop of the available research findings it is time to analyse the impact of priority sector lending in the process of economic development. Accordingly, it is attempted in this study to analyse the relevance of priority sector lending in the Indian context for the period involving both the pre and post liberalisation period.

Empirical Estimation and Analysis

In view of the aforesaid importance of Priority Sector Lending in the Indian context, this study has the following objective:

To understand the impact of Priority Sector lending by banks on inclusive growth in India and establish the relationship of Priority Sector lending on indicators of inclusive growth such as; Credit to GDP, GDP, Capital Formation in Household Sector, Total Capital Formation, Total Food grains Production, Employment in SSI sector and Output by SSI sector.

On the basis of the above mentioned objective, the following hypothesis was developed to be tested in the present study: The null hypothesis for the above test *H0: Coefficient of the parameter is not different from zero* that is the parameters for the test do not have the significant impact on the poverty level and the alternative hypothesis *H1: Coefficient of the parameter is significantly different from zero* that is the parameters have the significant impact on the poverty. Significance level for the study is set at 5%.

The required data for the analysis is obtained largely from the most reliable and official sources such as Reserve Bank of India website, India Development Report 2008 and other related sources. Economic Reforms in Indian economy were initiated in the year 1991-92. As such, to cover equal number of years of priority sector lending and inclusive growth during pre and post-Liberalisation period, data for the period from 1974-75 to 2007-08 has been analysed for understanding the trends. For the purpose of analysis the most popular statistical measure *Multiple Regression (OLS) Analysis* is used (Andrea Vaona, 2005, Andrea Vaonaand Roberto Patuelli, 2008 have also used the same kind of analysis for similar studies).

The objective of this section of the paper is to identify the determinants of Inclusive Growth which can be captured in Rural Poverty (RU_POV) (measured in percentage against that of the total population in rural areas and these figures are provided by the Census of India data) in India and ascertain the impact of Priority Sector Lending (PSL) on rural poverty in India. Priority Sector Lending in the Indian context refers to the bank credit under the directed lending towards the private firms and individuals which is an important parameter that determines the measure of development that can significantly contribute to inclusive growth (Andrea Vaona, 2005). Domestic Savings (SAV) (measured in Rupees in Crores) is included as a determinant in order to account for the argument that savings propels economic activity in the system at large and helps in inclusive growth process (Beck, Levine and Loayza 2000).Rural Employment is one of the significant measures of economic development and consequently of inclusive growth. A greater level of rural employment can be taken as evidence of greater economic development (Cole Shawn, 2007). In recognition of this argument, Employment in Rural Primary sector (EMP_RP) (expressed in million numbers) is included as one of determinants to study their impact on inclusive growth. Agricultural Production is another important determinant that affects the inclusive growth process in rural India. As a large population of weaker sections of the society still depends to a large extent on agriculture, Agricultural Production (AGRI_PRO) (expressed in Kilograms/hectare) determines their upward movement in the income ladder (Andrea Vaona, 2005 also considered production as an important variable in a similar study). Accordingly, agricultural production is also considered as a determinant in the analysis. There is also an indisputable argument that overall credit has profound impact on inclusive growth process (Andrea Vaona, 2005). In view of this, Credit to Gross Domestic Product (CRED_GDP) (measured as a ratio in percentage to GDP) is included as a determinant. If there is an increase in Per Capita Income (PCI) (measured as per capita NNP at factor cost expressed in Crores in Rupees) there certainly will be an increase in inclusive growth process. As such, Per Capita Income (as used as a determinant in a similar analysis by Andrea Vaonaand Roberto Patuelli, 2008, Srinivasan 1994, Streeten 1994, Sen 1992 and Sugden 1993) is commonly accepted measure of standard of living of people and consequently is a major factor that enhances inclusive growth and hence it is included in the analysis.

The model can be;

$$Y = \alpha + \beta_I X_I + \ldots\ldots\ldots\ldots + \beta_n X_n + \mu \qquad \ldots\ldots(1)$$

Accordingly, Rural Poverty can be better explained and estimated with the following version of equation;

$$RU\_POV = f\,(PSL,\ SAV,\ EMP\_RP,\ AGRI\_PRO,\ CRED\_GDP,\ PCI) + \mu \qquad \ldots\ldots(2)$$

In order to control for other factors associated with economic growth not linked to financial development, the regression results are presented by using a simple conditioning information set, including the constant, the logarithm of all explanatory variables. Due to potential nonlinearities, the natural logarithms of the regressors are considered (Levine, Loazya and Beck, 2000).

Accordingly, when we log-transform this model (also called a log-log, double-log) we obtain:

$$Log\ (RU\_POV) = \alpha + log(PSL,\ SAV,\ EMP\_RP,\ AGRI\_PRO,\ CRED\_GDP,\ PCI) + \mu \qquad \ldots\ldots(3)$$

α represents the *'Y intercept'*, $\beta_{1\ \ldots Ân}$ represent the respective regression coefficients for explanatory variables $X_{1\ \ldots\ldots}\ X_n$ and 'μ' represents the error term. Where, 'Y' represents the 'RU_POV', i.e, Rural Poverty and 'X_1', 'X_2', ..., 'X_{14} represent the predictor variables and 'β_1', 'β_2', ..., β_n' represent the partial regression coefficients of 'PSL' i.e, 'Priority Sector Lending', 'SAV'-Savings, 'EMP_RP'-Employment in Rural Primary sector, 'AGRI_PRO'-Agricultural production, 'CRED_GDP'-Credit to Gross Domestic Product and 'PCI'-Per Capita Income respectively. 'μ' represents the 'error term'. The results of analysis are presented in Table 3 for the period from the year 1977 to 2007. Inferring from the results of this analysis, it can be concluded that Priority sector lending has significant impact on rural poverty.

Table 3: Results of Regression Analysis - Impact of Determinants of Inclusive Growth

Variable	*Coefficient*	*Prob.*
Constant	-2.213583	0.7656
LOG (PSL)	0.310230	0.0059*
LOG (SAV)	-0.804166	0.0001*
LOG (EMP_RP)	-0.502652	0.3759
LOG (AGRI_PRO)	-0.286433	0.3869
LOG (CRED_GDP)	-0.831765	0.0016*
LOG (PCI)	1.803471	0.0016*
R-squared	*0.948572*	
Adjusted R-squared	*0.935715*	
Durbin-Watson stat	*1.923164*	
F-statistic	*73.77883*	
Prob(F-statistic)	*0.000000*	
Dependent Variable:	*LOG(RU_POV)*	

Note: * at 1% significance level Source: Outcome of analysis of this study.

Graphical presentation of the trend of priority sector lending in the pre liberalisation period from 1974-75 to 1990-91 and post liberalisation period from 1991-92 to 2006-07 is illustrated in Figure 1. It is clearly evident from the figure that priority sector lending has taken a gradually upward moving curve indicating a steady rise in the post liberalisation era.

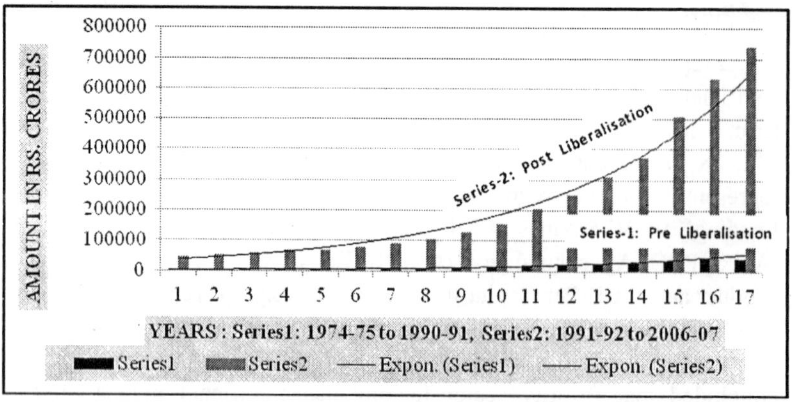

Fig. 1: Priority Sector Lending In India - Pre and Post Liberalisation

Source: Outcome of analysis of this study.

Further, the Nature and strength of the impact of the various determinants on Inclusive growth are captured in Table 4 here below:

Table 4: Nature and Strength of the Impact of Various

Explanatory Variable	*Correlation Trend*
Priority Sector Lending(PSL)	Positive and highly significant
Domestic Savings (SAV)	Negative and highly Significant
Employment in Rural Primary sector (EMP_RP)	Negative and insignificant
Agricultural Production (AGRI_PRO)	Negative and insignificant
Credit to Gross Domestic Product (CRED_GDP)	Negative and highly Significant
Per Capita Income (PCI)	Positive and highly Significant

Source: Outcome of analysis of this study.

A graphical presentation of the trend of the inclusive growth in India is presented in Figure 2. It is orchestrated by the rhythmic forward movement trends of the above discussed determinants during the study period. Rural Poverty is on a declining trend more pronouncedly during the post liberalisation period.

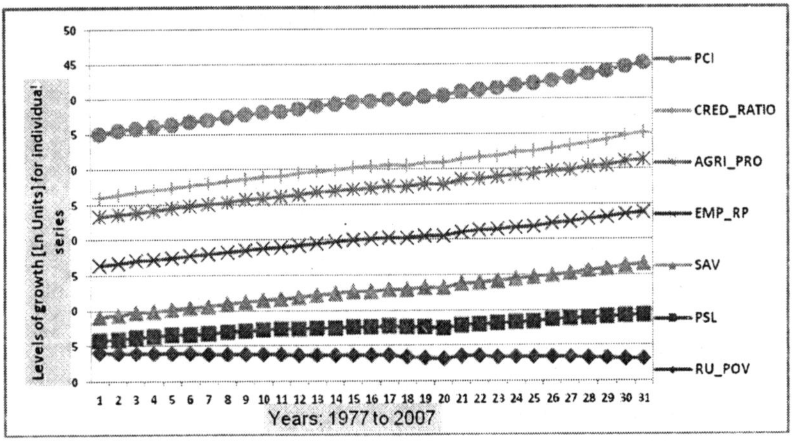

Fig. 2: Trend of Inclusive Growth in India.

Source: Outcome of analysis of this study.

Findings of the Study

The study found that Priority Sector Lending has a very high significant impact on inclusive growth, which is in line with the findings of Kraay (2004) and Beck, et al. (2007). Domestic Savings (in line with the conclusions of Levine, Ross; Loayza, Norman; and Beck, Thorsten, 1999), Credit to Gross Domestic Product (as established by Ayyagari, M., Demirgüç-Kunt, A. and Maksimovic, V, 2007b, Narasimham, 2002, Obstfeld 1994; Bencivenga and Smith 1991; Greenwood and Smith 1997) and Per Capita Income (as stated by Levine, 1998, 1999) are found to have significant impact on reducing rural poverty in India. The model developed in the study explains the trend of rural poverty (Lopez and Servén, 2004) to the extent of 93.5 per cent involving the important determinants such as Priority Sector Lending (Rajan and Zingales 1998), Savings, Employment in Rural Primary sector, Agricultural Production (Andrea Vaona, 2005), Credit to Gross Domestic Product (Andrea Vaona, 2005) and Per Capita Income (Andrea Vaona and Roberto Patuelli, 2008, Srinivasan 1994, Streeten 1994, Sen 1992 and Sugden 1993). Further, it is also demonstrated (Figure-2) that financial sector reforms have indeed had a positive impact on reduction of rural poverty.

Policy Choices and Conclusion

Undoubtedly, Priority Sector Lending in India has been largely influenced by directed lending approach of the Government policy in India. As such, there is a strong need to strengthen this policy approach for financing the priority sector. Further, in view of the findings I do not appreciate the measure of the government in allowing the (failing) banks in meeting the Priority sector lending obligation to park their shortfall in the Rural Infrastructure Development Fund as this has resulted in the gradual decrease in the priority sector lending when compared to total bank lending. Priority sector lending over a period of years in Indian banking has had clearly established a positive impact on inclusive growth. In view of the strong relationship between priority sector lending and inclusive growth, it is imperative on the policy makers in general and the governments in particular to make efforts to motivate the banks and financial institutions in increasing priority sector lending beyond the stipulations laid down by Reserve Bank of India. The banks in India are required to expand their efforts exponentially to reach out to the priority sector in providing fair and equitable financial assistance for achieving inclusive growth.

References

1. Aghion, P. and P. Howitt (1998), Endogenous Growth Theory, (MIT Press).
2. Aghion, P. and Bolton, P. (1997), A trickle-down theory of growth and development with debt Overhang, Review of Economic Studies, 64, 151–172.
3. Allen, F. and Gale, D. (2000), Comparing Financial Systems, (Cambridge, MA: MIT Press).
4. Amit K. Bhandari (2009), Access to Banking Services and Poverty Reduction: A State-wise Assessment in India, IZA Discussion Paper No. 4132, Indian Institute of Social Welfare and Business Management and IZA, IZA Bonn, Germany.

5. Andrea Vaona (2005), Regional Evidence on the Finance-Growth Nexus, working paper -#30, University of Verona, Department of Economic Sciences, Polo Zanotto, Viale dell. Università 4, 37129, Verona, Italy.
6. Andrea Vaonaand Roberto Patuelli (2008), New empirical evidence on local financial development and growth, Working paper -# 08-05, Decanato Della Facoltà di Scienze economiche, Via G. Buffi, 13 CH-6900 Lugano, Switzerland
7. Arun, T.G. and Turner, J.D (2002a), Financial liberalisation in India, in: Journal of International Banking Regulation, 4 (2), pp. 183-188.
8. Arun, T.G. / Turner, J.D. (2002b), Public Sector Banks in India: Rationale and Prerequisites for Reform, Annals of Public and Cooperative Economics, 73 (1), pp. 89-109.
9. Aslý Demirgüç-Kunt (2008), Finance and Economic Development: The Role of Government, Mimeo World Bank.
10. Ayyagari, M., Demirgüç-Kunt, A. and Maksimovic, V (2007b), Firm Innovation in Emerging Markets: Role of Finance, Mimeo World Bank.
11. Banerjee, A. and Newman, A (1993), Occupational Choice and the Process of Development,Journal of Political Economy, 101, 274–298.
12. Beck, T., Demirgüç-Kunt, A. and Levine, R. (2006), Bank Supervision and Corruption in Lending, Journal of Monetary Economics, 53(8), 2131-2163.
13. Beck, T., Lundberg, M. and Majnoni, G (2006), Financial intermediary development and growth Volatility: Do intermediaries dampen or magnify shocks?, Journal of International Money and Finance, 25(7), 1146-1167.
14. Beck, T., Demirgüç-Kunt, A. and Levine, R (2007), Finance, inequality and the poor, Journal of Economic Growth, 12(1), 27-49.
15. Beck, T., R. Levine and N. Loayza (2000), Finance and the Sources of Growth, Journal of Financial Economics, 58, pp. 261, 300.
16. Bell, Clive and Peter L. Rousseau (2001), Post-independence India: a case of finance–led Industrialisation?, Journal of Development Economics, Vol.65 pp.153-75.
17. Bencivenga, Valerie R., and Smith, Bruce D (1991), Financial Intermediation and Endogenous Growth, Review of Economics Studies, 58(2), pp. 195-209.
18. Bhide, M. G, Prasad, A, Ghosh, Saibal (2001), Emerging Challenges in Indian Banking, Working Paper Stanford University, No. 103, pp. 1-61.
19. Bonin, John P / Wachtel, Paul (1999), Toward Market-Oriented Banking in the Economies in Transition, in Blejer, Mario/ Skreb, Marko (ed.): Financial Sector Transformation: Lessons from Economies in Transition, Cambridge UK, pp. 19-92.
20. Boot, A.W.A. and Thakor, A (1997), Financial System Architecture, Review of Financial Studies, 693-733.
21. 22. Bourguignon, F (2003), The Growth Elasticity of Poverty Reduction; Explaining Heterogeneity across Countries and Time Periods, in Inequality and Growth: Theory and Policy Implications, ed. T. Eicher and S. Turnovsky, Cambridge, MA: MIT Press.
22. Boyd, John H. and Prescott, Edward C (1986), Financial Intermediary Coalitions, Journal of Economic Theory, April 1986, 3 8(2), pp. 211-232.
23. Burgess Robin and Rohini Pande (2003), Do Rural Banks Matter? Evidence from the Indian Social Banking Experiment, CMPO Working Paper Series No. 04/104.

24. Burgess Robin, Rohini Pande, and Grace Wong (2004), Banking for the poor: Evidence from India, Journal of European Economic Association, Vol. 3.
25. Cole, Shawn (2007), Financial Development, Bank Ownership and Growth-Does Quantity Imply Quality?, Harvard Business School, Working Paper
26. Commission on Growth and Development (2008), Growth Report: Strategies for Sustained Growth and Inclusive Development, Mimeo World Bank, Washington, DC.
27. Christopoulos, D.K. and Tsionas, E.G (2004), Financial development and economic growth: Evidence from panel unit root and co integration tests, Journal of Development Economics, 73, 55–74.
28. Demirgüç-Kunt, A. and Maksimovic, V (1998), Law, finance, and firm growth, Journal of Finance, 53, 2107–2137.
29. Deininger, K., and L. Squire (1998), New Perspectives on Old Issues: Inequality and Growth, Journal of Development Economics
30. Denizer, Cevdet, Desai, Raj M and Gueorguiev, Nikolay (1998), The Political Economy of Financial Repression in Transition Economies, Working Paper World Bank, pp. 1-32.
31. Dollar, D. and A. Kraay (2002), Growth Is Good for the Poor, Journal of Economic Growth, 7, pp. 195–25.
32. Demirgüç-Kunt, A. and Levine, R. (2001), Financial Structure and Economic Growth: A Cross-Country Comparison of Banks, Markets, and Development, (Cambridge, MA: MIT Press).
33. Galor, O. and Zeira, J (1993), Income distribution and macroeconomics, Review of Economic Studies, 60, 35–52.
34. Gamesman, P (2003), Impact of Priority Sector Advances on Profitability of Public Sector Banks in India, Journal of Financial Management and Analysis, 16 (2), pp. 14-27.
35. Gerald Epstein, Ilene Gravel (2007), Economic Policies, MDGs and Poverty, Financial Policy, Training Module No. 3, International Poverty Centre, Brasilia DF, Brazil.
36. Gerschenkron, Alexander (1962), Economic Backwardness in Historical Perspective, Cambridge, MA: MIT Press).
37. Goldsmith, R.W (1969), Financial Structure and Development", (New Haven, CT: Yale University Press).
38. Greenwood, Jeremy and Jovanovich, Boya (1990), Financial Development, Growth, and the Distribution of Income, Journal of Political Economy, 98(5, Pt.1), pp. 1076-1107.
39. Greenwood, Jeremy and Smith, Bruce (1997), Financial Markets in Development and the Development of Financial Markets, Journal of Economic Dynamics and Control, 21(1), pp. 145-186.
40. Guiso L, Sapienza P and Zingales L (2004a), Does Local Financial Development Matter?, Quarterly Journal of Economics 119: 929-969.
41. Guiso L, Sapienza P and Zingales L (2004b), The Role of Social Capital in Financial Development, American Economic Review, 94: 526-556.
42. Guiso L, Sapienza P and Zingales L (2006), The Cost of Banking Regulation, NBER Working Paper 12501.
43. Hanson, James A (2001), Indian Banking: Market Liberalisation and the Pressures

for Institutional and Market Framework Reform, Working Paper Stanford University, No. 104; pp. 1-37.

44. Ifzal Ali (2007), Inequality and the Imperative for Inclusive Growth in Asia, Asian Development Review, Vol. 24, no. 2, pp. 1"16.
45. Internal Working Group on Priority Sector Lending (2005), Draft Technical Paper, Reserve Bank of India, Rural Planning and Credit Department, Central Office, Mumbai, India.
46. Jaffe, Dwight/ Levonian, Mark (2001), The Structure of Banking Systems in Developed and Transition Economies, European Financial Management, 7 (2), pp. 161-181.
47. Jappelli T, Pagano M and Bianco M (2005), Courts and Banks: Effects of Judicial Enforcement on Credit Markets, Journal of Money, Credit and Banking, 37(2): 223-244.
48. Joshi, Vijay and Little, I.M.D (1997), India's Economic Reforms 1991-2001, Delhi et. al.
49. King RG and Levine R (1993a), Finance and Growth: Schumpeter Might Be Right, Quarterly Journal of Economics 108: 717-737.
50. King RG and Levine R (1993b), Finance, Entrepreneurship, and Growth, Journal of Monetary Economics, 32: 513-542.
51. Kraay, A (2004), When Is Growth Pro-Poor? Cross-Country Evidence, IMF Working Paper 4-47, International Monetary Fund, Washington, DC.
52. Kumbhakar, Subal C and Sarkar, Sucrate (2003), Deregulation, Ownership, and Productivity Growth in the Banking Industry: Evidence from India, Journal of Money, Banking, and Credit, 35 (3), pp. 403-424.
53. La Porta, R., F. Lopez-de-Silanes, A. Shleifer and R. W. Vishny (1998), Law and Finance, Journal of Political Economy, 106, pp. 1113-1155.
54. La Porta, Rafael, Lopez de Silanes, Florencio and Schleifer, Andrei (2002), Government.
55. Ownership of Banks, Journal of Finance, 57 (1), pp. 265-301.
56. Levine, R. and S. Zervous (1998), Stock Markets, Banks and Economic Growth, American Economic Review, Vol. 88, pp. 537-58 .
57. Levine, R (1998), The Legal Environment, Banks, and Long-Run Economic Growth, Journal of Money, Credit, and Banking, 30, pp. 596-613.
58. Levine, R (1999), Law, Finance, and Economic Growth, Journal of Financial Intermediation, 8, pp. 36-67.
59. Levine, Ross, Loayza, Norman and Beck, Thorsten (1999), Financial Intermediation and Growth: Causality and Causes, Mimeo World Bank.
60. Levine, Ross; Loayza, Norman; and Beck, Thorsten (2000), Financial Intermediation and Growth: Causality and Causes, Mimeo World Bank.
61. Lopez, H. and L. Servén (2004), The Mechanics of Growth-Poverty-Inequality Relationship, Mimeo World Bank.
62. Loayza, N. and Ranciere, R. (2002), Financial Fragility, Financial Development, and Growth, Mimeo, World Bank.
63. Marglin, Stephen and Juliet Schor (1990), The golden Age of Capitalism: Reinterpreting the Post War Experience, (Oxford University Press, New York).
64. Narasihmam, M. (2002), Economic Reforms: Development and Finance, (UBS Publishers' Distributors Ltd., New Delhi).

65. Obstfeld, Maurice (1994), Risk-taking, Global Diversification, and Growth, American Economic Review, 84(5), pp. 1310-29.
66. Paul Krugman (1995), Development, geography, and economic theory, (The MIT Press, Massachusetts).
67. Ray, Debraj (1998), Development Economics, (Princeton University Press, United States).
68. Raddatz, C (2006), Liquidity needs and vulnerability to financial underdevelopment, Journal of Financial Economics, 80(3), 677-722.
69. Rajan, Raghuram G. and Zingales, Luigi (1998), Financial dependence and growth, American Economic Review, 88 (3), pp. 559-586.
70. Ravallion, M (2001), Growth, Inequality and Poverty: Looking Beyond Averages, World Development 29(11), pp. 1803-1815.
71. Reddy, Y.V. (2002), Public Sector Banks and the Governance Challenge: Indian Experience, RBI Bulletin, May, pp. 337-356.
72. Report of R.V. Gupta Committee on Agricultural Credit through Commercial Banks in India, Reserve Bank of India Publications-Reports.
73. Report of the Advisory Committee on Flow of Credit to Agriculture, (Vyas committee), Reserve Bank of India Publications-Reports.
74. Report of the Expert Committee on Rural Credit in India, Reserve bank of India Publications-Reports.
75. Report of the IBA Working Group on Agriculture Credit in India, Reserve Bank of India Publications-Reports.
76. Schumpeter, Joseph A (1934), The Theory of Economic Development", 1912, translated by Redvers Opie, (Cambridge, MA: Harvard University Press).
77. Sen, Amartya (2000), Development as Freedom, (Anchor Books, New York).
78. Srinivasan, T.N. (1994), Human Development: A New Paradigm or Reinvention of the Wheel? American Economic Review, Papers and Proceedings 84(2): 238-243.
79. Streeten, Paul (1994), Human Development: Means and Ends, American Economic Review, Papers and Proceedings 84(2): 232-237.
80. Sugden, Robert (1993), Welfare, Resources, and Capabilities: A Review of Inequality Re-examined by Amartya Sen, Journal of Economic Literature.
81. Usai S and Vannini M (2005), Banking Structure and Regional Economic Growth: Lessons from Italy, Annals of Regional Science 39: 691-714.
82. Wade, R (1990) "Governing the markets", (Princeton: Princeton University Press).
83. White H. and E. Anderson (2001), Growth vs. Redistribution: Does the Pattern of Growth Matter? Development Policy Review 19(3), pp. 167-289.
84. World Bank (2005), Economic Growth in the 1990s: Learning from a Decade of Reform, World Bank, Washington DC.
85. World Bank (2006), India: Inclusive Growth and Service Delivery - Building on India's Success, World Bank Development Policy Review.

6

Enhancing Financial Inclusion through the Implementation of Self Help Group Bank Linkage Model

Jnaneshwar Pai Maroor and *Ashalatha. K.*

Introduction

Indian economy continues to suffer from the problems of poverty, sectoral divergences in growth and employment opportunities and a poor progress of various socio-economic indicators, despite of higher economic growth in recent past. Attaining the objective of hundred per cent financial inclusion is today one of the biggest challenges for Indian banking system. Greater Financial Inclusion shall be a catalyst for accelerating the pace of economic growth with equity. Financial inclusion can be relied upon to achieve inclusive growth which is one of the major objectives of 12th five year plan. There are various literatures which have studied the relationship between financial inclusion and economic growth and considered financial inclusion as a major determinant to economic growth. In fact there exists a two way relationship between financial inclusion and economic growth. On one hand, higher the financial inclusion, higher will be economic development. On the other hand greater infrastructural development and economic development facilitate higher financial inclusion.

Financial inclusion is the process of ensuring access to financial services and timely and adequate credit where needed by vulnerable Groups such as weaker sections and low income groups at an affordable cost. Financial inclusion also facilitates in efficient allocation of resources and enables the economy to maximise welfare by reducing the spread of informal source of avenues. A large number of earlier studies often suggest that development of the financial sector and better access to financial services are imperatives for facilitating economic growth with equity. Without an inclusive financial system, poor individuals and small enterprises have to rely on their limited savings and earnings to invest in their education and entrepreneurship to take advantages of growth opportunities (World Bank, 2008).

Achieving financial inclusion through formal banking system is a cumbersome task. Unavailability of adequate financial services like credit, insurances, and remittances to majority population at an affordable cost is a major roadblock for the growth of financial sectors. In this context, Micro-finance approach can be considered as an alternative solution to provide financial services to common section of the society. Micro-finance is the provision of thrift, credit and other financial services and products of very small amounts to the poor for enabling them to raise their income levels and improve their living standards. Microfinance consisting of micro credit, micro savings and micro insurance, is regarded as an important tool to reduce risk, poverty and vulnerability of common people. The micro finance sector started getting recognition in India after the launch of the self help group linkage model in the year 1992. Micro-finance through self help group bank linkage model can provide sustainable mechanism to meet the unmet financial needs of un-banked poor.

Rationale for Financial Inclusion in India

Impeded and higher cost of access to adequate financial services like credit, insurances, and remittances to majority population are major roadblocks for the growth of primary sectors like agriculture. Financial inclusion can create win-win environment for both customer and financial institution in an economy (Thorat, 2006). It enables customer to avail various kind of financial products for productive purposes. It also helps customers in availing micro remittance facilities, micro credit at an affordable cost. The Government also can use the bank accounts of people for providing various social security services for the vulnerable section of society. Thus, financial inclusion can be considered as prerequisite to achieve inclusive growth which would further helps in achieving sustainable economic growth.

Financial Inclusion in India: An Overview

Financial inclusion ensures ease of availability, accessibility and usage of formal financial system to all members of the economy (Sharma, 2008). Financial inclusion has been widely recognised as important means to achieve inclusive growth on India. During the post nationalisation of banking period, there has been spectacular progress in formal banking networks across the country. In the course of time, Reserve Bank of India has been adopting various measures like priority sector lending, KYC norms, banking correspondent model to ensure financial inclusion. In fact, measuring financial inclusion in a developing country like India is different from other developed countries. Financial inclusion can be measured in two ways. One is inclusion in the payments system i.e. having access to a bank account. The second type of inclusion is towards formal credit markets, thus requiring the excluded to approach informal and exploitative markets.

Previously various studies on financial inclusion have identified various factors which are responsible for financial exclusion in an economy. Some of these factors responsible for financial exclusion have been mentioned below:

- Lack of proper infrastructural development.
- Geographical factors: Remote and hilly areas.
- From demand side lack of awareness, income and asset constraints, limited literacy especially financial literacy and social exclusion act as major barriers.
- From supply side cumbersome documentation procedure, unavailability of diversified products and services, high transaction costs, and easy availability of informal credits are major barrier to achieve financial inclusion. (Thorat, 2007).
- Other factors like gender issues, nature of occupation, social security payment systems are also playing vital roles in influencing access to financial services. (World Bank, 2008).

Individual indicators like number of bank accounts, number of bank branches, size of credit and deposit to GDP are also used to measure the extent of inclusiveness of financial system. Financial services provided by various financial institutions like banks, postal saving banks, non banking finance companies; micro finance institutions are also form the basis to measure the level of financial inclusion in an economy. Number of bank account per thousand adults is considered as one of the common measure of financial inclusion.

Figure 1. Total No of Banking A/c s per 1000 adults

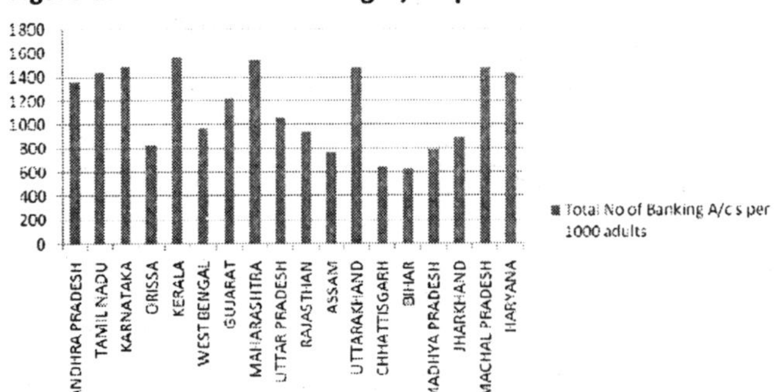

Fig. 1 represents financial inclusion in terms of total number of bank accounts per 1000 adults across various states for the year 2008. This figure depicts spread of financial inclusion across various states.

Sources: BSR report, Reserve Bank of India, Census of India.

SeLf Help Group Linkage Model and Financial Inclusion

In spite of Indian banking sector having witnessed a spectacular progress in spread of banking networks and extending financial outreaches across the country in the recent past, the relative decline in the supply of credit in rural areas poses the biggest challenge to achieve hundred per cent financial inclusion before Indian formal financial system. In this context, self help group bank linkage model launched by NABARD (1992) can be conceived as an alternative model to bridge the gaps which could not be filled up by formal banking system. It facilitates extending financial services to unbanked vulnerable section of society. NABARD led SHG bank linkage model is widely accepted as one of the largest and successful micro finance model in the world.

Three kinds of model are being emerged under SHG linkage programme. They are:

Model 1: SHGs are financed, guided and promoted by banks.

Model 2: SHGs are promoted by Non Government Organisations/ Government agencies but financed by bank.

Model 3: SHGs are promoted by NGOs but financed through financial intermediaries like NGOs or by any formal agencies.

Progress of SHG Linkage Programme in India

NABARD led SHG bank linkage programme witnessed a significant progress in the recent past. As on March 2011, total 6121147 SHGs were having Rs. 5545.62 cr savings with banks .On the other hand total 12253.51 cr loan have been disbursed to 1609586 SHGs and thereby registered 38.5% and 31.1% growth respectively. (Report by NABARD 2009-10). Overall progress under micro finance through SHG Bank linkage model from 2006-07 to 2009-10 has been given in the following Table 1:

Table 1: SHG Bank Linkage Model

Particulars		*2009-10*		*2010-11*		*2011-12*	
		No of SHGs	*Amount (crores)*	*No of SHGs*	*Amount (crores)*	*No of SHGs*	*Amount (crores)*
Savings of SHGs with Banks as on 31st March	Total SHGS	4160584	3512.71	5009794	3885.39	6121147	5545.62
	Out of which SGSY	956317	757.50	1203070	809.51	1505581	1563.38
Bank loan disbursed to SHGs during the year	Total SHGS	1105749	6570.39	1227770	8849.26	1609586	12253.51
	Out of which SGSY	188962	1411.02	246649	1857.74	264653	2015.22

Sources: Report on status of micro finance in India, NABARD.

Figure 2: Growth and progress of self help groups under SHG bank linkage

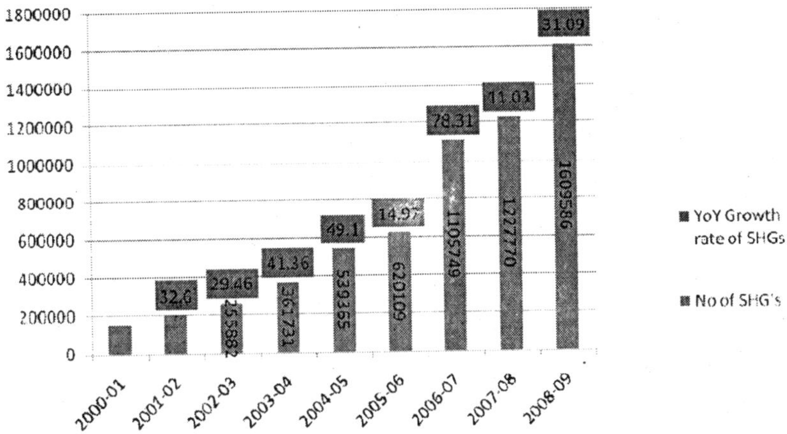

Source: www.indiastat.com.

Figure 2 represents the progress of SHG bank linkage programme from the year 200-01 to 2008-09. From the period 2000-01 to 2011-12, total number of SHG increased from 149050 to 1609586. The year 2010-11 witnessed a significant growth (78.31%) in total number of SHGs over previous year. The year 2008-09 registered a year on year growth of 31.09% for the number of SHG's under SHG bank linkage programme. SHG bank linkage programme has been recognised as one of the most successful and rapidly growing micro finance model to meet the promise to financial inclusion in India.

Figure 3: No. of SHGs across various states and level of financial inclusion

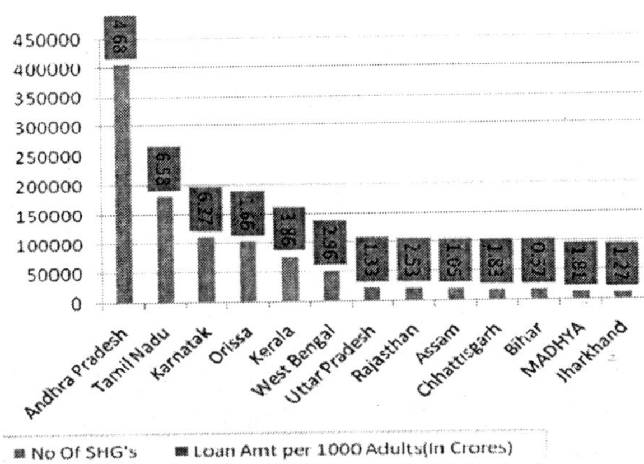

Sources: RBI, Census of India, NABARD

Figure 3 represents the spread of number of SHGs across various states and the level of financial inclusion in terms of credit deepening across them. The above figure depicts the close relationship between the level of credit deepening and the presence of absolute number of Self Help Groups across various states. States like Andhra Pradesh, Tamil Nadu, and Karnataka which had a higher presence of SHGs witnessed a higher level of credit deepening than states like Jharkhand, Bihar, Madhya Pradesh. It can be inferred from the figure that the spread of SHGs across the country along with the progress of formal banking network is skewed. Thereby leading to disparities in the levels of credit widening and credit deepening across various states.

Review of Literature

Sharma (2008), through cross country empirical study examined a close relationship between financial inclusion and development. Further, the study found a positive relation between financial inclusion and different socio-economic variables like income, inequality, literacy, physical infrastructures.

Kempson and Whyley (1998) argued that possibility of financial exclusion is more likely to occur in the lower income section of society than amongst others. Beside this, geographical factors and income inequality are also important factors in determining financial inclusion of a country.

Goodwin et. al. (2000) emphasised the role of level of employment of a country as another important factor of financial inclusion. Access to affordable financial services especially credit and insurance - enlarges livelihood opportunities and empowers the poor to take charge of their lives. Such empowerment aids social and political stability. Financial inclusion also imparts formal identity, provides access to the payments system and to savings safety net like deposit insurance. Hence it is considered to be critical for achieving inclusive growth; which itself is required for ensuring overall sustainable overall growth in the country. (Thorat, 2007).

Beck et. al. (2000), in their paper tried to evaluate empirically the relationship between level of financial intermediary development and economic growth. They observed a positive impact of financial intermediary development on the growth of total factor productivity which will lead to economic development.

Bekaert et. al. (2004), in their study examined a positive impact of equity market liberalisation on real economic growth. Further, they also observed the positive impact of capital account liberalisation and quality of financial institutions on economic growth.

Greenwood et. al. (1990), tried addressed two important issues in economic growth theories in a single model. They are relationship between economic growth and inequality and relation between financial structures and economic development. They argued that financial development facilitates economic growth as it gives high return on capital. On the other hand economic development also provides means to financial development.

A few empirical studies on the impact of SHG bank linkage model also revealed the importance of SHG model in achieving financial inclusion and inclusive growth in India. Puhazhendi and Satyasai (2000), studied the improvement in level of income of SHG members between pre and post SHG situations.

Chavan and Ramakumar (2002) in their study compared NGO led micro credit programme of various countries with state led poverty alleviation scheme and observed marginal improvement in member's income as a result of micro credit programme.

Puhazhendi and Badatya (2002), observed a significant improvements in the savings SHG members during post SHG situations. The programme also improves the borrowing pattern of SHG member households in terms of strengthening credit widening and credit deepening.

Sanghwan (2006), studied the extent financial inclusion across various states. He also tried to examine the role of SHG bank linkage programme in achieving financial inclusion. The study suggested a significant role of SHG led programme in achieving financial inclusion. Beside this, it also tried to examine the role of other factors like banking density, financial literacy and per capita income in achieving financial inclusion.

Sahoo et.al (2008), had attempted to develop index of financial inclusion to examine the progress of financial inclusion and various determinants of financial inclusion using secondary data from various sources. In their study, they observed a positive impact of infrastructure development, education; self help group formation on financial inclusion both from financial widening and deepening perspectives.

Model Specifications

Financial inclusion in an economy is determined by multiple factors like infrastructural development, economic development, type of financial products, financial literacy etc. Financial inclusion can be measured both from saving as well as credit aspects of financial inclusion. However, the present study attempts to measure the financial inclusion from credit widening and credit deepening aspects of financial inclusion. It also intends to study the role of various determinants of financial inclusion for 16 states for the period 2008. Secondary data for the study have been collected from various sources like Census of India, various report published by RBI, NABARD. In the regression analysis, two sets of regression equation have been fitted. There are four independent variables in the model. The selected independent variables are being taken based upon the various literatures on financial inclusion. Number of credit accounts and amount of credit/loan disbursed per 1000 adult populations has been taken as two dependent variables in the model. On the other hand level of economic development, financial literacy, branch density, percentage of credit linked SHG house hold is taken as independent variables. Per capita income, literacy rate are proxy variables of level of development and financial literacy respectively.

Model: $Cw = \beta_1 + \beta_2 x_2 + \beta_3 x_3 + \beta_4 x_4 + \beta_5 x_5 + u_1$ ....(1)

$Cd = \beta_1 + \beta_2 x_2 + \beta_3 x_3 + \beta_4 x_4 + \beta_5 x_5 + u_2$ ....(2)

Where, X_2 = Per capita income;

X_3 = Primary literacy;

X_4 = Branch density;

X_5 = No. of SHG groups having access to credit

β_1, β_1 are intercepts.

β_2, β_3, β_4, β_5, β_2, β_3, β_4, β_5 are co-efficients.

U_1 and U_2 are disturbances terms.

Table 2: Description of variables

Sl. No.	*Variables*	*Notation used*
1	No. of credit accounts per thousand adults.	Cd
2	Amount of loan disbursed per thousand adults.	Cw
3	Per capita income	X2
4	No. of persons having primary education per thousand adult population	X3
5	Population per branch (*Branch density*)	X4
6	No of SHG having access to credit through Self help group bank linkage programme	X5

Table 3: Correlation Matrix

Correlation matrix: 3.a Credit widening

	Cw	X2	X3	X4	X5
Cw	1				
X2	.5224	1			
X3	.4490	.1628	1		
X4	-.5778	-.8726	-.2714	1	
X5	.6098	.0379	.2489	-.1578	1

Correlation Matrix: 3.b Credit Deepening

	Cd	X2	X3	X4	X5
Cd	1				
X2	.7938	1			
X3	.2878	.1628	1		
X4	-.7851	-.8726	-.2714	1	
X5	.4066	.0379	.2489	-.1578	1

Table 3 presents the zero order correlation matrix to test the problem of multi collinearity problem in the model. The correlation matrix shows absence of correlation among selected exogenous variables.

Empirical Results and Findings

The objective of the study is to examine the role of SHG bank linkage model in achieving financial inclusion across various states. A cross sectional regression analysis was adopted to study the impact of selected independent variables on financial inclusion. The empirical results of two regression equation have been mentioned in the following table.

As depicted in the table, the R2 for equation (1) is 67.75%. +There exists a positive relationship between Credit Widening (Cw) with all the independent variables except for variable X4. This clearly describes that higher economic development, higher financial literacy and an effective SHG bank linkage programme facilitates higher financial inclusion across various states. The inverse relationship between Cw and X4 (Population per branch) describes larger expansion of branches lead to larger financial inclusion. The white test of heteroscadasticity also revealed the absence of heteroscadasticity in the model.

In case of equation (2), R2 is 78.38%. This explains that 78.83% of variation in financial inclusion in terms of financial deepening can be explained by the selected exogenous variables. The amount of loan disbursed per 1000 adult persons was taken as the measure of financial deepening. There exists a positive relationship between Financial Deepening with Per Capita Income, Financial Literacy, and an effective SHG bank linkage programme. At a 5% level of significance, both per capita income (X2) and SHG variables (X5) are found to be significantly affecting the amount of Financial Inclusion in terms of Financial Deepening.

Table 4: Regression Results

Dependent Variables Explanatory Variables	*No of Credit account per 1000 adult population*	*Amount of loan disbursed per 1000 adult population*
X_2	.0023126 (1.01)	.0000992 (2.08)**
X_3	.3470009 (1.25)	.0020767 (0.36)
X_4	-.0018425 (-0.31)	-.0000733 (-0.59)
X_5	.0004133 (2.89)*	6.90e-06 (2.31)**
Intercepts	.5343454 (0.00)	.7809542 (0.23)
R2	0.6775	0.7838

Note: Significance at *1%, **5%.

Conclusion

The present paper attempted to study the impact of self help group bank linkage programme in achieving financial inclusion across sixteen states for the period 2008. The multiple regression analysis method exhibited a positive and significant impact of Self Help Group bank linkage programme on financial inclusion in terms of credit deepening. The empirical analysis also revealed a positive impact of economic development and financial literacy on financial inclusion whereas branch density (population per branch) exhibited an inverse relationship with financial inclusion. Self Help group linkage model is one of the successfully operated models of Microfinance in India. Under this model, the SHGs are financed by bank without any collateral, peer group pressure is considered as collateral by the lenders. Self Help Group bank Linkage Model also helps to reduce transaction costs facilitates proper monitoring of funds by group members, economic empowerment of SHG members by collective decision making etc. In spite of the increased spread of formal banking network in the recent past, access to basic financial services are still beyond the reach of large sections of society. SHG bank linkage model exhibits the potential to provide an alternative mechanism to extend financial services to large unbanked sections of the society.

References

Basu Priya (2006), "Improving Access to Finance for India's Rural Poor", The World Bank, Washington.

Beck Thorsten, Ross Levine and Norman Loayza. (2000), "Finance and the Sources of Growth" Journal of Financial Economics 58 (1): pp. 261-300.

Bekaert, Geert, Harvey Campbell R and Lundblad Christian (2005), "Does financial liberalisation spur growth?" Journal of Financial Economics, Volume 77, July 2005, pp. 3-55.

Chavan pallavi and Ramakumar R., (2002), Micro-Credit and Rural Poverty: An Analysis of Empirical Evidence, Economic and Political Weekly, Vol. 37, No. 10 (Mar. 9-15, 2002), pp. 955-965.

Goodwin D., Adelman L., Middleton S. and Ashworth K. (2000), Debt, Money Management and Access to Financial Services: Evidence from the 1999 PSE Survey of Britain, 1999 PSE Survey Working Paper 8, Centre for Research in social policy, Loughborough University.

Government of India (2001): Census of India Report 2001.

Greenwood, Jeremy, and Jovanovic Boyan (1990), "Financial Development, Growth and the Distribution of Income." Journal of Political Economy 98 (5): 1076-1107.

NABARD: Annual Report, Various issues.

Puhazhendi V. and Satyasai K. J.S (2000), "Micro-finance for Rural People: An Impact Evaluation", NABARD.

Report of the Internal Group to Examine Issues Relating to Rural Credit and Microfinance (2005), Reserve Bank of India.

Reserve Bank of India (2008), Banking Statistical Return reports.

Reserve Bank of India, "Speeches published on Financial Inclusion".

Sahoo B.B, Mehrotra Nirupam and Nair Gopakumaran G. (2008): "Financial Inclusion-An Overview" Occasional paper-48, NABARD.

Sangwan S.S. (2008), "Financial Inclusion and Self Help Groups", NABARD.

Shahidur R. Khandker (2005): "Micro Finance and Poverty: Evidence Using Panel Data from Bangladesh", The World Bank Economic Review.

Sharma Mandira (2007), "Index of Financial Inclusion", Working paper, ICRIER, New Delhi.

Websites Referred

1. www.indiastat.com
2. www.rbi.org.in
3. www.nabard.org

7

Financial Inclusion in India – A Case Study of Belagavi City

N Maruti Rao **and** *Vishwanath Talwar*

Introduction

Government of India has taken number of steps to ensure vulnerable section of society should get access to financial services and products which includes setting up co-operative banks and State Bank of India, nationalisation of banks, Lead Bank Scheme, setting up of regional rural banks, promotion of Self Help Groups, etc. in spite of these efforts, in India, almost half the country is unbanked. Only 55 per cent of the population have deposit accounts and 9 per cent have credit accounts with banks. India has the highest number of households (145 million) excluded from Banking. There was only one bank branch per 14,000 people. Six lakh villages in India, rural branches of SCBs including RRBs number 33,495. Only a little less than 20% of the population has any kind of life insurance and 9.6% of the population has non-life insurance coverage. Just 18 per cent had debit cards and less than 2 per cent had credit cards. In the backdrop of this a study has been conducted to find out awareness about financial inclusion, financial products and services offered by banks, to assess the level of financial inclusion among vulnerable section of society and to understand the difficulties faced by banks and NGO. Belgaum city has been selected for the purpose of study.

Definition of Financial Inclusion

It is the process of ensuring access to appropriate financial products and services needed by vulnerable groups such as weaker sections and low income groups at an affordable cost in a fair and transparent manner by mainstream institutional players.

Objectives of the Study

1. To assess the level of financial inclusion among the vulnerable sections of society in Belgaum City.
2. To study the awareness level of the vulnerable section of society in Belgaum City about financial inclusion, financial products and services offered by the bank.
3. To offer suggestions for overall development of vulnerable sections of society though financial inclusion.

Research Methodology

The present study was intended to assess the level of financial inclusion among the vulnerable section of society in Belgaum City and also to study their awareness about financial inclusion, financial products and services offered by the bank and to understand the difficulties faced by banks in the area of financial inclusion. Five vulnerable areas of Belgaum city are selected Viz. Kasai Galli, New Gandhi Nagar, Gangwadi and *Vantamuri and 25 respondents from each vulnerable area* were randomly selected for the study. Face to face interview was conducted by using interview schedule to collect information from the respondents. Percentage was used to analyse data on demographic characteristics, level of financial inclusion and the awareness level of the respondents about financial inclusion, financial products and services offered by the banks.

Results and Analysis

The purpose of financial inclusion is delivery of banking services at an affordable price in a fair and transparent manner to the vulnerable sections o the society.

Socio-economic Status of the Respondents

The table 1 reveals that 72 per cent of respondents interviewed in selected survey areas were in the age group of 18 to 35 years. It is observed that 68 per cent of the respondents in the survey areas were male. Majority of the respondents were completed only primary level (48 per cent). Majority of the respondents were working as labour and house-made (48 per cent and 44 per cent respectively). It is noted that 92 per cent of the respondents were belonging to family monthly income range of Rs.1001 to Rs. 5000.

Table 1: Socio-Economic Profile of the Respondents

Socio-Economic Factors		*Respondents*							
		Kasai Galli		*New Gandhi Nagar*		*Gangwadi*		*Vantamuri*	
		Nos.	*%*	*Nos.*	*%*	*Nos.*	*%*	*Nos.*	*%*
Age	Below 25	09	36	12	48	07	28	10	40
	26-35	07	28	06	24	12	48	08	32
	36-45	05	20	03	12	04	16	04	16
	46-50	03	12	01	4	01	4	01	4
	Above 50	01	4	03	12	-	-	02	8
Gender	Male	25	100	19	76	16	64	17	68
	Female	-	-	06	24	09	36	08	32
Education	Illiterate	12	48	11	44	06	24	07	28
	Primary	06	24	08	32	15	60	12	48
	High School	04	16	02	8	03	12	04	16
	PUC	01	4	01	4	01	4	02	8
	Graduate	01	4	01	4	-	-	-	-
	Post Graduate	-	-	-	-	-	-	-	-
	Other	01	4	02	8	-	-	-	-
Type of occupation	Petty business	05	20	03	12	04	16	02	8
	Job	-	-	-	-	-	-	-	-
	Labour	20	80	19	76	15	60	12	48

contd...

Table 1 (contd...)

Socio-Economic Factors		*Respondents*							
		Kasai Galli		*New Gandhi Nagar*		*Gangwadi*		*Vantamuri*	
		Nos.	*%*	*Nos.*	*%*	*Nos.*	*%*	*Nos.*	*%*
	House made	-	-	03	12	06	24	11	44
Family monthly income	Below Rs. 500	-	-	2	8	1	4	-	-
	Rs. 505-1000	07	28	11	44	2	8	2	8
	Rs. 1001-1500	18	72	12	48	22	88	23	92
	Rs. 1501-2000	-	-	-	-	-		-	-

Source: Field work.

Financial Inclusion Status of the Respondents

The financial inclusion status of the selected respondents is discussed under the following headings.

Have a Bank Account

Table 2: Have A Bank Account

Particulars	*Respondents*								
	Kasai Galli		*New Gandhi Nagar*		*Gangwadi*		*Vantamuri*		*All Area*
	Nos.	*%*	*Nos.*	*%*	*Nos.*	*%*	*Nos.*	*%*	*Nos.*
Yes	07	28	04	16	03	12	01	04	15
No	18	72	21	84	22	88	24	96	85
Total	**25**	**100**	**25**	**100**	**25**	**100**	**25**	**100**	**100**

Source: Field work.

It is observed that (table 2) out of 100 surveyed respondents 85 per cent are having bank account whereas 15 per cent of respondents are not having the bank account.

Reasons for not Having Bank Account

Table 3: Reasons For Not Having Bank Account

Particulars	*Respondents*								
	Kasai Galli		*New Gandhi Nagar*		*Gangwadi*		*Vantamuri*		*All Area*
	Nos.	*%*	*Nos.*	*%*	*Nos.*	*%*	*Nos.*	*%*	*Nos.*
Distance	-		-	-	-	-	-	-	-
No money to save	12	66.7	12	57	7	31.8	6	25	37
Lack of awareness	02	11.1	09	43	15	68.2	13	54.2	39
Lack of advice	04	22.2	-	-	-	-	3	12.5	07
No identity cards	-	-	-	-	-	-	-	-	-
Lack of understanding	-	-	-	-	-	-	2	8.3	02
Total	**18**	**100**	**21**	**100**	**22**	**100**	**24**	**100**	**85**

Source: Field work.

Regarding the reasons for not having a bank account (table 3) majority of respondents in Kasai Galli and New Gandhi Nagar are not having money to save in bank account hence they have not opened bank account. Majority of respondents from Gangwadi and *Vantamuri* have not opened the bank account due to Lack of awareness. According to respondents, distance and not having identity card are not the route cause for respondents' not opening bank account. Seven per cent of respondents reported that due to lack of advice they could not open the bank account and two per cent of respondents are under lack of knowledge.

Awareness Level of the Respondents about no Frills Account

No-frills account (NFA) is financial product which allows financially excluded individuals to access banking services for the purpose of savings and also had credit feature in the form of overdraft facility. It is clear from the table 4 that 82 per cent of the respondents were unaware of no frills account.

Table 4: Awareness of No Frills Account

Awareness	*Respondents*								*All Area*
	Kasai Galli		*New Gandhi Nagar*		*Gangwadi*		*Vantamuri*		
	No.	*%*	*No.*	*%*	*No.*	*%*	*No.*	*%*	
Yes	02	08	05	20	01	04	-	-	08
No	23	92	20	80	24	96	25	100	92
TOTAL	**25**	**100**	**25**	**100**	**25**	**100**	**25**	**100**	**100**

Source: Field work.

PURPOSE OF USING NO FRILLS ACCOUNT

Table 5 : Purpose of Using No Frills Account

Purpose	*Respondents*								*All Area*
	Kasai Galli		*New Gandhi Nagar*		*Gangwadi*		*Vantamuri*		
	No.	*%*	*No.*	*%*	*No.*	*%*	*No.*	*%*	
No use	-	-	01	20	-	-	-	-	01
Saving	02	100	04	80	01	100	-	-	07
TOTAL	**02**	**100**	**05**	**100**	**01**	**100**	-	-	**08**

Source: Field work.

It is observed from table 5 that 12.5 per cent of the respondents were not using no frills account though they were aware of no frills account. However majority of respondents (87.5 per cent) of the respondents who are aware of no frills account were using the same service.

Source of Information About no Frills Account

Table 6: Source of Knowing No Frills Account

Source	*Respondents*								*All Area*
	Kasai Galli		*New Gandhi Nagar*		*Gangwadi*		*Vantamuri*		
	No.	*%*	*No.*	*%*	*No.*	*%*	*No.*	*%*	
Media	-	-	-	-	-	-	-	-	-
SHG	-	-	01	20	-	-	-	-	01
Bank	02	100	04	80	01	100	-	-	07
Others	-	-	-	-	-	-	-	-	-
TOTAL	**02**	**100**	**05**	**100**	**01**	**100**	-	-	**08**

Source: Field work

The table 6 reveals that bank employees are playing a critical role in creating the awareness and spreading message about no frills account. The table also reveals that media and Self Help Groups failed to act as source of information, the role which they are supposed to play.

Awareness Level of the Responents about Financial Services Offered by Banks after Opening an Account

The table 7 exhibits that majority (85 per cent) of the respondents were well familiar about deposits and saving after opening an account. It is noted that (54 per cent) of the respondents were familiar about pass books and cheque after opening an account. 67 per cent of the respondents were well familiar about loans and interest rates after opening an account. It is also noted that (76 per cent) of the respondents were well familiar about ATMs after opening an account. Only 4 per cent of the respondents were not familiar about insurance schemes even after opening an account.

Table 7: Awareness Level of the Responents About Financial Services Offered by Banks After Opening an Account

Awareness of Financial Service		*Respondents*								*All Area*
		Kasai Galli		*New Gandhi Nagar*		*Gangwadi*		*Vantamuri*		
		No.	*%*	*No.*	*%*	*No.*	*%*	*No.*	*%*	
Deposits and saving	Not familiar	-	-	-	-	-	-	-	-	-
	Just familiar	18	100	21	100	22	100	24	100	85
Pass book and cheque	Not familiar	06	33.3	06	28.6	09	40.9	10	41.7	31
	Just familiar	12	66.7	15	31.5	13	59.1	14	58.3	54
Loans and interest rate	Not familiar	03	16.7	03	14.3	07	31.8	05	20.8	18
	Just familiar	15	83.3	18	85.7	15	68.2	19	79.2	67
ATM	Not familiar	16	88.9	19	90.5	20	90.9	21	87.5	76
	Just familiar	02	11.1	02	9.5	02	9.1	03	12.5	09
Insurance schemes	Not familiar	18	100	20	95.2	21	95.5	22	91.7	81
	Just familiar	-	-	01	4.8	01	4.5	02	8.3	04
		18	**100**	**21**	**100**	**22**	**100**	**24**	**100**	**85**

Source: Field work.

Majority of the academicians are of the view that banks should set up service centres in vulnerable areas offering banking services. Whereas majority of non-academicians are of the view that Self Help Groups should play a key role in providing banking services to vulnerable sections of society and they also recommended setting up of exclusive lead bank focussing on vulnerable section of society. Both academicians as well as non-academicians suggested that bank should focus on providing Aadhaar Enabled banking services. Both academicians and non-academicians are of the view that Relaxation on know-your-customer (KYC) norms and Link between Banks and SHGs may not give better results if used as financial inclusion strategies (table 8).

Table 8 : Strategies for Financial Inclusion (Academician and Non-Academician)

Strategies for Financial Inclusion	*Acad-emician*	*%*	*Non-Acad-emician*	*%*	*All Respon-dents*	*%*
Service Centre in Vulnerable areas	13	52	05	20	18	36
Financial Literacy Camp	18	72	19	76	37	72
Relaxation on know-your-customer (KYC) norms	07	28	04	16	11	22
Aadhaar Enabled banking services	20	80	19	76	39	78
Key role by Self Help Groups	11	44	14	56	25	50
Lead Bank focusing vulnerable section	06	24	17	68	23	46
Link between Banks & SHGs	04	16	08	32	12	24
Total No. of Respondents	**25**	**100**	**25**	**100**	**50**	**100**

Source: Field work.

Suggestions

- As majority of respondents have not opened the bank account due to Lack of awareness. Further, majority of respondents were also unaware of no frills account. Therefore, the need of the hour is that banks in Belgaum city in association with Belgaum Municipal Corporation and Neemadi Kendra should organise financial literacy programme for the benefit of vulnerable section of society in vulnerable areas. This may help in creating awareness among vulnerable section of the society.
- Majority of the respondents who have opened bank account but are unaware of financial service offered by banks such as Pass book and cheque, ATM and Insurance schemes. In the light of this it is suggested that financial literacy camp should be organised to educate bank accountholders.
- The researchers are of the view that the vulnerable section of the society should open no frill account and this account should be tagged with Aadhaar Enabled payments.

- The researchers are of the view that the Neemdi Kendra should be restructured to enable it offer banking services to vulnerable section of the society at cost effective manner as it can prove to win-win model for all stakeholders.
- Banks should provide general ATM and overdraft facilities along with no frills account to encourage the account holders to actively operate the accounts.
- The accessibility of banking services is poor on an account of various constraints such as distance, no money to save and difficulty to understand the banking services. Therefore, it is recommended that banking service centres should be set up in residential areas where the vulnerable sections of society are living.
- Government should take various steps regarding a greater focus on credit rather financial services like saving and insurance although banks and financial institution and co-operative did provide facilities.
- Government should introduce new scheme to bring the socially excluded groups to be included in the financial sectors by offering low interest rates, credit facilities, low premium insurance schemes and pension scheme.

Conclusion

Financial inclusion and infrastructure should go hand in hand for all round development of vulnerable sections of society in order to ensure that they should have access to health, education, shelter, information and insurances apart from financial services. Banks should offer vulnerable actions of society no frill account with certain minimum common facilities. The services provided in this account should include deposit and withdrawal of cash at the bank branches as well as ATMs, credit of monetary benefits received under government schemes etc.

References

A. J. Vinayak, "Financial inclusion – The challenges ahead', Businessline, Mangalore, Augest. 29:

Dr. Debesh Roy, Assistant General Manager, NABARD, Financial Inclusion in India-Emerging Profitable Models".

Dr. K.C. Chakrabarty, Deputy Governor. Reserve Bank of India, Financial inclusion, keynote speech, St. Xavier's College, September 6, 2011.

Harun R Khan, ":Issues and Challenges in Financial Inclusion: Policies, Partnerships, Processes and Products" Keynote address, Indian Institute of Public Administration.

Reserve Bank of India, "Report of the Committee on Financial Inclusion", January 2008.

Sandeep Aggarwal, "Financial Inclusion: Understanding through Behavioural Perspectives", ZENITH International Journal Of Business Economics and Management Research Vol. 2 Issue 2, February 2012, pp. 225-229.

Sadhan Kumar Chattopadhyay. "Financial inclusion in India: A case-study of West Bengal", Paper presented at seminar.

8

An Analysis of the Performance of MGNREGP in Karnataka

M. Indira and *C. Anand*

Introduction

In September 2005, Indian Parliament enacted a remarkable piece of legislation – the National Rural Employment Guarantee Act (NREGA), later renamed Mahatma Gandhi National Rural Employment Guarantee Act (MGNREGA). The Act recognises employment as an entitlement and defines an obligation for the government – the obligation to provide, in each year, 100 days of wage employment at a stipulated minimum wage to all rural households whose members are seeking or willing to do unskilled manual work. Initially it was launched in 200 poorest districts during 2006-07 and later it was extended to another 130 districts during 2007-08. Since 2008-09, MGNREGP has been implemented in all the 600 non-urban districts in the country.

Special wage employment schemes for rural areas are not new in India; a variety of such schemes have been implemented since 1960. what is new in MGNREGP is that it is a special wage employment scheme with a binding obligation on the part of the government. Thus MGNREGP represents an explicit recognition by the government of its responsibility for ensuring availability of adequate employment for all workers.

The stated objectives of MGNREGP include not just creation of a social safety net for the vulnerable groups by creating a fall-back employment option but also stimulation of growth of the rural economy through a strengthening of the resource base in agriculture. In order to achieve the second objective the Act specifies a list of permissible works that can be undertaken for the purpose of providing wage employment under MGNREGP. These include water conservation and harvesting, building of irrigation works and canals, renovation of traditional water bodies (e.g., de-silting of tanks), land development, flood control and protection works, and improvement of "rural connectivity" (i.e., building of all-weather roads within rural areas). On one hand MGNREGP is expected to reduce rural poverty and on the other hand it is expected to have on indirect impact on the demand pattern in the rural areas.

There are two ways in which MGNREGP would increase money incomes of the rural poor. First, it would directly increase money incomes of workers from poor households in rural areas by generating additional wage incomes for them. Secondly, by increasing the demand for casual labour by paying a stipulated minimum wage, MGNREGP could conceivably have the effect of increasing the wage for casual labour in rural areas in general and thus increase the incomes of the poor indirectly. However the expected positive effects depend on how efficiently the money will be transferred to the identified beneficiaries.

The MGNEGP

The MGNREGP Act ensures, on demand, 100 days of employment in a year to a household at a minimum wage. It is based on the twin principles of universality and self-selection. The Act places enforceable obligation on the State and gives bargaining power to rural labourers. As a legal Right to Work, the NREG Scheme contrasts with previous employment generation schemes in several respects. First and the foremost, it bestows entitlements to workers – in the form of providing work for those who demand within a time frame (15 days of applying for work) at a guaranteed wage, which was not the case with earlier public works programmes. Second, the universal nature of the programme eliminates targeting errors. Third, the process of implementation and community involvement (in the form of social audits) is expected to reduce corruption and malpractices which formed a major weakness in earlier programmes. And finally, the guarantees enshrined in the Act are expected to ensure its implementation a binding responsibility of the government. (Mehrotra, 2008; Dhavse, 2004).

Given the focus on creating employment for unskilled workers by way of manual work, improvement of land and water resources formed an important part of the works undertaken. Water conservation, creation of water harvesting structures, and drought proofing (including afforestation and tree plantation) formed the top two activities in the order of priority in identification of public works. Improving land and micro and minor irrigation facilities (feeder channels, etc.) of marginal groups, especially SC, ST, and OBC communities, and those below the poverty line are also identified as important public works that would enhance productivity of land and provide long term asset base for the poor and the marginalised. Creation of flood protection mechanisms, renovation and restoration of water bodies are also part of the list of works which would enhance agricultural productivity and also strengthen the community resource base. Finally, rural connectivity (roads) is also part of permissible works as that would enhance communication and linkages with markets.

Apart from the focus on transforming the rural resource base, the implementation process of NREGS is expected to unleash a transformative potential in social relations and rural governance. At the center of implementation are three-tier Panchayat Raj institutions and Gram Sabha (the village community) plays a critical role in identifying and ratifying types of works to be undertaken in a village. Elected representatives of Panchayat, its official (Panchayat Secretary) and Rozgar Sevak (an NREGS worker – a dedicated field worker especially appointed for each Panchayat) have an important role in registering job seeker households, issuance of job cards, receiving job requests from workers, proposing suitable works for the approval of the Gram Sabha, monitoring of works, and timely payments. Functions at this level are scrutinised through a process of social audits, which again encompasses participation of the entire village community (Gram Sabha).

Salient Features of the MGNREGP

The NREGA extends to all rural areas of India, including Fifth and Sixth Schedule areas, except Jammu and Kashmir. The various provisions of the NREGA are the following: (i) it provides at least one hundred days of guaranteed wage employment in every fiscal year for at least one adult member of every household prepared to do unskilled manual labour at the wage rate specified by the state government; (ii) creation of durable assets and strengthening the livelihood resource base of the rural poor is an important objective of the scheme. The state council prepares a list of permissible works, as well as a list of "preferred works"; (iii) the programme may also provide, as far as possible, for the training and upgradation of the skills of unskilled labourers; (iv) wages may be paid in cash, in kind, or both, provided that at least one-fourth of the wages shall be paid in cash only; (v) employment shall be provided within a radius of five kilometres of the village where the applicant resides at the time of applying. In cases where employment is provided outside such radius, it must be provided within the block, and the labourers shall be paid 10 per cent of the wage rate as extra wages to meet additional transport and living expenses; (vi) in case the number of children below the age of six years accompanying the women working at any site is five or more, provisions shall be made to depute one women worker to look after such children. The person deputed for this shall be paid the statutory minimum wage; and (vii) a proportion of the wages, not exceeding 5 per cent, may be deducted as a contribution to welfare schemes organised for the benefit of labourers employed under the programme, such as health insurance, accident insurance, survivor benefits, maternity benefits, and social security schemes.

As specified in the act, for purpose of funding and the implementation of NREGA, the central government set up the National Employment Guarantee Fund. Individual state governments set up the State Employment Guarantee Fund for matching contribution under this scheme. The funding pattern, as laid down in the act, specifies that the central government's obligation would be to make payments of wages for unskilled manual workers under the scheme, up to three-fourths of the material costs of the scheme, including wages to skilled and semiskilled workers and a certain percentage of the total cost of the schemes determined by the central government. The state government shall have to bear the cost of unemployment allowance, one-fourth of the material costs, and the administrative expenses of the state council. Apart from the mandatory provision of resources required for the implementation of NREGA, its success in enhancing the "livelihood security" of rural households would critically depend on the effective implementation of the scheme.

MGNREGP provides for a multitier structure of authority for implementation and monitoring of the scheme with specified functions and duties for each authority. The agencies involved are Central Employment Guarantee Council, State Employment Guarantee Council, District Programme Coordinator, and the Program Officer appointed by the state government and the Gram Panchayat. The responsibility of the Gram Panchayat will be the identification, execution, and supervision of projects as per the recommendations of Gram Sabhas (village assembly). For accountability and transparency purposes, the Gram Sabhas are given the power to conduct a regular social audit of individual schemes. The structure of implementation as laid down indicates that a coordinated approach of different tiers of government or vertical coordination is critical for successful implementation of the scheme.

Also, the horizontal coordination across departments for programme identification and execution of work through Panchayat assumes critical importance.

Review of Related Literature

As the scheme is ongoing from 2006 onwards, various attempts have been made to analyse the performance of MGNREGA. Ramesh (2009) observed that the income levels of the workers have increased substantially and all the workers daily wage income was increased to two fold and in turn it helped in catering the minimum needs of the MGNREGA workers. The study also reveals that the expenditure before implementation of this scheme was met by indulging debts. So, it helped in easing out the debt burden to some extent after the implementation of the scheme. Pursty et.al (2009) reports that 80 per cent of informants agreeing to the fact that the standard of living of the people who have worked in NREGA has improved. It reconfirms strongly the hypotheses that NREGA has supplemented the income of worker households and 86 per cent of the workers feel that they are comfortable in having sufficient food after working in MGNREGA. It establishes the positive correlation between food security and MGNREGA. Indira Harway et.al (2008) observed that NREGA can reduce poverty at the bottom and empower the poor. If planned well, it can have highly positive output, income and employment multiplier effects on the local economy in the medium and long run. These works can also raise the multiplier co-efficient and accelerate the process of development subsequently. Anandharaja kumar (2010) observes that the income level of the scheme's women beneficiarys has increased after the implementation of MGNREA and the participation of women in the decision making of the family in regard to expenditure and saving has increased. Kareemulla et.al (2009) reports that the earnings from NREGA wages accounted for 32 per cent of the household income of those families who worked in the scheme as labourers. Purchase of food followed by expenses related to education of the dependents and health care was the major modes of utilisation of the earnings from NREGA. There seems to be a significant contribution towards household assets like fan, television and bicycle mainly by the savings of NREGA wages.

Objective

The Objective of this paper is to analyse the financial Performance of the MGNREP in Karnataka.

Methodology

The present paper is based on secondary data collected from the Annual Reports of Ministry of Rural Development, Government of India, Other references viz. relevant websites of Govt of India and Karnataka.

Progress of MGNREGP in India

Since the introduction of the programme during 2006-07 there is a continuous increase in the allocation of funds under the programme benefiting several lakhs of households in rural areas.

Table 1. Progress of MGNREGP in India (2006-2011)

Year	*Allocation of Funds (in lakhs)*	*Utilization (in lakhs)*	*percent of Amount Utilized*	*No. of HH P/E (in lakhs)*
2006-07	12.07	8.82	73.07	210.16
2007-08	19.27	15.85	82.38	339.09
2008-09	36.30	27.25	75.068	451.15
2009-10	45.68	37.90	82.96	525.30
2010-11	52.64	39.37	74.73	549.54

Sources: Ministry of Rural Development of Govt. of India.

Table 1 shows that the allocation has increased from mere Rs. 12 lakhs in 2006-07 to Rs. 52.64 lakhs by 2010-11. The number of households benefitted also increased from 210.16 lakhs to 549.54 lakhs. However an observation of the rate of growth in allocation and the number of households benefitted shows that while allocations increased by 336 per cent during the five years period, number of households increased only by 161 per cent. This shows that the growth in the number of households benefitted is not commensurate with the increase in allocation of resources, though the statistics indicate that out of the total allocations, nearly 75-80 per cent is actually spent. The percentage of actual spending to the allocations also shows fluctuations. In the first year of the introduction of the programme only 73 per cent was spent. But it increased to 82 per cent during the next year, i.e. 2007-08. However again it came down to 75 per cent during the next year though it increased to 83 per cent in 2009-10. Only around 75 per cent of the funds are spent during the year 2010-11.

District wise Allocation of Funds in Karnataka

Cumulative allocation of funds to different districts in Karnataka is presented in table 2. The data reveals that the total funds released up to 2010-11 was Rs. 160506 lakhs and out of this Rs. 59564 lakhs amounting to 37 per cent of the allocation was actually spent.

Table 2: Allocation of Funds under the MGNREGP in Karnataka Up to 2010-2011 (in lakhs)

Districts	*Total Availability (in lakhs)*	*Total Expenditure (in lakhs)*	*percent of Expenditure to total*
Bidar	4342	1618	37.27
Chitradurga	11732	8203	69.92
Davanagere	9790	5622	57.43
Gulbarga	9035	1245	13.78
Raichur	8655	6408	74.04
Belegaum	14318	8316	58.08
Bellary	3481	685	19.67
Chikkamagaluru	4460	1471	32.99
Hassan	4937	561	11.36
Kodagu	1461	482	32.97
Shimoga	5059	1718	33.96
Bagalakote	4800	1809	37.68

Districts	*Total Availability (in lakhs)*	*Total Expenditure (in lakhs)*	*percentage of Expenditure to total*
Bangalore	1281	34	2.63
Bangalore Rural	1767	556	31.45
Bijapur	8641	2650	30.66
Chamarajanagar	3235	631	19.5
Chikkaballapura	3088	1075	34.8
Dakshina kannada	1970	570	28.93
Dharwad	3905	1903	48.74
Gadag	3556	482	13.56
Haveri	5285	2787	52.73
Kolar	3720	2093	56.28
Koppal	9162	2147	23.43
Mandya	4316	753	17.44
Mysore	4876	109	2.23
Ramanagara	3465	1027	29.64
Tumkur	10473	1183	11.29
Udupi	1754	95	5.4
Uttarakannada	2695	1053	39.08
Yadgiri	5246	2280	43.46
Total	160506	59564	37.11

Sources: http://nrgea.nic.in

Among the districts, Belgaum received the largest amount of Rs. 14,318 lakhs. The other districts which received above Rs. 10,000 lakhs are Chitradurga and Tumkur. The poorer districts like Koppal, Bijapur, Raichur and Gulbarga received more funds during the past five years. Though allocations indicate the priority given, the actual amount reaching the target group will be indicated by percentage to the total money spent. Though the poorer district received more money, the percentage of utilisation is low. For example, in Chitradurga district, though it is one of the districts in the first phase of the programme, and received Rs. 11,732 lakhs, only about 70 per cent of the money was spent. Similarly Belgaum which received highest, amount spent only 58 per cent of the allocation. Koppal is another backward district where only 23.43 per cent of the funds were actually spent. Percentage of utilisation is more in Raichur (74 per cent) though it is also a backward district. Haveri, Kolar, Davanagare and Belgaum are the other districts with more than 50 per cent of the utilisation of the funds. Utilisation of funds is very low in developed districts like Bangalore, Mysore, Udupi, Mandya and Hassan compared to other districts.

Classification of Allocations under MGNREGP

MGNREG programme contains both project cost and administration cost. Cost of material, wage of skilled and semiskilled workers are covered under the project cost and the administrative cost includes the salary and the allowances of the programme officer, the supporting staff and work site facilities. These are determined by the central government. District wise money spent under different heads is presented in table 3.

Table 3. Percentage of Project cost and Administration cost Up to 2010-11 (Rs. in lakhs)

Districts	*Total Allocation*	*Project Cost*	*percentage of PC to Total Cost*	*Adm. Cost*	*Percentage of Adm. Cost to Total Cost*
Bidar	1618	1593	98.43	25	1.57
Chitradurga	8203	8121	99.00	82	1.00
Davanagere	5622	5532	98.39	90	1.61
Gulbarga	1245	1217	97.75	28	2.25
Raichur	6408	6353	99.15	55	0.85
Belgaum	8316	8174	98.29	142	1.71
Bellary	685	665	97.12	20	2.88
Chikamagalur	1471	1332	90.55	139	9.45
Hassan	561	526	93.83	35	6.17
Kodagu	482	474	98.37	8	1.63
Shimoga	1718	1626	94.66	92	5.34
Bagalkote	1809	1786	98.78	22	1.22
Bangalore	34	33	97.41	1	2.59
Bangalore Rural	556	539	97.04	16	2.96
Bijapur	2650	2600	98.13	49	1.87
Chamarajanagar	631	609	96.49	22	3.51
Chikkaballapur	1075	1031	95.91	44	4.09
Dakshina kannada	570	546	95.88	23	4.12

contd...

Districts	*Total allocation*	*Project Cost*	*percentage of PC to Total Cost*	*Adm. Cost*	*Percentage of Adm. Cost to Total Cost*
Gadag	482	464	96.27	18	3.73
Haveri	2787	2734	98.1	53	1.9
Kolar	2093	2067	98.74	26	1.26
Koppal	2147	2092	97.45	55	2.55
Mandya	753	718	95.38	35	4.62
Mysore	109	105	96.53	4	3.47
Ramanagara	1027	1022	99.56	5	0.44
Tumakur	1183	1123	94.94	60	5.06
Udupi	95	88	93.2	6	6.8
Uttarakannada	1053	995	94.44	59	5.56
Yadgiri	2280	2253	98.81	27	1.19
Total	59564	58259	97.81	1305	2.19

Sources: http://nrgea.nic.in.

From this classification it is clear that project cost includes the component of wages which goes to the beneficiaries in the form of wages and the administrative cost is the administrative component, though part of the expenditure spent on the onsite facilities helps the workers indirectly. In this context, an attempt is made to understand what percentage these two heads constitute in the total expenditure on the programme in different districts of Karnataka. Data presented in table 3 shows that project cost is more than 90 per cent in all the districts, though there are differences in the actual percentage. While Raichur district spent 99.15 per cent on project and only 0.85 per cent on administration, Hassan district spent about 94 per cent on project and 6 per cent on administration. The other districts with higher percentage of expenditure on administrations are Chikmagalur (9.45 per cent) Shimoga (5.34 per cent), Mandya (5.06 per cent) Udupi (6.8 per cent), Uttara Kannada (5.56 per cent) and Tumkur (5.06 per cent). Average administrative cost for the state was 2.19 per cent of the total allocation in the state. Chitradurga, Bagalkote, Kodagu, and Yadagiri are the districts with less than 2 per cent expenditure on administration. Ramanagara and Raichur have spent less than 1 per cent on administration of the programme.

Inter Linkages between the Expenditure, Poverty, Literacy and Irrigation status

MGNREGP was introduced with the twin objectives of producing rural employment to enhance the income earnings opportunities of the semiskilled and unskilled rural poor and development of rural infrastructure. In order to attain the objectives more amounts are to be spent in the districts with more poverty, less literacy and with least irrigation opportunities. The districts with more illiterates need greater allocation due to non-availability of skills and limited access to resources. similarly, drought prone areas which are rain-fed needs more attention due to non-availability of employment in the agriculture sector. Karnataka is one of the states with largest drought-prone areas and 52 per cent of the population is dependent on agriculture sector. According to NSSO estimates agricultural labour constitute 32 per cent of the labour force. Unemployment among agricultural labourers increased from 9.5 per cent in 93-94 to 15.3 per cent in 2004-05. This is one of the reasons for the implementation of MGNREGP in Karnataka.

An attempt is made to analyse the linkages among the actual money spent and the other development indicators like literacy status of the rural population, rural poverty and the net area irrigated. All the districts are ranked based on these indicators and the results are presented in the table 4.

Table 4. Districtwise ranking of Percentage of Utilisation, Rural Literacy, Rural Poverty and Irrigation

Districts	*Percentage of utilisation*	*Utilisation Rank*	*Rural literacy*	*Rural literacy Rank*	*Per-cent of BPL*	*BPL Rank*	*Percentage of Net irrigate area*	*Net irri Rank*
Bagalakote	37.68	10	64.8	23	29.82	19	55	4
Bangalore	2.63	29	78.57	5	22.00	11	19	23
Bangalore Rural	31.45	16	75.55	9	19.94	8	20	19
Belegaum	58.08	3	69.68	16	24.69	14	59	2
Bellary	19.67	21	62.6	26	24.29	13	44	7
Bidar	37.27	11	67	19	17.19	3	14	27
Bijapur	30.66	17	62.87	25	24.79	15	35	10
Chamarajanagar	19.5	22	57.52	28	38.86	25	35	11
Chikkabalapura	34.8	12	66.73	20	29.45	18	25	17
Chikamagalur	32.99	14	76.93	6	48.69	27	11	28
Chitradurga	69.92	2	70.68	15	19.08	6	19	21
Dakshina kannada	28.93	19	85.34	1	17.84	5	54	5
Davanagere	57.43	4	72.49	11	20.92	9	40	8
Dharwad	48.74	7	72.21	12	16.15	1	17	24

contd...

Table 4 contd...

Districts	*Percentage of utilisation*	*Utilisation Rank*	*Rural literacy*	*Rural literacy Rank*	*Per-cent of BPL*	*BPL Rank*	*Percentage of Net irri-gate area*	*Net irri Rank*
Gadag	13.56	25	71.89	13	19.12	7	19	22
Gulbarga	13.78	24	58.77	27	48.88	28	17	26
Hassan	11.36	26	72.78	10	30.69	20	26	15
Haveri	52.73	6	75.65	8	38.44	24	20	20
Kodagu	32.97	15	80.98	4	25.68	17	3	29
Kolar	56.28	5	69.22	17	31.82	21	17	25
Koppal	23.43	20	64.98	22	33.15	22	31	13
Mandya	17.44	23	67.48	18	17.81	4	55	3
Mysore	2.23	30	63.29	24	33.21	23	47	6
Raichur	74.04	1	55.19	29	53.35	1	38	9
Ramanagara	29.64	18	65.22	21	25.11	16	25	16
Shimoga	33.96	13	76.31	7	17.03	2	61	1
Tumakur	11.29	27	71.04	14	21.64	10	26	14
Udupi	5.4	28	83.91	2	24.14	12	33	12
Uttarakannada	39.08	9	81.22	3	40.31	26	24	18

The results show that in terms of percentage of utilisation of funds Raichur ranks number one, and in terms of poverty also, the districts ranks one with 53 per cent of population below poverty line. But in terms of irrigated area, it ranks 9 with 38 per cent of net area irrigated. This shows that in the case of Raichur which is a backward district has spent larger percentage of money allocated under MGNREGP and this is justified based on the existing socio-economic status of the district. But in the case of Chamarajanagar district, though the district is poor in literacy status (ranks 28 with 57.52 per cent of rural literacy) only 19.5 per cent of the allocated funds are utilised and the district has 38.86 per cent of the population below poverty line ranking 25. But the district has better irrigation facilities with 35 per cent of net irrigated area. Bangalore is another district with low utilisation, but with high rural literacy and low BPL population. Chikamagalur and Kodagu are not considered as least irrigated though only 3 and 11 per cent of the area is irrigated as these are plantation areas. Bidar which has only 14 per cent of the net area irrigated, ranking 27 also utilised only 37 per cent of the allocations. But Bidar ranks 3 in BPL population with 17 per cent of BPL population and 67 per cent of rural literacy. In this district, though agriculture is not supporting, the literacy levels of the population might have helped in finding employment opportunities leading to less utilisation of allocated funds. Same is not the status with Gulbarga where the utilisation of funds is low (13.78) despite less irrigation (17 per cent), higher poverty (48.88 per cent) and low literacy (58.77 per cent).

Summary and Conclusions

MGNREGP is a recent introduction to the employment generation programmes introduced in India by the central government and it is being implemented by the respective state government. The twin objectives of this programme are employment generation and promotion of infrastructure. An analysis of the financing of the programme shows that allocation increased from mere Rs. 12 lakhs in 2006-07 to Rs. 52.64 lakhs by 2010-11.There is a considerable variation across the districts in terms of allocation. One important observation is that though large amounts are allocated, the percentage of actual utilisation is low in some districts. Only in seven districts more than fifty per cent of the funds are utilised. Bangalore and Udupi Districts recorded least percentage of utilisation. The analysis also revealed that Raichur district which is ranking number one in utilisation is a poor district with largest number of population below poverty line. In this respect it can be concluded that the programme achieved social justice in providing employment in a district which is poor with largest number of illiterates. It is also observed that the districts with high literacy rate and low poverty and high irrigated area have recorded a utilisation of only five per cent. Due to large variations in the utilisation of funds, it is necessary to understand the administrative, socio political and economic reasons for the lower utilisation of funds in some districts though they are poor. Such an analysis will be able to suggest necessary policy changes to the existing patterns of allocation under the MGNREG programme across different districts in Karnataka.

References

Bhatia, Bela and Dreze, J (2006). Employment Guarantee in Jharkhand: Ground Realities, *Economic and Political Weekly,* 41(29), 198-202.

Dasagupta, S AND Sudarshana, M (2011).Issues in labour Market inequality and women's participation in India's National Rural Employment Guarantee Programme. *Working paper* No. 98, February.

Datt, G (1994). Poverty Alleviation through Rural Public Works: The Experience of Maharashtra Employment Guarantee Scheme. *The Indian Journal of Labour Economics,* 37(4): 659–665.

Drèze, J and Lal, S. Employment Guarantee: Unfinished Agenda, *The Hindu*, 13 July 2007.

Dreze. J, R Khera. and Siddhartha (2008). Corruption in NREGA: Myths and Reality, *The Hindu*, 16th January 2008.

Govt. of Karnataka (2011), Economic Survey of Karnataka (2010-11). Planning,

Programme Monitoring and Statistic Department: Bangalore. Govt. of India, Census Documents.

Govt. of India, Ministry of Rural Development (2008): The national Rural Employment Guarantee Act 2005 (NREGA)-Operational Guidelines, New Delhi.

Mohapatra, R et. al., (2008). The National Rural Employment Guarantee Act (NREGA) Opportunities and Challenges Natural Resource Management and Livelihood unit, Centre for Science and Environment, New Delhi

Murthy, S.P.S and Indumati, S. (2011) .Economic Analysis of MGNREGP in the Drought – prone States of Karnataka, Rajasthan and Irrigation – dominated State of Andhra Pradesh. *Agricultural Economics Research review*, 24: 531-536.

Rangaswamy, K and Kumar S.B. (2011).State Level Performance of MGNREGP in India :A Comparative Study. *International Multidisciplinary Research Journal*, 1 (10): 36-40.

Ravallion, M (1991). Reaching the Rural Poor through Public Employment: Arguments, Evidence and Lessons from South Asia. *The World Bank Research Observer* 6(2): 153–175.

Reddy, N.D and Upendranadh,C (2010). National Rural Employment Guarantee: Issues, Concerns and Prospects. *Oxfam India papers series* 5, September.

9

Financial Inclusion Under MGNREGA: A Revolutionary in Creation of Rural Community Assets and Poverty Reduction

V. Ramakrishnappa and *N. Krishne Gowda*

Introduction

A majority of the Indian population is living in rural areas with dependency on agriculture and allied activities for their livelihood. However, the Indian agriculture is largely depends on monsoons, the problem of poverty and unemployment are common phenomenon among most of the rural households. Recent assessments of poverty by the Planning Commission said that 278 million (34 per cent of the total population) of rural people were poor living with less than Rs. 22.4 a day in 2009-10 (Planning Commission, 2012). Growing poverty and unemployment have led to the fragmentation of land and an increase in number of agricultural labourers. Therefore, agricultural labour increased significantly from 7.08 million in 1981 to 121 million in 2008. On the other hand, *less than half of the households do not own farmlands in India, but still there exists other options for subsistence livelihood.* A recent National Health Family Survey (NHFS-3) reveals that 41.5% of Indian rural households do not own farmland. Further, the poor face absence of basic capabilities to function in society and lack opportunities such as access to employment opportunities and income earnings in rural areas.

Poverty reduction and creation of rural assets is one of the major goals of development policy in India since Independence. Various anti-poverty programmes and employment generation schemes have been in place for a long time now. Huge amount of resources have also invested in these programmes/polices for the welfare of rural poor. These programmes typically provide unskilled manual workers with short-term employment on public works such as irrigation infrastructure, afforestation, soil conservation and road construction. The rationale for workfare programmes rests on some basic considerations. The programmes provide income transfers to poor households during critical times and therefore enable consumption smoothing specially during slack agricultural seasons or years. In countries with high unemployment rates, transfer benefits from workfare programmes can prevent poverty from worsening, especially during lean periods. The major programmes which are related to rural development and benefit for rural poor are National Rural Employment Programme (NREP), Intigrated Rural Development Programme (IRDP), Rural Landless Employment Guarantee Programme (RLSEGP), Swarnjayanti Gram Swarozgar Yojana (SGSY), Sampoorna Grameen Rozgar Yojana (SGRY), Small Farmer's Development Programme (SFDP), Drought Area Development Programme (DADP), Minimum Needs Programme (MNP) and most recent one is Mahathma Gandhi National Rural Employment Guarantee Act/Scheme (MGNREGA). The most significant difference between the MGNREGA and the other schemes is that the MGNREGA provides the rural worker with 'the right to work'. This Act has the potential to provide livelihood to the teeming millions living Below Poverty Line in rural India (BPL) with guarantees at least 100 day's employment per year to every rural household. Against this background, in the present paper an attempt has been made to assess the extent of financial inclusion under MGNREGA for the development of rural economy.

Objectives

Major objectives of the study are:

1. To understand the implementation mechanism of MGNREGA and its features.
2. To analyse the trends in financial allocation for rural growth under MGNREGA at national level.
3. To assess the performance of MGNREGA in creation of durable productive assets and improvement of rural economy.

Sources of Data and Information

The study is exclusively based on secondary data/ information, which have been collected from various sources. The secondary information and data were obtained from Planning Commission, Economic Survey reports, journals, magazines, news papers etc. The data and information about MGNREGA has been also used from its official website of *www.nrega.nic.in.*

Implementation Mechanism and Salient features of the MGNREGA

The Government of India has adopted a multifaceted development strategy that promotes economic growth and also addresses the needs of the poor by ensuring their basic rights. National Rural Employment Guarantee

Act (NREGA) is a recent one enacted by India's United Progressive Alliance (UPA) Government on August 25, 2005 and came into force w.e.f. 2nd February, 2006. The Prime Minister of India Dr. Manmohan Singh described as 'NREGA is a landmark in our history in removing poverty from the face of the nation', after launching a programme in Hyderabad, Andhra Pradesh (The Hindu, Feb. 3, 2006). On 31st December, 2009, the Act was renamed by an Amendment as the Mahatma Gandhi National Rural Employment Guarantee Act. The Act was implemented in a phased manner with 200 districts in the first phase being notified on 2 February 2006, followed by another 130 from April 2007, and in the remaining districts with effect from 1 April 2008. The Act is now effective in the rural areas of the entire country, covering 619 districts. The Act guarantees 100 days of wage employment in a financial year to any rural household whose adult members are willing to participate in unskilled manual work. The Act is an important step towards realisation of the right to work and aims at arresting out-migration of rural households in search of employment simultaneously enhancing people's livelihood on a sustained basis, by developing the economic and social infrastructure in rural areas.

The MGNREGA scheme has been implemented through the Panchyat Raj Institutions (PRIs) across the country. MGNREGA has a five-tier structure of implementation starting from Grama Panchyat (GP) at the bottom to the Government of India at the top. GP is the nodal agency at the bottom level and played pivotal role in the implementation of the MGNREGA (Table 1). It is responsible for planning of works, registering those households which are entitled to get work, issuing job cards, allocating employment, executing 50 per cent of the works, and monitoring the implementation of the scheme at the village level. All these activities are to be done in consultation with the gram sabha. In view of the complexities and sheer volume of work, the implementation of the MGNREGA assigns a considerable organisational responsibility at the level of the Gram Panchayat. The rest 50% may be undertaken either by the taluk Panchayat or the district Panchayat or both. Taluk Panchayat monitors and coordinates the plans and works at the block level. Computer updating of MGNREGA works, muster roll entries, etc is done at the block level under the auspices of the MGNREGA programme officer. District Panchayat, in addition to implementing non-mandatory works, coordinates MGNREGA activities at the district level. Besides, it has the responsibility to prepare both the district annual plan and the five-year perspective plan. These two plan documents are the bases which guide the implementation of NREGA at the village level. These documents are prepared at the district level in consultation with the GP and block Panchayats.

Next in hierarchy is the state government which acts as a facilitator in the flow of MGNREGA funds and deployment of manpower. It has the responsibility to set up the State Employment Guarantee Council. The latter has the role to advice the government from time to time on MGNREGA implementation in the state. Besides, the council is also entrusted with the responsibility of monitoring and evaluation of the MGNREGA in the state. At the top of the hierarchy comes the central government. The Ministry of Rural Development, Government of India is the nodal agency for MGNREGA implantation. It has the responsibility to set up Central Employment Guarantee Council for receiving advice on programme implementation. It may also undertake independent evaluation and monitoring of the scheme. It has the responsibility to prepare the budget and disburse funds across states.

Table 1: Implementation Mechanisms of MGNREGA

Agency	*Responsibilities*
Government of India	• Ministry of Rural Development as Nodal Agency • Allocator of Funds • Monitoring and Evaluation
State Government	• Facilitator for Fund Flow • Regulator • Deployment of Manpower
District / Zilla Panchayat	• Coordination • Preparation of • Annual Plan and Perspective Plan • Design and Implementation of Non-mandatory works
Taluk Panchayat	• Coordination • Monitoring • Design and Implementation of Non-mandatory Works
Gram Panchayat	• Preparation of Village Plans • Identification • Design and Implementation of Works • Evaluation and Monitoring

The permissible works under the MGNREGA (Act as per Schedule I) in order of priority and include (i) water conservation and water harvesting; (ii) drought proofing (including afforestation and tree plantation); (iii) irrigation canals including micro and minor irrigation works; (iv) provision of irrigation facility, horticulture plantation and land development facilities to land owned by households belonging to the Schedule Castes (SCs) and Schedule Tribes (STs) or below poverty line (BPL) families; (v) renovation of traditional water bodies including desilting of tanks; (vi) land development; (vii) flood control and protection works including drainage in water logged areas; (viii) rural connectivity to provide all-weather access; and (ix) any other work which may be notified by the central government in consultation with the state government. The key features of the MGNREGA are:

1. Right based Framework and Time bound Guarantee: Adult members of a rural household, willing to do unskilled manual work, may apply for registration in writing or orally to the local Gram Panchayat. The Gram Panchayat after due verification will issue a Job Card. The Job Card will bear the photograph of all adult members of the household willing to work under MGNREGA and is free of cost. The Job Card should be issued within 15 days of application. A Job Card holder may submit a written application for employment to the Gram Panchayat, stating the time and duration for which work is sought. The minimum days of employment have to be at least fourteen. The Gram Panchayat will issue a dated receipt of the written application for employment, against which the guarantee of providing employment within 15 days operates. Employment will be given within 15 days of application for work, if it is not then daily unemployment allowance as per the Act, has to be paid liability of payment of unemployment allowance is of the States.

2. Labour Intensive Works, Employment and Wage Repayment: The main feature of the MGNREGA is focus on creation of durable assets that will enhance livelihood. Work should ordinarily be provided within 5 km. radius of the village. In case work is provided beyond 5 km. extra wages of 10% are payable to meet additional transportation and living expenses. Wages are to be paid according to the Minimum Wages Act 1948 for agricultural laborers in the State, unless the Centre notifies a wage rate which will not be less than Rs. 60/ per day. Equal wages will be provided to both men and women. Wages are to be paid according to piece rate or daily rate. Disbursement of wages has to be done on weekly basis and not beyond a fortnight in any case. Payment of wages is paid through Bank and Post Office Accounts. The ratio of 60:40 wage and material has to be maintained and contractors or machinery is not allowed strictly.

3. Transparency and Accountability: Conduct of social audit is one among the features of MGNREGA and this has to be done by the Gram Sabha. Grievance redressal mechanisms have to be put in place for ensuring a responsive implementation process. All accounts and records relating to the Scheme should be available for public scrutiny.

4. Other features: At least one-third beneficiaries shall be women who have registered and requested work under the scheme. Work site facilities such as crèche, drinking water, shade have to be provided. The shelf of projects for a village will be recommended by the grama sabha and approved by the zilla panchayat. At least 50 per cent of works will be allotted to Gram Panchayats for execution. Permissible works predominantly include water and soil conservation, forestation and land development works. The Central Government bears the 100 per cent wage cost of unskilled manual labour and

75 per cent of the material cost including the wages of skilled and semi skilled workers.

Financial Allocation and Assets Creation under MGNREGA

In the context of acute distress and deprivation in many parts of the country, the MGNREGA is the first step towards realising the right to work, which is included in the legal framework of Indian constitution. The new law impels to take clear responsibility for providing a social safety net for every poor rural household. It addresses urgent and immediate issues of hunger and deprivation, since it is this lack of livelihood, lack of food security and endemic poverty that sends rural households into the downward spiral of destitution. The budget allocation for this scheme has consistently risen from year to year. The budget outlay for MGNREGA was about Rs. 11, 300 crores, Rs. 12,000 crores and Rs. 16,000 crores for the year 2006-07, 2007-08 and for 2008-09, respectively. However, steadily it has been raised to Rs. 39,100 crores for the year 2009-2010, which marks an increase of 144 per cent over 2008-09 budget estimates. During 2010-11, the budget allocation for the MGNREGS was Rs. 40,100 (Economic Survey, 2010-11). During 2011-12 and 2012-13, the allocation of funds for MGNREGA has come down to Rs. 32,000 crore and it showing a dip of more than 20 per cent (Table 2). Decline in job demands is the main reason for dip in financial allocation. However, never in the history of India has a welfare programme of such scale been launched before. As the (MGNREGA enters its seventh year, its statistics are staggering. A total amount of more than Rs. 1.9 lakh crore (for seven years) has been allocated for the welfare of rural households and it is good prosperity.

Table 2: Financial allocation for MGNREGA

Year	*Amount (Rs/crores)*	*Percentage of variation against previous year*
2006-07	11300	--
2007-08	12000	6.19
2008-09	16000	33.33
2009-10	39100	144.38
2010-11	40100	2.56
2011-12	40000	-0.25
2012-13	32000	-20.00
Total	190500	

Source: Economic Survey reports and *www.indiabudget.nic.in*

The data on physical and financial performance of MGNREGA across States is available in the official website (http://nrega.nic.in). During the first year of implementation (2006-07) in 200 districts, a total of 2.10 crore household were provided jobs under the Act, but about 10.29 per cent of them could get 100-days of employment. The statistics reveal that about 3.39 crore rural households in 2007-08 were provided employment and 143.59 crore person-days were generated in 330 districts. During 2008-09, MGNREGA provided employment opportunities for more than 4.49 crore households as against 3.39 crore households covered in 2007-08 and and 215.63 crore person days have been generated across the country. During 2009-10, 5.26 crore households were provided employment under this scheme as against more than 4.5 crore during 2008-09. As per Economic Survey (2011-12) the scheme has provided jobs to 5.49 crore rural households during 2010-11 and generated 257.15 working days at national level. The progress of MGNREGA at national level during 2011-12 has shown in the Table 3. In 2011-12, 4.99 crore households were provided employment and 211.42 crore person days of work were generated. The participation of vulnerable groups (SC/STs) together accounted more than 40 per cent and women involvement is also high. According to the guidelines of NREGS, 30 per cent of work is reserved for women. The Table 4 clearly indicates that the share of women in the MGNREGA workforce was same (48 per cent) during last three years (2008-09 to 2010-11), though there was a noticeable increase from 40 per cent in 2006-01 to 43 per cent in 2007-08. Thus, almost half of the MGNREGA participants now are women and it is a healthy indication of growing participation of women over time. Other details such as expenditure, works completed and average wage rate have been furnished in the same table.

Table 3: Progress of MGNREGA in India during 2011- 2012

Sl No.	*Particulars*	
1.	No. of households who have demanded employment (in crore)	5.03
2.	Employment provided to No of households (in crore)	4.99
3.	Total No. of Person-days generated [in crore]	211.42
	(a) SCs	46.61 (22.04)
	(b) STs	38.38 (18.16)
	(c) Others	126.43 (59.89)
4.	The share of Women in the total No. of person-days (crore)	101.87 (48.18)
5.	Total No. of works taken up (Lakhs).	74.13
6.	No. of works completed (Lakhs).	15.01
7.	No. of works in progress (Lakhs).	59.12

Source: NREGA Implementation Status Report for the financial year 2011-12. *(http://nrega.nic.in)*

Note: Data in the brackets are percentages to total no. of Person-days generated (Sl no. 2).

Table 4: Progress of MGNREGA in India (2006-07 to 2010-11)

Sl. No.	*Particulars*	*2006-07*	*2007-08*	*2008-09*	*2009-10*	*2010-11*
1.	Employment provided to No. of households (in crore)	2.1	3.4	4.5	5.3	5.5
2.	Total No. of Person-days generated [in Crore]	90.5	143.59	216.3	283.6	257.2
3.	The share of Women in the total No. of person-days (%)	40	43	48	48	48
4.	Total expenditure (Crore)	8824	15857	27250	37905	39377
5.	No. of works completed (Lakhs).	3.9	8.2	12.1	22.6	25.9
6.	Average wage rate (Rs/day)	65	75	84	91	100

Table 5: Creation of productive assets under MGNREGA for the financial year 2011-12*

Type of works undertaken	*Physical assets created (in nos)*		*Percentage of against completed works*
	Taken up	*Completed*	
Rural Connectivity	1454767	189838	23.40
Flood Control and Protection	261670	41187	5.08
Water Conservation and Water Harvesting	1780062	140823	17.36
Drought Proofing	820912	59273	7.31
Micro Irrigation Works	425899	36886	4.55
Provision of Irrigation facility to Land Owned by SC/STs and other BPL families	790136	128972	15.90
Renovation of Traditional Water bodies	377583	45884	5.66
Land Development	643485	123019	15.16
Any Other activity Approved by MRD	246769	40359	4.98
Construction of Bharat Nirman Rajiv Ghandhi Sewa Kendra	25531	4980	0.61
Total	6826814	811221	100.00

* Up to January 2012

Source: NREGA Implementation Status Report for the financial year 2011-12. *(http://nrega.nic.in)*

The physical assets created include rural roads, flood and drought proofing measures like water harvesting, irrigation and land development projects, renovation of traditional water bodies and micro irrigation assets, among others. Nature and type of works have been undertaken under MGNREGA during 2011-12 and their progress is shown in the Table 5. During 2011-12, rural connectivity in the form of construction of village approach roads was the largest share of MGNREGA works at 23.4 per cent. The water conservation and water harvesting accounted for the second largest share of MGNREGA works at 17.36 per cent. This was followed by land development and provision of irrigation facilities for landowned by Scheduled Castes (SCs), Scheduled Tribes (STs) and small and marginal farmers, at 15 per cent each.

Bank/Post Office Account for Poor: a gateway to Financial Inclusion

To ensure timely payment, payment of wages is mandatorily done through the bank/post office beneficiary accounts. The number of new bank or post office accounts opened for wages under MGNREGA became a yardstick for measuring the success of this initiative. Nearly 10 crore accounts opened in banks and post offices for MGNREGA workers for their wage disbursement make this the largest financial-inclusion scheme of the rural poor. These accounts have also encouraged thrift and saving among some of the poorest families. Wage payment through the workers' accounts has helped to reduce leakages in wage payment. As per the Report of the Committee for Revision of MGNREGA Operational Guidelines, MGNREGA has generated more than 1,100 crore person-days of work at a total expenditure of over Rs.150,000 crores in a six years of time span. The share of SC/ST families in the work provided under MGNREGA has been 55 per cent and 45 per cent of workers are women. Average wages of workers have gone up by 54 per cent over the last five years (Shah, 2012). However a swift look at these figures, giving a kind of contentment in terms of that the socially backward groups like scheduled tribes, scheduled castes as well as women participated in the programme.

Conclusions

In the rural context where the economy is largely dependent on agriculture and allied activities, a large proportion of the rural population is dependent on the wages which they earn through unskilled manual labour. There are a number of distinct ways in which such a scheme tries to reduce poverty. The most direct and obvious way is by providing extra work opportunities and income to the poorest in rural areas (Dutta and others, 2012). The workers of MGNREGS are largely casual workers who are vulnerable and suffer from chronic poverty when there is inadequate labour demand. In this context, the MGNREGS is extremely important as they provide the community with income during critical times especially during lean agricultural seasons.

A large number of micro level studies have assessed the impact of MGNREGA and observed the positive impact on rural economy. In many parts of the country, spectacular successes have been recorded in water harvesting and road and land development works (Kareemulla, 2009; MPISSR, 2011; Aggarwal and others, 2012). Distress migration has been arrested in several areas (Kher and Nayak, 2009). People have started to feel that there is some level of impact at the individual household as well as village level. A study conducted in Karnataka by Pani and Iyer (2010–11) observed that a greater proportion of the income (from 48 per cent to 66 per cent for men and women), generated from MGNREGA tends to be spent on the rural economy. Every household has a potential to get Rs.12,000 per year as per new revised wage rate of MGNREGA. According to World Economic Forum Report (2012), MGNREGA scheme has improved access to financial services for farmers and holds a great scope for further agricultural and economic growth of the country. Thus, the MGNREGA has the potential not only to generate more employment directly and indirectly, but also to transform rural economic and social relations at many levels.

Unfortunately, the MGNREGA is also suffering from many critics. Delay in work and payment of wages, corruptions, poor quality of works and corruption are the biggest concern under the MGNREGA (Dreze *et al*, 2008; Gopal, 2009; Ravallian, 2012). The Comptroller and Auditor General of India has criticised dilution of the National Rural Employment Guarantee Act (NREGA) due to poor record maintenance, delayed payment of wages and non-payment of unemployment allowance. Therefore, the respective state governments and implementing agencies should take appropriate measures to prevent bottlenecks and need for effective implementation of MGNREGA on sustainable way.

References

1. Aggarwal, Ankita et al (2012): "Evaluation of NREGA Wells in Jharkhand", *Economic and Political Weekly,* 49(35): 24-27.
2. Ashok, Pankaj (2010): "Processes, Institutions and Mechanisms of Implementation of NREGA: Impact Assessment of Bihar and Jharkhand", *(http://www.nrega.net/pin/reports-and-resources/reports).*
3. Dreze and Reetika, Khera (2009): "The battle for employment guarantee", *Frontline*, Vol. 26(1), Jan. 03-16, 2009.
4. Drèze, Jean, Reetika Khera and Siddhartha (2008): "Corruption in NREGA: myths and reality", *The Hindu,* Tuesday, Jan 22, 2008.
5. Dutta, P., R. Murgai, M. Ravallion and M. V. Dominique (2012): "Does India's Employment Guarantee Scheme Guarantee Employment?", Policy Research Paper (WPS-6003), Washington, DC: World Bank.
6. Economic Survey (2010-11): *Economic Survey of India,* Ministry of Finance, Government of India.

7. Economic Survey (2011-12): *Economic Survey of India*, Ministry of Finance, Government of India.
8. Gopal, K S (2009): "NREGA Social Audit: Myths and Reality", *Economic and Political Weekly,* January 17, pp. 70-71.
9. Kareemulla, K., .S.K. Reddy, C. A. Rao, S. Kumar and B. Venkateswarlu (2009): "Soil and Water Conservation Works through National Rural Employment Guarantee Scheme (NREGS) in Andhra Pradesh—An Analysis of Livelihood Impact", *Agricultural Economics Research Review*, Vol. 22, pp. 443–50.
10. Khera, R. and Nayak, N. (2009): "Women Workers and Perceptions of the National Rural Employment Guarantee Act", *Economic and Political Weekly,* 43(17): 33-39.
11. Madhya Pradesh Institute of Social Science Research (2011): "Assessment of the Effectiveness and Impact of Kapildhara Sub-Scheme", MPISSR, Study Commissioned by Ministry of Rural Development and UNDP, Ujjain.
12. NFHS (2007): National Family Health Survey (NFHS 3) 2005- 06, International Institute for Population Sciences (IIPS), Mumbai, India.
13. National Sample Survey Organisation (2010-11). *Survey of MGNREGA*, NSSO, New Delhi.
14. Pani, N and C. Iyer (2011): "Evaluation of the Impact of Processes in the Mahatma Gandhi National Rural Employment Guarantee Scheme in Karnataka", National Institute of Advanced Studies (NIAS), Bangalore.
15. Planning Commission (2012): *Press note on Poverty estimates, 2009-10,* Government of India, New Delhi.
16. *Ravillion, M (2012):* "Corruption in the MGNREGS Assessing an Index", *Economic and Political Weekly,* 49(8): 13-15.
17. Shah, Mihir (2012): *Report of the Committee for Revision of MGNREGA Operational Guidelines,* Submitted to Ministry of Rural Development, Government of India
18. World Economic Forum Report (2012): *Putting the New Vision for Agriculture into Action: A Transformation is Happening*, Switzerland.
19. *www.indiabudget.nic.in* (financial allocations were obtained).
20. *www.nrega.nic.in.* (information and statistics obtained from the physical and financial status reports, circular of revised wage rates, implementation guidelines, etc.)

10

Financial Inclusion in India: Need for Concern to the Unprivileged

Santhosh Areekkuzhiyil and *Prajisha K.*

Preamble

Access to finance, especially by the poor and vulnerable groups, is an essential requisite for employment, economic growth, poverty alleviation and social upliftment. Further, financial inclusion will enable the poor and the rustics of our country to open a bank account to save and invest, to borrow and to repay, to insure and to take part in the credit. This will enable them to break the chain of poverty. Till 1960s, Indian banks were more conservative and inward looking, concerned with their profits. Banking services were greatly used by a segment of the people. Class banking was prevalent during those days. Majority of the banks were private commercial banks they are local oriented and primarily serving the business community. They had limited range of activities. They basically concentrated on selling their loans to those who are financially sound and are capable of providing security for their borrowings. The banks tend to positively appropriate their liabilities for keeping their funds safe and give modest interest on deposits. However, after the Nationalisation of 14 major commercial banks in 1969, Indian banks woke from their isolation, and evaluated the rapidly changing environment. The slogan during the Bank Nationalisation was 'transformation from class banking to mass banking'. The banking industry in India has undergone drastic changes during the last two decades. Reforms since the early nineties, has paved the way for the economic transformation of the country. India is an emerging economy that has experienced a rapid economic growth rate since the initiation of major economic reform in 1991. However, still large segments of the population suffer from poverty in India and economic inequality is widening over time (Datt and Ravallion 2002; Deaton and Drèze 2002; Dev and Ravi 2007; Suryanarayana 2008; Cain et al 2010).

Therefore, it seems that careful examination of the extent of financial exclusion across income groups in countries like India is of paramount importance. Second, India is the world's largest democracy and is federal in structure. Indian states are empowered with partial policy autonomy and there is diverse pattern of growth and development across states, which makes it more interesting to examine the issue of financial inclusion in India. This paper tries to explore the trend of inclusive financial growth in India and to identify the exclusion of rural people from formal financial services.

Background Literture

About 1.8 billion people in the world live in extreme poverty; almost half the world's population (2.8 billion) live on less than US $ 2 a day. There is a vast unmet gap in the provisions of financial services to the poor all over the world. Majority of these people depend for their credit needs on informal sources of finance for meeting livelihood and consumption needs. Financial inclusion refers to a process that ensures the ease of access, availability and usage of the formal financial system for all members of an economy. An inclusive financial system has several merits. It facilitates efficient allocation of productive resources and thus can potentially reduce the cost of capital. In addition, access to appropriate financial services can significantly improve the day-to-day management of finances. An inclusive financial system can help in reducing the growth of informal sources of credit (such as money lenders) that are often found to be exploitative. Thus, an all-inclusive financial system enhances efficiency and welfare by providing avenues for secure and safe saving practices and by facilitating a whole range of efficient financial services. The importance of an inclusive financial system is widely recognised in the policy circles and recently financial inclusion has become a policy priority in many countries. Initiatives for Literature on financial exclusion has defined it in the context of a larger issue of social exclusion of certain groups of people from the mainstream of the society. Leyshon and Thrift (1995) define financial exclusion as referring to those processes that serve to prevent certain social groups and individuals from gaining access to the formal financial system. Carbo et al. (2005) have defined financial exclusion as broadly the inability of some societal groups to access the financial system. According to Conroy (2005), financial exclusion is a process that prevents poor and disadvantaged social groups from gaining access to the formal financial systems of their countries. According to Mohan (2006) financial exclusion signifies the lack of access by certain segments of the society to appropriate, low-cost, fair and safe financial products and services from mainstream providers. A Government Committee on financial inclusion in India defines financial inclusion as the process of ensuring access to financial services and timely and adequate credit where needed by vulnerable groups such as the weaker sections and low income groups at an affordable cost (Rangarajan Committee, 2008). Thus, the definitions on financial inclusion/exclusion, conceptual as well as functional, provide an indication that financial exclusion occurs mainly among people who are at the margins of the society. Further, the literature on financial inclusion has also adequately pointed out that it is a complex phenomenon, having several dimensions. Therefore, an appropriate measure of financial inclusion has to be multidimensional. There is a vast literature on financial inclusion and the measure most commonly used by scholars is the number of banked persons, often proxied by the average number of bank accounts per 1000 population. Sarma (2008) has developed a multidimensional index of financial inclusion (IFI). This index incorporates information on three dimensions of financial inclusion, namely accessibility, availability and usage of banking services. IFI provides a better measure of financial inclusion than individual indicators such as those used in Beck et al. (2007). The literature on this has identified that the financially excluded population comprises marginal farmers, landless laborers, oral lessees, self-employed and unorganised sector enterprises, urban slum dwellers, migrants, ethnic minorities, senior citizens and women (Thorat 2007). The major reasons for financial exclusion include a low-income status, being unemployed, belonging to an ethnic group, living in remote or interior areas, suffering from illness or disability, lack of awareness, illiteracy and social segregation (Reynolds, 2003; Thorat, 2007). Further, countries with the highest level of income inequality and people with a history of bad debts have the highest levels of banking exclusion (Kempson et al. 2004). The literature has further identified supply-side factors in financial exclusion such as ineffective government intervention, procedural rigidities (Ferrari 2007), refusal by banks, identity requirements, onerous terms and conditions, bank charges and others, as their incidence is high in developing countries. In this context, there has been a widespread interest in minimising the incidence of financial exclusion and ensuring financial inclusion of the hitherto under-served population, given the obvious benefits of financial services for entrepreneurial firms and individuals. Theoretically, it is believed that financial development creates enabling conditions for growth through supply-led growth, as growth generates demand for financial products and leads to industrial growth (Rajan and Zingales 1998). Unfinancing of productive investment opportunities, business activities and trade always has negative consequences for growth and livelihoods, as it limits households ability to meet unexpected expenditures or invest in health and education (Commonwealth Finance Ministers Meeting, 2006). A developed financial system broadens access to funds. In its absence, people resort to high-cost informal sources (moneylenders). The lower the availability of funds and higher their costs, the fewer are the economic activities, resulting in lower economic growth.

'Financial exclusion' is invariably experienced by poorer members of society. Significant numbers of low income people are apparently excluded from financial services spanning a range of basic products that include credit, insurance, bill-payment services and deposit account facilities. In the UK until recently around 1.5 million (7%) of households lacked any financial products at all and a further 4.4 million (20%) were on the margin of financial services, typically with little more than a bank account. A number of aspects, or dimensions, of financial exclusion have been identified:

- **Access exclusion:** restricted access via the processes of risk assessment;
- **Condition exclusion:** where the conditions attached to financial products make them unsuitable for the needs of some people;
- **Marketing exclusion:** where some people are effectively excluded by targeted marketing and sales;
- **Self-exclusion:** people decide that there is no point in applying for a financial product because they believe that they would be refused. These beliefs can arise from many experiences and perceptions.

The financial inclusion assemblage is premised on the assumption that the 2.7 billion poor people in the world who do not currently have access to formal financial services are in need of such services (World Bank, 2010). Defined by an absence that is translated into a need, financial inclusion calls for scalable models of poor-appropriate financial technologies to serve these vast numbers, which can only be achieved by tapping mainstream financial markets. This results in a tension at the heart of the assemblage, between the 'financialisation of development' that constitutes poverty alleviation as the new frontier of capitalism, and the 'democratisation of capital' that promises access to financial services as one of the eradicators of global poverty (Roy, 2010).

The Reserve Bank of India (RBI) set up the Khan Commission in 2004 to look into financial inclusion and the recommendations of the commission were incorporated into the mid-term review of the policy (2005–06). In the report RBI exhorted the banks with a view of achieving greater financial inclusion to make available a basic "no-frills" banking account. In India, financial inclusion first featured in 2005, when it was introduced by K C Chakraborthy, the chairman of Indian Bank. Mangalam Village became the first village in India where all households were provided banking facilities. Norms were relaxed for people intending to open accounts with annual deposits of less than Rs. 50,000. General credit cards (GCCs) were issued to the poor and the disadvantaged with a view to help them access easy credit. In January 2006, the Reserve Bank permitted commercial banks to make use of the services of non-governmental organisations (NGOs/SHGs), micro-finance institutions, and other civil society organisations as intermediaries for providing financial and banking services. These intermediaries could be used as business facilitators or business correspondents by commercial banks. The bank asked the commercial banks in different regions to start a 100% financial inclusion campaign on a pilot basis. As a result of the campaign states or UTs like Pondicherry, Himachal Pradesh and Kerala announced 100% financial inclusion in all their districts. Reserve Bank of India's vision for 2020 is to open nearly 600 million new customers' accounts and service them through a variety of channels by leveraging on IT. However, illiteracy and the low income savings and lack of bank branches in rural areas continue to be a roadblock to financial inclusion in many states and there is inadequate legal and financial structure.

Rationale for the Study

Majority of the world's population - do not have access to formal financial services. As per the National Sample Survey Organisation (NSSO, 2005) about 73 per cent of the households in India were located in the rural areas. Since Nationalisation, the lending to the select elite in the urban areas gave way to lending to the rural masses. The policy makers recognised the fact that the potential of rural India should not be under estimated. The banks have to play a dual role in rural areas to institutionalise the rural savings for developmental activities as a part of commercial banking. Then the help in the social upliftment of the poor as a part of social banking. Eventhogh the number of banks which are try to augment the rural people's banking habits, the major portion of the households are excluded from the Black Box. This is an attempt to show the scope of rural sector and financial sector. Although there are many studies conducted in this area, it is a fertile ground especially developing countries like India.

Research Design

This study try to identify the trends in financial inclusion and the excluded portion of society from the formal financial background. In order to study the trend and other scope of this sector the study had used secondary data from Center for Monitoring Indian Economy(CMIE), Data from Bloomberg, Indiastat, National Income Statistics, Report of Indian Council for Research on International Economic Relations, etc. The present study limited to India, the data had collected for the last 10 years. The reminder of the paper scrutinised as the following sections (i) Data analysis (section 1, Financial Inclusion a cross word comparison briefly describes the Index of Financial Inclusion (IFI), section 2,Trend in financial inclusion, section 3, Analysis of households with in the financial boundary) (ii) Findings, (iii) Summing up.

Data Analysis

Index of Financial Incusion: A Cross World Comparison

The index of financial inclusion is a measure of inclusiveness of the financial sector of a country. It is constructed as a multidimensional index that captures information on various aspects of financial inclusion such as banking penetration, availability of banking services and usage of the banking system. The IFI incorporates information on these dimensions in one single number lying between 0 and 1, where 0 denotes complete financiai exclusion and 1 indicates complete financial inclusion in an economy. Sarma (2008) has developed a method of computing the IFI for several dimensions of financial inclusion. Based on the availability of comparable data, Sarma (2008) has computed the values of IFI using the three basic dimensions of financial inclusion—accessibility, availability and usage of banking services. Accessibility has been measured by the penetration of the banking system proxied by the number of bank accounts per 1000 population. In this paper we are comparing the financial inclusion index of India and other countries. Following table shows the contradiction of index of India and other countries.

Table 1: Index of Financial Inclusion

Spain	0.79	1
Germany	0.60	4
United Kingdom	0.43	17
United States	0.37	21
China	0.30	32
Brazil	0.21	44
India	0.17	50

Sorce: Indian Council for Research on International Relations 2011.

From the above table it is easily understand developing countries have low financial inclusion index when we compared to other developed countries. India has been ranked poorly, even below African countries like Kenya and Moracco, in the first-ever index of financial inclusion prepared by city - based think-tank ICRIER to find out the extent of reach of banking services in 100 country's of the world. India has been placed at the 50th spot, much above Russia but below China, in the index of financial inclusion (IFI) prepared by the Indian Council for Research on International Economic Relations (ICRIER).

Mandira Sharma (2008) studied the financial inclusion and development, he found that there is a direct relationship between financial inclusion index and human development index. As per that study the countries which have high financial inclusion index should have high Human Development Index (HDI).

Trend in Financial Inclusion

Financial Inclusion is a critical component of the inclusive growth envisaged for the overall development of the economy. The spread of banking facilities has been uneven in the country, throwing up challenges for achieving financial inclusion. Even after Nationalisation of commercial banks in 1969 and in 1980, a good proportion of households, specially rural, is still outside the coverage of the formal banking system. An inclusive financial sector would provide access to credit for all 'bankable' people and firms, to insurance for all insurable people and firms and to savings and payments services for everyone. Following table and figure shows the trend in financial inclusion for the last 10 years.

Table 2: Trend in Financial Inclusion

Year	*Number of Deposit A/c*	*Percentage of Change*	*Number of Credit Account*	*Percentage of Change*	*Number of Bank Officers*	*Percentage of Change*
2000-2001	428029197		94943329		35633	
2001-2002	439989348	2.79	56388379	-40.6	35517	-.32
2002-2003	446080712	1.38	59491187	5.502	68078	91.67
2003-2004	457258054	2.50	66390290	11.59	68645	.832
2004-2005	466792531	2.08	77150794	16.21	69969	1.92
2005-2006	485097771	3.92	85435381	10.73	70776	1.15
2006-2007	519199207	7.02	94442027	10.54	73199	3.42
2007-2008	581658012	12.02	106990180	13.28	77699	6.15
2008-2009	662302403	13.86	127056177	18.75	88802	14.28
2009-2010	790405412	19.34	145542331	14.54	101113	13.86

Source : RBI statistics.

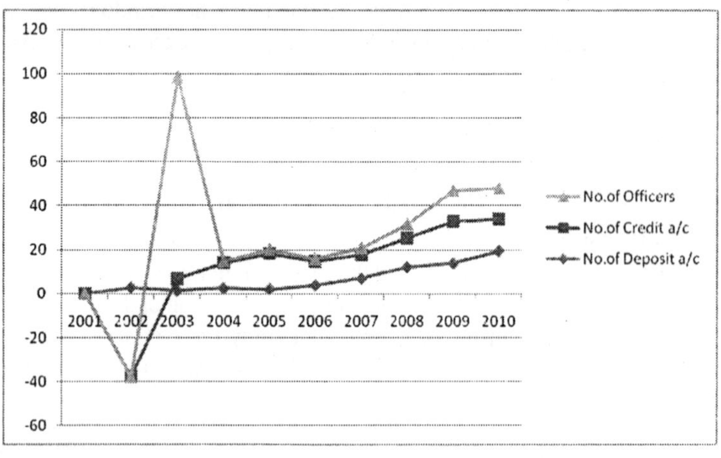

Fig. 1: Compared Growth Rate of Financial Inclusion.

ANALYSIS OF HOUSEHOLDS WITHIN THE FORMAL FINANCIAL BOUNDARY

There is clear distinction between access to formal finance and use of formal financial services. While access refers to timely availability of adequate financial services at a reasonable cost, use refers to the actual consumption of financial services. One may not use formal financial services, even if there is access, because of low reservation cost of informal financial services and/ or high relative prices of financial services compared to the prices of other goods (Kochar 1997, Claessens 2006). Access to formal financial services is a necessary, but not sufficient condition for use of formal financial services. Only those who use formal financial services can be referred as financially included, rest are financially excluded.

Table 3: Percentage of Households without Essential Financial Instruments

	Bank A/c	*Life Insurance*	*Health Insurance*
Rural	50.59	68.2	99.6
Urban	18.01	30.03	79.33
All India	45.23	50.10	90.67

Source: IISS Survey.

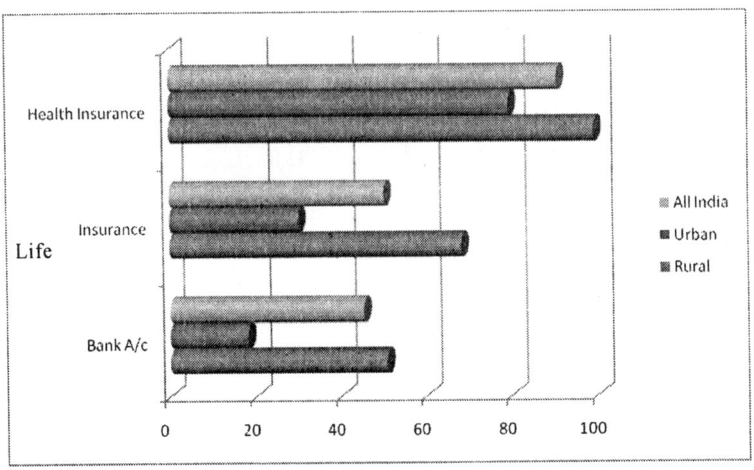

Fig. 2.

In the above table and figure it is clearly depicted that, in India 50.59 per cent of rural householders are excluded from banking services, 68.2 per cent from Insurance services and 99.6 per cent from health insurance services. Here it is shown that there is a wide disparity between rural households and urban households who have accessible to the most important formal financial service like banking service. The interesting fact is, majority of the population living in rural area. Hence the accessibility of financial inclusion of rural households can ensure the financial inclusion status of whole India.

Financial Inclusion and Rural People

At the heart of the financial inclusion assemblage are the 2.8 billion materially poor people the world over who are constituted as in need of financial services who are scattered in the rural area. financial exclusion is quite severe in India. Financial exclusion is disproportionately higher among the relatively rural households compared to their urban counterparts. Nonetheless, a significant percentage of urban households in India are also found to be financially excluded. As the earlier statistics of India reported the majority (near 75 per cent) of people living in rural area. But the percentage of people excluded from the formal financial services is more in this sector. The essential need for the most deprived rural people ,communities is supposedly the need for credit' (Servet, 2010). This need is thought to result from the absence of access to such services; it is a product of the financial inclusion assemblage and a precondition of its existence. In India Grameen Banks continue to insist to occupy the major portion of rural people to the formal financial boundary. Following table and graph shows the rural households which are excluded from the formal sources of financial services.

Table 4: Region –wise Excluded Rural Households from Formal Financial Sources (in lacs)

Region	*Total Households*	*Households Excluded From formal sources*	*Percentage to Total*
Northern	109.46	82.04	74.95
North Eastern	35.40	33.95	95.91
Eastern	210.61	171.14	81.26
Central	271.33	210.52	77.59
Western	103.66	58.07	56.02
Southern	161.56	92.49	57.25
UTs	1.48	1.33	89.86
Total	893.50	649.54	72.70

Source : IISS Survey.

Notes: (a) Northern Region—Haryana, Himachal Pradesh, Jammu and Kashmir, Punjab, Rajasthan;

(b) North-Eastern Region—Arunachal Pradesh, Assam, Manipur, Meghalaya, Mizoram, Nagaland, Tripura;

(c) Eastern Region—Bihar, Jharkhand, Orissa, Sikkim, West Bengal;

(d) Central Region—Chhattisgarh, Madhya Pradesh, Uttar Pradesh, Uttarakhand;

(e) Western Region—Gujarat, Maharashtra, Daman and Diu; and

(f) Southern Region—Andhra Pradesh, Karnataka, Kerala, Tamil Nadu.

(g) UTs - Pondicherry, Goa, Delhi, Andaman and Nicobar Islands, Chandigarh, Lakshadweep, Dadra and Nagar Haveli.

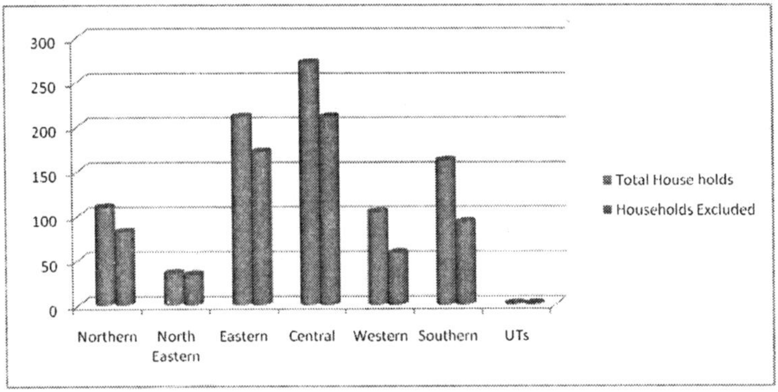

Fig. 3.

Although many Co-operative Banks, Regional Rural Banks, Nationalised banks and financial institution came in to existence, even now 72.7% of total rural households are excluded from all the financial services. Among them North Eastern Region population are the least (95.91) financially included area. The analysis further captures except Western ,Southern region all other region have less access to financial services. The Western region and southern region have has the highest access in banking services (43.98 and 42.75), followed by the East (18.74 per cent), North (25.05 per cent), Central (22.41 per cent) regions.

Table 5: Region Wise Aggregate Deposit and Credit (Amount in Crore)

		Rural			*Urban*		
		Offices	*Deposits*	*Credit*	*Offices*	*Deposits*	*Credit*
1.	**NORTHERN REGION**	5,559	111,451	86,429	10,753	1,124,736	937,832
	Haryana	851	16,440	18,883	1,904	119,024	85,570
	Himachal Pradesh	822	19,726	7,104	283	17,200	6,020
	Jammu & Kashmir	570	13,090	4,587	491	32,746	11,321
	Punjab	1,361	34,799	30,985	2,622	137,823	107,362
	Rajasthan	1,867	21,184	18,755	2,662	118,824	105,759
	Chandigarh	24	1,572	1,567	265	38,081	45,492
	Delhi	64		4,548	2,526	661,038	576,307
2.	**NORTH-EASTERN REGION**	1,235	19,055	8,177	1,140	77,006	25,877
	Arunachal Pradesh	51	1,758	401	37	3,211	924
	Assam	805	10,989	5,286	732	48,460	17,898
	Manipur	35	479	252	49	2,899	977

Table 5 (contd...)

		Rural			Urban		
		Offices	*Deposits*	*Credit*	*Offices*	*Deposits*	*Credit*
	Meghalaya	129	2,412	713	95	7,976	1,941
	Mizoram	54	481	263	47	2,611	1,037
	Nagaland	37	440	292	60	4,748	1,183
	Tripura	124	2,497	970	120	7,101	1,917
3.	**EASTERN REGION**	7,835	120,987	46,046	7,474	572,520	293,597
	Bihar	2,480	32,067	12,325	1,904	96,612	24,732
	Jharkhand	1,050	16,248	4,905	980	65,305	22,628
	Orissa	1,758	24,508	12,319	1,337	89,735	41,585
	Sikkim	55	1,133	467	29	2,516	799
	West Bengal	2,472	46,546	15,837	3,201	316,920	203,306
	Andaman and Nicobar Island	20	485	193	23	1,431	547
4.	**CENTRAL REGION**	8,344	121,779	65,684	10,095	563,967	246,904
	Chhattisgarh	698	9,917	3,436	758	51,452	30,375
	Madhya Pradesh	1,794	18,779	16,128	2,681	139,591	72,809
	Uttar Pradesh	5,214	80,410	41,336	5,970	331,589	129,675
	Uttarakhand	638	12,674	4,784	686	41,335	14,044
5.	**WESTERN REGION**	4,123	71,499	41,800	10,288	1,751,231	1,434,329
	Goa	188	7,132	1,240	280	27,918	8,009
	Gujarat	1,633	32,138	14,823	3,443	255,326	177,827
	Maharashtra	2,289	32,025	25,712	6,510	1,464,656	1,247,673
	Dadra and Nagar Haveli	11	193	24	28	1,386	488
	Daman and Diu	2	10	1	27	1,946	332
6.	**SOUTHERN REGION**	7,112	94,542	113,124	18,732	1,181,773	1,087,380
	Andhra Pradesh	2,633	28,416	44,119	5,059	295,044	311,231
	Karnataka	2,248	26,388	27,039	4,247	357,668	241,621
	Kerala	343	7,445	5,688	4,303	183,020	134,870
	Tamil Nadu	1,843	31,497	35,687	4,998	339,001	395,158
	Lakshadweep	8	154	24	4	372	27
	Puducherry	37	642	567	121	6,667	4,473
	ALL-INDIA	**34,208**	**539,314**	**361,260**	**58,482**	**5,271,232**	**4,025,919**

Source: Indiastat.

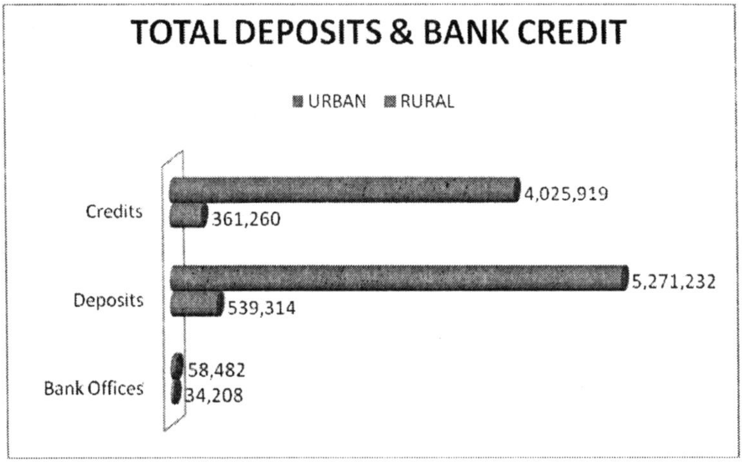

Fig. 4: Total Deposits and Bank Credit.

It can be observed that for the last 10 years a majority of total deposits and bank credit are mobilised from urban households. 4,025,919 crore credit is hold by Urban households and 361,260 crore holds rural households. In the case of deposits 5,271,232 crore acquired from urban households and 539,314 crores of deposits from rural households.

Findings

The study gives an indication that majority of the rural population doesn't have access to any formal financial instrument even though India entitled developing country. Financial inclusion trend showing an increasing trend but the rural people cannot address this trend. 'Developing financial system' it should be in the sense of access to a well functioning financial system, by creating equal opportunities then only it enables economically and socially integration and development.

Summing Up

Cooperative and Regional Rural Banks Acts and nationalisation of scheduled commercial banks, financial inclusion measures in India have led to physical expansion in the country. Unfortunately, the expansion has not brought about the necessary change in the backward and rural areas as financial services are yet to reach a vast majority of the population. Large multinational financial and technology companies are now looking for the fortune at the bottom of the pyramid, following C.K. Prahalad's seminar work on how corporations can eradicate poverty through profit. India's major portion of people are representing the rural sector. Hence in order to develop the nation we have to concentrate more on bottom level where the wide scope is lying.

References

1. Basu, Priya (2006), *Improving Access to Finance for India's Rural Poor.* Washington D.C.: World Bank.
2. Burra, Neera, Joy Deshmukh-Ranadive and Ranjani K. Murthy (2005), *Micro-Credit, Poverty and Empowerment.* New Delhi: Sage Publications.
3. Commonwealth Finance Ministers Meeting (CWFMM) (2006), 'Financial Inclusion- Information Document for Delegates', UK Department for International Development (DFID), Colombo, 12–14 September.
4. Dev, S. Mahendra (2006), 'Financial Inclusion: Issues and Challenges', *Economic and Political Weekly*, XLI(41): 4310–13.
5. Ferrari, Aurora (with Guillemette Jaffrin and Sabin Raj Shrestha) (2007), *Access to Financial Services in Nepal.* Washington D.C.: World Bank.
6. Ghate, Prabhu (2007), *Indian Microfi nance: The Challenges of Rapid Growth.* New Delhi: Sage Publications.
7. Gopinath, Shyamala (2006), 'Inclusive Growth: Role of Financial Education', *Reserve Bank of India Bulletin*, December, pp. 1517–21.
8. Government of India (1972), *Report of the Banking Commission.* New Delhi.
9. Rangarajan, C. (1996), "Rural India, the Role of Credit," *Reserve Bank of India Bulletin,* Reserve Bank of India, Mumbai.
10. Rangarajan, C. (2008), *Report of the Committee on Financial Inclusion,* Government of India, New Delhi.
11. Reserve Bank of India (1954), "All-India Credit Survey," Reserve Bank of India Bulletin, RBI, Bombay.
12. Reserve Bank of India (1954), "All-India Rural Credit Survey Report," Report of the Committee of Direction of the All India Rural Credit Survey, Bombay.
13. Reserve Bank of India (2010), "Report on Currency and Finance-2000-2010."
14. Reynolds, Faith (2003), 'Promoting Financial Inclusion', *Poverty*, 114: 1–7.
15. Royal Commission on Agriculture in India (RCAI) (1928), *A Report.* New Delhi: Agricole Publishing Academy.
16. Sharma, D.P. and V.V. Desai (1980), *Rural Economy of India.* New Delhi: Vikas Publishing House Pvt. Ltd.
17. Srinivasan, N. (2007), 'Policy Issues and the Role of Banking System in Financial Inclusion', *Economic and Political Weekly*, XLII(30): 3091–95.

11

Micro Finance Leads to Debt Trap

S. Mahendra Kumar and *S. Srinivasa*

Introduction

Micro finanace in India is growing rapidly and receiving increasing attention from the financial institutions, non-governmental organisations (NGOs) and the government, as an instrument that can transform lives of the poor. A vibrant and developed micro finanace sector can significantly influence the economic development and distribution of wealth in the country. Micro finance took roots in 1992-93 with the launching of the Self Help Group (SHGs)-Bank Linkage programme by National Bank for Agriculture and Rural Development (NABARD). India is a country of 5,93,643 villages as 70 per cent of its population resides in rural areas and the rural sector provides livelihood to about 72 per cent of the total population. They depend upon the agriculture. In addition to providing food and fodder to large population of human beings and livestock, respectively, agriculture is the main source of raw material for several key industries.

A number of studies begin with the All India Rural Credit survey in 1954; found that the rural poor had high levels of indebtedness and very limited bank access. The State Bank of India was set up in 1955 as facilitator to provide banking services to poor population, the 14 large commercial banks were nationalised in 1969, and the National Bank for Agriculture and Development (NABARD) was created in 1982. Each of the nationalised banks is deputed the role of lead banks in particular parts of the country and they are restricted of maintain justified ratios of urban and rural branches. A lot of cooperative banks and regional rural banks are created primarily to cater credit need of poor population in India.

India is one of the fastest developing country in the world. India's 'first world' economy is oriented to the very highest standards of globalise consumption, and formal sector incomes and life styles reflect this. By contrast, the real incomes and 'life styles' of the very poor, particularly in rural areas, are comparable very low. Micro-finance is often advocated as a solution to multiple social problems in India. Poor persons with access to credit can make investments in enterprises that bring them out of poverty.

Prof. Muhammad Yunus, of Bangladesh developed and founded the concept of micro finanace. He was awarded the Nobel Peace prize in 2006 for his contribution to institutions like micro finanace and Grameen Bank system. Nobel laureate Mr. Yunus founded the Grameen Banks in 1976 to make loans to poor Bangladeshis. Since then the Grameen Banks has issued more than $ 3 billion in loans to some 2.4 million borrowers. To ensure repayment, the bank uses a system of 'solidarity group'. Small informal groups apply together for loans and whose members act as co-guarantors of repayment and support one another's effort at economic self-advancement.

Gradually, the micro finanace institutions (MFIs) had become a 'poster boy' of financial inclusion in the last decade having built up a robust base of 2.6 crore clients and a sizeable impressive credit off-take. A latest report by Intellcap, an independent industry research firm, puts the total estimated demand for micro-credit in India at $ 51.4 billion (equalent of Rs. 240,000 crore). Another report by Bharat Micro finanace said the total outstanding loan portfolio grew from Rs. 3, 456 crore in 2007 to Rs. 11, 734 crore in 2009.

The Rs. 12,000 crore micro finance industry is mired in many wrong doings and controversies. The government must form a regulatory framework for the survival and disciplined functioning of this important industry, as the formal banking system has failed to reach out the poor and landless in the rural areas, the emergence of the micro finance industry-right from providing 'branchless banking', to easy-access to money-was seen as the best thing to have happened to the poor and un-banked in the country.

Faced with a liquidity crunch, micro finance companies have asked the Reserve Bank of India to direct banks to set up an emergency fund of Rs. 1,000 crore to help them tide over slowdown in their business. Sources said the Micro Finance Institution Network (MFIN) is trying to convince the Reserve Bank of India in this regard.

The micro finance sector has been reeling under a liquidity crisis after the Andhra Pradesh government issued an ordinance to control interest rate charged by micro finance institutions (MFIs) and also check the coercive recovery tactics adopted by these firms. From time to time, RBI had helped various sectors to deal with the money shortage. At the time of global financial crisis, the central bank had announced special liquidity injection measures for the mutual fund industry when it was facing a cash shortage.

Sources said the MFIN has has discussion with RBI seeking assistance. MFIN has requested RBI to ask the Small Industries Development Bank of India (SIDBI) and public and private sector banks to extend the funding.

MFIs offer credit to the poor after sourcing the funding from banks. While the banks lend the MFIs in turn change interest rates as high as 36 per cent. MFIs say high interest rate is charged because the cost associated to lending in rural areas is too high. The Andhra Pradesh ordinance on October 15 impacted the collections of MFIs.

The failure of banks to provide timely credit is forcing self help groups (SHGs) to borrow from micro finance institutions (MFIs) at excruciating rates of interest. "To meet RBI targets on priority sector lending, banks are taking the softer option of lending to MFIs instead of SHGs directly," according to NABARD Karnataka Chief General Manager Venkatesh Tagat. "As MFIs take responsibility for loan disbursal and recovery, this is an easy way out for banks," he added. According to NABARD estimates 5, 70, 000 SHGs have been linked with banks in Karnataka. But only one-third of these have been able to actively borrow from banks. While banks favour MFIs all over India, in Karnataka, the bias is particularly acute. According to NABARD data, banks lent Rs. 2, 600 crore to MFIs and just Rs. 1,000 crore to SHGs in Karnataka in 2009-10. In contrast, all-over India bank lending to SHGs at Rs. 14,450 crore, out weighed the funds given to MFIs at Rs. 10,700 crore, in the same period. Even Karnataka based commercial banks which lend generously to SHGs in other states are holding back here. Canara Bank and Syndicate banks lent just Rs. 42 crore and Rs. 34 crore respectively to SHGs in 2009-10 despite having excellent local network. Ironically, these banks respectively gave Rs. 142 crore and Rs. 189 crore to SHGs in Andhra Pradesh.

Review of Literature

Literature review for the study has been undertaken from various quarters, several books and Journals have been reviewed, Kittur, et al (2010) in their study on "Stree Shakti SHGs and Empowerment of women in Haveri District Karnataka" observed that the socio-economic conditions of the Stree Shakti women in the study area had increased after joining the Stree Shakti groups. Women members of Stree Shakti groups are able to purchase new house hold amenities, new agriculture implements due to changes of their occupational and income bringing capacity. And the scheme is able to develop the human dignity among the rural poor women. Babu Amjuth, et al (2005) in their study on "Poverty Alleviation and Empowerment Women-Role of Micro Credit" observed that access to credit is more important for the poor people than subsidies and it is denied to them. The practical difficulties stem from the discrepancy between the mode of operation followed by financial institutions and financing needs of house holds. More over banks are reluctant to lend to the poor because of lack of collateral and high transaction cost. Sharma Manohar (2002) study on "Impact of Micro Finance on Poverty Alleviation" observed that the spectacular growth of the micro finanace industry has been fueled not by market forces but by conscious actions of national governments, nongovernmental organisations (NGOs), and donors who view micro finance as an effective tool for alleviating poverty. This review indicates that impact studies themselves must be improved to make more accurate assessments of benefits.

Objectives of the Study

The study aims at the following objectives,

1. To examine the state wise number of MFIs clients and loan outreach in India,
2. To identify how microfinance leads to Debt Trap.

Methodology

The methodology for the study is based on both descriptive and analytical in nature the study is based on secondary data only. Secondary data was collected from the published articles, published documents, district gazettes, journals, books, periodicals and internet sources.

Theoretical Background

Under the trickle down theory in the planning process it was expected that women will equally benefit along with men. This has been believed by actual development. Prof. Kuznets is the first economist to study the income distribution empirically. He observes that in the early stages of economic growth relative income inequality increases, stabilises for a time and then decline in the later stage. This is known as the inverted U- shaped hypothesis of income distribution.

Table 1 : MFI clients and loan outreach (major states only)

States	*Client Outreach (No.)*	*Loan Portfolio (Rs)*
Andhra Pradesh	3653115	19445023878
Karnataka	1963373	11038481244
Tamil Nadu	1692560	5754100628
Orissa	1577600	5323529239
West Bengal	1540927	5298597926
Maharashtra	1169306	3840548354
Uttar Pradesh	533041	3469441228
Gujarat	416375	640302867
Kerala	382001	1277305126
Bihar	241651	90823380

Source: Micro Finance India, State of Sector Report, 2008.

Table 1 show that no. of client out reach and loan portfolio major states in India. Andhra Pradesh was the highest and also first place no. of client outreach which was 3653115 respectively. Karnataka was the second position as well as no. of client's outreach which was 1963373. Bihar was the lowest no. of outreach clients was just 241651 respectively.

Andhra Pradesh was the highest loan portfolio which was 19445023877 rupees, and Karnataka was the second position as well as portfolio which were 11038481244 rupees. In case Bihar was the lowest loan portfolio outreach which was just 90823380 rupees only.

Table 2 : Micro Finance Institution in India (2008)

Microfinance Institutions in India		
1.	Total No. of Microfinance Institutions in India	134
2.	Gross Loan Portfolio (US $)	2.1 Billion
3.	Average Loan balance per borrower (US $)	109.1
4.	Total Assets (US $)	3.0 billion
5.	Number of Active borrowers	16.1 million
6.	Total Deposits (US $)	88.6 million
7.	Number of depositors	1.2 million

Regulatory Steps in Micro Finance

One of the reasons why MFIs could get away by changing exorbitant interest rates is that there is no one to regulate them. But the Reserve Bank of India now has set up a panel headed by **J H Malegam** which will submit its report on the issue of MFI using coercive methods for loan recovery as well their interest rate practices by January end 2011.

When adverse news spread some borrowers stopped making even their usual repayments. There was talk of removing MFI loans from the priority sector category. The stock market regulator SEBI was also probing on SKS Micro finance, especially the way it sacked its CEO, the triggered the SKS stock price to crash spoiling hopes of other MFIs to raise money from the capital markets.

Like it or not, the micro finance sector has been gripped with a crisis of macro proportions. And the problem don't seem to go away in a jiffy like one would want it, which explains why MFIs were trying hard for emergency funding from banks. "We have not refused to fund MFIs, but have asked them to hold for a while. We are not turning down their proposals for funding, but we would rather wait for the RBI's Malegam Committee report as there will be more clarity after that. Besides, multiple lending created a bubble", as per Axis Bank President (Agri and Rural banking) S K Misra.

Misleading Borrowers

Various studies have pointed out that microfinance is not a magic wand that can automatically lift poor people out of poverty and access to credit is only the first step. But then the poor need the entire gamut of financial services from savings to insurance and livelihood services that span health, farming practices, education and financial literacy to break the shackles of destitution which calls for lot of innovations executed in large scale across the country.

Against this backdrop of growing criticism about MFIs charging very high interest rates and the coercive recovery methods developed by them, the high-powered Prime Minister's Economic Advisory Council (PMEAC) early this week strongly advocated for regulatory mechanism for the sector. The reason why there is a strong need for reform in the micro finance sector is that MFIs are already linked to the banking system. And if this link is to be strengthened then the MFIs need to modify some of their lending practices.

Though the government is slated to bring a bill on MFIs regulation in the parliament, a number of suicides by poor borrowers in Andhra Pradesh were blamed on functioning of MFIs and their usurious interest rates. RBI also set up a sub-committee to study the functioning and interest rate structures of MFIs, which prompted the government to defer the bill so that it could incorporate the recommendations of the RBI panel into it.

Many critics are of the view that the cost of lending indicated by MFIs in their advisements (generally around 18 per cent) don't add up the charges they put while advertising they low interest rates: "Over and above, they charge an upfront insurance fee, application fee which brings the effective rate to as high as 30 per cent (in the case of SKS)", according to Society for Elimination of Rural Poverty (SERP) CEO B Rajasekhar. At the same time, MFIs are looking at banks; they need about Rs. 1,000 crore, to bail them out hoping against hope. MFIs raise 75 per cent of their funding from (bank) borrowings and the remaining from equity and cash securities. Banks, which already have an exposure of over Rs. 30, 000 crore in MFIs, are shying away from funding MFIs after the recent controversy over malpractices in the sector involving poor borrowers being led to a debt trap and suicides, making it difficult for the micro-lenders.

Use of Coercive Methods

"These institutions are using quite coercive methods to collect", said Vasanth Kumar, the state's minister for rural development. "They aren't looking at sustainability or ensuring the money is going to income-generating activities. They are just making money".

Reddy Subrahmanyam, a senior official who helped write the Andhra Pradesh legislation, accuses micro finanace companies of making 'hyper profits of the poor', and said the industry had become no better than the widely despised village loan sharks it was intended to replace.

"The money lender lives in the community", as per Reddy Subrahmanyam. "At least you can burn down his house. With these companies, it is loot and scoot."

Indeed, some of the anger appears to have been fuelled by the recent initial public offering of shares by SKS Micro finance, India's largest for profit micro lender, which is backed by famous investors like George Soros and Vinod Khosla, a co-founder of Sun Microsystems.

One of India's leading social workers, Ela Bhatt, who heads the Self-Employed Women's Association, or SEWA, said micro finance firms had lost sight of the fact that the poor needed more than loans to be successful entrepreneurs. They need business and financial advice as well, she said. "They were more concerned about growth-not growth of the livelihoods and economic status of the clients, but only the institutions' growth", according to Ela Bhatt.

Mr. Mahajan, who is also the chairman of the micro finance Institutions net work, observes the industry was now planning to create a fund to help restructure the loans of the 20 per cent of borrowers in Andhra Pradesh who were struggling. He also said the industry, which has been reluctant to accept outside help, would share its client databases with the government and was negotiating restrictions on retail lending that did not go through the nonprofit self-help lending groups. The collapse of the industry could have severe consequences for borrowers, who may be forced to resort to money lenders once again.

Salient Features of Micro Finance Programme of Government of India

(a) **Arranging fixed deposits for MFIs/NGOs:** Under this scheme government of India arrange money to MFI/NGO like SIDBI for micro credit to poor.

(b) **Training and studies on micro-finanace programme:** Government of India would help SIDBI in meeting the training needs of NGOs, SHGs, intermediaries and entrepreneurs and also in enhancing awareness about the programme.

(c) **Institutional building for 'intermediaries' for identification of viable projects:** The government of India would help in institution building through identification and development of intermediary organisation', which would help the NGOs/SHGs in identification of product, preparation of project report, working out forward and backward linkages and in fixing marketing/technology tie-ups.

(d) **budgetary provision for the scheme during 10th plan:** There was a budgetary provision in 10th five year plan and hoping more funds in next plan.

(e) **Administrative arrangement:** A committee has been formed to control and monitor the administrative arrangement of MFIs/NGOs.

Latest Policy Announcement

Following funds and committee were set up:

1. RBI set up micro credit special cell in 1999.
2. Set up task force on supportive policy and regulatory frame work for micro finance in NABARD 1999.
3. Set up a Micro Development fund in NABARD with RBI and 11 commercial banks.
4. set up four informal group to examine various issue concerning micro finance delivery in 2002, which recommended to make the procedure of micro finance simple, make advances totally hassle free enhance micro finance, ensure sharing of experience among branches involved in micro finance.
5. Malegam Committee appointed by RBI to create regulatory frame work for micro finance institutions.

Conclusion

The Rs. 12,000 crore micro finance industry are mired in many wrong doings and controversies. The Government must form a regulatory framework for the survival and disciplined functioning of this important industry. One approach is to fix the margins of MFIs so that the margin they enjoy is not really too high. The margin should be adequate to cover the transaction cost and the risk element. It also depends on the rate at which they borrow and the rate at which they lend. One of the problems that have surfaced recently is that they have been indulging in multiple lending and large parts of the loans are given for consumption purposes. This is the model that will lend them in troubles. The whole idea of encouraging micro finance is to encourage credit for income generating activities. If the MFI'S do not come under regulation, this will definitely lead to Debt Trap.

References

1. Tiyas Biswas (2000), "Women Empowerment through Micro Finance: A Boom for Development", National Institute of Technology, Durgapur.
2. Rajesh Kumar Shastri (2009), "Micro Finance and Poverty Reduction in India (A Comparative Study with Asian Countries)", African Journal of Business Management, 3(4), 136-140.
3. Dr. H.T. Kittur and Sri. M. V. Shidaganal (2010), Strre Shakti SHGs and Empowerment of Women in Haveri District Karnataka, 24(277), Third Concept, New Delhi.
4. C.P. Chandan (2010), "Microfinance: A Tool for Rural Development in India, Indian Economy Article, 436/6.

5. Deccan Hearald, “Macro problems plague micro finance industry”, News paper, November, 22, 2010.
6. Deccan Hearald, News paper, Microfinance: Loan sharks driving village folks to suicide,” November, 25, 2010.
7. Deccan Hearald, “Banks drive Self-help groups into Micro finance debt trap”, News paper, December, 19, 2010.
8. Deccan Hearald, “Panel for cap on micro finance firms’ margins”, News paper, December, 20, 2010.

12

Micro Finance – A Tool for Financial Inclusion and Empowerment of Women: A Case Study of Chamarajanagara District, Karnataka

H.S. Niranjana Babu Reddy, Ashoka M.L. **and** *Deepu*

Introduction

Development is an issue in every economy when women are in included in this, efforts becomes more meaningful and useful. Micro finance plays an important role in empowerment of those who are poor and neglected in the society especially women. Though she represents more 48% of total world population, her contribution to the development of economy has not been recognised properly. With formation of self help groups by women especially in the rural areas has led to empower her community. Since from a very long period financial institutions completely neglected women and were not lending loans to women. Things are gradually changing with the successful repayment of loans in time to the banks by women members of self help groups, now banks and other financial institutions have changed their attitude because of her promptness in repaying the barrowed cum in time. Self help group concept basically emerged in Bangladesh in late seventies by Prof. Mohammad Yunis and later in nineties it was introduced to India also. SHGs are now important menas of giving credit to poor people and helps them to overcome from poverty traps. These SHGs consists of minimum 5 to 20 women members and are informal association of women. They are managed by elected leaders among themselves, they promote savings, and they lend money to members and are linked to the formal credit system, banks.

Micro finance programs have significant potential for contributing to economic and social empowerment to members of SHGs. Access to savings and credit can initiate or strengthen a series of interlinked and mutually reinforcing 'virtuoso spirals' of empowerment. Micro finance development has emerged as major strategy to combat the twin issues of poverty and unemployment that continue to pose a major threat to the polity and economy of both the developed and developing countries. So, micro finance is a way of financing to poor for their business, to alleviate their poverty, empowering them, giving socio economic benefits of sustainable way.

Micro finance has evolved as an economic development approach. Intended to benefit low-income women and men. The term refers to the provision of financial services to low-income clients, including the self-employed. Due to micro finance there are many possibilities have emerged including extending markets, reducing poverty and fostering social change.

Micro Finance: A Development Tool

In developing countries, people from lower income communities have innovative idea for their business, even an shop keeper of household products manufacturer, but they have no financial resources to implement their ideas, it lead them to more poverty and poor life standards. Hence, MFIs work for general financial services with this they provide insurance and payment services to their clients. MFIs not only financial intermediation but also providing social intermediation and social services to their clients. They include trainings, management development, and financial literacy activities.

Financial Intermediation

Financial intermediation is by far the most primary objective of MFIs because without loan/money social intermediations cannot work. Therefore, poor face barriers to access finance from general financial service institutions. MFIs in this regard, become a bridge to access finance and it result to poverty elevation, health care and education literacy.

Social Intermediations

Social intermediation is the process of building the human and social capital required by sustainable financial intermediation for poor. It covers the issues of group formations, leadership training and co-operative learning, which is the secondary role of MF for barrowers of MFIs. It establish on the basic of strong foundation of trust and co-operation. The ratio of social capital will increase with increase with increase in business activities among members, and financial transaction between lender and barrowers.

Enterprise Development Services

SHGs not all, support to barrowers, either in group or individual in different enterprise development services like marketing, business and accounting formation such as providing technical support to group or individual in start up of business, development and mattering ideas and maturing the skills. While, in transformation of enterprise, MFIs arrange trainings for their barrowers, workshops and get together for developing skills in their business area.

Social Services

MFIs role is productive in the life of men by offering financial services with supportive services. They play important role in sustainable human development and livelihood of the poor. Poor needs more than micro finance to address the problems of poverty and accessibility to other life needs like food, health, family planning, education, social support, network and so on.

Review of Literature

P. Jyothi (2010) conducted a study on "a study of SHG-microfinance initiative in Warangal district" and found that providing easy finance and microcredit has always been the primary objective of microfinance linkage. Micro finance in the form of SHG linkage model has been able to inspire hope in the; lives of thousands of rural peoplc, women in particular and enable them to contribute to their family well being through savings and enterprises.

BG Javali and Bagalkot (2009) in their paper "micro finance and women empowerment in Karnataka-a case study of koppal district", pointed out that micro credit is making a significant contribution to both the savings and barrowings of the poor especially the women and enforce financial discipline. Duce to credit extension by SHGs to their women members resulted in progressive change and benefited a lot and greater transformation of social outlook is found.

Dr. Kahnu Charn Dhir (2009) in their paper "women self help groups in empowering women", the issue has been analysed that for any social movement requirement role of catalyst in mobilising the members, assuring them of an affirmative result and making them well familiar with the possible means to accomplish the task. It is through SHGs that the women get an exposure to outside world. The resources and organisations' which are unseen earlier become accessible. Participations in SHGs increase their influence over economic resources and participation in economic decision making. Thus women SHG movement has accomplished the task of poverty reduction to a great extent.

Objectives of the Study

- The main objective of this study is to assess the degree of women empowerment.
- To assess whether empowerment is achieved through self help groups.
- To analyse socio-economic impact of SHGs on its members.
- To analyse economic impact of SHGs on members and their families.

Scope of the Study

The present study was conducted in Chamarajanagara district of Karnataka. Chamarajanagara is the southern-most district in the state of Karnataka, india. It was carved out of the original larger Mysore District in the year 1998. Chamarajanagara town is the headquarters of this district. According to the 2011 census Chamarajanagar district has a population of 1,020,962. Chamarajanagar has a sex ratio of 989 females for every 1000 males, and a literacy rate of 61.12%. It is the third least populous district in Karnataka (out of 30), after Kodagu and Bangalore Rural.

Sampling

For the purpose this research studies a sample size of 400 women, who are members of SHGs of chamarajanager taluk and kollegal taluk are selected. This district has the highest formation of SHGs in southern part of Karnataka.

Data Collection

For the present study primary data was gathered by schedule of questionnaire and sample members were asked questions on socio economic issues, members' monthly savings. Income level, domestic violence etc., and secondary sources include books and journals.

Tools for Analysis

Simple percentage statistical tool has been used to analyse the data and in some cases unprompted percentage has been used which fulfills the purpose of this study.

Limitations of the Study

This present study and analysis of data was done purely based on data provided by the members of SHGs when they are interviewed with a schedule of questionnaire and socio economic impact has not been seen physically witnessed. Sample size is only 400 which may not be sufficient to assess the accurate and actual result.

Data Analysis and Interpretation

Table 1: Age wise classification of respondents

Category	*Frequency*	*Percentage*
18-30	96	24
30-40	162	40.5
40-50	77	19.25
50 and above	65	16.25
Total	400	100

Source : Primary Survey.

Graphical Representation of the above Data

The above table is framed based on the age wise classification of the respondents. Out of the 400 respondents selected of the survey majority of

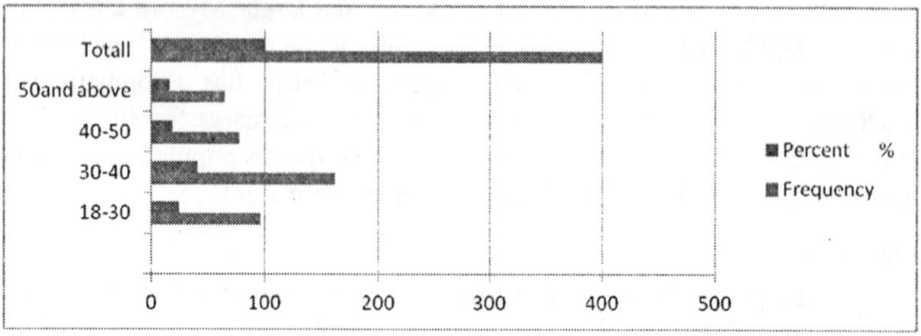

them belongs to age group 30-40 that is they account for 40.5 per cent, next is between 18-30 age group, followed by 40-50 age group with 19.25 per cent and at the end 50 years and above 16.25 per cent. it is interesting to observe that age group 30-40 in rural areas means women usually will be married, having two to three children, having full responsibility of running the family, caring for children education, elders health, and to maintain family. So this age group woman will have more responsibility on their shoulders.

Table 2: Caste wise Classification of Respondents

Category –caste wise	*Frequency*	*Percent (%)*
General merit	38	9.5
SC	112	28
ST	128	32
OBC	102	25.5
Cat I	20	5
Total	400	100

Source : Primary Survey.

Graphical Representation of the above Data

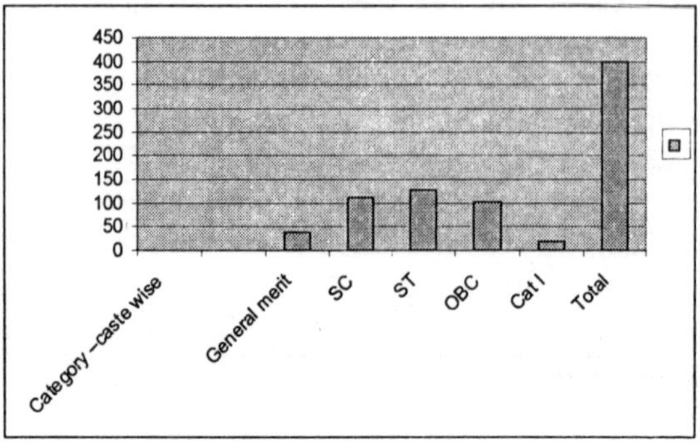

This table is constructed based on the caste wise classification of respondents taken for the survey. Out of 400 28 per cent of them belongs to SC category, 9.5 per cent general group, 32 per cent belongs to ST which is highest in the table, followed by 25.5 per cent OBC, and CAT-I with 5 per cent. In chamarajanagar where this survey was conducted in the selected villages of same taluk and also in kollegal taluk. Empowerment of women and rural poor becomes more meaningful if it can benefit all categories of people, because in every category we find poor people. So there by we can able to see balanced freqencies of respondents in SHGs.

Table 3 Classification of respondents based on education level

Education level	*Frequency*	*Percentage*
Illiterate	130	32.5
Primary	165	41.25
high school	66	16.5
puc	27	6.75
degree	12	3
Total	400	100

Source : Primary Survey.

Graphical Representation of the above Data

This above table is constructed based on the education level of respondents who are part of this survey. We can observe from the table

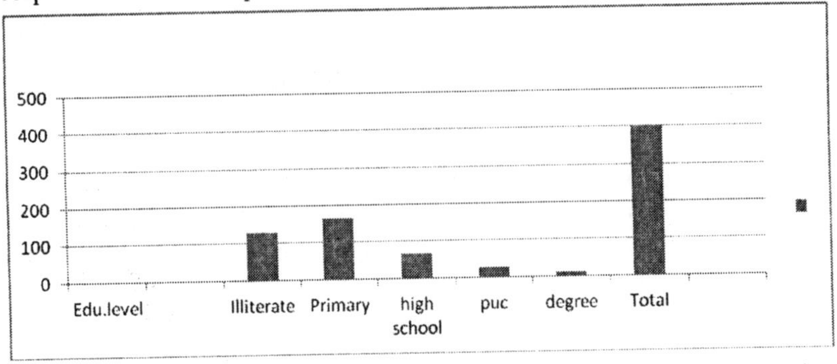

having classified based on illiterates accounts 32.5 per cent primary education about 41.25 per cent high school 16.5 per cent, PU education 6.75 per cent and rarely some degree holders also with 3 per cent. The economic and social background of the families will not permit to give education to girl child especially in the rural side. Education is the root cause for all kinds of opening up for opportunities. Those who are educated can access to facilities, financial services, health issues, and development issues more and more. But things are changing gradually everywhere to provide education sill long way to go in this regard.

Table 4: Classification of respondents based on occupation

Occupation	*Frequency*	*Percentage*
Personal service	70	17.5
Petty shop	54	13.5
Agriculture	188	47
Job	76	19
Others	12	3
Total	400	100

Source : Primary Survey.

Graphical Representation of the above Data

The above table is framed based on the occupation of respondents. Being dependence on agriculture segment more and more with recorded 47%

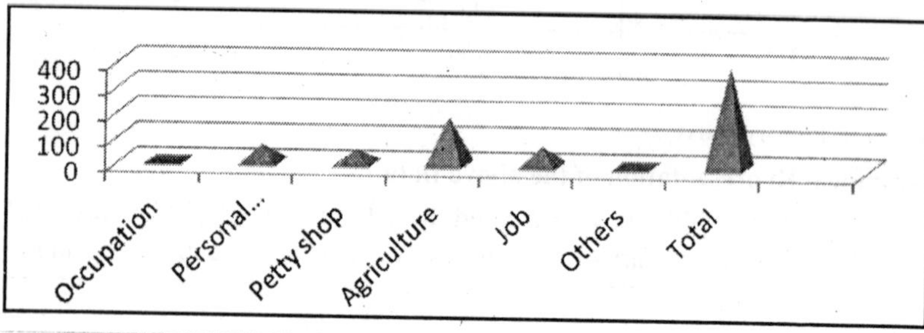

either working in their own fields or in others fields for wage earnings. Next personal services 17.5 per cent, running of petty shops at their homes is the other easy way of engaging in economic activities, going for small jobs in nearby towns identified 19 per cent, other unclassified accounts for 3 per cent. Since majority of them depend more on agriculture income generation is more depending on the rainfall. If the rain is good they get income otherwise miserable with no income and no scope for savings.

Table 5: Respondents Classification based on Income Level

Income level	*Frequency*	*Percentage*
0-2000	112	28
2000-4000	206	51.5
4000-6000	66	16.5
6000-8000	16	4
Total	400	100

Source : Primary Survey.

Graphical Representation of the above Data

In this table respondents were classified based on their income family income. In the first category 0-2000 there are 28% respondents, and in 2000-4000 51.5 per cent respondents which is highest in the above table, followed by 4000-6000 16.5 per cent and 6000-8000 only 4 per cent people. Since opportunities in the rural areas are limited they cannot earn more.

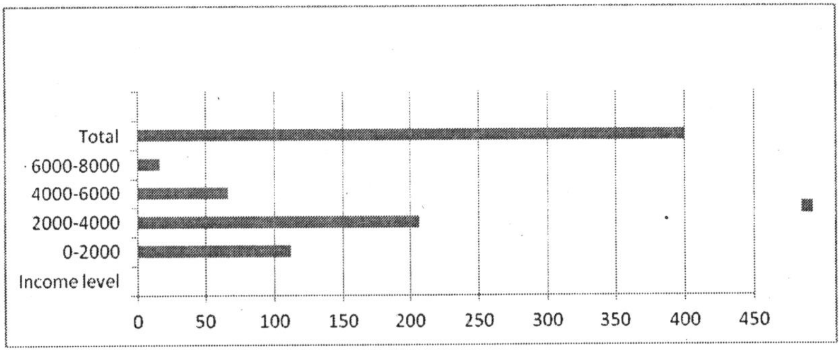

Table 6: Classification of Respondents based on Monthly Savings

Savings	*Frequency*	*Percentage*
100-200	20	5
200-300	30	7.5
300-400	66	16.5
400-500	108	27
500-600	152	38
600 above	24	6
Total	400	100

Source : Primary Survey.

Graphical Representation of the above Data

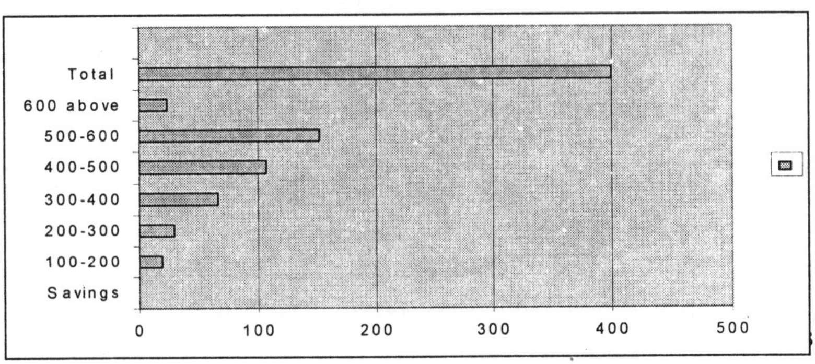

How much they save will decide what they can do in the future for their families. Here majority of people comes under 500-600 rupees savings bracket. Between 400-500 there are 27 per cent, in 300-400 16.5 per cent, 200-300 7.5 per cent, and 100-200 5 per cent.

Table 7: Classification of Respondents based on Loan Amount from SHG

Loan amount	*Frequency*	*Percentage*
Less than 5000	78	19.5
5000-10000	105	26.25
10000-15000	112	28
15000-20000	75	18.75
20000 and above	30	7.5
Total	400	100

Source : Primary Survey.

Graphical Representation of the above Data

The table is framed based on the loan amount taken from SHG from the respondents. Classified starting from less than 5000 with recorded 78 members,

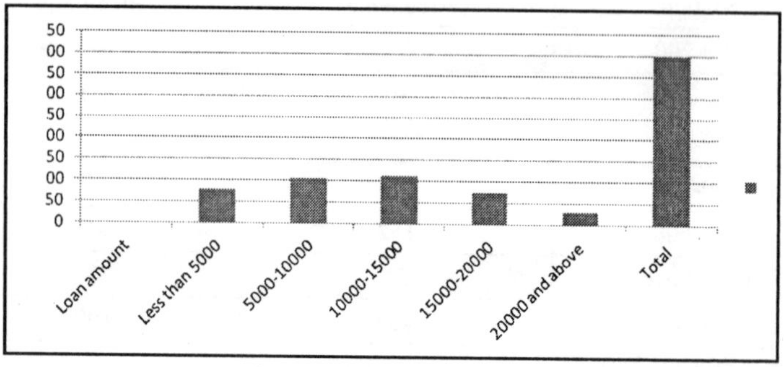

5000-10000 105 people, 10000-15000 112 respondents, between 15000-20000 there are 75, and at the end rupees 20000 and above there are 30 members. If loan has been taken SHGs means they have one financial service option with them and not going to private money lenders charging more interest rates.

Table 8: Social Impact of SHG on its Members

Social impact	***Percent unprompted***
Health aware	54
Education to kids	42
Reduce in domestic violence	76
Increase in Social status	96
	For 100

Source : Primary. Survey.

Graphical Representation of the above Data

This table has been constructed in order to assess the social impact of SHG on its members. To be a member in one group will yield many benefit

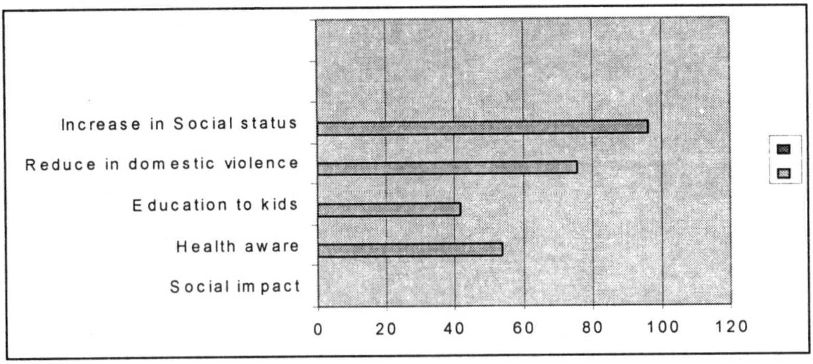

so also in case of self help groups. Due to membership in the group social interaction becomes more leads to awareness in health, finance, and change in the social status. It can be seen from the above table that members have expressed that their health awareness has increased 54 per cent, education giving to their kids by paying school fees in time by taking loan from self help groups 42 per cent, reduce in domestic violence 76 per cent and overall increase in social status 96 per cent members expressed their acceptance. This is the main issue of this article also.

Table 9: Economic Impact and Empowerment of Women through SHG

Economic impact	*Percentage Unprompted*
To be with group felt more secured	77
Communication	65
Financial service	90
Employment opportunities	82
Self confidence and esteem	70
Felt empowered?	95
Total	For 100

Source : Primary Survey.

Graphical Representation of the above Data

This table shows the expressions of the members about economic impact of to be a member of self help group by the respondents. Economic

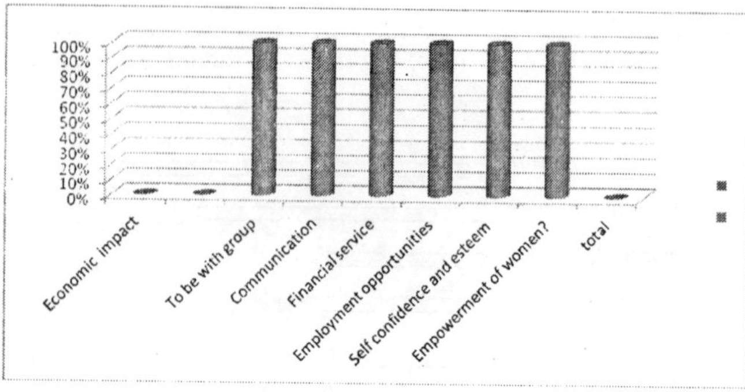

impact factor identified as to be with group brings them feeling of more secured is about 77 per cent, improve in communication system to hear and to be heard is 65 per cent, improve in accessing finance in case of need is 90 per cent which shows the success of self help groups to its members, increase in employment opportunities is about 82 per cent which means exchange of information between members has made this possible incase if they can't go for such jobs at least they can suggest to those who are in need of it in their villages, and 70% of the members are of the opinion that their confidence level and self esteem has increased due to their membership in self help groups. And lastly weather members feel that overall they empowered with SHG membership and by its activities is about 95% which shows economic impact and social impact on them.

Major Finding of the Study

- Women self help groups have become change agents by uplifting members family socio-economic status.
- Women feel more secured and economically strong by such SHGs membership.
- SHGs are not only a means of credit support but also flat form to share members family problems with others and to get solutions out of interactions.
- Due to membership in SHGs employment opportunities for them has increased.
- Capacity to save, ability to purchase and to manage their family financial problems has become possible.
- Due to in time availability of funds for health, children education has become reality.

- Interestingly domestic violence has become lesser due to women ability to take financial decisions at home.
- Overall members of SHG agree that it has positive impact on their socio economic conditions.

Recommendations

- Government must support more and more to these SHGs formation and in running them successfully.
- Institutions must come forward to train these women SHGs members to undertake small enterprises activates.
- Members' ability to earn and to save is needed to be increased.
- More MFIs, NGOs must actively participate in guiding poor women members of SHGs.
- Banks are needed to extend more credit facilities to these women SHGs.
- Banks must give separate education loans to children of SHG members who have successfully repaid their bank loans in time.
- Micro insurance must be extended to these SHGs.

Conclusion

To conclude, women empowerment is a big challenge in order to achieve inclusive growth which is possible through SHGs activities and its support to members. Family clashes, domestic violence reduces due to increase in the role of women in financial decision which is major move and direct impact of SHGs. Overall increase in socio-economic conditions of members of SHGs and empowering themselves through regular savings and timely credit support, rapid development becomes possible.

References

Bisoyi Tanuj Kumar, Rural Credit Regional Rural Banks and Mirco-Finance, 2010.

Deshmukh-Randive Joy 2004, womens Self-Help Group in Andhra Pradesh-participating poverty Alleviation in Action.

Fisher Thomas and M. S. Sriram, 2002, Beyond micro credit putting development Bank into micro-finance.

Gariyali C.K. and Yettivel S.K. 2003, Women own- The Self help Movement of Tamilnadu.

Govt. of India ministry of Finance 2008, Economic Survey, New Delhi India.

Micro finance-Self Employment and poverty Alleviation by Sangita Kamdar, Himalaya Publication.

Nadard-Annual Report 2007-08 SHG Bank linkage progress.

RBI 2007, Annual Report 2007, Report on trend and progress in Banking in India 2006-07.

Sa-Dhan-2008, "Quick Review" 2007-08 in India.

13

Financial Exclusion and Concomitant Social Exclusion: A Probe into the Financial Exclusion of Workers in Plantation Sector in Kerala

Rajesh R.

Introduction

Exclusion is the process and situation in which a section of the society is excluded from its mainstream with regard to the requirements and necessities of normal life which obviously includes deprivation of access to and attainment of basic amenities including education, health and livelihood. Financial inclusion that i.e. accessibility to financial assets like possession of bank account, savings habit, easy access to formal credit etc plays a very important role in enhancing the overall human development indicators thereby an inclusive growth. Financial inclusion could therefore be termed as the easy access to delivery of financial services at an affordable cost to every section in the society especially to the disadvantaged and those belonging to the low income bracket. By definition financial exclusion can be defined as the process of ensuring access to financial services and timely and adequate credit where needed by vulnerable groups such as weaker sections and low income groups at an affordable cost (Planning Commission, 2008). A society or community or group can be considered as financially excluded if they do not have access to mainstream formal financial services or assets like banking accounts, credit facility, insurance, remittances etc. (World Bank, 2008). Financial inclusion helps poor people to mitigate the risks they face as a result of unforeseen economic shocks like lack of job opportunities, failure of monsoon, drought situation and such other natural calamities. It also helps poor the access to financial services more easily. Financial inclusion also allows the poor to save money outside the house safely.

United Nation report (2006) states that "The stark reality is that most poor people in the world still lack access to sustainable financial services, whether it is savings, credit or insurance. Realising the need of financial inclusion for the upliftment of poor across the globe and in imporving their lives certain goals where set for achieving financial inclusion like access at a reasonable cost for all households and enterprises to the range of financial services for which they are "bankable," including savings, short and long-term credit, leasing and factoring, mortgages, insurance, pensions, payments, local money transfers and international remittances. Other goals include sound financial institutions guided by appropriate regulations, internal management systems, industry performance standards, and performance monitoring by the market, multiple providers of financial services, wherever feasible, so as to bring cost-effective and a wide variety of alternatives to customers which could include any number of combinations of sound private, non-profit and public providers etc.

In Indian vast sections of the society are excluded from attaining the basic amenities of life including decent housing, food, health and source of livelihood ultimately leading to social exclusion. Financial Exclusion is also one of the reasons attributed for social exclusion in Indian context. Easy access to finance by the poor and vulnerable groups is a prerequisite condition for poverty reduction and social cohesion. It plays a pivotal role in the creation of an inclusive society. Financial inclusion truly plays a very important role in the upliftment and empowerment of the vulnerable sections in the society like scheduled caste, scheduled tribe and other oppressed section of the society in the case of India. Post- Liberalisation period paved the way for increased liberalisation of financial sector and the easy accessibility to formal financial institutions to a large section of population in the country. But some what the trickledown effect failed to happen in this case i.e. the fruits of benefits failed to reach the downtrodden sections of the society as the access to such technology is restricted only to certain segments of the society. There is a growing divide in terms of financial inclusion, with an increased range of personal finance options for a segment of high and upper middle income population in the society whereas large section of the population who lack access to even the most basic banking services resulting in "financial exclusion" of majority of the citizens in our country. These people, particularly, those living on low incomes, are deprived of their access to mainstream financial products such as bank accounts, low cost credit, remittances and payment services, financial advisory services, insurance facilities, etc. ultimately leading to lesser savings, lesser options for credit, lack of insurance protection to life and property ultimately in financial exclusion.

Financial exclusion leads to non accessibility, non-affordability and non-availability of financial products resulting in fewer amounts of saving, skewed nature of access to formal source of credit and exposure to non-formal sources like money lenders who charge higher costs for credits (NABARD, 2009). Prolonged and persistent deprivation of banking services to a large segment of the population leads to a decline in savings habit and limited or no access to rural credit ultimately leading to social exclusion. Here arises the need for financial inclusion in a society like India where 37 per cent of the people belongs to the Below Poverty Line (BPL) category as per the Tendulkar committee report submitted to planning commission (2009).About 40 million households out of 89 million farm households in our country have no access to finance, whether formal or informal. For the remaining 45 million households, 40 per cent are having exposure to non-formal institution like money lenders in the form of outstanding debt obligations. More than Rs. 1.5 lakh crore was borrowed from traditional moneylenders in the year 2006-07 in the country. About 40 per cent of the urban population does not have access to financial services such as savings, credit and payment systems the situation is much worse in the case of rural areas (NSSO, 2007). In the case of migrants, the situation is even worse. Stringent and reluctant measures from the part of banks in providing credits in rural areas for farmers and agriculture labours remain as an important hurdle in the process of financial inclusion.

Research Problem

Though Kerala is an exception among the states in India with regard to equitable access to financial institution and thereby social development, there is inequity in financial inclusion instilling into various layers of social strata especially those in the lower rungs including the workers in the plantation sector, majority of the employed belonging to the scheduled caste (SC) and Scheduled Tribe (ST) community which are considered as outliers in the much hyped ‘Kerala Model of Development’ characterised by high human development index and low economic growth. Plantation sector consisting of tea, coffee, rubber, spices etc form the linchpin of the agriculture economy of the state by providing livelihood to millions and by providing revenue to state exchequer. Although workers in the plantation sector in Kerala are beset with manifold problems and the most serious among them is social exclusion of the workers owing to socio-economic (financial exclusion) factors which in turn manifests in the form of a vicious circle of poverty. Financial exclusion is playing a very important role in the dismal state of standard of living among workers in this sector. Financial assets like savings habit, access to bank accounts, provision for easy access to rural credit etc plays a very significant role in achieving financial inclusion and thereby overall improvement in livelihood is meager among the workers in plantation sector. Among the plantation workers the problem is much more pernicious in the spices sub-sector where households having access to bank account and formal credit is less than 10 per cent, the situation is not different in the case of workers in rubber sub-sector. Financial exclusion experienced by these communities is visible in all walks of their which in turn acts as an effective impediment to their advancement in education, health and livelihood, thereby hindering their social and economic development. This paper analyses the varied and complex dimensions of financial exclusion and concomitant social exclusion experienced by the plantation workers in the rubber and spices sub sectors.

Objective

- To understand the importance of financial inclusion among the workers in plantation sector in Kerala.
- To understand the extend of financial exclusion (inclusion) among workers in plantation sector in Kerala.
- To evaluate how financial exclusion leading to concomitant social exclusion in plantation sector in Kerala.

Materials and Methods

The paper is an attempt to situate the status of financial inclusion among the workers in rubber and spices plantations in the state. Primary data of 300 members from three plantations, 120 from spices plantations, 120 from small rubber plantations and 80 from large rubber plantations in Kerala are analysed for this purpose. Rubber plantations are sub divided into large and small plantation for sampling because about 90 per cent of the total rubber plantations in the state fall under the ambit of small plantations and the rest of the plantations fall under classification of large plantations. The number of respondents from each plantation was decided on the basis of number of plantations and their respective population proportion. Primary data was collected form Idukki, Kottayam, Pathanamtitta and Wayanad districts having high concentration of plantations in Kerala. Multi-stage random sampling was used for sampling. Cardamom and pepper plantation are taken as sampled spices planatation as majority of the spices plantation falls under these sub sectors. A structured interview schedule was used to obtain information about the quality of life as well as standard of living parameters. The data were subjected to plantation-wise comparison for understanding the differences if any in quality of life and standard of living. Statistical tools like correspondence analysis and Chi-square tests have been employed for in-depth analysis.

Results and Discussion

SECTION - I

Financial Exclusion among Workers in Plantation Sector

Financial Assets of Plantation Workers

Understanding the extent of financial exclusion among workers in plantation sector requires the assessment of ownership of financial assets among them. International agencies like USAID, UNDP clearly states that financial assets play a very important role in shaping and improving the livelihood of an individual or society. So the paper analyses the condition of financial assets including savings habit, average monthly income, possession of bank account, nature of indebtedness, source of indebtedness, purpose of indebtedness and amount of indebtedness and thereby understanding the degree of financial exclusion among the workers in rubber and spices plantation.

Average Monthly Income

Average monthly income is an important financial asset. 82 per cent of workers in spice plantation and 78 per cent of workers in large rubber

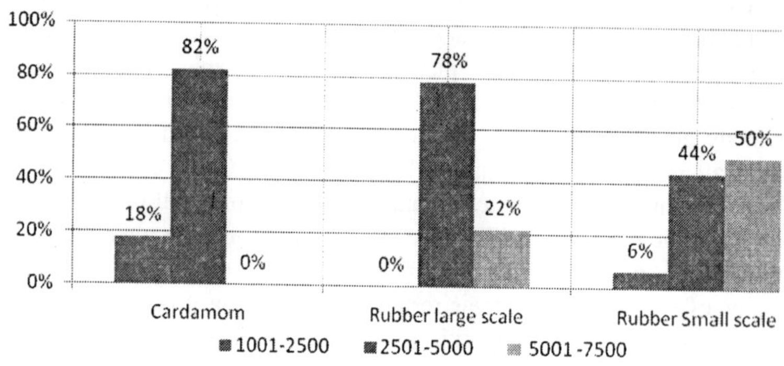

Fig. 1. Average Monthly Earnings

Source: Primary Survey (2011).

plantations earn between Rs. 2501–5000 (See Fig.1). It is significant to note that 50 per cent of the workers in small rubber plantations earn between Rs. 5001-7500. This kind of relatively good average monthly income earnings could be because of the high bargaining power of the workers as a result of the recent spurt in the price (five to six fold increases) of natural rubber in the international market making them to be better in the process of financial inclusion and thereby social exclusion.

Possession of Bank Account and Saving Habit

Among the plantations less than 10 per cent of the workers in spices plantations (Fig. 2) possess account in formal financial institutions

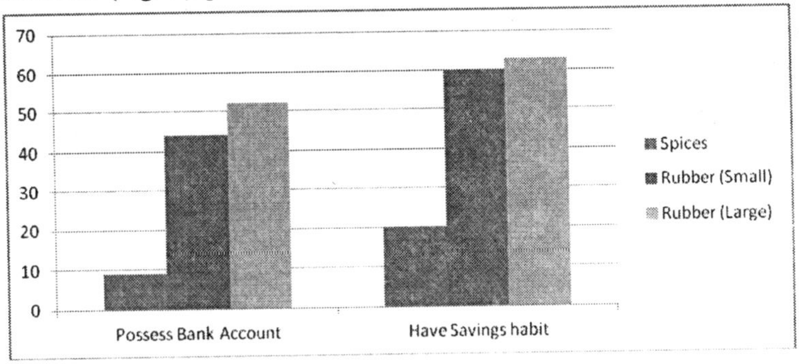

Fig. 2: Possession of Bank Account and Habit of Saving

Source: Primary Survey (2011).

like bank. The situation is much better in the case of rubber plantations. 52 per cent of the respondents in large rubber plantations possess bank account whereas in the case of small rubber plantations around 44 per cent of the respondents are having bank account as a financial asset.

Nature of Indebtedness

Nature of indebtedness explains that less than 5 per cent of the workers in spices plantations are exposed to loans from formal sources like commercial banks and the number of workers who are having debts in commercial banks in the case of workers in rubber large and rubber small plantations are little above ten per cent (Fig. 3). Majority of the workers in plantation sector irrespective of the type of plantation are expose to lending from private money lenders who charges exorbitant rate of interest thereby paving their way to immense misery.

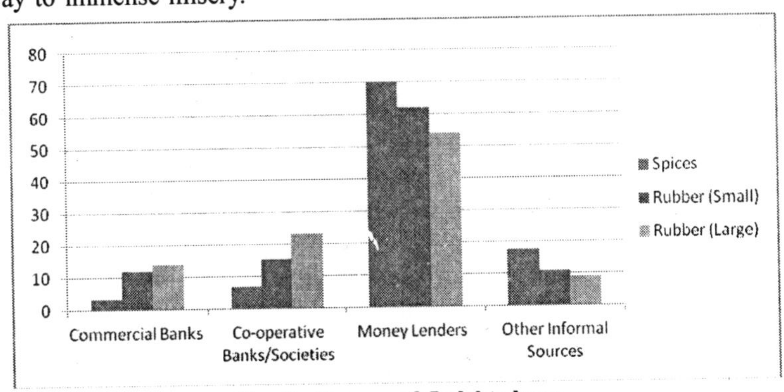

Fig. 3: Nature of Indebtedness

Source: Primary Survey (2011).

Lack of effective financial inclusion steps from the part of governmental agencies and organised financial institution like banks is reaching to the vulnerable sections could be clearly showcased in the present case. Too much of procedures, lack of enough mortgages, time consuming for getting loan sanctioned are some of the reasons attributed for the low exposure of workers in plantation sector to organised financial institutions.

Amount of Indebtedness

In the case of amount of indebtedness, majority of the workers have debt up to the tune of below Rs. 50000. 18 per cent of the workers in the

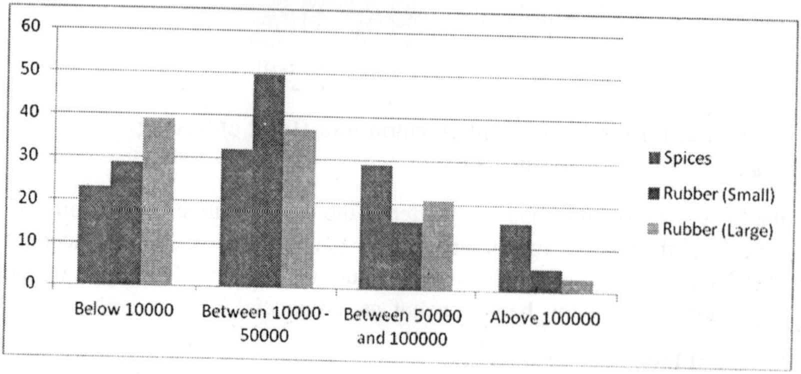

Fig. 4: Amount of Indebtedness.

Source: Primary Survey (2011).

spices plantation have a debt of Rs100000 and above which is really a matter of concern (Fig. 4). As explained earlier the low exposure of spices workers to formal credit sources clearly states that these borrowings have happened through informal credit sources like private money lenders who charges hefty amount as interest. Truly speaking indebtedness of this amount from informal sources forces workers force them to remain in a cycle of financial and social exclusion as they will be deprived of many other basic necessities.

Purpose of Indebtedness

Fig. 5 details the major purpose of indebtedness among workers in plantation sector. Meeting the medical expense of family is the major purpose of indebtedness among most plantations. The reasons that could be attributed for the situation are low income, lesser immunity and poor health conditions which make them prone to diseases.

Lack of health insurance protection and lack of provision for medical reimbursement is really hurting the budget of workers. Other important

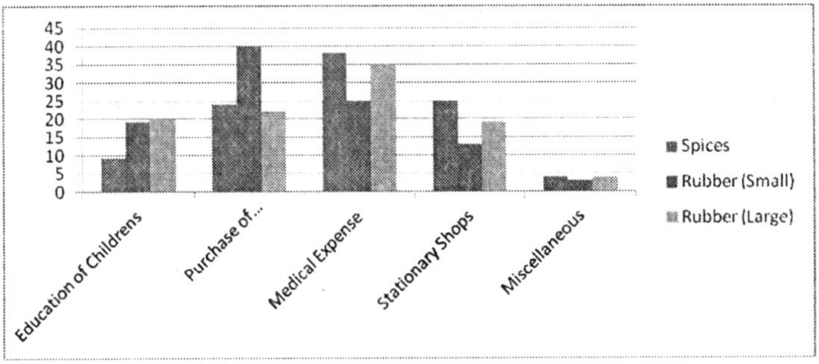

Fig. 5: Purpose of Indebtedness.

Source: Primary Survey (2011).

reasons for indebtedness are purchase of land /construction of house, education of children. Almost all the households have pending dues in stationary shops for purchasing daily household materials.

Type of Plantation and Financial Exclusion Index

Financial Exclusion Index was employed for measuring the relative financial exclusion among the workers in plantation sector. International agencies line UNDP, US AID etc. places financial assets like possession of bank account, habit of saving, nature, source and amount of indebtedness etc as important parameters in understanding the livelihood assets of vulnerable sections in the society. By understanding the financial assets of workers among plantation sector the variables identified where employed for measuring the Financial Exclusion Index on a 3 point scale.

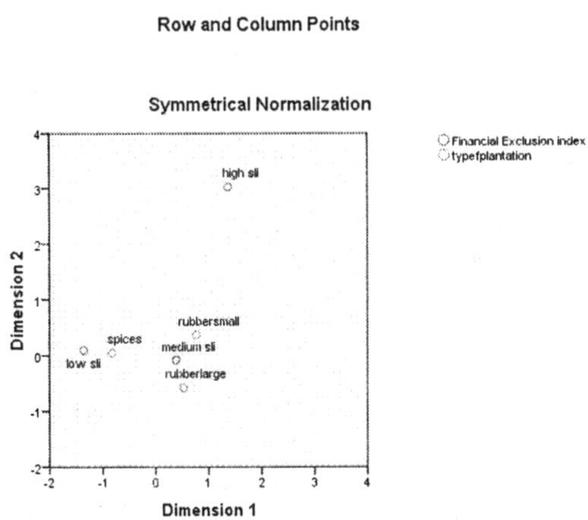

Fig. 6: Type of Plantation and Financial Exclusion Index.

Source: Worked out from Primary data.

The results a continuation of the earlier explanation depicts that workers in spices plantation falls under the ambit of low SLI in terms of financial exclusion i.e. the performance of workers in spices plantations are dismal in the financial assets scenario and in achieving financial inclusion. High amount of exposure to informal credit sources, low income, high amount of debt, low repayment capacity etc. are the major reasons for the low SLI among spices plantation workers (Fig. 6). Large and small rubber plantation workers fall under the range of medium SLI with small rubber plantation workers performing better moving forward. Lower amount of indebtedness, improved income etc. makes them better when compared to the rest of the workers in plantation sector.

Table 1: Chi-Square Tests Type of Plantation and Financial Exclusion

	Value	*df*	*Asymp. Sig. (2 sided)*
Pearson Chi-Square	25.608[a]	4	.000
Likelihood Ratio	30.274	4	.000
Linear-by-Linear Association	15.793	1	.000
N of Valid Cases	79		
(a) 4 cells (44.4%) have expected count less than 5. The minimum expected count is 24.			

Source: Worked out from Primary data.

This kind of difference in financial exclusion index is further evaluated with the help of Chi-Square test to bring out the significance. The Chi-Square value shows that there is significant difference in financial exclusion among the plantations i.e. there exist significant difference between rubber and spices plantations in terms of financial exclusion parameters (Table 1).

Section (II) Financial Exclusion and Concomittant Social Exclusion

Section II captures how financial exclusion forces them to be socially excluded or vice versa. Possession of financial assets and financial inclusion plays an important role in building an inclusive society. Obviously deprivation of financial assets results in social exclusion because of lesser saving and increased debt burden mostly from informal sources like money lenders. Educational attainmnet and possession of other basic assets of workers are captured for understanding the conmittant social exclusion because of financial exclusion in plantation sector.

Education Attainmnet

Workers in spices plantation fares badly when compared to workers in rubber plantation in the case of education attainment similar to the low SLI of financial exclusion among them. Majority of workers in spice plantation is not having even high school education which makes them very vulnerable in terms of livelihood options available with them. This is quite different in the case of workers in rubber plantation, where 50 per cent of the workers are having high school education; out of this 21.90 per cent have passed SSLC and three per cent of them having qualification up to plus two (Fig. 7). In addition to the low level of education the spices plantation lacks other types of skill for employability in other sectors. As tapping of rubber demands specific skill the workers in rubber plantations are treated as skilled workers.

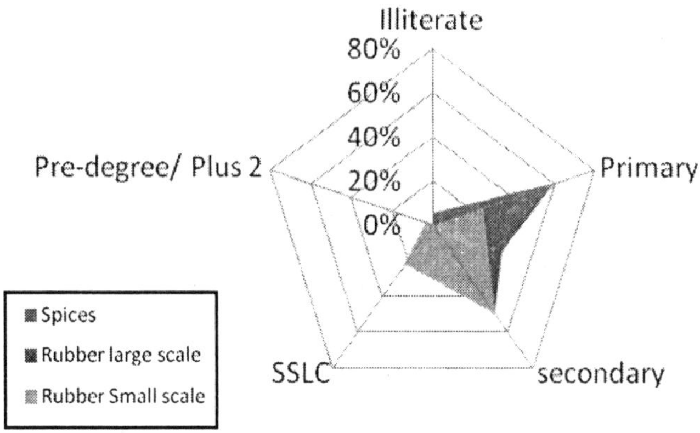

Fig. 7. General Education Attainments.

Source: Primary Survey (2011).

Possession of Other Basic Amenities

Further evaluation was made to understand the level of social exclusion resulted from the financial exclusion by analysing the possession of physical assets. Type of house, area of house, ownership of house, land holding pattern, sanitary facility etc. of workers was taken into consideration. Almost 90 per cent of the workers in the plantations live in their own houses. Whereas the workers in large scale rubber plantations stay in plantation quarters as most of them are from distant places or from neighboring states. The condition of workers in spices plantation are poor in this case also with about 80 per cent of the workers in spices plantation stay in kucha houses (Fig. 8). Low level of income and financial exclusion can be attributed as the major reasons for most of the workers in spice plantation to have kucha type of houses. In the case of large scale rubber plantation, the plantation itself provides housing accommodation which is of semi pucca in type.

The relatively higher income has enabled the tappers in small scale rubber plantation to have semi pucca houses. About 60 per cent of the

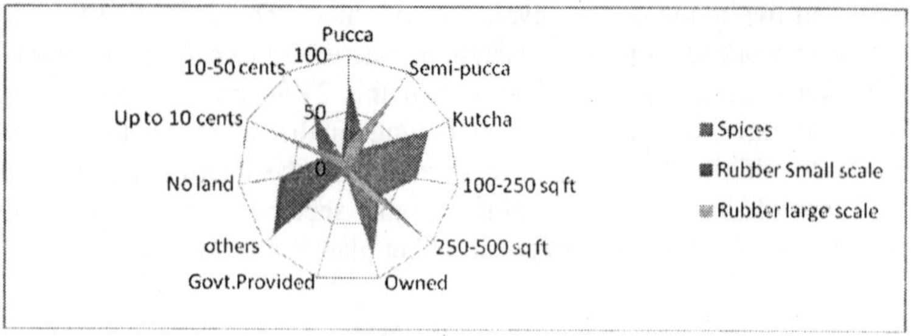

Fig. 8 Ownership of House, Type of house, Area of House and Land Holding Pattern.

Source: Primary Survey (2011).

workers in spice plantation own up to 10-50 per cents of land, whereas 62.5 per cent of the workers in large scale rubber plantations are not having any land at all (Fig. 8). Most of the workers in large rubber plantations are living in quarters provided by the plantation.

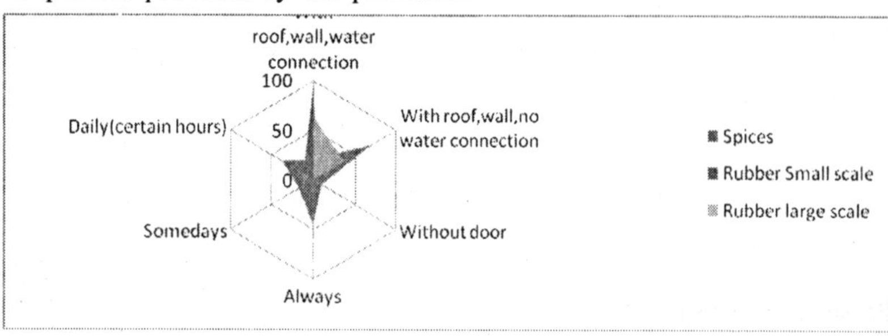

Fig. 9 Status of Availability of water for household purposes, Source of Fuel for cooking and Availability of Sanitary Facility.

Source: Primary Survey (2011).

Water is available round the clock in most of the rubber plantations whereas in spices plantations 33 per cent get access to water for only certain hours in a day (See Figure 9). Workers in plantations mostly depend on timber wood as a source of energy for cooking. Majority of workers in rubber plantation have toilets with roof, wall and water connection whereas in spices plantation 70 per cent respondents have toilets with roof, wall and no water connection. Overall possession of assets are poor in most of the plantation workers. Workers in spices plantations are more vulnerable to social exclusion when compared to workers in rubber plantations while comparing the overall performance of basic indicators stated above.

Conclusion

Overall indices for measuring financial exclusion and concomitant social exclusion explain the degree of financial and social exclusion among workers in plantation sector. Financial inclusion is necessarily a key to social inclusion. Higher the level of financial inclusion higher will be the social inclusion of the individual or society. Standard of living and quality of life are important determinants of social inclusion. Possession of financial assets plays prominent role in the process of financial inclusion thereby social inclusion. Workers in plantation sector are relatively poor in financial inclusion whether it is in the case of possession of bank account or savings habit or indebtedness. Poor performance of financial inclusion is quite visible in the educational attainment and overall poor asset building capacity of workers in plantation sector. Deliberate attempts from the part of government is needed for improving this dismal state of affair of workers when financial services are at door steps for the middle and upper middle class people. Strict directions should be given to banks in this purpose. Stringent action should be taken to those banks that decline to provide banking facility to the marginalised sections of the society. Provision of easy access to all banking services to the vulnerable sections should be made available in no time then only the dream of an inclusive society will get fulfilled.

References

1. A Financial System for India's Poor, 2005, Priya Basu, Economic and Political Weekly, No. 37.
2. Committee on Financial Sector Reforms (Draft Report), 2008, Planning Commission, Government of India.
3. Finance for All? Policies and Pitfalls in Expanding Access, World Bank Policy Research Report, 2008, World Bank, Washington DC.
4. NSSO (2007) Household Assets Holding, Indebtedness, Current Borrowings and Repayments of Social Groups in India, Ministry of Statistics and Programme Implementation Government of India.
5. Occasional Paper – 48, Financial Inclusion -An Overview, Department of Economic Analysis and Research, National Bank for Agriculture and Rural Development, 2009.
6. USAID (2005), "Report on Livelihood and Conflict Tool Kit for Intervention"
7. United Nations (2006), Building Inclusive Financial Sectors for Development" 1, Newyork.

14

Intensifying Financial Inclusion Strategies Between Public Sector and Principal Stakeholders

P.P. Sajimon

Introduction

One of the prime reasons of India's resilience to the global meltdown has been the strong regional diversity in its economic components that has largely insulated and diffused the challenges thrown by the global recession. Worldwide, we are observing substantive changes in finance and investment. The two decades of post reform period in India witnessed transformation of the economy in to a higher growth plane signaling the arrival of the country in the global stage. A number of these changes are reformist in nature while others due to economic pressure. Either way, financing and investment institutions have to respond rapidly and effectively to shield their territory, especially when fundamental predictions are impacted by international fallouts and domestic compulsions. How to survive and how to progress are the two indispensable questions for banking and investment institutions today. Financial inclusion as defined by the Reserve Bank of India is: "delivery of banking services at an affordable cost to the vast sections of disadvantaged and low income groups". Unrestrained access to public goods and services is the sine qua non of an open and efficient society. Financial markets in India have acquired greater depth and liquidity over the years. Steady reforms since 1991 have led to greater integration of India's economy with the world economy. Consequently the global economic crisis has impacted India's growth as well. The GDP growth for 2011-12 is expected to be only 6.9%, down from 8.4% in 2010-11. So while, there is a sturdy interconnected might which truss the Indian growth legend in concert and guarantee that the dissimilar regional economic apparatus work together their varied potential and interlace large inclusive aspirations.

Indian Financial markets and services are facing a much hard-hitting milieu as a consequence of crisis and its fall out together with numerous structural issues. Elevated funding costs, increased risks of defaults, soaring inflation and imperfect prospects for growth are all causal to a more challenging situation for the institutions. Combined with the likelihood of additional compliance obligations and an overall slowdown in the economy, financial institutions are facing a level of difficulty they have not seen for many years. As a result, many firms are being forced to place more emphasis on identifying newer growth opportunities as well as managing operating efficiencies. This means refocusing the operating models as well as premeditated customer and market strategies. The limited accessibility of capital means that both institutions and stakeholders are demanding that strategic decisions are correlated by legitimate evaluations of the alternatives. Economic growth of a nation to be sustainable, it requires all sections of the society included and participates in the growth process. As financial services institutions identified and practice new growth opportunities, that is, enormous fragments of the population, particularly the disadvantaged portions of the society, which have so far been neglected by financial services institutions and come under the classification of unbanked or financially excluded due to structural rigidities.

Looking around the globe, similar financial inclusion issues exist in other developing nations and different solutions have been used to address the problem in different areas of the world. South Africa – Mzansi Account: these are no frills bank accounts with a minimum number of transactions provided free. While about 18-20% of the population has a Mzansi account only about 50% of those are active - India too has a similar scheme and only about 10% of the people who signed up for the account are active. Sri Lanka – Palm top banking – This is another version of banking correspondent / mobile branches. Using Technology, Seylan Bank has introduced mobile teller services to enable customers to conduct basic transactions. Armed with a personal digital assistant, mini printer and cash, Seylan Bank's motorcycle-bound business development officers (BDOs) bring banking services to the heart of the Sri Lankan jungle. BDOs can open accounts, take deposits of up to Sri Lankan Rupees (LKR) 250,000 ($ 2,265), dispense cash of up to LKR 5,000 and provide services such as insurance and consumer finance. In the past, BDOs could conduct most of the same activities in remote areas, although it would require time-consuming trips back and forth between the branch and the customers. Brazil: Banking correspondent model has been very successful in Brazil and India has several socio-political and economic similarities.

Review of Literature

Finance is at the core of the development process backed by solid empirical evidence, development practitioners are becoming increasingly convinced that efficient, well-functioning financial systems are crucial in channeling funds to the most productive uses and in allocating risks to those who can best bear them, thus boosting economic growth, improving opportunities and income distribution, and reducing poverty. There is limited empirical studies have focused largely on the impact of financial development on growth, income inequality, and poverty reduction. The evidence strongly indicates that, when effectively regulated and supervised, financial development spurs economic growth, reduces income inequality, and helps lift households out of poverty (World Bank, 2008). Most cross-country evidence relates to the benefits of financial depth rather than to broad financial inclusion. Deep financial sectors are not necessarily inclusive ones, if financial access is tilted heavily toward the wealthy. Our lack of knowledge about the macro-level effects of financial inclusion stems, in part, from the challenges associated with measuring it on a consistent basis both across countries and over time based on surveys of users and potential users of those services (Cull, Robert, Aslý Demirgüç-Kunt, and Jonathan Morduch 2011).

According to Dr. Chakrabarty (2009), Deputy Governor, Reserve Bank of India1 "Economic growth in India has not been inclusive; unemployment and poverty remain high and a vast majority of the population remains excluded from health and education facilities." In order for growth to be inclusive, there needs to be not only the creation of economic opportunities, but also equal access to them. Inclusive growth can, thus, also contribute to poverty reduction by creating productive economic opportunities for poor and vulnerable groups. The magnitude of the impact is also large. Controlling for other relevant variables, almost 30 per cent of the variation across countries in rates of poverty reduction can be attributed to cross-country variation in financial development (Beck, Demirgüç- Kunt, and Levine 2007). Rangarajan Committee (2008) viewed financial inclusion as "The process of ensuring access to financial services and timely and adequate credit where needed by vulnerable groups such as weaker sections and low income groups at an affordable cost". Savings bolster stability at the individual and household level and, given their very large numbers, small savers potentially contribute to stability at the financial system level—though stability effects of savings at both levels could be explored in greater detail, especially at the level of the financial system (Dupas, Pascaline, and Jonathan Robinson. 2011). The various available literatures on financial exclusion define it in the as the social exclusion of certain groups of people from the mainstream of the society. Leyshon and Thrift (1995) defined financial exclusion as those processes that serve to prevent certain social groups and individuals from gaining access to the formal financial system. Carbo et al. (2005) defined financial exclusion as the inability (however occasioned) of some societal groups to access the financial system. According to Conroy (2005), financial exclusion is a process that prevents poor and disadvantaged social groups from gaining access to the formal financial systems of their countries. According to Mohan (2006) financial exclusion signifies the lack of access by certain segments of the society to appropriate, low-cost, fair and safe financial products and services from mainstream providers.

At the country level, evidence suggests that financial inclusion can lead to greater efficiency of financial intermediation (e.g., via intermediation of greater amounts of domestic savings, leading to the strengthening of sound domestic savings and investment cycles and thereby greater stability) (Prasad 2010). The "wrong" financial tools—or irresponsibly delivered financial services—have been correlated with adverse effects, such as lower levels of educational attainment, suggesting the importance of effective consumer protection in particular to ensure positive effects on micro stability (Zhan, Min, and Michael Sherraden. 2011). The benefits work not only through direct use of financial services, but through the indirect positive effects that financial development has on low income population segments, especially through labor markets. For example, careful empirical studies have shown that the deregulation of bank branching can not only intensify competition and improve bank performance, it can also boost the incomes of the poor, tightening income distribution by increasing relative wage rates and working hours of unskilled workers (Jayaratne, Jith, and Philip E. Strahan, 1996). Thus, greater financial inclusion in terms of access to credit might also coincide with greater stability at the level of providers of financial services. (Adasme, Osvaldo, Giovanni Majnoni, and Myriam Uribe. 2006).

Channelising the 'Unbanked' Prospects

Considering the large unbanked and under banked population in India, financial inclusion carries tremendous social appeal and presents a great economic prospect. The financially excluded sections comprise of marginal farmers, landless labourers, oral lessees, self employed and unorganised sector enterprises, urban slum dwellers, migrants, minorities and socially excluded groups, senior citizens and women. India has now risen to 1.53 lakhs making the country's high net worth individual (HNI) population, 12th largest across the globe. However, several million more households continue to be left out of this growth story. Economic prosperity has not yet penetrated to large sections of the urban poor and rural population. Of the estimated 365 million people living in urban areas in India 76 million are poor. In case of rural areas, more than 270 million people are below the poverty line. These vast sections of the Indian population are also the most neglected by financial services, having no access to savings, credit, insurance or any form of financial products. As per RBI, India still has 145 million households completely excluded from banking services.

Table 1 : Scenario of Financial Exclusion

Sl. No.	*Factors*	*Population*
1.	Deposit accounts	55%
2.	Credit accounts	5%
3.	Any kind of life insurance coverage	>20%
4.	Non-life insurance coverage	9.6%
5.	Number of demat accounts	1.6%
6.	Branches of Scheduled Commercial Banks (SCBs) and Regional Rural Banks (RRBs)	34,000
7.	Villages in India	600,000
8.	Completely excluded households	145 million

Overall growth of the economy has shown that social inclusion, growth and profitability can be achieved simultaneously. Couture their strategies to serve the masses, financial institutions shall be able to serve the society as well as create value for themselves. Hence, financial inclusion must be followed as a business opportunity rather than as a regulatory burden. International experience with financial inclusion and the success of domestic mobile telecommunications industry has sufficiently proven that achieving growth, tackling competition and social inclusion can go hand in hand. Indian financial services firms will benefit themselves and the society by developing focused strategies to augment the outreach of their services to attract the mass market explored and consider it as a potential business opportunity than as a regulatory mandate.

The substructure of the economic pyramid does at hand noteworthy enlargement vicinity for financial services institutions. The system to open worth at the floor of the pyramid will not be splintered through product innovation alone. What is needed is a fully-fledged service intention devoted to lower income markets that includes the vital means of new products and services, new distribution and service channels and new business processes. Financial Services firms shall also get support from the Government to further financial inclusion. In the 2012-13 Budget, the government has drawn up significant plans for financial inclusion initiative. Government has allocated Rs. 10,000 Crores to NABARD for refinancing of Regional Rural Banks. Government has extended 'Swabhimaan' (initiative to bring basic banking services to unbanked villages) to all villages with population of 1,000 and more in North Eastern region and all villages with population more than 2000 in rest of India. Government has also allowed Kisan Credit Card (KCC) to be used as ATM cards making it an effective instrument for making agricultural credit available to the farmers. UIDAI initiative which plans to create a unique identity to every Indian is likely to be used as a platform to directly send subsidy to beneficiary's bank account. Government is planning to roll out the pilot to 50 districts in next 6 months. While continued support from the Government shall remain the key, developing suitable business model to achieve financial inclusion shall be the responsibility of financial services institutions.

Acceleration of Inclusive Growth-Role of Financial Services and Institutions

Initiatives for financial inclusion have come from financial regulators, governments and the banking industry. While it is understood that financial services providers will be the key driving force for inclusive growth, it is important to understand and appreciate the key challenges and hindrances that have prevented us from achieving full-financial inclusion in the past. Inclusive growth has been on the agenda of the Indian government for a long time now, however, it still remains a distant dream for our country. Various public and private interventions have been undertaken in the past five decades to expand reach of financial services. However, these have met with limited success. Despite the efforts made so far, a sizeable majority of the population, particularly vulnerable groups, continue to remain excluded from the opportunities and services provided by the financial sector. The innovative loom for financial inclusion must aims at accelerated delivery and accomplishment of much deeper penetration of financial services in the country. It relies on partnerships between multiple stakeholders in this initiative and would be able to attain desired results only if all the stakeholders participate meaningfully in this initiative. There is no doubt that the new approach to financial inclusion will bring Regulators, Banks, Financial Institutions, Technology providers, together to create a vibrant eco-system for financial inclusion. Considering the scale of resources and transformation effort required for the financial inclusion, the government cannot alone complete the task of achieving 100% financial inclusion. The government shall be required to be facilitator to providing access to financial services is increasingly becoming an area of concern for policy-makers for the obvious reason that it has far-reaching economic and social implications.

Differentiated Models for Differentiated Initiation

The challenge today for financial services institutions is to move from a vend model that emphasises transaction processing and operational capabilities to one that focuses more effectively on the needs of customers, recognising they often vary across segments. They need to adapt their operating and tactical strategies according to their strategic positioning. Institutions will have to determine their area of operation and bring into line their business and operating models that best positions them to service customers. Hardly any institutions are responding to these new opportunities, but the industry as a whole remains largely unresponsive to the challenges of a more sophisticated, demanding and diverse customer base on one hand and the challenges of a financially poor-literate, culturally unique and diverse customer base on the other end of the spectrum. As competition intensifies, it is imperative for players to bring approaches and a set of economics that envelope and overwhelm the traditional economics and operating models. Some lessons can also be drawn from global examples of firms trying to solve the financial inclusion problem.

When we look in to the real issues behind financial inclusion, doubtlessly we can articulate that in accessibility of productive financial service is not because of the inability of saving but because of the reduction in credit. As we call credit is a financial service, at the same time the marginalised populations among the society are not confident to acquire credit due to nonexistence of innovative investment channels without any trepidation of trouncing. The diagram below shows public and private interventions to increase financial inclusion. It is clear that, deposits are more over the financial years under different schemes introduced by the financial sector of the country.

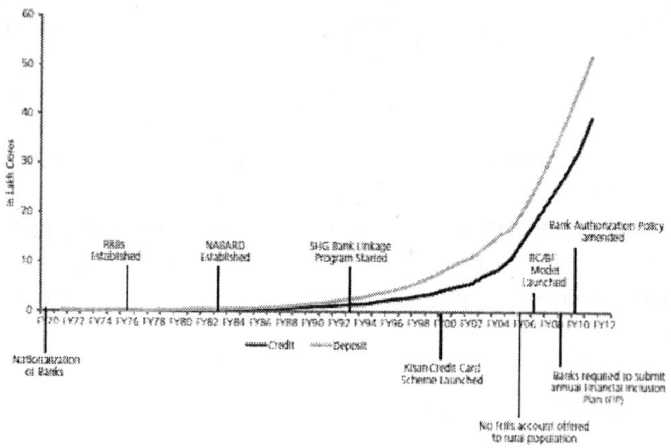

Source: Consolidated from various RBI publications, Reports on banking and finance.

Credit-deposit balance is important for financial inclusion. It is not only for the ingress but for a sustained and prolonged financial health of the people as well as economy. So, it is imperative to resolve the problem of lower credit acceptance owing to lack of confidence from the pro-poor families.

Secondly, the agriculture base forces the people from informal sector to exclude themselves from financial inclusion. They have a feeling that frequent uncertainties and volatility in price of their produces resist them to be part with financial products and services. Agriculture is already a neglected sector and nobody can guarantee an assured performance. The question of why majority of the population are excluded from financial inclusion is properly answered in this direction. Best part of the population is directly or indirectly connected with agriculture sector hence, they are excluded. So, policies and intervention from formal authorities and institutions are required for the stabilisation of agriculture sector and which ultimately leads to financial inclusion.

Thirdly, market volatility and knowledge imperfections play a vital role in financial exclusion. Both, income and instruments are affected by these two forces. The active participation from the stake holders necessarily required an ever increasing income and perfect knowledge on financial products. This is obviously needs literacy and financial literacy among the marginalised majority. The question is which literacy is inevitable? From my observation, a formal literacy naturally followed by financial literacy. Because literacy is an eye opener and it will work towards the right direction due to natural instincts.

Finally, social evils, social system, convention, tradition, greed of the urban population, educated discrimination, cultural diversities, gender issues, migration, concentration of economic power, political and administrative biasness, low standard of living, poor health, market failure, state failure, rural population growth, unemployment, geographical disparities etc. are the extraneous variables which negatively affect financial inclusion.

Thus it is my belief that, no model across the world has provided the ultimate solution. For a country as diverse as India it appears that a multi dimensional approach will be most suitable. Given the magnitude of the problem, multiple solutions may co-exist and may also be financially viable.

The Prospects and Challenges in Financial Inclusion

One of the biggest challenges of the past has been the lack of coordination and the limited number of stakeholders in the ecosystem. The initiatives were primarily driven by directives from RBI and the Banks were expected to play all the roles. There was limited coordination between the regulators i.e. IRDA, SEBI, NHB etc. and also limited role played by Technology and other Service providers. As a result, financial inclusion initiatives continued to be plagued with high-cost of delivery, lack of profitability for the players, poor participation from the financially excluded etc. whereas financial inclusion has been the priority of most regulatory bodies, there are unique structural challenges of the market that need to be addressed by the potential solutions. Urban population has a great credit opportunity, financial services institutions can take advantage of this by understanding the needs of the financially excluded and their futuristic mindsets. Challenges like lack of proper documentation with migrant workers, lack of customised products etc. to address financial inclusion in the urban setting. Contrasting this with rural India, the biggest challenge is the lack of infrastructure leading to a trust deficit. Even with severe structural disadvantages, farm income has been a big driver or rural wealth creation. Though rural economies lack sophistication, they are strong drivers of wealth creation in rural India. While many banks and financial institutions are experimenting with different models to bring financial products to rural market, none of the models so far have been scalable.

Table 2: Rural Challenges of Financial Inclusion

Sl.No.	*Factors*	*Percentage*
1.	Villages going without electricity	20%
2.	Villages without a Post Office	70%
3.	Telephone density	35.2%
4.	Literacy rate in rural areas	69%
5.	Non Performing Loans	7.7%,
6.	Rural area accounts for total of Indian population	70%
7.	Bank branches nationwide	30%

Source: (a) Census 2011 (provisional).
(b) Government of India: Financial Services, Banking, Financial Inclusion, 2011.
(c) Electricity access database 2008, IEA.
(d) Official India Post website (http://www.indiapost. gov.in/).

Table 2 shows the challenges of financial inclusion. At the same time, those are the opportunities yet to be explored. But the question is how? It requires a careful attention and analysis of the actual situation that what I explained above. So, challenges are the opportunities which lie in inverse direction. Government and financial institutions can work out a perfect strategy to invoke the participation of the pro-poor section especially from the informal economy. Much reliance upon introducing new, innovative products is not a perfect and accessible solution for the problem particularly proposed for a long run.

Technology – The Inevitable Transform for Financial Inclusion

Numerous efforts at upholding financial inclusion in the past have been reasonably flourishing at best, specifically due to profitability concerns. By substituting manual tasks with automated rule-based processing, banks can eliminate most of the human intervention and obtain cheaper and faster operations. Financial services firms will have to look at avenues to increase overall productivity to improve profitability and reduce operating costs. Efficiency in operations will help the firms better target their resources towards promoting financial inclusion and thus help in driving penetration. Similarly, increased penetration gives the firm economies of scale which in turn helps in reducing operating costs and increasing the utilisation of resources - driving productivity. In this paper, we evaluate the dual role that technology will play in achieving productivity as well as driving penetration. Technology helps in automating processes, managing risks, and freeing employees to interact with the customer who in turn helps in reducing costs and delivering an enhanced customer experience. It also helps connect with customers at their convenience through a channel of their choosing. The connectivity options provided by technology can enable firms to efficiently and effectively serve customers in outlying areas. This, in turn, will help banks in ensuring that they are able to successfully achieve the necessary and ambitious target set by RBI for financial inclusion as well as provide superior returns to their shareholders. Productivity and penetration are two key metrics of a bank, which act as complements to each other. By investing in increasing productivity, a bank can lower its cost of operations which may aid in increasing penetration in the unbanked segment. Similarly, penetration gives the bank economies of scale which in turn helps in reducing cost of operations and increasing the optimal utilisation of resources, and thus increasing productivity. Technology is a precondition for increasing productivity and increasing penetration. It helps connect with customers at their convenience through a channel of their choosing. Thus, the productivity improvements can enable banks to service those customers in a profitable and sustainable manner, helping drive and achieve the agenda of financial inclusion.

Public Sector and Stakeholders Affiliation

As banking services are in the nature of public good, it is essential that availability of banking and payment services to the entire population without discrimination is the prime objective of the public policy. Banks largely are expected to mitigate the supply side processes that prevent poor and disadvantaged social groups from gaining access to the financial system. Despite the risk, financing of first time entrepreneurs is a must for financial inclusion and growth. In particular, the role of the government would be more broad-based in this new approach for financial inclusion. On one side it would be required to play role of the facilitator to encourage the desire and ability of the firms to promote financial inclusion and on the other hand it would be required to play role of an enabler to empower the poor and needy people of this country to participate in this initiative. The broad objective of financial inclusion is to extend financial services to the poor as well as to create a sustainable ecosystem which will be effective and efficient to further the reach of financial services. The Government and RBI have undertaken several initiatives in the past to further the cause of financial inclusion and spread the fruits of economic prosperity. Nationalisation of banks, establishment of Regional Rural banks, Microfinance, Self Help Groups (SHG), Priority sector lending norms for banks – to name a few. While each of these initiatives has helped extend the reach of financial services, they have not been able to achieve the desired success and a lot still needs to be achieved. However, large portions of Indian population remain deprived of basic financial services such as credit, savings, insurance, payments and remittances and a number of social and economic factors continue to aggravate the situation. Following chart explains the problem of financial exclusion.

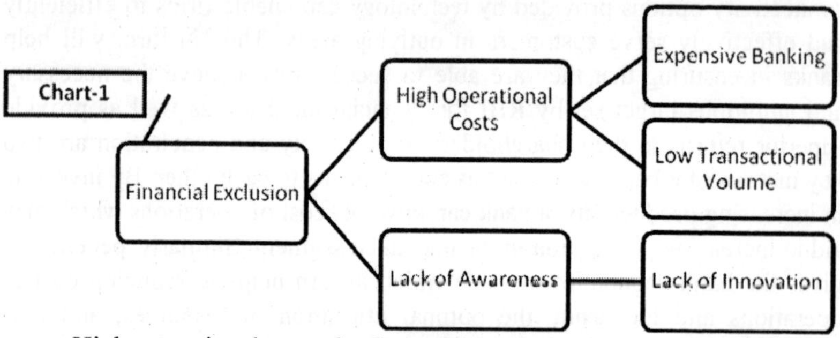

- High operational costs for financial institutions to provide services in rural areas, where transaction volumes and values are low.
- Expensive banking services and cumbersome documentation.
- Lack of awareness of financial products and services among large sections of the population on account of poor financial health and lack of education.
- Lack of innovation to develop financial products that are suitably tailored to cater the needs of the unbanked and poor.

The new approach for financial inclusion aims at accelerated delivery and accomplishment of much deeper penetration of financial services in the country. The new approach relies on partnerships between multiple stakeholders, which include; Central and State Government, regulators including RBI, IRDA, SEBI, PFRDA, NHB etc., financial services providers such as banks, insurance companies, mutual fund companies etc., other financial institutions, intermediaries and service providers such as NBFCs, IT service providers and telecommunication service providers, industry associations, NGOs and consumer organisations in this initiative and would be able to attain desired results only if all the stakeholders participate meaningfully in this strategy. Owing to difficulties in accessing formal sources of credit, poor individuals and small and macro enterprises usually rely on their personal savings or internal sources to invest in health, education, housing, and entrepreneurial activities to make use of growth opportunities.

Policy Suggestions

A new approach is being adopted that entails development of viable business model, development of innovative products and services, partnerships among broader stakeholders and more participative role from government.

(i) Focus on setting up extensive branch network to achieve scale i.e., frequent transactions that is associated with rural and low income regions.

(ii) Create a strong agricultural base for generating a regular flow of income and construct poise to the admittance credit.

(iii) Concentrate on banks as the nucleus of financial inclusion being coerced through regulatory channels to organise financial inclusion despite it being unviable to singularly reach the unbanked customer segment.

(iv) Ensure literacy and financial know-how among the marginalised majority.

(v) Target for horizontal growth strategies for expansion. Slender focus on innovation to develop complicated and stodgy products for poor and vulnerable groups of the society.

(vi) Use of Technology mostly as an enabler to enhance productivity and efficiency of the existing services rather than as an intrinsic tool to expand coverage and penetration.

(vii) Focus rural population as the target customer segments for financial inclusion.

(viii) Build a Partnership with stakeholders, technology providers, financial institutions and government institutions.

(ix) Confirm that the organisational architecture supports and creates institutions that can reach the low income and vulnerable groups of the society.

Conclusion

The extensive objective of financial inclusion is to broaden financial services to the poor to create a sustainable ecosystem which will be effective and efficient to promote the reach of financial services. Empirical evidence advocates that financial services to the poor have positive social impacts; nutrition, health, education, status of women etc. are all enhanced. Outsised fraction of population continue to be deprived of basic financial services such as credit, savings, insurance, payments and remittances and a number of social and economic factors continue to outbreak the situation. Access to financial services allows the poor to save money outside safely, put off concentration of economic power with a few individuals and helps in mitigating the risks that the poor normally face as a result of economic shocks. In the past, the efforts to achieve financial inclusion have been mostly through an environment centered mainly on banking institutions, have seen varied success in encouraging financial inclusion and have been providing diminishing returns over the last few years. Financial Literacy is the key to create awareness and provide impetus to financial inclusion initiative. The government should play an active role by encouraging financial education through the use of media on issues such as household budgeting, savings, insurance, pensions and investments–aiming to reach the massive unbanked population. In addition to coordinating the efforts of the various stakeholders, government shall be required carefully monitor the implementation of initiatives as well. Institutionally, studies shows that, expensive banking services and bulky documentation, high operational costs for providing financial services in rural areas characterised by low transaction volume and value. Providing right product to right customer is the key to success in any business and so is the case for financial inclusion. Lack of awareness of financial products and services among large sections of the population on account of poor financial health is the root cause. Therefore, products should be simple to understand and tailored to the needs to take financial services to poor and vulnerable groups.

References

1. Adasme, Osvaldo, Giovanni Majnoni, and Myriam Uribe. 2006. "Access and Risk: Friends or Foes? Lessons from Chile." World Bank Policy Research Working Paper 4003. Washington, D.C.: World Bank. May 2012.
2. Accion International (2009), Center for Financial Inclusion, Financial Inclusion Glossary, http://www.centerforfinancialinclusion.org/Page.aspx?pid=1941.
3. Allen, F., A. Demirguc-Kunt, L. Klapper, and M. S. Martinez Peria. 2012. "Policies to Expand Financial Inclusion." Development Research Group, World Bank, Washington, DC.
4. Aterido, R., T. Beck, and L. Iacovone. 2011. "Gender and Finance in Sub-Saharan Africa: Are Women Disadvantaged?" Policy Research Working Paper 5571, World Bank, Washington, DC.
5. Beck, Thorsten and Asli Demirgüç-Kunt. (2008). "Access to Finance: An Unfinished Agenda." The World Bank Economic Review 22(3): 383-396.
6. Beck, T., A. Demirguc-Kunt, and R. Levine. 2007. "Finance, Inequality, and the Poor." Journal of Economic Growth 12 (1): 27–49.
7. Beck and Brown (2011) for a discussion of the use of banking services in transition economies using the LITS data set.
8. Beck, T., A. Demirguc-Kunt, and M. S. Martinez Peria. 2007. "Reaching Out: Access to and Use of Banking Services across Countries." Journal of Financial Economics 85 (2): 234–66.
9. Chawla, M., G. Betcherman, and A. Banerji. 2007. From Red to Gray: The "Third Transition" of Aging Populations in Eastern Europe and the Former Soviet Union. Washington, DC: World Bank.

10. Chakrabarty, K.C., 2009, 'Banking: Key Driver for Inclusive Growth', Address delivered by at Clarity Through Debate' series organised by the Mint on August 10th, 2009 at Chennai, RBI Monthly Bulletin, September 2009.
11. Chen, S., M. Ravallion, and P. Sangraula, 2010. "The Developing World Is Poorer Than We Thought But No Less Successful in the Fight against Poverty." Quarterly Journal of Economics 125 (4): 1577–625.
12. Cull, Robert, Aslý Demirgüç-Kunt, and Jonathan Morduch, eds. (2011) Forthcoming. Banking the World: Empirical Foundations of Financial Inclusion. Cambridge, Mass.: MIT Press.
13. Clausen, B., A. Kraay, and Z. Nyiri. 2011. "Corruption and Confidence in Public Institutions: Evidence from a Global Survey." World Bank Economic Review 25 (2): 212–49.
14. Dupas, Pascaline, and Jonathan Robinson. 2011. "Savings Constraints and Microenterprise Development: Evidence from a Field Experiment in Kenya." NBER working paper 14693.
15. Cole, S., T. Sampson, and B. Zia. 2011. "Prices or Knowledge? What Drives Demand for Financial Services in Emerging Markets?" Journal of Finance 66 (6): 1933–67.
16. Demirgüç-Kunt, A., T. Beck and P. Honohan (2008) Finance for All? Policies and pitfalls in expanding access, A World Bank Policy Research Report, World Bank, Washington.
17. Deputy Governor, Reserve Bank of India at the HMT-DFID Financial Inclusion Conference 2007, Whitehall Place, London, UK, June 19.
18. Djankov, S., C. McLiesh, and A. Shleifer. 2007. "Private Credit in 129 Countries." Journal of Financial Economics 2 (84): 299–329.
19. Financial Inclusion Experts Group. (n.d.). G20 Financial Inclusion Action Plan.
20. Government of India (2006), Towards Faster and more Inclusive Growth – An Approach to the 11th Five Year Plan., Planning Commission.
21. Honohan, Patrick. (2008). "Cross-Country Variation in Household Access to Financial Services." Journal of Banking and Finance 32(11): 2493-2500.
22. Honohan, P. 2008. "Cross-Country Variation in Household Access to Financial Services." Journal of Banking and Finance 32: 2493–500.
23. Johnston, D., and J. Morduch. 2008. "The Unbanked: Evidence from Indonesia." World Bank Economic Review 22 (3): 517–37.
24. Joshi, D.P. (2010). India Securing Economic Growth with Equity - Steps to Universal Financial Inclusion. Brisbane.
25. Joshi, D.P. (n.d.). Session: Sample Survey and Methodology.
26. Jayaratne, Jith, and Philip E. Strahan, 1996. "The Finance- Growth Nexus: Evidence from Bank Branch Deregulation." Quarterly Journal of Economics 111, 639–70.
27. Keulder, C., and Naidoo, D. (2012). FinScope Consumer Survey. Namibia Consumer Launch. Namibia.
28. Prasad, Eswar S. 2010. Financial Sector Regulation and Reforms in Emerging Markets: An Overview. IZA Discussion Paper Number 5233. Bonn: Institute for the Study of Labor, October.

29. Ramesh. S and Preeti Sahai, (2007), Universal Fianncial inclusion in India: The Way forward., CAB Calling, July-September.
30. Rangarajan Committee (2008), Report of the Committee on Financial Inclusion, Government of India.
31. Reserve bank of India (2010), Report of Trend and Progress of Banking in India 2009-10, Mumbai.
32. Sarma, M. (2008), Index of Financial Inclusion, ICRIER Working Paper, August 2008.
33. Thorat, Usha (2007), Taking Banking Services to the Common Man – Financial Inclusion,
34. UN Publication. (2006). Building Inclusive Financial Sectors for Development. United Nations.
35. World Bank. 2008. Finance for All? (Policies and Pitfalls in Expanding Access). World Bank Policy Research Report. Washington, D.C.: World Bank.
36. Zhan, Min, and Michael Sherraden. 2011. "Assets and Liabilities, Educational Expectations, and Children's College Degree Attainment." Children and Youth Services Review 33(6): 846–54.

15

Financial Inclusion and Inclusive Growth in India: Issues and Implications

Siddaraju V.G

Introduction

Inclusive growth as the literal meaning of the two words refers to both the pace and the pattern of the economic growth. The literature on the subject draws fine distinction between direct income redistribution or shared growth and inclusive growth. The inclusive growth approach takes a longer term perspective as the focus is on productive employment rather than on direct income redistribution, as a means of increasing incomes for excluded groups. Inclusive growth is, therefore, supposed to be inherently sustainable as distinct from income distribution schemes which can in the short run reduce the disparities, between the poorest and the rest, which may have arisen on account of policies intended to jumpstart growth. While income distribution schemes can allow people, to benefit from economic growth in the short run, inclusive growth allows people to "contribute to and benefit from economic growth".

The 'inclusive growth' as a strategy of economic development received attention owing to a rising concern that the benefits of economic growth have not been equitably shared. Growth is inclusive when it creates economic opportunities along with ensuring equal access to them. Apart from addressing the issue of inequality, the inclusive growth may also make the poverty reduction efforts more effective by explicitly creating productive economic opportunities for the poor and vulnerable sections of the society. The inclusive growth by encompassing the hitherto excluded population can bring in several other benefits as well to the economy. The concept

"Inclusion" should be seen as a process of including the excluded as agents whose participation is essential in the very design of the development process, and not simply as welfare targets of development programmes (Planning Commission, 2007).

The Indian economy, though achieved a high growth momentum during 2003-04 to 2007-08, could not bring down unemployment and poverty to tolerable levels. Further, a vast majority of the population remained outside the ambit of basic health and education facilities during this high growth phase. In recent decades, economic and social inequalities have increased alongside high growth rates which have exacerbated regional inequalities. Over 25 per cent of Indians continue to live in abject poverty. As a result, Inclusive growth has become a national policy objective of the Union Government. The 11th five-year plan (2007 – 2012) envisions inclusive growth as a key objective. The Plan document notes that the economic growth has failed to be sufficiently inclusive particularly after the mid-1990s. It has identified agriculture, infrastructure, health care and education as critical areas for achieving higher inclusive growth. Thus, the Eleventh Plan Document tries to restructure the policies in order to make the growth faster, broad-based and inclusive by reducing the fragmentation of the society. Huge investments in agriculture, education and health, and rural infrastructure were the key elements of the inclusive growth strategy as envisaged. Broadly, the policies aim at increasing the income and employment opportunities on the one hand and on the other; it tries to finance programmes which are capable of making the growth more inclusive. In this context, the study has following three objectives. Firstly, to examine the role of financial sector in achieving inclusive growth in India, Secondly to analyse the causes and consequences of financial exclusion in India, finally how financial inclusion is one of important factor for the inclusive growth of the economy. The study is based on secondary data collected from various journals, government and RBI documents.

Inclusive Growth: Role of Financial Sector

There are supply side and demand side factors driving Inclusive Growth. Banks and other financial services players largely are expected to mitigate the supply side processes that prevent poor and disadvantaged social groups from gaining access to the financial system. Access to financial products is constrained by several factors which include: lack of awareness about the financial products, unaffordable products, high transaction costs, and products which are not convenient, inflexible, not customised and of low quality. Financial Inclusion promotes thrift and develops culture of saving and also enables efficient payment mechanism strengthening the resource base of the financial institution which benefits the economy as resources become available for efficient payment mechanism and allocation.

The empirical evidence shows that countries with large proportion of population excluded from the formal financial system also show higher poverty ratios and higher inequality. Financial stability, economic stability and inclusive growth with stability, it is not possible without achieving Financial Inclusion. Thus financial inclusion is no longer a policy choice but is a policy compulsion today. And banking is a key driver for inclusive growth. However, we must bear in mind that apart from the supply side factors, demand side factors, such as lower income and /or asset holdings also have a significant bearing on inclusive growth. Owing to difficulties in accessing formal sources of credit, poor individuals and small and macro enterprises usually rely on their personal savings or internal sources to invest in health, education, housing, and entrepreneurial activities to make use of growth opportunities.

The role of the financial sector in the financial inclusion efforts in India, date back to early 60s when the focus was on channeling of credit to the neglected sectors of the economy and weaker sections of the population. Starting with 1990s the focus shifted to strengthening financial institutions as part of financial sector reforms. The merits of financial sector reform need to be seen through the prism of what finance could do to harness the growth potential with stability, and financial inclusion represents a critical component of the policy process that intends to make the financial system serve the needs of the real economy. The 1990s also saw introduction of self-help groups – bank linkage programme and launch of Kisan credit cards in the country. The present phase of pursuing financial inclusion as a declared policy objective started in 2005. So, if financial inclusion efforts has been going on for that long, and clearly we have not succeeded, what is different this time and why are we talking so confidently about achieving universal financial inclusion now. It is because of the following reasons:

- The focus on inclusive growth which has become the mantra of the times;
- The Information and Communication Technology required by the formal financial sector for penetrating widespread unbanked areas in a cost effective way is now available;
- The realisation that the "Poor is Bankable". FMCG companies, telecom companies and other retailers are all concentrating on the untapped rural markets for growth. Formal financial sector players also have realised that vast untapped excluded areas have growth opportunities not only for low cost deposits/funds but also for other products such as micro-credit, micro-insurance, and micro-pension etc.

Financial Inclusion

Financial inclusion may be defined as the process of ensuring access to financial services and timely and adequate credit where needed by vulnerable groups such as weaker sections and low income groups at an affordable cost. Financial products and services are identified as basic banking services like deposits accounts, institutional loans, access to payment, remittance facilities and also life and non life insurance services. The following are the denotation and connotation of financial inclusion in India.

1. Affordable credit.
2. Savings bank account.
3. Payments and Remittance.
4. Financial advice.
5. Credit/debit cards.
6. Insurance facility.
7. Empowering SHGs (self help groups).

An inclusive financial system facilitates efficient allocation of productive resources and thus can potentially reduce the cost of capital. An all-inclusive financial system enhances efficiency and welfare by providing avenues for secure and safe saving practices and by facilitating a who le range of efficient financial services like easy day-to-day management of finances, safe money transfer etc. The govt. of India as well as the banking industry has recognised this imperative and has undergone certain fundamental changes over the last two decades. In fact, in order to address the issues of financial inclusion, the Government of India constituted a "Committee on Financial Inclusion" under the Chairmanship of Dr. C. Rangarajan. Not only in India, but financial inclusion has become an issue of worldwide concern, relevant equally in economies of the underdeveloped, developing and developed nations. Building an inclusive financial sector has gained growing global recognition bringing to the fore the need for development strategies that touch all lives instead of a select few.

The Committee on Financial Inclusion (Chairman, C. Rangarajan, 2008) defines financial inclusion as the "process of ensuring access to financial services and timely and adequate credit where needed by vulnerable groups such as weaker sections and low income groups at an affordable cost". Access to financial products is constrained by several factors which include: lack of awareness about the financial products, unaffordable products, high transaction costs, and products which are not convenient, inflexible, not customised and of low quality. Financial Inclusion promotes thrift and develops culture of saving and also enables efficient payment mechanism strengthening the resource base of the financial institution which benefits the economy as resources become available for efficient payment mechanism and allocation. The empirical evidence shows that countries with large proportion of population excluded from the formal financial system also show higher poverty ratios and higher inequality (Thorat, 2008).

It has been the endeavour of both the Government and the Reserve Bank to expand banking sector across the length and breadth of the country to ensure reasonably priced credit in a timely manner to all the deserving borrowers. Notwithstanding the significant expansion in bank network in unbanked areas after bank nationalisation in India, there are still large segments of the society that remain outside the financial system. A quick look at the data on the sources of loans and also percentage of persons having annual income less than Rs. 50,000 show that 28.3 per cent had bank accounts and only 13 per cent had availed of bank finance and even in higher income bracket exclusion existed (Tables 1 and 2). Hence, the recent focus has been on providing access to affordable banking services to every person.

Table 1: Earners having a bank account – 2007

Annual Income (Rs)	*Urban*	*Rural*	*Total*
< 50,000	43.1	26.8	28.3
50,000 – 1,00,000	75.5	71.2	73
1,00,000 – 2,00,000	91.8	87.4	89.9
2,00,000 – 4,00,000	95.5	93.6	94.9
>4,00,000	98.0	96.3	97.6
All	**61.7**	**38.0**	**44.9**

Source: Report on Currency and Finance 2006-08 (IIMS, 2007).

Table 2: Sources of Loans (Per cent of Indebted Earners)

Annual Income (Rs.)	*Banks*	*Money Lenders*	*Other institutional and Non-institutional source*	*Total*
< 50,000	13.0	34.0	52.1	100
50,000 – 1,00,000	34.5	19.6	45.9	100
1,00,000 – 2,00,000	49.3	12.0	38.7	100
2,00,000 – 4,00,000	51.6	11.8	36.6	100
>4,00,000	62.8	5.5	31.7	100

Source: Report on Currency and Finance 2006-08 (IIMS, 2007).

The process of financial inclusion in India can broadly be classified into three phases. During the First Phase (1960-1990), the focus was on channeling of credit to the neglected sectors of the economy. Special emphasis was also laid on weaker sections of the society. Second Phase (1990-2005) focused mainly on strengthening the financial institutions as part of financial sector reforms. Financial inclusion in this phase was encouraged mainly by the introduction of Self- Help Group (SHG)-bank linkage programme in the early 1990s and Kisan Credit Cards (KCCs) for providing credit to farmers. The SHG-bank linkage programme was launched by National Bank for Agriculture and Rural Development (NABARD) in 1992, with policy support from the Reserve Bank, to facilitate collective decision making by the poor and provide "door step" banking. During the Third Phase (2005 onwards), the "financial inclusion" was explicitly made as a policy objective and thrust was on providing safe facility of savings deposits through "no frills" accounts. A Synoptic View of Financial Inclusion is as under:

- Number of No-Frill Accounts – 3,30,24,761 at end-March 2009
- Number of rural bank branches – 31, 727 constituting 39.7 per cent of total bank branches (as on June, 31, 2009)
- Number of ATMs – 44,857 (as on May 31, 2009)
- Number of POS – 4,70,237 (as on May 31, 2009)
- Number of Cards – 167.09 million (as on May 31, 2009)
- Number of Kisan Credit Cards – 76 million (Source: CMIE publication 2007-08)
- Number of Mobile phones – 403 million (as on April 30, 2009) \out of which 187 million (46 per cent) do not have a bank account (*Source*: Cellular Operators Association of India)

The number of "no frills" accounts increased from 4, 89,497 at end-March 2006 to 3,30,24,761 at end-March 2009. Notably, the public sector banks account for the majority of these "no frills" accounts as at end-March 2009 (Table 3). Similarly, the number of credit as well as savings accounts per 100 adults has also shown increasing trend over the period 2002 to 2007.

Table 3: Progress of No Frills accounts in the Banking sector in India

Category	*March 31, 2006*	*March 31, 2007*	*March 31, 2008*	*March 31, 2009*
Public sector banks	3,32,878	58,65,419	1,39,09,935	2,98,59,178
Private sector Banks	1,56,388	8,60,997	18,45,869	31,24,101
Foreign banks	231,	5,919	33,115	41,842
Total	4,89,497	67,32,335	1,57,88,919	3,30,24,761

Source: Report on Trend and Progress of banking India – 2007 – 08.

Financial Exclusion

The concept of financial inclusion and its implementation has come a long way since the last two decades and the results are also quite fair. There have been much technological advances that have transformed the banking industry from traditional brick–and-mortar infrastructure like staffed branches to a system supplemented by other channels like automated teller machines, debit and credit cards, internet banking, online money transfer etc. The moot point, however, is that access to such technology and services are restricted to only certain segments of the society. There is a growing divide, with an increased range of personal finance options for a segment of high and upper middle income population and a significantly large section of the population who lack access to even the most basic banking services. This is termed as "Financial exclusion".

Financial exclusion can be geographical exclusion, exclusion on the grounds of charges, exclusion due to ignorance and also self exclusion. One of the oldest definitions by Leyshon and Thrift (1995) define financial exclusion as referring to those processes that serve to prevent certain social groups and individuals from gaining access to the financial system. According to Sinclair (2001), financial exclusion means the inability to access necessary financial services in an appropriate form. Exclusion can come about as a result of problems with access, conditions, prices, marketing or self-exclusion in response to negative experiences or perceptions. Carbo et al. (2005) have defined financial exclusion as broadly the inability (however occasioned) of some societal groups to access the financial system.

Causes of Financial Exclusion

Some of the important factors responsible for financial exclusion are given as under:

1. Terms and conditions

Different types of terms and conditions imposed by the bankers often deter people with low income and rural areas from opening bank account. In Canada, USA, France and India strict regulation is imposed on Opening balance and Minimum balance required for an account. This often goes beyond the budget of the low income people. Another area of obstacle is the conditions relating to the use of accounts. In Belgium for instance, accounts have been closed by banks because customers either use them too little or withdraw money too often.

2. Identity Requirements

Primary requisite of opening bank account is identity proof and witness. People mostly from rural areas don't have driving license or passport. In many cases, wrong information are given in their ration cards and voter I-cards, which make them illegible as proof. This problem is rife with the refugees and slum dwellers.

3. Psychological and Cultural Barriers

Rural people and low income people think transacting through banks is a cumbersome affair and banks charge highly. Sometimes they think that services offered by the banks are not meant for them. Such type of "Self exclusion" is far more important than direct exclusion by banks refusing to opening accounts. In England the Pakistani and Bangladeshi communities face religious barriers to banking, because, accounts overdrawn (even if inadvertently) is harmful under Islamic law.

4. Bankers' Approach

Bankers' attitude towards the rural folk and the marginalised mass is also not conducive. Sometimes these people are distracted by difficult financial terms used by the bankers and sometime by the apathetic attitude of the bankers.

Absence of banks in the vicinity of rural area is also one of the causes of exclusion.

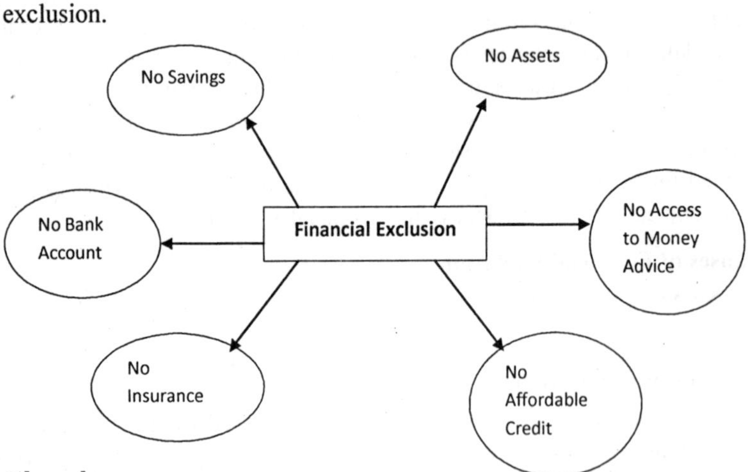

Bottlenecks

The bottlenecks and difficulties in achieving complete financial inclusion in our country are fairly well known. The major obstacles are:

1. The gigantic nature of the task, keeping in view the number of financially excluded people.
    - In India, almost half the country is unbanked.
    - Of the 6 lakh villages in India, only approximately 50,000 have access to finance.
    - India has the highest number of households (145 million) excluded from Banking.

- Only 10 per cent of the population has any kind of life insurance and 9.6 per cent of the population has non-life insurance coverage.

  This is not an India specific problem but a global one indeed. 2.5 billion Adults, just over half of world's adult population, do not use formal financial services to save or borrow.
- 2.2 billion of these unserved adults live in Africa, Asia, Latin America, and the Middle East.
- Of the 1.2 billion adults who use formal financial services in Africa, Asia, and the Middle East, at least two-thirds, a little more than 800 million, live on less than $5 per day. (Source: "Half the World is Unbaked", 2009, Financial Access Initiative).

  However, some of the critical indicators for access to finance in India along with benchmark indicators for selected high-income OECD member countries (Table 4) reveal that while there have been improvements during 2001-08 but it is still very adverse as compared to OECD economies.

Table 4: Getting Finance Indicators for India - 2001-08

Indicator	*2001*	*2002*	*2003*	*2004*	*2005*	*2006*	*2007*	*2008*	*Bench-mark (OECD)*
Branches per 1,00,000 people	6.42	6.33	6.25	6.26	6.33	6.37	6.35	6.6	10-69
ATMs per 1,00,000 people	-	-	-	-	1.63	1.93	2.4	3.28	47-167
Deposit accounts per 1000 people	416.77	421	418.7	426.1	432.1	443	459.5	467.4	976-1671
Loan accounts per 1000 people	50.99	53.9	55.84	61.88	71.42	78	83.59	89.03	248-513
Branches per 1000 km^2	22.18	22.3	22.41	22.57	22.99	23.5	24.13	25.49	1-159
ATMs per 1000 km^2	-	-	-	-	5.93	7.11	9.11	12.68	1-437

Source: Getting Finance in South Asia 2010, Kiatchai Sophastienphong, Anoma Kulathunga, The World Bank).

Note: The Benchmark Indicator ranges are for selected high-income OECD member countries (Australia, Canada, France, Germany, Italy, Japan, the republic of Korea, New Zealand and the United States).

2. Non-availability of appropriate banking technology till a few years ago. Lack of proper physical infrastructure, digital connectivity, etc. in some parts of the country. If Financial Inclusion is to take place, it can only be through Information and Communication Technology (ICT) based models.
3. Lack of proper Business Models. Banks still perceive this as a burden and an imposition and not as a viable Business Model.
4. Lack of cost effective scalable Delivery Models. There is no facilitating and effective Delivery Model especially when problems are encountered. Business Correspondent (BC) based Delivery Model is still in the evolutionary stage.
5. The costs of administering low value transactions and of financial intermediation are perceived to be on the higher side.
6. Planned, strategic and concerted efforts were lacking. It requires massive efforts from all stakeholders.

Effects of Financial Exclusion

Living without financial service and products is disadvantageous when the contemporary world is moving on cashless system depending on credit cards, debit cards, ATMs and Core Banking Solution (CBS systems). Exclusion imposes real cost on the excluded lot. The implication of the financial exclusion is much greater when the excluded mass is entrapped in the hydra headed cycles of poverty. This causes further social exclusion which is very much detrimental for the equitable growth of the world community. The following points describe disadvantages to the financially excluded mass:

(a) They pay higher charges in the absence of financial transactions like money transfer and cheque cashing etc.

(b) They take credit from non- institutional creditors at exorbitantly higher rate which exacerbate the harm already caused due to poverty.

(c) Lack of security in holding and storing money.

(d) The small business may suffer due to loss of access to middle class and higher-income consumers, higher cash handling costs and delays in remittances of money.

(e) Saving potential remains unexploited and unproductive from social point of view.

(f) General decline in investments.

(g) Increase in unemployment.

Who are the excluded?

The financially excluded sections largely comprise of:

- Marginal farmers.

- Landless labourers.
- Self employed and unorganised sector enterprises.
- Urban slum dwellers.
- Migrants.
- Ethnic minorities and socially excluded groups.
- Senior citizens and women, etc.
- Large pockets of population in North East, Eastern, and central regions of India.

Need for Financial Inclusion

Despite witnessing substantial progress in financial sector reforms in India, it is disheartening to note that nearly half of the rural households even today do not have any access to any source of funds-institutional or otherwise. Hardly one-fourth of the rural households are assisted by banks. Hence the major task before banks is to bring most of those excluded, i.e. 75 per cent of the rural households, under banking fold. But the task is not so easy since they are illiterate, poor and unorganised. They are also spread far and wide. What is needed is to improve their living standards by initiating new/increased economic activities with the help of banks, NGO's and local developmental agencies. To start with, it is necessary to develop a fair understanding of their profile. In addition, their perception about the bank and its services needs to be understood.

Hence, there is a need for the formal financial system to look at increasing financial literacy and financial counseling to focus on financial inclusion and distress amongst farmers. Indian banks and financial market players should actively look at promoting such programs as a part of their corporate social responsibility. Banks should conduct full day programmes for their clientele including farmers for counseling small borrowers for making aware on the implications of the loan, how interest is calculated, and so on, so that they are totally aware of its features. There is a clearly a lot requires to be done in this area.

Benefits of Financial Inclusion

- It paves the way for establishment of an account relationship which helps the poor to avail a variety of savings products and loan products for housing, consumption, etc.
- An inclusive financial system facilitates efficient allocation of productive resources and thus can potentially reduce the cost of capital.
- This also enables the customer to remit funds at low cost. The government can utilise such bank accounts for social security services like health and calamity insurance under various schemes for

disadvantaged. From the bank's point of view, having such social security cover makes the financing of such persons less risky. Reduced risk means more flow of funds at better rates.

- Access to appropriate financial services can significantly improve the day-to-day management of finances. For example, bills for daily utilities (municipality, water, electricity, telephone) can be more easily paid by using cheques or through internet banking, rather than standing in the queue in the offices of the service.
- Transfer of money can be done more safely and easily by using the cheque, demand draft or through internet banking.
- A bank account also provides a passport to a range of other financial products and services such as short term credit facilities, overdraft facilities and credit card. Further, a number of other financial products, such as insurance and pension products, necessarily require the access to a bank account.
- Lastly, the Employment Guarantee Scheme of the Government which is being rolled out in 200 districts in the country would bring in large number of people through their savings accounts into the banking system.

Tools of Financial Inclusion

To address the issue of financial exclusion in a holistic manner, it is essential to ensure that a range of financial services is available to every individual. These services are:

- a no-frills banking account for making and receiving payments,
- a savings product suited to the pattern of cash flows of a poor household,
- money transfer facilities,
- small loans and overdrafts for productive, personal and other purposes, and
- micro-insurance (life and non-life).

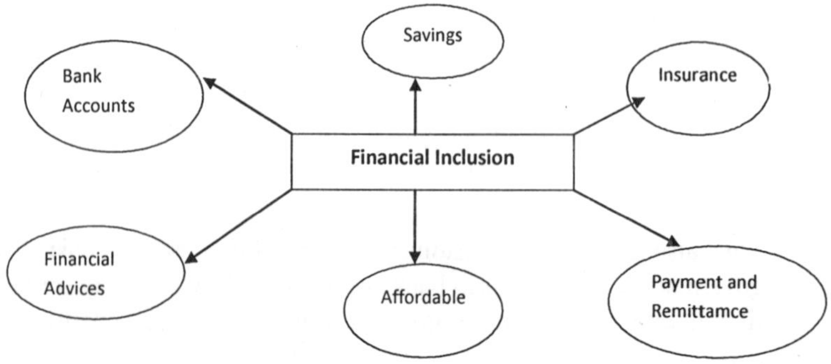

Meeting the Needs

To bring about a highly inclusive financial system, it is highly necessary that the current financial products are appropriate to the needs of low-income households. Following are some of the major points that are required to achieve success of the financial products.

Reducing barriers to access: Widening access requires overcoming the barriers presented by risk assessment as well as improving physical access. Using intermediaries to deliver financial products can overcome the problems of physical access. Telephone and computer-based services, however, are likely to reinforce financial exclusion as many excluded households lack these facilities.

Product design: The requirements of people without financial products are not unrealistic. For day-to-day money management they require a simple account which would allow them to retain tight control over their money. It should offer basic money transfer facilities, including a facility for spreading the cost of bills.

Products offering longer-term financial security should be simple and transparent so that users 'know where they are' and the costs associated with regulation compliance are low. They should be based on regular and automatic saving; flexible, so that products can be retained even during times of hardship; and give restricted access to the money saved. To reduce the likelihood of people cashing in long-term savings plans because of short-term needs for cash, long-term savings products could be used as collateral for small loans.

The key issue for home contents insurance is affordability and, in particular, options for spreading the cost of premiums across the year. Wider availability of simpler, cheaper products such as indemnity insurance (second-hand replacement value rather than new-for-old), or catastrophe-only policies could also widen access.

Moreover short-term credit facilities should also be offered: small, one-off, fixed-term loans rather than ongoing credit commitments such as credit cards or overdrafts; fixed, automatic repayments; and the use of technology in the distribution of loans and collection of repayments, which could reduce costs and therefore allow lower interest rates than are currently available from moneylenders.

Delivery systems: People on the margins of financial services want to deal with organisations which are financially secure, trustworthy and understand their needs. It is not, however, necessary for the same organisation to both provide the product and deliver it to the customer. Indeed, experience shows that the use of intermediaries offers many advantages. For example, many local authorities run *insure with rent* schemes for tenants wanting home contents policies, which they are able to offer at a substantial saving on similar policies bought direct or through a broker. The Post Office is also exploring a similar role as financial service intermediary, as are a small number of credit unions and housing associations. New technology offers some opportunities for product delivery at the end of the market. Electronic cards and electronic money transmissions are likely to be the most acceptable.

Encouraging take-up: Knowledge of and about financial products is remarkably low among households that are without them. This is compounded by marketing policies which reinforce the belief that financial services are 'not for the poor'. Measures to encourage take-up must, therefore, tackle the widespread mistrust which such households have of many financial providers, particularly those which are geographically remote. Use of trusted intermediaries could overcome these barriers. Targeted marketing and delivery of new products as they become available would also increase take-up. Equally, the language and cultural barriers faced by some potential users need to be taken into account.

There is also a need for an independent information and advice service. Lack of knowledge and experience of financial products renders some households especially vulnerable to mis-selling, as well as deterring them from taking up financial services.

Conclusion

Financial inclusion, though well recognised as a means for inclusive growth, is constrained by several factors in India. The banks are faced with high operating cost in extending the financial services to the remote areas. High maintenance cost of these accounts as well as small ticket size of the transactions is also adding to the problem. Further, reaching out to the illiterate people or people who can handle only the regional languages is also difficult without developing a suitable communication mode. The challenge also lies in offering a single loan product which is not based on or linked to the purpose of the loan, the collateral or assets held or income earned by the household but is purely based on cash flow and credit record of the household. With the arrival of banking technology and realisation that poor are bankable with good business prospects, financial inclusion initiatives will strengthen financial deepening further and provide resources to the banks to expand credit delivery. The banking technology initiatives meant for financial inclusion should be collaborative and innovative with an objective to reduce the transaction costs. Thus, financial inclusion along with the Governmental developmental programmes will lead to an overall financial and economic development in our country and as in the case for most developing countries, extending the banking services to everyone in the country will be the key driver towards an inclusive growth.

References

1. Chakrabarty, Dr K.C. (2009): "*Banking: Key Driver for Inclusive Growth*", *Address delivered at the Mint's 'Clarity through Debate' series in August 2009 at Chennai.*
2. Elena Ianchovichina and Susanna Lundstrom (2009), *Inclusive Growth Analytics: Framework and Application, World Bank.*
3. Government of India (2007), *Eleventh Five Year Plan Document, Planning Commission.*
4. Government of India (2008), *Committee Report on Financial Inclusion (Chairman: C. Rangarajan).*
5. Rangarajan, C, Padma Iyer Kaul and Seema (2007), "*Revisiting Employment and Growth*", *Money and Finance, September.*
6. Reserve Bank of India (2008), *Report on Currency and Finance, 2006-08.*
7. Thorat, U. (2008), "*Financial Inclusion and Information Technology*", *Delivered at WIPRO-NDTV Convergence Conference on "Vision 2020 - Indian Financial Services Sector.*
8. Thorat, U. (2008): *Inclusive Growth – the Role of Banks in Emerging Economies, lecture delivered at "Independence Commemoration Lecture, 2008" at the Central Bank of Sri Lanka, Colombo, 28 February.*

16

Evaluation of MGNREGA and Financial Inclusion in Indian Rural Development

Huchhe Gowda

Introduction

The paper analysis the first piece of legislation that compels the state to provide a social safety net for impoverished rural households, which is the Mahatma Gandhi National Rural Employment Guarantee Act (MGNREGA), is an Indian job guarantee scheme, enacted by legislation on August 25, 2005. The scheme provides a legal guarantee for one hundred days of employment in every financial year to adult members of any rural household willing to do public work-related unskilled manual work at the statutory minimum wage of Rs.100 per day. The Central government outlay for scheme is Rs. 40,100 crores in FY 2010-11.

The objectives of the study are to analyse the MGNREGA's implementations and its benefits to the rural people. The study shows that the myths and realities of the MGNREGA in the rural area. We used both primary and secondary data for this study. This act was introduced with an aim of improving the purchasing power of the rural people, primarily semi or un-skilled work to people living in rural India, whether or not they are below the poverty line. Around one-third of the stipulated work force is women. It was initially called the National Rural Employment Guarantee Act (NREGA) but was renamed on 2 October 2009.

Four years after it was introduced, the government has decided to rename its flagship rural employment programme after Mahatma Gandhi. PM Manmohan Singh announced on 2 October 2009, that the NREGA (National Rural Employment Guarantee Act) would now be called Mahatma Gandhi National Rural Guarantee Act. A government scheme is being named after the Mahatma after a long time. The government was earlier planning t name the scheme after one of the Nehru-Gandhi family members, initial inputs suggested. But that decision was changed. "NREGA has been aptly named after the Father of the Nation as he had always held the concept of Gram Swaraj in high esteem," said the PM during a celebration on the 50 years of Panchayati Raj in India.

The act was brought about by the UPA coalition government supported by the left parties. The promise of this project is considered by many to be one of the major reasons for the re-election of the UPA in the Indian general election, 2004. Dr. Jean Drèze, a Belgian born economist, at the Delhi School of Economics, has been a major influence on this project. The act directs state governments to implement MGNREGA "schemes". Under the MGNREGA the Central Government meets the cost towards the payment of wage, 3/4 of material cost and some percentage of administrative cost. State Governments meet the cost of unemployment allowance, 1/4 of material cost and administrative cost of State council. Since the State Governments pay the unemployment allowance, they are heavily incentives to offer employment to workers. However, it is up to the State Government to decide the amount of unemployment allowance, subject to the stipulation that it not be less than 1/4th the minimum wage for the first 30 days, and not less than 1/2 the minimum wage thereafter. 100 days of employment (or unemployment allowance) per household must be provided to able and willing workers every financial year.

Adult members of rural households submit their name, age and address with a photo to the Gram Panchayat. The Panchayat registers households after verification and issues a job card. The job card contains the details of the adult member enrolled and his/her photo. A registered person can submit an application for work in writing (for at least fourteen days of continuous work) either to the panchayat or to Programme Officer. Application daily unemployment allowance will be paid to the applicant. No discrimination between men and women is allowed under the act. Therefore, men and women must be paid the same wage. All adults can apply for employment.

- Adult members of a rural household are willing to do unskilled manual work may apply for registration to the local Gram Panchayat, in writing or orally.
- The Gram Panchayat after due verification will issue a job card. The job card will bear the photograph of all adult members of the household and is free of cost.
- A job card holding household may submit a written application for employment to the gram panchayat, stating the time and duration for which work is sought.

Time Bound Guarantee

- The gram panchayat will issue a dated receipt of the written application for employment. Against which the guarantee of providing employment within 15 days operates. If employment is not provided within 15 days, daily unemployment allowance, in cash has to be paid. Liability of payment of unemployment allowance is of the states.

- Work should ordinarily be provide within 5 km radius of the village or else extra wages of 10 per cent are payable.
- Wages are to be paid according to minimum wages. Disbursement of wages has to be done on weekly basis and not beyond a fortnight.

Transparency

All accounts and records relating to the scheme are to be made available to any person desirous of obtaining a copy of such records, on demand and after paying a specified fee.

Permissible Works

The MGNREGA achieves twin objectives of rural development and employment. The MGNREGA stipulates that works must be targeted towards a set of specific rural development activities such as: water conservation and harvesting, afforestation, rural connectivity, flood control and protection much as construction and repair of embankments, etc. Digging of new tanks/ponds, percolation tanks and construction of small check dams are also given importance. The employed are given work such as land leveling, tree plantation, etc. major sustainable works classification are.

- Water Conservation.
- Drought Proofing (including plantation and afforestation).
- Irrigation canals.
- Minor irrigation, horticulture and land development on the land of SC/CT/BPL/IAY and land reform beneficiaries.
- Renovation of traditional water bodies.
- Land development.
- Rural connectivity.

Funding

The scheme started from February 2, 2006 in 200 districts, was expanded to cover another 130 districts in 2007-2008 and eventually covered all 593 districts in India in April 1, 2008. The outlay was Rs. 11,000 crores in 2006-2007, and has been rising steeply, to Rs. 39,100 crores (140% increased amount respect of previous 2008-2009 budget) in 2009-2010. First a proposal is given by Panchayat to Block office then Block is deciding whether work would be sanction or not.

The central government bears the costs on the following items

- The entire cost of wages of unskilled manual workers.

- Seventy five per cent of the cost of material of wages of skilled and semi-skilled workers.
- Administrative expenses as many be determined by the central government, by the central government, which will include inter alia, the salary and the allowances of the Programme Officer and his supporting staff and work-site facilities.
- Expenses of the National Employment Guarantee Council.

The State governments bear the costs on the following items:

- 25 per cent of the cost of material and wages of skilled and semi skilled workers.
- Unemployment allowance payable in case the state government cannot provide wage employment on time.
- Administrative expenses of the State Employment Guarantee Council.

Implementation

The Comptroller and Auditor General (CAG) of India, in its performance audit of the implementation of MGNREGA has found "significant deficiencies" in the implementation of the act. The plan was launched in February 2006 in 200 districts and eventually extended to cover 593 districts. 4,49,40,870 rural households were provided jobs under NREGA during 2008-09, with an national average of 48 working days per household.

Seven Heady Years of MGNREGA

Though outcomes have at times fallen short of official claims, the scheme has done better than most expected. Going by the statistics available with the ministry of rural development, MGNREGA is the largest programme for providing employment in rural areas. Official statistics say that with 2.83 billion person days generated, 52.5 million households benefited from it in 2009-10, out of the 113.2 million households that had been issued job cards. Scheduled Caste/Scheduled Tribe (SC/ST) households accounted for 51.2% of total person days, and women for 49%. These are impressive statistics by any standard. Nonetheless, these need to be verified against independent evidence.

Though numerous field and micro-studies are available, very few large-scale surveys existed on the functioning of MGNREGA until the National Sample Survey Organisation (NSSO) decided to include it as part of its official employment-unemployment surveys. NSSO has now introduced a separate activity code (42) for all those working as wage labourers under MGNREGA. The 64th round of the survey (2007-08), the latest available, is large enough to provide a reliable estimate of MGNREGA work at both the national and state levels, and is fully comparable with the quinquennial round of 2004-05—the year immediately preceding the implementation of MGNREGA.

First, the broad results: According to NSSO, total employment generated by public jobs programmes in 2007-08 was 1.02 billion person days, 71% of the official estimate of 1.44 billion person days. At an average wage rate of Rs. 78.91 per day, this implies that the total wage bill was Rs. 8,040 crore, 74% of the official estimate of Rs. 10,738 crore. These definitely show an improvement over the usual claim that only 15% of government money reaches the people. But even a 25% leakage in MGNREGA wage payment is cause for concern.

How does this compare with pre-MGNREGA days, Public jobs programmes in 2004-05 generated 240 million person days of employment. In comparison, employment generated increased by 4.2 times in 2007-08. However, the increase varies across states and districts. Compared with phase I districts (the poorest 200), employment increased by more than 5.4 times in the 130 phase II districts, and by just 1.9 times in phase III ones. Considering that the districts in phase I and II were among the poorest, this also suggests that the largest expansion in employment generation happened in the poorest areas. Since these districts are also the ones where the programme was initially implemented, this may also represent strengthening of the delivery system over time.

However, there is considerable performance variation across gender and states. NSSO shows only 38% female employment compared with the official claim of 43%. The 200 poorest districts showed a marginal improvement in female employment, from 28% in 2004-05 to 36% in 2007-08. It actually declined in phase III districts. NSSO's estimate of SC/ST employment, however, was similar to official statistics.

In terms of state-wise distribution, four states accounted for 71% of total employment generated - Andhra Pradesh (28%), Madhya Pradesh (19.7%), Rajasthan (13.5%) and Chhattisgarh (9.5%). Andhra Pradesh itself showed a massive increase in employment from less than 10 million person days in 2004-05 to more than 270 million person days in 2007-08. The increase in Madhya Pradesh and Chhattisgarh was also impressive. On the other hand, Rajasthan, at 1.31 times, showed little improvement. Compared with these four, the poor states of Bihar, West Bengal, Assam, Jharkhand, Orissa and Uttar Pradesh together accounted for only 18% of the total employment generated.

These outcomes have had positive externalities on other areas. Not only have casual wages increased by 4.5% per year in real terms, MGNREGA has also led to a narrower gender gap in casual wages. As reported by NSSO, there is a negligible gender gap in public employment; but even in casual employment in other works, male wages were only 50% higher in 2007-08 compared with 58% in 2004-05.

It is obvious that in a short span of five years, MGNREGA has performed much better than what skeptics expected—in terms of the level of leakages, as well as inclusion for disadvantaged groups such as women and SC/ST households and poor districts. While these highlight the huge potential that the programme has, they also underscore its dependence on institutional structures and innovations in programme delivery, as in Andhra Pradesh. The huge gap across states in implementation is partly a result of governance. But it is also a reflection of political will.

Most skeptics agree that inflation and drought in recent years did not lead to massive protests partly because the rural population was insulated by MGNREGA's safety net. Such claims need to be verified. But the last general election is evidence that the scheme has paid rich political dividends.

MGNREGA Payment Woes: Bad to Worse?

To check corruption under the MGNREGA, the Centre is routing funds through banks and POs. But this has resulted in delayed payment and loss of faith in the system among people. Pradeep Baisakh argues the case for the earlier cash payment system. Apply for work, get work, and get paid on time". This is how the Mahatma Gandhi National Rural Employment Guarantee Act (MGNREGA) took off in February 2006. Various instruments like muster rolls and job cards were designed to keep the payment process transparent. However, it was soon realised that a good chunk of money was being siphoned off by officials and implementers.

Consequently, in a circular dated 21 January 2008, Ministry of Rural Development instructed the state governments that "opening of bank and post office accounts of all the NREGA beneficiaries must be done before April 1, 2008". The Government's primary concern was to rule out the possibility of officials/implementers/middlemen 'taking a cut' while disbursing the wages. All the states have officially adopted in the new system barring probably Tamil Nadu. However, subsequent surveys in Odisha (2007) and Jharkhand (2008), and observations from many other states like West Bengal highlight delay in delivery of wages as the most frustrating reason for people to lose faith in the scheme. By April 25, 2010, there was delay in delivering wages amounting to Rs. 1,355 crores (www.nrega.nic.in), of which, about Rs. 136 crores were paid after 90 days of delay, Rs. 156 crores in between 60-90 days, Rs. 466 crores between 30-60 days, and Rs. 596 crores between 15-30 days of delay. The total wage payment (unskilled) made during 2009-10 was about Rs. 25,000 crores. Consequently, 54 per cent of the wages did not reach the labour force on time, i.e., 15 days.

How Many Really Know of Job Scheme?

The awareness of the centre's ambitious rural job scheme-the Mahatma Gandhi National Rural Employment Guarantee Act (MNREGA) Varies across different regions of the state and only 56.33 per cent of the households are aware of the scheme. Evaluation of the impact of the processes in the in MNREGA in Karnataka (2011), show's the state government reveals that there have been delays in allotment of works and payment of wages, unevenness in the quality work, differences in wages for men and women and arbitrary process of assessing the labour.

The evaluation noted that awareness of the scheme was low in north Karnataka districts. Only about 19.27 per cent households of in northeast districts, comprising Bidar, Koppal, Gulbarga, Bijapur and Yadgir, and 25.75 per cent in northwest districts of Haveri, Belgaum, Gadag, Bagalkote, Davangere and Dharwad were aware of the scheme.

Awareness levels were more than 50 per cent in tribal dominated districts such as Raichur, Chitradurga and Bellary (51.20 per cent), southern Karnataka districts (75.29 per cent) and highest in Malnad districts (92.84 per cent). The study covered sample size of 2068 house holds in 22 villages across 10 districts in five regions. The scheme, which was launched in the State in 2006-07, was extended to the entire State in 2008-09. Under the scheme, a beneficiary is paid of Rs. 125 per day.

The awareness of 100 days entitlement a year of work was just 44.08 per cent among the households in the State. The northeast districts recorded the lowest awareness level at 9.86 per cent followed by northeast region (10.25 per cent), tribal belt (30.86 per cent), south (67.73 per cent), and malnad region (77.19 per cent).

Awareness about job cards was also dismally low in northeast region with 19.27 per cent against the State average of 56.33 per cent. Nothing existence of fake job cards, the study said "the phenomenon of job cards with a different number but of the same household is widespread across all regions". There were 29 per cent of job cards issued with different but same households in the State of which the highest was in the tribal belt (41.72 per cent). Around a fifth of the job card holders have not had a single day's employment under the scheme.

Unemployment Allowance

According to the study "the state government's record in paying unemployment allowances is very poor. The unemployment allowance is due for 76,773 workers". However, not a single worker was paid unemployment allowance in the state. As per the act, the payments must be made within 15 days of workers done.

Advantages of Shramik Cheque Book

- **Supplements the Job Card:** Since no written work is involved, the MGNREGA cheque book system adds another transparency safeguard without requiring additional time from the staff.
- **Personal possession:** In addition to Job card which a worker usually hands to the Rozgar Sevak for entering details of work, the labourer can keep the cheque book in his custody. He gets the seal from the Rozgar sevak, on the spot at the end of the day.

- **Helps illiterate labourers**: Inability to read a Job Card is a major reason for the exploitation of the poor labourers. The use of MGNREGA cheque book requires basic numeracy skills that almost all workers possess.
- **Equal opportunity to all labourers:** Since all beneficiaries are a fixed number of cheques (100 in this case), it is difficult for the Rozgar Sevak to be choosy about whom to employ and whom not to emplcy.
- **Makes inspection easy**: At the time of the inspection all one has to do is to check a Shramik coupon and ask the Rozgar Sevak how much the labourer has been paid. The amount can be quickly compared with the counter foils to see if the total amount is paid or not.
- **Psychological edge:** Till now the labourer had been running after the Pradaan or the Rozgar Sevak for work. This has created a sense of dependency for the labourer on the Rozgar Sevak or the Pradaan. With the cheque book system the Rozgar Sevak would be asking the labourer for the cheque as he has to balance his accounts book This balances the power equation between the two, and this sense of empowerment could easily be categorised as the strongest advantage of the cheque book.

Loopholes in the New System

The system works differently across states. In Rajasthan and Jharkhand, though the system of institutional payment has been put in place at least at the policy level, delays have been reported nevertheless. “In Chhattisgarh, it takes between one-and-a-half to two months to process payments,” says Gangaram Paikrai, a social activist.

In case of banks, although the process moves a bit faster, distance between villages and banks poses bottlenecks and exposes the system to many kinds of manipulation. For instance, the Utkal Gramya Bank (UGB) branch office is 15 km away from the Badabanki GP headquarters. Unaware of the bank transactions and schedules, villagers seek help from middlemen, mostly contractors, and pay for it. Frauds of this nature have come to light in Odisha and Jharkhand. Even in cases where the role of middlemen is limited, lack of knowledge about banking and overworked bank staff force the villagers to visit the banks at least 2-3 times to get what is rightfully theirs. This has been observed in Chhattisgarh, Odisha, and Jharkhand.

People cannot escape corruption in POs either. Jawahar Mehta, a Jharkhand-based social activist, says, “In Garhwa district, people complained that they had to give the postmaster 2% of their earnings while withdrawing wages from the local branch.” Gangaram Paikrai from Chhattisgarh says, “Post offices are often run by only one official. Naturally, it becomes very difficult to cope up with the task of payment under the MGNREGA.”

Old System vs. the New

Some studies suggest that the level of corruption in wage payment has gone down ever since the government started routing the funds through POs and banks. In their article "NREGA Wage Payments: Can We Bank on the Banks?", Anindita Adhikari, Kartika Bhatia write drawing facts from their survey in Karchana and Shankargarh blocks in Allahabad district of Uttar Pradesh and Mander and Angara blocks of Ranchi district of Jharkhand that 76% of the sampled workers confirmed the accuracy of the bank records. This, by any standards, is a fair delivery of wages.

But somewhere down the line, the very intent of MGNREGA is getting defeated. Each new mode of payment comes with its own inherent drawbacks. For instance, in the previous cash payment system, muster rolls and job cards were necessary documents to monitor payments and they were easily accessed by the poor labourers. Similarly, the open system of payment by 'roll call' of labourers was monitored by the community as was experimented in the Dungarpur (before the NREGA came into effect) and other areas of Rajasthan where Mazdoor Kishan Shakti Sangathan (MKSS) was at work.

Conversely, in the new system, documents are not easily accessible even by activists, let alone villagers in remote areas. It therefore weakens the community monitoring of wage payment of the scheme. The new system has rendered job cards meaningless and social audits, tedious. For instance, in Jharkhand, labourers come to know about the amount paid for the work done only when they receive the money from POs. In such cases, any underestimation of their work by junior engineers results in underpayment and the workers cannot even complain about it. Moreover, accounts are opened in the name of family heads which happen to be men, thus robbing a vast majority of the women workforce of its right over hard-earned money.

Local Problems Need Local Solutions

The wage payment monitoring system worked quite well in Andhra Pradesh as the state had designed its own mechanisms, not something imposed from New Delhi, to check corruption. Rajasthan, for example, was also performing fairly well in timely payment of wages and corruption was comparatively low. In an interface with CSOs at a training programme a year ago, former NRGEA Commissioner Manju Rajpal had said: "we were not in favour of introduction of the bank and post office payment system in NREGA as the direct cash payment system was working well with us. But the Centre made the new system mandatory leaving us no option but adopt it."

Currently, in states like Rajasthan where the system is performing well in overall implementation of the scheme, delayed payment is not uncommon. Richa of Janchetna Sansthan, Rajasthan, says, "Though the government has already developed the system for proper functioning of wage payment through banks and post offices, it is delayed by two or three months in several cases as the officials pass the buck from one institution to the other."

Outcomes so for

5 years of implementation of MGNREGA vindicates the self – targeting, demand based nature of the programme. It is also evident that nature of employment is seasonal and that the duration of employment sought varies according to the prevailing opportunities of employment offered under local agricultural practices and other alternative for   of employment and all job card holding families do not necessarily rec   t for the full 100 days of employment. Significant outcomes are as fol   s:

1. Increased employment opportunities f   he Rural Workforce.
2. Inclusive growth.
   - (i) Reach out the rural poor.
   - (ii) Increased women workforce par   pation ratio.
   - (iii) Share of SC/ST Households in employment.
   - (iv) Impact on minimum wages.
   - (v) Enhanced wage earnings.
   - (vi) Creation of productivity assets.
   - (vii) Training and financial inclusion.

Conclusion

Many criticisms have been leveled at the programme, which has been argued to be no more effective than other poverty reduction programmes in India, with key exceptions such as Rajasthan. The first criticism is financial. The MGNREGA is one of the largest initiatives of its kind in the world. The national budget for the financial year 2006-2007 was Rs. 11,300 crores (about US$ 2.5 bn and almost 0.3% of GDP) and now fully operational, it costs Rs. 39,100 crores in financial year 2009-2010. Funding was argued by Jean Dreze and others to be possible through improved tax administration and reforms, yet the tax-GDP ratio has actually been falling. There are fears the programme will end up costing 5% of GDP.

Though initial observations show good results, only time can tell its real impact. The concern is the more the system becomes complicated in vital components like wage payment, the more it drifts away from the common people's understanding. In such cases, the government, social activists, and the media occupy the centre-stage and debate and discuss to sort out the issues. Ironically, the poor stand on the periphery as they have little say on matters that affect them the most. This is not what the original rozgaar guarantee law envisioned. Just like other welfare schemes which are mostly government-driven, the MGNREGA may end up becoming an activists- or media-driven programme.

With the experience and learning of the past seven years, MGNREGA will be more effectively implemented. The scheme will continue to supplement income assets and bring long term tangible benefits to rural India.

References

1. Raj Krishna (1973), "Unemployment in India" *Economic and Political Weekly.*
2. Deaton A and J. Dreeze (2000), "Poverty and Inequality in India: A Re-Examination" *Economic and Political Weekly.*
3. Maheswari S.R. (1985), Rural development in India: A Public Policy Approach. Sage Publications, New Delhi.
4. Singh Katar (1999), Rural Development: Priniciples, Policies and Management, New Delhi.
5. *The Hindu* Wednesday May 04, 2011.

17

Rural Micro Finance and Women's Empowerment: A Case Study on Rural Women's Clients in Shivamogga District, Karnataka

B.T. Ramappa

Intoduction

Women are vital part of the Indian economy, constituting on third of the national labour force and forming a major contributor to the survival of family. Eighty nine per cent of total female labour involved in agriculture and allied industrial sector. Women have extensive workloads with dual responsibility for farm in general, and livestock and household production in particular. Women contribute considerably to household income through farm and non-farm activities as well as through work as landless labourers. Women generally have no control over land and other productive assets, which largely excludes them dependent on high cost informal sources of credit to secure capital for consumption and productive purposes.

Empowerment means that women live their own life in a way that think appropriate because of their condition of family circumstances, qualities and capabilities of which they themselves are the best judges. Empowerment of women encompasses many aspects such as economic opportunity, property rights, political representation, social equality, personal rights and so on. Historically the world over, either by law, the status of women is undermined by asymmetrical power relationships in decision-making, personal and social rights, access to resources and entitlement. Women in many countries still lack rights to inherit property, own land, get education, obtain credit, earn income, and control their fertility: they are still are still widely under-represented in involvement in decision making at the household. Ahmad

(1999) through a case study on thrift groups in Assam highlighted that women are coming to administration directly for their just rights and to address their grievance boldly. It proved that SHGs are successful in North East India even in the midst of insurgency. SHGs is a viable origination setup to disburse micro-credit to rural women for the purpose of making them entrepreneur and encouraging them enter into entrepreneur and encouraging them to enter in entrepreneurial activities.

Micro Finance sector has covered a long journey from micro savings to micro credit and then to micro enterprises and now entered the field of micro insurance, micro remittance, micro pension and micro livelihood. This gradual and evolutionary growth process has given a great boost to the rural poor in India to reach reasonable economic, social and cultural empowerment, leading to better life of participating households. Financial intuitions in the country have been playing a leading role in the micro finance programme for nearly two decades. Now they have joined hands proactively with informal delivery channels to give microfinance sector the necessary momentum. During the current year too, microfinance has registered an impressive expansion at the grass root level. Reserve Bank of India has defined Micro Finance as "Provision of thrift, credit and other financial services and products of very small amounts to the poor in rural, semi-urban, or urban areas for enabling them to raise their income levels and improve living standards." Micro Finance is a broad term that includes deposits, loans, payments services and insurances to poor. The concept of micro finance and micro credit are used interchangeably. Nevertheless, micro credit does not include savings; hence, micro finance is more appropriate term (Manimekalai, 2004). Today micro finance is very much in the agenda of public policy and it has been increasingly used as a vehicle for reaching the otherwise unreachable poor in the country. The need, therefore, is to share experience and materials, which will help in not only understanding successes and failures but also provide knowledge and guidelines to strengthen and expand micro finance programmes. The ultimate aim is to attain social and economic empowerment. Especially Women Economic Empowerment is so strong by Micro Finance through SHGs. Successful intervention is therefore, dependent on how each of these stages has been carefully dealt with and also the capabilities of the implementing organisations in achieving the final goal e.g. if bank credit delivery takes place without consolidation of SHGs, it may have problems of self-sustainability and recovery. A number of schemes under banks, governments offer direct credit to potential individuals without forcing them to join SHGs. Completion and classification of the communication materials in the directory is done based on this development process. The Eleventh Five Year Plan (2007-12) envisions inclusive growth as a key objective.

Objectives of the Study

1. To light on the impact of SHGs on savings and incomes.
2. To analyse the issues and challenges in microfinance for the development of Rural India.
3. To examine the progress of Women Self Help Group in Thirthahalli Taluk and Socio – Economic background.

Methodology

Flexible and mixed research design that combines quantitative and qualitative, and participatory methods is adopted to examine complex and comprehensive facts at individual, household and community levels. A mix of data gathering instruments (questionnaire, unstructured, focus group discussions, case story narrative, document analysis and review tools and site observations) were then employed to collects field data from five Gramapanchayat called as Kannangi, Bhandya, Thudur, Kudumalige and Hosahalli. 209 women Self Help Groups, 4529 women clients, selecting each 20 women client, total 100 women clients, who have been in the program for the past three and over years. In a multi-faceted examination, the results of the study, in general, revealed the existence of sufficient evidences that substantiate the possibilities of rural micro financing is not same and alike to all women however. Microfinance's potential effects are also dependent up on an array of issues ranging from institutional design, product diversification, triple role burden of women, livelihood assets of individual women, to the physical environment where rural women clients are leading their life. This study reveals both primary and secondary data.

Micro Finance and Women's Empowerment-Mahila Vikas Nidhi

It has been highlighted in various reports brought by the United Nations, apart from the HRD Index data published at regular intervals that despite the rapid strides made worldwide in the arena of science and technology, creation of wealth, etc. The plight of a large proportion of the world's population, mainly women continue to be pitiable. With this background, SIDBI has created a specially designed fund, The Mahila Vikas Nidhi (MVN) to cater to a structured programme for empowerment of women. A portion of the annual net profit of the bank is earmarked for the separate fund created for MVN.

Micro Finance – Sustainable Financial Intermediation Mechanism for Poor

While prevalence of poverty especially among women in developing countries is a major issue, there is also a growing awareness that poor people are ready and willing to emerge out of poverty if given assess to basic economic inputs in an enabling environment. This realisation has led to the growing support for micro finance programme that serve the poor people. Micro finance is being increasingly seen as a sustainable financial intermediation mechanism for the development of poor, particularly Women.

Salient Features of Micro-Finance Programme

1. Small loans, mainly for purchase of productive assets, working capital or for consumption.
2. Informal appraisal of borrowers and investments.
3. Collateral free, but with options like group guarantees or compulsory savings.
4. Access to repeat or larger loans based on repayment performance
5. Streamlined loan disbursement and monitoring system.
6. Low time lag getting loan.
7. Flexible saving products.

Development of SHG's

SHG is brain child of the government of Bangladesh, which was founded by Prof. Mohammed Yunus of Chittagong University, in the year 1975. When Mr.Yunus first started Gremeena Bank, he started giving loans to men, but the repayment rate was poor and Grameena Bank could not grow. He then observed that women were borrowing and repaying much better than men and he allowed women to take the lead. Today, more than 805 of Grameena Banks borrowers are women. In addition, women take the lead in the banks other ventures of telecommunications, handloom and energy production. There has been a major change in the country in the last 20years. In the years after independence, there was a multiplicity of political and economic interests. Now the economy is being increasingly dominated controlled by big global and single vision corporate interests.

The government as well as non government sectors and most recently, the corporate sectors involved themselves in SHG. It's fact that in few part of the country this has brought tremendous result but in most of the states the real situation is quite disappointing. The SHG model emerged in the 1980s and 1990s. With the tremendous support from the government of India, state governments, NABARD, the banking sector and NGOs, the movement spread like anything. Even such a situation arise that the Indian Government budget presentation has emphasised on SHG bank linkage each year as in many cases it gave the ruling party a political mileage. As per the report of NABARD, BY THE END OF March 2006 there were 3.37 million SHGs in India covering 40.95 million poor households (roughly 200 million people or 20 per cent of total population and 80 per cent of total poor population). As of March 2007, 2.92 million SHGs had received bank loans of Rs. 180, 410 million. But can we say it has really changed the fate of the poor women.

Table 1 : Progress under Microfinance in India – Savings of SHGs with Banks Region-wise/State-wiseAgency-wise position as on 31 March 2010 (Rs. lakhs)

		Commercial Banks		*Regional Bank*		*Cooperative Bank*		*Total*	
Sr. No	*Region/State*	*No. of SHGs*	*Saving Amount*	*No. of SHGs*	*Saving Amount*	*No. of SHGs*	*Saving Amount*	*No. of SHGs*	*Saving Amount*
A	**Northern Region**								
1.	Haryana	19167	9465.55	14063	1062.49	3532	234.51	36762	10762.55
2.	Himachal Pradesh	26908	2000.36	6660	849.28	16614	641.26	50182	3490.90
3.	Punjab	37576	3124.24	2825	216.14	4604	304.72	45005	3645.10
4.	Jammu & Kashmir	3511	266.83	437	17034	418	1534.66	4366	1818.83
5.	Rajasthan	96442	7549.18	61355	3360.67	55498	3345.23	213295	14255.08
6.	New Delhi	2191	234.85	Na	Na	Na	Na	2191	234.85
	Total	185795	22641.01	85340	5505.92	80666	6060.38	351801	34207.31
B.	**Northern Eastern Region**								
1.	Assam	77036	3662.24	121298	2637.95	20018	1059.75	298352	7359.74
2.	Meghalaya	7607	193.06	1834	132.51	2346	34.68	11787	360.25
3.	Nagaland	5419	151.37	Na	Na	507	183.00	5926	334.37
4.	Tripura	11244	574.34	15832	2660.60	4273	100.76	31349	3335.7
5.	Arunachal Pradesh	5173	71.51	1038	77.85	207	15.53	6418	164.89
6.	Mizoram	1765	44.23	2643	176.97	689	30.20	5097	251.4

		Commercial Banks		*Regional Bank*		*Cooperative Bank*		*Total*	
Sr. No.	*Region/State*	*No. of SHGs*	*Saving Amount*	*No. of SHGs*	*Saving Amount*	*No. of SHGs*	*Saving Amount*	*No. of SHGs*	*Saving Amount*
7.	Manipur	4973	118.44	4723	80.00	1135	20.12	10831	218.56
8.	Sikkim	1829	96.74	NA	NA	599	45.24	2428	141.98
	Total	115046	4911.93	147368	5765.88	29774	1489.28	292188	12167.09
C.	**Eastern Region**								
1.	Bihar	92616	6147.32	48208	2392.25	NA	NA	140824	8539.57
2.	Jharkhand	55252	6159.32	24172	1262.49	NA	NA	79424	7421.81
3.	Odisha	248873	10569.41	185309	18906.09	68990	6998.00	503172	36473.5
4.	West Bengal	304693	15476.46	171226	29358.99	171140	14651.40	547059	59486.85
5.	A & N Islands (UT)	511	18.10	NA	NA	3252	74.77	3763	92.87
	Total	701945	38370.61	428915	51919.82	243382	21724.17	1374242	112014.60
D.	**Central Region**								
1.	Chhattisgarh	42845	2199.47	50762	4626.75	20375	751.84	113982	7578.06
2.	Madhya Pradesh	98015	5745.42	60616	3435.34	19595	970.31	178226	10151.07
3.	Uttarakhand	22060	2295.70	10423	602.41	11514	4272.00	43997	7170.41
4.	Uttar Pradesh	189374	16665.25	237942	9567.55	2444	230.23	429760	26464.03
	Total	352294	26906.84	359743	18232.35	53928	6224.38	765965	51363.57

		Commercial Banks		*Regional Bank*		*Cooperative Bank*		*Total*	
Sr. No.	*Region/State*	*No. of SHGs*	*Saving Amount*	*No. of SHGs*	*Saving Amount*	*No. of SHGs*	*Saving Amount*	*No. of SHGs*	*Saving Amount*
E.	**Western Region**								
1	Goa	4768	3400.37	NA	NA	1977	248.94	6745	3649.31
2	Gujarat	96674	20313.52	44169	2097.13	27337	9779.50	168180	32190.15
3	Maharashtra	410864	29428.56	91762	703.82	268069	26695.64	770695	56828.02
	Total	512306	53142.45	135931	2800.95	297383	267245.08	945620	9266748
F.	**Southern Region**								
1	Andra Pradesh	1025638	97455.56	395965	26154.09	26613	19190.33	1448216	125528.98
2	Karnataka	219056	21224.22	157359	14304.26	158173	27176.84	134588	62705.32
3	Kerala	306422	322282.68	34190	849.88	53585	4423.76	394197	37556.32
4	Tamil Nadu	618627	69400.56	75202	4377.38	132881	16595.32	826710	90373.26
5	Puducherry	15786	1053.38	857	26.96	3080	206.62	19723	1286.96
	Total	2185529	221416.40	663573	45712.57	374332	50321.87	3223434	317450.84
	Grand Total	4052915	367389.24	1820870	129937.49	1079465	122544.16	6953250	619870.89

Table 2: Progress of SHGs in Karnataka (July 2008) (Rs. in crores)

Sr. No	*District*	*Saving accumulated*	*No. of Groups loan taken from the bank*	*Total loan taken from bank*	*Revolving fund released from bank*	*Loan amount distributed by SHG*	*Total repayment to SHG*	*Total repayment to bank*
1.	Bengaluru (U)	26.66	2979	41.97	1.445	58.62	53.42	37.18
2.	Bengaluru (R)	17.99	2645	20.73	1.4685	64.43	46.01	33.27
3.	Bagalkote	19.19	3460	15.11	1.9195	29.75	23.23	11.42
4.	Belaguam	44.43	9685	37.94	6.0699	57.74	48.18	31.95
5.	Bellary	22.25	4138	23.35	2.0485	32.83	25.61	20.66
6.	Bidar	15.34	2112	13.63	1.3695	35.59	29.03	12.87
7.	Bijapur	13.06	2505	10.9	1.8015	26.58	19.05	8.83
8.	Chamarajnagar	0.16	3096	25.59	1.8580	55.90	41.09	21.26
9.	Chikkamagalur	15.39	2634	13.47	1.4590	52.22	48.38	14.11
10.	Chikkaballapur	26.24	4163	15.18	2.2735	55.35	47.16	39.36
11.	Chitradurga	25.73	4335	27.25	2.8685	65.49	48.65	21.11
12.	Davanagere	22.52	3583	25.86	2.2150	46.25	30.06	14.43
13.	Dakshina Kannada	18.66	32948	49.09	1.8190	67.57	52.20	36.46
14.	Dharwad	11.07	1902	9.75	1.3520	10.74	9.20	4.97

Sr. No.	*District*	*Saving accumulated*	*No. of Groups loan taken from the bank*	*Total loan taken from bank*	*Revolving fund released from bank*	*Loan amount distributed by SHG*	*Total repayment to SHG*	*Total repayment to bank*
15.	Gadag	7.25	2361	8.53	1.5205	19.37	10.54	5.88
16.	Gulberga	42.26	5967	29.76	4.2500	115.62	79.98	31.01
17.	Hassan	30.08	5246	17.20	3.0250	138.25	106.31	40.28
18.	Haveri	19.98	3249	13.00	2.1300	93.91	59.60	19.62
19.	Kodagu	6.52	774	6.46	0.464	28.18	26.64	12.44
20.	Kollar	15.15	2220	14.33	1.964	44.22	41.19	16.90
21.	Koppal	9.40	2210	8.55	1.230	16.56	9.89	5.85
22.	Mandya	44.58	5553	36.42	3.107	131.69	109.85	45.44
23.	Mysore	27.53	4180	27.15	3.0765	84.12	74.10	38.15
24.	Raichur	14.87	3342	10.94	2.3800	27.33	13.07	6.47
25.	Ramnagar	23.82	3709	40.61	2.2035	88.53	63.34	54.36
26.	Shivamogga	17.09	3604	30.81	1.9400	75.78	72.73	25.26
27.	Tumkur	42.20	8259	62.66	4.7745	130.84	104.07	76.14
28.	Udupi	24.67	2461	31.36	1.3375	56.66	55.55	33.21
29.	Uttar Kannada	7.95	1476	6.10	0.8835	33.50	29.68	7.44
	Total	611.75	105242	685.37	65.00	1739.59	1372.63	729.37

Source: Women and Children Development Department, Bengaluru, Report-July 2008.

Status of Micro Finance in India 2009-10

Table 2 revealed that all groups have started savings; the total cumulative savings is Rs. 611.75 crores, 130000 SHGs have formed, in that 105242 are with bank linkages and Rs. 685.375 crores taken as loan from banks. The groups have received Rs. 65 crores as revolving fund released by the Government. The groups have distributed loan to its members amount is Rs. 1739.59 crores, in this 1372.63 crores repaid by the members, its 79 per cent of the loan has repaid it is good sign for development. Mandya, Belgium and Gulbarga, these districts have highest cumulative savings.

Mahila SHG and Bank Linkage in Thirthahalli Taluk

Economic development of our country can be achieved only through enlistment of the village folk consisting of farmers, women, artisans, etc. Finance being the lifeblood of every business venture, availability of adequate funds at reasonable terms is necessary to ensure speedy economic development of a village and economic empowerment of women.

SHG Members Set an Example in Self-Employment.

Details of Five Gramapanchyat-wise Selp Help Groups In Thirthahalli Taluk

In this study, SHGs have been selected for the purpose of conducting field study. The study period for this research study is between March 2000 to March 2012. In shivamogga district has been divided into 7 taluks is a lie under Thirthahalli taluk. As per 2011 household survey conducted by District of Rural Development Authortity more than 50% living below the poverty line.

Table: 3 Details Of Five Gramapanchyat-wise Women Selp Help Groups In Thirthahalli Taluk

Sl. No.	*Name of the G.P.*	*Total No of SHGs*	*Total Members*	*Total No of Women SHGs*	*Total No of Women Members*	*Total Amount of Savings (All)*
1.	Hosahalli	71	1042	52	918	4416241
2.	Kannangi	50	860	38	608	1941651
3.	Bhandya	39	2256	33	1780	2840951
4.	Thudur	25	388	20	356	11728
5.	Kudumalige	76	1008	66	867	5947122
6.	Total	261	5554	209	4529	15157693

Source: Primary Data andTaluka Panchayat Thirthahalli, District Commissioner Chu (4) CR 33/09-10, Dated 19-04-2010.

Table 3 reveals that the total number of panchayat in Thirthahalli is 38. Number of SHGs are 1202 its members are 25145. Among the Gramapanchayats' selected 5 Gramapanchayats' 50 Women SHGs, 100 members were randomly selected and for the field study. The areas covered Hosahalli, Kannangi, Bhandya, Thudur and Kudumalige. More specially, for culling out primary data, the direct personal interview method is followed. The total saving amount of Rs. 15157693 lakhs.

Above study through light on their Occupation to earn their livelihood. There are 160 members. Out of this total Average 50% – 60% members are agriculturists a few owns small area of land holdings and some are working as tenants. Even in this case though the lands have been granted by the Government, other process of confirming ownership is yet to be realised in many cases. Officialdom and Redtapisum appears to be the major factors in this regard. In this direction they have been exposed for exploitation by the concerned ones. In the village 20-25% members are engaged in petty business selling of bleeds, repairing and selling of locks, engaged in making plastic, flowers and selling etc in near by towns and villages. More than 10% are living on coolies i.e. wage in the lands of landlords/houses as labourers. The remaining comes under members of SHGs less than 10%.The table also points out that the annual income of members Rs. 6000 and below is 70% -80%. The persons in the annual income group per annum more than Rs. 6000 to less than Rs. 10000 stands at 10 -15%. Remaining 10-15% of members are getting an income of Rs. 10000 or more than 10000. This clearly indicates their economic status. Out of this it is easy to one to say that the majority live below the poverty line.

Table 4: Demographic Profile of Respondents

Educational Status		*Age*				*Marital Status*		*No. of years in microfinance programme*	
Level	*No*	*Range*	*No*	*Religion*	*No*	*Status*	*No*	*Years*	*No*
Illiterate	70	21-25	60	Hindu	10	Unmarried	4	5	51
Read and Write	10	26-30	10	Muslim	90	Married	78	3.5	26
Grade 1-4	06	31-35	02	Christian		Widowed	14	4.5	5
Grade 5-8	03	36-40	24	Others	100	Divorced	4	5	9
Grade 9-10	-	Above 41	04	-		-	-	4	
Grade 11-12	11	-	-	-		-	-	Over 5	
Total	100		100			Total	100		

Source: Primary data.

Nearly three-fourth 70 of the respondents is purely illiterate, while one half of the remaining can read and write only, typically reflecting the realities of rural women. Youths within the age range of 21 to 25 accounts for only 6% of the respondants.Young women's utilisation of rural microfinance is so limited perhaps due to lack of targeted products attracting such section of the population. Just over three-fourth of the total responds are Hindu and the remaining are followers of Muslim and others, matching with the study district population as more than 70 per cent of them are followers of Hindu. The number of married women dominates, some 4 widowed, 14 divorced and 4 unmarried women have been involved in the study. Such wide spectrum of age and marital status of respondents has been found important to examine the interests and challenges of different groups of the study population in utilising microfinance services.

Table 5: Household Profile of Respondents

	HH Headship		*Number of Household Members*				*Wealth Status of the Household*		
	Male	*Female*	*2 or less*	*3 to 4*	*5 to 6*	*Over 6*	*Very poor*	*poor*	*Middle*
No	75	25	12	65	15	8	15	25	60

The Residential and Wealth Status

In regards to household headship, 25 women are heading their respective households and husbands or elder sons head the rest 75. Above field study, indicate the residential status of SHGs in the villages' primary study. Out of 100 Members, more than 50% members of SHGs are having houses built Tiled roof andCement. Where as Tiled roof with Huts 10-25% of SHGs members, Average 10-20% SHGs members of the villages are in thatched houses, huts in many cases, the roofing is of gross and leaves, most of them are in deflected conditions. Respondents were also asked to indicate their households' current wealth status according to their own perception. As such, two-third (60) of the respondents perceived themselves as they are in the middle strata, 25 as poor and 15 as very poor. The lesson on gender dimension of rural microfinance is that, on one hand, relatively poor and very poor women among rural women themselves have gotten the opportunity for utilising services, opening the first gate to participate economically marginalised women. On the other hand, although a considerable number of poor and very poor women have participated in micro financing since the past four and over years, they reported that they did little improvement in terms of wealth status.

From the focus group discussions, it was found that women it very difficult for initiating the first-self group in selected village. As a first step, they started calling on selected women, who had similar 'thinking' an aspiration to be independent socially and economically. Then creating awareness about the benefits of SHG formation, savings, and micro credit activities. etc., was the second task. This was formed successfully by organising a meeting and collecting everyone at one place. An Animator/ Secretary were elected for thee group. In order to assist and support the secretary, represatives among the members were elected. The amount of money to be saved weekly or monthly was decided. Finally, information related to monthly membership fee, weekly/monthly meetings, opening a bank account, passing resolutions for all these were discussed. Transparency was established within the group members to avoid conflict. Then commenced savings and finally, the women opened a bank account and remitted money.

Problems Joining the Self Help Group and Other Work

Women in focus group discussions also shared the initial reactions of husband and family members to them joining as a member in SHG. Most of their family members questioned 'what is it that you are going to gain by joining as a SHG member? Men asked, 'If you go to the meeting, who will cook food at home? Who will look after the children? Who will take care of the house? The mother-in-law never showed any interest in taking over responsibility of their daughter-in-laws. Men started restricting, women for attending meetings held in the same village as most of the meetings were organised by men workers of the NGO. Men never wanted their wives to go away from their villages to the NGO's office for attending meetings. The villagers abused the SHG women by passing degrading comments on the streets and at bus stops whenever women 'dressed up' and went to attend meetings. It was really surprising to hear how these women solved all these problems within their family and could successful SHG member and an entrepreneur. They explained to their husbands and family members about what actually happens in the meeting. Initially all women finished their house work completely and then moved out of the house for attending training programmes and meetings. Such kind of tactics made women to get their support. Sudden increase in the confidence/knowledge level of women and their economic independence built trust and confidence in the eyes of men. The spirit within themselves made them solve all these problems and win their family's support.

Effects of Microfinance on Women's Empowerment

Empowerment assessment is extremely complex activity, in which the main challenges lie on reducing the various dimensions to a set of workable indicators. Having this in mind, the study tried to examine respondents' perception to empowerment indicators with respect to economic and social dimensions at individual, household and community contexts.

Activities/Business Financed by Loans of Respondents

Agriculture, Cattle Fattening, Diary Farming, Poultry, Handicraft,

Spinning, Trade, Micro goods Vending, Local Food and Beverages cloth selling and bangles selling etc.

Table 6: Effects of Microfinance on Respondents Income Level and Source

Effect of microfinance on Respondents'	*Increased Significantly*	*Increased Slightly*	*Stayed same*	*Total*
Income Source (s) diversification	40	40	20	100
Level of Income	45	50	05	100
Saving Capacity	55	40	05	100
Personal Cash Assets	45	45	10	100

Source: Primary data

Table 7: Respondents' Perception to Their Own Level of Confidence and Respectability

	Level of Confidence to Oneself		*Extent of Community Respect*	
	Before	*After*	*Before*	*After*
Very High	10	30	-	18
High	10	40	12	37
Medium	30	14	12	25
Low	20	08	50	05
Very low	30	-	10	05
Do not Know	10	8	16	10
Total	100	100	100	100

Source: Primary data.

Table 7 Women have also secured more freedom for movements than they did before. After they have been in microfinance programme, women have become freer than before and able to move by their own to market places, health, posts/centers, and other formal local institutions.

Table 8: Change in Respondents' Social Position after Joining the Microfinance Program

How do you rate change in your social position after joining MF Programme?	*Significantly Deteriorated*	*Deterio-rated*	*Remained Same*	*Do not know*
	Very Much	*Much*	*Little*	*Do not know*
If you are social, position has been improved or significantly improved, to what extent has the after joining MF Program?	30	50	6	14

Source: Primary data.

Table 8 few in number; women have also experienced adverse conditions in their social and economic status after they have been in the loan programme. Unlike to those, who have quite registered significant improvement in their social and economic status due to the programme, other women experienced deteriorating social and economic positions.

Before Joining SHGs

1. Women had no respect within their community.
2. Ample opposition was observed from tm the family members. As well neighbours.
3. Women had no knowledge about the outside world.
4. Women were not allowed to sit and talk on par with men.
5. Existence of disparities: educated and uneducated women.
6. Men had got a clear control over the women in their house. They treated women as slaves.

After Joining SHGs

1. After joining SHGs, women's opinions were considered and valued with respect to social problems or common issues prevailing in the village.
2. Women were given special respect at home.
3. Women were found with self-confidence.
4. Men encouraging women to attend meetings on time.
5. Men have realised the benefits of being a member of a SHG.
6. Women were economically independent after joining SHGs.
7. Parents and in-laws were also supportive and raised their hopes by providing extended cooperation.
8. Children are found really proud of their mothers. They say with a great pride that 'their mother is in a group'.
9. Women enjoy the respect provided to them in the village.

Conclusions

The findings of the study, in general, suggest the existence of sufficient evidences that substantiate the possibilities of microfinance program for empowering rural women. Empowerment is about change, choice and power. It is a process of change by which individuals and groups with little or no power gain the power and ability to make choices that affect their lives. Microfinance programs can only have tremendous impact on women's empowerment process if their products and services consider these factors. Therefore, this suggests the need to have more inclusive financial services that would allow the opportunity for more rural women to participate, which in turn could lead to have more effects in the process of women's empowerment.

References

Rangarajan Committee Report on Financial Inclusion rbi.org.in/scripts.

Dodkey, M.D.(1999), *"SHGs and Micro Credit, Sustaining Rural Women"*, Social Welfare, March, 45(12): 19-20.

NABARD (2004), Finacing Selp Help Groups:A Reference Handbook of NABARD, Bangalore, 4-5.

Lazar, D 7 Meganathan M. (2011), *Socio-economic Empowerment of Schedule Caste Women through Microfinance in Ramanathapuram*, district edited volume Shollapur and Naveen K Shetty, Microfinance and Sustainable Livelihood Promotions in India, EXCEL Publications New Delhi. 327-337.

Pavan K. Bhura: *Microfinance in India: A major link to ensure inclusive growth*, University of Delhi, India.

Elizabeth Rhyne: Microfinance in India, *'Micro-credit Is Imperiled in India by Defaults*" Published November 25, 2010 Re, Action International Washington.

Ahmad, M.A. (1999), *Women Empowerment: Self-Help Groups*, Kurukshetra, Vol. 47(7).

www.microfinancegateway.org

Government of Karnataka, (2005), *"Economic Survey, 2004-05", (Bangalore: Planning and statistical department)*

Dr. Ramesh T. "*Micro finance – A Drive to Combat Poverty*", "The Management Accountant" Nov. 2008, Vol. 43, No. 11, 822-826.

Government of Karnataka, Women and Children Development Department, Bengaluru, Report-July 2000.

www.http.yahoo.co.in *Status of Micro Finance in India 2009-10.*

Emerging Challenges, Tata McGraw-Hill, New Delhi.

Dr. R. Ponmurgan and Dr. S. Nadarajan, *Self –Helf Groups:Bank linkage programs,* Kisan World, Feb-2008

Rangarajan, C. (2008), *Report of the committee on financial Inclusion in India,* New Delhi, October, Mumbai.

http://www.microfinacefocus.com/

Nimal *A Fernando "Managing Microfinance risks: some observations and suggestions"*, Asian Journal of Agricultural and development, Vol. 4, No. 2.

Siddiqui Badruzzama, 3 "Priority Sectors Lending", A Journal on Rural Development, *Kurukshetra*, August 2002, Volume 50, No 10, New Delhi. pp. 14-18.

Government of Karnataka (1982), *"Karnataka State Gazetteer Part I"* (Ed. Kamath, Suryanath U) (Bangalore: Office of the Chief Editor, Karnataka Gazetteer Department), p. 823.

18

Role of Microfinance Interventions in Financial Inclusion: A Comparitive Study of Microfinance Models

Ramakrishna **and** ***K.V. Aiahanna***

Introduction

Most people in the developing world-the majority of the world's population - do not have access to formal financial services. Very few get benefited from savings accounts, loans, or convenient way to transfer money. Those who do manage to, say, open a bank account, are often faced with sub-optimal services. Households need access to finance for several purposes, the most important being for contingency planning and risk mitigation. Households build buffer savings, allocate savings for retirement (for example via pension plans) and purchase insurance and hedging products for insurable contingencies. Once these needs are met, households typically need access to credit for livelihood creation as well as consumption and emergencies (in the event that they do not have savings/insurance to fund them). Finally, wealth creation is another area where financial services are required. Households require a range of savings and investment products for the purpose of wealth creation depending on their level of financial literacy as well as their risk perception. Financial services for the poor, often referred to as microfinance, cannot solve all the problems caused by poverty. But they can help put resources and power into the hands of poor and low income people themselves, letting them make those everyday decisions and chart their own paths out of poverty. The potential is enormous, and so is the challenge. In other words, this vision is about inclusive financial systems, which are the only way to reach to the large number of poor and low-income people. The Rangarajan Committee Report- 2008 objects on Financial Inclusion that "Financial Inclusion may be defined as the process of ensuring access to financial services and timely and adequate credit where needed by vulnerable groups such as weaker sections and low income groups at an affordable cost."

Literature Review

Microcredit and microfinance are relatively new terms in the field of development, first coming to prominence in the 1970s, according to Robinson (2001) and Otero (1999). Prior to then, from the 1950s through to the 1970s, the provision of financial services by donors or governments was mainly in the form of subsidised rural credit programmers. These often resulted in high loan defaults, high lose and an inability to reach poor rural households (Robinson, 2001).RobinsonStates that the 1980s represented a turning point in the history of microfinance in that MFIs such as Grameen Bank and BRI2 began to show that they could provide small loans and savings services profitably on a large scale. They received no continuing subsidies, were commercially funded and fully sustainable, and could attain wide outreach to clients (Robinson, 2001). It was also at this time that the term "microcredit" came to prominence in development (MIX3, 2005). The difference between microcredit and the subsidised rural credit programmes of the 1950s and 1960s was that microcredit insisted on repayment, on charging interest rates that covered the cost of credit delivery and by focusing on clients who were dependent on the informal sector for credit (ibid.). It was now clear for the first time that microcredit could provide large-scale outreach profitably.

Research Problem and Objectives

There is currently a clear perception that there are a vast number of people, potential entrepreneurs, small enterprises and others, who are excluded from the financial sector, which leads to their marginalisation and denial of opportunity for them to grow and prosper. Financial inclusion is thus a key policy concern, because the options for operating a household budget, or a micro/small enterprise, without mainstream financial services can often be expensive. This process becomes self-reinforcing and can often be an important factor in social exclusion, especially for the communities with limited access to financial products, particularly in the rural areas. Microfinance intervention is considered an important component of development strategy to mainstream poor rural households with the formal financial system in India. With the able support of various agencies intervention has exponentially grown over the years. The increase in SHG clients taken together with the expanded outreach of the MFIs as led to an overall increase of 11.5 million clients during 2007-08. Net of adjustments more than 54 million clients are estimated to have been reached by the microfinance sector in different forms, with and expansion of 9.9 million during the year. While cross country aggregate indicators can help produces proxies for access by households and document barriers that prevent expansion of this access, only carefully conducted household surveys can provide us with in-depth information on the role on microfinance in providing sustainable access to finance for India's rural poor and its influence on the use of informal Sources for fulfilling their credit requirements. In this context this study tries to answer the following key research questions: How do the clients of the two main models of microfinance, the SHG model and the MFI model, differ? What is the average level of indebtedness to non-institutional sources among clients of different models of microfinance? Does the level of indebtedness to moneylenders depend on the type of microfinance model one is client of?

Research Methodology

In order to answer the above stated key research questions, we conducted a pilot survey indifferent blocks representing rural area .This survey was conducted among 59 households of twelve villages covering four blocks of the selected district. Although the choice of location is based purely on convenience basis, the selection of households is made such as to include both categories of respondents (members of SHGs as well as MFIs) relevant for our study. Primary data on different socio-economic aspects of the households and details of micro-financial services availed by them were collected directly from the clients through the structured questionnaire and personal interview. Qualitative information was collected through Focus Group Discussions (FGDs) and semi-structured interviews of the bankers, NGOs and MFIs operating in the area to understand the supply and demand sides of the problem of microcredit in the selected research area. The field study was conducted during March 2010 and further cross verification through field visits was done during June 2010. Considering complex nature of the field study, the data collected were processed and tabulated using a computer for analysis and interpretation. The collected data are subjected with the chi-square statistical test in order to fulfill the objectives of the study.

Results and Discussion

Grameen Group Model

The Grameen Group comprises of five members who guarantee each other's loans which are provided by microfinance institutions. The Grameen methodology originated in Bangladesh, where it was configured into a highly standardised loan product that allowed serving cost-efficiently poor people with small loan needs. Grameen approach targets entrepreneurial poor who invest ever growing loans into their small-scale businesses such as petty trade, poultry, milking cows and the like. In the recent years, the range, the range of microfinance products has widened considerably. Remittance services have been recognised as a critical service for the poor, many of which migrate temporarily and support their families from far. Microinsurance as a road to reduce vulnerability and not at least to reduce repayment risks of micro-loans, is an important financial service for the poor. Currently about 15 million poor are at least rudimentarily covered, mostly loan-linked (Sa-Dhan Quick Data 2008).

Microfinance-An Alternative Source of Formal Finance

Inadequacies in rural access to formal finance and the usurious terms of informal finance for the poor provide a strong need and ample space for innovative approaches to serve the financial needs of India's rural poor. Over the last decade, efforts have been made by the government, financial institutions, and Non-government Organisations (NGOs), often in co partnership, to develop new financial delivery approaches. These microfinance approaches have been designed to combine the safety and reliability of formal finance with the convenience and flexibility that are typically associated with informal finance. They typically involve providing thrift, credit another financial services and products of very small amounts to the poor, with the aim to raise income levels and improve living standards. What Microfinance Does and How? Microfinance is the provision of financial services on a small scale for target groups that have been excluded by the banks. Some providers started offering microfinance services way back in the 1970s, e.g. SEWA Bank in Gujarat. However, in the 1990s it gained momentum. At the core of microfinance is the provision of loans through group based methodology. In India, two principal concepts can be distinguished. Self Help Group (SGH) Bank Linkage Model The Self Help Group has between 10 and 20 members who pool savings and lend among themselves. It was first conceived by NGOs like MYRADA and PRADAN during the 1980s.Since 1996, NABARD mainstreams a nationwide bank linkage programme that offers additional i.e. beyond their own savings-credit to SHGs. Banks typically provide the group a loan amounting to four times the group's savings but, as the group matures, and based on the group's track record, banks are ready to lend more. Borrowed and saved funds are rotated through lending within the group using flexible repayment schedule (usually monthly repayment); SHG thus save, borrow and repay collectively.

Table 1 indicates that here was a vast increase in the amount of bank credit provided to the SHGs during this period. This includes credit provided by all three key institutions, namely commercial banks, Regional Rural Banks and cooperative banks. Of these, commercial banks have been instrumental in financing the largest number of SHGs till now.

Table 1: Cumulative Number of and Amount of Credit to SHGs, by Agency, 2010

Agency	*Cumulative number of SHGs*	*Cumulative amount of bank credit*
Commercial banks	1188040 (53.1)	698745 (61.3)
Public sector banks	1141570 (51.0)	643968 (56.5)
Private sector banks	46470 (2.1)	54777 (4.8)
Regional Rural Banks	740024 (33.1)	332215 (29.1)
Cooperative banks	310501 (13.9)	108795 (9.5)
All banks	**2238565 (100.0)**	**1139754 (100.0)**

Note: Figures in brackets indicates percentage share in total.
Source: NABARD (2010).

Table 2: Percentage of Households Reporting at least one loan Outstanding, by source

Source of Finance	*Percentages Households*
Formal Sources	**44.4**
Government	1.9
Cooperatives	26.1
Commercial banks	14.4
Other sources	5.6
Informal Sources	**68.0**
Landlord	1.4
Agricultural moneylender	4.6
Professional moneylender	53.1
Trader	0.9
Relatives and friends	7.4
Others	4.3

Note: The figures may not add up to 100 as there are households that have taken loans from more than one.
Source: NSSO (2010).

The data provided by the All India Debt and Investment Survey (AIDIS) in 2010 for Karnataka, we get a fairly similar picture of the predominance of informal sources in general, moneylenders in particular. We find that of the total number of rural households in the State, 68 per cent reported having taken at least one loan from informal sources and of these, 53 per cent reported at least one loan from professional moneylenders. Further, only 14.4 per cent of the rural households in the State reported at least one loan from commercial banks. Evidently, there was greater dependence on informal sources, particularly moneylenders in Karnataka.

Table 3: Percentage Distribution of Loans from SHGs, by Purpose

	Purpose	*Share in amount*	*Share in number*
1	**Directly income-generating activities**	**52.0**	**28.0**
	1.1 Agriculture	12.0	5.0
	1.2 Livestock	1.0	1.0
	1.3 Business/shop	39.0	21.0
	1.3.1 Silk business	14.0	6.0
2	**Consumption related activities**	**44.0**	**70.0**
	2.1 House construction	0.3	0.3
	2.2 Education	6.0	6.0
	2.3 Health	36.0	61.0
	2.4 Ceremonial expenditure	2.0	2.0
	2.5 Others	0.05	0.04
3	**Not reported**	**4.0**	**3.0**
	Total	**100**	**100**

Source: Primary data.

Table 3 shows that the Moneylenders in the region charged even higher rates of interest going up to 240 per cent per annum. Given the fact that most of the loans from SHGs were taken towards production related purposes we expect that any member borrowing from SHGs has to get a rate of return of over 24-36 per cent from her business venture in order to break even, which indeed is a high rate of return to be expected from the small business ventures that these women put their funds to.

Survey Findings and Discussion

Comparison of Alternative Microfinance Model Clients: In this study a modest attempt has been made to differentiate between the client characteristics of two main microfinance models prevalent in the study area.

Level of Literacy

The heads of the households interviewed were illiterate with 42 per cent reporting they had never been to school. The average completed years of education per household member was 4.9 years for the SHG clients 4 years for MFI clients. All the children aged between 5-14 years were reported to attending the school on a regular basis irrespective of the choice of the model of microfinance they made. As far as the literacy of microfinance clients is concerned, around half of the SHG clients were reported literate (attended formal school at least up to 5 the grade) which is slightly in higher side comparing MFI clients.

Housing

As far as average number of rooms is concerned; MFI clients scored less by 40 per cent with an average of 1.6 rooms compared to SHG clients with an average of 2.63 rooms per household. Comparing model wise, 37.5 per cent of SHG households live in Kachha houses whereas only 20 per cent of MFI clients have been reported to reside in the dwellings made up of non concrete walls and roof. Given the rural focus of our study, it comes as no surprise that over 95 per cent of our respondents live in the self-owned dwellings.

Landholdings and Sources of Income

A huge difference has been observed comparing the size of average land holdings per household which is quite low in case of MFI clients comparing to SHG clients. The reason for that cans be attributed to the fact that 62.5 per cent of SHG clients depend on agriculture as a primary source of their income that requires large landholdings. On the other hand, none of the MFI client has been reported engaged in farming. Only 25 per cent of the households were self employed among SHG clients. An interesting fact to note is that all the MFI clients were self employed engaged in dairy activities, owing small tea or tailoring shops and working as street hawkers. A part from farming, another major source of livelihood for SHG clients was wage labour.

Targeting Efficiency of Microfinance Programmes

On an average only 22.8 per cent of the sample households were found below the official Poverty Line for rural Uttar Pradesh. Below the poverty line for rural UP is defined as having per capital per month consumption under rupees 365.84.

Income and Consumption Expenditure

Average per capita monthly consumption expenditure for SHG clients was lower when comparing with that of MFI cliets which was approximately rupees 940.00. Another interesting feature to observe is that per capita monthly income of the household is lesser than the per capital monthly expenditure. The possible reason can be underestimation of reported income as the majority of households were engaged in agricultural or non-farm enterprises. However, there insignificant difference between SHG and MFI clients in regard to per capita monthly income. The explanation for this difference lies in the fact of difference in the primary source of income of the two groups. Majority of SHG clients were engaged in farming which is low return economic activity whereas most of the MFI clients are into the kind of business providing higher return on investments compared to agriculture.

Average Level of Indebtedness to Non-Institutional Agencies among Microfinance Clients

Non-institutional agencies played a major role in advancing credit to 81 per cent of the sample households. Among non-institutional agencies, professional money lenders and relatives were the two most important sources in the study area. They together accounted for almost 65 per cent of the outstanding cash dues. The loan from relatives was a major source of credit for social expenditures such as wedding in the family. Another noticeable feature was that such loans were interest free and required to be repaid only when any such event occurs in the family of the lender.

Conclusion

The basic idea of micro financing is simple-if poor people are provided access to financial services, including credit, they may very well be able to start or expand a micro enterprise that will allow them to break out of poverty. In totality, its focus is on eradication of poverty form gross level, women upliftment, creating small and medium enterprises and therefore takes care of development of any economy from within. Comparing two microfinance models in the research area reveals that the level of indebtedness to moneylenders is higher in the case of clients of MFI model. Such cases illustrate the difficulties MFI clients face, when they have unproductive financial requirements or they are compelled to ensure prompt and regular loan repayments through further borrowing from even money lenders. This makes poverty worse in the short run, and makes it harder to escape from poverty-and indeed can be source of poverty and inequality "traps".

Bibliography

1. Bansal, Hema, (2003), "SHG-Bank Linkage Program in Indian: An Overview", Journal of Microfinance, Vol. 5, Number 1.
2. Anil K Khandelwal, "Microfinance Development Strategy for India", Economic and Political Weekly, March 31, 2007.\Nachiket Mor, Bindu Ananth, "Inclusive Financial Systems - Some Design Principles and a case study", Economic and Political Weekly, March 31, 2007.
3. Srinivasan, N. (2008), Microfinance India-State of the Sector Report-2008, Sage Publications India Pvt. Ltd, New Delhi, India.
4. AIDIs (All India Debt and Investment Survey) (2002), "Various Rounds from 1961-2002," Ministry of Statistics and Programme Implementation, Government of India.

19

SHG-Bank Linkage Programme and Financial Inclusion in India

M.V. Dinesha and *Rajendra Prasad*

Introduction

By financial inclusion, we mean the delivery of financial services, including banking services and credit, at an affordable cost to the vast sections of disadvantaged and low-income groups who tend to be excluded. The various financial services include access to savings, loans, insurance, payments and remittance facilities offered by the formal financial system. Among the key financial services that are of great relevance here are risk management or risk mitigation services vis-à-vis economic shocks. Such shocks may be an income shock due to adverse weather conditions or natural disasters, or an expenditure shock due to health emergencies or accidents, leading to a high level of unexpected expenditure. This aspect of financial inclusion is of vital importance in providing economic security to individuals and families.

Financial inclusion is defined by various authors in different ways, and generally accepted to mean the delivery of banking services at an affordable cost to the vast section of disadvantaged and low-income groups. And although credit is the most important component, financial inclusion should also cover savings, insurance, payments and remittance facilities for these excluded segments of society (Mahendra, 2006).

The Rangarajan's Committee on financial inclusion defined it: "as the process of ensuring access to financial services and timely and adequate credit where needed by vulnerable groups such as weaker sections and low income groups at an affordable cost" (Kamath, 2007).

The banking industry has shown tremendous growth in volume and complexity over the last few decades. But despite making significant improvements in all areas relating to financial viability, profitability and competitiveness, there are serious concern that banks have been unable to include vast segments of the population into the fold of basic banking services - especially the underprivileged sections of society (Thorat, 2007). This has led to the emergence of Financial Inclusion as a strategy to bring these excluded people into the financial mainstream. Since banking services are considered to be in the nature of public good, it is essential that availability of banking and payment services to the entire population, without discrimination, be the prime objective of public policy.

Accordingly, since the late nineties, sophisticated and competitive services of a wide range of financial products and opportunities have become accessible to meet the emerging credit needs of these groups of people (Sangwan, 2008). By providing these services, the aim is to help them come out of poverty.

Finance has come a long way since the time when it wasn't recognised as a factor for growth and development. Today, however, it is recognised as an important factor, with financial inclusion accepted as a significant ingredient in the development of the economy. The major reasons for excluding the low income groups from access to formal institutions are (i) reliance on informal source of finance due to easy access, (ii) high cost in accessing formal financial services, (iii) non-price barriers such as identity of person, collateral security, distance between bank and residence, poor infrastructure, and (iv) behavioral aspects such as non-comfort with financial procedures, lack of understanding, etc.

Statistics show that the numbers of rural banks have increased over a period of time, i.e. the share of rural bank was 22 per cent during 1969 and had increased to 41 per cent by 2007. However, deposits and credit accounts are lower in rural households than urban households. Region wise analysis indicate that the population per bank has increased in rural areas in all the regions i.e. lower financial deepening; whereas in urban areas the population per bank decreased in all the regions, except the western region.

Reserve Bank of India (RBI, the Central Bank) took various initiatives to promote financial inclusion such as no-frill accounts, Know Your Customer (KYC) norms, use of local language, easy credit facilities through General Credit Card (GCC), involvement of rural intermediaries such as NGOs, SHGs and MFIs, and use of Information Technologies (ITs) etc. Unfortunately, despite this push, the rural population have not come forward and availed even the basic banking services (Agarwal, 2008).

Rationale for Financial Inclusion in India

Impeded and higher cost of access to adequate financial services like credit, insurances, and remittances to majority population are major roadblocks for the growth of primary sectors like agriculture. Financial inclusion can create win-win environment for both customer and financial institution in an economy (Thorat, 2006). It enables customer to avail various kind of financial products for productive purposes. It also helps customers in availing micro remittance facilities, micro credit at an affordable cost. The Government also can use the bank accounts of people for providing various social security services for the vulnerable section of society. Thus, financial inclusion can be considered as prerequisite to achieve inclusive growth which would further helps in achieving sustainable economic growth.

Financial Inclusion in India: An Overview

Financial inclusion ensures ease of availability, accessibility and usage of formal financial system to all members of the economy (Sharma, 2008). Financial inclusion has been widely recognised as important means to achieve inclusive growth on India. During the post nationalisation of banking period, there has been spectacular progress in formal banking networks across the country. In the course of time, Reserve Bank of India has been adopting various measures like priority sector lending, KYC norms, banking correspondent model to ensure financial inclusion. In fact, measuring financial inclusion in a developing country like India is different from other developed countries.

Financial Inclusion can be Measured in Two Ways

- One is inclusion in the payments system i.e. having access to a bank account.
- The second type of inclusion is towards formal credit markets, thus requiring the excluded to approach informal and exploitative markets.

Previously various studies on financial inclusion have identified various factors which are responsible for financial exclusion in an economy. Some of these factors responsible for financial exclusion have been mentioned below.

- Lack of proper infrastructural development.
- Geographical factors: Remote and hilly areas.
- From demand side lack of awareness, income and asset constraints, limited literacy especially financial literacy and social exclusion act as major barriers.
- From supply side cumbersome documentation procedure, unavailability of diversified products and services, high transaction costs, and easy availability of informal credits are major barrier to achieve financial inclusion (Thorat, 2007).
- Other factors like gender issues, nature of occupation, social security
- Payment systems are also playing vital roles in influencing access to financial services. (World bank, 2008).

Individual indicators like number of bank accounts, number of bank branches, size of credit and deposit to GDP are also used to measure the extent of inclusiveness of financial system. Financial services provided by various financial institutions like banks, postal saving banks, non banking finance companies; micro finance institutions are also form the basis to measure the level of financial inclusion in aneconomy. Number of bank account per thousand adults is considered as one of the common measure of financial inclusion.

Review of Literature

Sharma (2008), through cross country empirical study examined a close relationship between financial inclusion and development. Further, the study found a positive relation between financial inclusion and different socio-economic variables like income, inequality, literacy, physical infrastructures.

Kempson and Whyley (1998) argued that possibility of financial exclusion is more likely to occur in the lower income section of society than amongst others. Beside this, geographical factors and income inequality are also important factors in determining financial inclusion of a country.

Goodwin.et.al (2000) emphasised the role of level of employment of a country as another important factor of financial inclusion. Access to affordable financial services especially credit and insurance - enlarges livelihood opportunities and empowers the poor to take charge of their lives. Such empowerment aids social and political stability. Financial inclusion also imparts formal identity, provides access to the payments system and to savings safety net like deposit insurance. Hence it is considered to be critical for achieving inclusive growth; which itself is required for ensuring overall sustainable overall growth in the country. (Thorat, 2007).

Beck, et. al (2000), in their paper tried to evaluate empirically the relationship between level of financial intermediary development and economic growth. They observed a positive impact of financial intermediary development on the growth of total factor productivity which will lead to economic development.

Bekaert et.al (2004), in their study examined a positive impact of equity market liberalisation on real economic growth. Further, they also observed the positive impact of capital account liberalisation and quality of financial institutions on economic growth.

Greenwood et. al (1990), tried addressed two important issues in economic growth theories in a single model. They are relationship between economic growth and inequality and relation between financial structures and economic development. They argued that financial development facilitates economic growth as it gives high re return on capital. On the other hand economic development also provides means to financial development.

A few empirical studies on the impact of SHG bank linkage model also revealed the importance of SHG model in achieving financial inclusion and inclusive growth in India.Puhazhendi and Satyasai (2000), studied the improvement in level of income of SHG members between pre and post SHG situations.

Chavan and Ramakumar (2002) in their study compared NGO led micro credit programme of various countries with state led poverty alleviation scheme and observed marginal improvement in member's income as a result of micro credit programme.

Puhazhendi and Badatya (2002), observed a significant improvements in the savings SHG members during post SHG situations. The programme also improves the borrowing pattern of SHG member households in terms of strengthening credit widening and credit deepening.

Sanghwan (2006), studied the extent financial inclusion across various states. He also tried to examine the role of SHG bank linkage programme in achieving financial inclusion. The study suggested a significant role of SHG led programme in achieving financial inclusion. Beside this, it also tried to examine the role of other factors like banking density, financial literacy and per capita income in achieving financial inclusion.

Sahoo et.al (2008), had attempted to develop index of financial inclusion to examine the progress of financial inclusion and various determinants of financial inclusion using secondary data from various sources. In their study, they observed a positive impact of infrastructure development, education, self help group formation on financial inclusion both from financial widening and deepening perspectives.

Objectives of the Study

The present study was conducted with the following objectives.

1. To study the evolution of SHG-Bank Linkage programme in India.
2. To study the progress and impact SHG-Bank Linkage programme in India.

Methodology

The study is based on secondary data. Secondary data were collected from NABARD, RBI, and Economic survey.

Results and Discussion

The provision of financial services to rural poor, who constituted majority of the rural community, was the major area of policy concern world-wide including India in recent years. Historically, informal agencies like money lenders, traders, land lords, and solidarity groups of likeminded people played as financial intermediaries in the rural areas. They were rural based, and hence easily accessible and had the lowest transaction costs. With their local knowledge and close customer relationship they were able to meet all types of credit needs of rural peoples in time without collateral security. However, in the context of economic development and growing need for financial services, the informal agencies with their limited resources and exploitative terms were considered not suitable to meet credit needs of rural people. Until 1980s, attention was mostly focused on building up an alternative formal credit delivery system to replace the informal system.

The search for alternatives led to experimenting with a variety of formal financial institutions like cooperatives, specialised agricultural banks, rural banks, commercial banks, government sponsored project authorities and targeted cheaper credit projects'. The failure of all these formal financial institutions to replace informal agencies and to provide financial services to the rural poor on the cost effective basis prompted the international agencies like the world Bank, FAO, Aid agencies and NGOs to look into the appropriateness of practices and techniques adopted by the informal finance and the scope for linking them with the formal system. It was found that the poor tended to come together in a variety of informal forms for pooling their savings and dispensing small and unsecured loans at varying costs to group members on the basis of need.

Asia Pacific Regional Agricultural Credit Association (APRACA) – an association of the major agricultural banking and training institutions in the Asia and Pacific region was the pioneer in understanding an action research programme which led to promotion of linkage between banks and SHGs for rural saving mobilisation and credit delivery to the rural poor.

The guiding principles emerged from the experiment of pilot projects in different Asian countries under the Acton Research Prcgramme of APRACA are as follows:

- The rural people are capable of saving and offering excellent business opportunities for banks and lending to them is beneficial for both sides.
- SHGs as solidarity groups are capable financial intermediaries and linkage with tem facilities the financial services to the poor.
- SHGs contribute to facilitating screening of borrowers and ensure timely disbursement sand repayment of loans. SHG can exercise social pressure to enhance compliance with the loan repayment obligations.
- Linking saving with credit and applying market interest rates ensure financial viability and sustainability.
- SHGs reduce the dependence of the poor on money lenders and their exploitative terms.
- Banks and NGOs should encourage formation and developing of SHGs through training and empowering.

NABAARD as an apex body of agricultural credit was a pioneer in conceptualising and operational sing SHG-Bank Linkage Programme me as a strategy for delivering financial services to the poor on a sustainable basis. As a part of APRACA Action Research Project, it funded a project on "Savings and Credit Management of Self Help Groups" of an NGO Mysore Resettlement and Development Agency (MYRADA) in 1987. The research project yielded useful insights into aspects like dynamics of group formation, saving deposit potential, credit delivery mechanism, and group guarantee as collateral and repayment performance. Encouraged by the results of Action Research Project, NABARD in1988-89, undertook a survey of 43 NGOs spread over 11 states in India to study the functioning of SHGs and possibilities of SHG-Bank linkage.

Based on the findings of the studies in 1991-92, NABARD in consultation with ASPRACA and with the approval of RBI launched a pilot project aimed at linking 500 SHGs with the banks across the country. The pilot project was designed as partnership model of three agencies viz, SHGs, banks and NGOs. Under the pilot project 21 commercial banks were reviewed by a working group set up by the RBI in 1994, which led to adoption of SHG-Bank Linkage model for door-step banking for the poor.

In April 1996, the RBI announced the new policy and advised the banks to consider lending to the SHGs as a segment of priority sector advances and integrate it with the mainstream credit operations. Operational guidelines were developed based on the findings of pilot project and approved by RBI centered on group formation, size of group, criteria for selection, mode of linkage with banks, linkage models, and financial and administrative operations of SHGs and dynamics of group lending. As per the operational guidelines SHGs are informal groups formed on voluntary basis to attain certain collective goals both social and economic.

The following are guidelines issued to the banks for SHG-Bank Linkage

- The membership of the SHG group could vary between 10 and 20.
- The group should be inexistence for at least six months with successful savings and credit operations from their own resources.
- The group would be free to decide on selection of borrowers, interest rates and other terms and conditions of loans to members.
- The bank should finance groups as distinct entities, quantum of loan related to savings could be up to 4:1 without any collateral and savings should precede credit in the group.
- Support from voluntary/promotional institutions for group formation, training in group dynamics, accounting, cash management and technical skills should be used.
- The group is expected to meet regularly and all members are expected to participate in decision making.

Three broad models of SHG-Based Linkage propagated are as under;

Model I – SHGs formed and credit linked by banks directly. Bank takes initiatives in forming the groups, motivating and training them till they graduate to become eligible for bank financing Bank acts as both facilitator and financier.

Model II – SHGs formed by NGOs and other agencies and after graduation, become eligible for bank credit linkage. NGO acts as facilitator and bank as financier.

Model III –SHGs formed and financed by NGOs directly with financial assistance from banks NGO acts as facilitator and financial intermediary. Bank lends to NGOs for on lending to the SHGs.

Banks were however given freedom to formulate their own models for extending credit to SHGs. NABARD provided refinance to the banks to the extent of 100per cent of the credit provided by them to SHGs. Banks were expected to provide consolidate credit to supplement the resources of the SHGs to meet the credit needs of their members. The eligible credit line from the bank for a group would be based on the savings of its members with an outer limit of 1:4. There would be no collateral for bank loan. NABARD would also provide promotional and training support to banks for the SHG-Bank linkage programmes.

Progress under SHG-Bank Linkage Programme

Table 1: Progress under SHG-Bank Linkage Programme during 1996-97 to 2008-09

Years	*Number of SHGs Financed during the year (Rs. in lakh)*	*Bank Loan outstanding (Rs. In crore)*
1996-97	0.04	12
1997-98	0.06	24
1998-99	0.19	57
1999-00	0.82	193
2000-01	1.49	481
2001-02	1.98	1026
2002-03	2.56	2049
2003-04	3.62	3904
2004-05	5.39	6898
2005-06	6.21	11398
2006-07	11.06	12396
2007-08	12.28	16999
2008-09	16.09	22680

Sources: NABARD Report.

Initially there was a slow progress in the programme up to 1999 as only 32,995 groups were credit linked during the period 1992 to 1999. Since then the programme has been growing rapidly and the number of SHGs financed increased from 82,000 in 1999-2000 and further from 1,49,000 in 2000-01 to 16.09,000 in 2008-09. During the above period the bank loans disbursed to SHGs also witnessed a sharp increase from Rs12crore in 1996-97 to 193crore in 1999-2000. And further from 481 crore in 2000-01 to 22,680 crore in 2008-09.

According to Economic survey 2009-10 61,21,147 SHGs held savings bank accounts with total savings of Rs.5,545.62crore. The banks had the maximum share of Rs. 35,49,509 SHGs amounting to Rs. 27,72.99 crore. RRBs have saving accounts of 16,28,588 SHGs and saving amount of Rs. 1,989.75 crore. and co-operative banks have saving accounts of 9,43,050 SHGs with savings amount of Rs. 782.88 crore. More than 8.06 crore poor households were associated with banking system under the SHGs Bank Linkage programme. Over 90 per cent of the SHG's linked with banks were found to be exclusive women SHGs most of them were poor and assetles. Thus the SHG movement has proved to be an important instrument for financial inclusion particularly women hitherto by passed by the banking system.

Programme Impact

- Reduced the incidence of poverty through increase in income, and also enabled the poor to build assets and thereby reduce their vulnerability.
- Enabled households that have access to it to spend more on education than nonclient households. Families participating in the programme have reported better.
- school attendance and lower drop out rates.
- Empowered women by enhancing their contribution to household income, increasing the value of their assets and generally by giving them better control over decisions that affect their lives.
- Reduced child mortality, improved maternal health and the ability of the poor to combat disease through better nutrition, housing and health - especially among women and children.
- Contributed to a reduced dependency on informal money lenders and other non institutional sources.
- Facilitated significant research into the provision of financial services for the poor and helped in building "capacity" at the SHG level.
- Finally, it has offered space for different stakeholders to innovate, learn and replicate. As a result, some NGOs have added micro-insurance products to their portfolios, a couple of SHG federations have experimented with undertaking livelihood activities and grain

banks have been successfully built into the SHG model in the Eastern Region. SHGs in some areas have employed local accountants for keeping their books, and IT applications are now being explored by almost all for better management information sytems (MIS), accounting and internal controls.

Conclusion

There are more than 6 crore poor households in India, the existing number of SHGs will have to be increased manifold. The challenge before the SHG movement is not only to increase the number of SHGs to cover all the poor households but also sustain the existing ones to increase the extent of credit to the members substantially to improve standard of living.

Bibliography

1. Report of the committee on financial inclusion 2008, Government of India
2. Eleventh five year plan, Inclusive growth, planning commission, New Delhi.
3. Micro finance and financial inclusion, P.M. Mathew, *Yojana*, Jan. 2008.
4. Financial Inclusion, M.S. Modithaya, Sunrise Publications, New Delhi.
5. Banking sector reforms in India, R.K. Uppal and Rimpi Kaur.

20

Financial Inclusion and the Road Ahead

Navitha Thimmaiah and *Anitha C.V.*

Introduction

Access to finance by the poor and vulnerable groups is a prerequisite for poverty reduction and social cohesion. This has to become an integral part to promote inclusive growth. Financial inclusion denotes delivery of financial services to the most vulnerable and marginalised groups of the society at an affordable cost. The report of the committee on Financial Inclusion in India defines Financial Inclusion as the "process of ensuring access to financial services and timely and adequate credit where needed by vulnerable groups such as weaker sections and low income groups at an affordable cost. Blue book defines Financial Inclusion as "Universal access to a broad range of financial services, at a reasonable cost, provided by a diversity of sound and sustainable institutions. In India the main focus of financial inclusion is to promote sustainable development and generating employment in rural areas for the rural population.

Financial Inclusion concept has gained a greater significance in India due to the inclusive growth strategy of eleventh five year plan (2007-12) and the present twelfth five year plan (2012-17). It is not only the delivery of banking, but also other financial services like insurance, pension, remittance, mutual funds etc at affordable, through market driven costs. The provision of different types of financial services to the excluded population, for ensuring financial inclusion is depicted in Fig. 1.

NSSO data reveal that Out of 19.9 crore households in India, only 6.82 crore households have access to banking services. As far as rural areas are concerned, out of 13.83 crore rural households in India, only 4.16 crore rural households have access to basic banking services. In respect of urban

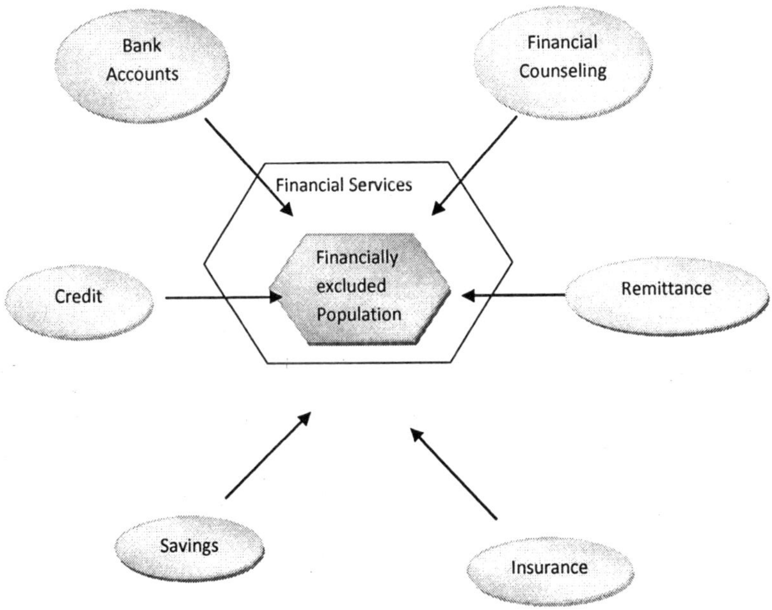

Fig. 1.

Source: Adapted from the Rangarajan Committee report.

areas, only 49.52% of urban households have access to banking services. Over 41% of adult population in India does not have bank account. 45.9 million farmer households in the country (51.4%), out of a total of 89.3 million households do not access credit, either from institutional or non-institutional sources. Further, despite the vast network of bank branches, only 27% of total farm households are indebted to formal sources (of which one-third also borrow from informal sources). Along with this India's central bank, RBI's data shows that as many as 139 districts suffer from massive financial exclusion with the adult population per branch above 20,000 and the unbanked population is higher in the poorer regions of the country, and is the worst in the North-Eastern and Eastern regions. It further states that only about 40% of the country's population has access to banking facilities. 2011 Census figures put the number of households having access to banking at 58.7%.

Thus in an emerging economy like India, financial inclusion becomes a question of both access to financial products and also the knowledge about their fairness and transparency. Many people who fall in the unbanked category are not adequately informed about the nature of the financial services that might be available to them. In this context proper delivery systems and information sharing mechanisms have become important for promoting financial inclusion.

Objectives

1. Highlight the concept of financial inclusion and measures take in the context of Indian economy.
2. Examine the strategies of financial inclusion in other developing countries and its relevance to India; and
3. To focus on best practices and thereby identify factors for effective and penetrative financial inclusion.

Methodology

The Present study is mainly based on secondary data. The required data has been taken from Reserve Bank of India, Indian Institute of Banking and Finance and Updated Master Office Files of Office of Registrar General and Census commissioner, Government of India. Simple tables and charts have been used for analysis purpose.

Literature Review

Nirupam Mehrotra and Puhazhendhi, et.al. Occasional Paper – 48 titled *"Financial Inclusion-An Overview"* attempts to present an overview of financial inclusion in India especially in rural areas and elucidates, discusses issues and concerns relating to financial inclusion in India. Finally, the paper ends with a section on future strategies to enable financial inclusion in a more meaningful manner.

Mahendra Dev's (2006) paper on *"Financial Inclusion: Issues and Challenges"* states that financial inclusion is important for improving the living conditions of poor farmers, rural non-form enterprises and other vulnerable groups. It also emphasis the role of SHGs movement and microfinance institutions in improving the financial inclusion.

In the paper by Laveesh Bhandari and Sumitha Kale (2008) titled *"Digital Payments and Financial Inclusion"* enough emphasis has been given to the present scenario and the paper has brought out the importance of embracing technology as a cost effective measure to improve financial inclusion. Payments through mobile phones have been suggested as the most appropriate measure.

Ramesh Pandi and Selvakumar (2012) paper titled *"Financial Inclusion"* find that penetration of both savings accounts and credit accounts in SCBs both in urban and rural area was low in the North-Eastern, Eastern and Central regions comparing to southern region. So it's recommended the government to take up structural programmes for balanced growth between regions.

In the paper titled "*100% Financial Inclusion : A Challenging Task Ahead*" Reena Agarwal (2007) stated that at present In India the focus of the financial inclusion is confined to ensuring a bare minimum access to a savings bank account without frills, to all. It throws a light on the Measures and consequences of financial inclusion and the major roadblocks towards achieving financial inclusion in India. It concluded by saying that financial inclusion will lead to financial development in our country which will help to accelerate economic growth.

Research Gap

Financial inclusion is an essential pre-condition to building uniform economic development, both spatially and temporally, and ushering in greater economic and social equity. The literature on Financial Inclusion reveals that Financial Inclusion both as a topic and movement has attracted the global attention in the recent years. Many of the works are in the background of Financial Inclusion - Issues and Challenges, Key providers of financial services, Barriers to the financial inclusion, Causes for financial exclusion, Technology role in financial inclusion etc. In this context the present study is just an addition to the existing literature. This tries to identify the factors for effective and penetrative Financial Inclusion, through focus on the measures, best practices, strategies of Financial Inclusion in India and strategies taken in other developing countries for Financial Inclusion.

Need for Financial Inclusion in India

Economic Objectives	*Social and Political Objectives*
Equitable growth	Poverty eradication
Mobilisation of Savings	Sustainable livelihood
Larger market for financial system	Wider inclusion in society
	Effective direction of good programmes

Effective Direction of Good Programmes

In order to achieve above objectives financial inclusion is needed in India.

Measures taken in the context of Indian Economy for Financial Inclusion

Inclusive growth has been a priority of the Government of India (GoI) over the past decade. The policymaking and regulating institutions like Government of India, RBI, IRDA, PFRDA (for micro pensions) have taken several measures and steps to bring the financially excluded people to the fold of the formal banking services. The most important among them are:

Business Correspondent (BC) and Business Facilitator (BF) Models

With the objective of ensuring greater financial inclusion and increasing the outreach of the banking sector, the RBI has permitted banks to use the services of NGOs / SHGs, MFIs and other civil society organisations as intermediaries in providing financial and banking services through the use of BF and BC Models vide their Circular of 25 January 2006.

The BC model allows banks to provide door step delivery of services especially 'cash in - cash out' transactions at a location much closer to the rural population, thus addressing the last mile problem. The list of eligible individuals/entities who can be engaged as BCs is being enlarged from time to time. For-profit companies have also been allowed to be engaged as BCs.

As a result, today in India Banking facilitators and Business Correspondents like *A Little World*, *Fino*, *Integra*, and *Eko* are active in the microfinance sector. They act as facilitators for banks by providing biometric cards to unbanked people and helping them to open new bank accounts in banks like State Bank of India.

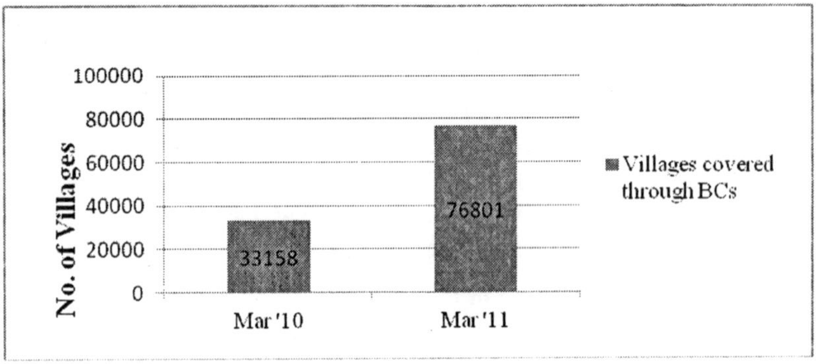

Chart 1: Villages Covered through BCs.

Due to the big push for BCs, no. of villages covered through BCs increased from 33,158 at end March '10 to 76,801 at end March '11 which is more than double and also the no of BCs/ BC Agents employed by banks increased from 33,042 at end Mar'10 to 96828 at end March '12.

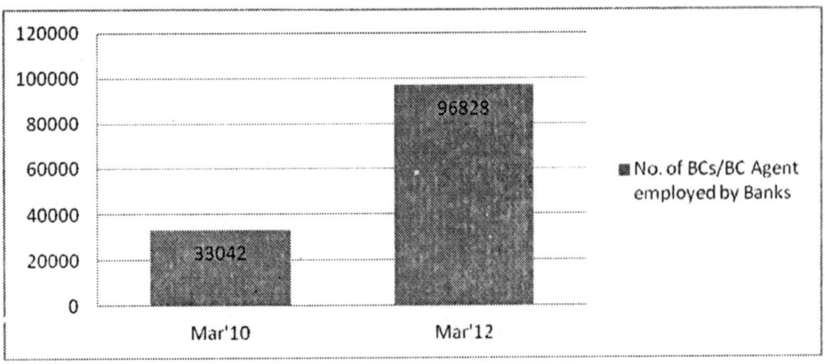

Chart 2: No. of BCs Employed by Banks.

Introduction of zero balance and no frills savings accounts

Introduction of zero balance and no frills savings accounts has a wonderful initiative of the Banks that has made opening of a bank account within reach of the poorest of the poor in the rural areas. A No Frills Account is one for which no minimum balance is insisted upon and for which there are no service charges for not maintaining the minimum balance.

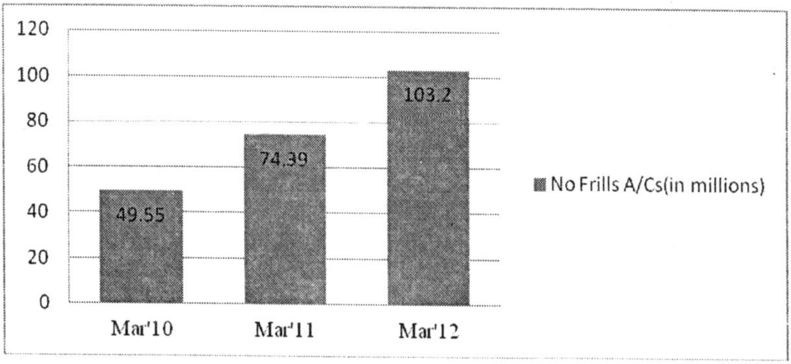

Chart 3: No Frills Account (in millions).

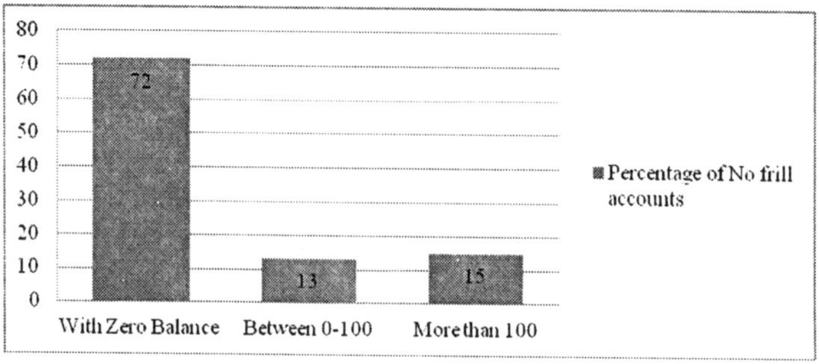

Chart 3: Percentage of No Frill Account.

Number of No Frills Accounts increased from 49.55 million at end March '10 to 74.39 million at end March '11and to 103.2 million at end March '12. But a perusal of sample zero balance and no frills savings accounts reveal that 72% A/Cs have zero or minimum balance even after one year of opening. Only 15% accounts had a balance of more than Rs. 100 thus leaving 85% of the new frill free accounts inoperative.

Overdraft in saving Bank Accounts

Banks were advised to give credit in the form of overdraft on saving bank account to its customer so that in case of small credit need like medical bill, any accidental charges etc. can be met. Because of this number of No frill accounts with overdraft (OD) increased from 0.13 million at end March '10 to 1.52 million at end March '12.

Simplification of Know your Customer (KYC) Procedures

In order to ensure that persons belonging to low income group, both in urban and rural areas do not encounter difficulties in opening bank accounts owing to procedural hassles, the know your customer (KYC) procedures for opening small accounts has been simplified in August 2005. The Reserve Bank has directed banks to make available all printed material used by retail customers in English, Hindi and the concerned regional language. RBI has also mandated that in rural areas the account holders can be identified by local officials.

Financial Inclusion Fund (FIF)

To support "developmental and promotional activities" with a view to securing greater financial inclusion, particularly among weaker sections, low income groups and in backward regions/ hitherto unbanked areas FIF was set up with NABARD with an overall corpus of Rs. 500 crore, with initial funding to be contributed by the GoI, Reserve Bank of India and NABARD in a ratio of 40:40:20.

Financial Inclusion Technology Fund (FITF)

FITF was set up with NABARD to enhance investment in Information Communication Technology (ICT) aimed at promoting financial inclusion, stimulate the transfer of research and technology in financial inclusion, increase the technological absorption capacity of financial service providers/ users and encourage an environment of innovation and cooperation among stakeholders.

Issuing of General Credit Cards (GCCs) and Kisan Credit Cards (KCCs) for Small Deposits and Credit

In order to help farmer's access timely and adequate credit the GoI, RBI and NABARD started Kisan credit card scheme in 1998-99. With a view of providing hassle free credit to customers without insistence on security purpose or end use of credit, banks were allowed to issue general credit cards akin to Kisan Credit Cards (KCC).

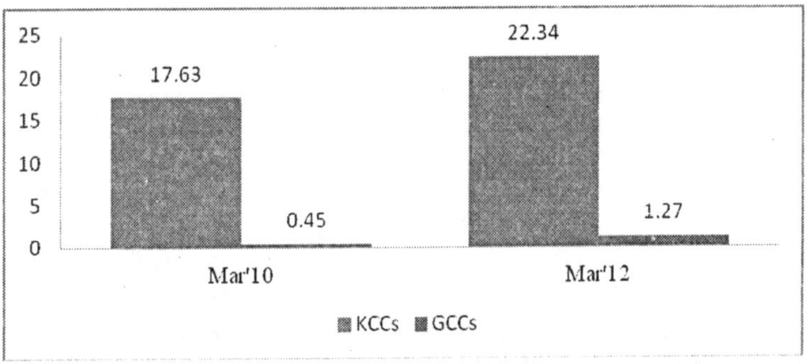

Chart 4: Kisan Credit Card and General Credit Card.

No of KCCs/GCCs increased from 18.08 million at end March '10 to 23.61 million at end March '12.

Removing usage Fee on ATMs for use of other Bank ATMs

Charges for using an ATM of another bank generally discouraged the customer from using the ATMs of other banks. Now there is more utilisation of the installed ATMs and it has also helped the customers from frequent unserviceability of the ATMs.

Setting of Biometric ATMs in Rural Areas for Catering to Illiterate Customers

RBI took a step ahead in order to include the rural illiterates in to the fold of financial inclusion by setting of Biometric ATMs in rural areas. Where Customers no longer have to rely on signatures or filling out documents - they can simply provide their fingerprints to authenticate themselves and access their accounts through specialised biometric teller machines (BTMs).

Pricing has been made free: Banks have been given the freedom to price their advances.

Opening of Branches in Unbanked Rural Centers

To improve banking penetration and financial inclusion rapidly in rural areas, according to the Monetary Policy Statement – April 2011 banks have been mandated to allocate at least 25 per cent of the total number of branches to be opened during a year in unbanked rural centres.

Use of Technology

Recognising that technology has the potential to address the issues of outreach and credit delivery in rural and remote areas in a viable manner, banks have been advised to make effective use of information and communications technology (ICT), to provide doorstep banking services through the BC model where the accounts can be operated by even illiterate customers by using biometrics, thus ensuring the security of transactions and enhancing confidence in the banking system.

Adoption of EBT (Electronic Benefit Transfer)

Banks have been advised to implement EBT by leveraging ICT-based banking through BCs to transfer social benefits electronically to the bank account of the beneficiary and deliver government benefits to the doorstep of the beneficiary, thus reducing dependence on cash andlowering transaction costs.

Promoting Financial Literacy

1. RBI has launched the project titled Project Financial Literacy with a objective of disseminate information regarding the central bank and

general banking concepts to various target groups, such as, school and college going children, women, rural and urban poor, defence personnel and senior citizens.

2. RBI advised to states and union territories to set up Financial Literacy and Counseling Centres (FLCC) in order to provide free financial literacy/education and credit counseling to people in rural and urban areas.
3. It also launched a site called "financial education" on November 14, 2007 commemorating the Children's Day with a aim of teaching basics of banking, finance and central banking to children in different age groups.
4. Recently, the Reserve Bank launched *'RBI Young Scholars Award'* Scheme amongst students undergoing undergraduate studies to generate interest in and create awareness about the banking sector and the Reserve Bank. Under the scheme, up to 150 young scholars would be selected through country-wide competitive examination and awarded scholarships to work on short duration projects at Reserve Bank.
5. A multilingual website in 13 Indian languages on all matters concerned to banking and the common man has been launched by the Reserve Bank on June 18, 2007.
6. RBI recommended for the Establishment of *Financial Stability and Development Council* to institutionalise the mechanism for maintaining financial stability.

National Rural Financial Inclusion Plan (NRFIP)

GOI thinking to set up of a mission mode with a target of providing access to comprehensive financial services to at least 50 per cent (55.77 million) of the excluded rural households by 2012 and the remaining by 2015 through rural/semi-urban branches of Commercial Banks and Regional Rural Banks.

Other Measures

- Canara Bank has a MoU with Government of Karnataka for implementation of Smart Card Technology for payment of NREGP wages and Social Security Pension in three districts namely, Bellary, Gulbarga and Chitradurga. It has installed *Bio Metric Voice enabled ATM* in sixteen semi urban locations all over the country.
- Banks have been mandated to open intermediary brick and mortar structure between the base branch and customer locations, which will lead to efficiency in cash management, documentation, and redressal of customer grievances and close supervision of BC operations.
- The corporation Bank adopted a branchless banking model in select

locations in four Southern States using a small Point of Transaction (POT) device developed by two local vendors using a bouquet of locally available ICT applications.

- GoI launched a programme named 'Swabhimaan' in February 2011, which aims at providing branch-less banking through the use of technology. The vision for this programme is social application of modern technology. Banks provide basic services including deposits, withdrawals and remittances using the services of *Business Correspondents*. This initiative also enables Government subsidies and social security benefits to now be directly credited to the accounts of the beneficiaries so that they could draw the money from the Business Correspondents also known as *Bank Saathi* in their village itself.
- The government has set a target of providing banking facilities to habitations having population of more than 2,000 by March, 2012.
- RBI advised banks to formulate a board approved Financial Inclusion Plan (FIP) for three years up to March 2013.

Upcoming Measures

- RBI recommended a combination of Brick-and-Mortar structure with Click-and-Mouse technology in extending financial inclusion especially in geographically dispersed areas.
- Multi-channel approach (Handheld devices, mobiles, cards, Micro-ATMs, Branches, Kiosks, etc.)
- Indian Bank will be opening 1,525 Ultra Small Branches comprising one clerk, one laptop and one Rural Development officer.
- The government decided to set up Rs. 800-crore fund to encourage banks to reach out to the financially excluded population and to compensate banks for costs incurred on providing no frills accounts in rural areas and other expenses incurred in reaching credit to unbanked areas. The new fund aims to bridge the viability gap in bank's arrangement for setting up branches in rural areas and also appointing business correspondents.
- The postal department put a proposal of Setting up a 'National Bank of India Post' before the GoI and RBI. It also took a step to install the ATMs on the premises of branch offices and thereby facilitate their saving account holders. Initially, the ATMs services will be available only at the post office ATMs but the department is mulling to extend its services at other ATMs too. DoP also making attempts to seek permission from the Reserve Bank of India to allow the dept to grant small ticket finances in rural areas.
- The committee on Financial inclusion has recommended that the

Government should constitute a National Mission on Financial Inclusion (NaMFI) comprising representatives of all stakeholders for suggesting the overall policy changes required and supporting stakeholders in the domain of public, private and NGOs sectors in undertaking promotional initiatives.

Best Practices on Financial Inclusion in India

Following are some of the best practices which have led to successful implementation of financial inclusion projects/initiatives.

Karnataka: Bellary- Pragathi Gramin Bank (Sponsor: Canara Bank)

Under this bank 628 villages were covered with 100 per cent financial inclusion. 8,26,173 families of SHG members were financially included. Two out of seven districts served by the bank have 100 per cent inclusion.

Gulbarga District – MGNREGA : The district has a population of 31.30 lakhs. There are 337 gram panchayts and 1363 villages. The total number of households is 3.89 lakhs out of which 2.15 lakhs households have been issued Job Cards under NREGA. 3000 works have been taken up during the 2007-08 as against 3259 works taken up in 2006-07. Till 2008, 62,313 accounts in post offices, 157,687 in commercial banks and 17,946 accounts in Co-operative banks have been opened. Almost 90 villages have banks and 752 villages have banks within 5 Km (51.17%), whereas 345 villages have banks within 5-19 km (25.97%).

Andhra Pradesh: East Godawari District MGNREGA

In East Godawari District the State Department of Rural Development and Department of Posts, A.P. Circle has entered into MoU for payment of wages through Post Office Saving Account. 4,17,154 postal saving accounts have been opened against 3.5 lakh persons reporting for NREGS works. The Programme Officers generate wage payment orders and issue cheques and hand them over to sub post masters every Monday. They also facilitate the sub post masters and branch post masters in receiving the cash. Every Friday the wage seekers withdraw amount from their postal accounts. Since inception, 77.2% of payments are being made within 15 days of closer of Muster Rolls.

Warangal District- Social Security Pension and REGS

Andhra Pradesh Government has embarked on a pilot project with six banks, viz., SBI, SBH, Andhra Bank, Union Bank, UTI Bank and AP Grameena Vikas Bank, to make payments of Social Security Pensions and AP Rural Employment Guarantee Scheme benefits to 50,000 beneficiaries in six Mandals of Warangal district through the use of business correspondents and contact less smart card/mobile technology. The state proposes to scale up the project to cover the nearly five million beneficiaries of the entire state in due course. The state has signed an MOU with banks and Institute for

Development and Research in Banking Technology (IDRBT) for the purpose. The state is also meeting the major portion of cost of the smart cards and also of the other devices used in the project.

Jharkhand: Dumka District – Payment of Wages

In Dumka District, payment of wages is made through Banks. On the basis of corrected Muster Rolls, cheques are transferred to respective banks. For smooth payment, accounts have been opened by the all the agencies in almost all the bank branches so that labourers get payments on the same day without any delay. District administration has also developed a system to ensure smooth payment through Post Office. Muster Rolls are collected and advice prepared accordingly. Fund assessment is made from particular day from each post office and the same amount is deposited in cash in the respective branch post office. A specific day is fixed for group of labourers for a particular group of schemes for wages payment through post office. Prior information is given to the labourers about the time and date of payment for a particular post office. On that particular day wages payment is ensured in the presence of respective Panchayat Sewak/ Rojgar Sewak/ Junior Engineer/Supervisor, etc.

Maharastra: Mumbai - Application of Core Banking Solution

Dharavi, Asia's largest slum is inhabited by lakhs of migrant labour from Tamil Nadu who do not have bank accounts. After the KYC norms (Know Your Costumer) were rationalised to enable opening of 'No Frills' Accounts, Indian Bank has opened a Core Banking branch in Dharavi Slums. The KYC of migrant labour can also be done at the home district in Tamil Nadu. As the bank has branches at the places from where the migrant labour has come, remittances to and fro have become very easy as they are just transfers between the accounts of the bank. Thus, the urban financially excluded have been given banking access and now it is found that many of the account holders who were otherwise spending on consumption have started saving. Thus, the core banking solution in banks become as a powerful remittance tool for the migrant labour.

Credit Counseling Initiatives

The counselling centres in the state of Maharashtra viz., 'ABHAY' counselling centre (an initiative of Bank of India); Disha Trust (an initiative of ICICI Bank Ltd.) and Grameen Paramarsh Kendras (an initiative of Bank of Baroda) showed a tremendous work by providing advices and guidance to the consumers problems arising out of multiple credit cards, personal loans, housing loans and loans from societies through a face to face meeting, over telephone, email, or by means of letters. Thus they help them to take up with the banks concerned for rescheduling/restructuring of loans.

Khopi Village ICT Model

The Khopi Village, Pune earned the distinction of becoming the first village in Maharashtra State to become 100% ICT Model Village as the Velu Branch, the base branch has confirmed that as on October 20, 2011, it has issued 279 bio-metric smart cards as against 242 households in the village.

Quick Look on the Developing Countries Strategies

Indonesia has long been a leader in microfinance and more recently in financial inclusion. Given the central importance of financial inclusion to the government's approach to poverty reduction, the recognition of the role of non bank financial institutions, and the need for coordination of different stakeholders, the Government of Indonesia assigned the Vice President's Office to coordinate with other line ministries and in close consultation with the bank of Indonesia. It led the formulation of a national strategy for financial inclusion: financial education, financial eligibility, supporting policies and regulations, intermediation facilities, and channelling and distribution.

In the Philippines, the national strategy has provided repeated opportunities to promote market oriented approaches to microfinance. Most recently in march 2011, President Benigno S.C. Aquino III used the 1998 national microfinance strategy as justification to end the practice of government direct lending by stating "we will work to institutionalise the national strategy for microfinance that was formulated in 1998. We will also make sure that microcredit will not be used as a tool for political patronage."

In Liberia, in part because key ministries were not involved at the highest level, but only at the technical level, the national strategy failed to be sufficiently owned by the government. As a result, it was not integrated into other national plans, nor was it put forward to key funders as a national priority.

In Madagascar, a difficult context in which to work has only become more difficult. High poverty rates, poor infrastructure, political instability, and limited institutional capacity have stalled the process of strategy implementation. There is an opportunity for a credible leader to step forward to take charge of the process. A quick update of the diagnostic and strategy, and a restructuring of the implementation team might be enough to get the process restarted.

In 2000, the central Bank of Brazil, in the face of mounting costs from processing of social transfer payments, began allowing banks to outsource some types of transaction processing to third party agents such as stores, post offices and pharmacies. Due to this 19 million new accounts opened just in four years.

Dakar declaration, June 2006: Over 300 senior stakeholders in Africa-donors, policymakers, and practitioners issued a declaration that included the following: 1. Reaffirm commitment to financial inclusion and to strengthening financial sectors in Africa by means of multi-stakeholders, participatory process that are nationally owned and managed and that include all financial sector stakeholders in the design and implementation of national or regional strategies for inclusive finance. 2. Highlight the fact that national strategy for building inclusive financial sectors in Africa should (a) Be flexible in their design, objectives, and implementation, (b) Take into account the unique local conditions existing in each country or region. (c) Consider and utilise lessons learned and best practices from countries around the world where national and regional strategies have been implemented and (d) If possible be included in broader financial sector strategies.

Future Options/Effective Factors

The BC model may not be commercially viable at the initial stage due to high transaction costs for banks and customers, the appropriate use of technology can help in reducing this. The need is to develop and implement scalable, platform-independent technology solutions which, if implemented on a large scale, will bring down the high cost of operation. Appropriate and effective technology, thus, holds the key for financial inclusion to take place on an accelerated scale. The BCs, who are the first level of contact for customers, have to be compensated adequately so that they too see this as a business opportunity.

Government should include all the key ministries and all the stake holders in the process of financial inclusion (Liberia case). It is important that adequate infrastructure such as digital and physical connectivity, uninterrupted power supply, etc. should be provided properly. The micro-credit and the Self Help Group movements are in their infancy and they still need to gather force, so the government should take some action which will strengthen the movement. Banks should institute systems of reward and recognition for personnel initiating, ideating, innovating and successfully executing new products and services in the rural areas. There is a need of collaboration and coordination across the 3 pillar or agencies of financial inclusion.

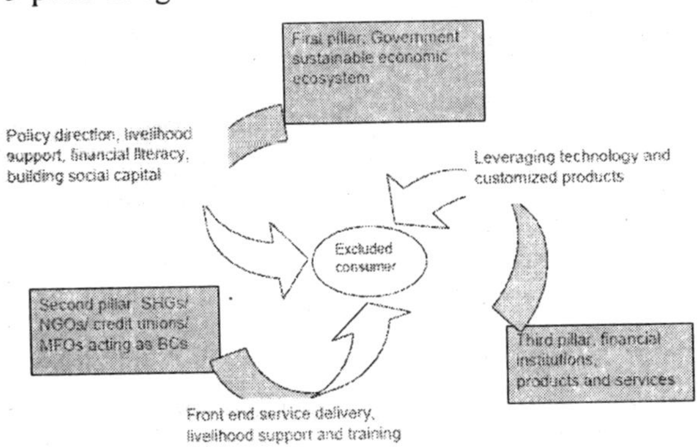

Fig. 2: Three Pillars of Financial Inclusion in India.

Financial Inclusion India is mainly aimed at bringing the rural farmers and vulnerable groups in to the fold of financial inclusion. This group contains more than 50% of illiterates, so the Government should take a serious action towards creating awareness among them with suitable means. Because once the fallacy is removed from the minds of the general public, they automatically will join the mainstream.

Concerted and structured effort by all stakeholders like RBI, Other sectoral regulators like SEBI, IRDA, PFRDA, etc., NABARD, Banks, Governments, Civil Societies, NGOs, etc. are enssential.

Adoption of multi-sector strategy like including Industry sector, retail sector, Banking, Government etc. in the process of financial inclusion. Aligning of financial inclusion strategy with other key national goals like poverty reduction, food security, etc., so that all work in tandem towards achievement of desired goals. Government and RBI should encourage the Banks in Infrastructure sharing amongst banks and other organisations which will help in lowering the operating cost and thus the cost benefit can be transferred to customers. It is evident from the literature that the hilly areas and rural areas are still exterior from financial inclusion process therefore GOI should give attention towards those areas. According to the FIndex 2012 report, prominent barrier to use formal bank accounts (globally) is not the absence of ultra low cost technology or absence of identification documents but having "not enough money" to save. In this regard GoI should take some measures to increase the capacity of saving of the people and also saving habits among them.

Conclusion

To sum up, Financial Inclusion is not an end but means to poverty reduction and economic growth. It is the road which India needs to travel towards becoming a global player. An inclusive growth will act as a source of empowerment and allow people to participate more effectively in the economic and social process. Financial access will also attract global market players to our country that will result in increasing employment and business opportunities. The measures taken by Government of India and RBI like BCs and BFs model, introduction of No frills account, biometric ATMs etc doing a wonderful work in bringing the financially excluded people to the fold of the formal banking services. But still 100% financial Inclusion is not achieved in India. In this regard the study found that a concerted and structured effort by all stakeholders, multi-sector strategy and the ICT are necessary in order to achieve 100% financial inclusion in India.

References

1. Presentation by Dr. K.C. Chakrabarty, Deputy Governor RBI, 26th Skoch Summit Mumbai, June 2, 2011.

2. Madurai, Karthikeyan Kothandaraman, *"Financial Inclusion in India"* (January 22, 2011).
3. Ramachandran, Dr Ramakrishnan, *"BFSI: Best Practices in Financial Inclusion"* (March 19, 2010). 22nd SKOCH Summit, 2010.
4. RBI Monthly Bulletin, May 2012.
5. Global Microcredit Summit, commissioned workshop paper, Nov. 14th-17th, 2011,Valladoid, Spain.
6. RBI, 2008, *"Financial Literacy and Credit Counselling Centres"*.
7. Report of the committee on Financial Inclusion, January 2008.
8. Gadewar A U (2007) Financial Inclusion: Issues and Challenges - Vinimaya January-March 2007 Vol. XXVII No. 4.
9. http://www.nabard.org/fileupload/DataBank/OccasionalPapers/OccasionalPapersonFinancialInclusion_080509.pdf.
10. http://hdl.handle.net/2259/485.
11. http://ssrn.com/abstract=1751020.
12. http://www.jstor.org/stable/4418799.
13. http://knowledge.nrega.net/744/2/Best_Practices_on_Financial_Inclusion_in_NREGA.pdf.
14. http://dx.doi.org/10.2139/ssrn.1745467.
15. http://articles.economictimes.indiatimes.com/2012-08-26/news/33402454_1_indian-bank-chairman-rural-banks-branches-in-rural-areas.
16. http://articles.economictimes.indiatimes.com/keyword/financial-inclusion.
17. http://articles.economictimes.indiatimes.com/2010-1014/news/27620251_1_financial- literacy-financial-inclusion-technology-fund-business-correspondents.

FIPs-Achievements at Glance

Particulars	*Year ended March 10*	*Year ended March 12*	*Progress- April 10 - March 12*
No. of BCs/BC Agents Deployed	33042	96828	63786
Banking Outlets through Branches	21475	24701	3226
Banking Outlets through BCs	32684	120355	87671
Banking Outlets-Through other Modes	99	2478	2379
Total Banking Outlets	**54258**	**147534**	**93276**
No Frill A/Cs (No. in Millions)	49.33	103.21	53.88
Overdraft- No Frill A/Cs (No. in Millions)	0.13	1.52	1.39
BC- ICT Based A/Cs (No. in Millions)	12.54	52.07	39.53
EBT A/Cs-through BCs (No. in Millions)	7.48	21.76	14.28
KCC (No. in Millions)	17.63	22.34	4.71
GCC (No. in Millions)	.45	1.27	.82

Source: Reserve Bank of India Records, June 8, 2012, Based on FIPs submitted by Banks.

21

Financial Inclusion and Inclusive Growth: A Case Study of Gandhian Model of Development Communication

B.P. Mahesh Chandra Guru, C.K. Puttaswamy* and *Nagaraju

Introduction

Several international conferences and publications have highlighted the need for inclusive growth and development across the globe over a period of time. The national constitutions have also emphasised the need for inclusive growth and development of women and weaker sections of the society across the globe. The Millennium Development Goals of U.N. have envisaged growth with equity in general and inclusive development of the disadvantaged sections of the society in particular. Gandhi was a great champion of inclusive growth and development of mankind in India. He had contributed the 'Sarvodaya Model of Development' which facilitates distributive justice in economy on humanitarian grounds. Development communication came to the Third World Countries in the 1960s as an important component of the development planning.

The quest for 'New Paradigm' in both development and communication has become a mission for academics as well as practitioners who are concerned about the inclusive growth and development of the mankind regardless of region, religion, caste, colour, creed and so on. A new upward movement for inclusive development has begun with the decentralisation of democratic system in Indian Republic on the basis of Gandhian ideology. The present article evaluates the Gandhian model of development communication which is widely regarded as the alternative paradigm of development communication in the world from the points of view of financial inclusion and inclusive growth.

Concept of Development

Development is the watchword of twenty first century planners in India and other developing nations. Every country perceives development in unmistakable terms as an irreversible process to maintain and raise the living standards of its people. Practically it is impossible to reach a consensus on a working definition of development. The western capitalist model of development aims to promote the positive and beneficial side of modern capitalism with emphasis focused on hedonism, consumption and individualism. There is continuous and unabated promotion of western type of political economy of capitalism which has expanded the industrial system and created a consumer society.

The stress was on economic development since almost all new born nations sought rapid strides in poverty alleviation after World War II. The western prescription of urbanisation, industrialisation, mechanisation, mobility, literacy, participation and empathy was embedded in what is called as the 'dominant paradigm of development'. This model has led to increasing concentration of resources, powers and privileges in the hands of a few which has resulted in high level of socio-economic inequity in India and other developing nations.

This fixation with the 'Dominant Paradigm' in the fifties and sixties slowly gave way for a critical evaluation of its efficiency and relevance. Today in all developing countries, development is considered to be a subject of special concern. The economic approach is being replaced with social, political and cultural matrix which emphasizes a new set of indicators of development. Mao, Gandhi, Schumacher, Beltran, Tehranian, Gunnar Myrdal, Amartya Sen et al questioned the wisdom behind the wholesale transfer and application of western model for the development of Third World Countries, where resource-man equation is very adverse and population is increasing very fast.

The inequalities created by material development must be compensated by meeting the social needs of the people and ensuring equality of opportunity over a wide range of human activity. The western model does not fit into the ground realities and requirements especially in the under-developed world. This model is often described as ethnocentric. India is basically a rural, agrarian and developing society. Indeed, this is true for the rural population of the Third World Countries as a whole. Even after six decades of national independence and planning, basic needs and infrastructural development sectors of our economy have remained neglected and malnourished since the policy makers have not understood the concept of the development which suits the Indian legacy, culture and context. National development in which the upward movement of the entire social system as a critical approach is inescapable in India.

"An entirely new orientation to development in which education as a critical input is inescapable. If education is to play a mediating role in social transformation, it must fulfill two conditions, namely (a) it must ensure people's confidence through democratic decentralisation and (b) it must be part of general plan for social development. Without an efficient and trusted mediating force and a delivery system resources are likely to go waste, leakages created, corruption encouraged and thus the objectives of development defeated," observes Njoku E. Awa (1989).

Concept of Development Communication

Development communication came to the Third World Countries in the 1960s as an important component of the development package. The pioneering research and writings of Daniel Lerner, Lucien Pye, Willbur Schramm et al., helped to launch the belief that systematic communication support to development programmes would brighten the prospects of the people of the Third World Countries. The creation of a climate suitable for increased production and serving as a prime mover in the economy was the essence of the ideology of development communication. Practically, all developing countries have accepted communication as an integral part of development planning.

A commonly used definition of development communication is the one given by Nora C. Quebral (1973) which reads: "Development communication is the art and science of human communication applied to the speedy transformation of a country from poverty to a dynamic state of economic growth that makes possible greater economic and social equality and the larger fulfillment of the human potential". While the Quebral definition remains a salient one, more recent definition reflect the thinking which has taken place over the past decade.

Romeo H. Gecolea (1982) observes: "Development Support Communication (DSC) may be broadly defined as an organisation's planned use of information and communication resources to help achieve its goals. Communication resources include manpower, money, facilities and equipment, communication materials and media. The organisations referred to are those whose chief objectives is to deliver development oriented services in rural areas i.e., services intended to improve socio-economic conditions among rural families. These organisations or agencies would typically possess a network of field workers who undertake educational or motivational activities as part of their duties. The fields they deal with could be in agriculture, rural health, fisheries, family planning, forestry, farm credit, rural industries and other concerns".

The Food and Agriculture Organisation (1969) more specifically defines development communication as the planned and systematic use of communication, through interpersonal and mass communication channels:

1. To collect and change information among all those concerned in planning a development initiative, with the aim of reaching a consensus on the development problems being faced and the options for their solution;
2. To mobilise people for development action, and to assist in solving problems and misunderstandings that may arise during project implementation;
3. To enhance the pedagogical and communication skills of development agents (at all levels) so that they may dialogue more effectively with their audiences;
4. And last, but by no means least, to apply communication technology to training and extension programmes, particularly at the grassroots level, in order to improve their quality and impact.

Since scholars use the terms 'development communications' and 'development support communication' interchangeable while others make a distinction between the two terms.

B.P. Mahesh Chandra Guru (1997) defines: "Development communication provides a conceptual and practical framework which is meant for accelerating the process of development in all spheres of human life in developing country settings. It broadly includes the integration of planned, organised and specific communication package into development planning and programme implementation at grassroots level. It is an approach to development that facilitates the flow of development education from and among beneficiaries, researchers, policy, administrators and extension personnel".

Scholars have defined all development-oriented information, education, motivation and persuasion activities of governmental, non-governmental and media organisations as development communication or development support communication. Broadly speaking, all development support communication programmes constitute the practice of development communication.

Communication and Development: Old and New Paradigms

The dissolution of the old colonial empires was brought about after the World War II. The scholars, scientists, technocrats and the leaders of the Asia, Africa, Latin America and Middle Eastern Countries explored alternative political alignments and economic arrangements. Some countries continued as the loyal members of the western block and many other countries were united under Non-Aligned Movement forum. The Third World Countries started implementing special programmes for the uplift of the rural people, tribals, women and weaker sections of the society on a priority basis. The governments invested in communications sector for the sake of popularising the beneficial effects of various welfare programmes and development projects. A considerable body of writing has developed over the years on socio-economic, political, cultural, technological and ethical issues in development and communication which can be classified broadly into two schools of thought, namely, a) 'Old Paradigm' and b) 'New Paradigm'.

Old Paradigm of Communication and Development

The western model was used to solve the backwardness of the Less Developed Countries (LDC) in the 1950s and 1960s. This was also called the 'dominant paradigm'. The advocates of this model were Daniel Lerner, Wilbur Scharamm, Rogers, Habermann et al.

Dannel Lerner (1958) argued: "The western model of modernisation exhibits certain components and sequences whose relevance is global. Everywhere for example, increasing urbanisation has tended to raise literacy raising literacy has tended to increase media exposure, increasing media exposure has gone with wider economic participation (per capita income) and political participation (voting). The model evolved in the west is a historic fact. The same basic model reappears in virtually all modernising societies on all continents of the world regardless of variation in race, colour, creed". Daniel Lerner described mass media as magic multipliers.

Wilbur Schramm (1964) had emphasised the need for economic development through progress in the industrial sector and sought to achieve national development through industrial development, urban development and market oriented economy. Wilbur Schramm stated that communication is a critical factor in the process of development.

Everett M. Rogers (1971) had perceived that: "Development is a type of social change in which new ideas are introduced into a social system in order to produce higher per capita incomes and levels of living through more modern production methods and improved social organisation". Rogers presented the 'diffusion model' that attempted to spread ideas or innovations across space and time.

New Paradigm of Communication and Development for Inclusive Growth

By the mid 1960s the belief had developed into a fairly coherent doctrine and was formalised at a seminar convened by the East West Centre in Honolulu, Hawali in 1964. The central tenets of the ideology of development communication were reduced to certain propositions, namely, (i) development is essentially the maximising of the goods and services, in a given society, (ii) the developing world is distinguished from the developed world, inter-alia, by the paucity of these goods and services, (iii) the people of the developing world should abandon their traditional ways and habits and follow the path of the developed world; and (iv) the quickest and most effective way of bringing about new consciousness among people was the application of technology-based communication.

Many scholars including Romero Beltran, Diaz Bordenave, Reyes Matta et al., led the attack in the 1970s on the ideology put forth by Daniel Lerner, Lucien Pye, Wilbur Schramm and Rogers on certain grounds, namely (i) development is not merely a quantitative or linear process. It should be based on fair and just distribution of the resources among people; (ii) the principal impediment to development within the Third World Countries was not the lack of communication but the prevalence of inequitable economic, social and political structures, both national and inter-national; (iii) the mass communication envisioned by Lerner and other champions of dominant paradigm only tended to replicate individualism and acquisitiveness of capitalist societies in the Third World; and (iv) the research data on which the champions of the dominant paradigm had constructed their development ideology did not reflect the realities and requirements of the Third World Countries.

Freire (1972) proposed a 'pedagogy of the oppressed' on the basis of (1) faith in people's ability to learn, to change and to liberate themselves from oppressive conditions of ignorance, poverty and exploitation; (2) direct contact of the learners with their own reality and its problems and analysis of the constraints imposed on them by social structure and official ideology; (3) elimination of differences between educator the educatee in so far as both are learners; (4) free dialogue; and participation in liberating action. Freire, indeed, focused his attention on alternative communication based on the needs of the beneficiaries and people in the Third World Countries.

Schumacher (1973) argues: "The poor of the world could not be helped by mass production, only through production by the masses". He prescribed a simple, cheap and free technology as against super-technology which has converted man into a slave deliberately". He also proposed intermediate technology based on the criteria of smallness, simplicity, capital cheapness and non-violence as an alternative in economic development. He indeed, thought of community – based, decentralised, localised and people-oriented communication approaches to development in the backward countries.

Kleinjans (1976) highlighted the human side of communication and development thus: "Science and technology can be borrowed, imported and adapted from abroad. But ultimately creatively from within is the only answer. For development, essentially is not a matter of technology or GNP, but the growth of a new consciousness, the movement of the human mind, the uplifting of the human spirit, the infusion of human confidence". Kleinjans has aptly concluded that the chief focus of development should be the attainment of collective welfare and not the multiplication of wealth of a few people.

Diaz Bordenave (1977) a Latin American champion of 'New Paradigm' remarked: "Media are more accessible to the participation of rural populations and government agents, technocrats and elites are learning to become receivers, the content of the messages is more relevant to rural people's problems and needs".

Sultana Krippendorf (1979) has written one of the most insightful analyses of the communication and development paradigm. She added that the western model assumed a passive, inert audience in the Third World Countries. According to her, the model made a number of wrong assumptions among which the Third World Countries were essentially folk societies with a homogeneous social base and low levels of economic aspirations.

Majid Tehranian (1979) who identified the periodic imbalance between our scientific and technological knowledge and moral and spiritual advances defined development as social learning and dialogue. He preferred a synthesis of moral, spiritual and cultural factors with economic development. He argues: "If theories and strategies of social development were torn away from the spiritual and cultural foundations of human life as they had increasingly been in an over-technocratic, over-programmed world we would run the risk of social decay and self-destruction". Tehranian has rightly identified the threats associated with the western model of development which was based on materialism. He has called upon the policy makers in the East to take into account vital factors and human values such as cultural ethos, spiritually, collective welfare and social justice while designing programmes for national development.

John Lent (1982) who also observed changes in the media scenario in the Third World Countries consequent on the wider acceptance of 'New Paradigm' records: "Out of the body of conceptualisation came a number of practical alternatives to older communication and development models, such as the ruralisation of bigger, formal media, the use of folk media and inter-personal communication patterns, the implementation of smaller media technology and reopening ancient lines of communication between Third World Nations".

Srinivas Melkote (1983) an Asian scholar writes: "The present process of development has under-developed a majority of individuals and groups especially in the Third World Countries".

Rajani Kothari (1984) has strongly argued for changing communication perspectives in the 1990s: "It (development communication) has to be thought of not as a specialised concern, but as part and parcel of the struggle for human liberation, freedom and justice, strengthening the struggles of communities and cultures, of national entities that are thought to be marginalised, and of already marginalised peoples within these and other societies. It should be communications that expose the hypocrisy of the rhetoric in international forums, which is in direct contrast to the same elites behavior in their own societies. Communication should be a process that contains the forces of backlash and promotes the forces of transformation and survival".

Vilanilam (1985) another prominent Asian scholar observes: "Today we have many buildings but millions still dwell on pavements. There is remarkable achievement in food production but millions are still left without proper food, cloth, etc. Production is also more but millions are still inadequately clothed; despite growth in number of schools millions remain unlettered. So mere growth without distribution is a curse rather than blessing. Because in a multi-tiered structure like ours the benefits of all plans and projects ought to go into the very same sectors where the benefits of the post efforts at growth had already accumulated".

Charles Okgbo (1985) an African scholar has expressed his disillusionment over the scenario of development communication in Africa thus: "Thus post World War II period saw the world in an optimistic mood about the prospects for the economic take off of new and developing nations. The media were also seen as an important stimulants in the expected development programmes. In a majority of the developing countries, however, development falls short of projections inspite of the handsome investment in modern media. The best that could be said was that some kinds of communication went with some kinds of development in some social situations".

R. Samarajiva (1985) noted: "One is reminded of the most significant change, that is, that communication and development was once the study of Third World peoples and societies by western researches for western policy purposes. Now, Third World scholars are active in the field".

Vijay Menon (1986) another Asian scholar concludes: "While the concept and practice of development are in a state of transition, and past notions do not reflect the reality and potential of the contemporary scene, policy makers and practitioners continue to operate on the basis of outdated and inappropriate assumptions. There is an urgent need to reconceptualise the meanings of development and communication and their relationship with each other. There is also need for development and communication theory to be systematically linked with economic theory and patterns of cultural change".

Fuglesang (1986) another advocate of 'New Paradigm' went to the extent of denouncing the role of mass media in social change and economic development of the people in the Third World in view of their elitist approaches and contents which benefited very few people. Fuglesang and Chandler lamented thus: "mass media have proved to be a string of rattling tin cans offering disinformation, educational irrelevance and noisy nothingness".

Nair and White (1987) further observe: "There is now realisation that the development process in the Third World context requires full participation of the people if there is to be commitment to development decisions. Sharing power through joint decisions making, blending and integrating indigenous and expert knowledge through dialogue are now viewed as more effective ways to seek solutions for micro-level problems. The focus on people's participation, and thinking about how development communication processes support that focus, is the current challenge for development planners and development communication scholars".

Rogers (1993) concludes: "In the 1980s debate about communication and development escalated. The question was whether it is development communication, communication for development, communication support for development or development support communication? This is perhaps a semantic issue, but out of this debate serious thinking of development communication began to turn around the worn out perspectives, ushering in new challenges for conceptualising communication processes, product and communicator roles. The quest for new paradigms in both development and development communication has become a mission for academics as well as practitioners".

Williams (2002) stated that the policy makers and people should think globally and act locally in order to protect local culture, environment and development of the people. The scholar suggested that local developmental interests should not be sacrificed for the sake of globalisation of development in the developing countries.

Servaes (2004) emphasised that communications media could not remain as means of entertainment and advertisement in modern society but should provide adequate education and guidance to the people on the ways and means of achieving national progress.

Nussbaum and Friedrich (2005) argued that educational communication and development communication disciplines have evolved over a period of time as prominent branches of human knowledge and advancement. The scholars have suggested that constant and continuous academic deliberations and scientific evaluations would boost the disciplines concerned all over the world.

Kim (2005) pointed out that grassroots level cultural communication and development support communication were essential in modern society in order to achieve the goals of cultural promotion and grassroots development. The study suggested that different cultural groups demand culture-specific and project-specific communication support in order to facilitate integrated development at the grassroots level on the basis of alternative development communication model.

Sen (2006) observed that in the age of market forces development of the marginalised sections of society was not brought about by the public and private sectors. The scholar pointed out that the attainment of national development should be based on social justice and economic equity in a developing country like India.

Many scholars in Asia, Africa, Latin America, Middle-East and other parts of the under-developed world have seriously thought of alternative approaches to communication and development to overcome the imbalance created by western model and to bring about just communication and development order. According to them, the essence of the ideology of development communication is the creation of a climate suitable for increased production and equitable distribution of goods and services. Development basically requires a fair and judicious distribution of the educational and economic products. The prevalence of inequitable social, economic and political structures is the principal impediment to development within the Third World. Experience has shown that development communication when used without concomitant changes in the structure of society, could lead to the strengthening of the status quo.

Concern for the quality of life, rather than the pursuit of economic goals, became the chief focus of attention of the champions of new paradigm of communication and development. The emphasis was laid on basic needs, infrastructure development, self-reliance, distributive justice, collective welfare, preservation of culture, environment protection, rural development and other vital areas of development. It was widely recognised that there was a need for a new model of development based on human values and perspectives of development that would fit into the requirements of the Third World Countries which shared an altogether different social, economic, political and cultural background. Thus, a new model called 'New Paradigm of Development' emerged on the basis of the philosophies of Freire, Schumacher, Diaz Bordenave, Fuglesang, Tehranian and others.

India has taken clear-cut decisions on the nature of the economic relationship between herself and the developed countries. By and large, success in the communication field has been dependent on the nation's own ability to mobilise its economic and technological resources. The communication media in India-newspapers, magazines, radio, television and film have shown rapid growth in the last 50 years of national independence. However, the mass media in India are urban-centered, urban-biased and elitist-oriented. These class-media have to be converted into the mass media in the true sense of the term. The rural masses have to largely depend on folk media, inter-personal channels and non-government organisations for development communication purposes. The tele-communication media and new communication technologies have been accessible to the rural masses in a commendable way. The Government of India have established Prasar Bharati Corporation which is responsible for controlling and regulating the satellite television channels in order to protect national environment, culture and security.

Gandhian Model of Development Communication

Mahatma Gandhi the great mass communicator and visionary of the twentieth century experimented with all aspects of human life practically. He was indeed, the foremost champion of inclusive growth and development of the mankind economically and otherwise. His model of development namely 'Sarvodaya' gains universal acceptance in the age of globalisation since it aims at facilitating inclusive economic development of the mankind across the globe. In fact, his thoughts in general and development model in particular covered every walk of human life. He strongly believed that India lived in her countryside and the western development model would be catastrophic. He wrote in Young India (1929): "What is the need of India following the path of industrialisation like western people? Western civilisation is urban-centered. It will be easy for small countries like England and Italy to become urbanised. It would be suitable for countries like America having less population. But India having a vast rural population and ancient traditions need not imitate western model".

Gandhi was also a champion of inclusive development and distributive justice. He had dreamt of Gram Swaraj (rural independence), Gramin Vikas (rural development) Sarvodaya (collective welfare) and Antyodaya (development of the poorest of the poor) as the foundations of national development. He wrote in Harijan (1942): "My idea of village swaraj is that it is a complete republic, independent of its neighbours for its own vital wants, and yet interdependent for many others in which dependence is a necessity. Thus every village's first concern will be to grow its own food crops and cotton for its cloth. It should have a reserve for its cattle, recreation and play ground for adults and children. It will have its own water works ensuring clean water supply. This can be through controlled wells or tanks. Education will be compulsory up to the final basic course. As far as possible, every actively will be conducted on the co-operative basis".

Gandhi drew his model from Bhagavadgita, Upanishads and other Indian religious scriptures and folk culture. He created a new style of communicating with the masses and eventually inducted them into the political culture. He also created significant meanings in his messages and conveyed a new egalitarian ethics for political relationships and mass participation. The meaning conveyed was a product of social activity and the idiom used was an 'individualised symbol' which became a powerful tool for mass communication.

The term 'Ram Raj' was used to project Gandhiji concept of a welfare society. Gandhiji explained it thus: "Ram Raj is the kingdom of righteousness. By Ram Raj I do not mean Hindu Raj. I mean by Ram Raj Divine Raj, the kingdom of god. Other symbolic expressions and idioms, namely Charkha (spinning wheel), Khadder (hand-spun cloth), Daridra Narayan (the poorest of the poor), Harijan (children of god), Satyagraha (struggle for truth and justice), Swadeshi (locally manufactured goods and services), Gram Swaraj (rural independence), Gramin Vikas (rural development), Swavalamban (Self-reliance), etc., were rooted in the socio-cultural experience of the masses and stimulated inter-personal communications.

Gnadhian mode helped influence the attitudes of the people and built a national movement for the attainment of freedom. The channels of communication for the dissemination of his ideas were traditional and inter-personal communication tools such as bhajans (prayer meetings), discourses (public lectures), processions (peace marches), demonstrations (truthful and non-violent opposition), agitations (peaceful and non-violent struggles), etc. He also edited young India, Harijan, Navjeevan and Indian Opinion which brought about tremendous awareness among the masses.

Mass communication does not occur only through the use of big media or new technology especially at the grassroots level in South India and other developing societies. The policy makers must realise that rural South India as well as India needs simple, low-cost, innovative, credible and participatory communication media and approaches which can meet the local needs. Our communication planners have to look into the traditional media of communication, inter-personal channels and non-government organisations which are rooted in the culture of our rural society.

Gandhiji rejected transformation of our higher culture into material culture. His system of communication was rooted in the Indian tradition and needs. He used his model of communication and development to solve the problems of the people very effectively. In view of this, Gandhiji's attempts at public education, organisation and development may be considered a holdover from the past. On the other land, Gandhian Participatory 'Sarvodaya Model of Communication and Development' can be an effective instrument of grassroots development in South India and Indian Republic. The policy makers must give a serious thought to Gandhian model of communication and development and re-design our grassroots communication system toward realising the dreams of Gandhiji such as self-reliance, self-rule, decentralisation of administration, distributive justice, rural development, uplift of the weaker sections, etc.

Conclusion

The poorest countries show no signs of catching up with the developed countries, despite the promised benefits of globalisation, and there are signs that rising inequality is becoming a permanent feature of the world economy. The middle strata of the developing countries, with incomes between 40 per cent and 80 per cent of the average in advanced countries, are thinner today than in the 1970s. Since 1990, growth in the global economy has averaged 2 per cent a year compared with 3 per cent a year in the turbulent 1980s and 5 per cent in the 1950s and 1960s. Growth in 2010 is around 4 per cent. Such a relatively modest rate can solve neither the North's labour market problems nor the South's poverty problems, nor will it allow for the narrowing of the North-South divide. The rules of global free trade have been drawn up in favour of the world's richest countries. Gandhian development ideology which lays emphasis on inclusive development financially and otherwise assumes great significance in the present times in order to bridge the communication and development gap between the advanced and less advanced countries.

Development communication is the premise of progress in our modern society. What is new is the realisation in today's increasingly democratising world, lack of development communication and restraints on the flow of information directly undermine development of every kind. The challenge facing the society today is how to widen the reach of development communication-how to make accessible to people everywhere and how to empower the people in every respect. It is here that the relevance of Gandhian development communication model assumes profound significance from the points of view of inclusive growth and development in India and other developing nations.

Hence long as the development communication system remains divorced from the overall objectives of grassroots development, the process of development will continue to bring about more under-development and the goal of empowerment of beneficiaries would remain unfulfilled. Participation of beneficiaries in the process of development communication planning would lend more authenticity, reliability and credibility. India needs a communication strategy which should be considered as a sub-system of the overall development system. Optimum use of all communication channels in proper combinations can certainly bring about development in the urban and rural areas.

The future agenda for inclusive development and communication at the national, regional and grassroots levels must deal with the process of people's participation in which related processes such as network building, resources allocation, policy making, systematic planning, inter-departmental coordination, integration of media (inter-personal, traditional and modern), effective supervision, responsible motivation, consultative communication, scientific evaluation etc are also addressed in order to revise the 'Dominant Paradigm' of development communication and reverse the process of under-development in India and other developing countries.

References

Awa, Njoku E (1989) Participation and Indigenous Knowledge in Rural Development, *Knowledge, Creation, Diffusion, Utilisation* 10(4):304-316.

Diaz-Bordenave, Juan E (1977) Communication and Rural Development. UNESCO, Paris, pp. 22-23.

Edger, D (2001) The Patchwork Nation: Rethinking Government –Rebuilding Community, Harper Collins Publishers, Sydney, Australia, p.152.

FAO. (1969) Toward a Strategy for Agricultural Development: FAO's Five Areas of Concentration. Rome, Italy.

Freire, Paulo (1972) Pedagogy of the Oppressed, Penguin, Harmondsworth.

Fuglesang, Andreas and Dale Chandler (1986) The Open Snuff Box: Communication as Participation, *Media Development* 2(1):2-4.

Gecolea, Romeo H (1982) Primer on Development Support Communication, Asia and Pacific Programme for Development Training and Communication Planning, UNDP, Bangkok, p.1.

Guru, Mahesh Chandra B.P, (1997) An Evaluation of Grassroots Level Development Communication System in Karnataka State, Ph.D Thesis, Mangalore University, Mangala Gangotri, Karnataka State, p. 31.

Harijan, July 27, 1942.

Kim, Young Yun (2005) Inquiry in Intercultural and Development Communication, *Journal of Broadcasting and Electronic Media,* 55(3):554.

Kleinjans, Everett (1976) Foreword, In Wilbur Schramm and Daniel Lerner (eds) Communication and Change: The Last Ten Years and the Next, University Press of Hawaii, Honolulu.

Kothari, Rajani (1984) Communications for Alternative Development: Towards a Paradigm, *Development Dialogue* No.1-2(1):13-22.

Krippendorff, Sultana (1979) The Communication Approach to Development: A Critical Review, In John A. Lent (ed) Third World Mass Media: Issues, Theory and Research, Studies in Third World Societies, Williamsburg, 9(1):71-81.

Lent, John A (1982) Grassroots Renaissance: Folk Media in the Third World, *Media Asia* 9 (1):9-17.

Lerner, Daniel (1958) The Passing of Traditional Society: Modernising the Middle East, Macmillan, New York, USA.

Melkote, Srinivas R (1983) Communication Gap in Development: An Ethical Perspective, *Media Asia* 10(2).

Menon, Vijay (1986) What Hope for the Future of Development Communication? *Media Development* No.2, pp. 5-6.

Nair, K.S. and Shirley A. White (1987) Participation is the Key to Development Communication, *Media Development* 34(3): 36-40.

National Policy on Education (1986) Government of India, New Delhi, India.

Nussbaum, Jon F. and Gustav Friedrich (2005) Instructional/ Development Communication: Current Theory, Research and Future Trends, *Journal of Broadcasting and Electronic Media,* 55(3): 578.

Okigbo, Charles (1985) Is Development Communication a Dead Issue?, *Media Development* No. 4(1): 23-25.

Quebral, Nora C (1973) What Do We Mean by Development Communication?, *International Development Review*, February, 1973, p. 25.

Rogers, E.M. and F.F. Shoemaker (1971) Communication of Innovations: A Cross-Cultural Approach, Free Press, New York, USA.

Rogers, Everett M (1993) Perspectives on Development Communication, In K. Sadanandan Nair and Shirley A. White (eds) Perspectives on Development Communication, New Delhi, India.

Samarajiwa, R (1985) Tainted Origins of Development Communication, Communicator, Indian Institute of Mass Communication. April-July, New Delhi, India.

Schumacher, F.F. (1973) Small is Beautiful: Economics As if People Mattered, Harper and Row, New York, USA.

Schramm, Wilbur (1964) Mass Media and National Development: The Role of Information in the Developing Countries, Standard University Press, Stanford, California, USA.

Schumacher, F.F (1973) Small is Beautiful: Economics As if People Mattered, Harper and Row, New York, USA.

Sean, MacBride (1980) Many Voices, One World, Report of the International Commission for the study of Communication Problems, UNESCO, Paris, p.198.

Sen, Amartya (2006) Development as Freedom, Anchor Books, New York, USA.

Servaes, Jan (2004) Multiple Perspectives on Development Communication, in Charles C. Okigbo and Festus Eribo (eds) Development and Communication in Africa, Rowman and Littlefield Publications, Toronto and Oxford.

Tehranian, M (1979). Development Theory and Communications Policy: The Changing Paradigms, In Voigt M.J. and G.T. Hanneman (eds) Progress in Communication Sciences Vol. 1, Ablex, Norwood, N.J, pp. 119-66.

Vilanilam, J.V (1985) Education and Communication, Kairali Books International, Trivandrum, India.

Williams, David Cratis (2002) Communication Perspectives on Relationships Between Globalism and Localism, *Communication, Globalism and Localism,* 53(1):1.

Young India, July 25, 1929.

22

Financial Inclusion of Women through Self Help Groups

Shashikala and *H.R. Uma*

Introduction

'A nation would not march forward if the women are left behind'

–Swami Vivekananda

Inclusive growth is often used interchangeably with a suite of other terms, including 'broad-based growth', 'shared growth', and 'pro-poor growth'. Growth is considered to be pro-poor as long as poor people benefit in absolute terms, as reflected in some agreed measures of poverty (Ravallion and Chen, 2003). In contrast, in the relative definition, growth is "pro-poor" if and only if the incomes of poor people grow faster than those of the population as a whole, which is an inequality decline. However, while absolute pro-poor growth can be the result of direct income redistribution schemes, for growth to be inclusive, productivity must be improved and new employment opportunities created. In short, inclusive growth is about raising the pace of growth and enlarging the size of the economy, while leveling the playing field for investment and increasing productive employment opportunities (DFID 2004). It is increasingly being seen as important to achieve of the Millennium Development Goals.

In many countries, poverty remains a very real global problem. The World Bank estimates that more than 2.5 billion people were living below the international poverty line of US$2 a day in 2005. In addition to having low incomes that are inadequate for maintaining a decent standard of living, poor people suffer from illiteracy, malnutrition, food insecurity, and poor health, vulnerability to external shocks, powerlessness and social exclusion. Women and children are disproportionately affected. For many poor people, finding a way out of poverty is limited by their inability to borrow or save money.

Financial services have failed to reach poorer populations for a number of reasons like, inadequate infrastructure, perceptions that lending to the poor is too risky to be commercially viable, inhibiting regulatory and legal environments and limited understanding and awareness of financial services by the poor.

In this regard, in 21st century the term financial inclusion was in lime light in the economic development of both developed and developing nations. Financial inclusion is important to achieve poverty reduction and empowerment of women. Financial inclusion is defined, "The process of ensuring access to financial services and timely and adequate credit where needed by vulnerable groups such as weaker sections and low income groups at an affordable cost" (Dr. C. Rangarajan). The Reserve Bank of India (RBI) said that financial inclusion is not restricted merely to opening of bank accounts and should imply provision of all financial services like credit, remittance and overdraft facilities for the rural poor. (Commission on Growth and Development 2008).

Moreover, financial inclusion emphasises the importance of creating an appropriate enabling environment to facilitate the provision of financial services to the poor household and the broader community. Access to finance can contribute to improved nutrition, housing and health, especially among female clients. By borrowing, saving or buying insurance the poor can plan for their future beyond the short term. They can build up assets and invest in Education and health. Financial services can help the poor cope in times of need and hardship. Beyond the severy tangible impacts, access to financial services promotes social inclusion and Builds self confidence and empowerment. Thus financial inclusion provides monetary fuel for economic growth and it is considered critical for achieving inclusive growth.

Financial Inclusion and Micro Finance

Financial Inclusion refers to delivering of banking services at an affordable cost to the vast sections of disadvantaged and low income groups who tend to be excluded from the formal banking channels. Despite widespread expansion of banking services during the last three decades, a substantial portion of the households, especially in rural areas, is at present outside the formal banking system. RBI spelt out its broad approach to Financial Inclusion as 'connecting people' with the banking system and not just the delivery of credit (RBI). These financial services are savings, loan, and, payment remittance facilities. Out of these three above mentioned important services if any one of the service is absent the entire concept will be considered as incomplete financial inclusion. Commercial Banks, RRBs, Cooperatives, Government, M.F.Is, SHGs, Post offices, NBFCs, NGOs, etc. are the provider of financial services and these have either adequate or inadequate presence in rural areas of the country (RBI 2006).

In this regard NABARD has played a very significant role for the promotion of financial inclusion in rural areas. SHG-Bank linkage programme was introduced by NABARD in the year 1992. SHG or micro-finance programme piloted by NABARD is one of the largest programme in the world and marginalised asset-less, resource-starved rural poor especially women in unbanked and under-banked rural areas are successful for unrestricted access to micro-credit and micro-insurance. Microcredit or microfinance, inclusive finance acknowledges that both bank and non-bank service providers have vital and complementary roles to play in providing financial services to the poor. Microcredit is the provision of small loans to poor people to assist in the development of small-scale businesses to address poverty and exclusion. Microfinance is the provision of a wider array of financial services including credit, savings and deposit services, payments and transfer services, and insurance products.

Hence, study reveals that households with access to microfinance are more likely to send their children to school and those children are more likely to stay in school for longer. Improvements in income and better access to credit, savings and insurance services can reduce the need to rely on children as laboure. Microfinance clients are overwhelming female, and the contribution of microfinance to women's empowerment is widely recognised. Microfinance can help to build women's self-confidence and assertiveness, often resulting in women obtaining greater decision-making power, control over assets, and mobility within both the delivered in conjunction with microfinance can lead to improved health outcomes, including more timely use of health care, greater awareness of health issues and prevention methods, and higher rates of child immunisation in client families compared with non-client families (B B Barik, 2004).

Over two-thirds of microfinance clients around the world are women. The strong participation of women in microfinance programs can be attributed to a number of factors. Women borrowers tend to have higher repayment rates relative to men and that when women are provided with access to finance, the whole household benefits, not just the individual client. Further more, targeting women is recognised as an effective mechanism to improve gender equality with in communities. Microfinance can enable women to diversify their income flows, accumulate assets and increase their economic activity. Women with access to microfinance can have greater control over their incomes and more power in household decision making. Through microfinance programs, women often gain new vocational skills, self-confidence and greater leadership, resulting in an enhanced ability to drive change within both the household and the community (Jha, B.K. 2008).

Self Help Groups

In this regard SHGs are playing predominant role in achieving children's health, education and women empowerment. The Microfinance programme envisages organisation of the rural poor into SHGs for building their capacities to manage their own finances and then negotiate bank credit on commercial terms. The origin of SHG can be traced back to early 1980s, SHGs has emerged as the most successful strategy, in the process of financial inclusion and empowerment of women. The rural women are the marginalised group of our society. Due to the presence of socio-economic constraints in the rural areas, women's potential for development remained far from fully utilised and they have been pushed further back into the social hierarchical system (Prasant Sarangi 2003). The rural poor and disadvantaged women were encouraged to inculcate banking habits through small savings and credit activities, which, at present has attained a global campaign in the name 'Bangladesh Grameen Bank' (Debotosh Sinha 2008).

Thus financial inclusion provides monetary fuel for economic growth and it is considered critical for achieving inclusive growth. Woman members of SHG were able to increase their disposable income, self/wage employment opportunities, standard of living through enhanced consumption expenditure and health care, saving potential and decision making power. As a result rural women members of SHG through financial inclusion were also able to achieve economic, social and political empowerment.

Women empowerment

The term empowerment refers to giving power to person or group for development. Empowerment of women should be a key aspect of all social development programs (World Bank, 2001). Although a considerable debate on what constitutes empowerment exists, Kabeer's (2001) definition, 'The expansion in people's ability to make strategic life choices in a context where this ability was previously denied to them' is more acceptable.

Empowerment are included in the eight indicators by Hashemi (1996): mobility, economic security, ability to make a small purchase, ability to make larger purchase, involvement in major decision, relative freedom from domination by the family, political and legal awareness, and involvement in political campaigning and protests.

Objectives

To analyse the financial inclusion of women through SHGs.

Methodology

Some of the criteria of financial inclusion and women empowerment mentioned above have been examined in this paper. For this purpose the study was conducted inthe taluk of H.D. Kote, one of the districts of Mysore, in Karnataka. To check whether women in this area are financially included an empirical study was carried out with hundred SHG members from H.D. Kote taluk with random sampling method of data collection.

Primary data has been collected through sample survey method, for which structured questionnaire and interview methods were used. With the help of these data efforts were made to see the role played by Self Help Groups in empowerment of women through that making them financially included. The questionnaire was coined in such a way that the respondents were to reveal their position before and after joining the Self Help Groups.

Result and Discussion

Table 1: Distribution of SHG members according to having Bank account

Sl. No.	*Parameter*	*Total*	*Percentage*
1.	Yes	83	83
2.	No	17	17
	Total	**100**	**100**

Financial inclusion is an important to poverty reduction and women empowerment. In this regard SHGs are significant role in financial inclusion for study area. Table 1 show the banking performance of SHGs in this taluk and also it refers to how many members having bank account and not having bank account about joining SHGs. The sample consists of 100 members. Out of this, majority of the members having bank account like 83% of the members having bank account, only 17% of the members are not having any bank account. It shows that SHGs are good performance in financially included.

Table 2: Distribution of SHG members according to Before and After joining having Bank account

Sl. No.	*Parameter*	*Total*	*Percentage*
1.	Before	11	13.2
2.	After	72	86.8
	Total	**83**	**100**

Table 2 shows the performance of before and after joining the SHGs. The Sample consists of 100 members; out of 100 members only 83 members are having bank account, in these out of 83 members only 13.2% of the members having bank account for before joining SHG.But after joining 86.8% of the SHG members are having bank account. It represents that after joining the SHG members are well performed in financially included. The reason for that, bank and NGOs are actively participating in promotion of SHGs.

Table 3 represents the receipt of bank loan in study area. Observation of the study 83% of the members are having bank loan. Only 17% of the members are not having any bank loan. Tough it shows that after joining SHGs majority of the members who are taken bank loan and taken up income generation activity like animal husbandary, poultry and other activities. So it leads to increase their income and standard of leaving.

Table 3: Receipt of Banks loan

Sl. No.	*Parameter*	*Total*	*Percentage*
1.	Yes	83	83
2.	No	17	17
	Total	**100**	**100**

Table 4 Purpose wise demand for credit in SHG members

Sl. No.	*Parameter*			*Total*
1.	Consumption	<5000	45	100
		>5000	55	
2.	Health	<5000	32	100
		>5000	68	
3.	Festival	<5000	70	100
		>5000	30	
4.	Repayment of old loan	<5000	73	100
		>5000	27	
5.	Business	<5000	35	100
		>5000	65	
6.	Children education	<5000	36	100
		>5000	64	
7.	Others	<5000	37	100
		>5000	63	

Table 4 represents purpose wise demand for credit in SHG members. The members took loans for different purpose like consumption, Health, Festival, Repayment of old loan, Business, Children education and others. 45% of the members having < 5000 Rs. credit for consumption purposes, followed by 32% for health, 70% for festival, 73% for repayment of old loan, 35% for business, 36% for children education, 37% for others. Remaining 55% of the members having >5000 Rs. Credit for consumption purposes, followed by 68% for health, 30% for festival, 27% for repayment of old loan, 65% for business, 64% for children education, 63% for others. Majority of people who have taken loan for > 5000 Rs. High income and middle income members who have taken loan for business and income generating activities purpose. Lower income members have taken loan for consumption and other purpose.

Conclusion

In this paper high lightened financial inclusion of women through SHGs in a developing country like India. Access to financial services and the subsequent transfer of financial resources to poor women enable them to become economic agents of change. Women become economically self-reliant, contribute directly to the well- being of their families, play a more active role in decision- making, and are able to confront systemic gender inequalities.

This study deals with micro finance as an important strategy for women empowerment and SHGs are helping women to be empowered. The program envisages organisation of the rural poor into SHGs for building their capacities to manage their own finances and then negotiate bank credit on commercial terms. In this regard Women Empowerment is an essential aspect of her being financially, socially, economically and politically included.

The impact of joining the SHG is well pronounced in H.D. Kote taluk. However, after joining the SHG the position of individual woman makes a change and financially included. So in this regard women empowerment leads to social and financial inclusion. This study observes that SHG has a positive impact on women empowerment and helps her to get financially, socially, politically and economically included. It is clearly visible in this empirical work.

References

1. Commission on Growth and Development (2008) Growth Report: Strategies for Sustained Growth and Inclusive Development, the World Bank.
2. DFID (2004) "What are Pro-Poor Growth and Why Do We Need to know?"
3. Femida Handy and Meenaz kassan (2004) Women's empowerment in rural India, paper presented as the ISTR conference, Toronto Canada.
4. Beijing (1995) Country paper India, 4th world conference on women,
5. Debotosh Sinha (2008) Self Help Group-Vehicle for women Empowerment (A Study in the sriniketan community Development Block of Birbhum District), Indian-J-soc-dev.
6. MD. Saiful Islam and Nourin Shabnam. (2005) "Women in development, A case study on selected rural areas of Bangladesh." Indian J Soc dev, Vol. 5 No.1.
7. Abhijit Sharma (2006). Study on Empowerment and Social Inclusion. World Bank's Social Development Group, Final Version: June 28, 2002. Yojana.
8. Jill Williams (2005) Measuring Gender and women's Empowerment using confirmatory Factor Analysis working paper.
9. Prasant Sarangi (2003) Self Help Groups-An Experiment in Orissa, Kurukhetra
10. Dr. M.S. Swaminathan (1995) Women's empowerment and men's enlightenment: twin challenges facing the Beijing conference, Kurukshetra.
11. Micro finance in India: (2005) Empirical evidence, alternative models and policy imperatives. Economic and Political Weekly.

12. B B Barik, (2004) financial inclusion and Empowerment of Indian rural households (bbarik2004@rediffmail.com)

13. Jha, B.K. (2008) in his empirical study entitled 'Role of Banking Services in Rural Entrepreneurship (A case study of Sultanpur District, U.P.)' published in 'Banking Finance', June compared the economic and housing conditions of rural entrepreneurs before and after the initiation of banking services.

23

Financial Inclusion and Unorganised Sector Workers

Mahesh R. **and** *Shamanth N.*

Introduction

Poverty is not merely insufficient income, but rather the absence of wide range of capabilities, including security and ability to participate in economic and political systems. Today the term 'bottom of the pyramid' refers to the global poor most of whom live in the developing countries. These large numbers of poor are required to be provided with much needed financial assistance in order to sail them out of their conditions of poverty. Accordingly, there is felt a need for policy support in channeling the financial resources towards the economic upliftment of resource poor in any developing economy.

A well functioning financial system empowers individuals, facilitates better integration with the economy, actively contributes to development and affords protection against economic shocks. The recent developments in banking technology have transformed banking from the traditional brick-and-mortar infrastructure like staffed branches to a system supplemented by other channels like automated teller machines (ATM), credit/debit cards, internet banking, online money transfers, etc. However, the access to such technology is restricted only to certain segments of the society. For a segment of high and upper middle income population and a significantly large section of the population who lack access to even the most basic banking services. This is termed "financial exclusion". These people, particularly, those living on low incomes, cannot access mainstream financial products such as bank accounts, credit, remittances and payment services, financial advisory services, insurance facilities, etc.

What is the present state of financial inclusion in India? A recent National Sample Survey (2007) reveals that out of 89 million farm households in our country, more than 40 million households have no access to finance, whether formal or informal. For the remaining 45 million households who have outstanding debt, more than 40 per cent of the debt comes from non-formal institutions such as moneylenders. Thus, in 2006–07, more than Rs. 1.5 lakh crore was borrowed from traditional moneylenders and not from the formal financial sector. Although we do not have similar detailed data for the urban areas, some estimates show that only 60 per cent of the urban households have bank accounts. This means that 40 per cent of the urban population does not have access to financial services such as savings, credit and payment systems. In the case of migrants, the situation is even worse. The NSS survey also shows that in recent years, the share of the traditional system of credit, such as moneylenders, may be increasing in rural areas and possibly also in urban areas.

Importance of financial inclusion arises from the problem of financial exclusion of nearly 3 billion people from the formal financial services across the world. The review of literature suggests that the most operational definitions are context-specific, originating from country-specific problems of financial exclusion and socio-economic conditions. Thus, the context-specific dimensions of financial exclusion assume importance from the public policy perspective. The operational definitions of financial inclusion, have also evolved from the underlying public policy concerns that many people, particularly those living on low income, cannot access mainstream financial products such as bank accounts and low cost loans, which, in turn, imposes real costs on them.

The main reason for financial exclusion is the lack of a regular or substantial income. In most of the cases people with low income do not qualify for a loan. The proximity of the financial service is another fact. The loss is not only the transportation cost but also the loss of daily wages for a low income individual. Most of the excluded consumers are not aware of the bank's products, which are beneficial for them. Getting money for their financial requirements from a local money lender is easier than getting a loan from the bank. Most of the banks need collateral for their loans. It is very difficult for a low income individual to find collateral for a bank loan. Moreover, banks give more importance to meeting their financial targets. So they focus on larger accounts. It is not profitable for banks to provide small loans and make a profit.

Financial inclusion mainly focuses on the poor who do not have formal financial institutional support and getting them out of the clutches of local money lenders. As a first step towards this, some of our banks have now come forward with general purpose credit cards and artisan credit cards which offer collateral-free small loans. The RBI has simplified the KYC (Know your customer) norms for opening a 'No frill' account. This will help the low income individual to open a 'No Frill' account without identity proof and address proof.

Unorganised Sector

The concept of an informal/unorganised sector began to receive world–wide attention in the early 1970s, when the International Labour Organisation (ILO) initiated serious efforts to identify and study the area through its World Employment Programme Missions in Africa. Since then, the informal sector has been the subject of several studies and seminars covering various aspects like its size, employment potential, its relationship with the formal sector, technological levels etc. In 1987, the Director General of the ILO submitted a report to the International Labour Conference on the "Dilemma of the Informal Sector." In it, he referred to the role of this sector in promoting employment, the absence of adequate laws for providing protection to workers in this sector, and the scope for application of international labour standards in this area.

The unorganised sector as that part of the workforce who have not been able to organise in pursuit of a common objective because of constraints such as casual nature of employment, ignorance and illiteracy, small size of establishments with low capital investment per person employed, scattered nature of establishments and superior strength of the employer operating singly or in combination.

India's workforce includes the self employed and employed in unorganised sector. The Ministry of Labour, Government of India, has categorised the unorganised sector workers under four groups in terms of Occupation, nature of employment, specially distressed categories and service categories.

(a) Occupation: Small and marginal farmers, landless agricultural labourers, share croppers, fishermen, those engaged in animal husbandry, in beedi rolling, labeling and packing, building and construction, collection of raw hides and skins, handlooms weaving in rural areas, brick kilns and stone quarries, saw mills, oil mills etc.

(b) Nature of Employment: Attached agricultural labourers, bonded labourers migrant workers, contract and casual labourers etc.

(c) Specially distressed categories: Toddy tappers, scavenger, carriers of head loads, drivers of animal driven vehicles, loaders, etc.

(d) Service categories: Domestic workers, barbers, vegetable and fruit vendors, newspaper vendors etc.

Objectives

- To know the reach of financial services in unorganised sector workers.
- To analyse the reasons for low usage of better financial services.
- To suggest measures to improve the reach with the help of various schemes.

Access to Financial Services and Growth of the Unorganised Sector

A free, multi-layered and well regulated national financial infrastructure is critical for the growth of the unorganised sector. It has been broadly observed that access to finance in the unorganised sector results in substitution of high cost debts by investment in productive assets, expansion of existing business and in value addition to the enterprise output with a direct positive impact on enterprise returns. Similarly, access to finance also has links to improvement in individual productivity by permitting individuals to move to higher levels of consumption of basic items, investment in education and skill building that determines future earning potential, specialisation in a few activities instead of over-diversification and an overall improvement in risk taking ability.

Finally, improved access to customised financial services also have a positive effect on the local economy through a general increase in wage labour opportunities and better utilisation of surplus labour. Improved access in this context is defined as the ability of economic participants (individuals and enterprises) to access a broad range of financial services (including access to capital-venture funds, credit, banking, investment, insurance and hedging instruments against price fluctuations) suited to their specific requirements.

Addressing Constraints of Capital for the Unorganised Sector

Reduction in the need for capital as well as increasing its availability is broadly constrained due to two reasons, Information Asymmetry and Difficulty of Access. Each of these reasons and the possible ways of addressing these issues are discussed in the following sections: Issues of information asymmetry lead to a high perception of risk by the investor/ financier, of adverse selection and moral hazard. The unorganised sector is characterised by the absence of complete financial records. The absence of registration under any specific regulation also contributes to the difficulty in verifying the risk associated with the provision of financial assistance/ capital to such enterprises. This is further compounded by the inability of most enterprises to offer any security in the form of collaterals, mortgages or guarantees for raising loans. Better information on tiny and micro enterprises performance and their financial health should eventually improve their commercial risk profile. As a result, tiny and micro enterprises might eventually require less equity and start getting more risk capital and other longer-term finance and investment.

Issues Related to Information Asymmetry can be Addressed through the following Methods

Group Lending Models Lending to the unorganised sector is often not collateralised and therefore, the lending by financial institutions actually constitutes equity. However, the returns from this high risk debt are limited for the lender, at the same time the promoter manages to raise 'capital' at extremely low rates. To address, group lending methods are commonly used. Such methods have been successfully able to address the issues of information asymmetry and have therefore, helped in making available financial resources to the unorganised sector. The two common group lending models that have demonstrated the capability of scaling are the Self Help Group model (SHG) supported by NABARD and the Joint Liability Group (JLG) model of Grameen Bank.

In such models, the issues related to information asymmetry are addressed through the knowledge of the group members about each other, moreover since the group members are jointly liable for all loans, it ensures that only the "good" borrowers band together to form an SHG or JLG which comes forward to take a loan.

There is a need to move towards extending credit and equity to individuals. However, there is insufficient understanding of the drivers of default and credit risk at the level of the individual in these models and there remains a need to invest in solutions that are able to build individual credit history. Investment in the creation of credit information bureaus could address this issue.

Credit Bureau

A credit bureau allowing sharing of credit information related to individuals between various lenders in any systematic manner could result in credit histories being used to make lending decisions. Such a bureau will require the existence of a unique national identifier Credit information tracking and sharing will enable lenders to provide incentives to members with good credit history and provides a strong deterrent to willful default. This will also facilitate transition to individual lending programmes from group lending over time. NABARD may play an important role in catalysing this initiative. Other developing economies are also investing in such institutions. The National Loans Register in South Africa is one such example. The bureau is a unique collaboration between the public and the private sector. It provides negative feedback on default behaviour of clients.

Supply Chain Financing

The sector is marked by lack of transparent credit information, limited sectoral data with high impairment propensity. Focusing on supply chain financing for certain industries could be a scalable model for delivering finance to this sector. Through this model investment in reducing information asymmetry can be limited to understanding few highly rated companies in a business to which the enterprise is a regular supplier or is a dealer of such a rated company. The enterprise can seek financing against the receivables from such a company or leverage that relationship even if on its own it does not have very strong financials.

Specialised Product or Industry Specific Banks

One way of addressing the 'lack of market information' issue is by creation of specialised Industry banks and financial institutions. Such banks can build specific skills in the particular sectors financed by them, also owing to their specialisation, these banks will be aware of the impact of macro and micro economic indicators on such industries. Sectoral knowledge also implies that the financial institutions understand the entire value chain and are able to identify bankable industry clusters.

Innovative Customised Financial Services

Some innovative approaches to address information asymmetry issues at a large scale for tiny enterprises and SMEs have been employed by Korean Banks like Woori and Kookmin. Kookmin Bank classifies un-audited companies which get a 'clean' opinion from accounting firms designated by it as a "Kookmin Green Company". The Bank pays up to 70% of the auditing fees of suchenterprises. A Kookmin Green Company applying for loans is provided with a wide range of services such as preferential lending rates, commission waivers as well as credit extensions.

Difficulty of Access

Besides, issues related to information asymmetry, access to finance for the unorganised sector is constrained by difficulty in accessing such financial services due to absence of banking channels. The transaction costs of servicing the unorganised sector are extremely high due to the low ticket size and high costs of processing, service and delivery.

In order to achieve ubiquity that is meaningful, models of outreach must have the ability to leverage local information while being cost-effective. Any strategy for universal access to financial services will have to address two key challenges ubiquity and the provision of a comprehensive range of financial services in the context of high transaction costs.

The two broad strategies that seem to be effective in this regard are:

Delivering Financial Services through Local Financial Institutions

Local Financial Institutions (LFIs) have emerged as a viable option to deliver financial services to the unorganised sector. LFIs are private, professionally run, community based entities engaged in the delivery of financial services. These entities could be set up either as a for-profit or a not-for-profit entity.

Such LFIs, being a community based institution, are aware of the intricate social structures in the area they operate and are also able to closely monitor the financial inflows and outflows of the enterprise. The biggest strengths of this form of financial organisations are its ability to remove information asymmetries and servicing the financial needs at a fraction of the costs of the formal financial institutions.

These LFIs work in close association with the formal financial institutions and, therefore, help in leveraging the relative strengths of banks (access to large capital and diversified risks) as well as the LFI (low transaction cost and local information).

Community Development Financial Institutions (CDFIs) broadly referred to as LFIs have been servicing the financial needs of the unorganised sector in USA. These CDFIs in addition to extending financial services to the poor entrepreneurs also help them develop financially sound business models. These Local Financial Institutions are better suited to asses risk, service it in a commercially viable manner and provide customised products. Presently, India has only 30 – 40 mature LFIs with a combined outreach of approximately three million households. There is a visible need to strengthen the existing LFIs and promote new LFIs to service the large unorganised sector. The following needs to be done in this regard:

Promoting venture capital investments for promotion of LFIs: There is a need to promote investment in such LFIs. One possible way is to make it attractive for venture capitalists to make investments to help set up such LFIs. This could be facilitated by creation of possible exit options for the venture capitalist. One possibility is the creation of a fund that provides the venture capitalist an option to exit at a predetermined price based on the rating of the LFI, through a leveraged buyout, by extending a long term debt to the entrepreneur for buying out the stake of the venture capitalist. This can be further facilitated if the LFIs are able to service all financial needs of the unorganised sector, raise capital from venture funds and other international investors, generate and distribute profits (dividends) and get listed on stock exchanges for accessing equity from general public and institutional investors.

Creation of training support for scaling up such LFIs: The growth in number and scale of LFIs can be facilitated by the existence of trained staff in adequate numbers for different roles in an LFI. Most LFIs are in the emerging phase and need continuous capacity building and mentoring support. LFIs typically recruit locally and provide on-the-job training. With rapid growth the need for a management cadre for scaled LFIs is increasing. There needs to be a systematic training strategy for the sector. Large LFIs will also need to build internal capabilities in risk management, asset-liability management and other financial aspects of the micro finance business.

Ways of Increasing Access to Financial Services

Creation of an Entrepreneurship Support Fund

Although, the measures reducing information asymmetry and enabling ubiquitous access will increase the availability of capital, the existence of a National Entrepreneurship Support Fund for enterprises in the unorganised sector could be catalytic in increasing flow of funds to this sector. Such approaches have been tried earlier but have met limited success. However, by a change in the design and role of such a fund, it is possible to meet the desired objectives. The equity investment should be made by the local financial institutions (LFI), with the proposed fund being used to provide a First Loss Default Guarantee to the LFI. This would facilitate the creation of markets, particularly if they combine resolution of information asymmetries with the function of providing risk-capital.

Provision of other Forms of Capital

The unorganised sector does not have access to other forms of capital such as subordinated debts, mezzanine finance, leveraged buyouts, acquisition financing and distressed debt etc. Such forms of capital become relevant in different growth phases of the enterprise. Securitisation of loans to Small and Medium-Sised Enterprises (SMEs): The capital market has traditionally been viewed as the exclusive marketplace for large corporations to raise funds through the issuance of stocks and bonds. With the growing sophistication of structured finance transactions, loan securitisation now makes it possible for small and medium-sised enterprises (SMEs) to access the capital market too. This should be available to tiny and micro enterprises also.

Knowledge about the Business

Banks lack the market knowledge and information about specialised sectors that form the unorganised sector. The branch led model may not be the most efficient approach in responding to the needs of a sector engaged in extremely diverse activities. In a typical branch banking model, banks and financial institutions do not always understand the nature of the business undertaken by entrepreneurs, and are, therefore, unable to assess the risk in extending financial services to such enterprises. Moreover, the current financial system is not geared to supporting new enterprises. There is a need for a systemic effort for developing training packages for the staff of the financing institutions for better assessment of the risks of such enterprises. Making available appropriate financial services is a function of specialised knowledge about the sector and requires the banking sector to expand its technical skills. Please refer to Annexure 3 for a detailed case study on Wells Fargo which has developed such skills.

Well-Defined Metrics

It has been suggested that the public sector character of several of the large participants in the financial system has led to very passive responses to the needs of finance for the underserved sectors and to the overall management of the institutions themselves. However, it is not obvious that privately owned banks within India either before or after nationalisation have sought to aggressively build new models to profitably serve the credit-constrained segments. While, within the corporate world in India and within

Banks outside India metrics such as shareholder value-add, detailed segment level performance reporting and balance score cards have played a key role in aligning the incentives of managements, within India these issues have not been given much attention. While longer run solutions may involve privatisation of banks and other financial institutions, the answer to better overall performance of the financial system may lie more within a better design of metrics of performance rather than in change of ownership – at least in the medium term.

Provision of a Range of Financial Services

Access to well-designed products that cater to various needs (growth as well as risk management) is critical for the overall development of the sector. However, most of the work that has happened in India has been geared towards increasing access to small loan amounts that may be used either for consumption or for enterprise purposes (typically livestock). While this is a critical need, there are gaps in access and availability of other financial services including insurance (life and non-life), savings, investment, remittance and derivatives. One of the main factors constraining the availability of a range of financial services has been the total absence of information on the unorganised sector. Although the existence of LFIs ensures that the risk associated with servicing the unorganised sector can be reduced, such local knowledge does not always inform product development.

Conclusion

In India unorganised sector represents large population, government has taken so many measures to bring unorganised sector under the umbrella of financial inclusion but it is found that the efforts of government are partly successful, reasons may be illiteracy, lack of awareness, poor saving habit, frequent migration from one place to another and easy access to local available loans etc. The recent actions taken by the government have been showing positive result but the proportion of the users of financial services are comparitively low when it compared to the whole sector.

To reach an end user the government has to come up with efficient policies to make a lay man to access various financial products and services then only the inclusive growth will be possible and can build economically strong nation.

References

Malhotra, Sandeep and Kamal Nigam, "Infrastructure Finance in India", ICICIresearchcentre.org and CAFS Working Paper, July 2003.

Pitman, Brian, "Leading for Value", Harvard Business Review, April 2003.

Basu Debashis, Growth Alchemy: Why Smaller Firms Fail to Find Finance and How Market – Based Solutions can Help, Indian Merchants 'Chamber-Economic Research and Training Foundation, (2004).

V. Saha, V., A. Kar and T. Baskaran, Contribution of Informal Sector and Informal Employment in Indian Economy, presented at 7th Meeting of the Expert Group on Informal Sector Statistics (Delhi Group) New Delhi, 2 - 4 February 2004.

24

Inclusive Growth of SHG's Through Project Based Approach-A Case Study of Pico Power Project in Banjarumale Tribal Area

P.N. Udayachandra, Vishal Pinto and *Sunil D'souza*

Introduction

Self Help Groups or SHGs represent a unique approach to financial intermediation in India. The approach combines access to low-cost financial services with a process of self management and development for the people who are in SHG movement. It is a village-based financial intermediary usually composed of between 10-20 local people. A Self-Help Group (SHG) is a registered or unregistered group having homogenous social and economic backgrounds, voluntarily coming together to save regular small sums of money, mutually agreeing to contribute to a common fund and to meet their emergency needs on the basis of mutual help. It is also a group of people who pool their resources to become financially stable by taking loans from the money collected by the group and by making everybody of the group self employed. The group members use collective wisdom and peer pressure to ensure proper end-use of credit and timely repayment. This system eliminates the need for collateral and is closely related to that of solidarity lending, widely used by microfinance institutions. Through Self-Help Groups, women are trained to save, plan and control their credit. Until the recent past, most of the women depending mostly on seasonal agricultural works but now women are able to get additional income through the income generation programmes adopted through the women groups. This has raised their economic status, social status and decision making power.

SHGs can work together to address issues that affect not only their own members, but others in the larger community but they need to be promoted and supported by funding agencies or by undertaking projects which involves all SHG members. Banjarumale Pico power project is such project which has involved all the local self help group members in establishing the project and which has resulted in overall development of the members.

Self Help Groups in Banjarumale

Banjarumale is the tribal area situated at near to Charmadi 9th cross, Belthangady Taluk, Dakshina Kannada District, Karnataka, India. Around 300 people live in this area without getting some basic facilities. SHGs were functional from the last 10 years. The Self Help Groups were introduced at the time of installation of Pico Power project. These groups contributed through labour sharing at the time of project installation and till its completion.

PICO HYDRO POWER

Pico Hydro projects are hydroelectric projects with power generation capacity of up to 10 KW. They generate power by converting water into electrical energy. The Project 'PICO HYDRO' was implemented with the objective of demonstrating the technical, managerial and economic feasibility of diffusing Pico Hydro Electric Technology for community use in remote hilly areas of Karnataka. Its positive environmental impacts are :

- Very little maintenance costs as the rotating parts are fully balanced and are not exposed to high temperatures unlike internal combustion engine based power packs.
- No recurring fuel costs-requires only water running down a slope for its operation.
- It can provide electricity to all typical domestic appliances. Power packs up to 1 KW (1000W) can be used for non-motive loads such as lighting, TV, Audio, Computer, water heating etc. Larger power packs can be used for motive loads such as refrigerators, mixer grinder, wet grinders etc. also.

Banjarumale Pico-power Project

History

Norvey citizens visited this tribal area last 10 years back and they promoted TIDE Company to install a hydro-power project. TIDE Company provided technical support to the installation of the project with the assistance of Shri Kshetra Dharmasthala Rural Development Project and Social Welfare Department of Karnataka Government and the Support and interest of the local people.

This power project is funded jointly by SKDRDP® and Government of Karnataka. Technical assistance was provided by the TIDE [Technology

Informatics Design Endeavour] Company and the construction was made through labour sharing by local SHG members. The basic philosophy is mutual help of sharing the resources and caring the members.

Table 1: Cost of the project

Sl. No.	*Sources of Capital*	*Amount (in Rs)*
1	Social welfare dept. of Karnataka	6,00,000
2	SKDRDP	1,50,000
3	Loan from Co-Op. Bank	1,00,000
4	Technology and labour force	3,50,000
	Total	12,00,000

Source: Primary Data.

Organisation and Management

For the installation, operation and managing the power plantation the tribal people farmed a committee named "Local Project Installation Committee" on 2001 this committee members provided labour assistance at the time of installing the project. This project was installed for the purpose of lightening all families of Banjarumale. So this is people's project installed for the purpose people's basic use and it is operated and maintained by the tribal people itself.

Maintenance

At the time of project installation Local Project Installation Committee borrowed Rs.1,00,000 loan from Co-Operative bank and at present the loan is totally cleared and they have the savings of more than Rs. 2,00,000. The savings made is used only for the purpose of repairs and maintenance of the power project plant. Two SHGs members appointed by Local Project installation Committee to operate the project technology and for them monthly Rs. 1000 [per head Rs. 500] given from savings made by committee members.

Table 2: Technical Aspects of PICO Power Project

1. Power estimated	8 KW
2. Water flow	65 ltr/sec.
3. Water cannel	0.65*0.30 mtr = 580 mtr.
4. Water tank	4.5*1.2*1.45 mtr. (1200 ltr capacity)
5. Pressure pipe	0.20 mtr. Diameter, 65 mtr. Long
6. Power plant	2.0*2.5*2.0 mtr. Building

Source: Primary Data.

Table 3: Machinery used in Power Plant

1. Turbine	3 jet Peltan
2. Governing	Electronic load controller
3. Generator	Induction generator
4. Generator speed	1500 RPM
5. Power Rating	8 KW
6. Voltage	240 volt
7. Excitation	Capacitor excitation
8. Face	Single face
9. Power factor	0.8
10. Frequency	50 Hz

Source: Primary Data

Table 4: Distribution of power

1. Cable	4000mtr Dressed wire through underground
2. Connected to	29 home + 1 temple
3. Operation	Local distribution only

Source: Primary Data.

The PICO Power project is people's project for their basic usage like lightening home, use of electronic devices like T.V. Tape recorder etc. The organisation and maintenance of project were undertaken by the Local SHGs members. The people's project by them for them is the feature of PICO Power project in Banjarumale. Considering the social role of a project in extending additional facilities for the SHG members, the study has been conducted with the following objectives.

Research Methodology

The study is analytical and based on the material collected from primary data and secondary data. Secondary data was collected from reference books, Research journals, Reports (i.e., RBI GOI,) and relevant internet sources.

Objectives of the Study

Following objectives are considered for the research study;

1. To study the impact of Pico Power Project in inclusive growth of SHGs.
2. To analyse after effect of the Pico Power project on SHG members.
3. To examine the Pre and Post socio-economic status of SHG members.

4. To analyse the possible role Project based approach in Inclusive Growth of SHGs.

Collection of Primary Data

To make the study practical and original, primary data was collected from individual respondents. Respondents are the SHGs members and from each family one member who is engaged in group activity was considered as sample for collecting primary data. Face to face discussion with the SHGs members was carried out.

Sample Size

Since the Population of Banjarumale Tribal area was comparatively less the sample size was confined to 64. This study is based on the sample of 64 family respondents, selected from 64 families in Banjarumale. Each family respondent selected on the basis of his/her membership in Self Help Group activities. The data was collected through questionnaires and the information collected reflects the true opinion of the SHGs members and is reliable.

Scope of the Study

The study was fully focused on Banjarumale Tribal area. The survey was conducted just to assess the impact of people's project on overall growth of the people involved in the project. The inclusive growth can be analysed in various dimensions. The project based approach is one such dimension. So there is enough scope for the further extension of study. The study can be undertaken in large scale by taking other projects.

Limitations

Following limitations are observed in the study:

1. As the information collected from primary data, its accuracy is subjective to the responses received.
2. Since the Project situated in remote area, regular field visits could not be made.
3. Technical aspects of the project not explained properly because local people are not much aware about the technical aspects of the project,

Organisation Profile

This chapter contains the profile of organisations that supported to install PICO Power project in Banjarumale Tribal area. PICO Power project is a Joint Social Enterprise. This project was established by Local Tribal people with the support of SKDRDP, TIDE Company, Government Department (Social Welfare Department) and Local PICO Power project installation committee.

Profile of Local Pico Power Project Installation Committee

This is the Committee of local Tribal people and they formed this committee to co-operate with the SKDRDP and TIDE Company. This committee came in to existence in the year of 2001 when the strategy framed by TIDE Company to install PICO Power project in Bajarumale. All Tribal people are the members of this committee; they elected a president for this committee and also a secretary, a joint secretary and a treasurer. The committee played a vital role in decision making process while installing PICO Power project.

The role of Local PICO Power project installation Committee:

1. Contributing to the project in terms of monetary as well as labour sharing activity,
2. Taking decisions in the favor of all Tribal people,
3. Selecting the workers for operate and maintain the power plant functions,
4. Collecting monthly Rs.100 from each family as repair and maintenance charge,
5. Opening a bank account in local co-operative bank for saving the money collected from members.

Profile of Tide Company

Technology Informatics Design Endeavour (TIDE) is an organisation devoted to sustainable development through technological interventions. It is a registered not-for-profit society set up in 1993 and registered under the Societies Registration Act. TIDE is an organisation devoted to promoting sustainable development through technological interventions. It shares a concept of development that meets the needs of the neediest. It is in harmony with the environment, permits grass root participation, uses local resources and builds local capacity. It also believes that development could be promoted through the introduction of new, environmentally benign technologies.

PICO HYDRO Power Technology

Project PICO HYDRO was implemented with the objective of demonstrating the technical, managerial and economic feasibility of diffusing Pico Hydro Electric Technology for community use in remote hilly areas of Karnataka and its positive environmental impact. Demonstration of decentralised PICO – HYDRO power plant as an eco-friendly technology to meet the energy needs of small communities in hilly areas of Karnataka Funded by Indo Norwegian Environmental Programme in Karnataka (INEP) and local NGOs during 1999 – 2001. The TIDE Company provided technical assistant to install the PICO project in Banjarumale tribal area.

Data Analysis

In this researcher has given the tabular analysis for the data collected through structured questionnaire and the analysis aspect focus on impact of Pico power project on inclusive growth of the SHGs members.

Table 5: Socio-Economic status of the Respondents

Sl. No.		*Factors*	*Frequency*	*In %*
1.	Age of the Respondents (In years)	18-20	14	21.88
		30-40	32	50
		40 & above	18	28.12
		Total	**64**	**100**
2.	Sex	Male	34	53.12
		Female	30	46.88
		Total	**64**	**100**
3.	Education	Up to 7th	39	54.24
		Up to 10th	19	26.27
		Up to PUC	3	4.24
		Diploma	1	1.70
		Graduation	2	2.54
		Total	**64**	**100**
4.	Members in a Family	Up to 3	32	50
		3 to 5	18	28.12
		More than 5	14	21.88
		Total	**64**	**100**
5.	Family Income (in Rs.)	Less than 10000	10	15.63
		10000-30000	20	31.25
		30000-50000	2	3.12
		50000-60000	32	50
		Total	64	100
6.	Occupation	Agricultural Labour	8	12.5
		Farmer	6	9.38
		Labour and Farmer	50	78.12
		Total	**64**	**100**

Source: Primary Data.

Table 6: Effects of SHGs Activity on inclusive Growth of the Respondents

Particulars	*Before undertaking the project*				*After undertaking the project*			
	Yes	*In %*	*No*	*In %*	*Yes*	*In %*	*No*	*In %*
House built	46	71.87	18	28.13	24	37.5	40	62.5
Faced basic need problem	50	78.13	14	21.87	0	0	64	100
Loan Borrowed	0	0	64	100	54	84.36	0	0
Purchase of Vehicle	0	0	64	100	6	9.4	58	90.6
Children going for School	0	0	64	100	32	25	48	75
Insurance Policy holders	4	6.25	60	93.75	58	90.62	6	9.38

Source: Primary Data.

Table 7: Effects of Pico Power projects on the Living Standards of Respondents

Electronic devices	*Before installing PICO power project*		*After installing PICO power project*	
	Respondents	*In %*	*Respondents*	*In %*
Radio	64	100	64	100
TV	0	0	26	40.63
Telephone/Mobile	0	0	32	50
Other (Mixy, Iron Box, Grinder etc.)	0	0	20	31.25

Source: Primary Data.

Table 8: Awareness about the Technical Aspects of the Pico Power Project

Technical aspects	*Aware*		*Not aware*	
	Respondents	*In %*	*Respondents*	*In %*
Technology used	10	15.63	54	84.37
Investment	48	75	16	25
Cost of production	48	75	16	25
Subsidy for project	44	68.75	20	31.25

Table 9: Self Help Group and Members in Banjarumale

Sl. No.		*Factors*	*Frequency*	*In %*
1.	Members from a family in SHGs	Up to 2	46	85.18
		2 to 4	08	14.81
		4 & above	0	
		Total	**54**	**100**
2.	Membership in SHGs (in years)	Less than 1	0	0
		1 to 3	12	22.22
		3 & above	42	77.78
		Total	**54**	**100**
3.	Purpose of Loan Barrowed	Agriculture	42	55.26
		House hold	24	31.58
		Purchase Vehicle	06	7.89
		Other purpose	4	5.26
		Total	**76**	**100**
4.	Performance of SKDRDP in Member empowerment	Excellent	08	14.81
		Good	46	85.19
		Average	0	0
		Poor	0	0
		Total	**54**	**100**
5.	Amount of loan can borrowed from Group	5000-20000	0	0
		20000-50000	12	22.22
		50000-60000	42	77.78
		Total	**54**	**100**
6.	Awareness about the Rate of Interest	Highly aware	0	0
		Aware	40	74.07
		Not aware	14	25.93
		Total	**54**	**100**
7.	Members opinion about interest rate	Highly Burden	30	55.56
		Partially Burden	16	29.63
		Not Burden	8	14.81
		Total	**54**	**100**
8.	Members Savings in Group	0 – 15000	0	0
		15000 - 30000	24	44.44
		30000 – 45000	30	55.56
		Total	**54**	**100**

Source: Primary Data.

Findings

This study is undertaken to identify how the Banjarumale Tribal people included in the inclusive growth activities as like the people who are leading standard life in the society. During the study a sample of 64 persons as respondent from 64 families of Banjarumale tribal area were chosen and the primary data is collected for the study. Following are the summary of findings made at the end of the study.

1. From each family (i.e., 64 families), one person has involved in the SHGs activities. This made them to save small amount of money for the necessary,
2. Tribal people Socio-Economic Status increased afte installing the Pico Power project,
3. Most of all Tribal people are living Above Poverty Line (APL) and all are having more than 3 acres of land and in that land they are cultivating commercial crops like; Rubber, Areca nut etc. and also they are engaged in wage earning works, but they are not involved in Socio-economic activities but the SKDRDP changed the culture of the tribal people by encouraging them in savings, enterprising activities etc.,
4. All Tribal people are Economically stable; more than 90% of the people in Banjarumale are having more than Rs.10,000 annual income but they were not engaged in economic activities like; savings, borrowings etc. From the last one decade SHGs introduced this activities in this area,
5. The income of the group member's is increasing and also the savings also has been increasing in the Group. All SHGs members built their house before joining the Groups, after joining Groups; they repaired, reconstructed their home. Members are not highly aware about the rate of interest on borrowing amount. They also feel that the rate of interest is a burden for them; they are not aware that the other Micro-Finance institutions are charging more than the what the rate of interest being charged to them,
6. All Tribal people contributed for the installation of the PICO Power project; in the form of labour sharing i.e., 100 man days from each family, Rs.7500 cash investment from each family,
7. All Tribal people participated in the Decision Making Process- before installing PICO Power project all Tribal people formed a 'Local PICO Power project installation committee'. Committee members and directors are the local Tribal people only. This committee took the decisions while installing the PICO Power project.
8. Power used only for the purpose of home needs like; Lighting, Operating electronic devices like T.V., Mixer-grinder, and Iron-box etc. and not for the agricultural purpose or supplying to the grid.
9. Power production is not consistent. Its production for the last decades

is coming down because power plants repair and maintenance was not systematically done and people are not competent to repair the machinery, repairs and maintenance are costly affairs,

10. Tribal people are aware about Socio-economic factors but not given much importance for Hygiene factors like; sanitation, clean water for drinking, health care etc. and also lack awareness about the government facilities for scheduled tribes,
11. The main problem for Banjaumale Tribal people are Transportation. No good transportation facility like; roads and public transportation is unavailable,
12. All Tribal people are satisfied with the PICO Power project and also with the Self Help Group scheme.

Suggestions

1. SHGs members should be provided with the basic knowledge about SHG scheme's, its importance and purpose,
2. SHGs office bearers should create awareness about the methodology of charging interest on loan amount to the members,
3. It is necessary to give much importance to Hygiene factors like; sanitation, clean water for drinking, and health care etc.,
4. To get the power supply at the summer season 'Power Grid' is necessary. The power grid also helps to use the power for 24 hours,
5. Local people to be trained on the technical aspects of the power plant minor repairs and maintenance,
6. Tribal people should raise their voice to get the facilities offered by the government especially to them,
7. Motivational training is necessary for the SHGs members to involve themselves in Economic activities like savings and borrowings and also on Entrepreneurship.

Conclusion

The very idea of Microfinance and Self Help Groups emerged as financial inclusion strategies and are moving towards enhancing sustainable livelihood and quality. In Banjarmale SHG members were encouraged install Pico Power project and this project lighten their life. The tribal people are now not only living with better social status but also have increased the quality of life style. It is ostensible that for most of the people in India the power is still a dream. Micro-hydro is a useful way of providing power to houses, workshops or villages that need an independent supply. For many remote areas that are beyond the reach of the national grid, micro-hydro is the better economic option. In this direction, Banjarumale PICO Power project is sustaining itself through the contribution of SHGs members. The project has improved their living standards and life style. Inferences and conclusions of this research study reveal that, for the rural development and overall development of the rural people the project based approach is more relevant and feasible.

Bibliography

1. Muralidhara S, Sriraghava T J, (2004), " *Environmental Studies*", First Edition, Samskruthi publishing house, S Chand and Company Ltd. Ramnagar, New-Delhi, pp. 121-134.
2. Dr. Mahesh Kumar, (2010), "Post Power Supply as Demand soars", *Facts for you,* Vol. 28, No. 8, p. 40.
3. Dr. Ramacharan T and Balakrishna S, (2010), "Impact of Self Help Groups on Women's Empowerment- A case study in Kanyakumari district", *Kurukshetra*, Vol. 57, No. 2, p. 31.
4. Dr. Seema Tyagi, (2010), "Strategic model for Effective functioning of SHGs, *Kurukshetra,* Vol. 57, No. 2, p. 17.
5. Dr. Tarun Bikash Sukai, (2010), "Tribal Development in India", *Kurukshetra,* Vol. 57, No. 2, pp. 3-9.
6. Premaakumara G.S, (2008), "Impact of power industry on economic development a mathematical analysis", *Kurukshetra*, Vol. 56, No. 4, p. 25,
7. Prof. Arjun Y Pangannavar, (2010), "Self Help Groups and Rural Poverty", *Kurukshetra*, Vol. 57, No. 2, p. 12.
8. Tangirala HSK, (2010), "SHG is a tool of Economic Development of Co-Operatives and its Members", *Kurukshetra,* Vol. 57, No. 2, p. 22.
9. http://www.edarural.com/documents/SHG-Study/Executive-Summary.pdf.
10. http://www.powerngo.org/shg.htm.
11. http://en.wikipedia.org/wiki/Self-help_group_(finance).
12. http://megselfhelp.gov.in/resources/GCS/SHG%20Defination%20Functioning%20etc.pdf.
13. http://www.tideorganisation.org.

25

Financial Inclusion and NPA with Reference to Commercial Banks of Dakshina Kannada and Udupi Districts: An Analysis

M. Chandramma and *Raghurama A.*

Introduction

After nationalisation, commercial banks in India have been directed to provide loans to the priority sector at concessional rate of interest and participate in government sponsored schemes by providing loan facilities at a subsidised rate of interest without insisting on collateral security. In this respect Financial Inclusion had taken place directly and indirectly by the banks through GOI and RBI. Financial inclusion is a process performed by the banks and the financial institutions with a aim to reach a vast segment of the population to provide basic banking facilities through their service with affordable cost. Many times most of the customers open bank accounts only to obtained loan. They obtained loan and due to various reasons they do not repay the overdues. The resultant feature is the non-performing assets. The Narasimham committee recommended reduction of gross NPAs to 5% by 2000, 3% by 2002 and net NPAs to 3.0 per cent by 2000 and to 0.0 per cent by 2002. Hence, this paper mainly aims to give a detail overview of defaulters socio-economic condition i.e. sex, age, literacy level, occupation, purpose of credit facilities availed.

The objectives of the study

- To study the overview of NPAs in Commercial Banks and to discuss the Socio-Economic conditions of the sample Defaulters of Syndicate bank and Karnataka Bank Limited in Dakshina Kannada and Udupi districts.

- To analyse the causes for poor recovery of loan by the defaulters and to offer suggestions having policy implications for the purpose of reducing NPAs.

Methodology and Statistical Tools

The study is based on primary data collected from the Defaulters of the sample banks of the study area through personal interview with the structured questionnaire. The primary data was collected between December 2006 and July 2007. Along with the primary data, secondary data have been utilised from books, journals and reports by visiting Libraries, Institutes of Bank Management, the proceedings of the Seminars, Conferences, Workshops and Symposia have been utilised.

These defaulters were selected on the basis of judgment sampling method. They include Small business, Agriculture, SSI, Non-SSI, Government employees, workers, helpers, SHGs, and Other type of loan defaulters. Organised data has been analysed with the help of different statistical tools like average and percentage.

Overview of NPAs in Commercial Banks

In common parlance, an asset becomes non-performing if it fails to contribute any income to the owners. An asset including a leased asset becomes non-performing when it ceases to generate income for the bank. Non-Performing Asset means an advance where payment of interest or repayment of instalments of principal or both remains unpaid for a period of more than six months. However with effect from March 2004, default status is given to a borrowed account if dues are not paid for 90 days.

As per the guidelines of Reserve Bank of India, income on loan assets is to be recognised on receipt basis (as against previous accrual basis). As per the RBI norms, a loan is considered to be NPA when borrower defaults on interest and/or principal repayments for two quarters. But from March 2004, a borrower who defaults on loan for one quarter is classified as defaulter and such loan is categorised as Non-performing Asset (Jeelan Basha, 2003). While many countries have tightened norms much earlier, RBI has adopted the system only from the year ending March 31, 2004. Similarly, Financial Institutions treat a credit facility as non-performing asset, if interest is overdue for more than 180 days instead of the present norm of 365 days.

Loans are the major output provided by banks, but they are a risky output, since there is always an ex ante risk for a loan to finally become non-performing. Non-performing loans (NPLs) can be treated as undesirable outputs or costs to a bank which will decrease the bank's performance.

The risk from NPLs mainly arises when the external economic environment worsens during economic depressionsControlling NPLs is hence very important for both an individual bank's overall performance and an economy's financial environment.

The Socio-Economic conditions of the sample Defaulters of Syndicate bank and Karnataka Bank Limited in Dakshina Kannada and Udupi districts eata relating to the literacy level of sample bank NPA beneficiaries and their banking habit has been colectural areas.eficiari The main respondents in this study are Defaulters from Syndicate Bank (SB) and Karnataka Bank Limited (KBL). The biographical variables such as age, gender, literacy level, type of business/ occupation and other variables such as name of the Bank branch where credit facilities are availed and type of credit facilities availed are discussed below. These variables may have a significant impact on the Defaulter's Socio-Economic conditions.

Defaulters are those respondents who availed loan facilities from the banks for business activities or personal purposes and not repaid their dues for more than 90 days and come under NPA category in Dakshina Kannada and Udupi districts.

Sex-wise Distribution of Sample Defaulters

A study on the sex-wise classification of sample defaulters of the banks becomes essential to know the differences in perception between the male and female sample defaulters about loan and their repayment attitude and also to know the extent of women involvement in the borrowing of loan from the banks for various purposes in the study region. The data relating to the sex-wise distribution of sample defaulters of banks is presented in Table 1.

Table 1: Sex-wise distribution of sample defaulters of the banks

Sex	*Banks*		*Total*
	KBL	*SB*	
Female	15 (14.7)	32 (23.7)	47 (19.8)
Male	87 (85.3)	103 (76.3)	190 (80.2)
Total	**102 (100.0)**	**135 (100.0)**	**237 (100.0)**

X^2 = 2.959 P= 0.085 NS Source: Survey data.

Note: Figures in the parenthesis denote percentages to the total number of sample defaulters of respective banks.

From an analysis of above Table 1.1 it can be observed that majority of (80.2 per cent) sample defaulters are male members who have initiated more discretion interest in borrowings than female defaulters It was also observed during the survey that the female defaulters neither borrowed for their own purpose and defaulted, nor did they aware of the overdues amount defaulted by them. Simply they put their signature on the loan agreement.

Chi-square analysis shows that, there is no significant difference in gender wise distribution of defaulters of banks. (X^2 = 2.959, P=0.085>0.05, NS)

Age-wise Distribution of Sample Defaulters

Knowing the age of sample defaulters is important in order to analyse and find out the different aspects of their loan borrowings and repayment behavior and also to know the problems faced by the defaulters. Keeping this in view, the study is carried out and the relevant data was collected and presented in the Table 2.

Table 2: Age-wise Distribution of Sample Defaulters

Age range (in years)	*Banks*		*Total*
	KBL	*SB*	
21-30	15 (14.7)	19 (14.1)	34 (14.3)
31-40	49 (48.0)	86 (63.7)	135 (57.0)
41-50	25 (24.5)	21 (15.6)	46 (19.4)
51-60	9 (8.8)	7 (5.2)	16 (6.8)
61-70	4 (3.9)	2 (1.5)	6 (2.5)
Total	**102 (100.0)**	**135 (100.0)**	**237 (100.0)**

X^2 = 7.425 P= 0.115 NS.
Source: Survey Data.
Note: Figures in the parenthesis denote percentages to the total number of sample Defaulter of respective banks.

It is largely evident from the above table 2 that, majority of the sample defaulters (57.0 per cent) belong to the age group ranging between 31 and 40 years. It can also be observed that a large number of sample Defaulters (19.4 per cent) are found in the age group ranging between 41 and 50 years. This may be due to the reason that generally the age between 31 and 40 is considered the highest income earning and saving period of life. There is no significant difference in the age of defaulters of the two banks (X^2=7.425, P=0.115>0.05 NS).

Literacy-wise Distribution of Defaulters

It is a well-known fact that the Defaulters of banks from Dakshina Kannada and Udupi districts because of their high literacy level are significantly different from Defaulters of banks of other places. Besides, the level of education and repayment of loan/installments are highly correlated. Data relating to the literacy level of sample bank Defaulters has been collected and presented in table 3.

Table 3. Literacy Wise Distribution of Defaulters of Banks

Level of Education	*Banks*		*Total*
	KBL	*SB*	
Below SSLC	42 (41.2)	52 (38.5)	94 (39.7)
SSLC – PUC	20 (19.6)	30 (22.2)	50 (21.1)
Below Graduation	21 (20.6)	24 (17.8)	45 (19.0)
Graduation	10 (18.6)	28 (20.7)	47 (19.8)
Other	0 (0.0)	1 (0.7)	1 (0.4)
Total	**102** **(100.0)**	**135** **(100.0)**	**237** **(100.0)**

X^2 = 1.420, P=0.841, NS.

Source: Survey Data.

Note: Figures in the parenthesis denote percentages to the total number of sample defaulters of respective banks.

It can be observed from the above table 1.3 that, 42 (41.2 per cent) of defaulters of KBL and 52 (38.5 per cent) Defaulters of SB have literacy level of below SSLC. 20 (19.6 per cent) defaulters of KBL and 30 (22.2 per cent) defaulters of SB have educational qualification ranging between SSLC and PUC, whereas 21 (20.6 per cent) defaulters of KBL and 24 (17.8 per cent) defaulters of SB have below graduation as their educational qualification.19 (18.6 per cent) defaulters of KBL and 28 (20.7 per cent) defaulters of SB are guaduates.

Therefore, it is worth mentioning that there is no significant difference in the defaulters educational qualification in both the public sector and private sector banks (P=0.841>0.05 NS). Thus, it is found that the literacy level and repayment habit among respondent defaulters in the two districts are generally low.

Occupation wise Distribution of Defaulters

The study relating to the occupation of the respondents is essential to know whether the beneficiaries of bank loan under NPA category have the capacity to repay the bank loan since occupation and income are related. It is also essential to know whether the economic activity of the respondents have any influence on their repayment and utilisation of bank loan. The study also becomes essential to know whether the defaulted borrowers have pursued any economic activity by utilising the loan productively and generated income to repay the loan. Keeping these objectives in mind the data on the occupation wise distribution of defaulted beneficiaries of both the sample banks has been collected and presented in table 4.

Table 4: Occupation Wise Distribution of Defaulters of Sample Banks

Occupation	*Banks*		*Total*
	KBL	*SB*	
Govt. Employees	17 (16.7)	39 (28.9)	56 (23.6)
Self Employment/ Business	70 (68.6)	81 (60.0)	151 (63.7)
Agriculture	2 (2.0)	1 (0.7)	3 (1.3)
Others	13 (12.7)	14 (10.4)	27 (11.4)
Total	**102 (100.0)**	**135 (100.0)**	**237 (100.0)**

X^2 = 5.323, P = 0.150, NS.
Source: Survey Data.
Note: Figures in the parenthesis denote percentages to the total number of sample defaulters of respective banks.

An analysis of above table 1.4 reveals that 151 Defaulters (63.7) of the sample Defaulters of both the banks are self-employed/ small and medium businessmen, small scale industrialists and professionals. This indicates that there is no significant difference in occupation among the Defaulters of both public sector and private sector commercial banks. More number of Defaulters are from self-employment category compared to Govt. employees, agriculture and others. They need the bank mainly for the loan facilities to run their business. Agriculturists along with others i.e. self help group members are the third major occupational group constituting 3 and 27 (1.3 per cent and 11.4 per cent) respectively. Chi-square analysis shows that there is no significant difference between the banks with respect to Occupation of the Defaulters ($X^2 = 5.323$ $p=0.150>0.05$, NS).

Credit Facilities Availed by Defaulters

Purpose for which defaulters borrowed loan

Branch Managers of the bank provide loans for different purposes to the beneficiaries. Some of these turn to NPAs. The Defaulters borrowed for different purposes belong to Agriculture and allied activities, small business, small scale units and others. Sufficient income generation is important for the repayment of loan. Therefore, the study becomes essential to know the purpose for which the Defaulters borrowed and the relevant data has been collected and presented in Table 5.

Table 5 : Purpose of loan availed by the Defaulters

Types of loan availed	*Banks*		*Total*
	KBL	*SB*	
Agriculture and allied	4 (3.92)	5 (3.70)	9 (3.79)
Small business	78 (76.4)	83 (61.4)	161 (67.93)
Small Scale units	3 (2.94)	8 (5.92)	11 (4.64)
Others	17 (16.66)	39 (28.78)	56 (23.6)
Total	**102 (100.0)**	**135 (100.0)**	**237 (100.0)**

X^2 = 6.717, P = 0.081, NS Source: Survey Data.

Note: Figures in the parenthesis denote percentages to the total number of sample defaulters of respective banks.

From the above table 5, it can be observed that majority of the defaulters (67.93 per cent) were found in small business category because D.K. and Udupi are commercial and trading centers where plenty of opportunities are available to the businessmen/women. Least of the defaulters (9.0 per cent) are found under Agriculture and allied activities. Other category includes personal loans and commercial loans which has a share of 23.6 per cent.

There is no significant difference in the purpose of loan availed by the defaulters. (X^2=6.717, P= 0.081>0.05, NS).

Defaulters Carrying on the Economic Activities at Present

Generally the performance of the loan repayment of the beneficiaries largely depends on the level of income generated by the borrowers, good intention in repayment of loan, collateral security given to the loan and action taken to regularise the non performing loans.

The study on defaulters carrying on business/agricultural activities presently becomes essential to understand their present activities, their repayment habit of the NPAs and their capacity to generate income to repay the NPAs. The data pertaining to this is presented in the following Table 6.

Table 6: Defaulters Carrying on the Activities at Present

Defaulters carrying on the activities at present	*Banks*		*Total*
	KBL	*SB*	
Not carrying activities	55 (53.9)	78 (57.8)	133 (56.1)
Carrying activities	47 (46.1)	57 (42.2)	104 (43.9)
Total	**102 (100.0)**	**135 (100.0)**	**237 (100.0)**

X^2= 0.351, P= 0.554 NS Source: Survey Data

Note: Figures in the parenthesis denote percentages to the total number of sample defaulters of respective banks.

An analysis of above table 1.6 reveals that 55 (53.9 per cent) of KBL and 78 (57.8 per cent) of SB defaulters are not presently carrying on any activities. This might be the reason for non-repayment of their over dues. There is no significant difference between the opinions of the defaulters of the two banks regarding activities pursued by them at present (X^2=0.351, P=0.554>0.05 NS).

It is clear from the study that more than half of the defaulters of both the banks are presently not carrying on any economic activities. It shows the strong reason for non repayment of their over dues.

To analyse the causes for poor recovery of loan by the defaulters and to offer suggestions having policy implications for the purpose of reducing NPAs.

1. Out of total 237 defaulters, 102 (43.0 per cent) defaulters represented KBL and 135 (57.0 per cent) defaulters represented SB.
2. A majority of the defaulters of both the banks are in the age group ranging between 31 and 40 years and majority of the defaulters are males in both the banks.
3. A majority of the defaulters (39.7 percentages) qualification is below SSLC. It shows that the literacy level is low among the defaulters of both the banks in the study region.
4. A majority of the defaulters of both the banks (63.7 per cent) are Self Employed/Business people. It shows that the majority of the defaulters of both the banks availed loan for small business purpose other than small scale industries, agriculture and other purposes.

5. A majority of the defaulters of KBL availed long term (44.1 per cent) loan as well as cash credit/ overdrafts (33.4 per cent) and other types of loan. Whereas majority of the defaulters of SB (65.2 per cent) availed only long term loan.
6. A majority of defaulters of both the banks are presently neither carrying on the economic activities for which they borrowed nor any other activity.

Conclusion and Suggestions

The conclusions were drawn as financial inclusion through distribution of loan does not fulfill the objective of Financial Inclusion because if the borrower unable to repay the loan for various reasons and turned as a defaulter is very much affected the profitability, liquidity position of the banks in the form of NPA. Therefore, for faster, sustainable and meaningful inclusive growth the Government of India and RBI should make a strong and vibrant policy for the distribution of loan and repayment of loan and find the permanent solution to minimise the NPAs.

References

1. Anthony Sounders (1997), "Financial Institutions Management – A modern perspective", Irvin Publications, Second Edition.
2. Balachandran G (1998), "The Reserve Bank of India: 1951-1967", New Delhi, Oxford University Press.
3. Banambar Sahoo (2002), "Banker's Handbook on NPA management", Hyderabad, S.P. Gogia (Asia Law House), Second edition.
4. Bank of Baroda (1981), "Overduwes in agricultural advances: a case study of Shadnagar branch, Andra Pradesh, Madras, Bank of Baroda.
5. Bidani S.N. (2002), "Management of Non-Performing Assets", New Delhi, Books Private Limited.
6. Datey V.S. (2003), "Law relating to Securitisation and Reconstruction of Financial Assets and Enforcement of Security Interest, 2002", New Delhi, Taxmann Allied Services Private Limited.
7. Dreze, Jean and Sen, Amartya (1990), "The Political Economy of Hunger", UK, Oxford Clarendon Press.
8. Dreze, Jean and Sen, Amartya (1995), "India, Economic development and Social Opportunity", UK, Oxford University Press.
9. Federation of Indian Chambers of Commerce and Industry, "Bank NPAs – Need for a new Perspective" (2003), New Delhi, Federation House.
10. Gokul B. Rathi and Smith M.Sanhane (2002), "Non-Performing Assets", Tanvi Publications, Pune.
11. Aastha Bhasin (2006-07), "Understanding Risks in Banking: A Note", Vinimaya, Vol. 27 (4), January-March.
12. Amutha R. (2004), "An Analysis of Non-Performing Assets in Banks", Indian Economic Panorama, Vol. 14 (2), July.

13. Androeas A. Jobst (2003), "Loan Securitisation and Moral Hazard-Is increased transparency more beneficial" The ICFAI Journal of Applied Finance, Vol. 9 (9), December.
14. Aruna Kumari A.V (2002), "Economic Reforms and Performance of Indian Banking: A cross structural Analysis", Indian Economic Panorama, Vol.12 (3), December.
15. Aruna Kumari A.V. (2003), "Indian Banking Vision 2010", Indian Economic Panorama, Special Banking Issue.
16. Arun Yuole (2004) "The Problem of NPAs", Yojana, November.
17. Ashok Wadhwa and Carlton Pereira (2003), "Asset Reconstruction Companies", Banking Finance, Vol. 16 (4), April.
18. Bagchi B.K. (2007), "Credit Counselling-A Pragmatic Solution", The Indian Banker, Vol. 2 (2), February.
19. Bagchi S.K. (2005), "Credit Risk Mitigation- Implications of Basel-II Prescriptions in Indian Banking", IBA Bulletin, Vol. 27 (12), December.
20. Baiju, S. and Gabriel Simon Thattil (2000), "Performance of banks with Non-performing Assets: An Analysis of NPAs", Yojana, Vol. 17 (3), March.
21. Balachandran Nair K.K (1999), "Banks and Non-Performing Assets", Southern Economist, Vol. 38 (14), November.
22. Balaji Prasad. P and Chandrashekhar.M (2003), "Challenges of Banking Industry and Services Marketing", Indian Economic Panorama, Special Banking Issue.
23. Banambar Sahoo (1999), "Rating of Banks on NPA Management", IBA Bulletin, Vol. 21(10), October.
24. Bhagavat T.K. (1990), "Management of Non-Performing Assets in Banks", Bank Economist Conference.
25. Bhaskar Gopal S. (2002), "Frauds Relating to Security Offered to Banks for Loan-Mortgage by Deposit of the Title Deeds (Equitable Mortgages)" IBA Bulletin, Vol. 24 (5), May.
26. Bhaskar Rao V.K. (2004) "Management of Non-Performing Assets in Commercial Banks", Banking Finance, Vol. 17 (2), February.
27. Bhaskaran S. (2005), "Securitisation, Boon or bane for public sector Banks?" Professional Banker, August, pp. 39-42.
28. Bodla B.S. and Richa Verma (2006), "Performance of Commercial Banks in India: A Sectoral and Temporal Analysis", Asian Economic Review, Vol. 48 (3), December.
29. Buvaneswari K. (2008), "Impact of securitisation on Banks" Monthly Public Opinion Surveys, Vol. L III (10), July.
30. Chachadi N.G. (1994), "Two Decades of Banking Development in Karnataka", Southern Economist, Vol. 33(15 and 16), Dec.1 and 15.
31. Chandrashekar A.R. (2001), "Banking business in the New Millennium: Challenges to the PSBs", SBI Monthly Review, Vol. 40 (4), April.

26

Cotton Farmers Perception Towards Weather Based Insurance in Davangere, Karnataka-A Case Study

Mahadevaswamy M., Sajan C.P. and *G. Kotreshwar*

Introduction

Agriculture plays a signification role in India economy in term of its GDP (14). Majority of Indian population depend on agriculture sector. Indian agriculture mainly depends on monsoon rain and farmers suffer high loses year by year due to monsoon rain shocks (15). In order to avoid this farmers depend on crop insurance. In recent year's effort have been made in Indian and other countries to encourage formal insurance market so that there is improvement in diversification of weather related income shocks. Index insurance refers to a contract whose payout is based on measuring local rainfall during key phase of the agriculture season. Weather based insurance is now available at a retail level in many parts of India, although this market is still in their relative new development in terms of product design and distribution.

Rain fall insurance is more essential because it reduces transactional costs and the farmer does not need to formally file a claim, and the insurance company does not need to do an inspection to estimate the amount of loss since rainfall data is observed in close to real time. This also means that claims can be calculated and disbursed quickly to farmer. Weather based insurance is developed on the foundation of universally acceptable parameter and farmers also take the compensation in the form of scientific manner.

Weather Based Insurance (WBI)

Weather based insurance is an alternative to traditional Crop insurance for agriculture products. Weather based insurance provides the compensation on the basis of rain fall data. The insurance companies obtain rain fall data on the basis of publically verifiable and standard measure, based on this information compensation is given. The main aim of weather based insurance is to protect the farmers against weather related shocks such as shortage or heavy rain fall. The main reason to develop weather based insurance is to avoid the adverse selection, minimise the administration cost and most important is quick compensation settlement to the farmers etc.

Crop Insurance

Crop insurance is oldest and traditional form of insurance. It was very popular in the beginning stage. However, over period of time, due to the implementation of new form of insurance like weather based insurance farmers preferred weather based insurance rather than crop insurance. This happened because in crop insurance the compensation was given only after proper examination of the crop field, and incase of natural disaster like floods the farmers had to claim within 48 hrs and if there is delay in claim by the farmers the insurance companies would refused to pay the compensation even if the farmers had paid the premium within the due time. The crop insurance also failed to re-structure their policy scheme which had lots of inconsistency. Crop insurance has some deficiencies like multiple agencies, adverse selection, lack of unique, reliable methodology for crop yield verification and reporting system, more administrative cost, difficulty to take the compensation, lack of quick settlement etc. these led to lose the faith on crop insurance in the mind of farmers due to which farmers had to depend on other insurance scheme like weather based insurance.

Comparison of Crop insurance and Weather Based Insurance

Particular	*Crop insurance*	*Weather based insurance*
Adverse selection and moral hazard	Yes	No
Transparence	Low	High
Premium	Highly subsidized or high	Market rate
Basis risk	Low	No
Administration cost	High	Medium
Formers documents submitted	Require	Not require
Field verification	Require	Not require
Compensation	Not unique	Unique
Patter	Conventional type of insurance	Modern and scientific type of insurance
Nature of the product	Rigid	Dynamic
Service perception of the formers	Not good	Good
Product types	Varieties	Only weather based insurance product
Claim settlement	Between 6 to 24 months	Less then 30 days

There are several potential features in the weather based insurance product which involved, however to attract the farmers in Karnataka investment is very essential and improvement has to be done in some area like adopted sophisticated technology for weather costing. In order to create harmonious relationship between the farmers and insurance companies there should be meteorological department in every district, Taluk and Grama panchayat to assess the distribution of rainfall. The installation of weather station attracts the farmers towards the weather based insurance.

Objective of the Study

The main objective of this survey is to study farmer's perception towards weather based insurance in Dhavangere district, Karnataka, since weather based insurance is relatively new concept to the Karnataka farmers.

Data Collection and Analysis

In order to fulfill the objective, the primary data was collected from the respondent through simple random sampling units structured questionnaire in some selected villages like Channagire, Harihara, Malebennuru, Arasikere and Chegateri. The sample size is 108. The respondent involved during the collection of data were uneducated farmers, educated farmers, younger farmers, aged farmers etc. the information differs from farmer to farmer based on their gender, age, education, level of knowledge, ready to take the risk etc.

It was observed that small growers were not much interested in purchasing the weather based insurance because of low income level which did not permit to purchase the weather based insurance even though it had less premium. Most of the dynamic farmers don't have the proper idea/ information about the weather based insurance, most of the farmers have not purchased the W.B.I. due to lack of knowledge regarding this particular insurance scheme.

Perception Process

The farmer's perception towards the weather based insurance can be identified by the perception model which is given in Fig. 1.

The above research model reveals the Karnataka farmer's perception towards weather based insurance product. According to this model the farmers are having two options to purchase the insurance product which is crop insurance or weather based insurance which is considered as the input process in the first level. Next level is cognition process. The cognition process means thinking process in these process farmers makes a discussion whether to purchase the insurance scheme or not. The discussion making is influenced by many factors such as farmer association, NGO's and other factors like family members, neighbors, friends' opinions etc. The final level is expressing their perception about the weather based insurance product it may be in three ways which are positive, neutral and negative with respect to weather based insurance product.

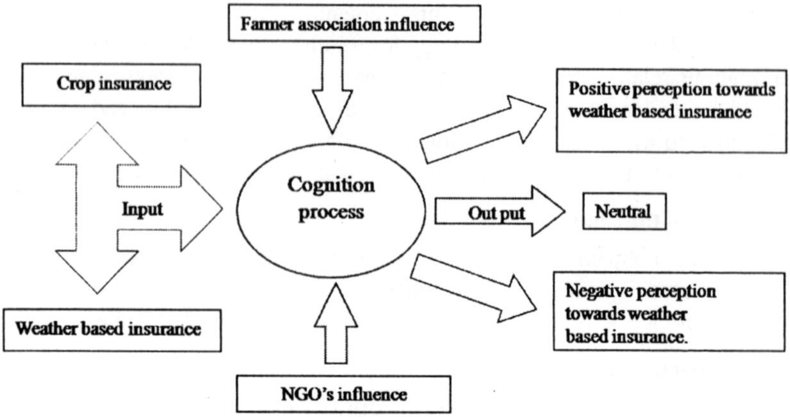

Fig. 1 : Perception Process.

Data Analysis and Interpretation

The Primary data collected from the respondent were analysed with the help of statistical tool (i.e. average), and the result are tabulated which is given in Table 1. Give the information of farmers' perception with respect to district gender, age, education.

Table 1: Perception of farmers in Davangere District

Partculars	*Categories*	*Freq-uency*	*Perc-entage*	*Positive perception*	*Negative perception*
District	Davangere	108	100	67	41
	Total	108	100	67	41
Gender	Male	89	82.41	53	36
	Female	19	17.59	14	05
	Total	108	100	67	41
Age	18-30	22	20.37	13	09
	31-50	47	43.51	28	19
	51 and above	39	36.12	22	17
	Total	108	100	63	45
Education	Educated: SSLC, PUC Degree, Post graduate	23	21.30	14	09
	Uneducated	85	78.70	53	32
	Total	108	100	67	41

Farmers' Perception with Respect to Gender

The survey was conducted in five villages. The questionnaire was carried out with respect to the gender, age and education among 108 farmers. In these 108 farmers 89 are male and 19 are female. In male farmers 53.94% of them showed their interest in accepting this scheme where as 46.06% showed negative response towards the weather based insurance. Among the female farmers 73.68% of them showed positive response and 26.32% showed negative response. The results obtained are given in table 2. The graphical representation of farmers response is given in Fig. 2. From graph one can clear say that, female farmers' perception to wards W.B.I. is more when compared to male farmers.

Table 2: Farmers perception towards WBI Scheme with respect to Gender

Categories	*Frequency*	*Positive perception*	*Negative perception*	*Positive perception (%)*	*Negative percepti on (%)*
Male	89	48	41	53.94	46.06
Female	19	14	05	73.68	26.32

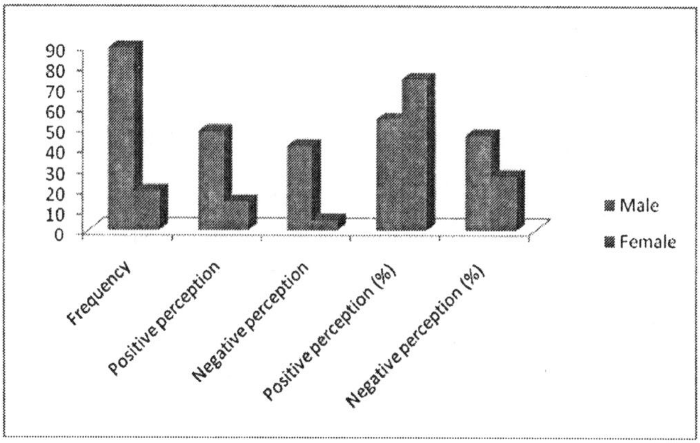

Fig. 2: Farmers perception towards WBI Scheme with respect to Gender

Farmers' Perception with Respect to Age

The response of farmers towards weather based insurance varies with respect to age. The results obtained are given in Table 3. Based on the results obtained we can say that the young and middle aged farmers showed more interest in weather based insurance scheme when compared to old age farmers. The graphical representation of variation of farmer's perception with respect to age is given in Fig. 3.

Table 3: Farmers Perception Towards WBI Scheme with Respect to Age

Categories	*Frequency*	*Positive perception*	*Negative perception*	*Positive perception (%)*	*Negative perception (%)*
18-30	22	13	09	59.10	40.90
31-50	47	28	19	59.57	40.43
51 and above	39	22	17	56.41	43.59

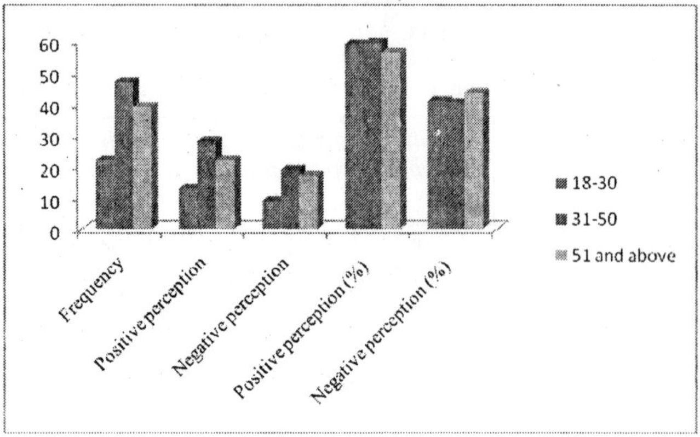

Fig. 3: Farmers Perception Towards WBI Scheme with Respect to Age.

Farmers' perception with respect to Education

Education plays a prominent role in perception of farmers towards weather based insurance. According to the survey conducted most of the farmers are uneducated. In the present case, among 108 farmers 85 are uneducated and 23 are educated. Among educated farmers 60.86% of them showed positive response and among uneducated 62.35% showed positive response. The results obtained are given in Table 4 and the pictorial representation of the perception of farmers with respect to education is given in Fig. 4.

Table 4: Farmers Perception Towards WBI Scheme with Respect to Education

Categories	*Freq-uency*	*Positive perception*	*Negative perception*	*Positive perception (%)*	*Negative percepti on (%)*
Educated	23	14	09	60.86	39.14
Uneducated	85	53	32	62.35	37.65

The overall opinion of the farmers of Davangere district is given in Table 5, the results clearly depicts that 67% of the farmers showed positive perception towards weather based insurance and 33% of them showed negative response.

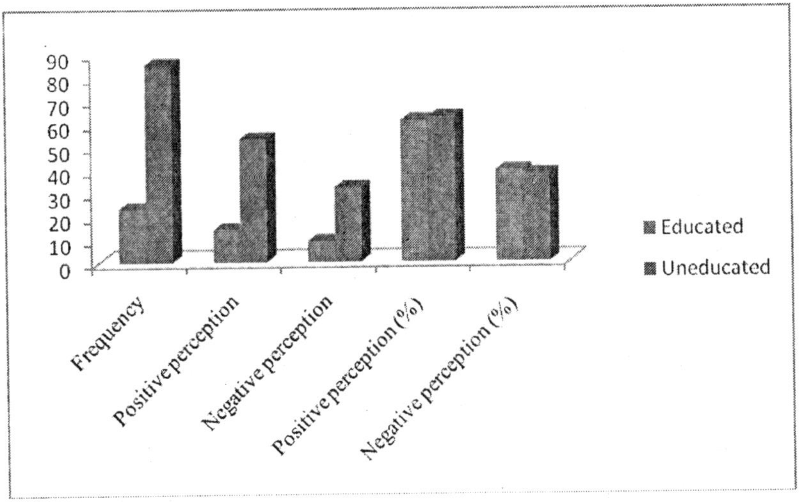

Fig. 4 : Farmers Perception Towards WBI Scheme with Respect to Education.

Table 5: Farmers perception towards WBI Scheme in Dhavangere District

Particular	*Positive perception*	*Negative perception*
Davangere District	**67**	**41**

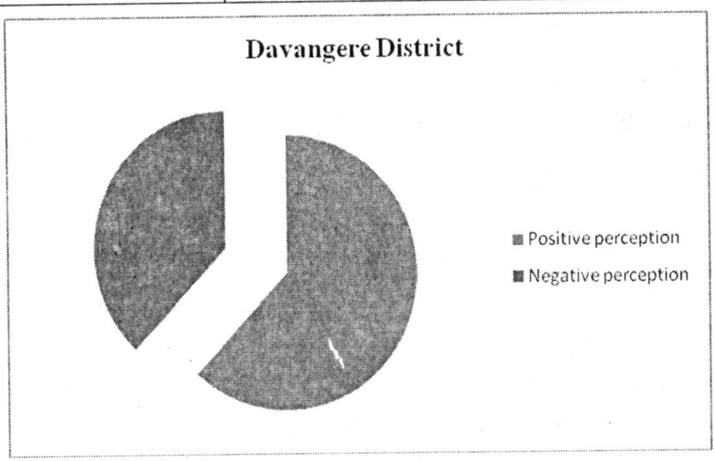

Fig. 5: Farmers Perception Towards WBI Scheme in Davangere District.

Conclusion

The study reveals that Karnataka farmers have faced the risk in the agriculture sectors since long time, in order to avoid its in agriculture sectors, government and private sectors have given its own contributions. Initially government and private sector insurance company have introduced the crop insurance scheme. It was quite suitable for long time but in present condition it has failed to create a positive perception towards crop insurance scheme due to lack of re-structuring policy, low indemnity level, localised calamities are not covered and lack of quick settlement. It was mainly quoted from the farmers when the primary data was collected. Apart from this, the farmers have positive perception towards the weather based insurance scheme. According to the farmers weather based insurance scheme have more benefit and are attractive to the farmers due to benefits involved in the policy. The policy is having more benefits to the farmers in term of quick settlement, rain fall can be independently verified and measured, compared to crop insurance scheme weather based insurance scheme is inexpensive, no field verification etc. Weather based insurance scheme is yet to create awareness in the state of Karnataka because some farmers do not have much knowledge about weather based insurance scheme even though they have purchased the scheme. The awareness programme is also conducted through NGOs or farmers association which can be more effective and suitable way to appreciate the farmers. Finally weather based insurance is not only solution for entire agriculture risk but at present situation as compared to Crop insurance scheme, weather based insurance scheme is much better to mitigate the risk.

References

1. Barnett. B.J. and Mahul. O (2008), "Weather Index Insurance for Agriculture and Rural Areas in Lower Income Countries".
2. Gine. X, Townsend. R and Vickery. J, (2007), "Patterns of Rainfall Insurance Participation in Rural India", A Research paper.
3. Hess, Ulrich (2003): Innovative Financial Services for Rural India: Monsoon-Indexed Lending and Insurance for Small holders, Agriculture and Rural Development Working paper 9, The World Bank (available at: http://www.climate-insurance.org/upload/ pdf/hess2003_ financial_ services_ rural_india.pdf) accessed on 12 October, 2008.
4. Hardaker, J.B., Huirne, R.B.M., Anderson, J.R., 1997. Coping with Risk in Agriculture. CAB International, Wallingford, UK.
5. Indian Agriculture: Towards Employment Guarantee and Poverty Reduction, Sage New Delhi, chp.7: 161-190. Singh, Surjit and M.S. Rathore eds. (2010): Rainfed Agriculture in India: Perspectives and Challenges Rawat Publications, Jaipur
6. Singh, Surjit (2009b): "Climate Change and Gender Concerns" a paper presented in a seminar organised by NORAD to review Norwegian Gender Action Plan 2007-2009, Olso, 9 March.

7. Singh, Surjit and R.L. Jogi (2008): Weather Insurance in Rajasthan: Some Grassroots Experiences a report submitted to Oxfam International (CENTAD), New Delhi.
8. Sinha, Sidharth (2004): "Agriculture Insurance in India: Scope for Participation of Private Insurers", Economic and Political Weekly, 19 June, 2605-2612.
9. Townsend, Robert (1994): "Risk and Insurance in Village India", Econometrica, 62: 539-592.
10. Townsend, Robert (1994): "Risk and Insurance in Village India", Econometrica, 62: 539-592. Vyas, V.S. and Surjit Singh (2005): Agriculture Crop Insurance: Performance and Needed Reforms, a report submitted to Agriculture Insurance Company of India, New Delhi.
11. Varangis, P., Larson, D., Anderson, J.R., 2002. Agricultural markets and risks: management of the latter, not the former. Policy Research Working Paper 2793. The World Bank.
12. Vyas, V.S and Surjit Singh (2006): "Crop Insurance in India: Scope for Improvement" Economic and Political Weekly, November 4.
13. World Bank (2005): Managing Agricultural Production Risk: Innovations in Developing Countries, Agriculture and Rural Development Department, report no. 32727-GLB, Washington D.C.
14. http://www.economicsfanatic.com/2012/03/agriculture-sector-can-propel-indias.html, http://www.indiareviewchannel.com/resources/2091-Contribution-agriculture-GDP.aspx Per Capita crude oil consumption, demand and geopolitics of oil ,US debt at staggering $22 trillion with debt to GDP at 147%. Will the federal reserve system continue to pile on government debt?, Debt with no ceiling for government sector, A case for long-term investment in agriculture
15. http://www.hdfcergo.com/rural/RainfallIndex.html.
16. www.economywatch.com.
17. http://www.indiareviewchannel.com/resources/2091-Contribution-agriculture-GDP.aspx.
18. http://www.indiareviewchannel.com/resources/2091-Contribution-agriculture-GDP.aspx.

27

Street Vendors in Urban Informal Sector: Financially Excluded or Included?

Prakruthi A.R., *Mamatha Kyatannanavar* and *Naveen Chandra C.B.*

Introduction

Access to finance, especially by the poor and vulnerable groups is a prerequisite for employment, economic growth, poverty reduction and social cohesion. Further, access to finance will empower the vulnerable groups by giving them an opportunity to have a bank account, to save and invest, to insure their homes or to partake of credit, thereby facilitating them to break the chain of poverty. However, in spite of a large network of the institutional credit system, it has not been able to adequately penetrate the informal rural financial markets and the non-institutional sources continue to play a dominant role in purveying the credit needs of the people residing in rural as well as urban areas. Thus, important challenge facing the banking sector is to extend financial services to all sections of society. Like others, the poor need a range of financial services that are convenient, flexible, and affordable and not just loans. At this juncture the introduction on "financial inclusion" comes from the recognition that this can serve the interests of both society and the banking system.

In the era of globalisation, the retail sector is the fast growing emerging sector after agriculture in India by providing employment. However, besides formal retail chain, small retailing including street vending has been one of the easiest ways to survive for working poor and is wide spread in the urban informal sector. Street vendors play very important role in urban India by providing employment and income and other aspects. They sell different kinds of goods such as clothes and hosiery, lather, moulded plastic goods and different kinds of household necessary goods, which are manufactured in small scale or home based industries where large numbers of workers are employed (Bhowmik 2001). However, studies reveal that street vendors face many problems regarding their social protection, working condition, credit accessibility, and their public space utilisation. Besides many legislation, policies like National Policy on Urban Street Vendors of 2004 and 2009, The Street Vendors (Protection Promotions of Livelihood) Bill 2007 and Street Vendors (Protection of Livelihood and Regulation of Street Vendors) Bill 2009, even though the status of street vendors not improved upon a satisfactory level. And still large majority of the street venders left out under the broad per view of financial inclusion. Against this background the paper is prepared with the following objectives.

Objectives of the Study

1. To highlight the socio-economic status of street vendors.
2. To reveal the financial accessibility of street vendors.
3. To offer some policy prescriptions.

Methodology

The study is based on both primary and secondary data. This study has been conducted on Street Vendors spreading in Mysore City of Mysore district of Karnataka State. The primary data has been collected through structured interview schedule. A total of 100 street vendors, were selected for the study through random selection. The secondary data were collected from available literature in books, journals, research reports, and other published materials related to the street vendors. The data were analysed by using the simple percentage, average and indices, wherever appropriate.

Street Vendors – A Brief Note

Street vending has been prevalent in our country since ancient times. Though most of these small venders were local people there were also include those who came from far off places like Afghanistan, Tibet and even China. Today this section of the urban employed is perhaps the most visible in the urban informed economy. A street vender is broadly defined as a person who offers goods or services for sale to the public without having a permanent built up structure but with a temporary static structure or mobile stall. Street vendors may be stationary by occupying space on the pavements or other public/ private areas, or may be mobile in the sense that they move from place to place carrying their wares on push carts or in cycle or baskets on their heads, or may sell their wares in moving bus etc. (Sharit K. Bhowmik, 2005).

There are 3 basic categories of street vendors:

(a) Stationary (b) Peripatetic and (c) Mobile.

(a) **Stationary vendors** are those who carry out vending on a regular basis at a specific location. Example : Those occupying space on the pavements or other public places and / or private areas either open/ covered with implicit or explicit consent of the authority. RMC market, Devaraja market, small market in Mysore City

(b) **Peripatetic vendors** are those who carry out vending on foot and sell their goods and services and includes those who carry baskets on their head/ slung on their shoulders and those who sell their goods on pushcarts

(c) **Mobile Street venders** are those who move from place to place vending their goods or mobile units on wheel.

There is a substantial increase in the number of street vendors in the major Asian cities. In India, the National Policy for Urban Street Vendors/ Hawkers notes that street vendors constitute approximately 2 per cent of the population of a metropolis. The total number of street vendors in the country is estimated at around 10 million (Bhowmik S K, 2005). Women constitute a large segment of their street vendors in almost every city in helping and supplementing their family income. Besides the employment context, street vendors also support urban rich and urban poor. Street vendors prop up urban rich to provide daily requirements as available on their doorsteps because some street vendors built up their profession in front of housing complexes (Tiwari, 2000). Street vending is not only a source of self employment to the poor in cities and towns but also a means to provide "affordable" as well as 'convenient' services to a majority of the urban population. They try to solve their livelihood issues through their own meager financial resources.

Result and Discussion

A large section of street vendors in Mysore city are those with low skills and who have migrated to Mysore cities in search of employment. These people take a street vending when they do not find other means of livelihood. Though the income in this profession in low, the investment is too low and the people do not require special skills or training. Hence for these people, men and women street vending is the easiest form for earning their livelihood.

Financial conditions of the street vendors in Mysore city are in miserable conditions, they earn enough to satisfy their hunger, however, less to save anything for their future. It came in to notice that most of the vendors have large families (number of dependents) to feed and save nothing or very less. The uncertainty of income due to the frequent removal/evacuation of markets make their life more miserable, also, this affects majorly to those who vend in weekly markets and removal of market for once means loss of income for the whole week.

Table 1: Demographic Profile of the Respondents

Particulars	*Categories*	*No of Respondents*	*Percentage of Respondents*
Gender	Male	59	59.0
	Female	41	41.0
	Total	**100**	**100.0**
Caste	SC	33	33.0
	ST	26	26.0
	Other	26	26.0
	Minority	15	15.0
	Total	**100**	**100.0**
Age	<20	5	5.0
	21-30	19	19.0
	31-40	40	40.0
	41>	36	36.0
	Total	**100**	**100.0**
Education	Illiterate	44	44.0
	Primary	29	29.0
	8-10	18	18.0
	>10	9	16.0
	Total	**100**	**100.0**

Source: Primary Survey.

The table 1.1 shows that out of 100 respondents studied 59 members are males and 49 members are females. The Caste compositions shows that out of 100 respondents interviewed, 33% of the respondents belonged to the Scheduled Caste, whereas 26% belong to the Scheduled tribes. The table also shows the distribution of the respondents according to their age. It reveals that 5% of respondents belong to the age group of 20 and below and about 19% of respondents belong to the age group of 21-30. But most of the respondent's i.e. 40% of respondents belongs to the age group of 31-40 and 36% of the respondents belong to the age group of 41 and above.

Educational background of the sample household is very important to describe as the bulk of their access to market, employment, credit, institutions, etc., is mainly dependent on the level of educational attainment by the sample respondents. Regarding the educational status is concerned the table shows that 29% of respondents were completed primary education. About 18% of respondents finished high school education and 16% of respondents studied above 10th or SSLC. The interesting fact is that 44% of the respondents are illiterate and despite being illiterate they are conducting their business that includes maintaining accounts having an inventory of goods bought and sold.

Occupational Pattern

Table 2 reveals the occupational pattern and regarding the occupation is concerned. It shows that 28 per cent of them are Vegetable/Fruits and about 40 per cent of them were engaged in sale of food items especially fast food and 23 per cent of them were doing other vending work. The items sold by vendors consist of a variety of goods. The non-perishable items include clothes, metal utensils, plastic goods, and leather goods etc. The perishable goods include vegetables, fruits, flowers, fish and cooked food. The preference of the vendors was for selling the perishable food items. They do so because the prices of these items are less compared to non-perishable items such as household and electronic goods and they also constitute mass consumption goods. The data shows that some cities have a greater proportion of vendors selling perishable goods (40%). The fruit vendors are in a better position than the vegetable vendors. The cost of fruits is higher than that of vegetables. The profit margin of fruit vendors is also quite high.

The working conditions of the street vendors of the Mysore city shows that almost all were involved in the activity for 5 to 6 days in the week. They sell their goods during most of the day or in the mornings and evenings. The activity was at its peak in the evenings as most of the office goers bought goods while returning home. The minimum time spent on street vending (including time spent on procuring the goods) was 8 to 10 hours every day. In some cases they spent 12 hours or more. The employing helpers on paid basis is very rare but 10% of the hawkers are assisted by their family members.

Table 2. Type of Occupations

Type of Occupation	*No of Respondents*	*Percentage of Respondents*
Vegetable/Fruits	28	28.0
Food	40	40.0
Garments	9	9.0
Others	23	23.0
Total	**100**	**100.0**

Source: Primary Survey.

Level of Income

The earning of street vendors depends on the products they sell, and it deviates from trade to trade, location to location, the volume of trade and terms of trade. It is seen that there are few of the vendors' income is quite high according to their business types, age of the business, location and product they sell. Interestingly, it is noticed from the data that income of garment vendors, vendors those who are selling fruits and food items deviates from vegetable vendors and small enterprises. But the profit margin of the vendors those who sell perishable goods like, vegetable vendors, fruit vendors, food vendors is quite impressive than others category of vendors. These vendors earn about 30 to 500 per cent profit of their daily sales.

Estimates of average earning of street vendors in 2000 by studies, referred to in the Report on Conditions of Work and Promotion of Livelihoods in the Unorganised Sector, 2007 of the National Commission for Enterprises in the Unorgnaised Sector (NCEUS), suggest that the vendors' earnings are very low although they vary from trade to trade and from location to location (GoI, 2009).

Table 1.3 shows that around 39 per cent vendors' per month income are between Rs. 3000 and Rs. 4500 while 21 per cent vendors' per month income fall into Rs. 4500- 6500 and 14 per cent of them earn a monthly income of more than 8500 and so on. Since street vending is not a licensed activity in Mysore city, street vendors face corrupt as the police. These vendors have to pay Rs. 2 or 3 every day to the beat constable in order to play their trade.

Table 3: Monthly Earning

Monthly Earning	*No of Respondents*	*Percentage of Respondents*
3000-4500	39	39.0
4500-6500	21	21.0
6500-8500	26	26.0
8500 >	14	14.0
Total	**100**	**100.0**

Source: Primary Survey.

Details of Banking Account

Individuals having a bank account are the first step of financial inclusion and the researchers have posed the question to the responds about the bank account and the result was alarming. Data reveal that out of 100 street venders surveyed only 36 of the respondents have formal bank account and rest of them transact with the other informal banking systems like, informal chit fund, money lender, friends, pawn brokers etc. It clearly shows that though government has introduced many policy measures to include large section of poor including unorganised sector workers like street vendors under financial inclusion the result is not worth mentioning. The government had given clear directions to banks to make arrangements to open no frills account to groups like street vendors, however in Mysore city most of the street venders have not utilised this facility much.

Table 4: Bank Account

Bank Account	*No of Respondents*	*Percentage of Respondents*
Yes	36	36.0
No	64	64.0
Total	**100**	**100.0**

Source: Primary Survey.

Do you have the saving habit?

Saving is one of the important yardsticks of economic inclusion. Due to lack of time and lack of awareness, the street vendors especially women do not really save, unless otherwise they are properly motivated and ensured some future returns/credit to overcome unexpected expenses. Same is the case of street venders. Table 1.5 shows that only 15 per cent vendors of total vendors manage by saving in formal sources banks, post offices where as 42 per cent vendors they manage their social protection by saving in informal chit fund and 7 per cent of respondents are saving in Self Help groups. However, interesting fact is that 34 per cent of respondents are not saving any money in any sources whether it is formal or informal. Because, of lack of time and unnecessary procedure to move a formal sector for the purpose of savings.

Table 1.5: Sources of Saving

Sources of saving	*No of Respondents*	*% of Respondents*
Bank/Post Office	15	15.0
Chit Fund	42	42.0
SHG	7	7.0
Other	2	2.0
Not Saving	*34*	*34.0*
Total	**100**	**100.0**

Source: Primary Survey.

Membership in SHG

Data reveals that 22.0 of the respondents are the member of Self help groups and they opine that due to lack of time, most of time they do not able to attend to the SHG meetings. Hence, for most of them except saving the regular amount ranging from 10 Rs. to 25 Rs. weekly they don't get opportunity to save in other formal sources and borrows money from SHGs. Most of them opine that main reason for joining SHG is to get loan and not to save money. Most of the women street vendors withdraw membership form the SHG due to nonavaliability of time to attend regular meetings of SHG

Table 6: Membership in SHG

Member in SHG	*No of Respondents*	*Percentage of Respondents*
Yes	22	22.0
No	78	78.0
Total	**100**	**100.0**

Source: Primary Survey.

Details of Borrowing

The monetary problem is compounded by the fact that the vendors have scarce resources for their trade and they need to obtain credit by borrowing. Most of the street vendors report having borrowed from money lenders who charge exorbitant interest rates (GoI, 2009). Hence, he instances of poverty that is haunting the street vendors compelled them to borrow money from various sources. Women vendors were in very less number when selling the cooked food is considered, which is supposed to be a better earning opportunity in the vending profession, but, also demand a high level of capital investment. Hence, very often they borrow money from moneylender which is a only option for them.

Table 7: Habit Borrowing

Habit of Borrowing	*No of Respondents*	*Percentage of Respondents*
Yes	92	92.0
No	8	8.0
Total	**100**	**100.0**

Source: Primary Survey.

According to the table 7 we could see that about 34 per cent of the respondents do not save in any sources, however about 92 per cent of people have the habit of borrowing money for many reason like purchasing products to sell, emergency, social function and family maintenance. Hence, it shows that though most of them borrow money even though most of them do not have the habit of saving. It is revealed from this present study that the purpose of borrowing is not only for their economic activities but they also borrow for their social security purposes. Thus, this section has pointed out that street vendors fall into debt trap due to high indebtedness.

Access to capital is an important economic linkage that ties street trade to the economy which affects the vendors' economic activities, profits, and potential business growth. Capital is needed for initiating the business and, later, for running and expanding the business through buying new merchandise. The table 1.8 reveals that only 9.0 of the respondents borrow money from formal sources like, post offices, banks, co-operatives etc., and during emergencies they too depend on money lenders for loan. About 58% of the respondents depend upon moneylenders for the loan and they sometime charge exorbitant rate of interest around 3-10 per cent per month. About 6 per cent of the respondents avail loan from other sources like traders, pawn brokers etc. Furthermore, some of the vendors are paying rate of interest on their indebtedness since 2-3 years who borrowed for their social protection purposes.

Table 8: Sources of Borrowing

Sources of Borrowing	*No of Respondents*	*Percentage of Respondents*
Bank/Post offices	9	9.0
Money lender	58	58.0
Friends/Relatives	19	19.0
SHG's	8	8.0
Others	6	6.0
Total	**100**	**100.0**

Source: Primary Survey.

Data reveals that there are many reasons for borrowing money from the moneylender. About 27% of the respondents reveal that they borrow money from moneylender due to its easy procedure and 67% of them opine that they borrow money due to its easy procedure, timely availability and another main reason that is one can get money in small amount also.

Access to Insurance/Micro insurance

Table 9: Persons Having Insurance

Insurance	*No of Respondents*	*Percentage of Respondents*
Yes	81	81.0
No	19	19.0
Total	**100**	**100.0**

Source: Primary Survey.

It is very interesting to note that even though 88 per cent of them are well knowledgeable about insurance scheme but only 19 per cent of them have been insured (Table 9). They opine that the main reason to not having insurance is unable to meet the ID proof formalities of financial institutions. Because some of them are migrants and they have no permanent residence in the city. Most of the street vendors are living in the slums of the city and they are neither the members of the registered trade unions or associations.

The street vendors have become an indispensable organ of the urban India. However, street vendors face some constraints such as lack of access to credit, adequate infrastructure, sufficient social security coverage and many other resources as other activities within the informal sector though they play very important actors in the urban informal economy by generating employment and supporting urban poor as well rich. The study reveals that the street vendors depend on the money lenders for credit accessibility as well as for social security purposes. Interestingly, the result shows that the street vendors are also forced to borrow at exorbitant rate of interest more so for the social security purposes that lead them to fall into a debt-trap situation, which is a matter of a deep concern.

Policy Suggestions

Based on the findings of the study, the following policy measures can be suggested for improving the economic condition of street vendors and thereby bring them on mainstream development.

As a first step of financial inclusion, saving behavior of the respondents should be improved and they can be empowered by providing microfinance through Self Help Groups, SGSY (Swarna Jayanti Gram Swarojgar Yojana) loans and other loans specially kept for small enterprises etc. The problem of moneylender is very much high among these people. Because, most of the households don't have the banking relationship like bank accounts, hence they don't avail loan from formal resources. Hence, they should be encouraged to open an account in the bank so that they can be freed from the clutches of money lenders. Starting a SHG operations and making them to open account in the bank lead to decrease in the working of money lenders in the colonies.

- Street vendors, being micro entrepreneurs should be provided with vocational education and training and entrepreneurial development skills to upgrade their technical and business potentials so as to increase their income levels as well as to look for more remunerative alternatives.
- There is need to introduce new products by the banks and financial institutions appropriate with the requirement of rural women. The customer-contact-programmers especially for women should be organised to disseminate the information of various schemes and financial needs of street vendors.
- The study reveals that there is need for more flexible loans. This would require a serious restructuring of financial products and marketing strategies. Some progressive financial institutions have introduced loan products with this greatly needed flexibility in order

to better suit the urban environment. There is a need to separate product exclusively for these families.

- With respect to credit, the Credit Guarantee Fund Scheme for Small Industries (CGFSI), designed by the Ministry of Micro, Small and Medium Enterprises, Government of India and the Small Industries Development Bank of India (SIDBI) may be extended to the street vendors. This scheme aims at resolving the problem of collaterals, and inducing banks to gradually move away from a completely risk-averse stance toward small scale industries. (GoI, 2009).
- Since most of the street venders lack proper address of correspondences and some of them are even migrants. Hence, to solve this problem there is a need to start a uniform identification number with a national identity card, which should lead to the creation of a credit bureau. So that, bad borrowers would be easily identified as in the formal banking sector, and formal banking institutions can lend loan to these people without much risk.
- There is a need to start separate co-operative bank in order to give special financial assistance to poor street vendors in urban areas.
- It is suggested that banks should come up with some special schemes for the vendors by reducing the procedural norms to extend the financial assistance to the vendors.
- It shall be the responsibility of the Government of India to take steps to ensure that street vending activities are carried out in accordance with street vending laws and also provide institutional designs; legislative frameworks and other necessary arrangements are put in place in conformity with the National Policy on Urban Street Vendor.
- At the higher education institutional level it shall make certain academic programmes accomplish with the students for the purpose of provide awareness to street vendors regarding financial plan, scheme and protections towards various street vendors.

Conclusion

The condition of street vendors is still miserable due to several reasons. They have no security for their old age thus have to work in order to feed them till they die. Also, most of them take money from money lender on higher interest rates in order to buy the goods. In short we can say that vending activity gives vendors, an opportunity to survive but survival is really costing them their lives. Today the street vendors have become inseparable part of our life and sustain their life and development is the responsibility of all. Hence, thinking of overall development of the street vendors is an urgent task.

References

Bhowmik, S.K. (2001): Hawkers in the Urban Informal Sector: A Study of Street Vendors in Seven Cities, National alliance of street Vendors in India (NASVI). www.streetnet.org.za/English/page10.htm

Bhowmik S K (2005): Street Vendors in Asia: A Review, Economic and Political Weekly May 28, June 4, 2005.

Tiwari, G. (2000): Encroachers or Services Provider?" *Seminar* 491, June, 2000. Available at: www.seminarindia.org.

GoI (2009): National Policy on Urban Street Vendors, 2009, Government of India Ministry of Housing and Urban Poverty Alleviation, New Delhi.

28

Microinsurance: A New Paradigm in Financial Inclusion

B.H. Suresh and *Amrutha Varshini V.*

Introduction

Microinsurance is generally, but accurately referred to as a new concept. It first appeared as a new financial service with microfinance but is now increasingly becoming an independent approach. Like regular insurance, microinsurance involves the pooling of risks across individuals who make small, regular payments in exchange for the promise of future compensation in the event of a financial loss. The "micro" refers to the fact that it targets the low income market through innovative cost structures, premium payment systems, terms of coverage and delivery modes.

Microinsurance can significantly assist the poor and low-income populations with managing some of their risks, but governments must meet their primary obligation to provide basic health services, fire fighting services, employment and education and so on.

The importance of microinsurance is undeniable in India, where a large percentage of the population lives below poverty line. Most of the people in this segment are illiterate and their level of awareness about insurance is very low. In order to facilitate penetration of microinsurance to the lower income segments, Insurance Regulatory Development Authority (IRDA) has formulated the microinsurance regulations 2005, which helped the distribution of insurance products that are affordable to the rural and urban poor and enabled microinsurance as an integral part of the country's wider insurance system.

Microinsurance mainly covers insurance products specifically designed to meet the challenges and needs of the poor. Although the risks faced by the poor are pretty much the same as most people, reality is that the poor are more vulnerable and susceptible to risks, unforeseen disasters and accidents tend to have a huge financial impact on them. Microinsurance provides the poor with the means of withstanding these shocks and being able to build up their resources and improve their standards of living. The microinsurance industry is still in the early stages of development with a small product range. Thus one can say that, microinsurance is a tool for the country's low income people to protect themselves from adversities. It will moderate financial risks and provide optimism to policy holders, helping them cope with financial emergencies. Microinsurance has been an integral output of microfinance and will assist the poor from being further impoverished as a result of adverse events. Further, efforts to enhance the provision of microinsurance services have become an important talking point if not necessarily a prominent feature of the Indian financial landscape in recent years. Its implications for reducing economic vulnerability amongst the low income strata of the population has, in many case, ensured that microinsurance is recognised as an essential aspect of financial inclusion. It is from this perspective that microinsurance is defined as "insurance that is provided to the low income segments of the population in accordance with generally accepted insurance practices".

Objectives of the Study

The main objectives of the present study are:

1. To understand the concept of microinsurance.
2. To know the various models of microinsurance.
3. To study the growth and development of micro-insurance in India.
4. To analyse the developments on the supply and demand sides of micro insurance.
5. To suggest some implementable suggestions for facilitation of desired growth and outcome of the microinsurance sector.

Concept of Microinsurance

Microinsurance, commonly called as insurance for the poor, has recently drawn the attention of practitioners in developing countries. In common parlance, microinsurance is the provision of insurance services to low-income households, which serves as an important tool to reduce risks for the already vulnerable population. There is no unanimously accepted definition of microinsurance despite its profound use and understanding across stakeholders and others. A simple definition of microinsurance is offered by Churchill (2006) is that it is an insurance that (i) operates by risk-pooling (ii) financed through regular premiums and (iii) tailored to the poor who would otherwise not be able to take out insurance. Microinsurance is defined as insurance that is accessed by the low-income population, provided by a variety of different entities, but run in accordance with generally accepted insurance practices. Importantly this means that the risk insured under a microinsurance policy is managed based on insurance principles and funded by premiums (International Association of Insurance Supervisors, 2007). Microinsurance is different from usual form of insurance. A macro definition of microinsurance states that it is the provision of financial protection contingent on the occurrence of predefined risk in exchange for an ex-ante premium payment affordable to the clients. In terms of micro definition, microinsurance is more complicated as there are different approaches. Micro as reference to low premium and low benefits may be affordable but it may not be effective enough to manage risks of different types of different categories of clients. Microinsurance is often believed to be an important component of a broader set of financial services under microfinance – making available financial services for poor households and enterprises to sustain their livelihoods. Basically there are two broad categories of microinsurance often commonly understood – one focused on extending social protection to the poor in the absence of appropriate government schemes and the other offering a vital financial service to low-income households by developing an appropriate business model that enables the poor to be a profitable (or sustainable) market segment for commercial or cooperative insurers. Microinsurance is also taken as group insurance that can cover thousands of customers under one contract. It requires an intermediary between the customer and the insurance company. This intermediary role has been played mainly by non-governmental organisation (NGO) and microfinance institutions (MFI). The role of intermediaries in growth of microinsurance in India is well documented. Currently around 135 million, or 5%, of low income people in developing countries are using microinsurance products. But the size of insurance market for low income groups is large and it constitutes about 1.5 to 3 billion potential clients (Microinsurance Centre, 2007). According to a research carried out by Swiss Re in 2007, most growth in the insurance industry over the past decade has come from the wealthy and middle income markets in emerging economies. Premiums grew by 3.3% globally and by 11.8% in the emerging markets in that year. Though partly this was due to a growing number of clients moving into the wealthy and middle income brackets in these countries, it is also attributable to insurance expanding into new markets. The number of people covered under microinsurance is estimated about 78 millions in 77 countries out of 100 less developed countries.

Microinsurance Delivery Models

One of the greatest challenges for microinsurance is the actual delivery to clients. Methods and models for doing so vary depending on the organisation, institution, and provider involved. As Dubby Mahalanobis states, one must be thorough and careful when making policies, otherwise microinsurance could do more harm than good in general, there are four main methods for offering microinsurance the partner-agent model, the provider-driven model, the full-service model, and the community-based model. Each of these models has their own advantages and disadvantages.

Partner agent model: A partnership is formed between the microinsurance scheme and an agent (insurance company, microfinance institution, donor, etc.), and in some cases a third-party healthcare provider. The microinsurance scheme is responsible for the delivery and marketing of products to the clients, while the agent retains all responsibility for design and development. In this model, microinsurance schemes benefit from limited risk, but are also disadvantaged in their limited control. Micro Insurance Centre is an example of an organisation using this model.

Full service model: The microinsurance scheme is in charge of everything; both the design and delivery of products to the clients, working with external healthcare providers to provide the services. This model has the advantage of offering microinsurance schemes full control, yet the disadvantage of higher risks.

Provider-driven model: The healthcare provider is the microinsurance scheme, and similar to the full-service model, is responsible for all operations, delivery, design, and service. There is an advantage once more in the amount of control retained, yet disadvantage in the limitations on products and services.

Community-based/mutual model: The policyholders or clients are in charge, managing and owning the operations, and working with external healthcare providers to offer services. This model is advantageous for its ability to design and market products more easily and effectively, yet is disadvantaged by its small size and scope of operations.

Development of Micro-insurance in India

Historically in India, a few micro-insurance schemes were initiated, either by non-governmental organisations (NGO) due to the felt need in the communities in which these organisations were involved or by the trust hospitals. These schemes have now gathered momentum partly due to the development of micro-finance activity, and partly due to the regulation that makes it mandatory for all formal insurance companies to extend their activities to rural and well-identified social sector in the country (IRDA 2000). As a result, increasingly, micro-finance institutions (MFIs) and NGOs are negotiating with the for-profit insurers for the purchase of customised group or standardised individual insurance schemes for the low-income people. Although the reach of such schemes is still very limited—anywhere between 5 and 10 million individuals—their potential is viewed to be considerable. The overall market is estimated to reach Rs. 250 billion by 2008 (ILO 2004).

The insurance regulatory and development authority (IRDA) defines rural sector as consisting of (i) a population of less than five thousand, (ii) a density of population of less than four hundred per square kilometer, and (iii) more than twenty five per cent of the male working population is engaged in agricultural pursuits. The categories of workers falling under agricultural pursuits are: cultivators, agricultural labourers, and workers in livestock, forestry, fishing, hunting and plantations, orchards and allied activities.

The social sector as defined by the insurance regulator consists of :

(i) Unorganised sector.

(ii) Informal sector.

(iii) Economically vulnerable or backward classes, and

(iv) Other categories of persons, both in rural and urban areas.

The social obligations are in terms of number of individuals to be covered by both life and non-life insurers in certain identified sections of the society. The rural obligations are in terms of certain minimum percentage of total polices written by life insurance companies and, for general insurance companies, these obligations are in terms of percentage of total gross premium collected. Some aspects of these obligations are particularly noteworthy. First, the social and rural obligations do not necessarily require (cross) subsidising insurance. Second, these obligations are to be fulfilled right from the first year of commencement of operations by the new insurers. Third, there is no exit option available to insurers who are not keen on servicing the rural and low-income segment. Finally, non-fulfillment of these obligations can invite penalties from the regulator.

In order to fulfill these requirements all insurance companies have designed products for the poorer sections and low-income individuals. Both public and private insurance companies are adopting similar strategies of developing collaborations with the various civil society associations. The presence of these associations as a mediating agency, or what we call a nodal agency, that represents, and acts on behalf of the target community is essential in extending insurance cover to the poor. The nodal agency helps the formal insurance providers overcome both informational disadvantage and high transaction costs in providing insurance to the low-income people. This way microinsurance combines positive features of formal insurance (pre paid, scientifically organised scheme) as well as those of informal insurance (by using local information and resources that helps in designing appropriate schemes delivered in a cost effective way).

In the absence of a nodal agency, the low resource base of the poor, coupled with high transaction costs (relative to the magnitude of transactions) gives rise to the affordability issue. Lack of affordability prevents their latent demand from expressing itself in the market. Hence the nodal agencies that organise the poor, impart training, and work for the welfare of the low-income people play an important role both in generating both the demand for insurance as well as the supply of cost-effective insurance.

Supply and Demand Side Developments

Supply of Micro-insurance

Recently, the ILO (2004a) prepared a list of products of all insurance companies, public as well as private, for the disadvantaged groups in India. Some of the observations made on the basis of the list are presented below:

1. Out of 80 listed insurance products, 45 (55%) cover only a single risk. The other products, covering a package of risks, mostly focus on 2 (20%) or 3 (18%) risks.
2. The available products cover a wide range of risks. However, the broad majority of the insurance products cover life (40 products or 52%) or accident-related risks. The health coverage remains very limited (12 products).
3. Most life insurance products (23 out of 42) are addressed to individuals. However, some products may be bought both by individuals and groups.
4. Most life insurance products (55%) have been designed to cover an extended contract duration ranging from 3 to 20 years.
5. Out of 42 life insurance products, 23 are pure risk products. The other 19 products propose various types of maturity benefits.
6. Out of the 12 currently available health insurance products, 7 have been designed and are restricted to groups.
7. Out of the total 12 health products, 7 products propose the reimbursement of hospitalisation expenses while the other 5 have chosen to narrow down the coverage to some specific critical illnesses.
8. Most of the health insurance products specifically exclude deliveries and other pregnancy-related illnesses. Most of these products also mention amongst their exclusion clauses, HIV/AIDS.
9. Most products whether life or non-life require a single payment of premium (i.e., a one-time payment) upon subscription.
10. Private insurance companies have three times more products than the public companies.

As per the IRDA statistics, the public insurance companies still play a predominant role in the present coverage of the rural and social sectors. This is only to be expected since the incumbent public insurers have been in the market for a number of years now.

Demand for Micro-insurance

On the demand side too, the ILO (2004b) has recently prepared an inventory of microinsurance schemes operational in India. Based on this list some of the observations are made below:

1. The inventory lists 51 schemes that are operational in India.
2. Most schemes are still very young, having started their operations during the last few years. Of the 39 schemes for which this information is available, around 24 schemes came up during the last 4 years, and about 7 schemes have operated for more than a decade.
3. As regards the beneficiaries, the 43 schemes for which the information is available cover 5.2 million people.
4. Most insurance schemes (66%) are linked with micro finance services provided by specialised institutions (17 schemes) or non-specialised organisations (17 schemes). Twenty two per cent of the schemes are implemented by community based organisations, and 12% by health care providers.
5. Life and health are the two most popular risks for which insurance is demanded: 59% of schemes provide life insurance and 57% of them provide health insurance. In SEWA's experience health insurance tops the list of risks for which the poor need insurance.
6. Twenty-five out of 37 schemes received some external funds to initiate their schemes. Twenty out of 32 schemes received external technical assistance in the form of advisory services, technical services, training or even referral services for their schemes.
7. In the majority of the schemes special staff had been recruited to manage the insurance activities. The other schemes kept relying on their regular staff while recognising them the additional responsibilities linked to the management of the scheme.
8. Most schemes (74%) operate in 4 southern states of India: Andhra Pradesh (27%), Tamil Nadu (23%), Karnataka (17%) and Kerala (8%), and the two western states (Maharashtra (12%) and Gujarat (6%)) account for 18% of the schemes.
9. 56% of schemes deal with one single risk.
10. Most schemes require single yearly premium at the time of subscription. Of the 43 schemes, 6 use a monthly payment for their contribution, while 2 others have linked the contributions to some other activities developed with their members (disbursement of loan etc.).
11. Most of the schemes rely on voluntary contribution, while 10 schemes imposed compulsory contributions, and 7 adopted a mix of voluntary and compulsory contributions (based on the type of service provided).

Suggestions

1. Many of the non government and nonprofit organisations are working in the field of microinsurance. These organisations must form a cartel

and government backing should be provided to the cartel so that they can work together with the support of the government for the upliftment of the poor and the weaker sections.

2. The IRDA must take necessary steps making it compulsory for the private players to have a target of doing a certain percentage of insurance as microinsurance which may be equal to some percentage of their sales.
3. The advertisements must be made in the local languages.
4. The microinsurance must be done in post offices and other government depots so that the transparency could be maintained.
5. Certain attractive rates of return schemes should be levied on microinsurance policies so that the money invested under the microinsurance policies could fetch good returns.
6. Microinsurance schemes can be made compulsory on the big corporate houses which can take insurance of their employees at a very cheap rate of premium.
7. The grievance handling cells must be made under the guidance and leadership of the gram and jila panchayats which can handle the queries, complaints, difficulties of the poor people and that too in a very short span of time.

CONCLUSION

Microinsurance in India is a new concept and in the real sense, is yet to be tested for conduciveness to the needs of the target segment. Microinsurance is an important component of financial services mainly available to the low income groups under different supply channels involved in microcredit. Although the current reach of microinsurance is limited, the early trend in this respect suggests that the insurance companies, both public and private, operating with commercial considerations, can issue a significant percentage of the poor. Serving low income people who can pay the premium certainly makes a sound commercial sense to insurance providers. Though India has experimented a lot with microinsurance, the sector is still driven by supply-led interventions. Moreover, the insurance providers, still, seek government subsidies and donor funding in order to achieve financial viability in preference to designing market-led, sustainable schemes. Hence, a strategic perspective towards microinsurance together with innovations in technology and assessment of client demand probably holds the key to the future of microinsurance in India.

Bibliography

Cohen, M. and Sebstad J. (2006), The demand for microinsurance in C. Churchill (ed.), Protecting the poor, A microinsurance Compedium, International Labour Organisation, Geneva.

Craig Churchill (2002) Trying to Understand the Demand for Microinsurance. Journal of International Development, Volume: 14, Issue: 3, pp. 381-387

Craig Churchill (2002) Trying to Understand the Demand for Microinsurance. Journal of International Development, Volume: 14, Issue: 3, pp. 381-387

Mirai Chatterjee (2005), "Microinsurance-A Note on State of The Art", pp. 1-6

Paul B. Siegel, Jeffrey Alwang, Sudharshan Canagarajah, (June 2001) "Viewing microinsurance as a Social Risk Management Instrument". pp. 1-34.

Rajeev Ahuja, Basudeb Guha-Khasnobis,, 2005, "Micro-insurance In India: Trends and Strategies for Further Extension", pp. 1-22

Thankom Arun, Susan Steiner (October 2008),"Microinsurance in the context of Social Protection", pp. 2-13.

Thankom Arun, Susan Steiner (October 2008), "Microinsurance in the context of Social Protection", pp. 2-13.

29

A Study on the Welfare of MGNREGS Members through Financial Inclusion in Coimbatore

M. Dhanabhakyam and *Swapna Kurian*

Introduction

MGNREGS was launched in Hooghly district on 2nd April, 2007. The MGNREG Act 2005 provides enhancement of livelihood security, giving atleast 100 days of guaranteed wage employment in every financial year household, whose adult members volunteer to do unskilled manual work. The basic objective of the act isto enhance livelihood security in rural area along with their other objectives like generating productive assets, ,empowering rural women, protection of environment, reducing rural –urban migration and foresting social equity among others. This act is an important step towards the realisation of the work to right. It is an enactment of the people, by the people and for the people.

Objectives

- To analysis the impact of MGNREGS members under financial inclusion.
- To find out the problem faced by the respondents without job under this scheme.
- To compare the performance appraisal of the respondents before and after implementing the scheme.

Hypothesis

Ho: There is no significant difference between the income of MGNREGS members before and after periods under financial inclusion.

Ho: There is no significant difference between the employments' (days) of MGNREGS members before and after periods under financial inclusion.

Methodology

The researcher has selected 150 respondents from Coimbatore city by convenient sampling method. The mean, weighted average rank method, percentage analysis, paired –t-test and chi-square analysis statistical methods are used for the study.

Sources of Data

This study is purely based on primary data and secondary data are collected from books, journals, magazines and websites.

Scope of the Study

In the developing scenario, the Indian government gives importance to poverty allegation and proper distribution of income to the public. Apart from that the government has introduced too much good schemes like PMRY, MGNREGS etc. to the layman for their improvement. In Indian population, more than 50% persons are lying below poverty line, *52 per cent of India's work force* is still engaged in agriculture for its livelihood and 74.04% persons are illiterate and India's unemployment rate stands at 9.4%. So in this scenario, these types of scheme and policy are very useful to layman for improving their income, standard of living and their self development also.

Limitation

- This study is limited to 150 respondents.
- The study area is limited to Coimbatore city.
- The accuracy of the data is depending upon the individuals.

Financial Inclusion in Indian Banking Scenario

Bank nationalisation in India marked a paradigm shift in the focus of banking as it was intended to shift the focus from class banking to mass banking. The rationale for creating Regional Rural Banks was also to take the banking services to poor people. The branches of commercial banks and the RRBs have increased from 8321 in the year 1969 to 68,282 branches as at the end of March 2005. The average population per branch office has decreased from 64,000 to 16,000 during the same period. However, there are certain under-banked states such as Bihar, Orissa, Rajasthan, Uttar Pradesh, Chhattisgarhi, Jharkhand, West Bengal and a large number of North-Eastern states, where the average population per branch office continues to be quite high compared to the national average. As you would be aware, the new branch authorisation policy of Reserve Bank encourages banks to open branches in these under banked states and the under banked areas in other states. The new policy also places a lot of emphasis on the efforts made by the Bank to achieve, inter alia, financial inclusion and other policy objectives.

One of the benchmarks employed to assess the degree of reach of financial services to the population of the country, is the quantum of deposit accounts (current and savings) held as a ratio to the adult population. In the Indian context, taking into account the Census of 2001, the ratio of deposit accounts to the total adult population was only 59%. Within the country; there is a wide variation across states. For instance, the ratio for the state of Kerala is as high as 89% while Bihar is marked by a low coverage of 33%. In the North Eastern States like Nagaland and Manipur, the coverage was a meager 21% and 27%, respectively. The Northern Region, comprising the states of Haryana, Chandigarh and Delhi, has a high coverage ratio of 84%. Compared to the developed world, the coverage of our financial services is quite low. For instance, as per a recent survey commissioned by British Bankers' Association, 92 to 94% of the population of UK has either current or savings bank account.

The National Rural Employment Guarantee Act 2005

In the background discussed above, the Indian parliament passed a revolutionary piece of legislation, i.e. the National Rural Employment Guarantee Act in 2005. Under this act, every household living in the most backward 200 districts of the country is guaranteed at least 100 days of wage employment in unskilled manual work. This legal commitment is a landmark event in the history of poverty reduction strategies in India. It is also a unique event in the pro-poor strategies in the world, as no country in the world has ever given a right of this kind to such a large population so far! The passing of the act is also a great success of the long struggle in which academics, NGOs, and even some policy makers participated. As discussed above, this act is expected to address the worst kind of poverty in the country, as it will provide unskilled wage work to the poor at the bottom, who have low risk bearing capacity and poor credit worthiness to take up self employment ventures and who have a strong preference for wage work. By guaranteeing them unskilled wage work at the minimum wages, the act is expected to create a significant impact in terms of eradication of their starvation and under nourishment on the one hand and reduction in their multiple vulnerability on the other hand.

The key features of the Act are presented in Appendix 1 at the end of the report. In brief, these features include (1) time bound guarantee of 100 days of work at a stipulated minimum wages to each household that demands unskilled manual work as well as payment of an unemployment allowance, which will be one third of the stipulated minimum wages, in the event the work is not provided in time, (2) other entitlements in terms of provision of minimum facilities at the worksite, medical treatment and compensation in the event of injury at work, unemployment allowance if work is not provided etc. (3) bottom up planning for works and their implementation, (4) a well designed institutional network for implementation and monitoring that includes Central and State level councils, Panchayati Raj institutions, government administration at different levels and people's organisations, (5) provision of regular fund flows and (6) social auditing of the scheme to ensure transparency and accountability. The Act has been implemented in the most backward 200 districts of the country. These districts are spread over 27 states.

Analysis and Interpretation

Table 1: Impact of MGNREGS Members in Financial Inclusion

Sl.No.	*Particular*	*Mean*	*Rank*
1.	Protection from Poverty	36.86	1
2.	Purchasing Power	32.25	4
3.	Family Income	33.66	3
4.	To Reduce the Distress to Migrate	36.00	2
5.	Standard of Living	31.00	5

The above table reveals that the protection from poverty is the first rank. To reduce the distress to migrate, Family Income and Purchasing Power are getting second, third and fourth rank respectively. The last and final impact of MGNREGS Members in Financial Inclusion is Standard of Living.

Table 2: Problem faced by the respondents without job

Sl.No.	*Particular*	*No. of respondents*	*Percentage*
1.	Seasonal Unemployment	30	20.00
2.	Children Education	35	23.33
3.	Family Income	30	20.00
4.	To meet the expenses	28	18.67
5.	Mental depression	27	18.00

The above table reveals that the respondents are getting more fear about children education under the unemployment period. The seasonal unemployment and income is the second faced by them. The meet the expenses and mental depression arising from the unemployment are other problems.

The table 3 shows that the before and after periods status of the respondents, the family income, savings, children education, employment and loan status are low performance in the before joining periods. The performance level is changed after implementing period. The family income and savings are increased from 52 to 77 respondents and from 57 to 75 respondents under 21%-50% slab rate. The children education media is drastically changed from Tamil media school to matriculation school. The employment rate is increased from 35 respondents to 40 and 20 respondents to 25 under 101<250 and 251<365 respectively and to ensure minimum 100 days employment to their members. The loan statuses of the respondents are partially completed from 15 to 25 respondents, and from 42-40 respondents are come under 41%-50% and 21% -40%.

Table 3: Performance Appraisals of the Respondents before and after Joining MGNREGS through Financial Inclusion

Sl. No.	*Particular*	*Category*	*No. of Respondent*		*Respondents*	
			Before	*After*	*Before*	*After*
1.	Family Income	0-20%	98	73	65.33	48.67
		21%-50%	52	77	34.67	51.33
2.	Savings	0-20%	93	75	62.00	50.00
		21%-50%	57	75	38	50.00
3.	Children Education (changing the education media)	Tamil Medium	105	95	70.00	63.33
		Matriculation	35	45	23.33	30.00
		CBSE,ICSE	10	10	6.67	6.67
4.	Employment (days)	0<100 days	95	85	63.33	56.67
		101<250	35	40	23.33	26.67
		251<365	20	25	13.34	16.66
5.	Loan status	0-20%	93	85	62.00	56.67
		21% - 40%	42	40	28.00	26.67
		41%-50%	15	25	10.00	16.63

The p value .000 is lesser than the table value 2.617 with a degree of freedom of 149 at 1% significant level. So the null hypothesis is rejected. Hence to conclude that there is a significant difference in the income of the beneficiaries before and after joining under the PMRY Scheme.

The p value .000 is lesser than the table value 2.617 with a degree of freedom of 149 at 1% significant level. So the null hypothesis is rejected. Hence to conclude that there is a significant difference in the Loan completed status of the beneficiaries before and after joining under the PMRY Scheme.

Suggestions

1. Most of the people aren't aware about this program so the government will conduct the awareness program and class to educate people.
2. The government makes wages difference among the workers on the basis of skilled, unskilled, age and work based.

Table 4: Ho: There is no Significant Difference between the Income of MGNREGS Members before and after Periods under Financial Inclusion

Particular		Paired Differences					t	df	Sig(2-tailed)
		Mean	Std. Deviation	Std. Error Mean	95% Confidence Interval of the Difference				
					Lower	Upper			
Pair	Income position before FI- Income position after FI	1.15833	.71002	.06482	-1.28668	-1.02999	-17.871	149	.000

Table 5: H0: There is no Significant Difference between the Employments' (days) of MGNREGS Members before and after Periods under Financial Inclusion

Particular		Paired Differences					t	df	Sig. (2-tailed)
		Mean	Std. Deviation	Std. Error Mean	95% Confidence Interval of the Difference				
					Lower	Upper			
Pair 1	Loan status Before FI– loan status After FI	-1.00000	.36668	.03347	-1.06628	-.93372	-29.875	149	.000

Conclusion

This study concluded that the MGNREGS member have a lot of improvement after joining the financial inclusion .They are very happy with this program. Majority population isn't aware about this program so the government should be conduct awareness program to the public. They have the positive energy and changes in children education, loan status, income, employment and savings mater. This program helps the public to reduce unemployment period problem and ensure minimum 100 days jobs to the public.

References

1. Abhay (2006), 'Status of National Rural Employment Guarantee Scheme in Raichur, (Karnataka). Satyagrah on 14-15 August 2007 at Raichur, Karnataka for NREGS.
2. Basu, Arnab K., 2011. "Impact of Rural Employment Guarantee Schemes on Seasonal Labor Markets: Optimum Compensation and Workers' Welfare," IZA Discussion Papers 5701, Institute for the Study of Labor (IZA).
3. Deaton, Angus S and Muellbauer, John, 1980. "An Almost Ideal Demand System," American Economic Review, American Economic Association, Vol. 70(3), pp. 312-26, June.
4. Impact of MGNREGS on Labour Supply to Agricultural Sector of Wayanad District in Kerala, Thadathil, Merin S, Mohandas, Vineeth, Vol. 25, Number 1, January-June 2012.
5. Kaushik Basu and Sanghamitra Das and Bhaskar Dutta, 2007. "Child labor and household wealth: Theory and empirical evidence of an inverted-U," Indian Statistical Institute, Planning Unit, New Delhi Discussion Papers 07-01, Indian Statistical Institute, New Delhi, India.

30

Empowerment of Woman Through Self Help Group – A Case Study of Mysore City

P.T. Dhamayanthi and *P.T. Bharathi*

Introduction

The deficiencies of the banking services to the poor through Government-sponsored programme led to the search for an alternative mechanism which would ensure a better credit delivery system for the poor. The successful experiment with micro-credit in Bangladesh and other countries encouraged our policy-makers to introduce this innovative method in India. Reorientation of the rural credit delivery system became necessary consequent upon the introduction of several banking sector reforms in the early nineties. The Committee on Banking Sector Reforms said, "Banking policy should facilitate the evolution and growth of micro-credit institutions/ including LABs which focus on agriculture, tiny and small scale industries, including such specialist institutions as may be promoted by NGOs for meeting the banking needs of the poor. Third-tier banks should be promoted and strengthened lo be autonomous, vibrant, effective and competitive in their operations (RBI 1998).

Micro-credit as the name itself indicates, is small amount of credit to lower income groups which comprise small and marginal farmers, landless labourers, petty shop owners, hawkers, fishermen, rural artisans, etc. The beneficiaries are those who in the normal course have great difficulty in having access to formal banking sector. It has very distinctive features which make it different from the approach adopted hitherto to reach the poor.

The Idea of Micro-finance has got long history. Micro finance is some form has been there since a very long time. Chit Funds, Nidhis, etc., are examples of informal micro-credit arrangements which played an important role in providing small amount of credit to the members of a group out of their own savings. The role of this informal arrangement has been rediscovered and a more systematic approach has been developed by forging a link between the formal and informal financial markets.

Self-help Groups

Poverty is a global phenomenon. Formation of Self-Help Groups is an attempt to create more opportunities for getting additional income and employment for the poor people. For the last three decades the women's movement across India gave emphasis on the promotion of grass-root level organisations for women's development. Women's Self-Help Groups arise as a result of the increasing emphasis on the promotion of grass-roots level organisations for women's development. SHGs strategy enables the women to participate in the ongoing development process at village level. Individual woman and women group not only benefited from the self-help groups but the families and community as a whole will be benefited from this. It is a well designed tool to empower rural women also. This is not only help them to alleviate their poverty but also help them to get economic and social empowerment. It also increases the members access to important services like education, health care etc. Members of SHG are more aware about their children education and health. Apart from economic and social empowerment the SHG households also show greater awareness and participation in local politics. It also helps them to familiarise with the banking system and NGOs.

Definitions of NGOs

According to UNO " a NGO is any non profit voluntary citizens group, which is organised on a local, national or international level. Task oriented and driven by people with a common interest. NGOs perform a variety of services and humanitarian function, bring citizens concerns to government advocate and monitor policies and encourage political participation through provision of information. Some are organised around specific issues such as human rights, environment or health. They provide analysis and expertise, serve as early warning mechanisms and help monitor and implement international arguments".

According to world Bank "NGOs as private organisation that pursue activities to relive suffering, promote the interests of the poor, protect – the environment, provide basic social services or undertake community development".

Role of NGOs in India

NGOs which started playing their role in the development process in India by assisting the target groups by way of helping them to adopt improved technology in agriculture and related activities soon felt the need for helping them to get credit from banks to finance their activities. In this process, they involved themselves in providing services like identification of beneficiaries, handling the loan formalities, supervising the end-use of loans and subsidies, procuring inputs and overseeing fulfilment of agreed repayment obligations (NABARD 1999). Subsequently, it was realised that informal organisational structure should be promoted to encourage thrift and self-reliance which led to the emergence of Self-Help Groups, which constitute today the informal arrangement through which the micro-credit system works.

Salient Features of SHGs

1. Self-help groups are homogenous groups formed by the poor to take care of both thrift and credit needs of the poor. They are essentially small groups having membership up to a maximum of twenty.
2. Majority of the groups formed are those of women.
3. They work on democratic principles. Each group has a president and a secretary and rotation of executives gives equal opportunities to all the members in managing the affairs of the group. Frequent meetings are held by the groups and decisions are taken after careful deliberations with regard to their savings, credit to be provided to the members, the activities to be financed through the credit, rate of interest to be charged for the loan given to the members, repayment period, etc.
4. SHGs follow the principle "savings first and credit later." It is mandatory that they should save. The minimum amount to be saved is fixed in some cases and in some cases it is left to the discretion of the members to decide the amount to be saved. The amount is deposited with the bank and used either as collateral for the loan raised from the bank or for building up an Emergency Fund from which small amounts of loans would be given as consumption loans. Unless the poor have access to institutional credit for meeting expenditure connected with health care, social or religious ceremonies, etc. they can never be free from the clutches of the money lenders.
5. Production credit is given to the members of the group out of the loans given to the group either directly or through an NGO under the Bank-SHG Linkage Programme.
6. The quantum of loan to be given to a member of the group is generally left to the discretion of the group. There is no uniform approach in this regard. The limit in each case depends upon the need and the capacity to repay promptly. Generally, the amount available as production credit is more than the amount available as consumption credit.
7. The activities for which SHGs make credit available are very large and diverse. They include both agricultural and non-agricultural activities

of various kinds. Apart from the activities undertaken at the individual level, group activities involving all the members of the group such as cattle rearing, sheep rearing, social forestry, management of common property resources may also be undertaken.

8. Repayment periods of micro-credit are very short ranging between ten to twenty-four months and repayments are in weekly/fortnightly/monthly instalments. Banks which directly lend to SHGs or to NGOs for on-lending to SHGs expect repayment over a period of three years. But SHGs fix shorter periods of repayment in order to recycle the funds to ensure that all the members who need credit get the benefit.
9. Regarding the interest rates, the groups are free to fix their own rates. Some groups lend at the same rate at which they borrow from the banks and some groups maintain margin and lend at a rate which is higher than the rate at which they borrow. In most cases the rates are very high ranging between 24 and 36 per cent like the usurious rates of moneylenders. But the interest earned remains with the group unlike in the case of borrowing from the moneylenders.

Apart from the SHGs, some NGOs like ASA (Activists for Social Alternatives) in Tamil Nadu, RDO (Loylam Bank of Rural Development and Organisation) in Manipur and SHARE (Society for Helping and Awakening Rural Poor Through Education) in Andhra Pradesh and the Oriental Bank of Commerce in Dehradun and Rajasthan have promoted groups of Grameen Bank Group (GBG) ...model (Rajaram Dasgupta, 2001). GBGs are different from SHGs in certain ways. The group is very small consisting of five members. The savings of members are deposited in a bank and the bank lends directly to the individual members. The group's responsibility is only to screen the borrowers and ensure prompt repayment of the loans. GBGs are not as popular as SHGs, though they serve the same purpose as SHGs).

Following are the NGOs Micro Finance to SHGs in Mysore City:

1. Ujjeevan
2. Sanghamithra
3. Sri. Keshthra Dharmastala Grameena Abhivrudhi (BKRDP)
4. Jana Lakshmi
5. Spandana
6. Grameena Koota Bangalore
7. Orgnaisatin for development programme
8. Sowharda Co-operatives etc.

OBJECTIVES

1. To study the Financial inclusion by the women empowerment through SHGs
2. To study the generation of micro finance by SHGs

3. To study the structure of SHGs.
4. To evaluate the Economic development of the members of the SHGs.
5. To analyse the income generating activities of SHGs.

Methodology of the Study

The study is based on both the primary and the secondary source of data. The primary data has been collected from the fieldwork in Mysore City. A structured questionnaire has used and the factors are tabulated through statistical tables. For the study 100 respondents have been selected from women on simple random sampling basis. Secondary data has been collected from published books, articles, Magazines and research papers etc.

The variables selected to study this case are age group, education, duration, amount of loan availed, occupation, employment generation, amount deposited, earnings, marital status and number of member remained and re-joined in SHGs.

Table 1: Age Group of Members in SHGs

Age	*No of Members*	*Percentage*
18 -25	10	10
26-35	25	25
36-45	50	50
46 and above	15	15

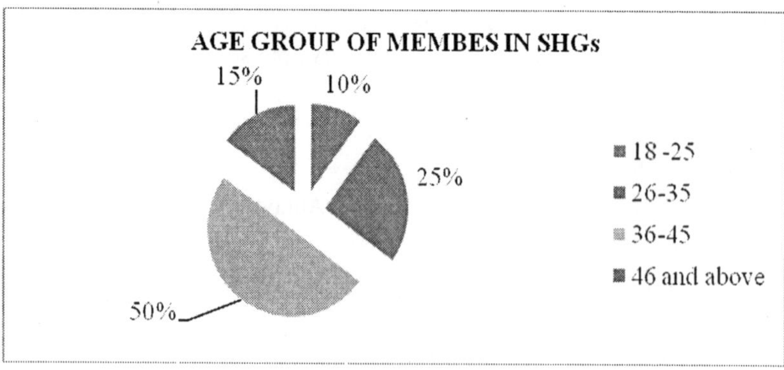

Table 1 consists of classification of members according to their age group. In this table age group of 18-25 is 10%, 26-35 is 25%, 36-45 is 50% and 46 and above 15%. It results 50% of members are in the age group of 36-45.

Table 2 : Education of Members Of SHGs

Education	*No of Members*	*Percentage*
Education	30	30
Less than S.S.L.C	60	60
P.U.C	10	10
Degree	nil	nil

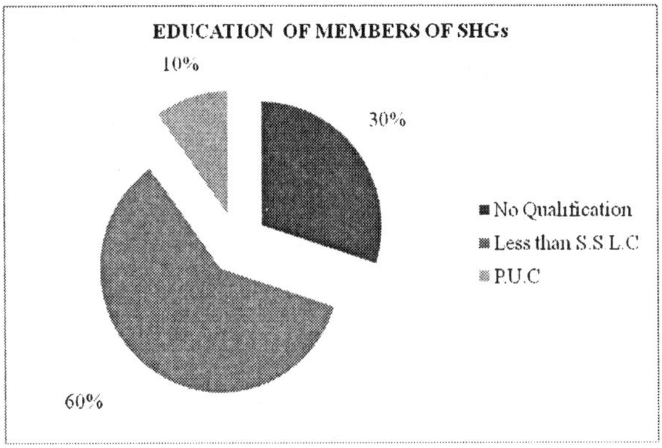

Table 2 Reveals Qualification of members of SHGs. Having no qualification are 30% of members, 60% members have less than S.S.L.C, 10% are of P.U.C and there are no members who have degree qualification.

Table 3: Duration of Members in SHGs

No. of years	*No. of members*	*Percentage*
1-2	10	10
3-5	40	40
5-10	50	50

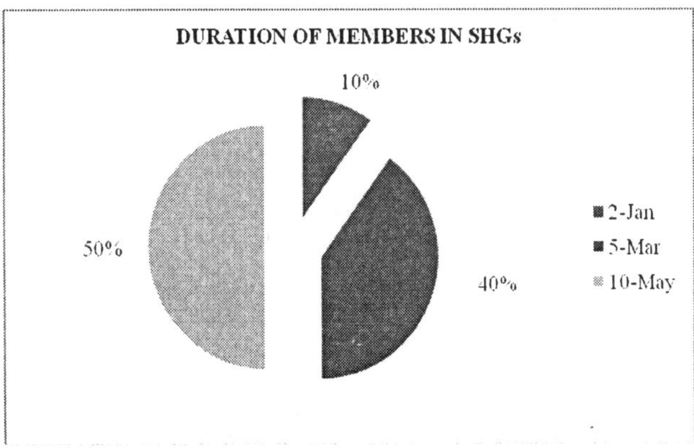

Table 3 Indicates the duration of members in SHGs. 10% of members joined with in 2 years, 40% of the members have joined with in 5 years, 50% of the members joined within 10 years.

Table 4: Amount of Loan Availed by the Members of SHGs

Loan availed	*No. of members*	*Percentage*
Less than 10,000	05	05
10,000-15,000	30	30
15,000-25,000	30	30
25,000-35,000	05	05
35,000-45,000	10	10
45,000 and above	20	20

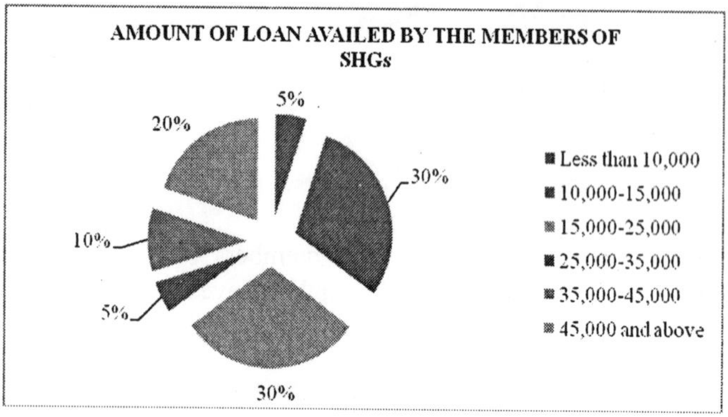

Table 4 consists of the members availed loan from any micro finance institutions. 5% of the members availed only Rs.10,000/- 30% of the members availed 10,000/- to 15,000/- 30% of the members availed Rs. 15,000/- to 25,000/-, 05%,10% and 20% of the members have availed 25,000/- to 35,000/-00, 35,000 to 45,000/- and 45,000/- and above respectively.

Table 5: Occupations of Members in SHGs

Occupation	*No. of Members*	*Percentage*
Business	75	75
Agriculture	10	10
House hold (No Business)	10	10
Working (No Business)	05	05

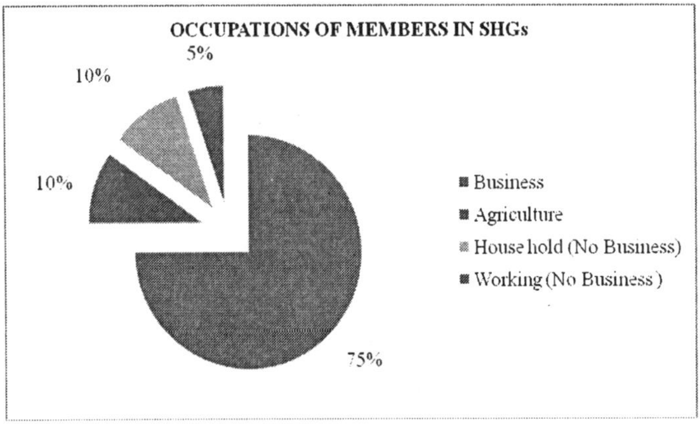

Table 5 reveals the occupation of the member of SHGs. 75% of the members undertaken Business, 10% of members doing. Agricultural activities, 10% are house hold and 05% are working and not doing any business. It specified that 85% of the members have under taken one or the other work.

Table 6: Employment Generated by the Members of SHGs

No. of Employees	*No. of members*	*Percentage*
Less than 1	27	27
Less than 2	60	60
Less than 4	13	13
5 and above	Nil	Nil

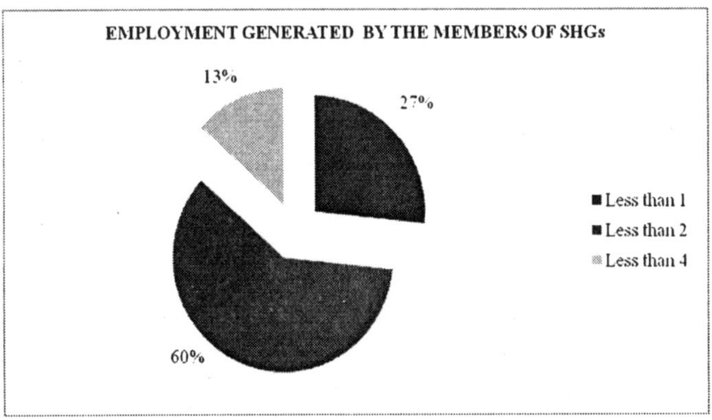

Table 6 Shows the employment generated by the members of SHGs. 27% of the members do business but employed any employees. 60% of members employed 1 or 2 employees, 13% of members employed 3 or 4 employees. Nobody hired 5 and more than 5 employees.

Table 7: Amount Deposited by the Members in SHGs

Amount of Deposited	*No. of members*	*Percentage*
100 and Less than 100	58	58
200 and Less than 200	37	37
More than 200	05	05

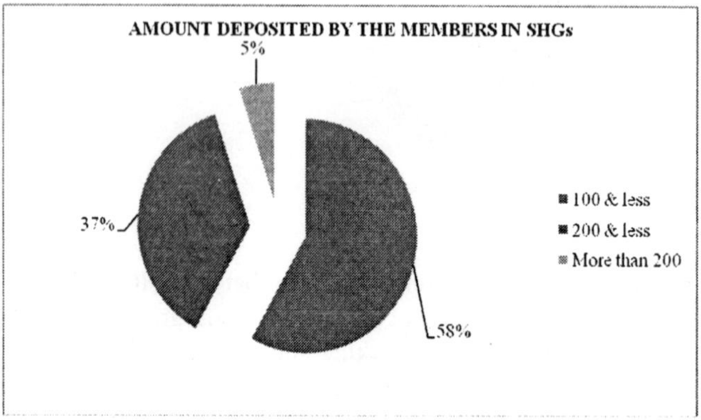

Table 7 consists of the deposits made by the members of SHGs. 58% of members deposited Rs. 100 and less, 37% of the members deposited 200 and less, 05 members deposit Rs. 200 and above.

Table 8: Earnings Per Month by the Members Of SHGs

Earnings	*No. of members*	*Percentage*
Up to 2000	19	19
2000-5000	35	35
5000-8000	26	26
8000 and above	20	20

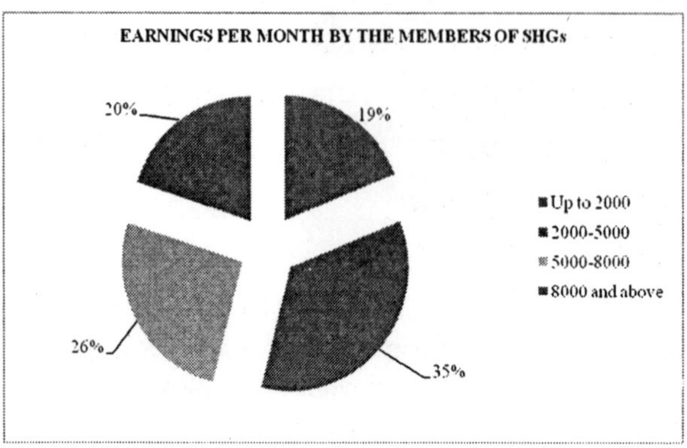

Table 8 reveals the earnings of the members of SHGs. 19% of the members earn less than Rs. 2000/-, 35% of members earn Rs. 2,000 to Rs. 5000/-, 26% of them are earning Rs. 5000-8000 and 20% of members earn Rs. 8,000 and above.

Table 9: Marital Status of Member SHGs

Marital Status	*No. of members*	*Percentage*
Married	95	95
Unmarried	05	05

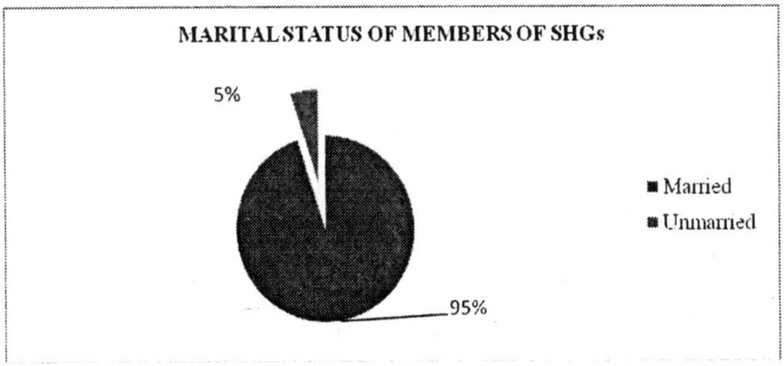

Table 9 Consists of marital status of the members of SHGs. Among 100 members 95 of the member are married and only 5% of them are unmarried.

Table 10: Number of Members Remains and re-joined

Status of members	*No. of members*	*Percentage*
Left	05	05
Not left	95	95

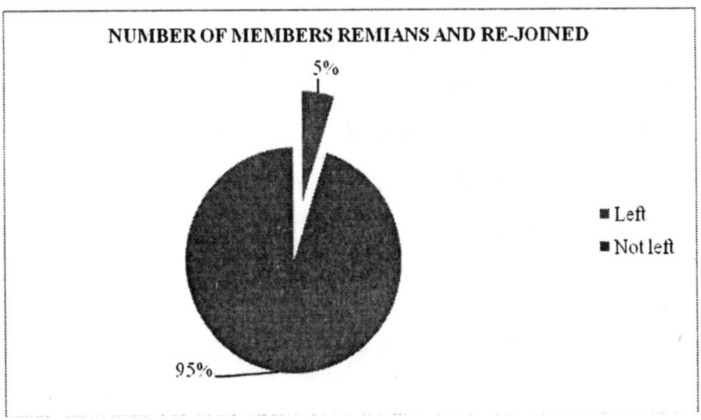

Table 10 throws light on the member who have left and the re-joined SHGs. out of 100 5% of the members who have left and made their relatives to join the SHGs.

Summary

- Most of the members of SHGs are fall under the age group of 36 to 45 that is 50.
- Married women are interested to be empowered because of high responsibility to earn more for children education, children Health, savings for the future maintenance of family etc., that constitute 95 per cent of members
- The qualification of most of the members is less than SSLC. Few among them are illiterates. But PUC and above are very less.
- 90% of women joined before 3 years.
- All the members of SHGs are availed the loan.
- 75% of the women used the money for their business and 10% agricultural activities 10%.
- 73% of members of SHGs employed employees
- 58% of members deposited Rs.100 and less than Rs.100, 37% deposited Rs. 200/- and less than Rs. 200, others have deposited more than Rs. 200
- 46% of women earn more than Rs. 5000/- and 20% earn more than Rs. 8,000/-
- 5% of members left the SHGs and replaced by their relatives.

Conclusion

Women empowerment through Micro Finance is considerably increasing. Now the earning capacity of the Women is increased. Every woman avail the loan from SHGs. The members are loyal toward the payment of their deposit as well as repayment of loan. They are able to acquire some household assets. They can run their family independently and they are self sufficient. The scheme is running effectively. It improved the social and economic conditions of the people who availed the benefit of the scheme. They are educated to some extent to know, how to bank the amount, how to avail the loan etc., they attend meetings regularly and come to know the recent developments. They are ready to face the risk and take decisions of their own.

Suggestions

1. Most of the women are from economically back - ward and illiterate. It is necessary to educate the members of SHGs. Educated women can know how to utilise the amount. It reduces the cost of maintenance

and better utilisation of the resources. This lead to the betterment of their family life.

2. There is a urgent need to reduce the existing rate of interests. To reduce the interest it is essential to start government organisations, to provide the funding to the members of SHGs.
3. It in necessary to provide the member of SHGs training to start the moderate business and other activities to become self-sufficient.
4. There is a need to make the members earn more than the repayment of installment.
5. It is necessary to create awareness among economically developed to contribute to the NGOs. the deposit can be assured with the minimum interest/or tax relief. It increase the lending capacity of NGOs.
6. More publicity is required so that every women from weaker section come under this scheme and enjoy the Benefit.

References

1. Biswas Manjari (2010). "The status of woman in India from antiquity to modernity" Abhijeet Publication Delhi.
2. G.D. Banerjee (2010). "Issues on rural finance infrastructure and rural development" Abhijeet Publication Delhi.
3. B.S. Sreekantaradhya (2004). "Banking and finance perspective on reform" deep and deep publication Pvt. Ltd., Delhi.
4. B. Suresh Lal (2009). "Human development in India" serials publications. New Delhi.
5. Prof. P. Venkatachalliah "A-Study on human empowerment through micro - credit in selected Taluks of Tumkur district.
6. Raghava D.H. "Socio economic empowerment of woman through NGOs based Micro-Finance."
7. Dr. T. Prasanna "Self-Help group and human empowerment: Issues and new imperatives.

31

Financial Inclusion through Microfinance and Self Help Groups

Raghavendra and *V. Basil Hans*

Introduction

Finance has come a long way since the time when it was not recognised as a factor for the growth. Today is attributed as the brain of an economic system and all economies are busy with making their financial system strong and efficient. Any problem in this sector will derail the process of development. The concept of financial inclusion has entered the domain of development. Financial inclusion is the process of ensuring access to financial services and timely and adequate credit to vulnerable groups such as weaker sections and low income groups at an affordable cost. It also means extending banking to the unreached and the excluded areas (Venkataramaraju and Ramesh, 2011). The term financial services include the entire gamut of savings, loans, and insurance and credit, payments. The financial system transfers resources from surplus to deficit units. The term financial inclusion is perceived in different ways. One view is that only access to credit is treated as financial inclusion and the other view is that all the services extended by financial institutions lead to financial inclusion. Despite critical importance of access to financial services for achieving equitable economic development, in most developing countries, a large segment of the population particularly low-income and vulnerable sections of the society has very little or no access to financial services from formal financial system. It is estimated that globally over two million people are currently excluded from the access to financial services (UN, 2006). They normally depend on their own limited resources or informal sources of finance at exorbitantly exploitative terms. Unless financial services is inclusive, the benefit of financial services is likely to elude many individuals and enterprises and thereby denying much of the population the benefit of growth opportunities. The emergence and growth of microfinance and self help groups (SHGs) should also be analysed in this context. The 'why' and 'how' of financial inclusion through microfinance and SHGs, their strengths and limitations are to be addressed and assessed critically. Therefore, the objectives of this paper are as follows:

- to know the structure, functioning and relevance of SHGs as a tool of financial inclusion and intermediaries of rural resource mobilisation.
- to understand the role of commercial banks in promoting SHGs in India.
- to study the role of SHGs in empowering the women.
- to suggest measures for regulating the lending activities of MFIs and SHGs to achieve inclusive growth.

This paper is based on the secondary data obtained from various published and unpublished works such as books, reports, journals, dissertations, magazines, and electronic web materials pertaining to microfinance, SHGs, banking etc.

Financial Inclusion

Although the buzz of the buzzword, "financial inclusion" seems to have settled down there seems to be still some 'newness' about it in terms of its application. Unfortunately, however, the depth and dimensions of the concept and philosophy of financial inclusion, in India seems to have been blurred because of its over-engagement with "bank linkage" and "no-frills account". The essence of financial inclusion is to ensure that a range of appropriate financial services rendered by the formal financial system is available to every individual and enable the individuals to access those services whenever needed. Accessibility is the key parameter of financial inclusion (Serrao,

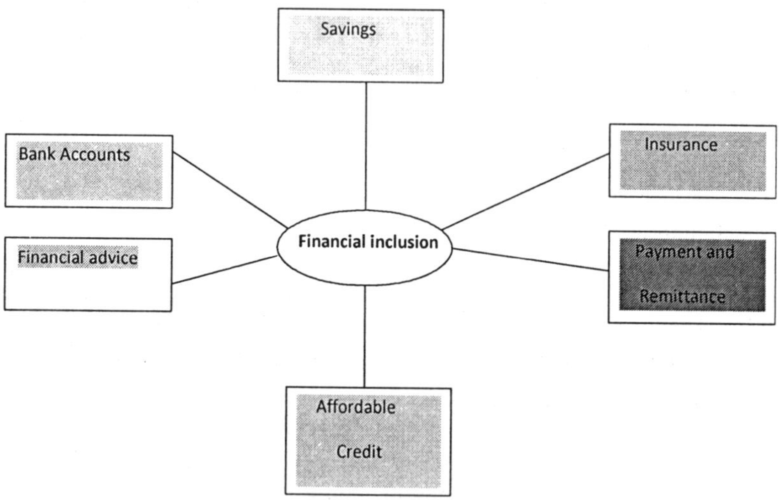

Fig. 1: Financial Inclusion – the Body.

Sequeira and Hans, 2011). The range of financial services include the entire gamut of financial products – cheque accounts, saving products, loans, debit cards, credit cards, insurance and healthcare services and the financial services such as payment services, remittance services and other transfer and advisory and counselling (Fig. 1).

Why a Policy of Financial Inclusion?

Now the question is why financial inclusion should be a policy. Can it happen on its own like the way goods and services are bought and sold? Why it cannot find a market of its own? Why so much importance is given to financial inclusion policy as a developmental tool? Poverty eradication being central to pro-growth and sustainable development policy, financial inclusion is central to such a policy. After 60 years of Independence in India, only 40 per cent of the population has a bank account and only about 10 per cent has some kind of insurance (Venkataramanaraju and Ramesh, 2011). What is livelihood 'security' for these people? What use is teaching 'growth' when the fruits of growth are not reaching them? Strong financial products and services are required to overcome shocks, fears and frustrations of the impoverished and to empower them.

Factors Affecting Financial Inclusion

The factors responsible for financial inclusion are varied and no single factor could explain the phenomenon. Broadly they can be classified as supply-side factors and demand-side factors. Supply side factors emanate from the structural operations of financial service providers. The major barriers are physical access, high charges penalties, and conditions attached to financial products, convenience of branch time, appropriateness of products and services, cumbersome procedure/documents required, collateral requirements, language, staff attitude, and cost and risk perception of financial institutions about the poor. The demand side factors mainly emanate from socio economic condition of financial service users. They include mainly lack of awareness, required, low income and low productivity leading to weak and non viable demand, lower social status resulting in social exclusion and financial illiteracy barriers and information asymmetry. Other factors affecting access to financial services to some extent are gender issues, age factor, legal hurdles and psychological and cultural barriers resulting in self exclusion. Most of these barriers are not there when these neglected sections of the society are to bank on micro financial institutions (MFIs) and SHGs.

Microfinance is the buzzword, a product of new alternative thinking and policy in the globalisation era (Hans, 2010). The concept is not new. Actually in some form or the other, the concept of microfinance has existed in almost each and every society. Throughout history, people in need of financial services, who lack the opportunity or ability to enter the formal financial markets, have designed micro saving and micro credit programmes without the intervention of outside institutions or agencies. It has only been in the four decades however, the serious efforts have been made to formalise these processes and services through the creation of micro financial institutions. Micro finance is one of those small ideas that turn out to have enormous implications when Mohammad Yunus, then Economics Professor, at Bangladesh University, started making small loans to local villagers in 1970s. It was unclear where the idea would go. Today Mohammad Yunus the Noble Laureate is a visionary in a movement that has spread globally providing small loans without collateral, collecting deposits, and increasingly selling insurance, all to customers who had been written off by commercial banks as being unprofitable. Occasioned by the institutional paradigm shift of the World Bank from heavy industrialisation to basic needs, rural development, human development and micro enterprises the non- governmental organisations (NGOs) got a renewed importance in political economy. SHGs as "development NGOs" arrived on the scene (Moniruzam, 2011).[1] Development from the bottom of the pyramid became the route, again.

Self Help Groups

Credit is one of the critical inputs for economic development and one of the three main challenges to input management in agriculture, the other two being physical and human (Jaysheela, et. al., 2008). The banking sector in India has undergone far reaching changes in terms of coverage, credit disbursement and banking technology in providing the banking services during the last four decades. After nationalisation of commercial banks, thousands of new banking centres even in the remote villages started appearing on the banking map of the country.

With the opening of branches in rural and urban centres, the number of bank customers increased substantially. The number of savings bank accounts has increased from 2.36 crore in 1971 to 42.91 crore as on March 2008. The total number of deposit accounts is 58.16 crore. While the urban and metropolitan branches have 18.29 crore savings bank accounts, the rural branches handle 13.30 crore accounts and semi-urban branches have 11.32 crore accounts (RBI, 2009). The number of borrowing accounts also has increased very impressively. The number of small borrowing accounts – amount borrowed being less than Rs. 10, 000 – was only 10.02 lakh in 1968. It has gone up to 9.45 crore in 2008. The total number of borrowing accounts now stands at 10.70 crore. The number of borrowing accounts handled by banks in Rural India is again much lower 3.04 to crore only. Considering the growing population, the number of people who remain unreached as bank borrowers could be certainly larger than those reached so far.

The development that has taken place in the Indian banking sector since nationalisation could be equated with voiceless growth the deprived are so many. According to All India Debt and Investment Survey 2002, money lenders' share in the debt of rural households has gone up from 17.5 per cent in 1991 to 29.6 per cent in 2002. More disturbing is the decline in the share of commercial banks during the same period from 33.7 per cent to 24.5 per cent. No attempt has been made to consolidate the banking system so as to develop a strong alternative to the money lender.

A significant innovation in the credit delivery system introduced in the recent years was the fostering of SHGs by the banks, either directly or in association with NGOs or the State. Extension of micro finance to the otherwise inaccessible sections of the rural society becomes feasible under this arrangement. The National Bank for Agriculture and Rural Development (NABARD) has played a crucial role in the propagation of this operational framework. Thus, access to finance especially by the poor and vulnerable groups is a prerequisite for employment, economic growth, poverty eradication and social cohesion. Further, access to finance will empower the vulnerable groups by giving them an opportunity to have a bank account, to save and invest, to insure their home or to partake of credit, thereby facilitating them to break the chain of poverty. In recent years, the idea of giving small loans to poor people has become the darling of the developing world, hailed as the long term elusive formula to propel even the most destitute into better lives.

Year 1991 saw the flood gates of liberalisation being opened by the Indian economy. There was euphoria all around and the vision of India moving into the ocean of globalisation was the talk of the town. However the poor and the voiceless bore the brunt of the advent of capitalism. Every sixth person in India was below the poverty line in 1997-98. Even the World Bank began to question the efficiency of economic growth in poverty reduction. Reaching to the poor people is a difficult task in India and nurturing them over a long period to improve their economic status and capabilities is an arduous task. But out of necessity and enterprise, those locked out of the banking world have found a way out. It is called Microfinance – the extension of small loans to individuals who are poor to qualify for the traditional bank loans, as they have no assets to be offered as guarantee. In India, Microfinance has worked largely through SHGs. Millions of poor and illiterate women in India are today using small loans to rewrite their present and future. These micro finance institutions include banks, non government organisations, refinance institutions and SHGs developing with small loans and deposits in rural, semi urban or urban areas enabling people to raise savings, productive investments and thereby their standard of living (Nadarajan and Ponmurugan, 2006).

Bankers in India have accepted the inevitability of extending microfinance through SHG- Bank Linkage as a last effective means of reaching out to the poor. As they are facing the challenge of minimising the menace of NPAs, they are in search of lending avenues where the profitability is high and NPA is low. Though profit maximisation is their prime goal, operating in an economy like India, they cannot afford to ignore the rural economy. Directed lending is apparently becoming slowly an unwelcome guest at the bank counters. Yet they can ill afford to shut their door for the rural customers, if a proper atmosphere is created for them to do banking business.

Taking off from the Mysore Resettlement and Development Agency (MYRADA) initiative of promoting credit management groups and subsequent NABARD experimentation of linking them with the formal credit delivery system, NABARD launched a pilot project by improving the access of poor to credit in February 1992. This could be considered as a landmark development in banking with the poor, as it formed the basis for the emergence of Self -Help-Bank Linkage programme, the most successful inclusive growth strategy so for in the Indian economy. These groups were originally called as the Savings and credit Groups [SACGs] and later rechristened as the Self-Help Groups (SHGs).

The physical and financial outreach of the programme has been impressive that there are more than 61 lakh saving-linked SHGs and more than 42 lakh credit linked SHGs and thus about 8.6 crore poor households are covered under the programme as on 31 March 2009. Today, the microfinance industry with over $60 billion in assets has unquestionably outgrown its charitable roots. Resentment is building up after the IPO of Swayam Krishi Sangham (SKS), India's biggest MFI. Its shares were launched at Rs. 1000 and have soared to Rs. 1400. Other MFIs are queuing up for fresh IPOs. A sector that started as a service to the poor now looks a money spinner, attracting private equity funds with no social aims whatsoever.

What are SHGs?

SHGs are small, cohesive and participating groups of the poor, who pool their thrift, regularly and the pooled thrift to make small interest bearing loans to members and in the process, learn the nuances of financial discipline. Subsequently, they graduate to access bank credit to augment their resources for lending to their members who are in need of financial assistance for meeting their emergent needs. Over the years, the pooled resources of the SHGs become a sizeable corpus, which supplemented by higher volume of bank credit can promote investments by the members in diversified livelihood activities, improving their standard of living. SHGs provide a forum to address various social issues, using their collective wisdom, peer pressure and strength (Deepika and Hans, 2011). It also helps in perpetuating folk, arts and culture.

An SHG is a group of about 20 people from homogeneous class, who come together for addressing their common problems. They are encouraged to make voluntary thrift on a regular basis. They use this pooled resource to make small interest bearing loans to their members. The process helps them imbibe the essentials of financial intermediation including prioritisation of needs, setting terms and conditions and accounts keeping. This gradually builds financial discipline and credit history for themselves, as the money involved in the lending operations is their own hard earned money saved over time with great difficulty. This is 'warm money'. They also learn to handle resources of a size that is much beyond their individual capacities. The SHG members begin to appreciate the fact that resources are limited and have a cost. Once the groups show this mature financial behaviour, banks are encouraged to make loans to the SHGs in certain multiples of the accumulated savings of the SHGs. The bank loans are given to SHGs without any collateral and at market interest rates. Banks find it easier to lend money to the groups as the members have developed a credit history. 'Cold money' or 'outside money' gets added to the own 'warm money' in the hands of the groups, which have become structures, which are able to enforce credit discipline among the members. The members have experienced the benefits of credit discipline by being able to save and borrow regularly without much hassle. The groups continue to decide the terms of loans to their own members. The peer pressure ensures timely repayments and acts as the "Collateral" for the bank loans.

SHGs and Financial Intermediation

Financial intermediation in simple words refers to a process of mobilising resources (deposits) and distribution (lending) activities of the financial institutions (SHGs). Here financial intermediary is an SHG and the process is borrowing and lending. Ultimate beneficiary is the low income group in the villages SHGs are considered as a strong alternative financial intermediary in the informal rural sector. Forming SHGs and carrying out financial intermediation through them, disproves the notion that the poor cannot save. The paper work is minimal, collateral is absent and interest margin remain within the community. This works on the organised and formalised social capital. The Linkage Programme promoted by NABARD is unique as it facilitates relationship banking practiced in other countries as compared to parallel banking practice in other countries. Under the relationship banking, improvements in the existing relationship between the poor and the banks are attempted with intermediation by the NGOs, who either play the role of promoters of SHG or financial intermediaries. The basic philosophy of the linkage models promoted by NABARD is to establish synergy between the banks, who have the financial strength and the NGOs who have the ability to mobilise the poor and build up their capacity to avoid loans from the banks. This is expected to facilitate the poor to graduate to a level from where they can access larger amounts of loan directly from the banks without the intervention of NGOs.

There are five types of SHG- Bank Linkages (Box 1).

BOX-1

Model 1 : SHGs promoted, guided and financed by banks. This model covers about 20 per cent of total of about 3.5 million groups that are linked to banks in India.

Model 2 : NGO forms the SHGs and performs financial intermediation role or lender to SHGs after servicing loan from bank. In this case, besides acting as the facilitator, the NGO also works as financial intermediary. Here the loan is given to NGOs by the bank for lending to SHGs/individuals. In this linkage model NGO would be legally responsible for the repayment and would bear the risk of non payment. Involvement of NGOs in micro credit system would have positive influence as they are grass root agencies with good information about borrowers thus, adverse selection and production of recovery could be avoided.

Model 3 : SHGs promoted by NGOs and financed by banks using NGOs/formal agencies as financial intermediaries. In this model, the NGO-MFI receives bulk of loan from the bank. The bank, in turn, delivers the same to groups and in the process charges service fee from SHGs. This model covers about 8% of total groups and expected to grow in future.

Model 4: Bank/ MFIs Federation/Community Based organisations-SHG Members.

Model 5: Recently piloted by NABARD for facilitating formation of SHGs in areas where there are no NGOs. It uses the services of committed individual volunteers identified by the bank branches. In all the above models the commercial banks and rural banks are expected to play an important role in providing financial services to the poor.

In India *Model 2* is very popular. What started as a local initiative by a few individuals with a social/ community objective to mobilise and channelise local resources has become a parallel organised banking phenomenon. SEWA Bank's Vyas says: "we found women begging us not to send them any letters or bank statements. They even asked us to keep their passbooks, as they did not want their husband to know they had money, as they would be pressurised to withdraw it More often than not, it would be spent frivolously on gambling or alcohol. Women will never beg, they live with dignity and pride." Vijayalaxmi Ramanna, Chairperson of CHETHANA says: "Woman in India will never lower their goals. They will always strive to raise their abilities to the height of their goals. When the SHG-NGO Bank Linkage touches the heart of every poor woman in this country, India will be transformed and we will see a prosperous and happy India. Micro finance will make her words come true.

V.K. Chopra, Chairman and Managing Director, Corporation Bank, admits, "Lending without any collateral by the commercial banks to the poorest of the poor in rural areas is very difficult as banks do not have the expertise or facilities in these areas. That is why microfinance institutions should step in. Today banks are flush with money. If micro financial institutions are strong banks will readily lend to them, that there are significant opportunities for banks in microfinance is more unquestioned.

Micro financing has been revolutionising the rural economy through the SHGs. The success of the concept of micro credit through SHGs has encouraged the government to use as an instrument to address the issues of poverty and unemployment (Ramakrishnan, 2007) with emphasis of local participation and decision-making. That way the bottom of the pyramid is being addressed through innovative strategies. Democratisation and decentralisation of finance for women empowerment is a revolution. Introduction of smart cards is a technological revolution. From financial management to environmental management and disaster management (e.g. rehabilitation during Tsunami); from Kisan cards to Smart cards, and from economic security to social security, the MFIs have travelled a long distance and the journey was worth it. They have moved with the times and moved along with the locals. Vikram Akula who started the SKS Microfinance in 1998 and who is now on Times list of people who shape our world, says, "There is already an MF revolution emerging in the villages and slums. It could be more than the green revolution."

Of late, this sector has attracted funds from global development financial institutions. They have invested approximately $300 million in this sector in about 25 transactions since 2006.This availability of capital in turn saw many socially–oriented entrepreneurs launching MFIs of their own. In all, over 3000 MFIs operate currently in India. This led many to draw comparisons between the credit card boom for the middle class and the poor man's credit mechanism, the microfinance industry. More importantly, the sector also seems largely immune to the global financial turmoil as it tends to operate on a regional basis. The SHG-bank linkage programme has made rapid progress in India (Table 1).

Table 1: SHG-Bank Linkage Programme

Year	*SHGs Financed During the year (In lakh)*	*Cumulative Number of SHGs Financed (In lakh)*	*Bank Loan Outstanding (Crore)*
2001-02	1.98	4.61	1026
2002-03	2.56	7.17	2049
2003-04	3.62	10.79	3904
2004-05	5.39	16.18	6898
2005-06	6.20	22.38	11398
2006-07	6.87	29.25	18047

Source: Progress of SHG Bank linkage in India, 2006-07, NABARD.

As on 2007, 50 commercial banks, 96 RRBs and 352 Cooperative banks were actively participating in the programme. The number of bank branches lending to SHGs was 35294. The SHGs credit linked with banks increased from 4.60 lakh in 2001-02 29.30 lakh in 2006-07. The cumulative outstanding increased from Rs.1026 crore 18,047 crore during this period. The saving amount outstanding of SHG members with banks was Rs. 2391 crore at the end of March 2007. Over 90 per cent of the SHGs linked with banks were found to be women SHGs. most of them were poor and asset-less. Thus, SHG movement has been instrumental in financial inclusion of women hitherto bypassed by the banking system. Regional distribution, however, has been so far, uneven (see Table 2). The region-wise analysis shows that southern region has achieved remarkable progress in the SHG bank linkage programme from the beginning of the project.

Table 2: Regional Distribution of SHGs Linked to Banks Percentage

Region	*2001(End March)*	*2006 (End March)*
Northern	3.4	5.9
North Eastern	0.2	2.8
Eastern	8.4	17.6
Central	10.9	12.0
Western	5.9	7.4
Southern	71.1	54.3
All India	100.00	100.00

Source: Progress of SHG Bank linkage in India, NABARD.

Data reveals that though the geographical disparity has declined over the years, there is still a greater concentration of the SHGs linked to banks in southern region. Other two regions which have significant share in SHGs linked to banks are eastern and central regions. However, what is noteworthy is that even other regions have made substantial progress and improved their share during the period

SHGs and Women Empowerment

The SHG movement in the country made the mission of women empowerment successful everywhere. The most identified contributions of SHGs to empowerment of women are –

(i) SHGs have provided poor women the access to economic resources like money and then by they enable the women to spend them or productive and consumption needs.

(ii) SHGs enabled women to participate in decision making on economic and financial issues like family income, consumption pattern, rising of loan, sale and mortgage of assets etc.

(iii) SHGs have enhanced the economic and social status of women at family and society level.

(iv) SHGs have given women opportunities of self-development through imparting them education, training and the practical knowledge. Working in the group is an opportunity for women to develop her.

(v) The SHGs made women to participate proactively involve in socio-political decision-making at local level through their participation in Village Gram Sabha, Panchayat meetings and other political activities.

(vi) SHGSs have changed mindset and vocation of women from house-keeper to organiser, manager and decision-maker and entrepreneur. Women learn skill and ability from the group.

(vii) SHGs changed the outlook of the women. As it brings unity and integrity among the members, it avoids or removes any type of disparities like caste, religion, language, age etc. It improved general welfare of family and community.

(viii) Most people manage to mobilise resources to develop their enterprises and their dwellings slowly overtime. Financial services could enable the poor to leverage their initiative, accelerating the process of building incomes, assets and economic security.

All is not well even with SHGs. A recent study undertaken among SHGs in Coimbatore (Tamil Nadu) (Palanivelu and others, 2011)[2] reveals that –

(i) Savings is increasing at a slow rate because of high incremental expenditure.

(ii) Majority of women face resistance from husbands in joining the group, some also from parents and others (including group members!)[3]

Drawing on the experience of two major NGOs in Bangladesh – Brac and Poshia – a research study (Moniruzzaman)[4] finds that lesser importance is being given to internal management of the groups. Also the performance of the groups on socio-political issues such as assertion of equal rights (e.g. gender equity) and resistance to social malpractices (as for example, in marriage and divorce) is quite low.

MFIs and SHGs need to have extended agenda today. Two points that we recommend here are –

- Mass financial literacy and its integration with mass functional literacy
- Literacy and education to include teaching/training/practising – portfolio management, entrepreneurship development in small and medium enterprises (SMEs), global networking and local governance

Need for Regulation

The rapid growth of MFIs has led to many concerns being raised, primarily around the rates charged by the lenders and usage of funds by the borrowers. In many cases, the lending rates range from an effective 25 per cent per annum to 32 per cent per annum. The interest rates charged are lesser than the interest charged by the money lenders and higher than the rate of interest charged by the commercial banking institutions. Experts like Mohammad Yunus are not in favour of profit oriented Micro financial institutions and are keen on government intervention on interest rate cap. MFIs are in the eye of the storm over the high interest rates they charge and the state governments' efforts to regulate them through the recent ordinance. In June the Governments in Andhra Pradesh and Kerala asked the MFIs to comply with local rules that regulate the money lending activity. A handful of MFIs are contesting this in court and last week Andhra Pradesh government passed an ordinance to regulate MFIs, one which stop short of capping interest rates.

Andhra Pradesh and Kerala governments have mandated NBFCs and MFIs to register under local money lending laws, which means the government has the right to cap / monitor interest rates charged to borrowers said India bulls securities research report. All these developments show that are mere substitute to money lending business and the money lending business of MFIs are under check. A sector that started as a service to the poor now looks a money spinner, attracting private equity funds with no social aims what so ever.

Are Money Lenders Still Dominant in Rural India?

These Southern states are worried about two things: the interest rates charged by the institutions and the possibility that borrowers could be coerced by goons hired by MFIs to make repayments. Andhra Pradesh has good reasons for worry about micro lending. Numbers from RBI show that over 53 per cent of loans are sourced from money lenders. Chennai follows, with money lenders accounting for 40 per cent of all borrowings. Money lenders account for more than 30 per cent of all lending in four more states Bihar, Manipur, Punjab and Rajasthan. Even today they are the dominant force in the rural credit market. If the activities of MFIs are controlled money lenders will regain their lost glory in the rural credit market.

Should Interest Rate of MFIs be Capped?

Should lending rates of Micro Finance Institutions (MFIs) – often 28-36 per cent – be capped? Some folks think so. Officials in Andhra Pradesh once closed down MFIs for usury, but the RBI came to the rescue, declaring there could be no cap on lending rates. Banning MFIs would only drive poor people into more expensive loan from money lenders. MFIs have provided finance to 20 million poor people, whom nationalised banks could not reach. But now capping has again come to the fore. The finance ministry has apparently told banks to ensure that MFIs to whom they lend cap their lending rates at 22-24 per cent. This directly contradicts the RBI policy that there should be no interest rate caps. Yunus says interest should be 10 to

15 per cent above the cost of raising the money, with anything beyond a red zone of loan sharking. “We need to draw a line between genuine and abuse”; “you will never see the situation of poor people if you look at through the glasses of profit making”; “we created micro credit to fight the loan sharks…we did not create micro credit to encourage new loan sharks”. He recently said to a gathering of financial officials at UN that micro credit should be seen as an opportunity to help people get out of poverty in a business way, but not an opportunity to make money out of poor people.

Micro financial institutions are relieved with the 26 per cent interest rate cap announced by RBI in its monetary policy. The apex bank had asked banks to ensure a margin cap of 12 per cent and an interest rate cap of 26 per cent for their lending to MFIs under priority sector loans. We expected worse in the wake of Andhra Pradesh Government’s campaign against so-called high interest rates and other irregularities. The RBI has now proved that it is on industry’s side said the Managing Director of a leading Hyderabad-based MFI While stating the broad framework of regulations suggested by the Malegam Panel was accepted, the RBI had in fact taken a more liberal view than Malegam Panel which felt that interest rates should be capped at 24 per cent.

After nearly 10 months of squeeze, banks are now turning positive about lending to MFIs. Some banks are actively processing loan application of credit starved MFIs which have been in red since the promulgation of the Andhra Pradesh Microfinance (Regulation and Money lending). Micro Financial Institutions in the country has shrunk by about 40 per cent a year after the crisis began to unfold in Andhra Pradesh. While the drop in portfolios and operations are quite discernible in major MFIs, many smaller ones are on the verge of disappearing.

India, being a large country known for its geographic and socio economic diversities, there is enough scope for many agencies to operate at different degrees of efficiency and sophistication. Knowledge, experience and skills combined together can build strong and progressive institutions (Hans and Deepika, 2011). MFIs and SHGs need not be considered as substitutes for banks but as grass root agencies and links to development banks. Poverty here is too deep rooted malady to be removed in a decade or so. The action programmes for poverty eradication is on. The bottom of the pyramid (BoP) of wealth is expanding and its peak at a much faster rate, reaching dizzy heights. Yet, it is also now being recognised that there is fortune at the BoP. SHGs as a powerful weapon of financial inclusion are one such instrument sharing the fortune of all those who survive at the BoP.

Conclusion

Micro-finance seems the most favoured route for poverty alleviation in rural India mainly for its novelty of accessibility. If participatory development is all that was needed to make financial inclusion a practicality then SHGs can do it for the people as is evident in women empowerment. The MFIs and SHGs cannot remain complacent. They need to innovate. While strengthening savings and stretching investments they need to practice sound managerial principles of portfolio management, interest rate management, risk management, entrepreneurship development in SMEs as well as local governance. More challenges lie ahead.

Notes

1. Yunus Model, (Grameen Bank) however, is not the first one in bottom- up approach, even in Bangladesh. An earlier attempt is the Comilla Model in 1959 launched by Pakistan Academy for Rural Development (renamed as Bangladesh Academy for Rural Development in 1971). The model envisaged rural empowerment through tow strategies; *one* intervention through infrastructure development and *two*, decentralisation of decision-making process. The model, however, failed.
2. Sample size: 150 respondents.
3. This goes to show that there is no collective and cooperative empowerment, if empowerment really means 'power to some one', 'power with', 'power within' and 'power to'.
4. Sample size: 248 members in six groups.

References

Adams, Dale W and Fitchett, D.A. (1992). *Informal Finance in Low Income Countries*, Oxford: West View Press.

Beatriz Armendariz and Jonathan Morduch (2007). *The Economics of Micro Finance*, New Delhi: Prentice-Hall of India Private Limited.

Chandreshekar, T.C. and Shivkumar S.C. (2009). "Micro finance for the Extreme Poor. A Study", *Southern Economist*, 48 (15):5-8.

Chakravarty, Saswati (2007). "*Celebrating the Bandhan of Microloans*", *The Economic Times*, December 25, Tuesday, 2007.

Deepika D. and Hans, V. Basil (2011). "Self Help Groups and Women Entrepreneurship Development: A Case Study in Karnataka", Paper presented at the National Seminar on Emerging Trends in Entrepreneurial Development, Besant Women's College, Mangalore, January 22.

Deepika and Hans, V. Basil (2011). "Inclusive growth and women in India – looking at MDGs', *International Journal of Social and Economic Research* (online), 1(1): 56-65.

Fernandez, Aloysius P. (2007). *A Microfinance Institution with a Difference, Economic and Political Weekly*, 42(13):1185- 1188.

Hans, V. Basil (2010). *Microfinance in India – From Financial to Social Intermediation,* In Rasure, K.A. (ed.), Rural Credit in the Era of Globalisation, Gurgaon: Madhav Books.

Hans, V. Basil (2009). *Innovations in Microfinance – Looking beyond Income Poverty*, Available at http://ssrn.com

Jayasheela, Dinesha P.T. and Hans, V. Basil (2008). "Financial Inclusion and Microfinance in India: An Overview". In Sohani, A K (ed.), *Financial Inclusion – Perspectives and Country Experiences*, Hyderabad: The Icfai University Press.

Joshi G.V. (2007). "Removal of Poverty in India: Can microfinance alone do it?", *Nitte Management Review*, 1(2): 1-17.

Karmakar, K.G. (2002). "Microfinance Revisited", *Financing Agriculture*, 34(2).

Khandelwal, Anil (2007). "Microfinance Development Strategy for India", *Economic and Political Weekly,* 42(13):1127- 1133.

Macfarquhar Neil (2010). "Microfinance is now big business", *Deccan Herald,* April 22, Thursday, 2010.

Moniruzzaman, M. (2011). "Group Management and Empowerment: Lessons from Development NGOs in Bangladesh", *Journal of South Asian Development*, 6(7): 67-91

Nair Ramachandra (2010)."Micro finance Bill skirts crucial Issues", *The Hindu Business Line*, June 11, Friday, 2010.

National Bank for Agriculture and Rural Development (2009). NABARD Annual Report, 2009.

Nadarajan, S. and R. Ponmurugan (2006). "Self-Help Groups: Bank Linkage Programme", *Kisan World*, 2(33), pp. 35-36.

Nayak, Gayatri (2010). "Macro challenges of micro lenders", *The Economic Times*, April 28, Wednesday, 2010.

Palanivelu P., Nandhini M., Usha M., and Krishnaveni V. (2011). "Poverty Eradication– Women's Self Help Groups", *SCMS Journal of Indian Management,* 8(11): 52-52.

Rangarajan, C. (2007). "Financial Inclusion: Some Key Issues", Lecture delivered at Mangalore University, Mangalore, August. 10, 2007.

Nair Ramachandra (2010)."Micro finance Bill skirts crucial Issues", *The Hindu Business Line*, June 11, Friday, 2010.

Ramanand, K.V. (2010). "Enhancing microfinance", *The Hindu Business Line*, August 26, Thursday, 2010.

Ramakrishnan, R. (2007). 'Micro Finance- Emerging Trends in Financial Management' April 17, available at http/www.Indianmbu.com/Faculty/column/FC557/fc557.html

RBI (2009). *Report of High level Committee Review the Lead Bank Scheme*, Mumbai: Reserve Bank of India.

Serrao, Manohar, V., Sequira, A.H., and Hans, V. Basil (2011). "Designing a Methodology to Investigate Accessibility and Impact of Financial Inclusion", Paper presented at the International Conference on Innovation and Inclusion in Banking: Issues, Strategies and Options, Department of Applied Economics, School of Development Studies, Kannur University, February 3-4.

Somnath, V.S. (2009). *Microfinance- Redefining the future,* New Delhi: Excel Books.

Swaminathan, S. Anklesaria Aiyar (2010). Do not cap microfinance lending rates, *The Economic Times*, September 22, Wednesday.

Thingalaya, N.K. (2007). " A microfinance model for rural India", *Nitte Management Review*, March 2007, 1(1), pp. 4-13.

Thingalaya N.K., Moodithaya M.S. and Shetty N.S. (2010). *Financial Inclusion and Beyond Issues and Challenges*, New Delhi: Acamedic Foundation.

United Nations (2006). *Building Inclusive Financial Sector for Development*. New York: UNO.

Venkataramaraju D. and Ramesh, S.V. (2010-11). "Financial Inclusion – Strategies and Regulations", *Journal of Accounting and Finance*, 25(1): 105-114.

32

Financial Inclusion and Self Help Groups in India

M. Dhanabhakyam and *M. Kavitha*

Introduction

Financial Inclusion or inclusive financing is the delivery of financial services at affordable costs to sections of disadvantaged and low income segments of society. It is argued that as banking services are in the nature of public good; the availability of banking and payment services to the entire population without discrimination is the prime objective of this public policy. The term "financial inclusion" has gained importance since the early 2000s, and is a result of findings about financial exclusion and its direct correlation to poverty. Financial inclusion is now a common objective for many central banks among the developing nations.

Financial inclusion broadly means the provision of reasonable financial services, viz., access to payments and remittance facilities, savings, loans and insurance services by the formal financial system to those who tend to be excluded. Since late nineties, the difficult and competitive financial services enable access to a wide range of financial products and opportunities to meet emerging credit needs. Realising the importance of Financial Inclusion even developed countries like the United Kingdom has been aggressively pursuing the same since 1997 and set up a Task Force in 2005, which continuously monitors the progress and advises the Government to expedite the programme. The Dependency and Indemnity Compensation (DIC) Board of Directors in US approved on November 2, 2006 the establishment of a DIC Advisory Committee on Economic Inclusion to advice the DIC for expanding access to banking services for underserved populations. The report of the Task Force in March 2007 (HM Treasury) defines financial inclusion as the access to appropriate financial services for every person for enabling him to:

- Manage his money on day-to-day basis, effectively, securely and confidently;
- Plan for future and cope with financial pressure in short term with the help of long term funds;
- Deal effectively with financial distress like long term sickness, unemployment, or family break down by availing money management advice and insurance.

Objectives of the Study

- To study the basic concepts related with financial inclusion.
- To study the model for financial inclusion.
- To know the Financial Inclusion and development indicator.
- To study the SHG approach and financial inclusion.

The Model for Financial Inclusion

Deepening the financial system and widening its reach is crucial for both accelerating growth and for equitable distribution, given the present state of development of our country. The model discussed below will be instrumental in bring hundred per cent financial inclusion in our country.

Stage I: Create Awareness and Financial Literacy

Intensive awareness, education and promotion drive to create an in-depth impact on the masses.

- Government should promote introduction of basic banking - relevance, services, merits as a topic in secondary and higher secondary classes in all education institutions.
- Government-sponsored publicity campaigns through all medias, radio; television; newspapers; village panchayat; movies; local stage shows etc.
- Banks should design and organise aggressive education cum promotion campaigns in unbanked parts of urban, semi-urban and rural areas to enhance financial literacy and awareness, as well as to remove the doubts and apprehensions that the masses have towards the banking sector.
- Banks should involve the knowledgeable and well-informed local inhabitants in such activities. This will help the banks to consolidate and ensure prompt and extensive response from the populace.
- Banks should gather support from the NGOs, retired bank personnel's, and academic institutions to reach the desired numbers within a limited span of time. Once the fallacy is removed from the minds of the general public, they automatically will join the mainstream. The all-round awareness and education simulation will drive them to open savings and current accounts. This will mark the beginning of basic banking in true sense.

Stage II: Basic Banking

The banks need to adopt a considerate approach towards this new clientele, to remove their qualms and disbeliefs. It is necessary that the basic banking should be comprehensive in scope and have attractive USPs that can lure people at large:

- All banks should allow no-frill accounts i.e. savings accounts which can be opened with a nominal amount of Rs. 5/- or even with zero balance. They should allow 6-7 withdrawals in the accounting period and should not restrict the number of deposits.
- RBI, along with banks, should toil hard to reduce the amount of paper work in relation to the opening of an account as well as in getting small credits. This would reduce the complexity and also speed-up the processing at banks.
- Banks should make sure that local people are positioned in the front offices, so that the general public does not have to endure language problem and does not have to suffer perceived/actual racial discrimination.
- It is all the more necessary for the banks that besides offering the conventional products and services they should set up teams who can understand the needs and requirements of the common man and design innovative products and services having greater suitability and desirability. Also, banks should work as one-stop store and offer diversified products in banking and insurance.
- Despite the risk, financing of first time entrepreneurs is a must for financial inclusion and growth. Banks should arrange and provide technical advice for these entrepreneurs. They will have to tone up their risk assessment and risk management capacities, and provide for these facilities.
- Banks should give free financial counsel to low income households and small entrepreneurs.
- The pricing of the product should be also done keeping in mind the pockets of the potential clientele. The cost burden should proportionately be shifted to high potential sectors, who can afford a little upswing in their banking cost.

Stage III: Innovative Strategies

Basic banking itself needs to be supported by innovative strategies, in order to improve the reach and reduce the operating cost of the banks:

- Infrastructure sharing amongst banks and other organisations will help in lowering the operating cost and thus the cost benefit can be transferred to customers.
- Bank should open small extension counters at organisation providing

public utility services such as local schools, primary health care centres, village mandies, and farmers associations, cold storages and warehouses, railway stations, bus stops etc.

- This should simultaneously be supplemented by mobile banks. Wherever it is not economical to set up a branch, credit camps/ loan 'melas' must be organised on weekly basis, to disburse small loans on easy terms.
- Greater use of technology should be made by the banks to improve their reach, speed of processing, as well as to cut down the operating cost. Last but not the least, the Government of India should initiate a civil rights law. Prohibiting discrimination by banks against low and moderate income neighborhoods. This will create a pressure on banks to play an important role in bringing financial inclusion in the country.

Financial Inclusion and Development Indicator

Recent data shows that countries with large proportion of population excluded from the formal financial system also show higher poverty ratios and high inequality.

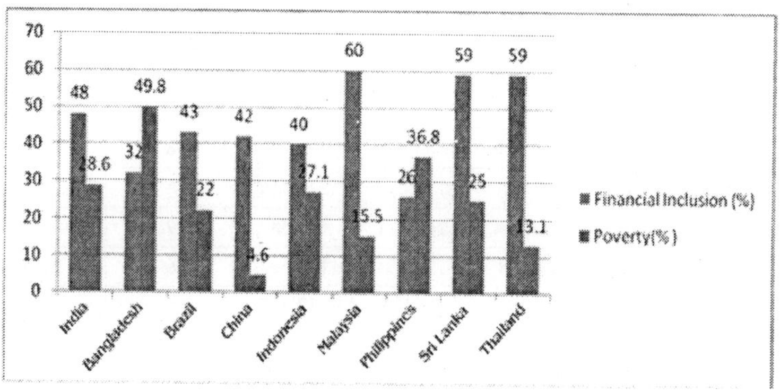

Fig. 1.

Source: World Bank.

SHG Approach and Financial Inclusion

As an innovative credit channel, the Self Help Group (SHG) approach was introduced in 1992, to link poor people with bank credit. Under this programme, about 40 million rural families have been linked with banks up to March 2007 (NABARD). The distinguishing feature of this approach as compared to other sponsored credit schemes is the learning the management of own money by the poor before availing bank loan. Moreover, the SHG approach does not involve any subsidy; hence, it is sustainable with its own strength. A number of studies have found that SHG approach reduces the transaction cost for banks and loan availing cost of borrowers. In financing SHGs, the requirement of collateral by banks has been replaced by peer group pressure and hence this approach has enabled social and economic inclusion of women by waiving the requirement of collateral. Some important highlights of SHG-achievements in India are as under.

(i) Upto March 2007, 2.925 millions SHGs and about 40.95 million families have been linked with bank credit.

(ii) Of the total SHGs, women groups are 86 per cent.

(iii) 0.686 million SHG linked with banks.

(iv) Rs. 664.3 million loan amount disbursed to SHGs.

(v) Average Bank Loan per SHG is Rs. 61000.

(vi) Bank loan of Rs. 180000 million provided to SHGs.

Table 1: State-wise cumulative credit linked SHGs

Sl. No	*States*	*2009*	*2010*	*2011*	*Percentage to Total in 2011*	*Percentage of adult covered under SHGs*
1.	Andhra Pradesh	49,2927	587,238	683,619	23	21.64
2.	Tamil Nadu	2,20,698	312,778	400,477	14	14.19
3.	Karnataka	163,198	224,928	317,636	11	14.52
4.	Orissa	123,256	180,896	234,451	8	15.58
5.	Maharashtra	71,146	131,470	225.856	8	5.63
6.	Uttar Pradesh	119,648	161,911	198,587	7	3,38
7.	West Bengal	92,698	136,251	181,563	6	5.54
8.	Rajasthan	60,006	98,175	137,837	5	6.78
9.	Kerala	60,809	86.985	117,913	4	8.03
10.	Assam	31,234	56,449	81,454	3	8.10
11.	Bihar	28,015	46,221	72,339	2	2.47
12.	Madhya Pradesh	45,105	57,125	70,912	2	3.16
13.	Gujarat	24,712	34,160	43,572	1	2.11
14.	Chhattisgarh	18,569	31,291	41,703	1	5.21
15.	Jharkhand	21,531	30,819	37,317	1	3.80
16.	Himachal Pradesh	17,798	22,920	27,799	1	10.91
17.	Uttarakhand	14,043	17,588	21,527	1	6.74
18.	Sub-total	1,591,350	2,199,616	2,873,035	98	7.78
19.	All India	1,591,350	2,238,786	29,24,786	100	7.57

Conclusion

Financial inclusion has been a catch phrase for the past few years. Increasing educational levels means more financial inclusion; therefore, a literate population must be created in order to create a meaningful financially included population. Innovation and out-of-the-box thinking are what has made the world what it is today. To empirically ascertain the determinants of financial inclusion, the state wise percentage adults in terms of saving and credit accounts were regressed. The person having low income and less geographical access to bank e.g., agricultural labourers, marginal and small farmers, migrant labourers, tribal and women may be excluded from the financial inclusion. The variable of percentage of adult covered in SHGs has also positive association with the level of financial inclusion especially in credit accounts. It suggests that SHGs can play significant role in achieving the financial inclusion especially for women and low-income families.

33

Implementation of Financial Inclusion- A Case Study of the Karnataka Bank Limited

Ramaprakasha N.

Introduction

India is a developing country. In order to achieve overall development and to attain prosperity great emphasis has to be given for Inclusive Growth i.e. equitable growth happening across all the sections of the society. The 12th Five Year Plan in India is focusing on *"Faster, Sustainable and more Inclusive Growth"* for the overall development of the nation. Financial Inclusion is one of the most crucial strategies to achieve Inclusive Growth in India. Financial Inclusion is deemed to have catalytic effect on inclusive growth. It aims at reducing the gap between various sections of the society by providing adequate and timely financial services at affordable cost to vulnerable groups such as economically weaker sections and low income groups at large. Banking is a key driver for Financial Inclusion and Inclusive Growth.

Definition of Financial Inclusion

The Reserve Bank of India (RBI) defines Financial Inclusion as *"The process of ensuring access to appropriate Financial Products and services needed by all sections of the society in general and vulnerable groups such as weaker sections and low income groups in particular at an affordable cost in fair and transparent manner by regulated mainstream institutional players".*

The primary motto of financial inclusion is each and every citizen of the country should have timely access to financial services such as banking, life insurance and non life insurance etc. at an affordable cost.

Objectives of the Study

The main objectives of this paper entitled "*Implementation of Financial Inclusion- a Case Study of the Karnataka Bank Limited*" are as follows,

- To carry out a comprehensive study at The Karnataka Bank Limited, to understand various initiatives implemented by the bank towards achieving financial inclusion in India.
- To identify the issues and challenges faced by The Karnataka Bank Limited with regard to implementation of financial inclusion in India.

Research Methodology

The study is **Descriptive** in nature. Primary data regarding implementation of financial inclusion at The Karnataka Bank Limited are collected through **Direct Interview** method by interacting with concerned Authority of Financial Inclusion Cell, Karnataka Bank Limited, Head Office Mangalore. Secondary data is collected by referring to Annual Reports of the Bank, Internet resources, Journals and various management journals. Primary data as well as Secondary data are then analysed thoroughly to achieve the required objectives of the study.

Company Profile-The Karnataka Bank Limited

The Karnataka Bank Limited is a private sector banking institution based in the town of Mangalore, in Karnataka, India. The Karnataka Bank was incorporated on February 18, 1924 as "The Karnataka Bank Limited" and commenced business on May 23, 1924. The Reserve Bank of India (R.B.I) has designated Karnataka Bank as an A-class scheduled commercial Bank.

As on 30-06-2012, the Bank now has national presence with a network of 506 Branches, 382 ATM outlets spread across 20 states and 2 union territories (totally 888 business outlets) and having 9 Regional Offices at Mangalore, Bangalore, Mysore, Shimoga, Hubli, Delhi, Mumbai, Chennai and Hyderabad.

The Bank has a highly dedicated team of around 6087 employees ably patronised by over 112863 shareholders and over 60 lakh clientele bases.

It is offering tailor made range of products and services in order to cater to diverse types of markets, trades, personal and corporate needs of the customers.

Having matured for more than 88 years in the Banking industry in India, The Karnataka Bank Limited has won the confidence of its Stakeholders namely Shareholders, Depositors, Employees, Customers and Society at large which has resulted in tremendous growth to become one of the premier private sector Banks in India.

Mission Statement

The Mission statement of The Karnataka Bank Limited is *"To be a technology savvy, customer centric progressive Bank with a national presence, driven by the highest standards of corporate governance and guided by sound ethical values".*

Table 1: Financial Results of Karnataka Bank Limited as on 30-06-2012

Business turnover	₹ 54259 Crores
Deposits	₹ 32547 Crores
Advances	₹ 21712 Crores
Owned funds	₹ 2598 Crores
Operating profit	₹ 510 Crores
Net profit	₹ 246 Crores
Proposed dividend	35 %

Awards and Recognition

- The Bank has bagged the **"Best Bank Award"** for **"Managing IT Risk"** under small bank category for the year 2010-2011, instituted by Institute for Development and Research in Banking Technology (IDRBT).
- The Bank has won **National Award**, it has been adjudged as the **"Runner-ups"** for the **"Best Banker for Customer Friendliness"** category among the mid-sised banks in India.
- Karnataka Bank Limited has recently bagged two of the IBA Banking Technology Awards 2011 instituted by Indian Banks Association. The bank has been adjudged as the **"Second Runner-up"** under **"Best Risk Management and Security Initiative" and** also the **"Second Runner-up"** under **"Best Financial Inclusion Initiative"** in the category of Private Sector Banks.

Initiatives Implemented by the Karnataka Bank Limited

Towards Achiveing Financial Inclusion in India:

- The Bank believes in Inclusive Growth and has full fledged, Core-Banking enabled 103 Rural Branches across India (20% of the total number of branches) and also it has taken up implementation of Financial Inclusion in 80 villages across Karnataka, Chhattisgarh and Andhra Pradesh.
- The Bank is utilising appropriate Information and Communication (ICT) based model using Business Correspondents (BC) Model in 69 villages for ensuring door step delivery of financial services and "*Brick and Mortar*" branch models in 11 Villages for extending banking services in every village having a population of over 2000.
- The Karnataka Bank Limited opened its First Financial Inclusion Branch at Kairangala (A small village in Dakshina Kannada District,

Karnataka), the Second branch at Horanadu (A Hindu holy town located in Chikmagalur District, Karnataka) and the Third branch at Arakere (A town located in Davanagere District, Karnataka)

- The Bank has implemented the Mobile Van Model of Financial Inclusion Resource Center (FIRC) in order to disseminate awareness on financial services available from banks to the general public and to facilitate financial education and financial literacy to the common man at the remotest village in the service area of the Bank. As on 31-03-2012 it has covered about 854 service area villages.
- The Bank has opened its first Financial Literacy Credit Counseling Center (FLCC) at B.C. Road, Bantwal by joining hands with Syndicate Bank and Vijaya Bank, as an institutional sponsorer, to provide education to the people residing in rural and urban areas regarding various financial products and services provided by the financial institutions and to provide financial counseling regarding responsible borrowing and dept counseling and restructuring.
- The Bank is a Trustee of the Karnataka Farmers Resource Center (KFRC) set up by State Level Bankers Committee (SLBC), Karnataka at Bagalkot, Karnataka. It acts as a resource center and provides bridging services to the farmers to develop their managerial capacities. It also coordinates the services of various service providers to provide training, consultancy, counseling and reference services.
- The Bank is also participating in the pilot project of the Government of Karnataka for Bio-Metric Smart Card based payment system (Electronic Benefit Transfer through Micro ATM's) for Mahatma Gandhi National Rural Employment Guarantee Scheme (MGNREGS) and Social Security Pension (SSP) beneficiaries covering Chitradurga, Yadgir and Bellary Districts in Karnataka.
- The Bank knows that "*Youths are the building blocks of a Nation*" hence to encourage savings habits among the Youths, the Bank has introduced two specialised "*No Frill Savings Bank Accounts*" namely, "KBL Kishore Savings Bank Account" exclusively for school children aged between 12 years and 18 years and "KBL Tarun Savings Bank Account" exclusively for students aged between 18 years and 25 years.
- The Bank knows that *"Women are the backbone of any society"* and has understood the significance of "*Women Empowerment*" in achieving Financial Inclusion and Inclusive Growth, hence it has an array of products and services exclusively for Women namely,
    - KBL Vanitha: A unique "*No-Frill Savings Bank Account*" exclusively for women which offers insurance coverage for jewelry worth ` 50,000/- with a host of other benefits also.

- KBL Mahila Udyog: Special loan scheme to promote Women Entrepreneurs.

- The Bank is offering specialised Loan schemes at reasonably priced interest rates to meet the credit needs of Agricultural workers such as,
    - KBL Agri Gold Loan and KBL Instant Agri. Credit: Loans for general agricultural purpose:
    - KBL Krishik Bhandar: Loan for general farmers.
    - KBL Krishik Pushpankur: Loans for establishment and maintenance of floriculture, nurseries and tissue culture activities.
    - KBL Krishik Sarathi: Loan for the purpose of purchasing "*Tractor*".
    - KBL Krishik Sinchana: Loan for the purpose of "*Irrigating*" the agricultural land.

Concept of Micro ATM's

- Micro ATM's are Bio Metric authentication enabled hand-held device (Point of Transaction) which can be used for the following purpose:
    - Cash Withdrawal and Cash Deposit
    - Balance Enquiry
    - Remittances
- Devices are operated by Business Correspondents (BC's) appointed by the Bank and Physical Currency would be handled by Business Correspondents and not a machine like a regular ATM's.
- All transactions require online Bio Metric authentication with the UIDAI (Unique Identification Authority of India).

Issues and Challenges

There are various issues and challenges with regard to implementation of financial inclusion in India. Some of them are discussed here in this paper,

Less Deposits and More Credit: Unlike the urban masses, the general rural masses have less Earnings and Savings. Naturally the Deposits in the rural bank branches are very less compared to the Credits taken from the Banks. In this situation recovering back the Loans/Advances given to the customers is one of the major challenges faced by the Karnataka Bank.

Increase in number of Inoperative Accounts: In the process of achieving financial inclusion the bank has taken up many innovative measures to increase the number of Bank Account holders across the Nation but this has also carried the risk of increased number of "*Inoperative Accounts*". A recent study has shown that the real financial inclusion in India is very low because around 40% of the newly opened bank account holders have used their accounts NOT even once a month! Thus merely making individuals open a Bank Account will not facilitate financial inclusion, the real financial inclusion takes place only when people utilise financial products and services offered by the Bank.

Issues with regard to Business Correspondents: Business Correspondents (BC's) acts as a bridge/ Agent between Bank and General Public. They connect both the "*Demand Side*" and "*Supply Side*" of the Banking industry. It may not be economically and technologically feasible for the bank to set up a full fledged "*Brick and Mortar*" branch at every village across India hence they utilise Business Correspondent's model to provide financial services to people residing in remote villages of the country. It is well known fact that Business Correspondent's (BC's) Model is one of the best suited models to achieve financial inclusion in India because of the several advantages it offers but it also carries some risks for the Bank. Some issues and challenges faced by the Karnataka Bank with regard to Business Correspondents model are :

- Managing the Business Correspondents and making them understand their jobs well.
- Fixing salaries and incentives for the Business Correspondents.
- Training the Business Correspondents.
- Security of Business Correspondents (BC's).
- Malpractices at Business Correspondents (BC's) Level.

Lack of Awareness and "*Resistance to Change*" with regard to financial services: Most of the people in rural and remote parts of the country are still unaware of the different financial services/products which are available in the market. Lack of proper knowledge regarding financial services and banking has resulted in "*Resistance to Change*" in the minds of people.

Technological Constraints: In order to achieve real financial inclusion appropriate Information and Communication Technology (ICT) must be effectively utilised. One of the major constraints of the ICT based BC model has been the technical problems associated with the model such as Malfunctioning of Hand held devices (Micro ATM's), Smart Cards, PoS (Point of Sale) Terminals, Limited number of technology service providers etc. These constraints can lead to erosion of confidence on the ICT based BC model. Hence these technological constraints need to be addressed quickly.

Security Concerns: It is known fact that in order to deliver financial services to customers, the bank is relying heavily on technology hence it is very essential to provide adequate security especially ICT security. Security related issues such as Frauds and Phishing can lead to decreased public confidence in the use of Electronic Fund Transfer further they could also lead to reputation risks. In order to overcome the security issues the Bank has to adapt stringent security measures. Again these cumbersome security procedures may deter customers using the products and using the electronic transactions! Thus achieving a proper balance between such apparently conflicting objectives is also one of the major challenges faced by the Bank.

Power supply and Network Connectivity: Most part of our country lack proper power supply and network connectivity. While banking transactions are enabled on a real time basis in urban centers, it is not so in case of rural centers. Normally it takes more time to complete banking transactions in rural/ remote centers due to poor internet connectivity and frequent power failures.

Conclusion

Financial Inclusion acts as a catalyst in promoting Inclusive Growth in India and Banks are the key drivers in implementing financial inclusion. The Karnataka Bank Limited is taking up many proactive and innovative measures in order to facilitate financial inclusion in India. There are various issues and challenges with regard to financial inclusion in India but as it is rightly said "*In Business Errors become Opportunity, Limitations stimulates Creativity, Propensity to experiment leads to New Products*", hence the various issues, challenges and limitations with regard to financial inclusion in India have to be converted in "*Opportunities*" for the overall development and prosperity of the country. The Karnataka Bank Limited reiterates its commitment to ensure the continuing appropriateness of its slogan "*Service with a Smile*" and "*Technology with a Human Touch*" in order to serve millions of its customers in an effective and efficient manner.

References

1. 88th Annual Report 2011-2012- The Karnataka Bank Limited.
2. Chakrabarty, K.C. (2011), "*Financial Inclusion- A Road India Needs to Travel*".
3. Chakrabarty, K.C. (2011), "*Financial Inclusion and Banks: Issues and Perspectives*", Key Note Address at FICCI-UNDP Seminar on "*Financial Inclusion: Partnerships between Banks, MFI's and Communities*", New Delhi.
4. Harun. R. Khan (2012), "*Issues and Challenges in Financial Inclusion: Policies, Partnerships, Processes and Products*", Key Note Address at Symposium on "*Financial Inclusion in Indian Economy*", Indian Institute of Public Administration, Bhubaneshwar.
5. www.karnatakabank.com
6. www.rbi.org.in
7. www.wikipedia.com

34

Financial Inclusion for Inclusive Growth – A Way Forward

Mohan Kumar T.P.R. Ramya and *R. Nakul*

Introduction

Financial inclusion may be defined as the process of ensuring access to financial services and timely and adequate credit where needed by vulnerable groups such as weaker sections and low income groups at an affordable cost. On 29.12.2003, Former UN Secretary-General Kofi Annan said "The stark reality is that most poor people in the world still lack access to sustainable financial services, whether it is savings, credit or insurance. The great challenge before us is to address the constraints that exclude people from full participation in the financial sector. Together, we can and must build inclusive financial sectors that help people improve their lives". According to the United Nations the main goals of financial inclusion are as follows:

1. Access at a reasonable cost of all households and enterprises to the range of financial services for which they are "bankable," including savings, short and long-term credit, leasing and factoring, mortgages, insurance, pensions, payments, local money transfers and international remittances.
2. Sound institutions, guided by appropriate internal management systems, industry performance standards, and performance monitoring by the market, as well as by sound prudential regulation where required.
3. Financial and institutional sustainability as a means of providing access to financial services over time.
4. Multiple providers of financial services, wherever feasible, so as to bring cost-effective and a wide variety of alternatives to customers

(which could include any number of combinations of sound private, non-profit and public providers.

5. Access at a reasonable cost of all households and enterprises to the range of financial services for which they are "bankable," including savings, short and long-term credit, leasing and factoring, mortgages, insurance, pensions, payments, local money transfers and international remittances
6. Sound institutions, guided by appropriate internal management systems, industry performance standards, and performance monitoring by the market, as well as by sound prudential regulation where required
7. Financial and institutional sustainability as a means of providing access to financial services over time
8. Multiple providers of financial services, wherever feasible, so as to bring cost-effective and a wide variety of alternatives to customers (which could include any number of combinations of sound private, non-profit and public providers.

Financial Exclusion

Financial exclusion is where the financial services are not available to the people. The rural people are very much excluded from having the financial services due to non availability of financial services in their areas or it may due to high cost for getting the financial services or non awareness about the availability of financial services. The poor people in rural as well as in urban are not able to get financial services still due to above reasons and also the huge formalities in availing the same. Financial exclusion includes-

- No savings;
- No insurance;
- No affordable credit;
- No access to monetary devices;
- No assets;
- No bank account.

Financial exclusion problem also includes the problems of financial discrimination and financial exploitation. The following are financially excluded:

- Poor people;
- Socially under privileged people;
- Disabled persons;
- Old as well as children;

- Women;
- Uneducated persons;
- Ethnic minorities;
- Unemployed people.

Financial Inclusion and Banks

Financial inclusion includes meeting the small credit needs of the people, giving them access to the payments systems and providing remittance facilities. For the purpose of financial inclusion it is highly required to ensure the following by the banking sector.

No frills accounts –RBI directed banks to offer a basic banking 'no frills' account with low or zero minimum balances and minimum charges to expand the outreach of such accounts to the low income groups.

Easier Credit Facility – Banks were directed to introduce a General Purpose Credit Card (GCC) facility up to Rs. 25,000.

Simpler KYC Norms – In order to ensure that the people belonging to the low income groups both in rural and urban areas, do not encounter difficulties in opening bank accounts 'Know Your Customer' (KYC) procedure is simplified for those accounts with balances not exceeding Rs. 50,000 and credits thereto not exceeding Rs. 1,00,000 in a year.

Use of Information Technology – Banks have been urged to scale up information technology initiatives for financial inclusion speedily while ensuring that solutions are highly secure, amenable to audit, and follow widely accepted open standards to ensure eventual inter-operability among the different systems;

Electronic Benefit Transfers (EBT) through banks – To encourage banks to adopt information and Communication Technology (ICT) solutions for enhancing their outreach RBI formulated a scheme to quicken the pace of adoption of the smart card based Electronic Benefit Transfer (EBT) mechanism by banks and rolled out the EBT system in the States that are ready to adopt the scheme. Banks are advised to work in co-ordination with the respective government departments at the Central and State levels to ensure that all State benefits are delivered to individuals only through bank accounts within a specific time frame.

Business – Correspondent (BC) Model – This model ensures a closure relationship between the poor people and the organised financial system. The RBI permits the banks to use the following as BCs.

- Non government organisations;
- Micro Finance Institutions;
- Retired bank employees;
- Ex-service men;

- Retired Government employees;
- Section 25 companies;
- Individual kirana/medical/fair shop owners;
- Individual Public Call Office (PCO) operators;
- Agents of small savings schemes of Government of India/Insurance companies;
- Individuals who own petrol pumps;
- Retired teachers;
- Authorised functionaries of well run Self Help Groups (SHGs) to linked banks; and
- Other civil society organisations;

Bank Branch and ATM Expansion Liberalised: RBI has permitted domestic scheduled Commercial Banks, other than regional rural banks, to open branches in tier 3 to tier 6 centres (with population up to 49,999 as on 2001 census) without having the need to take permission of RBI in each case. RBI also totally freed the location of ATMs from prior authorisation;

Project Financial Literacy: RBI has initiated a 'Project Financial Literacy' with the objective of disseminating information regarding the Central Bank and general banking concepts to various target groups. RBI's financial website line offers basics of banking, finance and central banking for Children of all ages. In a comic book format, RBI simplifies the complexities of banking, finance and central banking with the goal of making the learning fun and interesting;

Financial Literacy and Credit counseling: RBI has advised the convener-bank of each State Level Banks' Committee (SLBC) to set up a financial literacy-cum-counselling centre in any one district on pilot basis to provide free financial education to people in rural and urban areas on the various financial products and services while maintaining arm's length relationship with the parent bank and based on that experience to extend the facility to other districts in due course.

Financial Inclusion for Inclusive Growth

Financial inclusion is necessary for inclusive growth. Growth is inclusive when there is equality of economic opportunities. The seeds of financial inclusion were sown over 35 years ago when rural banks were established throughout the country. The branch network which was just 8000 in 1969 when banks were nationalised now has increased to more than 87000 because of the banking industry coming forward to take up social responsibilities. Still numerous villages do not have any access to the banking facilities.

Financial inclusion is integral to the inclusive growth process and sustainable development of the country. However, the financial inclusion models that banks come up with should be replicable and viable across the country. The Finance Minister said that although the banking network has rapidly expanded over the years, the key challenge would be to extend the banking coverage to include the large population living in 6 lakh villages in the country. Expressing his immense confidence in the Indian banking system to deliver on the plan for financial inclusion, Mr. Mukherjee said the system, which demonstrated its resilience in the face of the recent global financial crisis, should adopt strong and urgent measures to reach the unbanked segment of society and unlock their savings and investment potentials. To tap the fortune at the bottom of the pyramid, he recommended robust electronic transfers between bank branches located in the rural hinterland. This will facilitate the rural customers to transfer their income and conduct financial transactions seamlessly. He urged the private sector to support the designing of physical products including devices, software and financial services, training and capacity building so as to create a large manpower pool including business correspondents, and develop a business plan to tap the local talent that exists in the rural areas, on the lines of the e-choupal model.

Dr Janmejaya Sinha, Chairman, CII Taskforce on Financial Inclusion and Chairman (Asia Pacific), The Boston Consulting Group, said that 135 million of the 204 million households in the country face financial inclusion. Now, with 570 million people in the country being in the 0-25 age group, a very large segment would be entering the workforce in the coming years. Their financial inclusion at this stage would be of critical importance in the context of inclusive growth process and sustainable development. He further said that financial illiteracy is a key stumbling block in furthering financial inclusion. This has led to the financial illiterate segment making negative savings in many cases. He added that banks need to view the situation as not an obligation to be met but an opportunity that is to be weaved into their business strategies. He felt that a pro-active approach will see the banking network expanding in an all-inclusive manner like the telecom sector did. He also set a five point agenda for financial inclusion, which called for:

1. increasing overall consciousness of the need for financial inclusion;
2. increase in wireless and broadband connectivity in the rural areas to support rural banking;
3. spread of financial literacy programmes;
4. greater experimentation for financial inclusion through business correspondents, self-help groups, etc.
5. greater collaboration between the key stakeholders in the banking system.

Ms Chanda Kochhar, Chairperson, CII National Committee on Banking and Managing Director and CEO, ICICI Bank said with a low ratio of 1 bank branch for 16,000 people, financial inclusion is far-fetched today. But, the idea of financial inclusion should be broad-based, such that people are able to not only access credit, but also fetch various financial services and products through the banking access point. She also said that at the micro-level, the financial services providers should aim for a holistic approach that meets the different financial needs of the target customers, address not just rural but also large urban excluded segments, reduce cost of transactions with proper technology adoption, and support the development of support infrastructure.

In his Budget Speech for the year 2011-12 the Finance Minister stated that the Government has decided to provide appropriate banking facilities to the habitants having population in excess of 2000, as per 2001 census, by March 2012. For this purpose 73000 such habitants all over country have been identified and allocated to public sector banks, regional rural banks, private sector banks and co-operative banks for extending banking services by using the services of business correspondents and other models, with appropriate technology back up by March 2012. The banks have already covered 29000 villages by March 2011 and it is hoped that the remaining 44000 villages would be covered by March 2012. Self help groups are one of the few channels through which financial inclusion can be accelerated. The banks in general can do more bringing the banking services to the door steps of the under privileged through Financial Inclusion Plan.

Operational Guidelines

The Reserve Bank of India formulated 'Operational Guidelines on implementation of Electronic Benefit Transfer and its convergence with Financial Inclusion Plan' vide RBI/2011-12/153 and RPCD.CO.BC.FID No.16/12.01.019/2011-12, dated 12.08.2011 and issued to all scheduled commercial banks. These guidelines are expected to give a fillip to financial inclusion efforts and lead to a scalable and sustainable financial inclusion model.

The operational guidelines consist of five parts as below:

1. Financial Inclusion;
2. Electronic Benefit Transfer (EBT) Scheme using the "One District – One Bank Model";
3. Need for Convergence of Electronic Benefit Transfer and Financial Inclusion Plan;
4. Way forward for EBT implementation;
5. "One District-Many Banks-One Leader Bank" – model workflow.

Financial Inclusion

The key driver of our country's vision of inclusive growth is financial inclusion. RBI has adopted a 'Blank-led' model for ensuring financial inclusion to provide low cost, efficient, ICT based banking services utilising multiple delivery channels including intermediary low cost brick and mortar structures, branchless banking through Business Correspondents (BCs) and other modes like mobile vans, rural ATMs etc., so as to cover all the villages in due course. RBI, as a part of financial inclusion, initiates Governments to disburse social security payments through the banking channel leveraging Electronic Benefit Transfers for financial intermediation.

Electronic Benefit Transfers

In this model a designated bank has the mandate to disburse government payments at the doorstep of the beneficiary, electronically, through hand held devices using biometric smart cards at the locations of BCs of the bank. The following difficulties are expressed in scaling up 'one district – one bank model of EBT':

- No designated bank by itself may have the adequate branch/BC network to reach the entire District;
- Even if it is able undertake EBT, it may not be able to provide all financial services like deposits, OD, remittances and GCCs/KCCs to the customers;
- The designated bank may deploy BCs only 2 to 3 notified days in a month for disbursing the amount of social security payments in cash to EBT beneficiaries;
- It will take the freedom of people to bank with the bank of their choice keeping in view of better services etc.

Need for Convergence of Financial Inclusion and EBT

The operational guidelines insist the necessity for convergence of financial inclusion and EBT. Under 'One District – One bank Model' the leader bank is expected to extend all types of banking services to the residents of the area which is felt much difficult in attaining the object. Banks will not earn required amount of income unless they offer credit products. Since banks have invested in creating BC infrastructure for making EBT payments at the door steps of the beneficiaries they can provide banking services to non beneficiaries in those villages without any additional cost. At this stage of financial inclusion the intention of allocation of the unbanked villages, with population more than 2000, amongst various banks is to ensure that these villages are provided with at least one banking outlet for extending banking facilities comprising four products i.e., savings, credit, remittance and insurance. For the financial inclusion model to be a success it is necessary that there is a convergence between the EBT and the Financial Inclusion Plan model.

Way Forward for EBT Implementation

- One district – many banks – one leader bank model may be adopted henceforth for EBT implementation;
- There is no prohibition for adoption of 'one district –one bank' model

approach where the model exists and is already working provided one bank is in a position to provide whole range of minimum banking services under this dispensation;

- The State Governments should not stipulate any condition that prevents EBT accounts from being used for other banking transactions;
- The State Government shall designate a nodal department for administration of each social benefit schemes. The provisions of MOU signed between Government Agency and the banks should be consistent with the extant guidelines and notifications of RBI.
- Achieving full financial inclusion is crucial for implementation of EBT and direct transfer of subsidies. SLBC should prepare plans to cover all unbanked villages including population less than 1000, the allocation of these villages may be done on the basis of geographical proximity;
- Once banking services are extended to all villages under the financial inclusion plan, convergence between the EBT scheme and FIP would automatically realised;
- Once UID is issued to all the villagers, a 'model' will emerge where the customer will have the option to transact with the bank of their choice in any village by using UID enabled Micro ATMs. This will reduce their dependence on cash and lower costs for transactions.

"One District-Many Banks-One Leader Bank" – Model Workflow

The model workflow framed by the operational guidelines for 'One district-Many banks-One leader bank' is as follows:

- The State Government is to select a Leader Bank for EBT for a district and designate a nodal department for coordination at the district level;
- State Government is to make MOU with the leader bank for the particular district;
- Leader bank is to make arrangements with other participating banks in the District on revenue sharing contract;
- Nodal department is to give the list of beneficiaries to the leader bank;
- Leader bank is to distribute the list of beneficiaries among all participating banks;
- Participating banks are to appoint to select the technology provider and deploy BC/CSPs in all villages;
- BC/CSPs are to enroll all beneficiaries, participating banks to open accounts and issue smart cards;
- Nodal Department is to open a savings account with the leader bank;
- Nodal Department is to provide files electronically containing the details of beneficiaries each month and arrange for crediting the required amount into the SB Account with the leader bank;

- Leader bank is to arrange for crediting the amount electronically to other participating banks;
- Participating banks are to credit the beneficiary accounts on the same day and send confirmation to the leader bank;
- Leader bank will confirm credit to the nodal department;
- The funds are now at the disposal of the beneficiaries for use as per their requirements;
- MIS reports are to be provided by the participating banks to leader bank and in turn the leader bank is to submit report to the nodal department;
- Reconciliation with the nodal department is to be done by the leader bank preferably on daily basis, but at least on weekly basis;
- Developments in the implementation of EBT are to be mailed to DCC/ BLBC level every month by the leader bank. Any policy or structural issues in the implementation is to be discussed at SLBC (State Level Banker's Committee) level.

'One District-Many Banks-One Leader Bank' model, if implemented will able to achieve the 100% of the financial inclusion in the country though it will take some time.

Conclusion

The discussion made above clearly shows that financial inclusion if highly required for inclusive growth of the country to enable the people to get equality of economic opportunities. Awareness in this regard is to be created. Ministry of Corporate Affairs is conducting various awareness programs through professional institutes and other bodies in capital market all over the country especially in rural areas and the people are much benefited. In the same way the awareness program in this program may be conducted in all over the country so that the financially excluded people may get the benefit of economic opportunities. The ICWAI institute may initiate the same with RBI.

References

1. www.rbi.org
2. www.pib.nic.in
3. Operational Guidelines for implementation of Electronic Benefit Transfer and its convergence with financial inclusion plan issued by Rural Planning and Credit Department, Central Office, RBI.
4. 4.http://en.wikipedia.org
5. http://www.taxmanagementindia.com/visitor/member_profile.asp?ID=8914

35

Obstacles for Financial Inclusion Among the Tribes: An Empirical Study in Chamarajanagara and Mysore Districts of Karnataka

O.D. Heggade and *Puttaraja*

Introduction

In this chapter an attempt is made to identify and analyse the obstacles for the financial inclusion of tribes which hamper their socio-economic empowerment. This is a case study based on primary data collected by using an interview schedule. It deals with the case of four tribes namely Jenukuruba, Kadukuruba, Soliga and Yarava who live in and closer to the National Reserve Forest Area of Nagarahole, Bandipura, and B.R. Hills spread over in southern part of the Mysore and Chamarajanagara districts in Karnataka state. The tribal population is highly deprived and exploited thus, it is a very backward segment of Indian society. The tribes of India are subject to a high degree of social exclusion on account of assigning them a low caste status; whereas the Indian tribes also suffer from economic exclusion from the mainstream economy on account of their isolated living and absence of modern educational capability and skills as well as other physical and economic resources. Therefore the tribal people of India suffer from socio-economic exclusion as well as financial exclusion.

Conceptual Framework

Financial inclusion means delivery of banking services and credit at an affordable cost to the vast sections of disadvantaged and low income groups. The various financial services include savings, loans, insurance payments, remittance facilities and financial counseling/ advisory service by the formal financial system. An open and efficient society is always characterised by the unrestrained access to public goods and services. As banking services are in the nature of public goods, financial inclusion should therefore be viewed as availability of banking and payment services to the entire population without discrimination of any type. Dr. C. Rangarajan Committee Report, (2008, p. 33).

According to the European Foundation the concept of social exclusion refers to "The process which individuals or groups are wholly or partially excluded from full participation in the society in which they live". Various scholars of the sociology and anthropology have shown interest in studying the causes and consequences of social exclusion. On the whole social exclusion is a practice, which is an obstacle to full participation of all the people or group of people in the societal process and thus a welfare depressant. On the whole as C.J. Sonowal has observed social exclusion shows the following features of a 'society at large or individual at least'; '(i) inability to participate effectively in economic, social, political and cultural life, (ii) distance of alienation from the so called mainstream society. iii) isolation from major social mechanisms which produce or distribute social resources (C.J. Sonowal; p. 125).

The C. Rangarajan Committee Report (2008) has defined the concept of financial inclusion as "the process of ensuring access to financial services and timely and adequate credit where needed by vulnerable groups such as weaker sections and low income groups at an affordable cost"

The means of financial inclusion implies more and more access to all individuals to institutional credit and financial services for the purpose of productive and social purposes. The Rangarajan Committee (2008: p.1) observed that;

"The essence of financial inclusion is in trying to ensure that a range of appropriate financial service is available to every individual and enabling them to understand and access those services. Apart from the regular form of financial intermediation, it may include a basic no frills banking account for making and receiving payments, as a savings product suited to the pattern of cash flows of poor household, money transfer facilities, small loans and overdrafts the productive personal and other purposes, insurance (life and nonlife) etc".

The term 'financial exclusion', the opposite of 'financial inclusion' is defined by the Dr. C. Rangarajan Committee (2008: p. 1) as " There is growing divide, with an increased range of personal finance options for a segment of high and middle income population and significant large section of the population who lack access to even the most basic banking services. This is termed 'financial exclusion'. These people, particularly, those living on low incomes, cannot access mainstream financial products such as bank accounts, credit, remittances and payment services, financial advisory services, insurance facilities etc".

The idea of financial inclusion is very powerful and socially important. The achievement of financial inclusion helps to promote personal/individual development/empowerment. This all important aspect is explained by Dr. C. Rangarajan Committee Report (2008; p. 34) as under "… the term financial inclusion is perceived in different ways under different contexts. There is a view that only access to credit is treated as financial inclusion whereas the other view that only access to credit is treated as financial inclusion whereas the other view includes all the services extended by the financial institutions. That apart, financial inclusion by banks and other institutions must target, apart from personal/private "investment requirements of individuals and groups, the universal public investment requirement necessary for development of infrastructure, social sector services, public utilities and productive forces/capacity building efforts, etc. Thus financial inclusion may well be all about money and finance, but with the ultimate objective of directly abolishing the state of social exclusion in the economy".

The study of financial inclusion by the UN (2006) has set the following as its main goals:

(a) Access at a reasonable cost of all households and enterprises to the range of financial services for which they are "bankable", including savings, short and long term credit, leasing and factoring, mortgages, insurance pensions payments, local money transfers and international remittance.

(b) Sound institutions, guided by appropriate internal management systems, industry performance standards and performance monitoring by the market, as well as by sound prudential regulation where required.

(c) Financial and institutional sustainability as a means of providing access to financial services over time.

(d) Multiple providers of financial services, where feasible, so as to bring cost-effective and a wide variety of alternatives to customers (which could include any number of combinations of sound private, non-profit and public provider).

Literature Review

Traditional economic theory deals with interrelationship between finance and economic development. This part of economic theory has evolved the past 150 years. The classical theory of economic growth has examined the significance of an investment function in commencing and increasing the rate of economic growth but, however, it has not dealt with the different sources of finance available in capitalist economy.

Adam Smith (1776, 1998) had expressed the view about the significant and crucial contribution of high density of banks in Scotland for invigorating stimulating development of the Scottish economy.

For the first time Joseph A. Schumpeter (1912, 1992) has analysed the role of commercial banks in financing economic development. One of his hypotheses is an entrepreneur's use of bank credit to finance innovations is empirically found true. The Schumpeter theory of economic development lays foundation for bank financing for corporate enterprises. It does not deal with the need for and significance of financing individuals, particularly those who are poor, to come out of their poverty through self employment activities. In the early 20th Century Joseph A. Schumpeter contends that technological innovations and their successful implementation is prompted and stimulated by well-functioning banks. More specifically Schumpeter argued that creation of credit through the banking system is an essential source of entrepreneurs capability to drive real growth by funding and employing new combination of factor use.

Jude L. Fernando (1997), in his study on empowerment of women by means of micro credit-based income generation programmes is a new orthodoxy in the development discourse. In this article he appraises this phenomenon in a broader historical context. It shows how women's interests are being subsumed by and subordinated to the priorities of mainstream development in ways detrimental to the radical aspirations of the NGOs' empowerment project. In addition is a critical evaluation of the current approaches used in studies on micro-credit and empowerment. These studies have mostly focused on the final outcome of micro-enterprise rather than the process through which they are achieved. This study based on field research in Bangladesh, demonstrates that widely documented success of micro – enterprises are a result of the activities of the very institutions that are considered to be oppressive to women. In this process, NGOs contribute to further legitimisation of the same institutions that their micro-enterprises desire to transform.

Mahendra Dev S. (2006) in his study on "Financial Inclusion; Issues and Challenges", examined that financial inclusion is important for improving the living conditions of the poor farmers, rural nonfarm enterprises and other vulnerable groups. Financial exclusion, in terms of lack of access to credit from formal institutions, is high for small and marginal farmers and some social groups. Apart from formal banking institutions, which should look at inclusion both as a business opportunity and social responsibility, the role of Self-Help Groups (SHGs) movement and micro finance institutions is important to improve financial inclusion. This requires new regulatory procedures and de politicisation of the financial system.

Identification of Research Gaps

Some of the important research gaps in the study of financial exclusion/ inclusion include the following.

1. The factors contributing to the financial exclusion/inclusion differ across the countries in the world. This is the reason for existence and continuation of financial exclusion in a large number of countries of the world. Thus, an investigation of the socio-economic and politico-cultural causes for financial exclusion in different countries and in different regions of a country like India become essential.
2. Indian strategy from Eleventh Plan has accepted the goal of financial inclusion for the purpose of poverty alleviation and bringing the economically poor, the religious minority communities and vulnerable groups into mainstream of the society. Thus the government of India has initiated a number of dialogues and policy initiatives with the RBI and other public sector financial institutions to achieve the goal of financial inclusion. This impact of the change in the financial sector policy deserves further research.
3. The nature and extent of financial exclusion exist across the sex (female), across different regions, across various occupations (organised and unorganised sector), different regions (progressive and backward regions). Therefore the problem of financial exclusion has to be studied in all these perspectives.
4. There are few studies on the inclusion and exclusion of the tribes in the development process particularly on the north eastern tribes. But, on the tribes of Karnataka and particularly in Mysore and Chamarajanagara Districts, the studies on inclusion and exclusion particularly on financial inclusion for tribal development not undertaken.

Results and Discussion

The present study is based on primary data. The sample size is one hundred. Of these, 55 tribal households are selected from Mysore district and 45 households are selected from Chamarajanagara district. The four major tribes namely Jenukurba (30), Kadukuruba (20), Soliga (30) and Yarava (30), are selected for the study. The data is collected by using an interview schedule by the researcher from six Hadies/Podus namely Attagullypura colony, Melukamenahally, and Mookahally colony of Chamarajanagara district and Shettyhally, Hosahally-A and B hadies and Yashodharapura hadies of the Mysore district. The field study was under taken during January to March 2012.

The Yashodharadapura where the soliga tribe lives, is located 4 kms away from Hunsur town (Taluka headquarter), and Shettyhally, 20 kms away from Hunsur town and Hosahlly A and B hadi, is located 12 kms away from H.D. Kote town (Taluka headquarter), where Soliga, Jenukuruba, Kadukuruba and Yrarava tribes live, in Mysore district.

The Attagullipura tribal colony, where the soliga tribe lives, is located 18 kms away from Chamarajanagara town (District headquarter), Mookahally and Melukamenahally Colony where Soliga, Jenukuruba and Kadukuruba tribes live, is located 12 kms away from Gundalpet town (Taluka headquarter) in Chamarajanagara district. These tribal settlements are connected by road. There is a public and private transport plying between hadis/podus and towns.

The geographical proximity influences the people of the inter land of a town or city the sample tribes in both the case study districts live at short distance from small towns which have health and educational infrastructure as well as the economic infrastructure like public transport, public road, public telephone, post office, agriculture market, banks, and tiny and small scale industries. Even though, the sample tribes are not highly influenced by the nearby small towns and their economy. This is clear from the data related to employment level and pattern (Table 2). The level and variety of banking practices of the tribes (Table 5) the mode of saving habits of the sample tribes (Table 6). In other words there are no urban influences on the tribal society and economy in our case study region.

Demographic Profile of the Case Study Tribes

In the total tribal population of these two districts, 44,151 and 31,505 are the selected four tribes in Mysore and Chamarajanagara district respectively which is 16.27% and 29.69% of the total tribes.

Table 1: Demographic Profile of the Selected Tribes in Mysore and Chamarajanagara Districts

Sl. No.		*No. of Hadies*	*No. of Families*	*Total Tribal Population*	*Jenu Kuruba*	*Kadu Kuruba*	*Yarava*	*Soliga*
Mysore District								
1.	H.D. Kote	114	4841	23368	16761	2430	1547	2630
2.	Hunsur	51	2916	13071	11329	00	93	1649
3.	Mysore	01	104	518	0	0	0	518
4.	Najangudu	05	247	1235	1195	0	0	40
5.	Piriyapatna	30	1201	5959	5783	0	0	176
	Mysore Total	**201**	**9309**	**44151**	**35068**	**2430**	**1640**	**5013**
Chamarajanagara District								
1.	C.R. Nagara	24	1052	6001	-	-	-	6001
2.	Gudlpet	29	1048	4119	1355	750	-	2014
3.	Kollegal	80	3176	19506	-	-	-	19506
4.	Yalandur	10	462	1879	-	-	-	1879
	C.R. Nagara Total	**143**	**5738**	**31,505**	**1355**	**750**	-	**29400**
	Grand total	**344**	**15047**	**75656**	**36423**	**3180**	**1640**	**34413**

Source: ITDP Office Report of Mysore and Chamarajanagara Districts-2010.

The Table 1 shows that H.D. Kote and Hunsur talukas have highest tribal population in Mysore district than the other talukas. That means in these talukas in 165 (82%) tribal hadies 7757 (83.38%) families are settled which consist of the 36,439 (82.53%) tribal population with good mixture of the four tribes in Mysore district. The Mysore, Nanjanagudu, Piriyapatna talukas have less tribal population and mix of the above said tribes. Among the selected tribes Jenukurubas (primitive tribe) are the highest in number than the others. In Chamarajanagara district Soliga is the major tribe. They are living in 143 podus of the 5530 (96.37%) families which consist of 29400 (93%) population and spread over in the four talukas. Kadukuruba and Jenukuruba tribes are very less in numbers and there is no Yarava tribe in the Chamarajanagara district. Comparatively Mysore district has highest in numbers of tribes and good mix of all the four tribes. In both the districts all the selecetd tribes are unevenly distributed, because of the unequal spread of the forest and different cultural and ethnic nature of the tribes.

Table 2. Sources of Employment of the Sample Tribes (In Percentage)

Districts	*Chamarajanagara*				*Mysore*				
Tribes	*JK*	*KK*	*Soliga*	*Average*	*JK*	*KK*	*Soliga*	*Yarava*	*Average*
Sample Size	10	10	25	45	20	10	05	20	55.0
Wage Labour	97	95	97	96.33	98	90	95	85	92.0
Agriculture	50	60	54	54.66	52	65	48	65	57.5
MFP Collection	17	30	45	30.66	40	32	20	20	28.0
Animal Husbandry	15	20	17	17.33	20	30	15	35	25.0
Self Employment	01	00	09	3.33	02	05	15	10	9.25
Govt.Jobs	10	08	06	08.00	12	06	05	05	07.0
Migration	60	65	54	59.66	70	60	50	62	60.5

Source: Compiled from Primary Data.

Of one hundred sample tribal households nearly 85-98% of the Jenukuruba, Kadukuruba, Soliga, and Yarava tribes work as wage labourer in Mysore district. Whereas 95-97 per cent of Jenukuruba, Kadukuruba and Soliga tribes in Chamarajanagara district work as wage labourer. That means wage labour is major form of labour supply among tribes. Next agriculture tends to be the major source of employment of all the four sample tribes in both the districts (Table 2). This is because nearly 35-50 per cent of the total sample tribal households do not own agricultural land. Nearly 50-75 per cent of the total sample tribal households do not have appropriate land records. Thus 40-60 per cent of the tribal households suffer from unemployment and underemployment problems. It indicates that the tribal rehabilitation programme in Mysore and Chamarajanagara districts is still not complete and it is not tribal friendly (Table 4).

The dependency of sample tribes on Minor Forest Produces (MFP) collection and animal husbandry for their livelihood is marginal. The Jenukuruba and Kadukuruba tribes in Mysore district and Soliga as well as Kadukuruba tribes in Chamarajanagara district still relay upon income derived from MFP collection than the other two tribes like Jenukuruba and Yarava in the study area (Table 2).

The self employment programme has not made any significant impact on tribes in the case study region. Although the state government as well as NGOs (VGKK and SVYM), offer short duration courses on vocational education and training. The response of the youth of the four sample tribes is highly discouraging (Table 2).

The sample tribal population has not taken advantage of job reservation policy of the State, since the level of education and skill formation and training level is very low and qualitatively is very poor. So, they are unable to take advantage of the periodic recent developmental schemes implimented by various State and Central government (Table 2).

All the four sample tribes of the Mysore and Chamarajanagara districts show a high degree of migration characteristics. It was reported that, 50-70 per cent of the different tribal labour migration (Table 2) to Coorg and neighbouring districts in Karnataka and Nilagiri and Coimbatore districts of Tamil Nadu State.

Migration of tribal labour from subsistence agriculture to capitalist plantation economy is a recent emerging trend probably since 30 years. The migration of tribal labour from rural to rural area enable more wage income leading to improved and better food security and availability of cheap or low cost labour to the plantation owners. In recent past, they prefer to migrate to the neighboring coffee plantation, since the employment available help them to overcome income poverty and famine (O.D. Heggade and Puttaraja: 2011).

Nearly 50 to 70% of the tribal families earn between Rs. 2500-Rs. 5000 per month through a combination of wage employment, MFP collection, and animal husbandry etc. (Table 3). That means on an average each tribal family has 2 to 3 adult working members. Thus each family person earns an average Rs. 750 – Rs. 1250 per month. However the income carried by the tribal family is unstable and very low throughout the year. Thus the incidence of income poverty and human poverty on the sample tribal households in southern Karnataka is very high. This is the major problem responsible for the lack of participation in financial inclusion activities.

Table 3: Monthly Income of the Tribal Families (in Rupees)

Districts	*Chamarajanagara*				*Mysore*				
Tribes	*JK*	*KK*	*Soliga*	*Average*	*JK*	*KK*	*Soliga*	*Yarava*	*Average*
Below Rs. 2500	04	03	05	04	05	02	03	02	03.00
Rs. 2500-5000	70	65	60	65	75	60	50	58	60.75
Rs. 5000-7500	15	20	25	20	18	25	30	25	24.50
Rs. 7500-10,000	10	08	08	08.67	02	10	12	10	08.50
Above Rs. 10,000	01	04	02	02.33	00	03	05	05	03.25
Total	100	100	100	100	100	100	100	100	100

Source: Compiled from Primary Data

A small number, that is 20-24.5% of the total sample households in Chamarajanagara and Mysore districts respectively, earn more than Rs. 5000 – Rs. 7500 per month. In this category of income earners, more number of Soliga, Yarava, and Kadukuruba tribes are found. In this sense, the Jenukuruba tribe in both the case study districts is economically highly backward and thus, Jenukuruba across to financial inclusion with the modern financial intermediaries is not existent.

Table 4: Size of Land Holdings and Source of Income for Agricultural Operation (in Per cent)

Districts	*Chamarajanagara*				*Mysore*				
Tribes	*JK*	*KK*	*Soliga*	*Average*	*JK*	*KK*	*Soliga*	*Yarava*	*Average*
< 2 Acre	10	15	32	19.00	11	12	08	12	10.50
2-4 Acre	35	35	20	30.00	30	38	30	35	33.25
Above 4 Acre	05	10	02	05.66	11	15	10	18	13.50
No Land	50	40	46	45.33	48	35	52	35	42.50
No Land Records	70	75	65	70.00	75	70	50	60	63.75
Institutional Source	05	10	20	11.66	08	10	15	20	13.25
Non Institutional Source	65	72	60	65.66	75	65	55	60	63.75

Source: Compiled from Primary Data.

On an average 40 to 50 per cent of the tribal households own agricultural landholdings between 0.10 to 4 acres (43.75% in Mysore district and 49% in Chamarajanagara district). The total numbers of sample households which own more than 4 acres of agricultural land are in more number in Mysore district rather than in the Chamarajanagara district (Table 4). It may also be observed that the land owning tribal households in the case study regions have made inroads into institutional sources of credit and banking services. Whereas, those households which do not own land as well as, those tribal households which do not possess appropriate legal Title Deeds to their land do not have access to institutional source of credit and banking services (Table 4).

Table 5: Banking Practices of Tribes (In Percentage)

Districts	*Chamarajanagara*				*Mysore*				
Tribes	*JK*	*KK*	*Soliga*	*Average*	*JK*	*KK*	*Soliga*	*Yarava*	*Average*
Accounts Open	20	25	30	25.00	25	30	35	40	39.5
Transactions	18	15	20	17.66	18	24	25	26	23.25
Know about M. B.I	01	02	05	2.66	01	01	02	02	1.50
Use of M.B.I	00	00	01	0.33	00	00	01	01	0.50
Loans Received	15	20	25	20.00	20	25	30	26	25.25
Loans Repayments	05	06	08	6.33	05	10	15	12	10.50
Response of Bankers	Good	Good	Good		Good	Good	Good	Good	

Source: Compiled from Primary Data.
(**Note:** M.B.I- Modern Banking Instruments).

It may be observed from Table 5 that, the financial inclusion process of the tribes has begun and it is in its nascent stage in both Chamarajanagara and Mysore districts. About 25 per cent of the sample tribal households in Chamarajanagara districts and on an average 39.5 per cent of the tribal households in Mysore district have bank accounts in public sector banks like Cauvery Kalpataru Grameena Bank State Bank Of Mysore, Vijaya Bank and private sector banks like Karnataka Bank... etc.

Nearly 17.66 per cent and 23.25 per cent on an average of total sample tribal households in Chamarajanagara and Mysore districts have started using various kinds of banking services in conducting financial transaction and about 20 per cent in Chamarajanagara district and 20-25 per cent in

Mysore district sample tribal households have availed bank loans. About 6.33 per cent in Chamarajanagara district and 10.5 per cent in Mysore district the tribal borrowers have repaid loans (Table 5).

The entire tribal households have expressed their happiness about the bankers response to open bank accounts and avail bank loans. However only a negligible number of tribal households in both the districts have reported that they are aware and using services/instruments like ATM/credit and debit cards, cheques, MT, overdrafts, DD., etc. The major reason for ,nearly 97.3 per cent of the sample tribal households in the case study districts are not using banking instruments due to their acute poverty and near obstacles of integration between tribal economy and mainland economy. This suggests that, the need for increasing the avenues for economic interaction between tribes and non tribes in the study region.

Table 6: Mode of Savings of the Tribes (In Percentage)

Districts	*Chamarajanagara*				*Mysore*				
Tribes	*JK*	*KK*	*Soliga*	*Ave-rage*	*JK*	*KK*	*Soliga*	*Yarava*	*Ave-rage*
Postal Savings	02	04	05	3.66	02	05	10	08	06.25
Micro Saving	01	02	35	12.66	02	02	05	05	03.50
Pigmy Deposits	00	00	00	00.00	00	00	00	00	00.00
Fixed Deposits	00	00	00	00.00	00	00	02	02	01.00
LIC	03	02	05	03.33	02	03	10	03	04.50

Source: Compiled from Primary Data.

Broadly, two trends may be observed about savings behavior of the four observed tribes of Mysore and Chamarajanagara district. They are:

1. A small number of tribal households have undertaken postal and micro savings in this respect, 35 per cent of Soliga households in Chamarajanagara district have undertaken micro savings, because of successive working of the SKS micro finance in Attagullipura colony.
2. It is discouraging to note that, the tribal households in general have not purchased pigmy deposits or fixed deposits from the nationalised banks (Table 6). This empirical data show again that there is a direct link between extreme poverty and financial exclusion.

Table 7 shows that the women SHGs movement is fairly successful among all the four sample tribes in the case study region, all though, the loan repayment by the women members of the SHGs is low among all the sample tribes of Chamarajanagara and Mysore districts. In terms of other indicators of financial inclusion like membership of the SHGs formation of

Table 7: Performance of Women SHGs (In per cent)

Districts	*Chamarajanagara*				*Mysore*				
Tribes	*JK*	*KK*	*Soliga*	*Ave-rage*	*JK*	*KK*	*Soliga*	*Yarava*	*Ave-rage*
Membership	52	54	45	50.33	56	57	48	53	53.50
Savings	52	54	45	50.33.	56	57	48	53	53.50
Loans	29	32	38	33.00	40	45	32	46	40.75
Profits Received	52	54	45	50.33	56	57	48	53	53.50
Repayment	10	12	15	12.33	15	20	22	25	20.50
Interest to Continue	40	45	40	41.66	50	40	40	42	43.00

Source: Compiled from Primary Data.

the tribal women savings and borrowing behavior, profit received is vary sustained improvements in the employment income generation, integration process between tribal economy and mainland economy will help to further create and develop Bank-SHGs network for the benefit of tribal. About 41.66 per cent in Chamarajanagara district and 43 per cent in Mysore district of the sample households have shown interest to continue to be part of the working of women SHGs. The equal partnership at household level which is an important tribal culture value has supported the attempts to bring tribal women under the SHGs network.

Conclusion

The foregoing analysis of obstacles for financial inclusion among tribes in southern Karnataka reveals that the continued existence of subsistence tribal economy increased alienation or shifting of tribes from Forest to mainland, failures in tribal resettlement and redevelopment programmes, lead to extreme poverty unemployment and underemployment, shortage of civic amenities and thus poor quality of life of the tribes, all these factors of underdevelopment results in extremely low level of tribal human resource development. Thus the tribal underdevelopment and threats to their life and livelihoods do not provide opportunities for financial inclusion initiatives among the tribes. Thus, there are, as it is already explained supply side and demand side constraints to bring tribes under financial inclusion process. The State should make efforts to reduce or remove them.

It was also revealed in this study that increased employment opportunities, job securities, encouragement to undertake sustainable agriculture and facilitating labour migration among tribes to help to initiate financial inclusion process in tribal societies and economy. In many of the tribal settlements there are no grampachayat (Rural Self Governments). Thus, like other mainland villages, the tribal settlement (Popu/hadi) do not receive development grants from the government of India under its umbrella programme MGNREGP, and other programme under state government except ITDP which are not well devised and adequately funded. Therefore based on the present study we conclude that, among four tribes like Kadukuruba, Jenukuruba, Soliga and Yarava, in southern Karnataka, financial inclusion process is just begun and is in its nascent stage.

References

1. Alaysius P. Fennandez (1997) Micro Finance Institutions with Difference, Economic and Political Weekly, Vol-42 (13): pp. 1185-1189
2. Atkinson Rob, Divoudi Simin (2000), The Concept of Social Exclusion in European Union, Context Development and Possibilities. Journal of Common Market Studies-38(3): 427-448.
3. GOI (2008), Report of Committee of Financial Inclusion (New Delhi; Planning Commission Government of India). Chairman Dr. Rangarajn.
4. Mahendra Dev S. (2006), Financial Inclusion: Issues and Challenges Economic and Political Weekly Vol. 31, No. 16, April.
5. O.D. Heggade and Puttaraja (2011) Migration of tribal labour : A Case Study of Rural-Rural Migration in Karnataka. Vol. VII, No. 3, Journal of Rural Development and Social Change Odyar publications Mysore.
6. Schumpeter Joseph (1912), (1992) The Theory of Economic Development, translated by Reveres Opine, with new introduction by E. Elliot, Transaction Publishers, New Brunswick.
7. Smith Adam (1776), (1998), An Enquiry into the Nature and Causes of Wealth of Nations: London; UK.
8. Sonowal C.J. (2008), Indian Tribes and Issue of Social Inclusion and Exclusion, Studies in Tribes and Tribals, 6 (2): p. 125. Kamal Raj Enterprises, New Delhi.
9. United Nations (2006), Building Inclusive Financial Sector for Development; (New York: United Nations Organisation).

36

Financial Inclusion and Microfinance: A Micro Perspective

Dinesha P.T., Kiran Kumar P. and *Nanjunda D.C.*

Introduction

The financial institutions of India have shown tremendous growth in volume and complexity during the last four decades. Despite making significant improvements in all the areas relating to financial viability, profitability and competitiveness, there are concerns that banks have not been able to include vast segment of the population, especially the underprivileged sections of the society, into the fold of basic banking services. Thus, important challenge facing the banking sector is to extend financial services to all sections of society. Hence, this lead to the emergence of Financial Inclusion as a strategy to bring so called excluded people in to the mainstream. The introduction of financial inclusion comes from the recognition that this can serve the interests of both society and the banking system. As a complementary to this, micro-finance through self help groups can work as a powerful tool to fight poverty became the effective approach of financial inclusion, not only in India but in the entire developing world.

Keeping the above facts in view, this paper has the following objectives:

- To examine the impact of Self Help Groups on financial inclusion of women;
- To analyse the problem faced by the women in accessing the financial services and suggest policy prescriptions.

Data Base and Research Design

The study is based on both secondary and primary data. The primary data were collected by canvassing the structured interview schedule for the sample households of 240 in Dakshina Kannada district of Karnataka State. The sample members of SHGs of three different promotes, i.e. NGO, Cooperative and Government were interviewed for collection of primary data. From each promoter, the members of SHGs belonging to the Scheduled Caste (SCs), the Scheduled Tribes (STs) and Others (Other castes including Other Backward Castes and minorities) were considered as the target group members. Further, an attempt has been made to include members of different income groups that are Low Income groups, Medium Income groups, High-income groups and Very High income groups. From each promoter 80 SHG members consisting 40 members from each district 20 members from each taluk 10 SHG members from each village were selected for the interview. The total size of the sample SHG members was estimated at 240 from the four chosen taluks of the district. The data were analysed by using the simple percentage, average and indices, wherever appropriate. In this study the researches has taken only social and income groups for analysis.

Research Issues

The detailed review of literature at regional, national and international level reveals that there are two important views on the efficacy on the impact of SHG microfinance on poverty reduction and financial inclusion. Most of the studies speak about the positive side impact of microfinance on poverty reduction, but there are also some studies which question the ability of microfinance in empowering women and combating poverty. Studies like Carr et al (1996), Harper (1998), Dadhich (2001), Suarshan Synghal (2002), Venkatarao (2009), Reddy Narasimhalu (2009), Vimala (2009) and Tankha et al (2005), Purohit (2003), Isebelle (2006) and Jayasheela and Palanna (2005) showed that participation of women in women organisations like SHGs has changed their lives economically, socially and politically and SHG's has become the effective approach of financial inclusion. Ramakrishna and Krishnamurthy (2005) revealed that SHGs recorded better scores in credit worthiness, banking habits, loan repayments and freed them from moneylenders. There are some studies conducted which speaks about some negative points of microfinance in empowering women and reducing poverty. A study by Hulme et al, (1996) Rajsekar (2004), Joanna (2000), Kamal Vatta (2003) and Gupta et al (2010) showed that just because women are clients of MFIs do not mean they will automatically become empowered and it is generally accepted that it is not a silver bullet to the problems of poverty reduction or financial inclusion and women's empowerment. Moyle et al (2006) in his study found some negative appraisals of pressure, challenges and stress for most of the SHG members.

After in-depth review of the literature on empowerment, a very few studies have been dealt with social and income groups. The impact of SHG microfinance also differs by social groups such as Scheduled Caste (SC), Scheduled Tribe (ST) and others. The impact of SHG microfinance also differs among different income groups such as Low Income groups, Medium Income groups, High income groups and Very High income groups. Against this background, the present study made an attempt to compare the performance of different social groups and income groups and draw correct policy suggestions for sustaining the reduction in poverty through financial inclusion.

Result and Discussion

Financial Inclusion through Economic Empowerment

Credit is one of the critical inputs for economic development. Its timely availability in the right quantity and at an affordable cost goes a long way in contributing to the well-being of the people especially in the lower rungs of society. Thus access to finance, especially by the poor and vulnerable groups is a prerequisite for employment, economic growth, poverty reduction and social cohesion. Further, access to finance will empower the vulnerable groups by giving them an opportunity to have a bank account, to save and invest, to insure their homes or to partake of credit, thereby facilitating them to break the chain of poverty. In the study areas, there are several NGOs, Government organisations/ departments and Co-operatives have been found busy with mobilisation of the neglected women, build their capacity and place them on mainstream development through a plat form known as SHG. Therefore, an effort has been made to examine the impact of micro finance programme (SHG movement) on economic empowerment of women and thereby financial inclusion. The economic empowerment of SHG members is observed in terms of changes in their savings behavior, occupations after joining SHG, income changes and changes in assets, both livestock and households etc.

(a) Savings Behaviour of SHG Members

Saving in the formal sources like, banks/post offices is considered as the first step of financial inclusion. In SHG's operation without savings, access to micro credit is not possible. An important aspect of SHG is that how their savings and credit are managed to build women's economic empowerment. As per the byelaws of SHGs, a member of particular group is expected to save some specified amount of money at least for a period of six months or so from the date of their membership. Against the amount of savings by the members, the credit will be provided for consumption and investment needs. Therefore, savings and credit management are the key activities of SHG. If they are able manage them properly, they will be successful in doing the business. In no presence of banking facilities and lack of awareness, women do not really save; unless otherwise they are properly motivated and ensured some future benefits or access to credit.

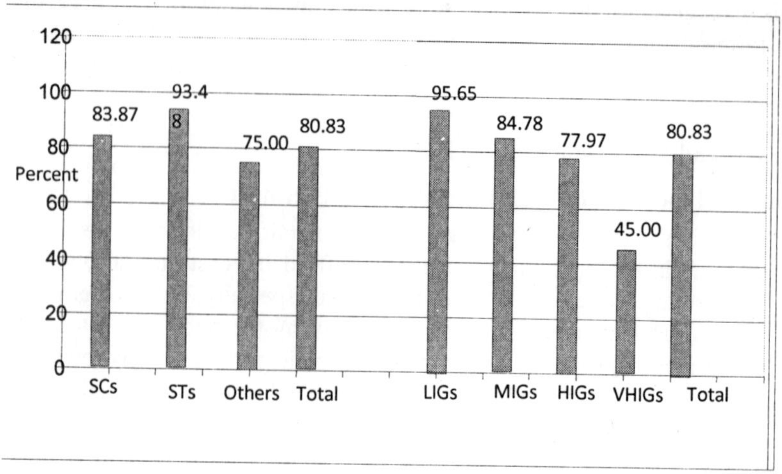

Fig. 1. Distribution of SHG Members Who Started Savings only after Joining SHG by Social and Income Groups.

Note: LIGs: Low income groups; MIGs Medium income groups; HIGs: High income groups; VHIGs: Very high income groups.
Source: Primary Survey.

Income groups are defined in terms of the total household income: less than Rs. 40, 000 as the low income group; Rs. 40001-80000 as the medium income group; Rs. 80001 to 1, 20,000 as the high income groups and more than Rs. 1, 20, 001 as very high income group. This classification is based on the frequency of the sample households in each category.

The data provided in Fig. 1 presents the percentage of SHG members who started saving only after joining the group. The data show that the proportion of SHG members who started saving only after becoming member of the group was as high as 80.83 per cent, and the rest had started saving even before their joining the group. This is not uniform across social and income groups. The proportion of women who started saving only after joining the group was as high as 93.5 per cent in respect of STs and 83.9 per cent in respect of SCs as against Others who accounted for 75 per cent. In the case of income groups, it has been found that the proportion of members who started saving only after joining the group tended to decline as the level of income of the household tended to increase. This means that the proportion of such members was found to be higher in the case of the households of low income groups as compared to those of very high income group households.

(b) Changes in Savings

Another important area of economic impact on the part of the SHG member's domain is the changes in their average savings. The provision of micro credit tends to enable some members to take up some petty business which in turn enable to save more, in addition to compulsion and regular saving practices of them. The data proved in Table 1 indicate the proportion of SHG members reporting that their savings and saving practices have been improved a lot after joining SHG. A close of 80 per cent of the SHG members has reported that their savings have gone up after joining SHG. This figure varies across different promoters, social and income groups. The data show that, only after joining SHG, a greater improvement in savings has been observed among those SHG members belonged to SC/ST households as compared to that of Other households and among those SHG members belonged to the income poor households as compared to that of the income rich households. This is indeed good sign because it enables them to access more credit and which can be used to take some petty business and thereby generating more income, which in turn contribute to increased savings with SHG or in non-SHG sources savings.

Table 1: Distribution of SHG Members with Increase in their Savings after Joining SHG by Promoters, Social and Income Groups (%)

Particular	*Increased in Savings after Joi8ning SHG*		*No. of Sample SHGs*
	Incereased	*Not Increased*	
Social Groups			
SCs	87.1	12.9	62
STs	76.1	23.9	46
Others	76.5	23.5	132
All	79.2	20.8	240
Income Groups			
Low Income Groups	87.0	13.0	23
Medium Income Groups	82.6	17.4	138
High Income Groups	76.3	23.7	59
Very High Income Groups	55.0	45.0	20
All	79.2	20.8	240

Source: Primary Survey.

(c) Changes in Occupation

Occupational change is one of the important immediate impacts of the provision of microfinance, if the consumption of needs of credit is fulfilled. A great majority of the SHG members accessed micro credit for consumption purpose, as most their basic needs, food, education, health, housing, etc., are not yet fulfilled. Once these are satisfied, then they go for investment and consequent impact on occupational changes. Table 2 presents data on the proportion of SHG members who have changed their occupational structure after joining SHGs in the study areas. The data show that a little more than one-third of the SHG members have felt that their occupational structure was changed after joining SHG. The change was in favour of better paid self-employment. This is not uniform across different social and income groups.

Table 2: Distribution of SHG Members who have changed their Occupation after Joining SHG by Social and Income Groups (%)

Particular	*Occupation Changed/ not changed after joined SHG*		*No of Sample SHGs*
	Changed	*Not Changed*	
Social Groups			
SCs	32.3	67.7	62
STs	32.6	67.4	46
Others	39.4	60.8	132
All	36.3	63.7	240
Income Groups			
Low Income Groups	17.4	72.6	23
Medium Income Groups	34.8	65.2	138
High Income Groups	49.2	50.8	59
Very High Income Groups	30.0	70.0	20
All	36.3	63.7	240

Source: Primary Survey.

It has been observed that a larger proportion of members of SHG b belonging to Other (39.4%) have reported that their occupation was changed as compared to those belonging to SCs (32.3%) and STs (32.6%). This means that the change in the occupational structure was more glaring in respect of others as against SC's and ST's. This is due to the fact that as the consumption of needs of SC/ST-SHG members have not fulfilled, they have accorded less priority for investment and consequent change in the occupational status was expected to be limited as compared to those belonged to Other households whose consumption needs are found to be relatively better met.

It has been observed across the SHG households with different levels of income groups that the income poor households have expectedly reported that the change in their occupational structure was limited as most credit was used for consumption purpose, as compared to those households with high income groups. Generally, the income rich households take more credit for investment purpose and less for consumption purpose as compared to the income poor households.

(d) Changes in Income

Table 2 provides data on the perception of whether there is an increase income or not after joining SHG by the sample SHG members.

Table 3: Distribution of SHG Members Reporting their Income Increased/ Not Increased through SHG by Social and Income Groups (%)

Particular	*Increase in Assets after Joining SHG*		*No. of Sample SHGs*
	Incereased	*Not Increased*	
Social Groups			
SCs	59.7	40.3	62
STs	58.7	41.3	46
Others	61.4	38.6	132
All	60.4	39.6	240
Income Groups			
Low Income Groups	47.8	52.2	23
Medium Income Groups	59.4	40.6	138
High Income Groups	69.5	30.5	59
Very High Income Groups	55.0	45.0	20
All	60.4	39.6	240

Source: Primary Survey.

It is evident from the data that a larger proportion of SHG members (60.4%) have opined that their income has increased after joining SHG. Such perception was varied across different social and groups. Across social groups, the proportion of SHG members reporting their increased income was higher for those SHG members belonging to Other household (61.4) as compared that of SC (59.7) and ST (58.7) households. No significant variation, however, was observed in this regard. This shows that most of the SC and ST- SHG members used the bulk of the micro credit for consumption purpose as their most basic needs are not yet fulfilled by default. The data show that as the income of the SHG households tended to rise, the proportion of SHG members saying that their income levels have gone up after joining SHG, by and large, tended to increase, except in respect of very high income group households, mostly due to prior hike in their income levels. This is quite possible that the income poor SHG households are more likely to use micro credit to meet their basic needs as compared to the income rich SHG households. It can be noted that more than one-third SHG members have felt that their income have not gone up due to variety of reasons.

The data show that out of those who felt that their income levels were not increased, a great majority of them use utilised micro credit for consumption purpose. A larger proportion of SHG members were constrained to make of micro credit for IGA due to illiteracy (22.9%) and no land (18.9%) followed by no permission by her husband (15.8%). In case of land as one of the reasons, the proportion of SHG members reporting no land as one of the reasons was higher for SHG members belonged to SCs and STs as compared to Others. All those who have reported that their income levels have not been increased are not due to the use of micro credit for consumption purpose. There is a strong will to make use of micro credit for productive purpose, but is not made possible due to no land, illiteracy or lack of awareness and no permission by her husband or in-laws.

(e) Changes in Assets Possession

An increase in income of the sample SHG households, *a priori*, tends to result in an increase in asset possession, including livestock and household assets. An improvement in asset acquisition due to micro financed activities and income generation thereof is also one the important its impact on economic domains of their life. If large number of assets is acquired because of her joining to SHG, she would be further respected; her demands and voices are properly herd by the head of the household or all other members. The data provided in Table 4 show that the proportion of SHG members who felt that there was an improvement in their assets, both livestock and

Table 4. Distribution of SHG Members Reporting the Changes in Assets Possession after Joining SHG by Promoters, Social and Income Groups (%)

Particular	*Increase in Assets after Joining SHG*		*No. of Sample SHGs*
	Incereased	*Not Increased*	
Social Groups			
SCs	54.8	45.2	62
STs	58.7	41.3	46
Others	62.1	37.9	132
All	59.2	40.8	240
Income Groups			
Low Income Groups	78.3	21.7	23
Medium Income Groups	58.7	41.3	138
High Income Groups	58.6	41.4	59
Very High Income Groups	45.0	55.5	20
All	59.2	40.8	240

Source: Primary Survey.

households, was estimated about 59.2 per cent. Across different social and income groups, it was higher for those SHG members belonged to Other (62.1) households followed by SCs (54.8) and STs (58.7). For different income group households, it has been observed that the proportion of SHG members reporting an improvement in their assets after joining SHG tended to decline as the income of the households tended rise. This is quite possible that when there is an increase in income of the income poor households, there will be an improvement in the base of their assets.

(f) Repayment of Loan

The repayment of loan out of their earnings may also reflect economic empowerment of women. There are several instances where the members of SHG attempted to repay the loan by way of borrowing, in which case they are reduced to debtor, leading to disempowerment.

Table 5: Distribution of Members with Sources of Repayment of Loan by Social Groups and Income Groups

Particular	*My Income*	*Husband Has given*	*My Income + Husband has Given*	*Total*
Social Groups				
SCs	67.74	19.35	12.90	(100%)62
STs	60.86	17.39	21.73	(100%)46
Others	56.81	18.18	25.00	(100%)132
Total	60.41	18.33	21.25	(100%)240
Income Groups				
Low Income Groups	39.13	26.08	34.78	(100%)23
Medium Income Groups	71.73	15.94	12.31	(100%)138
High Income Groups	50.84	11.86	37.28	(100%)59
Very High Income Groups	35.00	45.00	20.00	(100%)20
Total	60.41	18.33	21.25	(100%)240

Source: Primary Survey.

The data provided in Table 4 illustrate that the proportion of members repaying the loan amount out of their earnings was found to be relatively higher among those SHG members belonged to SC (67.74%) and ST (60.84%) households as compared to others (60.41%) households. Whereas, in the case of income groups, it was higher for the SHG members of Medium (71.73%) and High income (50.84) households as compared to Low Income (39.13%) and Very High (35.0%) income households.

Policy Prescriptions

Based on the findings of the study, the following policy measures can be suggested for better functioning of SHGs and their sustainability to ensure financial inclusion and bring them on mainstream development:

- It is suggested that to address financial inclusion effectively banking system has to develop a holistic approach in creating awareness about financial products, education, and advice on money management, debt counselling, savings and affordable credit. The banks need to redesign their business strategies to incorporate specific plans to promote financial inclusion of low-income group treating it both a business opportunity as well as a corporate social responsibility.
- Simple procedure and right encouragement from the financial agencies may enable women to form more and more SHGs in their locality. The financial institutions including various government departments should give wider publicity on the availability of credit facilities and others benefits that can be offered to the SHGs.
- The members of SCs/ STs and low-income group households have not invested much micro credit on agriculture and related IGA's. Hence, most of them are facing the financial problem. The main problem of them is the lack of land. Even though these communities have some amount of land they are not suitable for cultivation. It is in mostly hilly regions and even irrigation facility is not good. Thus for time being training should be given them to concentrate on much IGA's other than agriculture related like tailoring, soap, phenoel making Agarbathi making since it does not need any land.
- It can be suggested that motivational campaign may be conducted for inculcating saving habit in the minds of the members. The campaign shall provide the exposure of savings, its future benefits, how the savings of members are utilised for rotation among the members, how the amount of groups' savings form a base for getting government sponsored scheme for income generating activities and the benefits to the individual member. The members who would like to save more should be encouraged to save in other avenues like pigmy, post office, bank etc.
- Most of the SHG members especially low income groups avail micro credit for consumption purpose only. It is much more in and among SC and ST members. It is partly because many of the households have limited access to basic infrastructural facilities and also limited access to food grains obtained from PDS. Thus government should think in this direction and should provide basic infrastructural facilities like electricity, water supply, house and adequate provision of food grains through PDS. The promoters should create awareness among

the SC/ST and low income members to reduce consumption expenditure and concentrate on investment expenditure.

- Special attention should be given to SC, ST and low income groups. Promotes have to motivate their and respective members to change their occupation infavour of better paid self employment.
- There must be an exclusive department or cell to handle micro credit, instead of this issue being handled merely under priority sector lending because the latter also covers larger and broader credit needs beyond the scope of those living below poverty line. Bank must recruit and post women staff to serve rural areas pacifically the micro credit clientele most of whom are women. The sensitisation process of bank staff towards needs of those living in poverty especially women and their credit worthiness must be continuous and it should become mandatory on the part of the Human Resource development in the banking sector.

Conclusions

Microfinance has drawn attention to an entire sector of borrowers who had been previously poorly served by the formal financial sector. The 'SHG – Bank Linkage' programme plays a predominant role in the financial inclusion of poor. But there is a need to strengthen the SHG-Bank Linkage Programme to fully mainstream it with the commercial banking system. The variations in performance across the regions, both in terms of reach and quality needs immediate attention. SHG- Microfinance has drawn attention to an entire sector of borrowers who had been previously poorly served by the formal financial sector. But the provision of micro credit is not a magic bullet to bring about far-reaching changes in the life of the women and there are no hundred per cent guarantees that microfinance always leads to empowerment of women and poverty eradication. The variations in performance of SHGs across the social and income groups need immediate attention. Government has to take proper initiative, so that the spread of SHGs movement can be streamlined across the country. At the same time banking system has to develop a holistic approach in creating awareness about financial products, education, and advice on money management, debt counselling, savings and affordable credit to make microfinance a sustainable strategy.

References

Carr Marilyn, Martha Chen M. and Renana Jhabvala R. (1998): '*Speaking out Women's Economic Empowerment in South Asia'*, Vistaar Publications, New Delhi.

Dadhich C.L (2001): 'Micro-finance–A Panacea for Poverty Alleviation: A Case Study of Oriental Grameen Project in India', *Indian Journal of Agricultural Economics*, Vol. 56, No. 3, pp. 419-421.

Gupta, Parameshwara A, Syed Rahmathulla and Shankar S.L. (2010): 'Impact of

Microfinance: A Critical Analysis', *Southern Economist*, Vol. 48, No. 18, pp. 29-32.

Harper, Malcolm (1998): '*Profit for the Poor: Cases of Microfinance*', Oxford and IBH Publishing Company Private Limited, New Delhi.

Hulme, David, Montgomay, Richard, Debapriya Bhattacharya (1996): 'Credit for Poor in Bangladesh: The BRAC and TrDEP'. In David Hulme and Paul Mosely (Eds), 'Financing Against Poverty' Vol. 2, Routledge Publisher, London.

Isabelle Guerin, (2006): 'Women and Money: Lesson from Senegal', *Journal Development and Change,* Vol. 37, No. 3.

Jayasheela and Palanna V.K. (2005): 'Role of Self-Help Groups in Enhancing Sericulture Productivity: A case study in Karnataka'. *SEDME,* Vol 32, No 1.

Joanna Ledgerwood (2000): '*Sustainable Banking with the Poor-Microfinance Handbook: An Institutional and Financial Perspective*' The World Bank, Washington D.C.

Kamal Vatta (2003): 'Microfinance and Poverty Alleviation', *Economic and Political Weekly,* Vol. 38, No. 5.

Moyle, Dollard and Biswas (2006), 'Personal and Economic Empowerment in Rural Indian Women: A Self-help Group Approach', *International Journal of Rural Management*, 2, Sage Publications.

Rajasekhar D. (2004): '*Microfinance, Poverty, and Empowerment of Women: A Case Study of two NGOs from Andrapradesh and Karnataka*', ISEC Publications, Bangalore.

Ramakrishna R. and Krishna Murthy B., (2005): 'Microcredit for the Rural Poor through Self Help Groups', *Co-operative Perspective*, Vol 38, No.3, pp 48-59.

Reddy, Reddeppa A. and K. Narasimhalu (2009): 'SHG in India: A Tool for Urban Poverty', *Southern Economist*, Vol. 48, pp. 39-40.

Suarshan, Synghal (2002): 'Taking Micro-credit to Women', *Financing Agriculture*, Vol. 34, No. 2.

Tankha, Ajay Rewa Shankar Misra and Prabhat Labh (2005): 'Case for Microfinance in India', *Mainstream,* Vol. XLIII, No. 16, pp. 3-6.

Venkatarao P (2009): 'Role of SHGs in the Empowerment of Women' *SEDME,* Vol. 35, No.1, pp. 29-45.

37

Prespectives in Women Empowerment through Microfinance Intervention -A Study in the Rural India of Chamrajnagar District in Karnataka State

Rajendraprasad N.L.

Introduction

Chamarajanagar district was formed in 1988; it was originally a part of Mysore district. It is located in the extreme south end of Karnataka. Since it lies in the border, it links Karnataka with Tamil Nadu and Kerala. The district consists of 4 taluks, 16 hoblies, 424 inhabited villages and 85 uninhabited villages. Most of the district lies in the leeward region of the Nilgiris. The four taluks of the district are Chamarajanagar, Gundlupet, Kollegala and Yelandur. The town of Chamarajanagar is the head quarters of the district. The net district income at current prices of 2009-10 is Rs. 14,4405 lakhs. Chamarajanagar has a number of credit and non credit co-operative societies along with commercial banks which provide financial assistance to the people.

The primary of occupation in the district is farming, mainly mulberry cultivation and sericulture. The agrarian nature of the district brings out the requirement for irrigation facilities. Since the district being sparsely irrigated, it is highly dependent on the seasonal rainfall. Other than the farming activities there are 21 factories in the district providing employment to a number of people.

Area and Demographic Features

Chamarajanagar district has a total area of 56,9901 hectares out of which

1.76 lakh hectares consists of the net sown are, 31% is the cultivable area in the district (Fig. 1), approximately only 35% of which is provided with irrigation facilities (Table 1). The irrigation facilities include canals, tanks, wells, bore wells and lift irrigation. Area under mulberry cultivation is 7960 (Karnataka, 2007-08) hectares. The majority of the area consists of widespread forest.

Objectives of the Study

The specific objectives of this paper are:

1. To study the growth pattern of various types of Self Help Groups in Karnataka.
2. To study the formation, nurturing and structure of women Self Help Groups.
3. To analyse the functioning, performance and sustainability of women Self Help Groups.
4. To examine and evaluate the impact of women Self Help Groups on the social and economic status of its members.
5. To analyse the functional linkages of woman Self Help Groups with governmental, nongovernmental and para-statal organisations.
6. To document various government schemes introduced towards Self Help Groups and suggest suitable policy measures.

Importance of the Study

The SHG – Bank Linkage programme has been one of the most rapidly expanding credit programmes of recent times and not much study has been undertaken to assess the programme in many Karnataka districts till date hence there is need for an conducting proper survey for empowerment of women through micro finance.

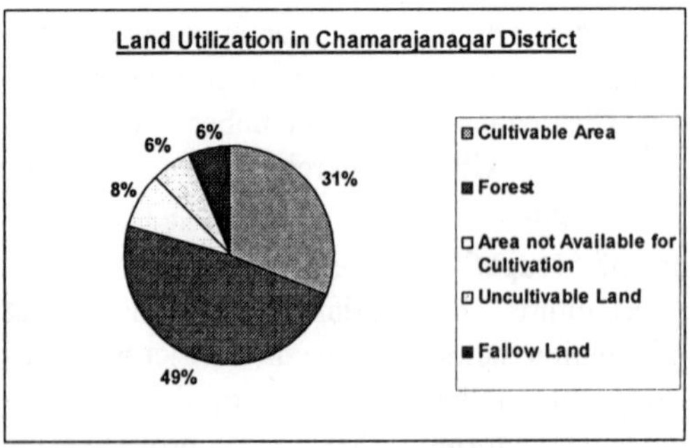

Fig. 1. Distribution of Land.

Source: Chamarajanagar District at a Glance 2009-10.

Table 1: Total Share of Net Sown and Net Irrigated Area

Taluks	*Geographical Area (in Hectares)*	*Share of Net Sown Area to Geographical Area*	*Share of Net Irrigated Area to Net Sown Area*
Camarajanagar	123078	44.68	34.67
Gundlupet	140607	36.84	17.44
Kollegala	279743	21.69	36.31
Yelandur	26473	33.67	124.39
Total	569901	30.95	34.70

Source: Computed using Chamarajanagar District at a Glance, 2009-10.

The irrigation facilities are mainly concentrated in Yelandur. As per the agricultural Census of 2009-10, the total number of farmer's holdings was (Karnataka, 2007-08) 197781 over an area of 211658 hectares. The marginal and small farmers (0-2 hectares) had 87% of the land holdings while the semi medium farmers (2-4 hectares) had 10% and the medium and big farmers (greater than 4 hectares) had the remaining minority of 3% approximately.

The total population of the district is 965462 (Chamarajanagar District at a Glance 2009-10) as per the 2001 census, out of which the total number of males is just a fraction more than 50%. 817372 of the total population reside in the rural area. The total number of workers in the district is 448369 in number. Of this total 27.7% (Chamarajanagar District at a Glance 2009-10) are cultivators, 43% are agricultural labourers, 4.4% are workers in household industry and 24.9% are engaged in other services.

The literacy rate of the district as per 2001 census is 50.9% (Chamarajanagar District at a Glance 2009-10) (Table 2) which is way below that of the state level. The literacy rate of the urban population is much higher reaching a total of 70.9% as compared to 47.2% of the rural population.

Table 2 : Demography of Chamarajanagar District

Taluks	*Area in sq. km*	*Inhabited Villages*	*Demographic Features*		
			Density per sq km	*Total Literacy Rate*	*Sex Ratio*
Camarajanagar	1226.67	171	275	49.2	983
Gundlupet	1392.88	140	153	49.4	984
Kollegala	2785.82	85	121	53.9	951
Yelandur	266.34	28	293	49.6	966
Total	5101	424	189	50.9	971

Credit Scenario

Banking and Financial Institutions

NABARD has come out with a detailed plan consisting of the financial requirements for 2009-10 pertaining to each sector. According to these projections, the total amount of credit required for the agriculture sector was estimated at Rs. 318 crores with crop loans constituting about 54% of the total. A sum of Rs. 52 crores is required to carry out allied activities such as dairy farming, sheep and goat rearing. Also, non-farm sector and agro-processing needed credit to the tune of Rs.11 crores and Rs. 2.8 crores respectively together adding up to 4.2% of the total as in Table 3

Table 3: Sector-wise PLP Projections (2009-10) Chamarajanagar District, Karnataka (Rs. Lakhs)

Sl. No.	*Sector*	*Financial Projections*
1.	Crop Loan	17159.00
2.	Term Investment for Agriculture and Allied Activities	5203.18
3.	Total Investment under Agriculture and Allied Activities (1+2)	22362.18
4.	Non-Farm Sector	1061.25
5.	Agro-Processing	280.60
6.	Other Priority Sector	8100.00
7.	Total Priority Sector (3+4+5+6)	31804.03

Source: PLP 2009-10, Chamarajanagar District, NABARD.

Performance of Credit Agencies

Credit availability is a critical factor which determines the development of agriculture and farming sector in the district. Therefore, it is necessary to have an adequate and continuous supply of credit for which there exist a number of financial institutions in Chamarajanagar district.

Deposits

Chamarajanagar district had a total of 153 bank branches which mobilised deposits to the tune of Rs. 59984.73 lakhs as on 31.3.2008 as in table 4.

CBs – Commercial Banks.

RRBs – Regional Rural Banks.

DCCBs – District Credit Co-operative Banks.

PACS - Primary Agricultural Cooperative Societies.

PCARDBs - Primary Co-operative Agriculture and Rural Development Banks.

KSFC – Karnataka State Financial Corporation

Table 4: Deposits Mobilised in Chamarajanagar District (Rs. Lakhs)

Agency	*No. of Bran-ches*	*Deposits*			*Growth over 2007 (%)*	*Percentage to total (as on 31.03.08)*
		31.03.06	*31.03.07*	*31.03.08*		
CBs	39	31543.34	39751.18	47471.73	19	80
RRBs	22	6649.38	8085.09	8736.14	8	16
DCCBs	5	1235.36	1507.10	1553.18	3	3
PACS	82	NA	NA	NA		
PCARDBs	4	4.88	1.90	0.20		0
KSFC	1			412.00		1
Total	153	39428.08	49349.79	59984.73		100

Source: PLP 2009-10, Chamarajanagar District, NABARD.

The total mobilised deposits of the district increased by 21% during 2007-08 out of which, CBs had a growth of 19% with deposits amounting to Rs. 475 crores. The district has a maximum of 82 PACS. The 22 RRBs present in the district (including Cauvery Kalpatharu Grameena Bank) registered a growth of 8%. Despite having one PCARDB in each taluk, the deposit over the year 2007-08 reduced from Rs.1.90 to only 0.20 lakhs.

Credit

Credit plays an important role in an agrarian district like Chamarajanagar with a rural population of 85%, 24% of them being agricultural labourers. The details pertaining to loans outstanding can be found in table 5.

Table 5: Loans Outstanding Pertaining to Chamarajanagar District (Rs. Lakhs)

Agency	*No. of Branches*	*Loans Outstanding*			*Growth over 2007(%)*	*Percentage to total (as on 31.03.08)*
		31.03.06	*31.03.07*	*31.03.2008*		
CBs	39	30688.83	38758.04	46577.58	20.00	76.00
RRBs	22	4377.55	5162.19	6609.65	28.00	11.00
DCCBs	5	3669.34	2183.29	3812.02	75.00	6.00
PACS	82	3101.12	3644.05	1312.38	0.00	2.00
PCARDBs	4	1870.50	2061.12	2182.59	6.00	4.00
KSFC	1	926.50	810.71	802.89	0.00	1.00
Total	153	44633.84	52619.40	61297.11		100.00

Source: PLP 2009-10, Chamarajanagar District, NABARD.

The maximum loans advanced were by CBs followed by RRBs in the district. While there was an increase of 20% in CBs, the loans outstanding went up by 28% in RRBs. Except for PACS and KSFC, all other agencies registered a growth with majority of the growth seen in DCCBs (75%).

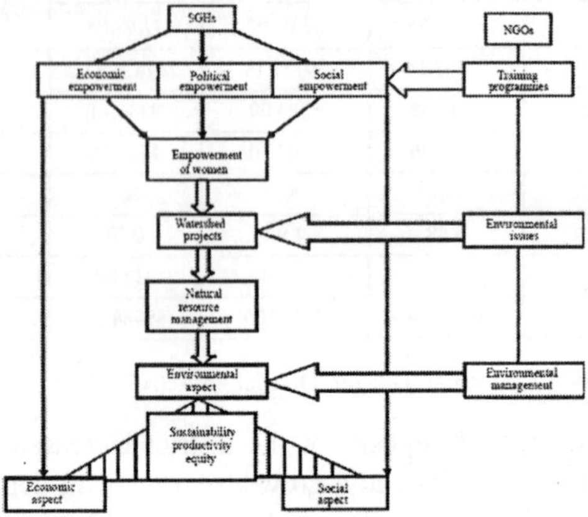

Fig. 2. Relationship between NGOs and SHGs to attain sustainable development.

Credit Deposit Ratio

Credit deposit ratio show the loan amount as against the deposits received. The details of bank wise CDR can be seen in Table 6.

Table 6 : Credit Deposit Ratio (CDR)

Sl. No.	*Agency*	*31.03.2006*	*31.03.2007*	*31.03.2008*
1.	CBs	97.29	97.50	98.12
2.	RRBs	61.05	63.84	76.00
3.	DCCBs	297.03	144.86	245.00

Source: PLP 2009-10, Chamarajanagar District, NABARD.

All the major agencies showed an increase in the CDR during 2007-08. While the rise in CDR of CBs was moderate, the RRBs saw a significant rise in their CDR (from 63.8% to 76%) during 2007-08. The CDR of DCCB jumped to 245% from 144.8% due to a poor deposit base and infusion of borrowed funds for financing.

Micro Finance

Micro finance is a major source of credit in the district. It comprises of SHGs (Self-Help Groups, see Table 7), NGOs, Farmers' Club and Credit packages for Women. The status of micro finance profile in the district is shown below:

Table 7 : SHGs and Related Information

No. of Blocks in the district	4
No. of Blocks where SHGs exist	4
Total No. of Blocks where SHGs are credit linked	4
No. of NGOs in the district	30
No. of NGOs participating in the linkage programme	27
No. of Additional NGOs to be roped in during 2008-09	3
No. of Government/other agencies participating	5
No. of Government/other agencies likely to participate	2

Source: PLP 2009-10, Chamarajanagar District, NABARD.

As far as SHGs are concerned about 624 new SHGs were formed in the district during 2007-08 taking the cumulative SHGs to 10,208. Credit linked SHGs are present in all the taluks of the district and 1900 fresh SHGs were credit linked with an amount of Rs.1437.91 lakhs during 2007-08. These SHGs mainly have women members. A number of initiatives have been taken by the government through the Women and Child Development Department (WCDD) so as to raise the status of poor women in the district by establishing Stree Shakti Groups. The WCDD provides employment assistance by implementing Udyogini programme. 3700 SHGs have been set-up under Stree Shakti Programme out of which 2988 groups have access to bank credit amounting to Rs. 2247.58 lakhs. Entrepreneurship development among women has been encouraged by the introduction of a package of programmes called Yeshaswini. In addition, NGOs guide and help rural women to take up micro enterprises. A total of 4050 loans were provided to women amounting to Rs.11420.16 lakhs during 2007-08.

Farmers' Club

The Farmers' Club consists of people who assist banks to build relations with borrower farmers. This helps in promoting SHG of farmers and bringing efficiency in banking activities. A total of 134 clubs were launched as on March 2008. These clubs take initiative in conducting training programmes, help banks in recovering loans so as to make available fresh loans to farmers and assisting farmers to adapt to new technology.

Financial Inclusion

Apart from the regular form of financial intermediation, financial inclusion includes a basic 'no-frills' banking account for making and receiving payments, a savings product suited to the pattern of cash flows of a poor household, money transfer facilities, small loans and overdrafts for productive, personal and other purposes, insurance etc. Although the banking network seems to be adequate, many villages do not have access to banks due to poor connectivity.

In order to ensure that the entire district is having access to financial services, RBI advised banks to make available a basic banking 'no-frill' account with low or no minimum balance, relaxation in KYC norms, provide General Purpose Credit Card (GCC) facility upto Rs. 25,000 at their rural and semi-urban branches.

Government of India (GoI) created two funds; Financial Inclusion Fund (FIF) and Financial Inclusion Technology Fund (FITF), and is operationalised by NABARD. FIF is meant for meeting the cost of developmental and promotion interventions, whereas FITF is meant to meet the cost of technology adoption. Each fund will have an overall corpus of Rs. 500 crore.

SHG Bank Linkage Programme (SBLP) movement was launched by NABARD and a total of 10,208 groups opened SB accounts in Chamarajanagar district. Kisan Credit Card Scheme provides hassle free short term credit to farmers and Swarozgar Credit Card Scheme was introduced to provide hassle free credit to artisans for investment and working capital credit requirements.

Policy Initiatives and Credit Innovations

Government of India, State Governments, RBI and NABARD have taken policy measures for the development of agriculture and rural sectors. Also NABARD and financing banks have brought about certain innovations in credit delivery systems. Some of the important policy measures/innovations are mentioned below:

Policy Initiatives by GoI

- National Rural Employment Guarantee Scheme is extended to all the rural districts.
- Agriculture Debt Waiver (for small farmers and marginal farmers) and Debt Relief (for other farmers) Scheme covering direct agriculture credit, implemented.
- National Agriculture Insurance Scheme (NAIS) to continue in its present form for kharif and rabi 2008-09 and a crop insurance scheme for tea, tobacco and spices to be introduced next year.

Policy Initiatives by Government of Karnataka

- 5 lakh irrigation pump sets will get free power with effect from 01-08-2008 and a provision of Rs. 2050 crore has been made for the same in the budget.
- An integrated plan will be prepared to supply drinking water to all Gram Panchayats and urban areas from lakes and rivers.
- SHGs will get financial support at 6% interest.
- The social security pension and wages under NREGP will be disbursed through the use of Smart cards in each village of Bellary, Chitradurga and Gulbarga districts.

Policy Initiatives by RBI

- Guidelines on Priority Sector Lending (PSL) revised, enlarging the scope of PSL.
- Limits for loans under DRI scheme raised from Rs. 6500 to Rs. 15000 and that for housing loan under the scheme from Rs. 5000 to Rs. 20000.

Policy and Development Initiatives of NABARD

- "Farmers' Technology Transfer Fund" created to support programmes, workshops/seminars on technology transfer, marketing of agriculture produce, imparting training on new technologies or agriculture practices.
- NABARD continues to provide consessional refinance at 3.5% and 4.5% respectively to SCBs and RRBs providing crop loan (unto Rs. 3 lakh) to farmers at 7% per annum.
- Krishak Saathi Scheme introduced to provide refinance to banks to provide loans to farmers to free themselves from the clutches of money lenders.

Credit Innovations

Credit innovation undertaken by NABARD comprises of Kisan Credit Card Scheme, Swarozgar Credit Card Scheme, SHG-BLP and Gramin Tatkal Scheme. The Kisan Credit Card Scheme seeks to provide timely and adequate

NABARD Rating of Level of Coverage of SHGS in Karnataka (2008-09) (No. of SHGs for every 1,000 households)

Good		Moderate		Low	
District	No.of SHGs	District	No.of SHGs	District	No.of SHGs
Dakshina Kannada	116	Chamarajanagar	62	Haveri	49
Shimoga	87	Davanagere	61	Bangalore (Urban)	47
Chikmagalur	87	Hassan	61	Bijapur	45
Gulbarga	83	Gadag	61	Belgaum	45
Uttara Kannada	80	Tumkur	59	Bagalkot	35
Dharwad	79	Kolar	57	Koppal	33
Kodagu	79	Bellary	55		
Bidar	79	Raichur	54		
Mysore	78	Bangalore (Rural)	51		
Chitradurga	72				
Udupi	70				
Mandya	69				

Source: SHG-Bank Linkage in Karnataka - 2007-08, NABARD Regional Office, Bangalore.

credit for agricultural activities. Swarozgar Credit Card scheme also provides credit, but for investment purposes. The SHG-Bank Credit Linkage has provided formal financial services and established bank credit networks for over 5.8 crore poor households. Another important scheme of the NABARD is the Gramin Tatkal Scheme which seeks to provide financial assistance to rural families.

Women's empowerment can be measured by factors contributing to each of the following i.e. their personal, economic, familial, and political empowerment. Household and interfamilial relations are to be included which is believed to be a central locus of women's dis-empowerment in India. To understand the change women undergo in becoming empowered we look at the above aspects. Various studies show that the women have been empowered based on factors such as income, households, political, decision making etc.

Conclusion and Suggestions

This study has shown that, the concept of SHG is a better mechanism for easy availability of microcredit to rural women and helps them to uplift their social and economic status. Their involvement in family decisions is enhanced. Microcredit facility enables women to own tools and means of production to upgrade their skills and improve their business. After encouraging habit of savings among women, group loans for specific economic purposes are provided. Most of the poor women use this money at first, for domestic needs, to support their families. Aided by microcredit, women are now running canteens, catering units, cooking for schools, tailoring etc.

Women have realised that they have an important role to play in the family and confident about achieving their goals set for their families and make major decisions, thus implying an increase in the influence of women in decision making in their households. Though most of the residents in the village are Muslims, who were once not allowed to move out of their houses, they now have an opportunity to socialise with people being one of the objectives of the SHGs. They move around the village to shops and other places and also travel torelatives when they desire to showing that there is an increase in women's mobility and participation in social activities.

The women are enlightened and educated on various issues – political, to handle finances, to talk freely in public and are aware of the present happenings. They are encouraged and motivated to grow in the society. Therefore it can be concluded that there is an increase in their awareness and knowledge.

The Eleventh Five Year Plan (2007-2012), in its reference to Self Help Groups has several recommendations. The Plan suggests to arrive at the actual cost of lending to small rural borrowers through scientifically sampled

Therefore it can be concluded that there is an increase in their awareness and knowledge.

The Eleventh Five Year Plan (2007-2012), in its reference to Self Help Groups has several recommendations. The Plan suggests to arrive at the actual cost of lending to small rural borrowers through scientifically sampled studies. No interest rate ceilings are to be imposed on the banks by the government. A free interest rate regime and competition should be recognised as the primary means of ensuring reasonable interest rates. The Fixation of cost of dispensing credit is to be best left to the commercial judgment of the borrowing MFIs and the lending institutions. Creating a database and monitoring system for interest rates being charged by the MFIs as a prelude to reduce the interest rates without introducing rate caps. Rating of MFIs by external agencies, use of IT solutions and transparency in pricing of credit to lower interest rate charged by the MFIs, close integration of NABARD's programme with those of the State Governments, enlargement of equity capital of MFIs by inviting venture capital, foreign equity participation and equity support from NABARD are some of the policy measures mooted.

In Karnataka too NABARD has initiated several schemes and interventions during the year 2007-08. Under the financial support category the interventions are General Refinance Scheme, Refinance Scheme for financing matured SHGs for Farm Production nd Investment Activities, Scheme for Better access to credit to Joint Liability Groups (JLGs), Scheme for Support to mFIs, Scheme for Capital/Equity Support to mFIs, Revolving Fund Assistance to mFIs for on-lending to SHGs. Under the Promotional and Developmental Initiatives the interventions are Scheme for Capacity Building of stakeholders, Grant assistance for promotion and credit linkage of SHGs, Scheme for Capacity Building of SHGs, Scheme for Micro Enterprise Development Programme, Scheme for Technology Upgradtion support to NGOs, Scheme for Pilot Project on Processor Cards and branch automation, Scheme for Pilot Project on 'e-Grama', Scheme for Supporting SHG Federations, Scheme for Scheme for financial assistance to banks for rating of MFIs, Scheme for Documentation and Dissemination and Scheme for Felicitation of Best Performance.

NABARD intended to promote 30,000 new SHGs, link another 40,000 fresh SHGs and repeat link 75,000 SHGs in the State during 2008-09 in Karnataka. NABARD's consensual strategy measures for 2008-09 in the State were increasing per group credit for SHGs, promotion of SHGs in low and moderate density districts, compilation of data of inactive and active SHG accounts, rejuvenation of inactive groups, undertaking Micro Enterprise Development in innovative activities, supporting SHG Federations, capacity building of Business Facilitators, arranging Financial Education campaigns, encouraging Technology adoption for service delivery and facilitating coordination among various agencies. The Karnataka State Budget Plan 2009-10 in its reference to microfinance envisages to form 2000 Self-Help Groups of fishermen and provide them with assistance of Rs.10 crore will be provided. It intends to provide marketing facilities for the products made by these self-help groups, build office-cum-sale complexes and '*Streeshakthi Bhavans'* in every taluk.

Apart from garnering savings and providing credit, the SHGs should be encouraged to add services such as provision of personal or family insurance to the families of the members, providing insurance to the dairy and other livestock of the members, assisting members and their families in obtaining essential civic documents such as ration cards, voter cards. They can also help the members to avail Government provisions such as old-age pensions, widow and disability pensions to the members or their family members.

The government should give directions to all its Departments and their extension agencies to give priority and preference to SHGs/NGOs nurturing SHGs when disseminating information and technology. The dissemination process should be designed keeping in mind the educational and aptitude level, the limited mobility of the SHG members. The Departments should especially encourage any direct approaches from SHGs for guidance and information. Facilities like travel, stipend, stay, board and other necessary inputs should be provided to SHG members who approach these agencies for guidance as far as possible.

NGOs should focus and train members who have not yet undertaken the responsibility of *prathinidhi* or haven't yet undertaken maintenance of accounts. Such members should occasionally be pursued to chair the Groups' meetings to overcome their inhibitions. Similarly extra books can be provided to such members so that they can undertake shadow or parallel accounting of their groups and eventually gain competence to undertake that responsibility. More persistent efforts have to be made by the NGOs to persuade SHGs to undertake literacy drives for their members and other basic skills such as calculations and comprehending bank documents.

Vocational training in SHGs has to be made more relevant NGOs and SHGs should arrange for consultation with professional management agencies in order to ascertain the appropriate types of employment opportunities to SHG members in their areas. They should also approach local industrial entrepreneurs for obtaining at-home work opportunities to the members. These entrepreneurs could also be induced to conduct or sponsor skill acquisition or training programmes for SHG members. Entrepreneurships are also to be scaled up or developed especially among non-agricultural members. Micro Enterprise Development in innovative activities is also being encouraged by NABARD.

References

1. Chamarajanagar District at a Glance 2009-10.
2. Denise M. Lucy, Jayati Ghosh, Edward Kuwaja (2008), Empowering Women's Leadership: A case study of Bangladeshi Microcredit Business, Dominican University of California, Sam Advanced Management Journal, 31-50.
3. Karnataka at a Glance 2007-08.
4. Microcredit: One of Many Intervention Strategies, CGAP,http://www.cgap.org/p/site/c/template.rc/1.9.2413/
5. Ritu Jain, (2003), "Socio-Economics Impact Through Self Help Groups", Yojana, Vol. 47, No. 7, pp. 11-124. JASON CONS and KASIA PAPROCKI (2010), Contested Credit Landscapes: microcredit, self-help and self-determination in rural Bangladesh, Third World Quarterly, Vol. 31, No. 4, pp. 637–654.
6. Rosintan D.M. Panjaitan Drioadisuryo, Kathleen Cloud (1999), Gender, self employment and microcredit programs: An Indonesian case study, Quarterly review of economics and finance 39, 769-779.
7. Smith, D.H. and K. Pillheimer (1983), 'Self-Help Groups as Social Movement Organisations: Social Structure and Social Change', Research in Social Movements, Conflicts and Change, Vol. 5 No. 2.

38

Financial Inclusion and Technology

Sri. Oscar Abhishek

Introduction

Financial transactions become a very important part of our lives. We take special care while we transact in our bank, insure our life, invest and while we borrow. All these financial services today are done instantly with the use of latest technology. Our country has witnessed dramatic transition in the area of technology. Today the world without technology is almost impossible. Technology has become a part and parcel of our daily lives, may it be in our work, in our travel or in our dwellings technology today has captured a greater significance in our life.

Even though technology has become so important in availing financial services, this is only restricted to urban areas or metros. The rural part of our country comprises of around 72% of our total population. These people who live in rural areas do not have adequate access to financial services and also are not aware of the same. Even though they are provided with some financial services like loan facilities, deposits, savings etc. the mode used are traditional and unorganised. There is a greater need for these sections of the society to be provided with technology enabled financial services which are more swift and systematic.

"Financial Inclusion is the delivery of financial services to all the classes of people in a fair, transparent and equitable manner at affordable cost". It also means extending banking and other financial services at an affordable cost to the vast sections of disadvantaged and low-income groups.

Low-income Indian households in the informal or subsistence economy often have to borrow from friends, family or usurious moneylenders. They have little awareness and practically no access to insurance products that could protect their financial resources in unexpected circumstances such as illness, property damage or death of the primary breadwinner. They also have very low awareness on savings and investment options available.

Expectations of poor people from the financial system is security and safety of deposits, low transaction costs, convenient operating time, minimum paper work, frequent deposits, and quick and easy access to credit and other products, including remittances suitable to their income and consumption. Technology application is the answer to all the requirements of the financially excluded. With the use of latest technology financial services can be reached to untapped segments of poor and low income groups living both in urban and rural areas.

It is now well understood that commerce with the poor is more viable and profitable, provided there is ability to do business with them. The provision of uncomplicated, small, affordable products supported by technology can help bring low-income families into the formal financial sector. Taking into account their seasonal inflow of income from agricultural operations, migration from one place to another, and seasonal and irregular work availability and income, the existing financial system needs to be designed to suit their requirements. Mainstream financial institutions such as banks have an important role to play in this effort, not as a social obligation, but as a pure business proposition.

Objectives

- To analyse the reasons for the ineffective functioning of traditional methods of services used for financial inclusion.
- To know about the areas of concern (focus) before providing technically supported financial services.
- To know the latest technological up gradations available for the effective implementation of financial inclusion.
- To suggest measures for overcoming the hindrances of using technology.

Methodology

The data for the study was collected from the secondary sources like journals, news papers and various websites.

The study-An update

Financial inclusion in rural and under developed areas is a great matter of concern today in our country. Financial services can be provided to the rural sections of the society effectively only with the use of recent technological upgradations. Financial facilities should more importantly be included in three priority areas requiring serious attention, that is: access to banking, access to affordable credit, and access to free face-to-face money advice.

While considering the banking sector, 52 per cent of Indians do not have bank accounts. Thus, even though we have made great strides in the development of our financial markets, large sections of the population do not avail of the basic financial services in India. In rural India, there are around 4 branches per 100,000 people and less than 1 branch per 100 square kilometres of land area. These numbers alone are sufficient to infer that the simple task of accessing the nearest bank branch is often the most severe challenge. Not surprisingly, the IISS survey results of households who have bank accounts reveal that access is the most important factor in choosing a particular bank.

In particular, 45 per cent of the rural household, 28 per cent of the urban and 38 per cent of all India households have admitted that access and availability are the main factors determining their choice of a particular bank.

Table 1: Percentage of Households without Essential Financial Instruments

	Without Bank Accounts	*Without Life Insurance*	*Without Health Insurance*
Rural	59.59	68.30	98.58
Urban	36.67	45.40	94.72
All India	52.41	61.10	97.39

Source: IISS survey, 2007.

Coming to the urban areas, the urban poor population in the country is estimated to be nearly eight crore whereas the slum population hovers around four crore. The urban economically backward people comprises of migrants, poor and the not-so-poor, who criss-cross the country in search of jobs and better life for themselves and their families. They take up non-contractual and non-permanent jobs, such as, house help, security guards, daily wage labourers, hawkers staying on the streets, and petty workers Most of the working population in urban areas work under utterly deplorable conditions in unorganised sector with a very few livelihood options. More than 40 per cent of adult Indian urban population has no access to a bank account (this figure would be more if multiple accounts held by individuals are factored), and, thereby depriving them of savings, credit, remittance and other financial service facilities from the formal financial system.

Apart from having no bank accounts they are unaware about the importance of savings, investment in profitable avenues and also availing loan facility at a cheaper or reasonable rate of interest. One of the main reasons why these people have no bank accounts is due to non-availability of genuine identity or address proofs with them which becomes a major set back. Also lack of cohesion among the inhabitants of urban slums, irregular incomes and migration among the workers to and from rural areas are some of the reasons why low income population of urban areas is financially excluded.

It is entirely possible that households choose not to deal with formal financial institutions and also with technologically upgraded transactions. This could be for a number of reasons:

(a) lack of awareness about formal institutions.

(b) lack of financial literacy.

(c) ineffective financial services that do not address the specific requirements of the financially excluded, etc.

(d) Location of banks/financial institution branches being far from the village.

(e) Most of the economically backward classes are illiterates and also they do not know how to operate a computer or an internet.

(f) Mobile supported transactions also face the same kind of a problem as most of the mobile users in the unorganised sectors only know to pick and disconnect the call. Other operations are totally confusing and they do not even tend to learn the same out of ignorance.

(g) One of the main problem for financial inclusion through traditional financial institutions or banks is that they require proper documents for address and identity proof of a customer who transacts with them which is not found in the low income unorganised groups. As a result they do not want to open an account, borrow, save or invest in any banks or financial institutions.

We find that more than 95 per cent of the households are aware of banks as well as that of the benefits from banking. The figure is not very different across rural and urban households, nor does it differ between households who have bank accounts and those who do not have bank accounts.

Banks and financial institutions too have not ventured aggressively into rural areas because of several reasons, few of which may be:

(a) seasonal income of labour.

(b) high transaction cost per account opened.

(c) lack of awareness which increase the promotional cost for banks and financial institutions to create awareness and make them understand the usage and importance of financial services.

(d) high credit risk due to seasonal income in rural areas and lack of proper identification and communication addresses as most of them keep changing houses and cities.

(e) high rates of illiteracy etc.

When does financial exclusion make a huge difference? It occurs when households are forced to avail of funds, often caused by emergencies, from informal sources. First, households that do not have bank accounts are forced to borrow increasingly from moneylenders and these loans attract high interest rates. Much of the problem is in the fact that more than 90 per cent of the employment in India is in the unorganised sector. This means that much of the insurance and pension services are not being provided through the employer. Also, much of the unorganised sector labour is poor. Thus, not only are the poor not introduced to financial services by their employers, they are also less aware of the benefits of these services. Indeed, according to the data, a household where the primary income earner is in the unorganised sector is less likely to have any sort of insurance cover. Furthermore, approximately 20-25 per cent of the households, who currently do not have life insurance cover, did have insurance earlier. This is because some policies have matured while some others have simply been discontinued. There are two major reasons for low insurance cover–high costs (both monetary and otherwise) and two, financial illiteracy/awareness.

The basic idea of the financial Inclusion initiative is to extend banking and other financial services to the un-banked, under banked and underdeveloped rural and low income groups of urban population. The rural communities that reside in remote regions were the target beneficiaries of the scheme.

Information technology should enable banks and financial institutions to provide services that have the following business requirements:

Banking services such as deposits, withdrawals and funds transfer are to be provided. Each customer must be identified uniquely by some means especially fingerprints. Biometric authentication using fingerprints proved to be more secure than Personal Identification Numbers (PIN) authenticating. As most customers are illiterate, they would not be able use PINs to authenticate themselves (in some pilots it was noticed that the rural customers who could not keep their PIN secret had written it down on the card itself!). Both online and offline transactions must be possible. Balance enquiry and mini-statement showing last ten transactions must be possible at all terminal located.

The need of the hour is developing a suitable cost-effective model to serve the under-privileged and in the process banks also stand to gain by way of newer business opportunities.

Focus Areas for Financial Inclusion

Before we discuss about the technological aspects for financial inclusion it is necessary to throw light on certain important areas which requires special focus. Some of which may be:

Community Banking

At present, banks are offering the services only through their branches.

The branches have not been opened at far flung areas, leaving a gap in meeting the requirement of rural masses. The time and cost involved in this exercise can't be afforded by the rural persons. Thus all the rural population is not financially included. But opening a branch at every village is not feasible and viable due to the inadequate power supply, non–availability of digital network for the seamless connectivity and migratory nature of the village population.

Business Correspondent / Facilitator Model

Majority of financially excluded groups are from poor, socially under privileged, disabled, old as well as children, women, uneducated, ethnic minorities and mobile population. The only way to include the leftover segment to banking stream is to reach them at their place of residence or work i.e. by providing doorstep banking through cost effective technology driven model Business Correspondents/ Business Facilitator (Private/ Public) with the use of technology will provide the desired result. The model will be successful only if it has the acceptability and confidence of the rural folks. BCs and BFs need to be involved as they are not only operating in a similar domain, but they also have high acceptability and respectability in the area. Tie up arrangements with banks which has wherewithal ability to finance, accounting etc. with the BC and BF that has a better ability to handle the last mile activities will help in increasing the outreach of financial inclusion initiatives. The model will benefit society as a whole. It will uplift the social and financial excluded poor thus developing the society as a whole. The petty savings of the poor will be brought into the banking stream.

Under the 'Business Facilitator'; model, banks may use intermediaries, such as, NGOs/ Farmers' Clubs, cooperatives, community based organisations, IT enabled rural outlets of corporate entities, Post Offices, insurance agents, well functioning Panchayats, Village Knowledge Centres, Agri Clinics/ Agri Business Centers, Krishi Vigyan Kendras and KVIC/ KVIB units, depending on the comfort level of the bank, for providing facilitation services. Such services may include:

(i) Identification of borrowers and fitment of activities.

(ii) Collection and preliminary processing of loan applications including verification of primary information/data.

(iii) Creating awareness about savings and other products and education and advice on managing money and debt counseling.

(iv) Processing and submission of applications to banks.

(v) Promotion and nurturing Self Help Groups/Joint Liability Group; and

(vi) Follow-up for recovery.

In addition to activities listed under the Business Facilitator Model, the scope of activities to be undertaken by the Business Correspondents will include:

(i) Disbursal of small value credit.

(ii) Recovery of principal/collection of interest.

(iii) Collection of small value deposits.

(iv) Sale of micro insurance/mutual fund products/ pension products/ other third party products.

(v) Receipt and delivery of small value remittances/other payment instruments.

As these services are not intended to involve the conduct of banking business by business facilitators, no approval is required from RBI for using the above intermediaries for facilitation of the services indicated above.

In engaging such intermediaries as Business Correspondents, banks should ensure that they are well established, enjoying good reputation and having the confidence of the local people. Banks may give wide publicity in the locality about the intermediary engaged by them as Business Correspondent and take measures to avoid being misrepresented.

Customer Education

Persons in unbanked remote villages are situated in the far flung areas still depend on local moneylenders and are denied of the affordable banking services. The role of BC/BF in the present model is an important one. They are not only the first point of contact with the customers but they are required to educate the customer also about the benefits of having an account with the bank. The strength of public domain like strong banks with the reach of the private agencies to the far flung areas. Some of the agencies can be out of NGOs, Farmers Clubs, SHG, Co-operatives, Community Based Organisations; IT enabled rural outlets of corporate entities. The role of Bank's Farmer Training Colleges and Information Kiosks will be in addition to the BC and BF Model for Financial Inclusion.

Credit Counselling

Credit counseling is important for ensuring success of farmers in the remote areas. They must be informed the credit facilities available in the bank to meet out their various needs crop loan, loan for farm mechanisation as well as personal loans to meet out petty needs. The BC/BF can play an important role in spreading the credit schemes and by providing them credit counseling to choose from the various options available to them.

Technology can be effectively used in reaching financial services to the rural areas as well as economically backward classes of urban areas. By introducing technology enabled services for making payments, buying groceries, depositing and withdrawing cash, availing insurance facility, loan facility etc the financial industry can reach the untapped or the neglected sector with low cost service devices which mutually benefit eachother. Further in this paper we would be discussing about various options available for providing financial services with the help of latest technology. Some of the popular devices are discussed below:

Smart phones:

Before knowing in detail about how smart phones help in financial transaction, let us throw light on associations called Credit Unions.

What is a Credit Union?

Credit unions are member-owned, savings-led financial cooperatives. They provide an array of financial service products, including savings, credit, insurance and remittances, to meet the evolving needs of people from all socioeconomic levels. Credit unions worldwide provide members opportunities such as starting small businesses, growing farms, building family homes and educating their children.

Let us now know what does World Council of Credit Unions which plays a significant role in providing technology based financial services to rural and backward areas

World Council of Credit Unions (WOCCU) is the global trade association and development agency for credit unions. World Council promotes the sustainable development of credit unions and other financial cooperatives around the world to empower people through access to high-quality and affordable financial services. Worldwide, 53,000 credit unions provide services to more than 188 million credit union members in 100 countries. They have mobilised US$1.2 trillion in savings and shares to finance a loan portfolio of US$960 billion. World Council introduces new tools and technologies to strengthen credit unions' financial performance, governance, outreach, product quality and product diversity. It also advocates on behalf of the global credit union system before international organisations and works with national governments to improve legisla-tion, regulation and supervision.

The increasing popularity of transaction and payment services through cell phones has revealed the tremendous potential to expand financial inclusion through mobile technology. These "electronic money" models have already improved the lives of millions by reducing the need to carry cash or spend time travelling over long distances to reach the nearest point of service for deposits or withdrawls, payment of insurance premiums, payment of bills etc. Nonetheless, successful models linking electronic money to interest-bearing savings, loans and other financial services have been limited. Worldwide, 2.5 billion people still lack access to these basic financial products. For four decades, World Council of Credit Unions has used a savings-led model to bring financial services to the rural and underserved poor. Traditionally, this meant setting up a credit union or branch office and drawing people in from the community. In many areas, however, population density did not support a new credit union branch office, World Council's approach focuses on building national, regional and international credit union networks and capitalising on existing ones. By pooling interests and negotiating as a collective group, credit unions that otherwise may not be able to afford mobile technology gain access at a lower cost, and their members benefit from additional products, points of service and lower fees. Each mobile solution is designed to expand the credit unions' reach and provide increasing levels of financial access to the unbanked and underserved.

In some countries, credit union field officers travel to rural and remote communities on a scheduled weekly or monthly basis to provide services. The field officers use credit union-linked **smart phones** to enroll members and conduct financial transactions, such as balance inquiries, deposits and withdrawals, in real time.

In these and other communities, credit unions have arranged with local member-merchants to install **point-of-sale (POS) devices** in their shops, joining an agent network that provides both payment and financial services. Members only need to swipe a debit card to access their credit union account at the local business. By leveraging the merchants' existing infrastructure, the credit union expands the hours of financial access from one or two hours weekly (or monthly) to the merchants' daily business hours. Personal **cell phones** can connect members to their credit union's network to make or receive payments and access their accounts 24 hours a day, seven days a week. When a credit union network connects with larger payment or financial networks, members gain even more access points and services outside the credit union system.

In order to expand financial access beyond the credit union walls, World Council developed the field officer model in which rural credit union staff take financial services directly to homes and businesses in remote, underserved communities. The addition of smart-phone technology has improved the efficiency of financial transactions and reduced operational costs, providing more frequent opportunities to open and access member accounts in real time during field officer visits. In the field officer model, credit union employees visit rural communities on a weekly or monthly schedule to enroll new members, collect deposits, perform withdrawals, process small loan applications, disburse microloans and receive loan payments. Credit unions select communities using a route-costing tool developed by World Council that identifies profitable markets. Oftentimes, if at all, these markets have only had access to high-interest loans or informal community savings groups.

When World Council first launched the model, field officers recorded transactions by hand and reentered them into the credit union database at the end of their daily circuit. Field officers now use a tailored smart phone software applica-tion that wirelessly connects to the credit union server to process transactions and provide members real-time access to their accounts. In areas with little or no cell phone connectivity, the smart phone encrypts and stores transaction data offline and later synchronizes it with the credit union's system using batch processing. In the field, handheld wireless printers provide members with receipts that have up-to-date account balances after each transaction. Printed receipts increase transparency and customer satisfaction while reducing potential for fraud.

The use of smart phones not only increases the efficiency and accuracy of field officers, but also improves the credit union's overall image and ability to attract more members. Credit unions have found that previously unbanked individuals are more trusting of the credit unions. Many have subsequently joined, moved their money into savings accounts, taken out progressively larger loans and accessed additional financial products to help manage their evolving financial needs.

2. Smart Cards

A smart card is a plastic card about the size of a credit card, with an embedded microchip that can be loaded with data, used for telephone calling, electronic cash payments, and other applications, and then periodically refreshed for additional use. Presently, various types of cards are floated by various Banks. Debit Cards, Credit Cards, Kisan Credit Cards, Swarojgar Credit Card, Artisan Credit Card, Bhumiheen Kisan Card,

Kisan Samadhan Card, Laghu Udyami Trade Card, etc. are some of the cards issued by various banks. There is a felt need to replace these individual purpose specific cards to a single card containing all the possible features.

An ideal card needs to have all the features as detailed below:

- Card to contain the full particulars of the account holder with limits sanctioned/available, balance outstanding, photo, finger prints, etc. with provision for data updation and the unique citizenship number, if any allotted in future.
- Cover working capital, consumption loan and OD Limits.
- Card should be operable both in online and offline systems.
- Operable in ATMs/POS/POTs.

There are two kinds of smart cards. They are:

1. Contact Smart cards: Contact smart cards have a contact area of approximately 1 square centimetre (0.16 sq in), comprising several gold-plated contact pads. These pads provide electrical connectivity when inserted into a reader, which is used as a communications medium between the smart card and a host (e.g., a computer, a point of sale terminal) or a mobile telephone. Cards do not contain batteries; power is supplied by the card reader.

2. Contactless smart cards: A **contactless smart card** is any pocket-sised card with embedded integrated circuits that can process and store data, and communicate with a terminal via radio waves. These cards require only proximity to an antenna to communicate. The card should be issued to all the underprivileged as a matter of routine after taking care of the KYC norms as applicable. If cards are issued free of cost only one card from any Bank should be provided and holding of more than one card from different banks should be avoided. If consumer needs more cards from different banks, it must be on chargeable basis.

The cards should also be used for:

- Providing Govt. benefits/subsidy/services to the customer.
- Getting the required information of the customers on his family.
- Making utility payments.
- Micro credit / micro insurance facilities.

The fruits of technology should thus be made available to the underprivileged by providing them with a multi-purpose proximity / near field contact/contactless (RFID) Smart card for availing the basic banking facilities along with other benefits Government propose to provide for their upliftment. The data needs to be updated in one common smart card that need to facilitate carrying out transactions at POS/POT/ATMs and Branches. Through the Business Correspondents, using hand held or mobile 'Point of Transaction' terminals the banking should be taken to the doorsteps of the downtrodden. User friendly, (e.g. voice enabled / local language user interface etc.) Point of Transaction models using bio-metric authentication need to be put in use for benefiting the illiterate customers to effect their transactions.

Online and Offline Model

Depending upon the topography and availability of infrastructure, two models are envisaged for meeting the requirements of the Bank and the customers.

Highlights of Online Model

In view of the expansion of network connectivity even in the remote areas by way of GSM/GPRS/CDMA besides WIMAX facility, Banks may go in for an online model which needs to have the following features:

1. All the Banks, having internet Banking facilities may explore using the channel for the updation of transactions. The Internet Banking channel would enable online updation of transactions. The authorised Bank official/business correspondent will be provided with separate User-id and Password for enabling transactions by the customers.
2. Specific accounts (like accounts of a particular branch / accounts opened in a specific area) can be attached to operator with daily limits.

3. In view of the high illiteracy prevailing in the rural areas, a convenient medium like a proximity / near field contact / contactless smart card has to be used.
4. The card will hold personal particulars of the customer along with his finger prints (at least two fingers say right and left index fingers).
5. Card will have amount outstanding, along with last 5 or 10 transactions in the account.
6. For enrolment of customers, a small kit containing a laptop, finger printer reader, web camera, small printer, etc. may be used to capture the details of the account –holders for opening no-frill accounts. This will be a onetime affair in each village and the villages may be revisited for enrolment periodically.
7. For the operations of the accounts, a small hand held device (or set of devices) called "Point Of Transaction" (POT) like 'Point of Sales Terminals' with facility to authenticate fingerprints, contactless smart card reader/writer, receipt printer has to be used.
8. The terminals preferably to be voice enabled in the regional language so that the accountholders will know what transactions the customer has made and the amount.

- Receipts for transactions (preferably in local language) are to be given then and there.
- Business Correspondents/facilitators may be used for operations.

Following transactions at the minimum are to be enabled:

- Balance Enquiry.
- Statement of Account.
- Cash Withdrawal.
- Cash Receipt.

In course of time, the facilities may be improved or enhanced.

Precautions to be taken

- Customers may be allowed to operate their account only through the cards given to them.
- Business facilitator has to be given suitable threshold limit for cash transactions.
- Suitable procedures to be evolved for operation during holidays.

Offline Model

- Offline mode on lines of online model without connectivity is envisaged in remote areas.
- The accounts will be opened similar to online model with usage of proximity/near field/contactless smart card.

- The transactions will be done through a "Point of Transaction (POT)" device (or set of devices) using Business correspondent/bank officials.
- The transaction terminal (POT) will record all the transactions happened during the day and will be uploaded into the CBS system at the end of the day or at pre-defined intervals.
- Before start of the day, the transaction terminal will be refreshed and made in sync with the CBS system. Facility will be available in the device for updating the entries in the proximity / near-field contactless smart card given to the customers.

In today's payment systems scenario in India, a normal magnetic stripe card that is used for debit or credit cards. The magnetic stripe card holds the customer's primary account number (PAN), name and some authentication information (such as enciphered PIN). No account balance information is held in the card. These cards facilitate only online transactions. However, the business requirements for this initiative demanded that offline transactions should be accommodated since connectivity is poor in rural India. This meant that the card needed to carry the account balance to allow offline transaction facilities. Therefore, the option of a smart card was designed. The smart card is to carry biometric (fingerprint) identification details, customer information and bank account information. However, since the card should also possibly be used with other existing financial networks, a magnetic stripe was also needed in the card. So a chip and pin solution was needed.

The fingerprint template was stored in the card so that every time the customer wanted to do a transaction, a fingerprint scanner could extract the image and terminal could compute the template for feature matching. The biometric validation process could either take place at:

The card: The biometric fingerprint template is held within the card. The terminal reads the fingerprint and creates the template. The templates are compared within the card using the intelligence within the card.

The terminal: The terminal reads the biometric fingerprint and convert it to a template and it is compared with the template stored read from the smart card. The terminals do have memory requirements and limitations.

The back-end host: The back-end stores both the image and the template. The comparison is made with the biometric template stored within the smart card. This solution is costly in terms of telecommunication costs since the fingerprint template needs to be communicated to the back-end host over wired or wireless telecommunication networks for every transaction the customer makes.

1. Micro ATMs: The presence of ATMs mostly found in Metro/Urban centers and banks are not keen to install ATMs at Rural/Semi Urban centers on account of high investment and low transaction volume. In order to make the ATMs viable at these centers, there is a need to deploy low cost ATMs with basic features such as cash withdrawal and balance enquiry and should be located at places where rural folk pays frequent visits such as petrol pumps, mandis etc. It is convenient and cost effective compared to paying visit to the bank branch located at nearby center.

Micro-ATMs are biometric authentication enabled hand-held device (also known as a Point of Transaction [PoT] terminal). Micro-ATMs will primarily perform following functions:

- Cash withdrawal
- Cash deposit
- Balance enquiry
- Remittances

Business Correspondents (BCs) appointed by the banks will operate these devices. The physical currency would be handled by this Business Correspondent and not a machine like a regular ATM. All transactions will require online biometric authentication with the UIDAI authentication server in order to be processed.

1. Biometric ATMs: The penetration of ATMs into Rural / Semi-urban areas may not serve the envisaged purpose unless it is put to use by illiterates/semi-literates whose presence is predominant in rural areas. The existing ATMs are not being used optimally by rural folk on account of PIN and Password related issues. Introduction of Biometric ATMs enables the illiterate and semi-literate customers to avail ATM facilities on par with literate customers. Under this, Thumb impression of the cardholder will be scanned and transfer the same to central server as one time measure. ATM dispenses cash and other services only after verifying the thumb impression of the cardholder with that of finger print available with the bank's server. Bio-metric ATMs are going to play an important role in the remote rural areas in the ensuing years.

2. Mobile ATMs are designed for providing ATM facility to the rural folk as well as other customers. The Van would move to the pre-determined places and also accessible to Biometric card holders. Opening of accounts also can be undertaken during the visits to the rural areas. This can be used at weekly shandis/markets effectively.

All the above initiatives warrant the banks to invest substantial amount on infrastructure besides recurring expenditure. The distribution of financial products and services at the lowest rung of the pyramid requires a low-cost model that allows accepting and making of a large number of micro payments to and from the poor. The high intermediary cost of the banks is a stumbling block to reach the poor, which need to be addressed. Hence, it is warranted the banks to search for the following alternate models to extend Branchless Banking across rural India.

High Operating Costs and Low Business Volume are the major constraints of the banks in extending banking services especially in remote rural and inaccessible areas through Branch Banking Model. To address this issue, RBI permitted the banks to make use the services of Business Facilitators and Business Correspondents to take banking to un-banked areas in a most cost effective Manner.

Today our focus should be to simplify technology so that it can operate on any platform. The technology solution to the business needs should be user-friendly without much third-party or IT vendor intervention or support requirement for operating the same. In this context, the banks need to redesign their business strategies to incorporate specific plans to promote financial inclusion of low income group, treating it both a business opportunity as well as a social responsibility.

We can achieve our goal of inclusive growth if all the available resources including technology and expertise available with the banks, the support of the government, the optimum utilisation of the Micro Finance Institutions (MFIs), NGOs and SHGs are geared towards including more people under the banking net. Various studies reveal that even the relatively low margins on high volumes can be profitable.

2. Point of Sales Device (POS device): Agent banking includes the use of POS devices at local merchants that give members debit card access. Both members and nonmembers can use POS devices for transaction and payment services.

Some credit unions have installed POS devices in local mom-and-pop shops, gas stations, agricultural input providers and restaurants to increase the points of service and hours in which members can access their accounts and other transaction and payment services.

Biometric cards use fingerprints to validate that the cardholder is the card owner. Biometric cards serve as effective identification cards for individuals who lack other forms of formal identification like name, father/ husbands name, age, occupation, annual income etc. or are illiterate. Biometric cards can be combined with smart cards to prevent use of the card in financial transactions by individuals who are not the card owner, making transactions more Secure.

Thereafter, impressions of all the ten fingers are captured and stored. The data thus captured is stored in the chip embedded in the bio metric card and handed over to the account holder. The advantage of the card is that instead of pin number it recognises and authenticates transactions on the basis of fingerprints of the account holder It is safe, as it allows only the account holder on matching his fingerprints to carry out any transaction. The biometric card has 15 slots, meaning thereby that the bank can offer 15 different financial products to the cardholder like savings, term deposit, recurring deposit, Loan product, Insurance etc. Once the card is issued to the customer, it is ready for operations. These BC will move to the customer with the hand held device (Point of sale machine (POS) which also works as a storage device. The POS gets activated only after the BC identifies himself with the agent card provided to him. Once the POS machine gets activated the account holder can start transacting after completing his identification process–inserting his card, matching the fingerprints etc. On completion of each transaction, the POS generates a receipt in duplicate, of which one copy is given to the account holder. At the end of the day, the agent goes to a nearest telephone landline point and uploads the data to the CBS server. Once all the active POS machines are settled, the technology provider will come to know about all the transactions carried out on POS machines. This process helps in tracking the POS not settled.

Measures to be taken for the effective usage of technology by rural and urban low income groups:

1. **Customer education:** This can be the best thing to make people actively participate in the usage of technology for availing financial services. Customer education can be given by the business correspondents or the bank/financial institutions representative.
2. Repeated field officers visits to address the problems faced by the rural mass and helping them solve the same.
3. Live demonstrations and allow the customers also to practice and learn the usage of technology enabled devices such as ATM'S, biometrics, mobiles etc.
4. **No frills account:** This is an account offered especially to these lower income groups for encouraging them to open bank accounts even by maintaing less cash balance or zero balance as they may not have regular income. No additional charges would be levied for not maintaining the minimum or average balance and other additional charges too will be waived off. When such accounts are opened people will be naturally encouraged to transact with the help of technology repeatedly.
5. **Low cost:** One of the major areas which the financially excluded mass would focus on is the cost of operating the technology supported devices.They should be provided with those kind of financial services like fund transfers, bill payments, mobile banking etc. free of cost so that they are motivated to do the transactions with the help of hand held devices.
6. **Local language:** The technology used like ATM'S, POS devices etc should deliver the receipt and make announcements about the type of transaction made in local languages. This also may be one of the reasons for increased technology enabled transactions.

Conclusion

Financial inclusion to the economically backward classes and unorganised sector of rural and urban areas can only be possible with the effective implementation of technology.

Banks and financial institutions have a major role in extending banking facilities to rural areas for inclusive growth and availability of financial facilities to common man across the country. In this context, commercial orientation may be important for achieving financial inclusion. From policy makers focused on development, to bankers and FIs willing to reach out to the poor, to vendors providing technology-enabled financial inclusion platforms, everyone needs to understand the fact that financial services has to be reached to all the classes of people for which they all have to work in a brisk pace along with integrated efforts which can surely do wonders in servicing the financially excluded mass. On the other hand, IT industry will also need to collaborate with a renewed focus beyond short-term sales maximisation of hardware and software. To that effect, efforts are needed for agreeing on industry standardisations for technologies relevant for building platforms for financial inclusion, such as micro atm's, biometrics, etc. Industry standardisation is also relevant in this context. While it can lead to network externalities that will play a crucial role in technology adoption, it also has spillover effects as it initially leads to economies of scale and catalyses innovation.

An overwhelming majority of rural India, and a significant portion of urban India, do not avail of financial services. While availing of any service is a matter of choice in a market economy, it is mandatory for society to allow access to all services for the entire population. Unfortunately, as we have discussed in this paper, while most are aware of the benefits of the various basic financial services, few are able to partake of them because of the way these services are delivered in India. The transaction costs of availing financial services are simply too large for them. Once the transaction costs are brought down to a minimum, the distribution of these services can then be determined by the pricing of such services. The decision to save in banks should be driven by the return on savings and not by the cost of visiting the bank; insurance bought should be governed by their premiums and not by the difficulty of making payments on the premiums. As we have demonstrated, technology can play a major role in reducing the cost of availing financial services. The current information and communication technology opens up new avenues of service delivery that are cheap and can be customised to the needs of everybody. The objective of the technology should not be simply to increase value to those already in the market place for financial services and the objective of the regulator should not be to restrict anything that is too innovative. The system has to encourage experiments in limited geographical spheres and with select groups of people, under strict monitoring, to see how different mechanisms can work. In addition to satisfying all the characteristics of a credible payment system, these experiments must encourage the excluded from participating in the use of these mechanisms. This latter is very important–the objective is not one that earns more revenue from existing market participants but increase the number of participants. Hence the use of latest technology contributes a lions share in servicing maximum number of participants and helping them obtain various financial services that are available in a quick and cost-effective manner.

References

1. (Carr, A technological approach to financial inclusion:Problems and sollutions, July-Sept 2007).
2. Unions, W.C. (n.d.). Using mobile technology to expand financial inclusion. *The Credit Union Experience.*
3. Indian Banks Association. (n.d.). How to leverage technology for broad basing financial inclusion initiatives. *Approach paper on it enabled financial inclusion.*
4. http://articles.timesofindia.indiatimes.com/2011-03-07/software-services/28665085_1_financial-inclusion-indian-banking-system-banking-services.
5. http://www.idfresearch.org/Financial-Inclusion-0901.pdf-How can technology facilitate financial inclusion in India? A discussion paper.
6. http://www.livemint.com/2009/11/26232941/Mobile-phone-technology-key-to.html.
7. http://en.wikipedia.org/wiki/Smart_card.
8. http://en.wikipedia.org/wiki/Point_of_sale.

39

Financial Inclusion: Reaching the Unreached

R. Nagabhushan

Introduction

Access to financial services plays a critical part in development by facilitating economic growth and reducing income inequality. Inclusive financial systems allow poor people to smooth their consumption and insure themselves against economic vulnerabilities, from illness and accidents to theft and unemployment. Financial access enables poor people to save and borrow-allowing them to build their assets, to invest in education and entrepreneurial ventures, and thus to improve their livelihoods. Inclusive finance is especially likely to benefit disadvantaged groups such as women, youth, and rural communities. For all these reasons financial inclusion has gained prominence in recent years as a policy to improve the lives of the poor (World Bank, 2012).

Financial inclusion has become one of the most critical aspects in the context of inclusive growth and development. The importance of an inclusive financial system is widely recognised in policy circles and has become a policy priority in many countries. Several countries across the globe now look at financial inclusion as the means to more comprehensive growth, wherein each citizen of the country is able to use earnings as a financial resource that can be put to work to improve future financial status and adding to the nation's progress. The Eleventh Five Year Plan (2007-12) envisions inclusive growth as a key objective. The Plan Document tries to restructure the policies in order to make the growth faster, broad-based and inclusive by reducing the fragmentation of the society. It clearly stated that 'The development of rural India is an imperative for inclusive and equitable growth and to unlock huge potential of the population that is presently trapped in poverty with its associated deprivations'. Growth is inclusive when there is equality of economic opportunities. Financial inclusion makes growth broad based and sustainable by progressively encompassing the hitherto excluded population. Financial inclusion is no longer a policy choice but a policy compulsion. Financial inclusion is an important process to attain the goal of inclusive growth. Access to finance by the poor and vulnerable groups is a prerequisite for poverty reduction and social cohesion. In fact, providing access to finance is a form of empowerment of the vulnerable groups. The objective of financial inclusion is to extend the scope of activities of the organised financial system to include within its ambit people with low incomes. Through graduated credit, the attempt must be to lift the poor from one level to another so that they come out of poverty. The essence of financial inclusion is in trying to ensure that a range of appropriate financial services such as savings, loans, remittances and insurance services is available to every individual and enabling them to understand and access those services. India has, for a long time, recognised the social and economic imperatives for broader financial inclusion and has made an enormous contribution to economic development by finding innovative ways to empower the poor. Starting with the nationalisation of banks, priority sector lending requirements for banks, lead bank scheme, establishment of regional rural banks (RRBs), service area approach, self-help group-bank linkage programme, etc., multiple steps have been taken by the Reserve Bank of India (RBI) over the years to increase access to the poorer segments of society. In spite of these measures almost half the country is unbanked. Achieving financial inclusion in a country like India with a large and diverse population with significant segments in rural and unorganised sectors requires a high level of penetration by the formal financial system. This paper tries to analyse how far the policy of financial inclusion has been successful in reaching the hitherto unreached population.

Need for the Study

Despite broad international consensus on the importance of financial inclusion as a powerful social development instrument, it is estimated that over two billion people continue to be financially excluded from the formal financial sector. With over 135 million financially excluded households, India is home to the world's largest financially excluded population after China. Only 34 per cent of the Indian population is currently engaged with the formal financial sector and the urban rural divide is very apparent. If usage intensity of a savings account is considered as a true indicator of financial inclusion rather than mere ownership, then the financial inclusion percentage will certainly be much lower. RBI Annual Report (2012) quoting a World Bank Report observes that India has scored poorly on financial inclusion parameters when compared with the global average (Table 1). India also scored poorly in respect of credit cards, outstanding mortgage, health insurance, adult origination of new loans and mobile banking. "Financial inclusion remains a substantially unfinished agenda," said the report. Given that the vast population of the country is still financially excluded, this makes an interesting study. This paper tries to analyse how far the policy of financial inclusion has been successful in fulfilling its objectives.

Table 1: Key Statistics on Financial Inclusion in India (per cent)

	Share of adults with an account at a formal financial institution	*Adults saving in the past year using a formal acco-unt*	*Adults originating a new loan in the past year from a formal financial institution*	*Adults with a credit card*	*Adults with an outstanding mortgage*	*Adults paying for Health Ins-urance*	*Adults using mobile money in the past year*
India	35	12	8	2	2	7	4
World	50	22	9	15	7	17	7

Source : Policy Research Working Paper, 6025, World Bank, 2012.

Methodology

The study is based on the secondary data collected from various sources such as the RBI, XIth Five Year Plan Document, Mid Term Appraisal of the XIth Plan, Report of the Committee on Financial Inclusion and several other sources. Statistical tables have been used to show the progress made in recent years with respect to financial inclusion.

Financial Inclusion: What is the Need?

The Report of the Committee on Financial Inclusion (2008) defines financial inclusion as the process of ensuring access to financial services and timely and adequate credit where needed by vulnerable groups such as weaker sections and low income groups at an affordable cost.

The correlation between financial inclusion and economic growth has long been widely recognised: low financial inclusion impedes economic growth. Access to easy and affordable credit by the disadvantaged social groups is acknowledged as a key criterion for poverty alleviation and reducing social inequity. Such unfettered access enables the financially excluded population to build savings, carry out investments, avail safe and low-cost credit and perhaps most importantly it enables the poor to mitigate risks of income seasonality, illness and employment loss. However despite broad international consensus on the importance of access to finance as a powerful poverty alleviation tool, it is estimated that over 2 billion people globally continue to be excluded from the formal financial sector. Financial exclusion relegates the poor to a subsistence livelihood and increases the probability of their being dependant on social welfare schemes thereby increasing the burden on the economy. Difficulty in accessing credit from formal financial institutions leads these disadvantaged groups to depend on non-formal sources including local un-regulated credit providers especially for non-productive consumption oriented expenses e.g. medical emergencies, social ceremonies and marriages etc. Financial exclusion also has an adverse national economic impact as it precludes large sections of the population from micro-entrepreneurship opportunities thereby restricting them from becoming economically productive and increasing their contribution to the national GDP in a bigger way.

The objective of Financial Inclusion is to extend financial services to the large hitherto unserved population of the country to unlock its growth potential. In addition, it strives towards a more inclusive growth by making financing available to the poor in particular.

Government of India wishes to directly transfer subsidies on LPG, fertilizers and kerosene to the bank accounts of the beneficiaries. Besides, there are at least 32 other schemes including MNREGA where the benefits are intended to be transferred to the beneficiaries by way of electronic transfers. This has necessitated bringing in the hitherto unreached population to the ambit of banking. Extension of banking and other financial services to the rural areas will also facilitate and, in fact, accelerate the economic development of such areas.

Financial Inclusion: A Few Concerns

RBI believes that nothing represents the extent of human face of the banking than the progress it makes on the goal of financial inclusion (RBI Annual Report 2012). Financial inclusion was adopted as a formal agenda for Indian banking following the Report of the Committee on Financial Inclusion under the Chairmanship of Dr. C. Rangarajan in 2008. The Report noted that 51 per cent of farmer households did not access credit, either from institutional or non-institutional sources. Further, despite the vast network of bank branches, only 27 per cent of total farm households were indebted to formal sources (of which one-third also borrow from informal sources). Access to formal institutional credit amongst farm households was as low as 4.1 per cent in North-Eastern, 18.2 per cent in Eastern and 22.4 per cent in Central Regions.

A World Bank study by Asli Demirguc-Kunt and Leora Klapper (April 2012) is revealing about the dismal state of financial inclusion world-wide and even more so in India. Providing an analysis from a newly developed Global Financial Inclusion Database (Global Findex), that is drawn from survey data covering 148 countries shows that only half of the world's population hold accounts with formal financial institutions and only 9 per cent have taken out new loans from a bank, credit union or microfinance institution in the past one year. This study also shows that India scores rather poorly on financial inclusion parameters than the global average (Table1). In India, only 35 per cent of people had formal accounts *versus* an average of 41 per cent in developing economies. India also scored poorly in respect of credit cards, outstanding mortgage, health insurance, adult origination of new loans and mobile banking.

Reserve Bank of India Initiatives

India with 135 million households is home to the second largest financially excluded population, after China. As only about 5% of the nearly 6 lakh villages in the country were having bank branches and there were 296 under banked districts in the under banked states in the country, the Government of India had undertaken a major initiative aimed at financial inclusion by extending the reach of the banking and other financial services to the hitherto unserved areas. As per the announcement made in the Budget 2010-11, the Government initiated the process of extending banking services through new bank branches and banking correspondents (BCs) in the habitations with population of 2000 and more as per 2001 census. Under the Financial Inclusion Plan (FIP) under implementation, around 73,000 villages having population of 2000 and above have been provided with banking services by March, 2012. The Business Correspondents and the new bank branches opened in these villages would also provide services in the adjoining areas.

Financial inclusion has been accorded high importance by the Reserve Bank to aid the inclusive growth process for the economy. There have been formidable challenges in this area such as bringing sections of society that are financially excluded within the ambit of the formal financial system, providing financial literacy and strengthening credit delivery mechanisms. A brief analysis of the progress made under FIPs of banks shows that penetration of banks in rural areas has increased manifold. As against 21,475 brick and mortar branches of these banks in rural areas as in early March 2010, banks are now providing banking services in rural areas through 1,38,502 outlets comprising 24,085 rural branches, 1,11,948 BC outlets and 2,469 outlets through other modes. No-frills accounts have increased to around 99 million with an outstanding balance of above 87 billion with the addition of about 50 million new no-frills accounts since April 2010. (Reserve Bank of India Monetary Policy Statement 2012-13).

In pursuance of the announcement made in the Monetary Policy Statement of April 2010, the roadmap to provide banking services in every village with a population above 2,000 was finalised by state level bankers' committees (SLBCs). Under the roadmap, 74,414 villages with population above 2,000 were identified as unbanked, which were allocated to various banks, including regional rural banks (RRBs) for providing banking services by March 2012. Banks have covered 74,199 (99.7 per cent) of these unbanked villages.

In recent years, the RBI has taken several initiatives to push financial inclusion high on the agenda of Indian banking. It required banks to provide no-frills accounts, tried to improve the outreach of Indian banking through the business facilitator and business correspondent (BC) models and set up the goal for banks to provide access to formal banking to all 74,414 villages with a population over 2000. In June 2012, the process was refined further by advising all banks to prepare road maps covering all unbanked villages with population of less than 2000 with banking services. Yet, the RBI's assessment is that financial inclusion remains a substantially unfinished agenda. This is also suggested by independent appraisals through analysis of the banking data, evaluation studies and outreach activities. Latest figures indicate that there are over 110,000 BCs employed, which is not a large number in context of the under banked villages that exist.

Business Correspondent: The RBI had adopted the Information and Communication Technology (ICT) based agent bank model through BCs for ensuring door step delivery of financial products and services since 2006. The list of eligible individuals/entities who can be engaged as BCs is being enlarged from time to time. For-profit companies have also been allowed to be engaged as BCs.

No Frills Accounts: Following the Reserve Bank directive in November 2005, no-frills accounts have been accepted by banks as one of the important pillars of financial inclusion. Such accounts opened with nil or very low minimum balance have the potential to effectively combat credit rationing and provide the much-needed finance to a large section of the under-privileged population. In order to further encourage such accounts, the Reserve Bank in August 2012 asked banks to rechristen these as 'Basic Savings Bank Deposit Account', with a view to remove the stigma attached to earlier name and to integrate them as part of basic baking services. It also issued specific guidelines to bring about uniformity on basic banking services across banks. It specifically removed altogether the requirement of any minimum balance and has asked banks to offer deposit and withdrawal of cash at bank branch as well as ATMs. The number of no-frills accounts by banks had increased to 103 million by March 2012.

Priority Sector Lending: Priority sector lending aims at encouraging and enhancing credit availability to sectors of the economy that would otherwise find it difficult to get credit from banks. Agriculture and micro and small enterprises (MSE) are two major sectors that receive priority sector lending apart from education, housing etc.

Opening of Bank Branches: Government has been aggressively pursuing the expansion and strengthening of the bank branch network in the country, thereby providing access to financial services to all strata of the society. In view of the continued need to set up the opening of branches in rural areas so as to meet the objectives of increasing banking penetration and financial inclusion rapidly, Government issued detailed strategy and guidelines on financial inclusion in October 2011, vide which it was, inter-alia, advised to banks to open bank branches by Sept. 2012 in all habitations of 5,000 or more population in under banked districts and 10,000 or more population in other districts. As per reports received from the Convener Banks of State Level Bankers Committees (SLBCs), of the 3905 bank branches to be opened, 739 bank branches have been opened by end of April, 2012.

Regional Rural Banks (RRBs) were also advised to work out branch expansion plan such that there is an increase of 10% in bank branches in 2011-12 and also in 2012-13 over the respective previous years. As per provisional data received, RRBs opened 914 branches during 2011-12. RRBs propose to open 1845 branches under the plan in 2012-13.

Swabhimaan-the Financial Inclusion Campaign: In order to extend the reach of banking to the rural hinterland, Banks were advised in 2010-11 to provide appropriate banking facilities to habitations having a population in excess of 2000 (as per 2001 census) by March, 2012 under Swabhimaan campaign. Swabhimaan aims at providing branchless banking through use of technology. Banks provide basic services like deposits, withdrawals and remittances using the services of Business Correspondents. The initiative enables Government subsidies and social security benefits to be directly credited to the accounts of the beneficiaries and who wou!d be able to draw the money from the Business Correspondents in their village itself. As per reports received from State Level Bankers Committee (SLBC) Convener Banks, out of 74,398 such villages identified, 74,194 villages have been covered by March, 2012. Further in terms of Finance Minister's Budget Speech 2012-13 it has been decided to extend the Swabhimaan campaign to habitations with population of more than 1000 in North Eastern and hilly States and to other habitations which have crossed population of 2,000 as per census 2011. Accordingly Banks have been advised to initiate steps for providing banking facilities in habitations with population of 1000-2000 in North Eastern and hilly States and to habitations of 1600-2000 in all States/ UTs by March, 2013.

Establishment of Ultra Small Branches: Considering the need of close supervision and mentoring of the business correspondent agents by the respective bank branch and to ensure that a range of banking services are available to the residents of such villages, it has been decided that Ultra Small Branch be set up in all villages covered through BCA under financial inclusion. Ultra Small Branch would comprise of a small area of 100-200 sq. feet where the officer designated by the bank would be available with a lap top on predetermined day and time in a week. While the cash services would be offered by the BCA, the bank officer would offer other services to be offered by the bank undertake field verification and follow up the banking transactions. The BCA shall also operate from such premises. The periodicity and duration of visits can be progressively enhanced depending upon business potential and reviewed periodically.

Banking Facilities in Unbanked Blocks: In order to provide banking facilities in unbanked blocks, the Government in July, 2009 identified 129 unbanked blocks, of which 91 blocks were in North East States and 38 in other States. With the persistent efforts of the Government, the number of unbanked blocks were brought down to 71 as on 31.3.2011, and by March 2012, banking facilities have been provided in all the unbanked blocks either through Brick and Mortar Branches or Business Correspondents Model or mobile banking. As a next step it has been advised to cover all those blocks with BCA and Ultra Small Branch which have so far been covered by mobile banking only.

Electronic Benefit Transfer: Electronic Benefit Transfer (EBT) is one of the products offered under Financial Inclusion in which benefits are directly credited into the account of beneficiary who can then withdraw it from the bank branch or the ATM or the Micro ATMs. Government in its strategy and guidelines on financial inclusion has advised banks that benefits in the areas covered under Financial Inclusion must be transferred electronically into the accounts of the beneficiaries. The Convener Banks of SLBC have been advised to take up this matter in the SLBC meeting and the roadmap for Electronic Benefit Transfer in respect of each of the 32 schemes under which subsidies are provided by Central Government must be finalised.

GIS: A Geographical Information System (GIS) is being developed for mapping of all the branches in the country so as to enable the banks to determine the deficit areas of banking. Pilots have already been done for Mewat and Bulandsahar districts.

Findings and Suggestions

A look at the figures on financial inclusion seems very impressive in isolation. As indicated above, while India has made enormous strides towards greater financial inclusion, there is a long way to go; about 500,000 villages are yet to be provided with banking services. By RBI's own admission the work on financial inclusion to make available basic amenities for the poor is still lacking in some parts of the country and efforts need to be made to broad base the achievements. The BC model has not been very effective in addressing financial inclusion needs. The model, by itself, cannot serve the financial inclusion objective. BCs cannot substitute the services and the customer confidence that the brick and mortar bank branches provide. Also, most BCs are not adequately trained in the use of technology, knowledge of bank products and processes and have not imbibed the customer service culture. There is a need for mainstreaming financial inclusion. To improve the access of the poor to banking, banks need to open branches to provide low-cost intermediation with simple structures, minimum infrastructure for operating small customer transactions and supporting up to 8-10 BCs at a reasonable distance of 2-3 kms. This will lead to efficiency in cash management, documentation and redressal of customer grievances. As far as the No frill accounts are concerned over three-fourths of such accounts are dormant. This raises the question whether the blanket supply-side thrust to financial inclusion is workable. For financial inclusion to work, it is necessary to replace the bank or the service provider approach with customer-centric approach.

To make financial inclusion far reaching and more inclusive the following suggestions may be looked into:

- Financial Inclusion literacy plays an important role in making financial inclusion policy more effective. Awareness in general, coupled with financial awareness on opening and operating accounts, must accompany the financial inclusion initiative.
- Banks should prepare comprehensive plans to cover all villages, through a mix of branchless banking and bricks and mortar branch banking. They should speed up enrolment of customers and opening of UID-enabled bank accounts. It envisages putting in place a system that enables routing of all social benefits to bank accounts electronically as also seamless cash transfer to the poor, as and when the government replaces the age-old system of subsidy and public distribution system with cash transfers.
- As mentioned earlier, banks must provide a minimum four products—a no-frills savings account with an overdraft facility, a pure savings product, entrepreneurial credit and remittance services, and new products tailored to income streams of poor borrowers and according to their needs and interests. Banks must be able to offer the entire suite of financial products and services to poor clients at attractive pricing.
- Banks should effectively leverage ICT solutions so as to cut down the cost. This can be done through innovative methods of banking. Mobile banking can prove to be a very cost effective way of banking.
- It is important that adequate infrastructure such as digital and physical connectivity, uninterrupted power supply, etc., is available.
- Mindset, cultural and attitudinal changes at grass roots and cutting-edge technology levels of branches of banks are needed to impart organisational resilience and flexibility. Banks should institute systems of reward and recognition for personnel initiating, ideating, innovating and successfully executing new products and services in the rural areas.

Table 2: Progress of Scheduled Commercial Banks in Financial Inclusion Plan

Particulars	*March 2010*	*March 2011*	*March 2012*
No of BCs/BC Agents deployed	33,042	57,329	95,767
No of Banking outlets in villages with population above 2,000	27,353	54,246	82,300
No of Banking outlets in villages with population less than 2,000	26,905	45,937	65,234
Total number banking outlets in villages	54,258	1,00,183	1,47,534
No-Frill Accounts			
Number (millions)	50.3	75.4	105.5
Amount (Rs. Billion)	42.6	57.0	93.3
Number of Kissan Credit Card Accounts (millions)	15.9	18.2	20.3
Number of General Purpose Credit Card Accounts (millions)	0.9	1.0	1.3
Number of ICT Based Accounts through BCs (millions)	12.6	29.6	52.1

Source: Reserve Bank of India Annual report 2011-12.

Table 3 : An Overview of the Extent of Financial Inclusion in India

Parameters	*Percentage (Age 15+)*
Accounts at a formal financial Institution	35%
Accounts at a formal financial Institution, female	27%
Accounts at a formal financial Institution, income, bottom 40%	27%
Accounts used to receive wages	8%
Accounts used to receive government payments	4%
Accounts used to receive remittances	2%
Saved at a financial institution in the past year	12%
Loan from a financial institution in the past year	8%
Loan from family or friends	20%
Debit card	8%
Credit card	2%

Source: Global Findex, World Bank, 2012.

40

Role of Banks in Achieving Financial Inclusion: A Case Study of State Bank of Mysore in Mysore District

Kempe Gowda G.N. and *Nadeesha H.K.*

Introduction

Increasing Globalisation has resulted in increasing remittance throughout the world. The updated technology can no long more exclude the people from the view point of utilisation. Today, the banking industry has shown tremendous growth in volume and complexity. As banking services are in the nature of public good it is essential that availability of banking and payment services are provided to entire population in an egalitarian manner. In India, focusing on inclusive growth, financial inclusion has been used as one of the major component to achieve this stipulated target.

Financial Inclusion has become a buzzword internationally – even in developed financial markets there are concerns about those excluded from the banking system. The barriers to access to formal banking system have been identified as relating to culture, education (especially financial literacy), gender, income and assets, proof of identity, remoteness of residence and so on. Efforts are being made by the authorities – especially banking regulators to improve access to affordable financial services through financial education, leveraging technology and generating awareness.

In India the focus of the financial inclusion at present is confined to ensuring a bare minimum access to a savings bank account without frills, to all. Internationally, the financial exclusion has been viewed in a much wider perspective. Having a current account/savings account on its own, is not regarded as an accurate indicator of financial inclusion. There could be multiple levels of financial inclusion and exclusion. At one extreme, it is possible to identify the 'super-included', i.e., those customers who are actively and persistently courted by the financial services industry, and who have at their disposal a wide range of financial services and products.

At the other extreme, we may have the financially excluded, who are denied access to even the most basic of financial products. In between are those who use the banking services only for deposits and withdrawals of money. But these persons may have only restricted access to the financial system, and may not enjoy the flexibility of access offered to more affluent customers.

Financial inclusion is intended to connect people to banks with consequential benefits. Ensuring that the financial system plays its due role in promoting inclusive growth is one of the biggest challenges facing the emerging economies. Financial inclusion is a global task where inclusive growth can't ignore the financial services. Now a day's financial inclusion is a common and priori objective for many developing countries. Access to well functioning financial system, by creating equal opportunities, enables economically and socially excluded people to integrate better into the economy and actively contribute to development and protects themselves against economic shocks (vighneswara and vijayalakshmi).

Definition

Financial Inclusion

- Financial inclusion refers to a process that ensures the ease of access, availability and usage of the formal financial system for all members of an economy.
- Financial inclusion is the process of ensuring access to appropriate financial products and services needed by all sections of the society in general and vulnerable sections and low income groups in particular at an affordable cost.

Financial Exclusion

Financial exclusion refers to a process whereby people encounter difficulties accessing and/or using financial services and products in the mainstream market that are appropriate to their needs and enable them to lead a normal social life in the society in which they belong.

Bank nationalisation in India marked a paradigm shift in the focus of banking as it was intended to shift the focus from class banking to mass banking.

The rational for creating Regional Bank was also to take the banking services to poor people. Though, in India, half of the population still unbanked. The data provided by the committee on Financial Inclusion had measured the extent of exclusion i.e., 51.4% of farmer households are financially excluded from both formal /informal sources.

The extent of exclusion is as high as in Centre, Eastern and North Eastern region which concentrate 64% of all financially excluded farmer households in the country. Therefore, in order to bring them into development mainstream with providing affordable financial services both fiscal and monetary actions need to be undertaken in the Indian context. This paper is an attempt comprehend and distinguish the significance of financial inclusion in the context of a emerging economy like Karnataka as well as India wherein a large population is deprived of the financial services which are very much essential for overall growth of a state/country.

Kofi Annan (Former secretary general of United Nations) had made his statement that (December 2003) "The stark reality is that most poor people in the world still lack access to sustainable financial services, whether it is savings, credit or insurance. The great challenge before us is to address people from full participation in the financial sector. Together, we can and must build inclusive financial sector that help people improve their lives.

Dimension of Inclusion

1. *Penetration*
   - per cent of all households that use services.
   - per cent of households living in rural with no banking facilities.
2. *Affordability*
   - costs to use service.
   - minimum requirements (for opening account).
   - fees associated with service.
3. *Convenience*
   - days to complete transaction.
   - documents required.

Physical proximity

Table 1: Full range of financial services

Credit	*Saving*	*Insurance*	*Payments*
Personal Consumer Credit card Education Mortgage Home improvement Micro enterprises Business Assets leasing	Saving account Current account Certificate of deposits Pension Youth saving others	Life Health Property Disability Agriculture crop Credit life	Money transfer International transfer Bill payments Government transfers Benefit transfers ATM / debit cards e-payments

Source: Secondary data.

Measures taken towards financial inclusion:

- Co-operative movement,
- Setting up of SBI,
- Nationalisation of banks,
- Lead bank scheme,
- Regional Rural Bank,
- National mission of financial inclusion,
- Financial inclusion promotion and development fund,
- Financial inclusion and technology fund,
- Setting up of a committee on financial inclusion,
- Self help groups,
- No frill accounts,
- Service area approach,
- BC and BF model for inclusion approach.

In such a situation, to measure the level of inclusion there should be require to use a multi-dimensional approach which measure the accurate representation. Therefore, the present study aims to provide the information on how inclusion is being achieved by using different data provided by different sources. The study analyse the financial inclusion aspects on the basis of accurate data compiled through commercial banks, RRBs, SHGs. Identifying the level of financial inclusion in Mysore and the trends and issues by using different dimensions is a key researchable issue in this empirical research.

Significance of the Study

In India, financial inclusion first featured in 2005, when it was introduced by K.C. Chakraborthy, the deputy Governor of the RBI. Since, in order to meet the 100% financial inclusion in India both fiscal and monetary actions have been undertaken by the Government of India as well as Reserve Bank of India. The fiscal action like MG-NREGA has greater potential to link the banking services to the poor. In India, almost half of the country is unbanked. Therefore, there are ample opportunities to achieve financial inclusion in India and we can make entire population bankable. The present study is focused on the efforts of State Bank of Mysore towards financial inclusion in Mysore district. To know the level of financial inclusion in the district a multi dimensional approach is used in this study.

Literature Review

With a view to evaluate the objectives of the study, it was considered desirable to have an idea of the findings of some of the earlier research studies and the methods adopted therein. In this part a brief review is made of the previous studies, which are focused on financial inclusion and performance of financial institutions.

Minakshi Ramji (2009) in the study on "Financial Inclusion in Gulbarga, Finding Usage in Access" examined that bank accounts have been typically opened to receive government assistance mostly under the MG-NREGP. The awareness among rural with respect to use of banking services remain low. Therefore, the government programs like MG-NREGP have the greater potential to include large number of households access to accounts not often lead to usage. After the drive force to achieve financial inclusion in Gulbarga, NO FRILL ACCOUNTs were restricted to those needing bank accounts for wage payments under the MG-NREGP scheme only. The BC model provides doorstep delivery of banking services, encourage non-official users of bank accounts make greater use of their accounts. Finally the researcher concluded that the driving effort for financial inclusion in Gulbarga failed to reach a number of people. The access does not mean usage, simply opening bank account without training and marketing may result in additional cost for banks without any benefits to the community.

Usha Thorat (2007) reported that banks are entering into agreements with India post for using post offices as agents for branchless banking. Setting up of financial literacy centre and credit counseling on a pilot basis, launching a national literacy campaign, forging linkages with informal sources with suitable safeguards through appropriate legislation, evolving industry wide standards for IT solutions, facilitating low cost remittance products are some of the initiatives currently under way for furthering financial inclusion.

Tejani Rachana (2010) in the article titled "Financial inclusion and performance of rural co-operative banks in Gujarat" evaluated that in the group 23 states for which a 3-dimensional INDEX OF FINANCIAL INCLUSION has been estimated that led to Kerala with highest value of IFI followed by Maharashtra and Karnataka. Gujarat was lagged behind at 11th place. There is significance impact of occupation on having the bank account. But those who are land labours and are doing lower level jobs don't have account. The researcher finally concluded that through RRBs and PACCs have good coverage but most of them are running into losses. The instrument like KCC issued under it, has shown declining trends. The wide penetration of PACCs across the nation as well as villages would act like a catalyst while pursuing the objective of 100% financial inclusion.

Muthiah Manoharan P. and Krishnaveni Muthiah (2010) found limited access to affordable financial services such as savings, loans, remittance and insurance services to the vast majority of the population in the rural area and unorganised sector is believed to be a constraint to the growth impetus in these sectors. The behavioral pattern shows that many people were not comfortable with formal financial services. The reasons were difficulty in understanding language, various documents and conditions that come with financial services etc.

Research Gap

Financial inclusion is intended to connect people to banks with consequential benefits. Ensuring that the financial system plays its due role in promoting inclusive growth is one of the biggest challenges facing the emerging economies. In India, both monetary and fiscal policy has been working towards inclusive growth vis-à-vis financial inclusion. The earlier works on financial inclusion were focused only on the banking coverage rather than usage behavior. There were few studies been made on account of financial inclusion in Karnataka and very rare studies in Mysore district which used a single dimension i.e., banking penetration. But access to banking services does not mean usage. Financial services should channelise through increasing marketing operation. Thus, the present study aims to use the multidimensional approach to analyse the financial inclusion in Mysore district. Identifying the level of financial inclusion in Mysore district and analyse the trends and issues by considering different dimensions is a key researchable issue in this empirical study.

Research Objectves

1. To study the measures taken by the banks for financial inclusion.
2. To analyse the different dimensions of financial inclusion in Mysore district.
3. To investigate the efforts of the SBM towards financial inclusion in Mysore district.
4. To compare Mysore taluk with H.D. Kote on different aspects of financial inclusion.

Methodology for the Study

The data required for the study was collected from both primary and secondary sources. The primary data was collected from the banks and from the people using structured questionnaire. The secondary data was collected from the published journals, SBMs annual reports, books and various websites. The samples were selected by administering convenience sampling technique. The total numbers of samples were 200.

Nature and Sources of Data

The study is based on both primary and secondary data. The data is compiled from the households by direct interview. The data on different aspects like sources of income of households, number of account holders in the family, level of knowledge on banking habits, transaction, credit and debit records, insurance, information on ATM card, MG-NREGA, transport facility is collected in a precise manner.

Scope of the Study

Secondary data on SBMs performance in Mysore district for the year 2011 is collected from the various sources. Two taluks of Mysore district

H.D. Kote and Mysore taluk have selected for the study. The rational is H.D. Kote which is recognised as most backward taluk in Mysore district and Mysore taluk is most developed as per HPCFRRI report.

A Profile of State Bank of Mysore

STATE BANK OF MYSORE was established in the year 1913 as Bank of Mysore Ltd. under the patronage of the erstwhile Govt. of Mysore, at the instance of the banking committee headed by the great Engineer-Statesman, Late Dr. Sir M.Visvesvaraya. Subsequently, in March 1960, the Bank became an Associate of State Bank of India. State Bank of India holds 92.33% of shares. The Bank has grown progressively, right from its inception and has declared uninterrupted profits from the beginning. "MYSORE BANK", as it is popularly known, is constantly committed to serve its customers.

Branch Network

The Bank has a widespread network of 707 branches (as on 31.03.2011) and 22 extension counters spread all over India which includes 6 Small and Medium Enterprises Branches, 4 Industrial Finance branches, 3 Corporate Accounts Branches, 6 specialised Personal Banking Branches, 10 Agricultural Development Branches, 3 Government Business branches, 1 Asset Recovery Branch and 8 Service Branches, offering wide range of services to the customers.

Business Profile

Total deposits of the Bank as at the end of March 2011 is **Rs. 43225 Crores** and the total advances stood at Rs. 34442 Crores which include **export credit** of **Rs. 1260 Crores.** The Bank is a major player in foreign exchange dealings also and has achieved a merchant turnover of over Rs. 34342.96 Crores and a trading turnover of over Rs. 37658.49 Crores for the year ended March 2011.

Results and Discussion

The heritage district Mysore is well known for its historical and cultural remarks. Mysore district comprises 1350 revenue villages and currently 42 banks are working throughout the district. The number of bank branches is 360 in that 52 branches have been established through the SBM. In order to achieve the financial inclusion in rural area, SBM nominated 5 Business Correspondents to increase the banking habits in rural populace. In Mysore district, 298 ATMs are established for customer service in that 70 ATMs that is about (70/298%)are established by the SBM.

Financial inclusion has become a top task due to the emergence of inclusive growth strategy. SBM is the lead bank in the district and serves all communities in an egalitarian manner in order to uplift the economic condition of marginalised communities in the district. It advanced 2,229 lakhs for SC and ST communities in the total advancement of 3, 6036 lakhs during March 2012. It is working together with Self Help Groups and nearly 2, 8743 Self Help Groups have been linked with SBM in Mysore district.

Deposits

Total Deposits increased from Rs.38880 crores in March 2010 to Rs. 43225 crores in March, 2011 registering a growth of over 11% (Rs. 4345 crores). The focus was predominantly on CASA deposits which grew by over 21%. The Bank continued to restrict the growth of bulk deposits. Cost of Deposits declined to 5.56% from 6.01%, mainly owing to increase in CASA share from 31.06% to 33.97%.

Kalyan (Mybank Raithamitra): Krishi Kalyan provides for simultaneous sanction of crop loans and produce loans facilitating farmers to avoid distress sale and fetch remunerative prices for their produce.

SME Sector

While continuing with all the existing products and schemes introduced to take care of the varying financial needs of the sector, the Bank has introduced during the year, several new schemes for micro and small enterprises viz., - MYBANK-SME Welcome, DALLMILLS PLUS, SBM DOCTOR PLUS, and SME Shoppe. Bank also entered into tie-up arrangements with reputed truck and tractor manufacturers for extending hassle-free loans to transport operators and farmers. Micro Sector Collateral Free loan scheme provides for sanction of loans up to Rs.10.00 lakhs without any collateral security or third party guarantee, (increased from Rs. 5 lakhs).

Branch Expansion

The Bank opened 17 General Banking Branches and one Cash Management Branch during the year. The total branch network of branches as on 31st March 2011 stood at 707 for India, which includes 571 branches in the State of Karnataka.

Smart Cards

To promote Branch-less Banking, Smart Cards are introduced in rural areas enabling the card holders to avail banking facilities in remote places under the Business Correspondent Model. Besides facilitating normal banking business, these cards enable the beneficiaries to receive payments under MGNREGA and Social Security Pensions (SSP) even in remote villages where no banking facilities are available. The Bank has participated in implementing financial inclusion Programme by issue of Smart Cards for the purpose of Electronic Benefit Transfer (EBT) payments in Bellary and Chitradurga Districts.

Saral Savings Bank Account (No Frills Account)

This account comes with very low minimum balances as well as low/nil charges, to cater to the needs of individual from the vast sections of population who are, otherwise, not fulfilling certain conditions of our existing Savings Bank requirements;

Table 2: SBM Criteria to Open no-frill Account

Purpose	To enable the common man to open/ maintain bank account at no cost.
Eligibility	Individuals of 18 years and above.
Available at	Presently in Rural Branches only.
Initial Deposit amount	Rs. 10/-
Minimum balance to be maintained	Zero.
Minimum balance /amount	If the value of business connection including interalia, the other liability products like Recurring Deposit or Term Deposit, exceed Rs. 10,000/- the account will be upgraded to normal SB account.
Rate of Interest	As applicable to Savings Bank from time to time.
Operation of the account and applicable charges	Cheque facility will not be extended on this account. Withdrawals will be made through withdrawal forms. Maximum 4 withdrawals per calendar month. No restrictions on deposits in the account.
Account opening procedure	Extant procedure for opening a SB account will be applicable.
Whether ATM card facility/ standing instructions/ overdraft facility is available?	Not available.
Nomination	As applicable to deposit accounts.

Source: SBMs annual report 2011.

Table 3: No Frill Account Holders in the Selected Samples

Mysore Taluk				*H.D.Kote Taluk*			
Total respondents	*100*	*Male* 69	*female* 31	*Total respondents*	*100*	*Male* 62	*Female* 38
Number of account holders	68	52	16	Number of account holders	51	42	09
No frill accounts	23	17	06	No frill accounts	17	14	03

Source: Primary data

The above table reveals that the number of account holders in Mysore taluk is 68 out of a sample of 100 in that 52 are males and 16 are females. The number of no frill account holders among them is 23, out of which 17 are males and 6 females. Where as in H.D. Kote the number of account holders are 51 in that 42 are males and 09 females. The number of no frill account holders among them is 17 in that 14 and 03 are males and females respectively. It is found that the criteria of no frill account have still not reached many households in both the taluks and it is very low particularly in H.D. Kote taluk. It is found that only few households have opened no frill accounts and they were made under MG-NREGA programme. This implies that the bank's role towards financial inclusion in H.D. Kote taluk has been minimal. Mysore taluk has shown improving trends where as H.D. Kote taluk has not achieved to a greater extent due to rare banking penetration and low level of financial literacy as observed during data collection. Further, the data clearly reflects that financial inclusion of women is very low in both the taluks indicating gender disparities.

Automatic Teller's Machine

An ATM is a machine in which routine banking transactions can be done by customers on their own without any intervention of Bank Staff. The Bank has 785 ATMs and all are networked. The SBMs ATMs are part of over 26814 ATMs of the State Bank Group as on 31.01.2012. In Mysore district 298 ATM cash withdrawal points are established by nearly 42 banks among which 70 ATM points are established through SBM. State Bank Group ATM Cards is available to the customers without any charge for the first year and Annual Service Charge of Rs. 100/- will be levied from second year onwards.

Table 4: ATM Cardholders in the Selected Samples of Study Area

Mysore Taluk				*H.D.Kote Taluk*			
Total respondents	*100*	*Male*	*female*	*Total respondents*	*100*	*Male*	*Female*
		69	*31*			*62*	*38*
ATM holders	16	14	02	ATM holders	04	04	00

Source: Primary data.

It is found that the usage behavior of banking technologies like ATM card is very poor in H.D. Kote taluk compared to Mysore taluk where only 16 account holders have ATM cards in Mysore taluk and 04 in H.D. Kote taluk respectively out of 100 samples considered for this study. The female ATM holders are nil in H.D. Kote taluk in the selected samples. This situation implies that both the taluk accounted low financial inclusion in terms of using of updated banking gadgets and dismal situation in case of females.

Internet Banking Services

The Internet banking portal of SBI bank enables both retail banking and corporate banking customers to operate their accounts across India, removing the restrictions imposed by geography and time. It's a platform that enables the customers to carry out their banking activities from their desktop, aided by the power and convenience of the Internet.

Mobile Banking Services

State Bank Freedom–Your Mobile Your Bank

The service is presently available on java enabled mobile phones over SMS/ GPRS/ WAP as also non java phones with GPRS connection. The service can be availed over the free GPRS facilities offered by various mobile service providers.

The following functionalities will be provided:

- Funds transfer (within and outside the bank –using NEFT).
- Enquiry services (Balance enquiry/Mini statement).
- Request services (cheque book request).
- Bill Payment (Utility bills, credit cards).
- M Commerce (Mobile Top Up, Merchant payment, SBI life insurance premium).

Advances

Total advances of the Bank reached Rs. 34442 crores in March 2011, registering a growth of over 15% over the previous year. The focus was predominantly on small loans including micro/ small enterprises, agricultural sector and other retail sector, which recorded a growth rate of over 23% year on year. While SBMs priority sector advances recorded a growth of over 28% year on year, loans to micro and small enterprises grew by over 47%. Under personal segment, housing loans grew by Rs. 386 crores and vehicle loans grew by Rs. 57 crores. The Bank has lent Rs. 3658 crores to MSE sector, Rs. 5378 crores to Agriculture, Rs. 2981 crores to housing, and Rs. 560 crores to Education.

Table 5: SBMs Taluk wise advances during 2011-12 in Mysore District

Taluk	*Allocation (in crores)*	*Percentage*
Mysore	1192.55	51%
Periyapatna	303.55	13%
Hunsur	234.36	10%
Nanjangud	194.24	8%
K.R. Nagar	145.21	6%
T. Narsipur	136.44	5%
H.D. Kote	92.56	4%

Source: SBMs Annual Report 2011.

The above table reveals that SBM advanced Rs. 2,909.76 crore among all the seven taluks during 2011 financial year. In that, Mysore taluk had got major portion in the total allocation where H.D. Kote stood at least place in terms of total allocation advanced by SBM during 2011. This situation reveals the story that the efforts of SBM towards financial inclusion is very poor in H.D.Kote taluk where it got only 4% in the total allocation advanced by SBM during financial year 2011.

Other Dimensions of F I Used in this Study

Table 6: Analysis of the other Dimensions Concerned in this Study

Mysore Taluk				*H.D. Kote Taluk*			
Total respondents	*100*	*Male* *69*	*Female* *31*	*Total respondents*	*100*	*Male* *62*	*Female* *38*
Insurance holders	79	57	22	Insurance holders	68	49	19
Average distance	8km			Average distance	14km		
SHGs linkage	19			SHGs linkage	13		
Leading banks in the taluk	SBM, CGB and Karnataka Bank			Leading banks	SBM and CGB, Vijay Bank		

Source: Primary data.

In Mysore taluk, the number of insurance holders is 79 out of 100 samples selected in this study where as 68 insurance holders out of 100 samples were found in H.D. Kote taluk. The project like SHGs has the greater potentiality to reach the number of rural female beneficiaries through its banking linkage program. In this empirical study, 19 and 13 female respondents are being linked to SHGs in Mysore taluk and H.D. Kote taluk respectively. Only SHGs linkage program has shown improving trends in both the taluk and it is the only program which introducing the banking habits to the rural women. Self Help Groups are the carriers of micro finance. It is found that SHG initiatives are emerging as one of the powerful tools for rural transformation. It is certainly more sustainable and would deliver better if supported by state and NGOs. It is found that financial inclusion is being achieved through insurance and SHGs linkage programs in both the taluks.

It is found that the average distance of bank branches in Mysore and H.D. Kote taluk is 8 km and 14 km respectively. Both the taluks have experienced with rare banking penetration where villagers need to walk number of miles to meet the nearest branch. Many villages have crossed 5000 population and don't have any branch for their resource transformation.

Conclusion

It is a fact that Mysore district yet to reach number of miles in order to make the entire district bankable. State Bank of Mysore is extending financial services to all the taluks in the district but has not achieved the target to a larger extent. The Regional Rural Bank namely Cauvery Kalpatharu Grameena Bank has achieved significant growth in terms of branch expansion and number of account holders in that bank followed by Karnataka Bank. The taluk like H.D.Kote is experiencing rare banking penetration and low level of financial literacy and behind in all dimensions considered in this study. However, financial illiteracy, time consumption, high cost, distance etc., continue to be a road block to financial inclusion in many areas. Consequently, many banks are not adopting full fledged financial inclusion plan. The BC and BF models for financial inclusion approach need to be implemented rigorously and market channels have to be strengthened in the district particularly in H.D.Kote taluk. Only SHGs linkage program, MG-NREGA and insurance have shown improving trends in both the taluk and particularly SHGs is the only program which is introducing the banking habits to the rural women. Self Help Groups are the carriers of micro finance. The fiscal action like MG-NREGA has greater potential to link the banking services to the poor. Therefore financial services should channelise through increasing marketing operation thereby increasing banking habits among rural households.

Suggestions

The following are the suggestions recommended from this study to various beneficiaries like Banks and the Government:

- Many villages in the district have crossed above 5000 population but don't have banking facilities. Therefore banks need to establish branches in such villages.
- Banks should appoint business correspondent to disseminate its service to the unreached area.
- State Bank of Mysore can extend number of branches thereby reach the number of households throughout the district.
- But the bank should take special steps in the taluks like K.R. Nagar, T. Narsipur and H.D. Kote taluk because these taluks have not achieved significant growth towards financial inclusion.
- The BC and BF model for inclusion approach have to be strengthened further.
- The government should include financial literacy in the curriculum of schools and colleges.
- The government should pay all the social security payments through the bank account of the beneficiary. This would enhance the banking

habits among villagers and thereby pave the way for financial inclusion at gross root level.

- The national program like MG-NREGA has the greatest potentiality to reach the number of beneficiaries through the banking linkage activities. It has to be strengthened further and need to reduce the malpractices while implementing the program in the villages.

Bibliography

1. B. Sujatha, "Financial Inclusion – Concepts and Strategies" ICFAI University Press.
2. Report of "Committee on Financial Inclusion", Report submitted by Committee Headed by C. Rangarajan.
3. "Taking Banking Services to Common Man – Financial Inclusion" – Commemorative Lecture by Shri V. Leeladhar, Deputy Governor, Reserve Bank of India at the Fedbank Hormis Memorial Foundation at Ernakulam on December 2, 2005.
4. "Financial Inclusion – The Indian Experience" speech by Smt. Usha Thorat, Deputy Governor, Reserve Bank of India at the HMT-DFID Financial Inclusion C Whitehall Place, London, UK on June 19, 2007.
5. Fernandez, Aloysius P. (2006) -'The Role of Self Help Affinity Groups In Promoting Financial Inclusion of Landless and Marginal/Small Farmers' Families' MYRADA Bangalore.
6. Kempson, E. (2006) Policy Level Responsible To Financial Exclusion in Developed "Economies: Lesson for Developing Countries, Paper Presented at the conference, Access to Finance: Building Inclusive Financial Systems, World Bank, Washington, DC.
7. Basu, Priya (2005), "A Financial System for India's Poor". *Economic and Political Weekly,* September 10, 2005. pp. 4008-4012
8. Usha Thorat (2007). Financial Inclusion - the Indian Experience. Financial Inclusion Conference. London. BIS Review.
9. Vighneswara Swamy and Vijayalakshmi, "Role of Financial Inclusion for Inclusive Growth in India – Issues and Challenges".
10. http://www.planetd.org//financial-inclusion-in-india/
11. http://www.hindu.com/stories/2006073103551500.htm

41

Financial Exclusion: Causes and Consequences

Bhavya Shri B.

Introduction

The concept of financial inclusion is not old to India, the implementation of this concept was before few decades back and it as shown some positive results also. The banking industry have undergone some fundamental changes by adopting new technologies like introduction of insurance, debit and credit cards, internet backing, online money transformation system, ATM and many more things. In spite of all these developments some group of the society are far from not only from the advanced financial services but even from the basic services like access of personnel account. This is known as financial exclusion.

This group of society can be excluded from the behavior and regulations of financial institutions. Sometimes they get self excluded because they may not like the financial products offered by the institutions or they may assume that even if they apply they may not the service.

The term financial exclusion mainly refers to poor community of the society. Financial exclusion is the major concept of societal exclusion. Societal exclusion is the process by which people are discriminated on the basis of caste, race, age, HIV status, migration status etc. Thus the people who suffer from societal exclusion they are automatically excluded from the financial services.

Thus concept of financial inclusion has become world wide concern and it is very essential not only to under developed countries but important to developing and developed countries. Building of financial inclusion will create world wide recognition and this strategy should be developed to not only touch few lives but all lives in the world.

In particular, a number of other dimensions of financial exclusion have been identified (Kempson and Whyley, 1999a, 1999b):

- ***Access exclusion***: the restriction of access through the processes of risk assessment;
- ***Condition exclusion***: where the conditions attached to financial products make them inappropriate for the needs of some people;
- ***Price exclusion***: where some people can only gain access to financial products at prices they cannot afford;
- ***Marketing exclusion***: whereby some people are effectively excluded by targeting marketing and sales;
- ***Self-exclusion***: People may decide that there is little point applying for a financial product because they believe they would be refused. Sometimes this is a result of having been refused personally in the past, sometimes because they know someone else who has been refused, or because of a belief that 'they don't accept people who live round here'.

Objectives

1. To the features of financial exclusion form the view of stake holders
2. To know who are actually financially excluded.
3. To identify the main factors of financial exclusion.
4. To identify the causes of financial exclusion.
5. To show the effect or consequences of financial exclusion.
6. To show how wide the financial exclusion is spread.

Methodolgy

The whole paper work is purely based on secondary data i.e. literature review. Here paper first identifies the features of financial exclusion from the view point of stack holders then identifies what are the main causes of the financial exclusion and what are its effects and lastly it tries to explain how financial exclusion is spread across the country.

History of Fiancial Exclution

The term financial exclusion was first coined in 1993 by geographers who were concerned about limited physical access to banking services as a result of bank branch closures (Leyshon and Thrift, 1993). Throughout the 1990s there was also a growing body of research relating to difficulties faced by some sections of societies in gaining access to modern payment instruments and other banking services, to consumer credit and to insurance.

There was also concern about some people lacking savings of any kind. It was in 1999 that the term financial exclusion seems first to have been used in a broader sense to refer to people who have constrained access to mainstream financial services. Since then, a number of commentators have added their views of how financial exclusion should be defined. These include both academics and policy makers.

Features of Finacial Exclution from the View of Stake Holders

- ***True exclusion:*** this implies that many numbers of people are not able to access the financial products.
- ***Cost Exclusion:*** this means that some portion of the population is not able to meet the cost of the products.
- ***Unfair transaction:*** charging of high interest rate and charging some commission for ending of transaction.
- ***Unsafe products:*** It is mainly concerned with some products which does not give fair return on investment.

Who are Actually Excluded?

Financial inclusion is important to know whether every individual is getting appropriate financial services and help them to understand and access the financial services. Apart from regular financial services every individual should be aware and should access innovated financial products only then they can come out from financial exclusion.

Inclusion of finance does not mean every one who are included should access the products but they should have an ability to choose the relevant product which suites them.

In order to promote the financial inclusion the people who wish to access but denied to access should be addressed. There are situations where the individuals desire to access the services but they cannot access them. This can be seen in the countries like India which is having vast population they suffer from geographical dimensions. Inaccessibility, distance and infrastructure hinder financial inclusion.

Another factor which should be addressed is social exclusion. This is actually created when the people of one area or group faces the problem of poverty, unemployment, poor housing facility low income.

Main Factors that Influence Fiancial Exclution

- Lack of financial literacy is on of the important factors that are leading to financial exclusion. People with limited knowledge of financial products get sacred to investment on them because they assume that investing on those products may lead them to incur loss so it is very essential to spread the knowledge of financial products and the methodology in dealing them.
- Poverty is also a factor which will lead to financial exclusion lack of income will not allow the people to access the financial services and sometimes they may not have a proper asset to get loan from the financial institutions.

- Unemployment is another factor which leads to financial exclusion which often leads to poor qualification of credits and subsequently incurs low income.
- Various other factors like language problem, distance, psychological problem, cultural issues, availability of time or alternative products all these may drives to financial exclusion.

Causes of Fiancial Exclution

There are many factors which are causing financial exclusions and these factors are grouped into three category. They are:

1. Societal factors
2. Demand factors
3. Supply factors

Societal Factors

The various types of societal factors like caste, age, gender, poverty causes financial exclusion because lack of income or lack of knowledge regarding the financial products. This group of factors includes the broader socio-economic and demographic trends such as the ageing population, changing labor market structures, and political trends such as the transfer of risk and responsibility from state and employers to individuals. These also include liberalisation of financial markets, when people start getting various types of financial products they get confused and make some people difficult to access financial products and they remain out the boundary of financial exclusion.

The structural changes of labors markets, the inflexibility of job security is indirectly leads to unemployment which then leads to low income which then finally leads to financial exclusion.

Financial exclusion is also effected by demographic factors such as increase of diverse and young people leaving home at the young age and the tendency of the youth who this it is waste to invest on financial products.

Demand Factors

There are various obstacles which are not allowing people to access the various financial products offered by the institutions these may include:

1. Low level of financial literacy.
2. Consumer trust and confidence.
3. low levels of consumer awareness of the need to plan and provide for the future, or shop around for better deals.
4. Impact of external factors.

On demand side people may not access to financial products due to some psychological and cultural factors. Usually the group of elderly age may often think bank is the only place where they can safely keep their funds because of the fear of loosing their money. People are deterred from opening an account if it does not have an overdraft facility to ease access to money paid in. Delays in clearing cheques paid into an account mean that people cannot have instant access to any money paid in (Anderloni, 2003).

The only true measure of the success of financial capability interventions is whether are to be effective. Therefore, our strand of work in this area focuses on undertaking innovative research that provides real insight into how consumers behave in financial markets and identifying the interventions that are actually effective at promoting positive consumer behaviours.

The demand side causes for financial exclusion are as follows:

1. Low level of income: The population which is currently live below the poverty line cannot access or demand for the financial products and even they may not have stuffiest amount for the purpose of deposit.

2. Lack of financial literacy: Lack of financial literacy means improper knowledge on financial products. Low understanding capacity and low knowledge on mathematical calculation may lead to poor knowledge of financial products.

3. High cost: the terms and conditions of the services charges like transaction cost, high service cost will lead the poor population excluded from finance.

4. Misconception on financial institutions: Most of the times the poor population may think the financial products are not there cup of tea.

Supply Side

Sometimes the way that the financial institutions works is they may exclude some of the people from obtaining the services from them. The main obstacles are:

1. Basic economics of access
2. Inefficient regulation

On the supply side people may not be allowed access the financial services due their poor credit history, unstable employment or those who fail credit scoring system. The people who do not have a proper identity requirement may also fail to access products this mainly affects the migrated population who do not have a stable identity card. The countries which do not have a standard identity card may relay on pass port or driving license. Even the terms and conditions prescribed the instructions may become an obstacle to access the financial products that may be like minimum balance to open an account, transaction charges, monthly charges and many more.

However, even if these policies were 100% successful, the basic economics of access means that large numbers of consumers will always be economically unviable for mainstream financial providers. Radical, sustainable and innovative solutions are needed to meet the needs of these consumers. For example, we are working on the concept of social investment bonds to increase the pool of sustainable loan capital for third sector organisations such as credit unions and charities.

The supply side barriers of financial exclusion are as follows:

1. Location: Lack of transportation to reach the financial institutions which are located in far distance, poor infrastructure, inadequate numbers of financial institutions are creating financial exclusion.

2. Lending risk: Lending to the population which does not have credit worthiness is highly risky so the institution may avoid them and they leads to financial exclusion.

3. Poor credit record: The group of people who have poor credit records, bad past experience during the collection of loan will always lead them to be financially excluded.

4. Bank requirements: The valid identity cards will play a very important role in financial inclusion but when we look the poor or rural population they fail to have a proper identity proof which often makes them financially excluded.

Other Causes of Fiancial Exclution

Lack of Apporpriate Products: The financial institutions lacks in developing appropriate products for all the groups of the society. People with middle income group wants to access the services but looking the product cost and design they think even if they apply they may be rejected. So when the customers are not aware of the products which are suitable to them they try to come out from the financial institutions.

Affordability: It is also one of the most important obstacles for the use of financial services by the low income population. Some time they afford for the investment and suffer when they are charged for the use of those services. For e.g. The premium charged on the insurance policy is often high. A survey of savings and investments for low-income consumers concluded that 'the less money you have to save and invest, the more likely you are to pay a premium for the industry's savings and investment products – if you have access to them at all.' (Vass, 1997).

Psycological Barriers: Sometimes banks look disinterested with the people who have low income, even though banking societies have a positive shine. Some portion of the low income population tries to save their income in an informal way because they think that the institution may look them down when they deposit very few amount in their account.

Financial exclusion could be looked at in two ways:

Lack of access to financial services which could be due to several reasons such as:

- Lack of sources of financial services in our rural areas, which are popular for the ubiquitous money lenders but do not have (safe) saving deposit and insurance services.
- High information barriers and low awareness especially for women and in rural areas.
- Inadequate access to formal financial institutions that exist to the extent that the banks couldn't extend their outreach to the poor due to various reasons like high cost of operations, less volume and more number of clients, etc. among many others.
- Poor functioning and financial history of some beleaguered financial institutions such as financial cooperatives in many states which limit the effectiveness of their outreach figures.
- Primary Agricultural Cooperative Societies (PACS), which number around one lakh are also often exclusionary, as their membership is restricted to persons with land ownership. Even to their members, not many PACS offer saving services.

Lack of access to formal financial services in both rural and urban areas, but is a larger issue in cities and small towns. The distinction between access to formal and informal services is crucial to understand, as informal financial markets suffer from several imperfections, which the poor pay for in many ways. Some attributes of informal financial services, due to which there is exclusion, are:

- High risks to saving: loss of savings is an easily discernible phenomenon in low income neighbourhoods in urban areas.
- High cost of credit and exploitative terms: credit against collateral such as gold is even more expensive than the effective interest rates, similarly, rates paid by hawkers and vendors who repay on daily basis are very high.
- High cost and leakages in money transfers: the delays in sending money home through all informal channels add to these.
- Near absence of insurance and pension services: life, asset, and health insurance needs. Another key aspect of financial exclusion is the lack of "financial education and advice". (nabard.ogr- SBI)

Consequences of Financial Exclusion in India

Financial exclusion is not a new problem even now we can observe wide range of population do not have access to financial services. However the consequence of access to the use of financial products like insurance, credit and many more have become serious than what it was in the past. Being the small portion of financial excluded have become more serious.

The consequences of financial exclusion on the individual and the society must not be underestimated. Those unable to access finance for enterprise development or personal consumption have greater difficulties in integrating socially and economically. No access to financial services may bar people from accessing vital services and activities, including employment, as some companies pay their employee's wages by electronic transfer only. Equally, financially excluded people can have difficulty participating in mainstream social activities and events specific to their cultural reference group. Financial exclusion also results in less ability to face financial shocks and unexpected expenses. People excluded from savings services are more vulnerable to theft, as they are forced to keep their cash and savings at home. Moreover, people excluded from financial services such as cheques and transfers by the mainstream financial sector are likely to turn to institutions that offer these services at a much higher price. This is also true for access to credit, as people who are refused credit from mainstream financial institutions are forced to turn to private intermediaries or informal moneylenders, who charge more and offer less favorable conditions, further exacerbating their vulnerability and exclusion, and putting them at risk of becoming over-indebted.

The consequences of financial exclusion are as follows:

Bank Facilities

Lack of banking facilities will create more problems, because people now make heavy use of banking facilities which helps to have a fast transaction. Lack of bank account or banking services may leads complexity in the management of cash and safety of cash. It is important to know that lack of banking facilities is not only apply to those who do not have current account, but also people who have only account facilities and far from advanced financial services. The impact of this is as follows:

- People without banking account may face difficulties in encashment of their cheque which is drawn by the third party. In this situation the people who do not have banking facility have to pay some fee to encash their cheque.
- Lack of bank account may make the bills payment more costly.
- The cost of banking services will be high to the person who does not have a continuous relation with the institution than the person who has close relation with the bank. The services which is occasionally done like tax payment, money order from the bank counter, cashing cheques and may more will be expensive than the customer of the bank.

- Being out of formal method of saving may create problem, because the people who follow informal method may rarely get benefits from tax advantage and interest rate than the people who follow formal method of saving.
- Some times the people who follow informal method of saving do not have security for the amount saved by them.
- In the absence of credit facilities savings will only be the last path to meet uncertain situations. So if proper savings are not done they may not be able to meet even the household expenses.
- Saving is the important resource for the people to supplement their income during the old age. If proper saving is not done it may lead to poverty.

Pension

- Those without any private pension provision are forced to rely totally on a state retirement pension linked to prices, rather than incomes, which may need to be topped up with means-tested social security benefits. This can be problematic for many older people, who are strongly resistant to claiming income related benefits and who are prepared to face the stigma of doing so only as a last resort (see, for example, Finch and Elam, 1995). However, even the state retirement pension topped up with Income Support and other means-tested benefits is not intended to provide more than a basic minimum income that covers no more than essentials and has little leeway for unforeseen expenditure.
- People, who have made inadequate private pension provision, rather than none at all, also face a problem. People in these circumstances risk falling into the trap of having too small a pension on which to live comfortably, but too high an income from a private pension to qualify for state-benefits. As a consequence, they are little better off than those who have made no private pension provision at all. Also they must live with the knowledge that they have been penalised in old age for their thrift earlier on in life.

Magnitude of Fiancial Exclusion in India

Financial exclusion is experienced by both developing and developed economies alike. The World Bank estimates that 2.7 billion people, over half the population of the developing world, live on less than US$2 a day. Reserve Bank of India data shows that as many as 139 districts suffer from massive financial exclusion in India, with the adult population per branch in these districts being above 20,000 and only 3 per cent with borrowings from banks. On the assumption that each adult has only one bank account (which does not hold good in practice, so that actual coverage is likely to be worse) on an all India basis, 59 per cent of the adult population in the country has bank accounts. 41 per cent of the population is, therefore, unbanked. In rural areas the coverage is 39 per cent against 60 per cent in urban areas.

The unbanked population is higher in the poorer regions of the country, and is the worst in the North-Eastern and Eastern regions. Out of 203 million households in the country, 147 million are in rural areas 89 million are farmer households. 51.4 per cent of farm households have no access to formal or informal sources of credit while 73 per cent have no access to formal sources of credit. (nabard.ogr- SBI)

According to the NSSO data, the total 45.9 million farmer households in the country (51.4%), out of a total of 89.3 million households do not accesses credit, either from institutional or no institutional sources. Further, despite the vast network of bank branches, only 27% of total farm households are indebted to formal sources (of which one-third also borrow from informal sources). Farm households' not accessing credit from formal sources as a proportion to total farm households is especially high at 95.91%, 81.26% and 77.59% in the North Eastern, Eastern and Central Regions respectively. Thus, apart from the fact that exclusion in general is large, it also varies widely across regions, social groups and asset holdings. The poorer the group, the greater is the exclusion.

Conclusion

It is important to know that financial exclusion is not absolute concept rather than separate from the financial services due to the reason of poverty. People vary with the extent of using financial services. People who have just banking account transaction are also called as financially excluded. Among the three types of financial exclusion i.e. demand, supply and social factors. The demand and supply problems can be easily identified and remedial actions can be implemented.

Financial exclusion is closely related with social exclusion and the relation is demonstrated throughout the country. So people should at least have access to basic banking transaction and be socially included. There is also a widely made argument that access to banking is important for the economic development of a country (World Bank CGAP). Policy makers should consider financial exclusion issues in all courses of action regarding social exclusion or poverty.

Exclusion from mainstream financial services can be costly. Annualised interest rates in the alternative financial sector are often as high as 200%, and a family that uses cheque-cashing outlets to convert its paychecks into cash can easily devote 3% of its income just to obtain this simple service. In recent years, several policy measures have been implemented in an effort to increase the percentage of low-income households using mainstream financial services. In many cases, however, these measures have not directly addressed the fundamental causes of financial exclusion, the measures have been quite limited in scale or scope, or the effectiveness of the measures has not been carefully assessed.

Finally the main policy which as to be implemented to come from the social and economical consequences of financial exclusion is to fill the gap of financial information in the society. People should be educated regarding to trade financial products, the spread of negative information regarding loss on investment on financial products should be reduced. Research on the impact of financial exclusion on people facing it is essential to better understand the financial inclusion issue and its place and necessity within the wider frame of the social inclusion policy of a country. Moreover, that knowledge is essential to underline and justify the important role that financial institutions corporate social responsibility can play to ensure financial inclusion. All stakeholders (researchers, NGOs, financial institutions and policy makers) should therefore aim to carry out or/and finance further research on the subject.

Bibliography

1. Financial service provision and prevention of financial exclusion (European Commission).
2. Anderloni, L. and Carluccio, E. (2006) 'Access to Bank Accounts and Payment Services', in Anderloni L, E Carluccio and M Braga, New Frontiers in Banking Services: Emerging Needs and Tailored Products for Untapped Markets. Berlin: Springer Verlag.
3. Kempson, E., J. Caskey, C. Whyley and S. Collard (2000): "*In or Out*?" London: Financial Services Authority.
4. Report of the Committee on Financial Inclusion in India (Chairman: C. Rangarajan) (2008), Government of India.
5. Kempson, E. (2006): "Policy Level Response to Financial Exclusion in Developed Economies: Lessons for Developing Countries", Paper for Access to Finance: Building Inclusive Financial Systems, World Bank, Washington, May.
6. Kempson, E. (1997). Understanding financial exclusion. (Unpublished.)
7. Thorat Usha (2007), "Financial Inclusion –The Indian experience" RBI Monthly Bulletin, Dec. 2007, pp. 1165-1172.
8. Financial Exclusion: Concept, Nature and Extent by Mahendra Mishra.
9. Mohan, Rakesh (2006), Economic Growth, Financial Deepening and Financial Inclusion, Reserve bank of India, bulletin, November 2006, pp. 1305-1319.
10. Duvvuri Subbarao (2010), "Financial Inclusion; Challenges and Opportunities" RBI Monthly Bulletin, Jan 2010, pp. 1-10.
11. Conroy, J. (2005), APEC and Financial Exclusion: Missed Opportunities for Collective Action? Asia-Pacific Development Journal, 12(1), June 2005.
12. Carbo S., Gardener E.P., Molyneux P., 2005. *Financial Exclusion.* Palgrave MacMillan.

13. Rangarajan Committee, 2008, "Report of the Committee on Financial Inclusion", Committee Report.
14. Sinclair S.P., 2001. "Financial Exclusion: An introductory survey", Report of Centre for Research in Socially Inclusive Services, Heriot-Watt University, Edinburgh.
15. Satya R. Chakravarty and Rupayan Pal Measuring Financial Inclusion: An Axiomatic Approach.
16. Reserve Bank of India. Government of India: *Economic Survey* (various years), Government of India New Delhi.

Web Site Links

http://www.european-microfinance.org/cause-et-consequence_en.php

http://www.scribd.com/doc/77545057/6/Causes-of-Financial-Exclusion

http://www.nabard.org/departments/pdf/seminar/State%20Bank%20of%20India%20-%20Documentation.pdf

http://www.smeworld.org/story/money/indian-financial-inclusion-scenario.php

http://www.scribd.com/doc/47323243/2/CONSEQUENCES-OF-FINANCIAL-EXCLUSION

http://www.publicnet.co.uk/features/2008/10/24/tackling-financial-exclusion/

http://www.jrf.org.uk/publications/understanding-and-combating-financial-exclusion

http://www.igidr.ac.in/pdf/publication/WP-2012-013.pdf

http://india.microsave.org/node/1270

42

Financial Inclusion and Inclusive Growth through Microfinance in India

V. Basil Hans

"*There are six things one needs: roti, (food), kapada (clothing), makan (housing), primary health, primary education and primary banking*"

– Ela Bhatt (Mother of Micro-finance in India, Founder of SEWA).

Introduction

India's deficits in social sector and the recent economic slowdown are well-known. There are several gaps in attaining the Millennium Development Goals (MDGs). The Eleventh Five Year Plan gave a country-wide call for "faster and more inclusive growth". The Key challenges spelt out in the Approach Paper to the Twelfth Five Year Plan (2012-2017) clearly indicate the vision for social-economic and political empowerment across sectors and sections (Hans, 2012a). Therefore, it is necessary to have a re-look at the philosophy and agenda of "inclusive growth". At the same time we need to take into account the progress in the sphere of "financial inclusion", particularly through the empowering tool of "micro-finance" in India. Although the objective is to assess the impact of micro-finance on 'growth' the broader issues are that of 'development', i.e. whether micro-finance has succeeded in achieving economic growth with change, taking into account even the related aspects like 'management', governance etc. The present article is a small attempt in that direction.

Financial Inclusion – Concept, Structure, Strategies and Growth

What most developing countries have realised in recent times is that poverty is largely an issue of sustainability or its absence. Poor are those who lack access to sustainable financial resources or services like savings, credit and insurance (Venkataramaraju and Ramesh, 2011). Inaccessibility results in isolation and exclusion from the very process of growth. This negates the attempts at poverty eradication and ensuring livelihood security to all because looking at 'development' from the prism of democracy it requires the involvement and contribution of the people, by the people and for the people. According to the United Nations the main goals of inclusive finance are as follows (en.wikipedia.org, 2012):

- Access at a reasonable cost of all households and enterprises to the range of financial services for which they are "bankable," including savings, short and long-term credit, leasing and factoring, mortgages, insurance, pensions, payments, local money transfers and international remittances
- Sound institutions, guided by appropriate internal management systems, industry performance standards, and performance monitoring by the market, as well as by sound prudential regulation where required
- Financial and institutional sustainability as a means of providing access to financial services over time
- Multiple providers of financial services, wherever feasible, so as to bring cost-effective and a wide variety of alternatives to customers (which could include any number of combinations of sound private, non-profit and public providers).

Despite the critical importance of access to financial services for achieving equitable economic development, in most developing countries, a large segment of the population particularly the low-income and vulnerable sections of the society has very little or no access to financial services from formal financial system. It is estimated that globally over two million people are currently excluded from the access to financial services (UN, 2006). They normally depend on their own limited resources or informal sources of finance at exorbitantly exploitative terms. Unless financial services are inclusive, the benefit of financial services is likely to elude many individuals and enterprises, thereby denying much of the population the benefit of growth opportunities. The emergence and growth of micro-finance and its corollary, the self help groups (SHGs) should also be analysed in this context. The 'why' and 'how' of financial inclusion through micro-finance and its strengths and limitations are to be addressed and assessed critically.

Essentially inclusion is active (productive) contribution of the people for their economic security, sustainability and well-being. Financial inclusion, thus, is not merely an exercise of lifting people above the poverty line, but also a safety net against future economic shocks and disturbances. The impact of measures for financial inclusion, therefore, has to be assessed and analysed in a multi-dimensional framework, including individuals, households, communities and regions; food, nutrition, health, education and entitlements; work, wages and productivity; and assets (wealth), income and welfare at all levels. In combating poverty both means and end become significant. Rightly therefore, a positive impact of micro-finance may be a better education or nutritional status, accumulation of productive and consumptive assets (including entrepreneurship), women empowerment, networking of local organisations, mobilisation of resources, mobility of people etc. The net result is creating a plan(k) of inclusive growth contributing to quantitative and qualitative growth of human capital, physical capital and social capital (Jayasheela, 2007). Financial inclusion is never complete, without individual, social and institutional sustainability, simultaneously. It is enabling and enveloping people who are the victims of vulnerability, disparity, division and marginalisation.

The Rangarajan Committee (2008) defined the concept of financial inclusion as "the process of ensuring access to financial services and timely and adequate credit where needed by vulnerable groups such as weaker sections and low income groups at an affordable cost". In a restricted sense, it means extending banking to the unreached and the excluded areas (Venkataramaraju and Ramesh, 2011). More and more access to financial and institutional credit services is the very purpose of financial inclusion (Heggade and Rashmi, 2012). Financial inclusion, thus, is a working solution to the opposite phenomenon of "financial divide" or "financial exclusion". Accessibility – and not simply availability and affordability – is the key parameter of financial inclusion (Serrao, Sequeira and Hans, 2011) and a pre-requisite of poverty reduction and social cohesion (Jayasheela, Dinesha and Hans, 2008; Dubey, 2011). The diversity and range of financial services matter for making accessibility a reality. The range of financial services include the entire gamut of financial products – cheque accounts, saving products, loans, debit cards, credit cards, insurance and healthcare services and the financial services such as payment services, remittance services and other transfer and advisory and counselling. According to NABARD by including "no frills banking account" as well as value added services like insurance to the regular form of "financial intermediation", the objective is to develop a "comprehensive financial inclusion". The reach and returns from such inclusive policy and programme depend, largely on "financial literacy" and "financial counselling" and "financial education" (even as a part of consumer education)[1] which by themselves are vital issues and challenges in the pursuit of financial inclusion.

Including people in any financial programme or development activity, is to make them more responsive and responsible to their own livelihoods. Comprehensive financial inclusion ensures combining of endogenous and exogenous factors that initiate a process of empowerment at the household level (say decision-making in the family) to the level of the community (say management of common property resources) and the region. Well-designed financial education initiatives can reduce demand-side barriers to more effective financial inclusion and can empower vulnerable individuals economically, so that they can better manage household resources and develop income generating activities (Messy and Monticone, 2012). Coupled with timely reforms at the supply-side, this enhances the status of financial inclusion and paves the way for inclusive growth. That is the reason why financial inclusion strategies need to be 'revolutionary' (Arunachalam, 2008). While retaining the growth urge and development impulses, the beneficiaries have to help themselves to move beyond income poverty. The stakeholders (borrowers, savers, banks, cooperatives, service providers, and the civil society) have to develop mechanisms of "social intermediation" as well. The habits of social investment and intermediation will come into play here. There is need for investing in social values in individuals and communities, values basically summarised as fundamental human rights, social cohesion and sustainability (Hans, 2008).

With manifold needs and multiple stages of saving-investing-spending and varied agencies in financial inclusion there have to be different approaches and strategies too. Pragmatically, the following strategies could help (Naidu, Krishna and Nanduri, n.d.)

- Segmentation of the poor.
- Operating through client associations.
- Innovative technologies.
- Customised product/service design.
- Multi-stakeholder partnerships.
- Apex body.

Segmentation should be made on the basis of occupation (e.g. salaried/ self-employed; vendors, auto-drivers etc) and income-flow patterns, as well as credit needs, nature of risk, bankability etc. Client associations need to be rural or urban specific in terms of culture, costs and clientele. It could be an existing social or cultural association or a new one for the purpose of mobilising financial resources. Technologies should be in-built to the system of finance, ranging from a simple mobile banking to ATM, smart card operating system, kiosks etc. Products and service destining and delivery must be interwoven with the needs, size and spatial distribution of the segments. For example, a self-employed person like vegetable vendor will be happy with daily/weekly loans, whereas a teacher with monthly loans, sex workers may need health loans/insurance and so on. Multi-stakeholder partnership gives provides for structure, strength and networking of the financial system, with its agencies like banks, Non Governmental Organisations (NGOs), Micro Finance Institutions (MFIs) etc., smoothly. Besides organising the resources and their flows, it ensures shared resources, risks and returns.

The need for an apex body for the federal system of finance needs no overemphasis. For enlisting the support and cooperation of all stakeholders and fair game-play an agency like the NABARD is needed.

United Kingdom was one of the forerunners of the system of financial inclusion (2004). India picked up in the same year. The Reserve Bank of India (RBI) set up the Khan Commission in 2004 to look into financial inclusion. In the report RBI exhorted the banks with a view of achieving greater financial inclusion to make available a basic "no-frills" banking account. In India, financial inclusion first featured in 2005, when it was introduced by K.C. Chakraborthy, the Chairman of Indian Bank. Mangalam Village[2] became the first village in India where all households were provided banking facilities. Norms were relaxed for people intending to open accounts with annual deposits of less than Rs. 50,000. General credit cards (GCCs) were issued to the poor and the disadvantaged with a view to help them access easy credit. In January 2006, the RBI permitted commercial banks to make use of the services of non-governmental organisations (NGOs/SHGs), MFIs, and other civil society organisations as intermediaries for providing financial and banking services. These intermediaries could be used as business facilitators or business correspondents by commercial banks. The bank asked the commercial banks in different regions to start a 100 per cent financial inclusion campaign on a pilot basis. As a result of the campaign states or Union Territories like Pondicherry, Himachal Pradesh and Kerala announced 100 per cent financial inclusion in all their districts. The vision of RBI for 2020 is to open nearly 600 million new customers' accounts and service them through a variety of channels by leveraging on IT. However, illiteracy and the low income savings and lack of bank branches in rural areas continue to be a roadblock to financial inclusion in many states and there is inadequate legal and financial structure.

In India the drive for financial inclusion has thus far, involved ensuring access to at lest one zero minimum-balance 'no frills' savings bank account to every household. At least one district in each state has been brought under the purview of this drive with public sector taking the lead and SHGs being active partners in a linkage programme. This has succeeded in bringing the poverty and the needy into the fold of formal (organise) sector of finance to seize the opportunities of systematic and productive saving, borrowing and investing.

Inclusive Growth – Perspective and Prospects

Inclusive growth – implying an equitable allocation of resources with benefits accruing to every section of the society – is apparently a utopian concept and hence elusive. Yet for developing countries like India, already under the influence of the 'welfare state' concept, inclusive growth is ideal and practical. It is being built into the schema of planned economic development. Inclusive growth is also referred to as "broad-based growth", "shared growth" and "pro-poor growth", although these terms can be clearly distinguished form one another. Basically it implies an equitable allocation of resources and benefits accruing to all sections of society, both in the short-run and long-run (Hans and Deepika, 2011).

While traditional problems of inequality and poverty are still the core issues of development, in the globalisation process it is imperative that faster and healthy growth has to be inclusive. Better utilisation of resources focussing on human development needs amalgamation of growth-increasing and equity-ensuring polices and action. The concept of inclusive growth has its origin and dimensions of the concept of inclusive growth as also its socio-economic impact, as it directs the strategists. There are also people's expectations from inclusive growth, given the characteristic of dualism in the developing economies.

The planned economy of India saw a sudden U-turn from 1990 (Aziz, 1996). In the 1990s, while poverty eradication still remained a plan objective, the economy was opened for the philosophy and practice of liberalisation, privatisation and globalisation, as a response to the huge balance of payments deficits, heavy external borrowings etc. of the country. New and more growth opportunities emerged for consumers as well as producers. Globalisation, however, did not guarantee equal pace and pattern and return of growth endeavours and enterprises for all. While the overall growth rate was impressive ranging from 6 to 9 per cent, agricultural sector almost stagnated at 2 to 2.5 per cent growth. Institutional and infrastructural deficits in development came to be highlighted. The rural populace felt the brunt of 'divide' and disparity leading to marginalisation and 'exclusion'. The problems of girls and women in terms of educational and health deficits etc became issues of debate, discussion and policy formulation. This led to the emergence of concepts and catch phrases like "growth with a human face", "gender empowerment" and emphasis on human development and its indicators like mean years of schooling, expected years of schooling, life expectancy at birth and per-capita national income etc.

The Eleventh Five Year Plan boldly and brightly focussed on the problem of exclusion, the very subtitle of the Plan document being "Towards Faster and More Inclusive Growth". There is no retracting from planning rather protracting its tools and techniques for the realisation of the inclusion agenda. The emphasis is not only on "growth in income" but also on its outcomes for the poor. The Plan singled out "the type of growth", rather than growth *per se*, as an important element of inclusive growth strategy. The growing acceptance of concepts like inclusion and exclusion to explain inequality, discrimination and deprivation by us is itself indicative of inadequacies among various conceptual tools in vogue earlier (Hans, 2010a; Thorat 2011). It is new growth philosophy that addresses the issues of development and disparity at one stroke. It is a programme of co-governance of people. Citizens, beneficiaries of programmes and users of infrastructure are now treated as co-designers of the concerned methodologies. Reforms in governance are focussing on the effective and efficient delivery of public services (Hans, 2011; Vayunandan and Mathew, 2003). Governance is now being recognised as the instrument both for growth and gender equity. Governance first and last is about the exercise of power to achieve political, social, and other objectives. Governance can easily be embedded in empowerment and ensuring good governance is strategically included in inclusive growth philosophy and policy. In India, where half the population is female, women empowerment approach to development brings turnaround of gender role – a shift from 'women for development' to 'women in development' (Hegde and Hans, 2012).

While efforts are on at making administration accountable and citizen-friendly, social, cultural, political and technological factors are considered together with the economic determinants of development. More than introducing new schemes and programmes governments appear more inclined in giving facelift to the existing ones in order to make them more meaningful with political correctness and economic wisdom for people's prosperity by participatory approach. Aspirations and actions for affirmation, autonomy, devolution, decentralisation, ICT initiatives and e-governance along with minimum (yet critical) state intervention have become the 'bounded' growth curriculum today. Convergence of managed globalisation and good governance are attempted in the counter of inclusive growth.

Micro-finance: Initiatives and Impact

The inclusive growth perspective being people-centred approach includes all the dimensions of development in a holistic and synergic manner. To achieve the goal of inclusive growth micro-finance was introduced to meet small financial needs of poor, strengthening of rural sector, development of entrepreneurial activities, employment, economic growth, social cohesion, financial sustainability, eradication of global poverty and human capital development. Micro-finance[3] is thus, an innovative tool to articulate social justice in economic growth perspective through financial inclusion.

The Declaration of Micro Credit Summit held in Washington D.C. in 1997 defined micro-credit programmes as those "extending small loans to poor people for self-employment projects that generate income, allowing them to car for themselves and their families." A micro-finance is a financial cum employment (peer) support programme. NABARD in 2000 defined micro-finance as the "provision of thrift, credit and other financial services and products of very small amounts to the poor in rural, semi-urban or urban areas enabling them to raise their income levels and improve living standards". It is a financial business for market business for individual and the group.[4]

A borrower can take a loan, make a product, sell it and make profit, and save in the group that again helps borrowers/investors. It is a circular flow of credit where members partake-take-make. The salient features of micro-finance thus are:

- Very small loans: amount and duration-wise.
- Loans offered without collaterals.
- Formation of borrower groups.
- Focus on rural/urban poor.
- Loans for income-generation through market.
- High frequency of repayment.
- Private mechanism of NGO or SHG control/management as far as funds, rules and regulations etc.

Traditional banking and financial services in India, howsoever, vast and vibrant it could be was criticised as being largely target and supply driven. The financial products/services were not flexible and user-friendly both in design and delivery. Corruption, unproductive borrowing and high rate of default made the formal financial sector (including banks and co-operative societies) unsuccessful in mitigating poverty. It had failed to recognise the divergence between the hierarchies of credit needs and credit availability. Typical micro credit for the poorer sections of the society was lacking. Now the self help groups and MFIs (MFIs[5]) emerged to fill this gap. With both governments and NGOs focussing on people's empowerment through group-based approach the road to financial inclusion was paved. The main inspiration came from Bangladesh (Grameen Bank Model, 1976) where more than 70 per cent of rural households had financial access compared to about 5 per cent in India. Different models of micro-finance are in operation, the SHG-Bank linkage model (launched in 1992 by NABARD) being the most popular and viable. There followed a momentous growth of MFIs, SHGs etc.

The key factor in rapid growth in micro-finance business is reduction in transaction costs. They enable the poor the break the vicious circle of poverty/usury and convert to the virtuous circle of well-being (Biradar, Naik and Pargonda, 2010). Recognising micro-finance as an important instrument to fight poverty the United Nations declared 2005 as "International Year of Micro Credit".[6]

The RBI said that critical exclusion (in terms of credit) is manifest in 256 districts across 17 states and one Union Territory, with a credit gap of 95 per cent and above. With the phenomenal growth of SHGs, more than 409 lakh poor households gained access to micro-finance by March 2007 (Dinesha and Jayasheela, 2008). India's MFIs reached 76.6 million in 2009 with about 9 million clients during the year. Between 2007-08 and 2008-09 there was a growth of 60 per cent over the previous year. More than 50 per cent of low income households are covered by some form of micro-finance product.

The total outstanding micro-finance loans posted a growth rate of 30 per cent or 359.39 billion over the previous year's level of 229.54 billion. The SHG loan outstanding increased by Rs. 71.5 billion with an addition of 6.9 million clients. MFIs so far reached 234 of the 331 poorest districts identified by the government (Naaraayana, 2009).

Subsequently there has been a lull, nay a downward trend as reported in the "Global Microscope on the Microfinance Business Environment, 2011". Borrowers' base growth decreased from 43 per cent to 7.5 per cent and the growth rate of loan portfolio size from 76 per cent to 7.2 per cent. The Andhra Pradesh micro-finance crisis is an alarming bell for India as a whole (Azad, 2011).

What is special about micro-finance is that it leads not merely to financial inclusion but slowly but steadily to social inclusion and empowerment too. The success stories of many SHGs of women amply demonstrate this. Micro-finance has energised social mobility and developed social capital through financial and entrepreneurial progress and contributions. Negotiating or negating problems of gender bias, illiteracy, lack of basic facilities like food and housing is now possible, with resilience. Subsidiary occupations to women, development of small agribusinesses, progress in women leadership and skill management are signs of sustainable diversification and modernisation. Micro-finance has been revolutionising the rural economy through the SHGs (Hans, 2010b). Economic empowerment has changed the economic environment in most villages of India with SHGs emerging as avenue for sustainable development not only initiating and monitoring micro-credit programmes and micro enterprises but also enhancing the degree of equality of members, decision-makers and beneficiaries in the democratic, economic, social and cultural spheres of life (Seerengarajan and Narasimhan, 2008).

Unfinished Tasks in Inclusive Growth

Poverty reduction is a long-term process of elimination of the dependency of the poor on social/political receipts (and relations?), and of vulnerability with respect to changes in their environment. Therefore, real impact of micro-finance lies in creation of strong and substantial resources and assets with long-term income flows that have bearing on the sustainable livelihood of the poor.

Essentially the success of any micro-credit programme depends on knowledge, access to and management of resources, creation of assets, rise in family income as well as social status, individually and collectively. Micro-finance needs to combat all forms of poverty – income poverty and human poverty as well. While in many cases it has enhanced knowledge of poverty it has not solved the poverty of knowledge or the lack of social infrastructure and social security. Many experts in the field of micro-finance attribute this to weak 'capital' base of MFIs, capital to include financial, physical, intellectual and social capital. Even where financial capital has grown the life of the poor has not correspondingly improved due to many contingencies or risks.

The traditional forms of risk management such as self insurance and mutual insurance are now either inadequate or inappropriate. Disaster management for instance is part of financial management, though still 'natural'. Econometric models of resource mapping, risk mapping and insurance coverage are now required. The mismatch between needs of the insurers and the insured must be corrected, putting 'priorities' against 'profits' (Dinesha and Jayasheela, 2008). Losses and financial burden coupled with poor resource planning has led many farmers to be 'victims' of borrowing, inadvertently. This is unfortunate as we are transforming credit from 'informal' to 'formal' structure. Micro-finance, today, no doubt is an 'industry' in terms of size, structure and volume of business, and has made rapid strides in the hitherto un-banked and under-banked areas of the country. But some of the practices followed by certain lenders have subjected the sector to greater scrutiny and need for stricter regulation. In addition to the problems of less transparent pricing and low financial literacy there are a few emerging concerns like cluster formation, insufficient funds, multiple lending and over-indebtedness which are arising because of the increasing competition among the MFIs (Arena, 2011). There are also interest rate controversies (in fact a turmoil in micro-finance industry)[7] and problems of drop-outs of group members, marginal decline in women SHGs – and hence fall in savings and funds as reported from Tamil Nadu, recently – (Hans, 2012b) and so on. In the light of the challenges we may look into the following aspects for rejuvenating micro-finance revolution in India.

- Need to move from 'targets' to 'needs' for better identification and coverage of beneficiaries and fine tuning of credit processing.
- Lessening the perception of non-customised risk tendency.
- Developing micro-insurance as inbuilt stabilisers in the micro-finance system.
- Realisation of full potential of women, especially illiterate and less educated one.
- Promoting rural infrastructure management through local initiatives and partnerships of capital and labour.
- Expanding entrepreneurial training and development programme to create viable ventures.
- Ensuring steady wage employment, on or off farm.
- More push to savings to create more confidence, contribution and credit-worthiness within the group.
- Effective supervision, monitoring and management of operations both in Bank-Linkage Programme and MFIs.

Hans, V. Basil (2010a). Inclusive Growth in India: Dimension and Directions. In Rasure, K.A. (ed.), *Inclusive Growth – Challenges and Opportunities*, Oxford book Company, Jaipur.

Hans, V. Basil (2010b). Microfinance in India – From Financial Intermediation to Social Intermediation. In Rasure, K.A., *Rural Credit in the Era of Globalisation*, Madhav Books, Gurgaon.

Hans, V. Basil (2011). "Managing ICT for Rural Development in India – Initiatives and Inferences", *Artha Journal of Social Sciences*, 10(2): 85-105.

Hans, V. Basil (2012a). Gendered Response to Key Challenges in the Twelfth Five Year Plan. In Aquinas, P.G. and Ashalatha (eds.), *Development Challenges in the 12th Five Year Plan*, Justice K.S. Hegde Institute of Management, Nitte.

Hans, V. Basil (2012b). Entrepreneurship and Women Empowerment in India (in Kannada). In: Jayasheela et.al (eds.), *Mahila Sabaleekaranadalli Swa-Sahaaya Gumpugala Paatra Ondu Aarthika Vishleshane* [Role of Self Help Groups in Women Empowerment: An Economic Analysis], Global Research Publications, New Delhi.

Hans, V. Basil and Deepika (20110. "Inclusive Growth and Women In India – Looking at MDGs", *International Journal of Social and Economic Research*, 1(1): 56-65.

Hegde, Shakila and V. Basil Hans (2012). "Women Representation in Local Governance: Impact on Decentralised Democracy". Paper presented at the National Policy Conference on Social Exclusion in India: Self Governance, Development Politics and Autonomy Movements, Centre for the Study of Social Exclusion and Inclusive Policy, University of Mysore, August 22-23.

Heggade, O.D. and Rashmi H.N. (2012). "Empowering Rural Women through Financial Inclusion", Journal of Development and Social Change, 8(3):194-204.

Jayasheela (2007). Impact of Micro-finance on Poverty Alleviation and Women Empowerment: A Study in Dakshina Kannada, Project Report, Mangalore University.

Jayasheela, Dinesha P.T. and V. Basil Hans (2008). Financial Inclusion and Microfinance in India: An Overview. In Sohani, A.K. (ed.) Financial Inclusion – Perspectives and Country Experiences, ICFAI University Press, Hyderabad.

Messy, Flore-Anne and Chiara Monticonne (2012). "The Status of Financial Education in Africa', OECD Working Papers Finance, Insurance and Private Pensions, July 1. No.25, OECD Publishing.

Naidu, Rajesh, C. H. and Sai Krishna Nanduri (n.d.). "Strategies to overcome Challenges and Financial Inclusion of Urban Poor", Institute of Rural Management, Anand. Retrieved from https://www.irma.ac.in/others/winner.pdf, September 11, 2012.

Naaraayana, Naagesh (2009). "India microfinance records 30% growth: state of the sector report", Retrieved http://www.microfinancefocus.com/news/2009/10/26/india-microfinance-records-30-growth-state-of-the-sector-report/, September 14, 2012.

Raghavendra and V. Basil (2012). "Micro Finance Institutions and Interest Rate Controversy", Working Paper.

Seerengarajan R. and A.T. Narasimhan (2008). Self-Help Groups – A Viable Alternative for Sustainable Development. In: Rathakrishnan, L. (ed.), *Empowerment of Women through Entrepreneurship*, Gyan Publishing House, New Delhi.

Serrao, Manohar, V., Sequeira, A.H., and Hans, V. Basil (2011). "Designing a Methodology to Investigate Accessibility and Impact of Financial Inclusion", Paper presented at the International Conference on Innovation and Inclusion in Banking: Issues, Strategies and Options, Department of Applied Economics, School of Development Studies, Kannur University, February 3-4. Retrieved from http://ssrn.com, September 11, 2012.

Thorat, Sukhadeo (2011). "Growth, Inequality and Poverty during 1983/2005: Implications for Inclusive Policy", *The Indian Economic Journal*, 59(1): 3-39.

United Nations (2006). Building Inclusive Financial Sector for Development, New York: UNO.

Vaunandan, E. and Dolly Mathew (2003) (eds.), *Good Governance initiatives in India*, Prentice-Hall of India Private Limited, New Delhi.

Venkataramaraju D. and S.V. Ramesh (2011). "Financial Inclusion – Strategies and Regulations", Journal of Accounting and Finance, 25(1): 105-114.

Other:

http://en.wikipedia.org/wiki/Financial_inclusion#Financial_inclusion_in_India (September 11, 2012.

Index